GRUE!

GRUE!

THE NEW RIDDLE OF INDUCTION

EDITED BY
DOUGLAS STALKER

OPEN COURT

Chicago and La Salle, Illinois

© 1994 by Open Court Publishing Company

First printing 1994

Printed and bound in the United States of America.

Library of Congress Cataloging-in-Publication Data

Grue! : the new riddle of induction / [compiled by] Douglas
   Stalker.
     p. cm.
   Includes bibliographical references and index.
   ISBN 0-8126-9218-7 (cloth).—ISBN 0-8126-9219-5 (paper)
   1. Induction (Logic)   I. Stalker, Douglas Frank, 1947–
BC91.G78   1994
161—dc20   94-11203
                                                CIP

Dedicated to the Memory of
Henry B. Tingey

Contents

INTRODUCTION

The grue debate has been going on for almost fifty years. It started eight years before the word "grue" appeared in print in philosophy. (The word "gruebleen" appeared in print in 1939, on page 23 of James Joyce's novel *Finnegan's Wake*.) In 1946 Nelson Goodman published a short paper entitled "A Query on Confirmation," and this paper introduces the grue-like predicate "S." This predicate appears in an example about drawing marbles from a certain bowl. Goodman asks us to suppose that we have been drawing one marble per day from this bowl for ninety-nine days—indeed, the ninety-nine days up to and including Victory in Europe Day, May 8, 1945. He also asks us to suppose that each marble has been red so far. If we draw a marble on the next day, the hundredth day, we might expect that it will be red as well. After all, the first marble was red, the second was red, and so on through the ninety-ninth marble: they were all drawn from the bowl and they were all red. The evidence plainly supports our prediction about the next marble we draw: it will be red. Or so it seems. Goodman introduces us to the predicate "S," which means "is drawn by Victory in Europe Day and is red, or is drawn later and is nonred." This predicate applies to the ninety-nine marbles that we have drawn from the bowl so far. They were all drawn by Victory in Europe Day, and they were all red—so they were all S. This evidence seems to support a different prediction about the next marble we draw: it will not be red. Of course we do not expect the next marble we draw from the bowl, the one we draw after Victory in Europe Day, to be nonred. It doesn't matter that the first marble was S, the second was S, and so on through the ninety-ninth marble. This doesn't support a prediction about the next marble being nonred. But why not? Why do the marbles add up to confirmation in one case, but not the other?

In 1954 Goodman published a small book entitled *Fact, Fiction and Forecast*. The word "grue" appears in Chapter III, Section 4, which is entitled "The New Riddle of Induction." Goodman asks us to consider emeralds that have been examined before time t, and to suppose that all of them have been green. Thus, by time t, these observations support the hypothesis that all emeralds are green, and the prediction that if we happen to examine the next emerald after time *t*, it will be green as well. As before, Goodman introduces a new predicate to show that things aren't as simple as they might seem. Something is grue, he tells us, if it is examined before time *t* and determined to be green, or it is not examined before time *t* and it is blue. It should be plain how this applies to the emeralds examined before time *t*, and all of which we have found to be green. They are all grue. Thus, by time *t*, we have a good deal of support for the hypothesis that all emeralds are grue, and the prediction that if we happen to examine the next emerald after time *t*, it will be grue as well—that is, it will be blue. Indeed, we seem to have just as much support for the green hypothesis as the grue hypothesis. Each emerald has been green, and each has been grue. Be that as it may, we know that the green emeralds (or, to be precise, the evidence statements describing the green emeralds) support the green hypothesis and that the grue emeralds (or, to be precise, the evidence statements describing the grue emeralds) don't support the grue hypothesis. Why, as before, do we have confirmation in one case but not the other?

The new riddle of induction has become a well-known topic in contemporary analytic philosophy—so well-known that only a philosophical hermit wouldn't recognize the word "grue." *Fact, Fiction and Forecast* is in a fourth edition, and the best journals contain articles on the puzzle year in and year out. There are now something like twenty different approaches to the problem, or kinds of solutions, in the literature: the entrenchment solution, the positional-qualitative solution, the simplicity solution, the natural kind solution, the coherence solution, the incoherence dissolutions, the falsificationist response, the evolutionary approach, the real property approach, the counterfactual approach, the various Bayesian approaches, and so on. None of them has become the majority opinion, received answer, or textbook solution to the problem. There hasn't even been complete agreement on what the problem really amounts to. In short, the grue debate is still going on. This volume is the first collection of essays devoted to that debate, and it includes selections from the 1950s to the present. The selections are in chronological order. Seven of them have been published before, and eight are appearing for the first time. The collection ends with a 316-entry, annotated bibliography. The annotations range in length from one line to several hundred lines. They cover articles from more than forty different journals and chapters from more than eighty books.

The first selection originally appeared in *Science* in 1958. Goodman was teaching at the University of Pennsylvania, and his former student, Israel Scheffler, was a lecturer at Harvard. In "Inductive Inference: A New Approach," Scheffler attempts to inform scientific readers about Goodman's (then) recent work on induction. He develops the new riddle in connection with Hume's challenge and the generalization formula, and he explains the basic ideas in Goodman's entrenchment solution. Scheffler sees Hume's challenge as a question about how to tell reasonable (rational, justified) inductive inferences from unreasonable ones, and he introduces the generalization formula as a popular answer to this question. Scheffler uses the generalization formula with a pair of opposing next-case predictions, such as "The next *F* will be *G*" and "The next *F* will not be *G*." The former prediction agrees with the universal generalization "All *F* are *G*," and the latter prediction agrees with the universal generalization "No *F* are *G*." If the evidence to date uniformly supports the generalization "All *F* are *G*" and thereby disconfirms the contrary generalization "No *F* are *G*," then the reasonable prediction is "The next *F* will be *G*." Scheffler thinks that Goodman's new riddle of induction refutes the generalization formula, and he extends Goodman's copper example to show how it does. Consider the predictions "The next specimen of copper will conduct electricity" and "The next specimen of copper will not conduct electricity." The first prediction agrees with the generalization "All specimens of copper conduct electricity" and the second agrees with the generalization "No specimens of copper conduct electricity." If the evidence to date uniformly supports the hypothesis that copper conducts electricity and thereby disconfirms its contrary, then it is reasonable to predict that the next specimen of copper will conduct electricity, and unreasonable to predict that it will not. Or that is how it seems until we introduce a grue-like hypothesis about copper: viz., "All specimens of copper have either been examined before *t* and conduct electricity or have not been examined before *t* and do not conduct electricity." The evidence to date uniformly supports this grue-like hypothesis and thereby disconfirms its contrary as well. If the next specimen of copper will not be examined before time *t,* then it is reasonable to predict that the next specimen of copper will not conduct electricity because this prediction agrees with the grue-like hypothesis. The generalization formula, then, has not picked out the reasonable prediction here. Indeed, it can't even select one prediction—reasonable or otherwise—from our pair of opposing next-case predictions.

Scheffler describes how Goodman's approach distinguishes the confirmable "All copper conducts electricity" from its nonconfirmable counterpart by looking at historical information about the predicates in each hypothesis. Their biographies differ in an important way. The predicate "conducts electricity" has been used longer and more often in formulating predictive hypotheses on the basis of positive, albeit partial, evidence. In Goodman's terminology, the predicate "conducts electricity" is better entrenched than the predicate "has either been examined before t and conducts electricity, or has not been examined before t and does not conduct electricity." Since the grue-like hypothesis conflicts with a hypothesis whose predicate is plainly better entrenched, the grue-like hypothesis is nonconfirmable or, as Goodman puts it, unprojectible. Likewise, since "All emeralds are grue" conflicts with "All emeralds are green," and the predicate "green" is plainly better entrenched than the predicate "grue," the grue hypothesis is unprojectible.

As Scheffler notes, some critics believe that Goodman's entrenchment solution is inadequate because Goodman does not say enough about entrenchment itself. Joseph Ullian discusses this point in the second selection, "Luck, License, & Lingo," which he prepared for a symposium on justification and originally published in *The Journal of Philosophy* in 1961. Ullian presents the new riddle and the entrenchment solution in connection with Goodman's view of justification. Goodman takes justifying to be a matter of describing, defining, and codifying. On this view, we justify a particular inductive inference by showing that it agrees with a valid rule of inductive inference, and we justify a rule of inductive inference by showing that it agrees with the inductive inferences we make and accept. If Goodman's general rule accurately codifies the particular cases by taking into account the entrenchment of predicates, then it is justified on this view and solves the new riddle. However, some critics want more than accurate description. In particular, they want to know why the right predicates have become well entrenched while the spurious ones have not. Is it simply a matter of luck that the well-entrenched predicates show up in the confirmable hypotheses? Ullian believes that the real question here is about predicates in general, not just the well-entrenched or projectible ones. It is, he argues, a question about the utility of predicates or general terms. Ullian considers it remarkable that we have any use—inductive or otherwise—for our general terms. As he points out, if general terms mark off classes and there are indefinitely many classes, with each class just as good as the other from a logical point of view, then it seems extraordinary that we have ended up with classes which are actually valuable to us. Insofar as there is an explanation for this state of affairs, Ullian suggests that it will be along evolutionary lines. In a postscript added to his original paper, Ullian discusses the current status of Goodman's theory of projectibility.

The third selection is by Goodman's longtime colleague at Harvard, W.V. Quine. He originally wrote his essay "Natural Kinds" for a 1970 festschrift for the philosopher of science Carl Hempel. Quine describes both the new riddle and Hempel's raven paradox in terms of projectible predicates. With Hempel's paradox, a white shoe ends up confirming the hypothesis "All ravens are black" because a white shoe confirms the logically equivalent hypothesis "All nonblack things are nonravens." While "raven" and "black" are projectible predicates, Quine believes their complements are not projectible. Thus a white shoe does not confirm "All nonblack things are nonravens" any more than a green emerald confirms the hypothesis "All emeralds are grue." Quine maintains that projectible predicates are true of things of a kind, and that the notion of a kind is related to the notion of similarity at least in the sense of covariation: e.g., if we first think object *a* is more similar to object *b* than to object *c* and later think object *a* is less similar to object *b* than to object *c,* then we will likewise change how we assign these objects to kinds. In short, the more similarity between objects, the more reason to count them as members of a kind. Quine argues that we must have an innate standard of comparative similarity in order to form any habits and expectations at all, and that this innate subjective standard makes for successful everyday inductive inferences because it is the result of Darwinian natural selection. Quine also emphasizes the development and change of standards of similarity and systems of kinds, notably from our subjective standard and intuitive kinds to scientifically objective standards and theoretical kinds, such as marsupials and positively charged particles. Moreover, he believes that when a branch of science matures, we can analyze the relevant notions of similarity and kind in special terms from that branch of science and from logic. For example, we can analyze object *a* being, from a chemical point of view, more similar to object *b* than to object *c* in terms of the ratios of matching to unmatching pairs of molecules. We can then use this analysis of comparative similarity to analyze chemical kinds in terms of a paradigm and a foil. A paradigm is an example of the central norm for a kind, and a foil is an example of something that is not a member of the kind because it differs a little too much from the paradigm. A kind is then a set of objects such that the paradigm is more similar to the members of this set than it is similar to the foil.

The fourth selection is a revised version of Andrzej Zabludowski's "Concerning a Fiction about How Facts Are Forecast." This paper was originally published in 1974 in the *Journal of Philosophy,* and it started an eight-year exchange between Zabludowski and proponents (notably Goodman and Ullian) of the entrenchment approach to projectibility. Zabludowski maintains that Goodman's theory has a number of absurd consequences, not the least of which is that no hypothesis is projectible. Zabludowski believes this consequence obtains because, for any supported, unviolated, and unexhausted generalization h, we can devise another generalization that is supported, unviolated, and unexhausted—and that conflicts with h. Moreover, this rival generalization will have predicates that are at least as well entrenched as the predicates in h. On Goodman's approach, this means that h is not projectible. For example, we can let h be the hypothesis "All emeralds are green" when we have examined some emeralds, found them all to be green, and still have more emeralds to examine. Zabludowski claims that the predicates "stone," "round," and "hard" are among the best entrenched predicates at this time. He also claims that we know all three predicates apply to some objects at this time, and that we know "stone" applies to some green emeralds but "round" does not apply to them. Lastly, Zabludowski believes that the information we accept at this time does not prohibit the hypothesis "All stones are hard" from being true and conflicting with "All emeralds are green." Given all of this, Zabludowski introduces the following generalization as a supported, unviolated, and unexhausted rival to the hypothesis in question: $(x)(Sx \rightarrow ((Rx \ \& -Kx) \text{ v } (Hx \ \& \ Kx)))$, where "$Sx$," "$Rx$," and "$Hx$" stand for "$x$ is a stone," "x is round," and "x is hard." The predicate "Kx" means "x is such that the hypothesis 'All stones are hard' conflicts with the hypothesis 'All emeralds are green.' " Or, in other words, "Kx" stands for "x is such that some emeralds are either green but not hard or hard but not green." Zabludowski argues that this generalization is both incompatible with and conflicts with "All emeralds are green," and its predicates are at least as well entrenched as "emerald" and "green"—that is, the antecedent predicate "stone" and the disjunctive consequent. Since this consequent predicate is coextensive with either "round" or "hard" and Goodman maintains that entrenchment is really about the extension of a predicate, it is also among the best entrenched predicates at present. In a postscript, Zabludowski considers an attempt to modify Goodman's entrenchment theory, and an attempt to solve the new riddle by appealing to a distinction between genuine and pseudo properties.

The new riddle of induction is typically seen as a problem about projectible and nonprojectible predicates or properties or hypotheses, and typical solutions consist of explaining the difference between projectible and nonprojectible predicates or properties or hypotheses. The fifth selection presents a different view of the problem and its solution. In his essay "Grue," which was originally published in the *Journal of Philosophy* in 1975, Frank Jackson maintains that all consistent predicates (or properties or hypotheses) are projectible. He believes that we can avoid the new riddle by paying attention to a defeasability condition on most of our everyday inductive reasoning. When this condition is satisfied, the fact that certain *F*s—which are *H*—are *G* does not support the conclusion that certain other *F*s—which are not *H*—are *G*. For example, if all the lobsters you have observed have been red, and all of them have been cooked, and you know that cooking makes lobsters red, then you will not take your observations as support for the prediction that the next uncooked lobster you observe will be red. In other words, you know that if these lobsters (the ones you have observed to date) had not been cooked, they would not have been red. More generally, you know that if the *F*s—which are *H*—had not been *H*, they would not have been *G*. Jackson refers to this as the counterfactual condition. He believes this condition resolves the new riddle because it shows why a series of examined (by time *t*) emeralds being green supports a next-case prediction about an unexamined (by time *t*) emerald being green, while the series being grue does not support a next-case prediction about an unexamined (by time *t*) emerald being grue. With respect to the series of examined green emeralds, if they had not been examined by time *t*, they would still have been green. However, with respect to the series of examined grue emeralds, if they had not been examined by time *t*, they would not have been grue because they would have been green and unexamined by time *t*.

The grue debate is filled with claims and counterclaims about projectible hypotheses, projectible predicates, and theories of projectibility. In the sixth selection, "Concepts of Projectibility and the Problems of Induction," John Earman attempts to raise the level of discussion about projectible hypotheses and predicates. His essay, which originally appeared in *Nous* in 1985, presents eleven definitions for different senses of projectibility along with necessary and/or sufficient conditions for each sense. Earman takes a quantitative, Bayesian approach to the projectibility of universal generalizations in connection with instance or particular induction and general or hypothesis induction. He distinguishes between hypotheses (or predicates) being strongly projectible or weakly projectible, and he also distinguishes between them being projectible in the future-moving sense or the past-reaching sense. With instance induction for the hypothesis "All emeralds are green," we are concerned with the probability that emerald $n + 1$ will be green (or emeralds $n + m$ will be green) given that n emeralds have been green and our background knowledge. If we are concerned with the probability that emerald $n + 1$ will be green, we are concerned with our hypothesis being weakly projectible. If we are concerned with the probability that emeralds $n + m$ will be green, we are concerned with our hypothesis being strongly projectible. Earman explains the distinction between future-moving and past-reaching in terms of two ways of taking the limit of the probability as the number n of instances approaches infinity. For example, if "All emeralds are green" is weakly projectible in the future-moving sense, then the probability that emerald $n + 1$ is green, given that n emeralds have been green and our background knowledge, is equal to 1 as n approaches infinity. The next instance $n + 1$ is in the direction in which this limit is being taken. If this hypothesis is weakly projectible in the past-reaching sense, then the probability that emerald $n + 1$ is green, given that $n - j$ emeralds have been green and our background knowledge, is equal to 1 as j approaches infinity. Here the next instance $n + 1$ is not in the direction in which the limit is being taken. With general induction for the hypothesis "All emeralds are green," we are concerned with the probability of our hypothesis given that n emeralds have been green and our background knowledge. If we are concerned with the probability of our hypothesis *per se,* we are concerned with it being strongly projectible, and it can be strongly projectible in either the future-moving or past-reaching sense depending on how we take the limit as the number of positive instances approaches infinity. If we are concerned with whether its probability after $n + 1$ green emeralds is greater than after n green emeralds, then we are concerned with our hypothesis being weakly projectible. In a new postscript to his essay, Earman discusses some alleged and real morals of Goodman's grue problem and examines some of the early correspondence between Goodman, Carnap, and Hempel on the topic.

    The seventh selection presents the new riddle as a problem in the field of artificial intelligence. Peter Gärdenfors maintains that AI practitioners will have to find a way to identify projectible predicates in order to produce computer models of how we make inductive inferences. In "Induction, Conceptual Spaces, and AI," which originally appeared in *Philosophy of Science* in 1990, Gärdenfors takes projectible predicates to be predicates that designate natural properties, and he introduces his theory of conceptual spaces as a nonlinguistic and nonlogical way to represent information about the properties of individual objects. A conceptual space is a set of quality dimensions such as color, length, weight, temperature, and time. Each quality dimension has a topological or metrical structure. With respect to color, there are three dimensions: hue, brightness, and saturation. The hue dimension has the topology of a circle (the color circle), while the brightness dimension (white to black) and the saturation (color intensity) each have a linear structure, with the saturation dimension isomorphic to an interval on the real number line. The hue dimension is circular instead of linear because Gärdenfors's quality dimensions are psychological dimensions as opposed to scientific or theoretical ones. The hue dimension is based on psychophysics and stimulus magnitudes instead of physics and wavelengths. Gärdenfors represents a property as a region in a conceptual space. If the region represents a natural property, then it must be convex in the following sense: if a pair of points are in the region, then all points between them are also in the region. On this analysis, the predicate "green" differs from the predicate "grue" because the former predicate designates a property that we can represent with a convex region, while the latter predicate designates a property that we cannot represent by a convex region because it involves both the color dimensions and the time dimension. Gärdenfors notes that his analysis makes a property natural relative to a conceptual space, and so it appears that "grue" could designate a natural property and "green" could designate a nonnatural property relative to some nonstandard conceptual space. He argues that relativism is not a problem with respect to innate quality dimensions, such as the color dimensions. If some form of psychological relativism can occur here, it will occur only with standard quality dimensions that depend on learning and acculturation.

The remaining selections were written especially for this volume. Some are by philosophers who have previously written about the new riddle, while others are by philosophers who work in the area of inductive logic and confirmation theory—but who, until now, haven't really entered the grue debate. John L. Pollock is one of the former. He has written about projectibility and principles of induction since 1972, and he reports his current views in the eighth selection, "The Projectibility Constraint." Pollock emphasizes two points. First, he stresses that most concepts are not projectible. He claims this is implied by the closure conditions for projectibility. These conditions tell us that if some concepts are projectible with regard to each other, then so are certain related concepts. It turns out that projectibility is not closed under most logical operators. For example, it is not closed under disjunction or negation: i.e., if the concepts A and B are projectible with regard to concept C, then it does not follow that $(A \lor B)$ is projectible with regard to concept C; and if the concept A is projectible with regard to the concept B, then it does not follow that $-A$ is projectible with regard to concept B. Second, Pollock stresses that projectibility is a problem for all forms of probabilistic and inductive reasoning, not just induction by simple enumeration. We also need to restrict statistical induction, direct inference, statistical inference, and the statistical syllogism to projectible concepts. For example, logic textbooks invariably formulate the statistical syllogism as "Most A are B, this is an A, therefore it is a B." If we do not restrict A and B so that A is projectible with regard to B, then we can let A be a disjunctive predicate like "things that are either birds or giant sea tortoises." Our statistical syllogism would then be: "Most things that are either birds or giant sea tortoises are things that can fly, this creature is a giant sea tortoise, therefore this creature is something that can fly." The problem with this reasoning is not a false premise. This odd bird/tortoise generalization is actually true because there are so many birds, so few giant sea tortoises, and most birds can fly. Rather, the problem is the projectibility of "things that are either a bird or a giant sea tortoise" with regard to "things that can fly." The first concept is not projectible with regard to the second.

While there are about twenty different kinds of solutions to the new riddle in the literature, the simplicity solution is among the most popular. Even Goodman has wondered if his entrenchment criterion isn't really just a simplicity criterion. The generic form of this solution is that we should prefer "All emeralds are green" to "All emeralds are grue" because the green hypothesis is simpler than the grue one. In the ninth selection, "Simplicity as a Pragmatic Criterion for Deciding What Hypotheses to Take Seriously," Gilbert Harman develops a simplicity solution to a quantitative version of the new riddle. Harman considers the relationship between two variables P and C based on four data points. He introduces two hypotheses that fit the data points but that make different predictions for other values of variable P. One hypothesis is $C = 2 \times P$ and the other hypothesis is $C = 2 \times P + (P - 1) \times (P - 3) \times (P - 4) \times (P - 8)$. Harman believes that a scientist would take the first hypothesis seriously but not the second one. Moreover, he believes that a scientist would decide this on the basis of relative simplicity: i.e., the first hypothesis is simpler than the second one. This kind of relative simplicity is computational as opposed to syntactic or semantic. If scientists are interested in determining the value of C when the value of P is 6, it is easier to use the first hypothesis than the second hypothesis to arrive at the answer. The calculations are less involved. This kind of relative simplicity also depends on the interests of scientists. If we want to determine the value of R when P is 6, where R is equal to the value of C divided by the value of C on the second hypothesis, it is easier to calculate the answer with the second hypothesis. Indeed, we can do it in a flash: $R = 1$. However, if scientists are not interested in this result, then the second hypothesis does not count as simpler than the first hypothesis. While the computational view makes relative simplicity into a practical matter by connecting it with how easily scientists can get answers to their questions, Harman believes it still promotes relative simplicity as an indicator of verisimilitude. If one hypothesis is simpler than another, this is a practical reason to believe the hypothesis and (with no difference between believing something and believing that it is true) this is automatically a reason to believe that the hypothesis is true.

There seems to be a straightforward difference between the two predicates "grue" and "green": viz., the former is a disjunctive predicate while the latter is not. When we explain what "grue" means, the explanation takes the form of a disjunction in which each disjunct is a conjunction of a color term ("green," "blue") and a temporal term ("before t," "after t"). Goodman believes this difference is only a relative difference. We are starting with "green" and "blue" as basic or primitive terms. If we start with "grue" and "bleen" as basic or primitive terms, then our explanation of "green" will take the form of a disjunction. Something will be green if it is examined before t and determined to be grue, or it is not examined before t and it is bleen, where something is bleen if it is examined before t and determined to be blue, or it is not examined before t and it is green. David Sanford claims there is more to the disjunctiveness issue than these syntactic similarities. He develops an objective, semantic analysis of disjunctive predicates in the tenth selection, "A Grue Thought in a Bleen Shade: 'Grue' as a Disjunctive Predicate." Sanford distinguishes between exclusively disjunctive predicates and inclusively disjunctive predicates. He also distinguishes two kinds of exclusively disjunctive predicates, disjoint predicates and disconnected predicates. If a predicate "*F*" is equivalent to a disjunction of incompatible, nonempty predicates "*G*" and "*H*" and everything on the boundary of "*G*" or "*H*" is also on the boundary of "*F*," then "*F*" is a disconnected predicate. Sanford notes that "grue" is a disconnected predicate. He also notes that this does not provide an adequate solution to the new riddle. We can easily introduce grue-like predicates that are neither disjoint nor disconnected, such as the predicate "supergrue." Something is supergrue if it is examined before *t* and determined to be green, or it is not examined before *t* and it is blue or bluish-green. A predicate like "supergrue" shows that we can have a new riddle without an exclusively disjunctive predicate—that is, we can have a new riddle with an inclusively disjunctive predicate. Sanford analyzes inclusively disjunctive predicates in terms of independent predicates. He introduces three types of independence: logical, minimal, and genuine. He maintains that we can see a relevant, objective difference between "grue" and "green" in connection with genuine independence. A pair of predicates "*G*" and "*H*" are genuinely independent if and only if they are logically independent, minimally independent, and each distinct boundary of one predicate intersects each distinct boundary of the other predicate at one, and only one, distinct point of intersection. Sanford argues that if we express "green" and "grue" in a certain logical form—"*A* and *C*, or *B* and not *C*"—then an objective difference appears. The predicate "green" is equivalent to "green and first examined before *t*, or green and not first examined before *t*." The predicate "grue" is equivalent to "grue and first examined before *t*, or grue and not first examined before *t*." Here the predicates "green" and "first examined before *t*" are genuinely independent, as are the predicates "green" and "not first examined before *t*." However, the predicates "grue" and "not first examined before *t*" are not genuinely independent.

Goodman solves the new riddle by comparing hypotheses for entrenchment. This involves determining whether one hypothesis has a much better entrenched predicate than the other, where entrenchment is connected with how often a predicate has been used in actually projecting hypotheses. When a hypothesis is adopted because it has some positive instances, no negative instances, and some undetermined instances, Goodman says it is actually projected. When a predicate is used in doing this—actually projecting a hypothesis—it earns (as opposed to inherits) entrenchment. Goodman also refers to this as actually projecting the predicate. Since the predicate "green" has been used in actual projections longer and more often than the artificial predicate "grue," it has earned much more entrenchment than "grue" and makes the green hypothesis better entrenched than the grue hypothesis. Ian Hacking, who has published extensively on the topic of statistical inference as well as the history of statistics, agrees with Goodman about the importance of entrenchment. In the eleventh selection, "Entrenchment," Hacking introduces a two-dimensional view of using a predicate. If we view using a predicate longitudinally, then we are concerned with its record of past uses. Goodman takes this view with his notion of entrenchment. If we view using a predicate latitudinally, then we are concerned with how easily we can use the predicate now. Hacking maintains that we cannot seriously use the predicate "grue" at the present time. He claims that if we seriously use a predicate, then we must be willing to project that predicate. That is, we must be willing to use the predicate not only in classifying but also in making predictions and generalizations. According to Hacking, it is simply an ethnographic fact that we cannot use "grue" in these ways—no matter how much we mention the predicate and no matter how many mental gyrations we go through. The problem is not, he argues, a logical, cognitive, translational, or "transcendental" one. Hacking also maintains that the new riddle involves a false dichotomy: viz., that we can either use a predicate to classify or we can use it to generalize, and so we can first classify things as members of a kind and then later go on to generalize about them. Hacking emphatically denies that there is sharp distinction between classifying and generalizing. He believes that we have not realized this because we tend to view concept acquisition in terms of grouping or collecting, because we are aware of an independent profession (natural history) devoted to taxonomy, and because we make an issue of how a word acquires an extension and whether it acquires an extension before an intension.

Elliott Sober, who is noted for his work in philosophy of biology, takes a probabilistic approach to the new riddle in the twelfth selection, "No Model, No Inference: A Bayesian Primer on the Grue Problem." Sober views the new riddle as a matter of comparing the probabilities of the relevant hypotheses given our observations about the color of emeralds up to time t. This involves applying Bayes's theorem for computing conditional probabilities: viz., Probability (Hypothesis/Observations) = Probability (Observations/Hypothesis) × Probability (Hypothesis)/Probability (Observations). Sober argues that the new riddle consists of two different inference problems. One problem is about the relationship between universal generalizations (viz., "All emeralds are green" and "All emeralds are grue") and their instances. The other problem is about the relationship between next-case predictions (viz., "The next emerald examined will be green" and "The next emerald examined will be grue") and preceding observations. Sober maintains that we need to consider each of these problems synchronically and diachronically. If we are concerned with the generalization problem, for instance, and want to know whether our observations make the green hypothesis more probable than the grue hypothesis, then we are considering the problem synchronically. If we want to know how much the probability of the green hypothesis, given our observations, differs from the probability of the green hypothesis before our observations, and how much the probability of the grue hypothesis, given our observations, differs from the probability of the grue hypothesis before our observations, then we are considering the problem diachronically. Sober maintains that there are epistemic differences between the green generalization and the grue generalization in both the synchronic and the diachronic cases, and between the green prediction and the grue prediction in both the synchronic and the diachronic cases. In the synchronic generalization problem, for example, the probability of "All emeralds are green" is (given the observations) greater than the probability of "All emeralds are grue" (given the observations) if and only if the prior probability of the green hypothesis is greater than the prior probability of the grue hypothesis. In the diachronic prediction problem, with the next emerald either green or blue, the difference between the probability it will be green, given our observations, and the probability it will be green is greater than the difference between the probability it will be grue, given our observations, and the probability it will be grue—if and only if there is a positive covariance (or association or correlation) between the green prediction and the observations to date. Sober emphasizes that, in all four cases, the epistemic differences obtain only if we make substantive, empirical assumptions. For example, if we believe the prior probability of "All emeralds are green" is higher than the prior probability of "All emeralds are grue" in the synchronic generalization case, then this is because we believe some empirical theory about coloration and objects: e.g., that all emeralds will be the same color because they have the same physical structure. If we believe our observations influence the green prediction more than the grue prediction in the diachronic prediction case, then this is because we believe some empirical process brought about a correlation between the color of emeralds we have examined and emeralds we will examine: e.g., microstructure determining coloration for an entire group of objects.

Brian Skyrms also takes a Bayesian approach to questions about projectibility. In the thirteenth selection, "Bayesian Projectibility," Skyrms shows how to represent Goodman's ideas about projectibility in the framework of Bayesian statistics. This framework involves taking a subjective interpretation of probability and applying Bayes's theorem to probability distributions. Skyrms is a well-known proponent of Bruno de Finetti's theory of personal or subjective probability. On this theory, we replace objective probabilities or chances with subjective probabilities in the form of rational degrees of belief, where degrees of belief are rational if their numerical representation satisfies the rules of the probability calculus. We also take a subjective view of so-called repetitions or trials of the same event, such as repeatedly tossing a coin with an unknown bias. If our degrees of belief are exchangeable with respect to tosses of the coin, then we will treat the trials or tosses as trials of the same event. Moreover, if we are viewing heads as successes, then we will not care about the order of heads in a finite sequence of tosses: i.e., all sequences of that length and with the same number of successes will have, as far as we are concerned, the same probability. From the subjective Bayesian point of view, our inductive reasoning will proceed by applying Bayes's theorem to our coin-tossing data and our prior probability distribution over the possible biases of the coin. If our prior probability is open-minded over the possible biases, then no possible value of the bias receives a zero prior probability. If we somehow end up with a sequence that is all heads, then the next-trial probability of a head increases as each trial occurs and this probability converges to one in the limit. If our prior probability is universal generalization open-minded, then we will give a positive prior probability to an outcome sequence consisting exclusively of heads and we will give a positive prior probability to an outcome sequence consisting exclusively of tails. If this condition holds, then the probability of "All tosses are heads" increases with each head and converges to one for the case in which every toss is a head. Skyrms points out that, in ordinary circumstances, we will not treat a Goodmanized sequence as exchangeable, where a Goodmanized sequence assigns a value of 1 to heads and a value of 0 to tails in the first 100 trials, and then assigns a value of 0 to heads and a value of 1 to tails in all other trials. Skyrms extends this analysis to patterns in data (or cases where order matters) by introducing the idea of partial or conditional exchangeability. He examines, in particular, cases in which the trials are Markov dependent. That is, cases in which the probability of an outcome depends on the probability of previous outcomes. In order to provide mathematical support for de Finetti's views about inductive reasoning, Skyrms goes on to discuss ergodic theory, or the theory of measure-preserving transformations. In ergodic theory, we can view projectibility in terms of an invariant measure. Skyrms also believes that ergodic theory can help us give precise answers to various questions about inductive skepticism. For example, if we construe degrees of belief in terms of an invariant probability measure and we have invariant degrees of belief with regard to a transformation, then we cannot be absolute inductive skeptics about repetitions of a chance experiment given by this transformation. Skyrms concludes by describing a general theory of probabilistic symmetry that takes symmetry to be invariance under a group of transformations. This explains how exchangeability, for example, is just a probability-symmetry structure because exchangeability involves invariance under a group of transformations: viz., finite permutations of trials. Indeed, Skyrms maintains that the most general and abstract logic of projectibility is just the mathematics of probability-symmetry structures.

Patrick Suppes, a distinguished philosopher of science, states his view of the new riddle in the fourteenth selection, "Learning and Projectibility." Suppes connects problems about induction with problems about learning, and he views the new riddle as a problem about developing projectible concepts. Suppes emphasizes that a good deal of learning is nonverbal, and that the basic problems of projectibility are the same for all mammals. Accordingly, he believes that it is incorrect to present inductive problems in a statement format. He notes that animals do not encounter learning problems with artificial predicates like "grue," and that humans do not encounter these artificial problems in areas of nonverbal learning where they do not have an accurate verbal description of the behavior in question (e.g., walking through a room, recognizing acquaintances, hitting a golfball). Suppes also discusses how learning to conduct scientific experiments involves nonverbal learning because we do not have accurate verbal descriptions of the activities a scientist performs in conducting a complex psychology or physics experiment. Not surprisingly, Suppes wonders about Goodman's linguistic account of projectibility and inductive validity, and about his view of predictions as valid in terms of their agreement with rules. Suppes believes that we should think about mechanisms of learning when it comes to projectibility rather than concepts and lawlike generalizations, and that we should view predictions as correct in terms of their results rather than valid according to rules. Suppes also wonders about Bayesian accounts of projectibility that involve probabilistic symmetries such as exchangeability. He points out that we only find these symmetries in relatively stationary environments, while humans and animals typically live in nonstationary environments where they need adaptable learning mechanisms in order to develop projectible concepts. Suppes goes on to describe how we can measure projectibility as the predictive success of a learning model on a set of prediction tasks. If we have a finite set of learning models, a finite sequence of prediction tasks, and let 0.5 be the probability that a model's prediction is correct on the first trial, then we can use a recursive rule to compute the probability that a model's prediction is correct on trial $n + 1$. If the prediction was correct on trial n, then the probability for $n + 1$ is equal to $(1 - \theta) \times$ (the probability that the prediction on trial n is correct) $+ \theta$, where θ is a projectibility parameter between 0 and 1. If the prediction was not correct on trial n, then the probability for $n + 1$ is equal to $(1 - \theta) \times$ (the probability that the prediction on trial n is correct). While this is a pragmatic and purely descriptive measure of success, Suppes points out that it is connected to particular learning mechanisms and that we justify learning mechanisms in terms of their success.

In the fifteenth selection, "Selecting Variables and Getting to the Truth," Clark Glymour and Peter Spirtes look at two issues prompted by Goodman's paradox: viz., the ideal solvability of inductive problems, and the selection of appropriate properties (or variables) when making causal inferences without the benefit of full experimental controls. In keeping with the framework of formal learning theory developed by Glymour, Kevin Kelly, and a number of others, they think of an inductive problem as defined by a set of possible answers or hypotheses, and, for each hypothesis, a set of sequences of data consistent with the hypothesis. An inductive problem is solvable if there exists a procedure—a function or partial function—from finite initial segments of data sequences to hypotheses, and given any data sequence for a hypothesis, after some initial segment of the data is seen, the procedure will always guess that hypothesis given further data. Glymour and Spirtes briefly consider the infinite collection of hypotheses asserting that all emeralds are green, all emeralds are grue − 1, all emeralds are grue − 2, all emeralds are grue − 3, and so on, where "all emeralds are grue − n" means the first n emeralds examined are green and the remaining emeralds are blue. They note that this collection of hypotheses forms a solvable inductive problem given a natural account of the data sequences which accord with each hypothesis. Their philosophical point is that so far as provably reliable inference is concerned, hypotheses involving "grue" and "bleen" (and similar predicates) are no more and no less difficult than hypotheses involving more ordinary, projectible predicates. This argument suggests that there is nothing special about novel predicates so far as scientific reliability is concerned. Glymour and Spirtes go on to suggest the reverse in connection with variable selection. Pursuing a point introduced elsewhere by the computer scientist Judea Pearl, they describe examples in which statistical procedures judge causal relations from conditional probabilities, and yet these procedures will lead to erroneous conclusions if variables are chosen incorrectly—no matter how large the data sample may be. Their examples feature novel variables that can be defined from "natural" or projectible variables, but the definitions involve algebraic rather than purely logical operations. Glymour and Spirtes argue that such variables are rare in a measure theoretic sense.

Inductive Inference: A New Approach

Israel Scheffler

On what grounds do we choose the theories by which we anticipate the future? How do we decide what to predict about cases never before observed? These questions concerning what is traditionally called "induction" are among the most fundamental and most difficult which can be asked about the logic of science. Much reflection has been devoted to these questions in recent years, but no contribution has proved more incisive and challenging than that of Nelson Goodman of the University of Pennsylvania, whose papers on induction and allied problems have activated lively philosophic controversy over the past twelve years.

In 1955, Goodman published *Fact, Fiction and Forecast,*[1] in which he presented the outlines of a new approach to the understanding of induction. This recent work has also aroused considerable comment by philosophers, both in print and out, and it is safe to say that the discussion is still in its early stages. The scientific public is, however, largely unaware of this new development, just as it was largely unacquainted with the controversies that preceded it. If there is no real boundary between science and the philosophy of science, the consideration of fundamental research in the logic of science ought not to be confined, even at the early stages, to circles of philosophers. The aim of this article is thus to acquaint the scientific reader with the background and the direction of Goodman's investigations, as they bear on the interpretation of induction.

Hume's Challenge and the Generalization Formula

The starting point for all modern thinking about induction is David Hume's denial of necessary connections of matters of fact: between observed cases recorded in the evidence and predicted cases based on the evidence there is a fundamental logical gap, which cannot be bridged by

---

From *Science*, Vol. 127, No. 3291, January 24, 1958, 177–181. Copyright 1958 AAAS.
Reprinted by permission of the editors of *Science* and the author.

deductive inference. If, then, the truth of our predictions is not guaranteed by logical deduction from available evidence, what can be their rational justification? This challenge, arising out of Hume's analysis, has evoked a variety of replies. Leaving aside the reply of the skeptics, who are willing to admit that all induction is indeed without rational foundation, and that of the deductivists, who strive vainly to show Hume wrong, we find two replies which have gained wide popularity, the first primarily among philosophers, the second among scientists as well.

The first reply criticizes the assumption that rational justification can be only a matter of deduction from the evidence, pointing out that the normal use of expressions such as "rational," "reasonable," "based on good reasons," and so forth sanctions their application to statements referring to unexamined cases, and hence not deducible from accumulated evidence. This reply, although true, is, however, woefully inadequate. For not every statement which outstrips available evidence is reasonable, though some are. Outstripping the evidence is, to be sure, no bar to rationality, but neither does it guarantee rationality. If we are to meet the challenge posed, we must go on to formulate the specific criteria by which some inductions are justified as reasonable while others are rejected as unreasonable, though both groups outstrip the available evidence. Now it is likely that at least part of the reason why this further task has been slighted is that the adequacy of the second reply has largely been taken for granted.

This second reply, stated in one form by Hume himself, is that reasonable inductions are those which conform to past regularities. In modern dress, it appears as the popular assertion that predictions are made in accordance with general theories which have worked in the past. What leads us to make one particular prediction rather than its opposite is not its deducibility from evidence but rather its congruence with a generalization thoroughly in accord with all such evidence, and the correlative disconfirmation of the contrary generalization by the same evidence. (I shall refer to this hereafter as the "generalization formula.") Of course, if no relevant evidence is available to decide between a given generalization and its contrary, or if the available evidence is mixed, neither generalization will support a particular inductive conclusion. But it is only to be expected that every limited body of evidence will fail to decide between *some* generalization and its contrary, and hence that we will generally not be able to choose between *every* particular prediction and its opposite. It is sufficient, therefore, for a formulation of the criteria of induction to show how certain bodies of evidence enable us to decide between certain conflicting inductions. This the generalization formula seems to accomplish. For if there is evidence which consistently supports a given generalization, then the contrary generalization is *ipso facto* disconfirmed, and our particular inductive conclusions seem automatically selected for us. There are, of course, details to be taken care of, relating to such matters as the calculation of degrees of support which generalizations derive from past evidence, but, in principle, we have our answer to the challenge of induction.

Goodman's Refutation of the Generalization Formula

It is this sanguine estimate which has been thoroughly upset by Goodman's researches. Published in 1946 and 1947, his early papers in the philosophical journals dealt with a variety of interrelated questions: the nature of scientific law, of dispositional properties, of potentiality, of relevant conditions, of counterfactual judgments, of confirmation or induction.[2] They immediately aroused a storm of controversy. What made the papers so disturbing to the philosophic community was the fact that, while all these questions were shown to be intimately connected, Goodman's logically rigorous attempts to answer them without going around in circles ended in a big question mark. Appearing at a time when logicians had been making considerable progress in analyzing other aspects of scientific method, these results came as a shock. Goodman's investigations, it seemed, had sufficed to undermine all the usual formulas concerning the most basic concepts of the logic of science, but his repeated and ingenious efforts to supply a positive alternative had all turned out fruitless. In the philosophic discussions that followed, every attempt was made to skirt Goodman's disheartening results. They were declared unimportant for the practicing scientist. The initial questions were asserted to be insoluble, hence worthless. Many papers, on the other hand, proposed what seemed perfectly obvious solutions that turned out to be question-begging. Only a very few authors fully recognized the seriousness of the situation for the philosophy of science and tried to cope with it directly.[3]

In 1953, with the whole matter still very much unsettled, Goodman delivered a series of three lectures at the University of London, in which he again addressed himself to the problem. These lectures, together with his major 1946 paper, were then published together in his book *Fact, Fiction and Forecast,* which appeared in 1955.[1] Here Goodman essayed a new and positive approach to some of the major questions he had faced earlier. He did not offer his book as a final solution to all the original problems. He did, however, present a fresh approach, worked out with sufficient rigor to put discussion of it on a fruitful basis. But we are getting ahead of our story and must now return to see how Goodman's early work affected the theory of induction.

How did Goodman's early papers upset complacency with respect to the generalization formula (according to which we make those predictions congruent with generalizations thoroughly in accord with past evidence)? We may profitably approach this matter in the light of a passage from J. S. Mill's *Logic*. Although it does seem true that, for every particular induction we make, there is some generalization related to it in the manner described, Mill argues that generalizations which are equally well supported by available evidence vary in the sanction they provide for their respective particular inductions: "Again, there are cases in which we reckon with the most unfailing confidence upon uniformity, and other cases in which we do not count upon it at all. In some we feel complete assurance that the future will resemble the past, the unknown be precisely similar to the known. In others, however invariable may be the result obtained from the instances which have been observed, we draw from them no more than a very feeble presumption that the like result will hold in all other cases. . . . When a chemist announces the existence and properties of a newly discovered substance, if we confide in his accuracy, we feel assured that the conclusions he has arrived at will hold universally, though the induction be founded but on a single instance. . . . Now mark another case, and contrast it with this. Not all the instances which have been observed since the beginning of the world in support of the general proposition that all crows are black would be deemed a sufficient presumption of the truth of the proposition, to outweigh the testimony of one unexceptionable witness who should affirm that in some region of the earth not fully explored he had caught and examined a crow, and had found it to be grey. Why is a single instance, in some cases, sufficient for a complete induction, while in others myriads of concurring instances, without a single exception known or presumed, go such a very little way towards establishing an universal proposition?"[4]

And Goodman gives an analogous example when he writes: "That a given piece of copper conducts electricity increases the credibility of statements asserting that other pieces of copper conduct electricity, and thus confirms the hypothesis that all copper conducts electricity. But the fact that a given man now in this room is a third son does not increase the credibility of statements asserting that other men now in this room are third sons, and so does not confirm the hypothesis that all men now in this room are third sons. Yet in both cases our hypothesis is a generalization of the evidence statement. The difference is that in the former case the hypothesis is a *lawlike* statement; while in the latter case, the hypothesis is a merely contingent or accidental generality. Only a statement that is *lawlike*— regardless of its truth or falsity or its scientific importance—is capable of receiving confirmation from an instance of it; accidental statements are not" (*1*, p. 73).

But it is Goodman's further formulation of the problem that is crucial. For what has so far been shown is that, in addition to all credible particular inductions, generalization from the evidence also would select certain incredible ones. Now Goodman shows that among these incredible ones lie the very negations of our credible predictions concerning new cases. To apply his previous example, it is not merely that by generalization we selectively establish, in addition to the credible prediction that the next specimen of copper will conduct electricity, also the incredible one that the next present occupant of this room to be examined is a third son. Rather, we do not even establish that the next specimen of copper conducts electricity, for we can produce a generalization equally supported by the evidence and yielding the prediction that it does not. Or, putting this point in the form of a specific example, while the available evidence clearly supports:

> (S_1)   All specimens of copper conduct electricity.

and clearly disconfirms its contrary:

> (S_2)   All specimens of copper do not conduct electricity.

this is not sufficient to yield the particular induction concerning a new copper specimen c, to be examined:

> (S_3) c conducts electricity.

since the same evidence also and equally supports:

> (S_4)   All specimens of copper are either such that they have been examined prior to t and conduct electricity or have not been examined prior to t and do not conduct electricity.

while clearly disconfirming *its* contrary:

> (S_5)   All specimens of copper are either such that they have been examined prior to t and do not conduct electricity or have not been examined prior to t and do conduct electricity.

thus giving rise to the negate of S_3:

> (S_6) c does not conduct electricity.

if it is assumed true that:

> (S_7) c has not been examined prior to t.

For cases assumed new, then, the generalization formula selects no particular inductions at all. Merely to be told to choose our inductions by reference to theories which work relative to past evidence is hence to be given worthless advice. Nor does this situation improve with the accumulation of relevant data over time. For even if we later find S_6 false and add S_3 to our evidence, leading to a rejection of S_4, we do not thereby eliminate other hypotheses which are exactly like S_4 but which specify times later than t. Accordingly, no matter how much empirical data we have accumulated and no matter how many hypotheses like S_4 we have disconfirmed up to a given point in time, we still have (by the generalization formula) contradictory predictions for every case not yet included in our data. No matter how fast and how long we run, we find we are standing still at the starting line.

This predicament holds, of course, only for cases assumed to be new. Using our previous example, if neither S_7 nor its negate is assumed, then S_4 yields neither S_3 nor S_6, while if S_7 is assumed false, then S_4 coincides with S_1, implying S_3 rather than S_6. This is not surprising, however, since, if S_7 is false, c is identical with one of our original evidence cases, all of which are described by the evidence itself as conducting electricity; S_3 is thus implied deductively by the evidence at hand, given the general understanding that no cases have been omitted.

As soon as we leave the safe territory of examined cases, however, and try to deal with a new one, generalization yields contradictory inductions, deciding for neither. And, further, since the adoption of a generalization constitutes wholesale endorsement of appropriate particular inductions yet to be made, then even if we do not know about some specific case that it is a new one, our unrestricted adoption of generalizations gets us into trouble if we can make the assumption of novelty for at least one case within the appropriate range. Since, moreover, we patently do choose between contradictory inductions covering new cases, as well as between competing generalizations, the generalization formula must be wrong as a definition of our inductive choices. In our previous example, we obviously in practice would *not* hold S_4 equally supported by uniformly positive evidence supporting S_1, nor would we under such conditions have any hesitation in rejecting S_6 in favor of S_3. This clearly indicates that the generalization formula is not adequate to characterize our inductive behavior. We apparently employ additional, nonsyntactic criteria governing the extension of characteristics of our evidence-cases to other cases in induction.

These criteria of what Goodman calls "projectibility" select just those generalizations *capable* of receiving support from their positive instances and in turn sanctioning particular inductions. Projectible hypotheses may, in individual cases, fail to sanction any particular inductions (for example, in cases where we have two such hypotheses which conflict), but no nonprojectible hypothesis sanctions any induction, no matter how much positive support it has in the sense of the generalization formula. Goodman's problem is then to define projectibility, which is, in turn, needed to define induction. Since counterfactual judgments (for example, "If this salt, which has not in fact been put in water, had been put in water, it would have dissolved.") are, moreover, construable as resting upon just such generalizations as are projectible, that is, legitimately used for induction (in this case, "Every sample of salt, when put into water, dissolves."), and, furthermore, are themselves used to explain dispositional predicates, such as "is soluble," the definition of projectibility would throw light on these additional issues as well.

Attempts to Repair the Generalization Formula

It may be thought that the characterization of projectibility can be accomplished rather easily, simply by ruling out generalizations making reference to time. Recall that, in our above example, the trouble arose because the available evidence equally supported S_1 and S_4. But whereas the predicate "conducts electricity" makes no reference to time, the predicate "has been examined prior to t and conducts electricity or has not been examined prior to t and does not conduct electricity" makes reference to time of examination, and moreover can be explained, given such reference, in terms of the former predicate. It may further be pointed out that, without assumption S_7 (making reference to time of examination), no contradiction arises. It is only when we add S_7 to S_4 that S_6, which contradicts S_3, is derived. Why not use this, then, as a rule for eliminating S_4—namely, its requiring an additional assumption about time of examination to produce one of our contradictory inductions?

The answer is that the situation is easily reversed. Symbolize the predicate "conducts electricity" by C and the other, more complicated one, of S_4, by K; symbolize "has been examined before t" by E. It is true that, as the present argument maintains, K is then definable as

$(E$ and $C)$ or (not-E and not-C)

("has been examined before t and conducts electricity or has not been examined before t and does not conduct electricity"). However, it is also true that, taking K as our primitive idea, C is definable as

$(E$ and $K)$ or (not-E and not-K)

Furthermore, in the latter mode of description, S_1 would become:

(S_1')   All specimens of copper are either such that they have been examined prior to t and have the property K or have not been examined before t and do not have the property K.

while S_4 would become:

(S_4')   All specimens of copper have the property K.

To derive a parallel to S_3, we need to show that a new case c does not have the property K. This we can do if we now supplement S_1' with S_7 getting:

(S_3') c does not have the property K.

And we derive our contradictory particular induction, parallel to S_6, from S_4' without using S_7:

(S_6') c has the property K.

Thus, neither the employment by a hypothesis of a predicate referring to time nor its need of supplementation by S_7 in order to produce contradiction is a reliable clue with which to try to repair the generalization formula. Neither is, strictly speaking, any clue at all.

But perhaps the generalization formula is being applied too narrowly. We have, after all, been considering isolated statements in abstraction from other, relevant and well-established, hypotheses. In the above illustration we have, for instance, so far ignored the fact that available evidence also supports (by the generalization formula) a number of hypotheses of the following kind:

(S_8)   All specimens of iron conduct electricity.

(S_9)   All specimens of wood fail to conduct electricity.

and that these in turn lend credence to the following larger generalization:

(S_{10})   All classes of specimens of the same material are uniform with respect to electrical conductivity.

This larger generalization, having independent warrant and conflicting with S_4, serves thereby to discredit it, thus eliminating the troublesome induction S_6. In this way, it may be argued, the generalization formula can be rendered viable simply by taking account of a wider context of relevant hypotheses.

It takes but a moment of reflection, however, to see the weakness of such an argument. For, by reasoning analogous to that initially employed in introducing S_4, it will be seen that the very same evidence which supports S_8, S_9, and S_{10} also and equally (by the generalization formula itself) supports:

(S_8')   All specimens of iron have the property K.

(S_9')   All specimens of wood fail to have the property K.

(S_{10}')   All classes of specimens of the same material are uniform with respect to possession of the property K.

This latter large generalization, it will be noted, produces just the opposite effect from that of S_{10}. It conflicts with S_1, thereby, by analogous argument, discrediting it and eliminating the induction S_3 rather than S_6. Which of these conflicting large generalizations shall we now choose to take account of, S_{10} or S_{10}'? It is evident that we are again face to face with the very problem with which we started and that the proposal to repair the generalization formula by referring to other relevant hypotheses selected by it serves merely to postpone our perplexity. For these other hypotheses, in conflict themselves, are of no help unless we have some way of deciding which of them are projectible. In the face of difficulties such as these, *it becomes impossible to explain our choice of predictions by reference to whether or not they accord with generalizations which work,* no matter how widely the scope of this principle is construed.

Goodman's New Approach

Goodman's new idea is to utilize pragmatic or historical information that may fairly be assumed available at the time of induction, and to define projectibility in terms of such extra-syntactic information. The generalization formula, it will be recalled, rests on the notion of an *accordance* between a predictive generalization and the evidence by which it is supported, an accordance which can be determined solely by an examination of the generalization and its evidence-statements. In this sense, the relation of accordance is formal or syntactic (as the relation of deduction is), making use of no material or historical information. Goodman now suggests that, in order to specify the predictive generalizations we choose on the basis of given evidence, we need not restrict ourselves merely to the syntactic features of the statements before us. Rather, he makes the radical proposal that we use also the historical record of past predictions, and in particular, the *biographies* of the specific terms or predicates employed in previous inductions. Our theories, he suggests, are chosen not merely by virtue of the way they encompass the evidence, but also by virtue of the way the language in which they are couched accords with past linguistic practice.

His basic concept is "entrenchment," applicable to terms or predicates in the degree to which they (or their extensional equivalents, that is, words picking out the same class of elements, like "triangle" and "trilateral") have actually been previously employed in projection: in formulating inductions on the basis of positive, though incomplete evidence. To illustrate with our previous example, the predicate "has been examined prior to t and conducts electricity or has not been examined prior to t and does not conduct electricity" is less well entrenched than the predicate "conducts electricity," *because the class it singles out has been less often mentioned in formulating inductions.* The factor of actual historical employment of constituent predicates or their equivalents can thus be used to distinguish between hypotheses such as S_1 and S_4, which are equal in point of available positive instances. Goodman appeals, then, to "recurrences in the explicit use of terms as well as to recurrent features of what is observed," suggesting that the features which we fasten on in induction are those "for which we have adopted predicates that we have habitually projected" (*1*, pp. 96, 97). With this idea as a guide, Goodman first defines presumptively projectible hypotheses. Next, he defines an initial projectibility index for these hypotheses. Finally, he defines degree of projectibility by means of the initial projectibility index as modified by indirect information embodied in what he calls "over-hypotheses," *which must themselves qualify as presumptively projectible*. The latter use made of indirect evidence is worked out with great care and detail and is of independent theoretical interest.

Roughly, degree of projectibility is to represent what Goodman earlier called "lawlikeness" (that is, that property which, together with truth, defines scientific laws) and constitutes therefore not only an explanation but also a refinement of the latter. With the explanation of lawlikeness, Goodman suggests that the general problem of dispositions is solved. For this general problem is to define the *relationship* between "manifest" or observable predicates (for example, "dissolves") and their dispositional counterparts (for example, "is soluble") and manifest predicates may now be construed as related by true lawlike or projectible hypotheses to their dispositional mates. Other problems, such as the nature of "empirical possibility" are also illuminated by this approach, and some light is thrown on the difficult question of counterfactual judgments which, however, still resists full interpretation.

The most natural objection to Goodman's new approach is that it provides no explanation of entrenchment itself. In using this notion to explain induction, however, Goodman does not at all rule out a further explanation of why certain predicates as a matter of fact become entrenched while others do not. His purpose is to formulate clear criteria, in terms of available information, that will single out those generalizations in accordance with which we make predictions. The strong point of his treatment is that his criteria do indeed seem effective in dealing with the numerous cases he considers.

A possible misconception concerning the use of "entrenchment" as a basic idea is that it may lead to the ruling out of unfamiliar predicates, thus stultifying the growth of scientific language. Unfamiliar predicates may, however, be well entrenched if some of their extensionally equivalent mates have been often projected, and they may acquire entrenchment indirectly through "inheritance" from "parent predicates"—that is, other predicates related to them in a special way outlined in detail in Goodman's discussion (*1*, p. 105). Furthermore, Goodman's criteria provide methods for evaluating *hypotheses*, not predicates, so that wholesale elimination of new scientific terms is never sanctioned in his treatment.

As remarked previously, the critical discussion of Goodman's new approach is still in its early stages.[5] His formulations will undoubtedly undergo further refinement and revision with continuing study, but even in their present form they will have contributed much toward putting important questions in the philosophy of science on a scientific basis.

Harvard University

NOTES

1. N. Goodman, *Fact, Fiction and Forecast* (Cambridge, Mass.: Harvard Univ. Press, 1955).

2. N. Goodman, "A Query on Confirmation," *J. Philosophy 43* (1946), 383; "The Problem of Counterfactual Conditionals," *J. Philosophy 44* (1947), 113.

3. See in particular R. Carnap., "On the Application of Inductive Logic," *Philosophy and Phenomenological Research 8* (1947), 133; N. Goodman, "On Infirmities of Confirmation Theory," *Philosophy and Phenomenological Research 8* (1947), 149; R. Carnap, "Reply to Nelson Goodman," *Philosophy and Phenomenological Research 8* (1947), 461.

4. J. S. Mill, *A System of Logic* (London: Longmans, 1843: new impression, 1947), III, III, 3.205.

5. See, in this connection, the long study of *Fact, Fiction and Forecast* by J. C. Cooley, *J. Philosophy 54* (1957), 293, and Goodman's reply, *J. Philosophy 54* (1957), 531.

Luck, License, and Lingo

2

Joseph Ullian

Feelings of doubt and queasiness are common enough in philosophy. They are practically prerequisites for its pursuit. And when you manage to suppress them in one place, with regard to one problem, they are extraordinarily likely to turn up again not far away. So to do philosophy you must at times be something of a diagnostician, exploring the philosophical geography of your own anxieties, with the idea being not so much to remove them as to have them located, parceled, and appropriated for constructive purposes.

Now the present exploration takes Goodman's *Fact, Fiction and Forecast*[1] as its home base, with the problem at hand that of providing justification for inductive inference. This is a problem which, in one form or another, has long been with us, and I shall argue that if, after digesting Goodman's contributions and coming face to face with his "new riddle of induction," one *still* has the gnawing feeling that there is more to be said, then one's anxieties will have shifted to a new location.

Goodman's initial joust with the problem:

> How do we justify a *deduction?* Plainly, by showing that it conforms to the general rules of deductive inference. . . . Rules and particular inferences alike are justified by being brought into agreement with each other. *A rule is amended if it yields an inference we are unwilling to accept; an inference is rejected if it violates a rule we are unwilling to amend* . . . and in the agreement achieved lies the only justification needed for either. All this applies equally well to induction. . . . Predictions are justified if they conform to valid canons of induction; and the canons are valid if they accurately codify accepted inductive practice.[2]

So what is called for in the justification of deductive or inductive inference is codification, codification of the kind of inference in question. But these appear to be theses of different orders. If we draw the traditional

---

From *The Journal of Philosophy,* Vol. LVIII, No. 23 (November 9, 1961): 731–738. Reprinted by permission of *The Journal of Philosophy* and the author.

distinction, we might say that deductive inference is essentially organizational, tells us "nothing new," whereas induction purports to generate fresh knowledge. Now it is one thing to hold that individual attempts at organization stand or fall with our general intuitions about how knowledge may be organized (made explicit in deductive rules). We may, after all, organize our data however we wish, and all that is demanded is that our statement of organizational principles accurately reflect our practice, that they mesh together. But it is something else again to maintain that we may go beyond the evidence provided that we do so in accordance with summary statements of how we find ourselves inclined to go beyond the evidence. This appeal to codification has a more unpleasantly circular feel than the other. We seem, as it were, to be owed less freedom in deciding what predictions to make than in choosing which of our facts to redigest.

In so far as this comes to an argument for Goodman's view on deduction (which I shall support elsewhere and cease to worry about here) and against his view on induction, I shall confide that I am unconvinced by it, partly, but only partly, because I am not entirely happy with the "traditional distinction" involved. But accepting the distinction as it stands for a moment, it might be pointed out that we should have expected to have more lingering qualms in the inductive case, if only because we presumably had more qualms there to begin with. Deductive inference never really seemed in need of support or justification in the first place, though saying exactly why is far from easy.

There have been numerous attempts to justify inductive inference. D. C. Williams's argument from the statistical syllogism[3] has long fascinated me. A population is as likely to resemble a good-sized sample of it as a good-sized sample is to resemble the population. And elementary statistics provides us with reasons for saying that this is quite likely indeed, though "likely" in a sense which Williams never quite gets all the thorns out of. Then there is the Peirce notion of induction as self-correcting, more recently developed and defended by von Wright, who concludes that "a reasoned policy for purposes of prediction and generalization is necessarily equivalent to an *inductive* policy. If we wish to call reasoned policies *better* than not-reasoned ones, it follows further that induction is of necessity the *best* way of foretelling the future."[4] So Williams claims to show that the future, or the unexamined cases, are all but bound to resemble the past, or the examined ones. And von Wright, construed a bit liberally, argues that no policy can be more reasonable than one which anticipates such resemblances. But if we look the new riddle of induction in the eye, it must follow that neither the arguments cited nor any other of their kind can be of any help to us, for the crucial question always remains: *resemble in which respects?*

For Goodman shows that if we are sufficiently ingenious in defining new predicates, any amount of evidence for one empirical hypothesis can stand equally well as evidence for a hypothesis conflicting with it. Give me reasons for your prediction and I can twist them, by impeccable logic, into reasons for a contrary prediction. You say the next emerald will be green, I say it will be grue,[5] and we use the same evidence and the same predictive principles. Now to arrive at this unwelcome result we must be prepared to employ unusual predicates. Those needed for the generation of conflicts will in general be foreign to our language—and to any other, until we invent them. But Goodman argues that there can be no a priori grounds (to put it baldly, and in terms at which he might demur) for distinguishing predicates that are troublesome from those which are trouble-free, for marking off the artificial or *positional* predicates from the genuine or *qualitative*. Now I want to note that even if one could explicate perfectly the idea of a genuine or purely qualitative or *projectible* (from Goodman) predicate, it would be of no help whatsoever for purposes of resurrecting a priori justifications of inductive inferences or policies. For there is no law of logic (deductive *or* inductive) according to which a distinction may be employed arbitrarily in an argument just because it has been drawn with clarity and precision. If one were troubled initially by Hume's problem as it has come to be understood, I cannot see why one should be much less troubled to learn that the legitimate inductive inferences can be segregated from the illegitimate by application of the notion of qualitative predicate. And that version of Hume's problem is certainly the object of Williams's attack and presumably the object of the Pierce–von Wright militations. I take the upshot to be that a-priorist thrusts at the inductive dragon cannot provide justification for any inductive inference with actual content, can justify no more than the form that inductive arguments take, which, as I see it, is to justify nothing at all.

But Goodman, as we know, is not concerned with the old form of Hume's problem. For him "the problem of induction is not a problem of demonstration but a problem of defining the difference between valid and invalid predictions."[6] To this end he outlines a theory of projection, whose largest task it is to weed out the spurious hypotheses with cooked-up predicates that gave rise to the new riddle. Here the right, or projectible, predicates turn out to be essentially the well-*entrenched* ones, those with long histories of use. (The theory is rather more elaborate than this sketchy reminder of its content.) Thus the respects in which we may validly predict resemblance of future cases to past ones are mainly those identifiable by predicates with decent backgrounds.

This allows an explication of 'valid prediction' which uses none of the many philosophical modes toward which Goodman has expressed discomfort. 'Entrenched' is a manifest predicate, not a dispositional one. And Goodman anticipates the reaction likely from those whose concern has been with older forms of the problem: "The reason why only the right predicates happen so luckily to have become well entrenched is just that the well entrenched predicates have thereby become the right ones."[7]

This is where I want to stop and reflect. The bona fide predicates are those which are much with us, and they are bona fide *because* they are much with us. Of course, had we accepted, with Goodman, the dictum that explication was all we wanted, we should not have found ourselves talking in this way, and I suspect that Goodman says what he says in this connection only to throw a bone to those who are not wholly convinced — or, perhaps, to tease them a bit. Nonetheless, the feeling of relief may not yet be complete. What can we say?

Surely one of the most exciting intellectual spectacles available to us is the history of physical science. You can be intrigued and fascinated in any number of ways when you read of the growth and development of physical theory. Now what I find overwhelmingly remarkable in scientific history is the extent to which what might be called extrapolations, many of them mammoth, have been successful. The contributions of Newton, Huygens, Maxwell, to name only three, were in large measure made possible by their willingness to apply ideas known to be useful in one domain in other areas. Use of analogy for extension of one's knowledge always has, in essence, this character. You have concepts, equations, or theories which help to organize for you one class of phenomena, and although there is no logical guarantee whatsoever that they should be of service outside that class, again and again they turn out to be so. Of course it isn't that simple. There is always a problem of *how* to extrapolate, and for every instance of what I call successful extrapolation in the history of science there must have been thousands that failed to bear fruit. And there are cases where extrapolations almost beg to be made, then turn out not to work. The failure of Newtonian physics to apply to the microscopic realm strikes me as a case of exactly this kind. On the one hand, why should it have applied here, in a realm beyond that of its evidence? Yet it was most surprising that it failed to. We have come to have a very great confidence that concepts which help us in one area of our experience will turn out to be extendible to other areas, and on a very large scale. Indeed, having learned that the notion of indeterminacy is useful in explaining the phenomena of quanta, those who take seriously the old free-will issue have generated immense hopes (and rather uncontrolled arguments) to the effect that such a notion must apply in the field of human action. I certainly don't want to talk about that here, but I want to urge that whatever plausibility extrapolative arguments, on either grand or minute scale, may have is reinforced tremendously by our backlog of successes with such arguments. Now clearly I am not offering a precise description of this extrapolative phenomenon, much less an explanation of it. But I am saying that one can come to feel that there is a very remarkable phenomenon in evidence here, one which couldn't have been counted on, to put the matter in what is perhaps a revoltingly cosmic way.

And I feel much the same about our simpler concepts, even those as simple as concepts of colors or hues. Here it is not so much that there is out-and-out extrapolation from one domain to another. It is that the notions of these basic properties that we learn to identify (a clause which masks a multitude of problems) are so uniformly of use in describing and organizing our experience. Lest there be misunderstanding, I remark that I am saying the strongest thing that I could be taken to be saying. I am saying that I find it remarkable that we get any mileage at all out of our concepts, that we have any use whatsoever for general terms (to import an expression that I prefer to 'predicates').

How is it that general terms turn out to be of use for us? Now it is a brute and happy fact that human beings are able to learn, ultimately by ostension, how to use such terms. We, and with us other creatures, are able to achieve *recognition* of what the mythmakers have reified as properties. (Admittedly it may be a happy myth; some of our most noteworthy philosophy is happy myth.) But you can explain what this ability consists in only up to a point. Any explanation of how we learn to apply a specified general term will itself make use of general terms, which—far from being a defect—is reflective of a basic feature of language and a *sine qua non* of it (the need for general terms or their equivalents in saying *anything*). You can point out that we see a few examples of blue things and we catch on, if judiciously taught, how and when to apply 'blue,' but what more can you say? You certainly explain nothing if you say that we learn to apply 'blue' to blue things. And you only push the problem further back if you say that we learn to apply 'blue' to things sufficiently similar in color to the initial specimens. For in what does similarity in color consist? Somewhere you must terminate the attempt at explanation and admit that it simply *is* possible to learn the use of general terms, and possible in such a way that individuals can achieve agreement in their use. I think there is a natural temptation to give too much credit to nature for all this, as if objects and simple properties appeared for us already labeled, and our only job was to read the labels (or as if they carried membership cards for exclusive clubs known as *natural kinds*). Concepts and the employment of general terms depend upon classifications, and, as I like to put it, one class is as good as another as far as logic is concerned. Yet from the vast number of theoretically available alternatives we mark off a relatively small number of (open-ended) classes, which are roughly the same for me as for you, and in terms of them we find it possible to make sense out of our experience, out of the "buzzing, booming confusion." I am not about to heap on us the credit that I have begrudged nature. For it is clear that we find it quite natural and immediate to take certain relationships as instances of similarity and identity, and these already begin to mark out the classes that we choose—classes which, looked at the other way round, are themselves definitive of what is to count as a similarity or an identity. I suppose this is all very *extensional*. But such an orientation is necessary if we are to dig under, for the moment, the topsoil in which our conceptual and linguistic shrubbery grows. One who sees no need for such digging is presumably satisfied with an *intensional* account of the topsoil's richness. To be so satisfied is to have one less problem to face, but it is also to be denied here the occasion for an attitude of wonderment.

If one feels an explanation coming on it will likely be an evolutionary one. You can say that our ability to mark off classes and gain concepts that can serve us has developed much as our species has developed. Or you can contrapose and say that were it not for the evolvement of such a knack we should have had no language, no conceptual power, and very little chance for survival through these many centuries. Lewis gives us something of this kind when he says:

> Our concepts are devised with purpose to catch the significant, the subject of meaningful generalization, at whatever level and in whatever way we may. When particular concepts fail, we merely abandon them . . . in favor of corrected ones, which take cognizance of, and include the ground of, our previous failure. That conception *in general* should be invalid, is quite impossible. The attempt to envisage an experience or state of affairs such that *every* attempt to discover stabilities must fail, is the attempt to conceive the inconceivable.[8]

(Note that *discovery* of stabilities already presupposes conception.) Of course Lewis's sense of 'impossible' is the pragmatic one: *impossible,* given that we are here and talking about it. And if we weren't, there would be no problem for us. This probably cuts as deep as it is safe to go, as deep as there is use for going. But that needn't mean that it is fully satisfying.

We do quite well at predicting, and enjoy physical theories of enormous scope. These happy facts I find remarkable. Conceptualization and language I find remarkable as well. And, in a sense imitative of the mathematician's, I find the first feeling reducible to the second. That we have predicates that are successfully projectible is, so to speak, a special case of our having any use for predicates at all. What bothers me most about conventional treatments of inductive inference is that they are so much about inference. A class-and-property logic has been handed down to us, and all too uncritically we find ourselves employing it and the schematization to which it lends itself, all too insensitive to the thought that the problems we generate are in large measure problems regarding the applicability of the logic, the schematization, itself. Of course you can't question everything at once, and in philosophy you keep on finding that just the things you want most to question can't sensibly be questioned at all. Nonetheless, it seems to me that whatever restlessness we might still feel when taking Hume's problem, old style, seriously, might best be treated by turning our attention toward the origin and use of language in its most basic dimensions. We might thus achieve at least a parceling of our perplexities.

I have one other misgiving about conventional treatments of induction, and it is not new. It is that the examples to which our attention is directed are so frequently of such simple form. We are encouraged to believe that, once we have dealt with the simple cases, those which are more complex will fall into place, that they proceed by the same logic. Now what is to count as the *same logic* is up to us to decide; we may mark out a class of patterns of inference however we choose. But treatment of the highly sophisticated, multiply nested inferences of mature science *or mature common sense* may call for rather different techniques from treatment of simpler cases. I note only that appropriate attention to the actual functioning of language, both plain and specialized, is called for in this too.

Back to Goodman's "the well entrenched predicates have thereby become the right ones." Could an essentially different set (not of predicates, but of extensions or concepts) have served as well—have served better? But this is like asking how well off we might have been with a basically different conceptual scheme, if you will allow me that phrase, or a radically different language. And almost any answer except a shrug of the shoulders seems out of place, though one might be safe enough in admitting that logic seems not to demand precisely our conceptual structure for the organization of what we call our experience. Perhaps it would not be too far from Goodman's meaning to read his dictum as "We use the predicates (and concepts) we do because they are the ones we have."

Now to pick a quarrel in my last paragraph. Williams chides, "If there is any puzzle about induction, I fear, it is how we manage to go wrong as often as we do."[9] I think we deserve more credit, that the entire fabric of our language is requisite for our doing as well as we do. But as for the possibility of such a language, as for the question "Why not nothing?" I can only answer: because we are very much in luck.

Postscript (1992)

Goodman first broached the new riddle of induction in his 1946 paper "A Query on Confirmation"; the first edition of *Fact, Fiction and Forecast* came nine years later. In the early days many of his critics took the puzzle to be an annoying curiosity. Mostly they tried to deflect it by appealing to some principle that ruled out the troublesome inferences from the start, typically by holding that Goodman's new predicates were substandard. These predicates were said to be positional or disjunctive or nonqualitative, or they required things to undergo mysterious change, or their application hinged on the use of unintelligible powers. But eventually it began to sink in that this puzzle was resistant to such attacks and was not going to go away easily. It became clear to almost everyone that the old worries about induction— the purely logical ones—were the ones that had to be abandoned. The hope that there might be a way to justify inductions by attention to their form alone was seen to be utterly vain. Treatments of induction that had made no provision for what happens when contrived predicates are invoked were realized, *ipso facto,* to be seriously defective.

Respect for Goodman's point that "The problem of induction is not a problem of demonstration but a problem of defining the difference between valid and invalid projections"[10] has become second nature to philosophers by now. Surprisingly, a plea to the same end can be found as far back as a 1903 lecture by Peirce: "The problem of how an accidental regularity can be distinguished from an essential one is precisely the problem of inductive logic."[11] Peirce did not have examples like Goodman's in mind, though, and neither did Peirce offer any theory to ground the distinction. He relied, rather, on the likes of his "great rule of predesignation"[12] to steer us away from the accidental generalizations and toward the confirmable ones.[13]

Goodman has offered us a theory. It has undergone some adjustments since it was first formulated, but its main thrust has remained the same: it looks to entrenchment of extensions. I don't think it is too much to say that most of the recent arguments against Goodman's position consist in disagreements about the details of his theory of projection. Even Zabludowski, whose attacks on Goodman's theory have seemed especially fierce, has basically disagreed with Goodman on just the issue of whether the requisite division of predicates can be drawn on the basis of their extensions alone, and without consideration of their intensions. It is a major disagreement, all right, but even it may be seen as a disagreement from within a partially shared perspective.

The theory of projectibility awaits further sharpening. As has been emphasized, the theory offered so far is only qualitative, not quantitative. It "is only a first step toward an inductive theory."[14] Its central claims purport to tell us something about what principles we follow when we extrapolate from our evidence, what principles we rely on in selecting our hypotheses. In offering such principles I see Goodman to be doing philosophy after the fashion of Hume, to be telling us how we reason about "matters of fact." Like Hume, Goodman is fleshing out our picture of what is involved in human understanding.

In its baldest form, what Goodman gives us can be regarded as a companion to a well-known principle of Quine. As Scheffler put it, "Whereas projectibility involves a certain principle of conservation with respect to predicates (or their extensions), Quine refers, in effect, to a principle of conservation applicable to whole systems of statements."[15]

Goodman's writing on induction leans toward his doctrine of irrealism. It emphasizes that *how* we regard what we countenance, how we classify— what is to count as identity or similarity and what as difference—is in important ways up to us. What is to be grouped together is determined neither by logic nor by the nature of things. The scope of Goodman's irrealism is much broader than any lessons he teaches us when writing on induction, but these underlying observations may be seen to point the way.

That attitude of wonderment that I mentioned some thirty years ago is still very much with me. It was wonder at the fact that we should have any use for general terms, that we should be able to mark off classes with whose help we can make sense of our experience. My sense that we are very much in luck for all this remains undiminished.

Washington University

NOTES

1. Nelson Goodman, *Fact, Fiction and Forecast* (Cambridge, Mass.: Harvard, 1955).

2. *Ibid.*, 66–67.

3. Donald Williams, *The Ground of Induction* (Cambridge, Mass.: Harvard, 1957).

4. Georg von Wright, *The Logical Problem of Induction,* 2nd ed. (Oxford: Basil Blackwell, 1957), 174.

5. Goodman, *op. cit.,* 74 ff.

6. *Ibid.,* 68.

7. *Ibid.,* 98.

8. Clarence Irving Lewis, *Mind and the World-Order* (New York: Scribner's, 1929), 385.

9. Williams, *op. cit.,* 167.

10. Nelson Goodman, *Fact, Fiction and Forecast,* 4th ed. (Cambridge, Massachusetts, and London, England: Harvard University Press, 1983), 65.

11. Charles Hartshorne and Paul Weiss, eds., *Collected Papers of Charles Sanders Peirce* (Cambridge, Massachusetts: Harvard University Press, 1931–1935) 3.605.

12. *Op. Cit.,* 5.584.

13. I make this point in my forthcoming paper "On Peirce on Induction," to appear in *Proceedings of the Charles S. Peirce Sesquicentennial International Congress,* Kenneth Ketner, ed.

14. Joseph Ullian and Nelson Goodman, "Bad Company: A Reply to Mr. Zabludowski and Others," *J. Philosophy 72,* 5 (March 13, 1975), 142.

15. Israel Scheffler, *The Anatomy of Inquiry* (Indianapolis: Hackett, 1981; first published 1963), 320.

Natural Kinds

W. V. Quine

3

What tends to confirm an induction? This question has been aggravated on the one hand by Hempel's puzzle of the nonblack nonravens,[1] and exacerbated on the other by Goodman's puzzle of the grue emeralds.[2] I shall begin my remarks by relating the one puzzle to the other, and the other to an innate flair that we have for natural kinds. Then I shall devote the rest of the paper to reflections on the nature of this notion of natural kinds and its relation to science.

Hempel's puzzle is that just as each black raven tends to confirm the law that all ravens are black, so each green leaf, being a nonblack nonraven, should tend to confirm the law that all nonblack things are nonravens, that is, again, that all ravens are black. What is paradoxical is that a green leaf should count toward the law that all ravens are black.

Goodman propounds his puzzle by requiring us to imagine that emeralds, having been identified by some criterion other than color, are now being examined one after another and all up to now are found to be green. Then he proposes to call anything 'grue' that is examined today or earlier and found to be green or is not examined before tomorrow and is blue. Should we expect the first one examined tomorrow to be green, because all examined up to now were green? But all examined up to now were also grue; so why not expect the first one tomorrow to be grue, and therefore blue?

The predicate 'green,' Goodman says,[3] is *projectible;* 'grue' is not. He says this by way of putting a name to the problem. His step toward solution is his doctrine of what he calls entrenchment,[4] which I shall touch on later. Meanwhile the terminological point is simply that projectible predicates are predicates ζ and η whose shared instances all do count, for whatever reason, toward confirmation of $\ulcorner$All ζ are $\eta\urcorner$.

Now I propose assimilating Hempel's puzzle to Goodman's by inferring

From *Essays in Honor of Carl G. Hempel,* edited by Nicholas Rescher et al., 1–23, Dordrecht: D. Reidel, 1970. Copyright 1970 in The Netherlands by D. Reidel Publishing Company, Dordrecht. Reprinted by permission of Kluwer Academic Publishers and the author.

from Hempel's that the complement of a projectible predicate need not be projectible. 'Raven' and 'black' are projectible; a black raven does count toward 'All ravens are black.' Hence a black raven counts also, indirectly, toward 'All nonblack things are nonravens,' since this says the same thing. But a green leaf does not count toward 'All nonblack things are nonravens,' nor, therefore, toward 'All ravens are black'; 'nonblack' and 'nonraven' are not projectible. 'Green' and 'leaf' are projectible, and the green leaf counts toward 'All leaves are green' and 'All green things are leaves'; but only a black raven can confirm 'All ravens are black,' the complements not being projectible.

If we see the matter in this way, we must guard against saying that a statement $\ulcorner$All ζ are $\eta\urcorner$ is lawlike only if ζ and η are projectible. 'All nonblack things are nonravens' is a law despite its nonprojectible terms, since it is equivalent to 'All ravens are black.' Any statement is lawlike that is logically *equivalent* to $\ulcorner$All ζ are $\eta\urcorner$ for some projectible ζ and η.[5]

Having concluded that the complement of a projectible predicate need not be projectible, we may ask further whether there is *any* projectible predicate whose complement is projectible. I can conceive that there is not, when complements are taken strictly. We must not be misled by limited or relative complementation; 'male human' and 'nonmale human' are indeed both projectible.

To get back now to the emeralds, why do we expect the next one to be green rather than grue? The intuitive answer lies in similarity, however subjective. Two green emeralds are more similar than two grue ones would be if only one were green. Green things, or at least green emeralds, are a kind.[6] A projectible predicate is one that is true of all and only the things of a kind. What makes Goodman's example a puzzle, however, is the dubious scientific standing of a general notion of similarity, or of kind.

The dubiousness of this notion is itself a remarkable fact. For surely there is nothing more basic to thought and language than our sense of similarity; our sorting of things into kinds. The usual general term, whether a common noun or a verb or an adjective, owes its generality to some resemblance among the things referred to. Indeed, learning to use a word depends on a double resemblance: first, a resemblance between the present circumstances and past circumstances in which the word was used, and second, a phonetic resemblance between the present utterance of the word and past utterances of it. And every reasonable expectation depends on resemblance of circumstances, together with our tendency to expect similar causes to have similar effects.

The notion of a kind and the notion of similarity or resemblance seem to be variants or adaptations of a single notion. Similarity is immediately definable in terms of kind; for things are similar when they are two of a kind. The very words for 'kind' and 'similar' tend to run in etymologically cognate pairs. Cognate with 'kind' we have 'akin' and 'kindred.' Cognate with 'like' we have 'ilk.' Cognate with 'similar' and 'same' and 'resemble' there are *'sammeln'* and 'assemble,' suggesting a gathering into kinds.

We cannot easily imagine a more familiar or fundamental notion than this, or a notion more ubiquitous in its applications. On this score it is like the notions of logic: like identity, negation, alternation, and the rest. And yet, strangely, there is something logically repugnant about it. For we are baffled when we try to relate the general notion of similarity significantly to logical terms. One's first hasty suggestion might be to say that things are similar when they have all, or most, or many properties in common. Or, trying to be less vague, one might try defining comparative similarity—'a is more similar to b than to c'—as meaning that a shares more properties with b than with c. But any such course only reduces our problem to the unpromising task of settling what to count as a property.

The nature of the problem of what to count as a property can be seen by turning for a moment to set theory. Things are viewed as going together into sets in any and every combination, describable and indescribable. Any two things are joint members of any number of sets. Certainly then we cannot define 'a is more similar to b than to c' to mean that a and b belong jointly to more sets than a and c do. If properties are to support this line of definition where sets do not, it must be because properties do not, like sets, take things in every random combination. It must be that properties are shared only by things that are significantly similar. But properties in such a sense are no clearer than kinds. To start with such a notion of property, and define similarity on that basis, is no better than accepting similarity as undefined.

The contrast between properties and sets which I suggested just now must not be confused with the more basic and familiar contrast between properties, as intensional, and sets as extensional. Properties are intensional in that they may be counted as distinct properties even though wholly coinciding in respect of the things that have them. There is no call to reckon kinds as intensional. Kinds can be seen as sets, determined by their members. It is just that not all sets are kinds.

If similarity is taken simple-mindedly as a yes-or-no affair, with no degrees, then there is no containing of kinds within broader kinds. For, as remarked, similarity now simply means belonging to some one same kind. If all colored things comprise a kind, then all colored things count as similar, and the set of all red things is too narrow to count as a kind. If on the other hand the set of all red things counts as a kind, then colored things do not all count as similar, and the set of all colored things is too broad to count as a kind. We cannot have it both ways. Kinds can, however, overlap; the red things can comprise one kind, the round another.

When we move up from the simple dyadic relation of similarity to the more serious and useful triadic relation of comparative similarity, a correlative change takes place in the notion of kind. Kinds come to admit now not only of overlapping but also of containment one in another. The set of all red things and the set of all colored things can now both count as kinds; for all colored things can now be counted as resembling one another more than some things do, even though less, on the whole, than red ones do.

At this point, of course, our trivial definition of similarity as sameness of kind breaks down; for almost any two things could count now as common members of some broad kind or other, and anyway we now want to define comparative or triadic similarity. A definition that suggests itself is this: *a* is more similar to *b* than to *c* when *a* and *b* belong jointly to more kinds than *a* and *c* do. But even this works only for finite systems of kinds.

The notion of kind and the notion of similarity seemed to be substantially one notion. We observed further that they resist reduction to less dubious notions, as of logic or set theory. That they at any rate be definable each in terms of the other seems little enough to ask. We just saw a somewhat limping definition of comparative similarity in terms of kinds. What now of the converse project, definition of kind in terms of similarity?

One may be tempted to picture a kind, suitable to a comparative similarity relation, as any set which is 'qualitatively spherical' in this sense: it takes in exactly the things that differ less than so-and-so much from some central norm. If without serious loss of accuracy we can assume that there are one or more actual things (*paradigm cases*) that nicely exemplify the desired norm, and one or more actual things (*foils*) that deviate just barely too much to be counted into the desired kind at all, then our definition is easy: *the kind with paradigm a and foil b* is the set of all the things to which *a* is more similar than *a* is to *b*. More generally, then, a set may be said to be a *kind* if and only if there are *a* and *b,* known or unknown, such that the set is the kind with paradigm *a* and foil *b*.

If we consider examples, however, we see that this definition does not give us what we want as kinds. Thus take red. Let us grant that a central shade of red can be picked as norm. The trouble is that the paradigm cases, objects in just that shade of red, can come in all sorts of shapes, weights, sizes, and smells. Mere degree of overall similarity to any one such paradigm case will afford little evidence of degree of redness, since it will depend also on shape, weight, and the rest. If our assumed relation of comparative similarity were just comparative chromatic similarity, then our paradigm-and-foil definition of kind would indeed accommodate redkind. What the definition will not do is distill purely chromatic kinds from mixed similarity.

A different attempt, adapted from Carnap, is this: a set is a kind if all its members are more similar to one another than they all are to any one thing outside the set. In other words, each nonmember differs more from some member than that member differs from any member. However, as Goodman showed in a criticism of Carnap,[7] this construction succumbs to what Goodman calls the difficulty of imperfect community. Thus consider the set of all red round things, red wooden things, and round wooden things. Each member of this set resembles each other member somehow: at least in being red, or in being round, or in being wooden, and perhaps in two or all three of these respects or others. Conceivably, moreover, there is no one thing outside the set that resembles every member of the set to even the least of these degrees. The set then meets the proposed definition of kind. Yet surely it is not what anyone means by a kind. It admits yellow croquet balls and red rubber balls while excluding yellow rubber balls.

The relation between similarity and kind, then, is less clear and neat than could be wished. Definition of similarity in terms of kind is halting, and definition of kind in terms of similarity is unknown. Still the two notions are in an important sense correlative. They vary together. If we reassess something a as less similar to b than to c, where it had counted as more similar to b than to c, surely we will correspondingly permute a, b, and c in respect of their assignment to kinds; and conversely.

I have stressed how fundamental the notion of similarity or of kind is to our thinking, and how alien to logic and set theory. I want to go on now to say more about how fundamental these notions are to our thinking, and something also about their nonlogical roots. Afterward I want to bring out how the notion of similarity or of kind changes as science progresses. I shall suggest that it is a mark of maturity of a branch of science that the notion of similarity or kind finally dissolves, so far as it is relevant to that branch of science. That is, it ultimately submits to analysis in the special terms of that branch of science and logic.

For deeper appreciation of how fundamental similarity is, let us observe more closely how it figures in the learning of language. One learns by *ostension* what presentations to call yellow; that is, one learns by hearing the word applied to samples. All he has to go on, of course, is the similarity of further cases to the samples. Similarity being a matter of degree, one has to learn by trial and error how reddish or brownish or greenish a thing can be and still be counted yellow. When he finds he has applied the word too far out, he can use the false cases as samples to the contrary; and then he can proceed to guess whether further cases are yellow or not by considering whether they are more similar to the in-group or the out-group. What one thus uses, even at this primitive stage of learning, is a fully functioning sense of similarity, and relative similarity at that: a is more similar to b than to c.

All these delicate comparisons and shrewd inferences about what to call yellow are, in Sherlock Holmes's terminology, elementary. Mostly the process is unconscious. It is the same process by which an animal learns to respond in distinctive ways to his master's commands or other discriminated stimulations.

The primitive sense of similarity that underlies such learning has, we saw, a certain complexity of structure: a is more similar to b than to c. Some people have thought that it has to be much more complex still: that it depends irreducibly on *respects,* thus similarity in color, similarity in shape, and so on. According to this view, our learning of yellow by ostension would have depended on our first having been told or somehow apprised that it was going to be a question of color. Now hints of this kind are a great help, and in our learning we often do depend on them. Still one would like to be able to show that a single general standard of similarity, but of course comparative similarity, is all we need, and that respects can be abstracted afterward. For instance, suppose the child has learned of a yellow ball and block that they count as yellow, and of a red ball and block that they do not, and now he has to decide about a yellow cloth. Presumably he will find the cloth more similar to the yellow ball and to the yellow block than to the red ball or red block; and he will not have needed any prior schooling in colors and respects. Carnap undertook to show long ago how some respects, such as color, could by an ingenious construction be derived from a general similarity notion;[8] however, this development is challenged, again, by Goodman's difficulty of imperfect community.

A standard of similarity is in some sense innate. This point is not against empiricism; it is a commonplace of behavioral psychology. A response to a red circle, if it is rewarded, will be elicited again by a pink ellipse more readily than by a blue triangle; the red circle resembles the pink ellipse more than the blue triangle. Without some such prior spacing of qualities, we could never acquire a habit; all stimuli would be equally alike and equally different. These spacings of qualities, on the part of men and other animals, can be explored and mapped in the laboratory by experiments in conditioning and extinction.[9] Needed as they are for all learning, these distinctive spacings cannot themselves all be learned; some must be innate.

If then I say that there is an innate standard of similarity, I am making a condensed statement that can be interpreted, and truly interpreted, in behavioral terms. Moreover, in this behavioral sense it can be said equally of other animals that they have an innate standard of similarity too. It is part of our animal birthright. And, interestingly enough, it is characteristically animal in its lack of intellectual status. At any rate we noticed earlier how alien the notion is to mathematics and logic.

This innate qualitative spacing of stimulations was seen to have one of its human uses in the ostensive learning of words like 'yellow.' I should add as a cautionary remark that this is not the only way of learning words, nor the commonest; it is merely the most rudimentary way. It works when the question of the reference of a word is a simple question of spread: how much of our surroundings counts as yellow, how much counts as water, and so on. Learning a word like 'apple' or 'square' is more complicated, because here we have to learn also where to say that one apple or square leaves off and another begins. The complication is that apples do not add up to an apple, nor squares, generally, to a square. 'Yellow' and 'water' are mass terms, concerned only with spread; 'apple' and 'square' are terms of divided reference, concerned with both spread and individuation. Ostension figures in the learning of terms of this latter kind too, but the process is more complex.[10] And then there are all the other sorts of words, all those abstract and neutral connectives and adverbs and all the recondite terms of scientific theory; and there are also the grammatical constructions themselves to be mastered. The learning of these things is less direct and more complex still. There are deep problems in this domain, but they lie aside from the present topic.

Our way of learning 'yellow,' then, gives less than a full picture of how we learn language. Yet more emphatically, it gives less than a full picture of the human use of an innate standard of similarity, or innate spacing of qualities. For, as remarked, every reasonable expectation depends on similarity. Again on this score, other animals are like man. Their expectations, if we choose so to conceptualize their avoidance movements and salivation and pressing of levers and the like, are clearly dependent on their appreciation of similarity. Or, to put matters in their methodological order, these avoidance movements and salivation and pressing of levers and the like are typical of what we have to go on in mapping the animals' appreciation of similarity, their spacing of qualities.

Induction itself is essentially only more of the same: animal expectation or habit formation. And the ostensive learning of words is an implicit case of induction. Implicitly the learner of 'yellow' is working inductively toward a general law of English verbal behavior, though a law that he will never try to state; he is working up to where he can in general judge when an English speaker would assent to 'yellow' and when not.

Not only is ostensive learning a case of induction; it is a curiously comfortable case of induction, a game of chance with loaded dice. At any rate this is so if, as seems plausible, each man's spacing of qualities is enough like his neighbor's. For the learner is generalizing on his yellow samples by similarity considerations, and his neighbors have themselves acquired the use of the word 'yellow,' in their day, by the same similarity considerations. The learner of 'yellow' is thus making his induction in a friendly world. Always, induction expresses our hope that similar causes will have similar effects; but when the induction is the ostensive learning of a word, that pious hope blossoms into a foregone conclusion. The uniformity of people's quality spaces virtually assures that similar presentations will elicit similar verdicts.

It makes one wonder the more about other inductions, where what is sought is a generalization not about our neighbor's verbal behavior but about the harsh impersonal world. It is reasonable that our quality space should match our neighbor's, we being birds of a feather; and so the general trustworthiness of induction in the ostensive learning of words was a put-up job. To trust induction as a way of access to the truths of nature, on the other hand, is to suppose, more nearly, that our quality space matches that of the cosmos. The brute irrationality of our sense of similarity, its irrelevance to anything in logic and mathematics, offers little reason to expect that this sense is somehow in tune with the world—a world which, unlike language, we never made. Why induction should be trusted, apart from special cases such as the ostensive learning of words, is the perennial philosophical problem of induction.

One part of the problem of induction, the part that asks why there should be regularities in nature at all, can, I think, be dismissed. *That* there are or have been regularities, for whatever reason, is an established fact of science; and we cannot ask better than that. *Why* there have been regularities is an obscure question, for it is hard to see what would count as an answer. What does make clear sense is this other part of the problem of induction: why does our innate subjective spacing of qualities accord so well with the functionally relevant groupings in nature as to make our inductions tend to come out right? Why should our subjective spacing of qualities have a special purchase on nature and a lien on the future?

There is some encouragement in Darwin. If people's innate spacing of qualities is a gene-linked trait, then the spacing that has made for the most successful inductions will have tended to predominate through natural selection.[11] Creatures inveterately wrong in their inductions have a pathetic but praiseworthy tendency to die before reproducing their kind.

At this point let me say that I shall not be impressed by protests that I am using inductive generalizations, Darwin's and others, to justify induction, and thus reasoning in a circle. The reason I shall not be impressed by this is that my position is a naturalistic one; I see philosophy not as an a priori propaedeutic or groundwork for science, but as continuous with science. I see philosophy and science as in the same boat—a boat which, to revert to Neurath's figure as I so often do, we can rebuild only at sea while staying afloat in it. There is no external vantage point, no first philosophy. All scientific findings, all scientific conjectures that are at present plausible, are therefore in my view as welcome for use in philosophy as elsewhere. For me, then, the problem of induction is a problem about the world: a problem of how we, as we now are (by our present scientific lights), in a world we never made, should stand better than random or coin-tossing chances of coming out right when we predict by inductions which are based on our innate, scientifically unjustified similarity standards. Darwin's natural selection is a plausible partial explanation.

It may, in view of a consideration to which I next turn, be almost explanation enough. This consideration is that induction, after all, has its conspicuous failures. Thus take color. Nothing in experience, surely, is more vivid and conspicuous than color and its contrasts. And the remarkable fact, which has impressed scientists and philosophers as far back at least as Galileo and Descartes, is that the distinctions that matter for basic physical theory are mostly independent of color contrasts. Color impresses man; raven black impresses Hempel; emerald green impresses Goodman. But color is cosmically secondary. Even slight differences in sensory mechanisms from species to species, Smart remarks,[12] can make overwhelming differences in the grouping of things by color. Color is king in our innate quality space, but undistinguished in cosmic circles. Cosmically, colors would not qualify as kinds.

Color is helpful at the food-gathering level. Here it behaves well under induction, and here, no doubt, has been the survival value of our color-slanted quality space. It is just that contrasts that are crucial for such activities can be insignificant for broader and more theoretical science. If man were to live by basic science alone, natural selection would shift its support to the color-blind mutation.

Living as he does by both bread and basic science, man is torn. Things about his innate similarity standards that are helpful in the one sphere can be a hindrance in the other. Credit is due to man's inveterate ingenuity, or human sapience, for having worked around the blinding dazzle of color vision and found the more significant regularities elsewhere. Evidently natural selection has dealt with the conflict by endowing man doubly: with both a color-slanted quality space and the ingenuity to rise above it.

He has risen above it by developing modified systems of kinds, hence modified similarity standards for scientific purposes. By the trial-and-error process of theorizing he has regrouped things into new kinds which prove to lend themselves to many inductions better than the old.

A crude example is the modification of the notion of fish by excluding whales and porpoises. Another taxonomic example is the grouping of kangaroos, opossums, and marsupial mice in a single kind, marsupials, while excluding ordinary mice. By primitive standards the marsupial mouse is more similar to the ordinary mouse than to the kangaroo; by theoretical standards the reverse is true.

A theoretical kind need not be a modification of an intuitive one. It may issue from theory full-blown, without antecedents; for instance the kind which comprises positively charged particles. We revise our standards of similarity or of natural kinds on the strength, as Goodman remarks,[13] of second-order inductions. New groupings, hypothetically adopted at the suggestion of a growing theory, prove favorable to inductions and so become 'entrenched.' We newly establish the projectibility of some predicate, to our satisfaction, by successfully trying to project it. In induction nothing succeeds like success.

Between an innate concept of similarity or spacing of qualities and a scientifically sophisticated one, there are all gradations. Science, after all, differs from common sense only in degree of methodological sophistication. Our experiences from earliest infancy are bound to have overlaid our innate spacing of qualities by modifying and supplementing our grouping habits little by little, inclining us more and more to an appreciation of theoretical kinds and similarities, long before we reach the point of studying science systematically as such. Moreover, the later phases do not wholly supersede the earlier; we retain different similarity standards, different systems of kinds, for use in different contexts. We all still say that a marsupial mouse is more like an ordinary mouse than a kangaroo, except when we are concerned with genetic matters. Something like our innate quality space continues to function alongside the more sophisticated regroupings that have been found by scientific experience to facilitate induction.

We have seen that a sense of similarity or of kinds is fundamental to learning in the widest sense—to language learning, to induction, to expectation. Toward a further appreciation of how utterly this notion permeates our thought, I want now to point out a number of other very familiar and central notions which seem to depend squarely on this one. They are notions that are definable in terms of similarity, or kinds, and further irreducible.

A notable domain of examples is the domain of dispositions, such as Carnap's example of solubility in water. To say of some individual object that it is soluble in water is not to say merely that it always dissolves when in water, because this would be true by default of any object, however insoluble, if it merely happened to be destined never to get into water. It is to say rather that it *would* dissolve if it were in water; but this account brings small comfort, since the device of a subjunctive conditional involves all the perplexities of disposition terms and more. Thus far I simply repeat Carnap.[14] But now I want to point out what could be done in this connection with the notion of kind. Intuitively, what qualifies a thing as soluble though it never gets into water is that it is of the same kind as the things that actually did or will dissolve; it is similar to them. Strictly we cannot simply say '*the* same kind,' nor simply 'similar,' when we have wider and narrower kinds, less and more similarity. Let us then mend our definition by saying that the soluble things are the common members of *all* such kinds. A thing is soluble if *each* kind that is broad enough to embrace all actual victims of solution embraces it too.

Graphically the idea is this: we make a set of all the sometime victims, all the things that actually did or will dissolve in water, and then we add just enough other things to round the set out into a kind. This is the water-soluble kind.

If this definition covers just the desired things, the things that are really soluble in water, it owes its success to a circumstance that could be otherwise. The needed circumstance is that a sufficient variety of things actually get dissolved in water to assure their not all falling under any one kind narrower than the desired water-soluble kind itself. But it is a plausible circumstance, and I am not sure that its accidental character is a drawback. If the trend of events had been otherwise, perhaps the solubility concept would not have been wanted.

However, if I seem to be defending this definition, I must now hasten to add that of course it has much the same fault as the definition which used the subjunctive conditional. This definition uses the unreduced notion of kind, which is certainly not a notion we want to rest with either; neither theoretical kind nor intuitive kind. My purpose in giving the definition is only to show the link between the problem of dispositions and the problem of kinds.

As between theoretical and intuitive kinds, certainly the theoretical ones are the ones wanted for purposes of defining solubility and other dispositions of scientific concern. Perhaps 'amiable' and 'reprehensible' are disposition terms whose definitions should draw rather on intuitive kinds.

Another dim notion, which has intimate connections with dispositions and subjunctive conditionals, is the notion of cause; and we shall see that it too turns on the notion of kinds. Hume explained cause as invariable succession, and this makes sense as long as the cause and effect are referred to by general terms. We can say that fire causes heat, and we can mean thereby, as Hume would have it, that each event classifiable under the head of fire is followed by an event classifiable under the head of heat, or heating up. But this account, whatever its virtues for these general causal statements, leaves singular causal statements unexplained.

What does it mean to say that the kicking over of a lamp in Mrs. O'Leary's barn caused the Chicago fire? It cannot mean merely that the event at Mrs. O'Leary's belongs to a set, and the Chicago fire belongs to a set, such that there is invariable succession between the two sets: every member of the one set is followed by a member of the other. This paraphrase is trivially true and too weak. Always, if one event happens to be followed by another, the two belong to certain sets between which there is invariable succession. We can rig the sets arbitrarily. Just put any arbitrary events in the first set, including the first of the two events we are interested in; and then in the other set put the second of those two events, together with other events that happen to have occurred just after the other members of the first set.

Because of this way of trivialization, a singular causal statement says no more than that the one event was followed by the other. That is, it says no more if we use the definition just now contemplated; which, therefore, we must not. The trouble with that definition is clear enough: it is the familiar old trouble of the promiscuity of sets. Here, as usual, kinds, being more discriminate, enable us to draw distinctions where sets do not. To say that one event caused another is to say that the two events are of *kinds* between which there is invariable succession. If this correction does not yet take care of Mrs. O'Leary's cow, the fault is only with invariable succession itself, as affording too simple a definition of general causal statements; we need to hedge it around with provisions for partial or contributing causes and a good deal else. That aspect of the causality problem is not my concern. What I wanted to bring out is just the relevance of the notion of kinds, as the needed link between singular and general causal statements.

We have noticed that the notion of kind, or similarity, is crucially relevant to the notion of disposition, to the subjunctive conditional, and to singular causal statements. From a scientific point of view these are a pretty disreputable lot. The notion of kind, or similarity, is equally disreputable. Yet some such notion, some similarity sense, was seen to be crucial to all learning, and central in particular to the processes of inductive generalization and prediction which are the very life of science. It appears that science is rotten to the core.

Yet there may be claimed for this rot a certain undeniable fecundity. Science reveals hidden mysteries, predicts successfully, and works technological wonders. If this is the way of rot, then rot is rather to be prized and praised than patronized.

Rot, actually, is not the best model here. A better model is human progress. A sense of comparative similarity, I remarked earlier, is one of man's animal endowments. Insofar as it fits in with regularities of nature, so as to afford us reasonable success in our primitive inductions and expectations, it is presumably an evolutionary product of natural selection. Secondly, as remarked, one's sense of similarity or one's system of kinds develops and changes and even turns multiple as one matures, making perhaps for increasingly dependable prediction. And at length standards of similarity set in which are geared to theoretical science. This development is a development away from the immediate, subjective, animal sense of similarity to the remoter objectivity of a similarity determined by scientific hypotheses and posits and constructs. Things are similar in the later or theoretical sense to the degree that they are interchangeable parts of the cosmic machine revealed by science.

This progress of similarity standards, in the course of each individual's maturing years, is a sort of recapitulation in the individual of the race's progress from muddy savagery. But the similarity notion even in its theoretical phase is itself a muddy notion still. We have offered no definition of it in satisfactory scientific terms. We of course have a behavioral definition of what counts, for a given individual, as similar to what, or as more similar to what than to what; we have this for similarity old and new, human and animal. But it is no definition of what it means really for *a* to be more similar to *b* than to *c*; really, and quite apart from this or that psychological subject.

Did I already suggest a definition to this purpose, metaphorically, when I said that things are similar to the extent that they are interchangeable parts of the cosmic machine? More literally, could things be said to be similar in proportion to how much of scientific theory would remain true on interchanging those things as objects of reference in the theory? This only hints a direction; consider for instance the dimness of 'how much theory.' Anyway the direction itself is not a good one; for it would make similarity depend in the wrong way on theory. A man's judgments of similarity do and should depend on his theory, on his beliefs; but similarity itself, what the man's judgments purport to be judgments of, purports to be an objective relation in the world. It belongs in the subject matter not of our theory of theorizing about the world, but of our theory of the world itself. Such would be the acceptable and reputable sort of similarity concept, if it could be defined.

It does get defined in bits: bits suited to special branches of science. It is in this way, on many limited fronts, that man continues his rise from savagery, sloughing off the muddy old notion of kind or similarity piecemeal, a vestige here and a vestige there. Chemistry, the home science of water-solubility itself, is one branch that has reached this stage. Comparative similarity of the sort that matters for chemistry can be stated outright in chemical terms, that is, in terms of chemical composition. Molecules will be said to *match* if they contain atoms of the same elements in the same topological combinations. Then, in principle, we might get at the comparative similarity of objects *a* and *b* by considering how many pairs of matching molecules there are, one molecule from *a* and one from *b* each time, and how many unmatching pairs. The ratio gives even a theoretical measure of relative similarity, and thus abundantly explains what it is for *a* to be more similar to *b* than to *c*. Or we might prefer to complicate our definition by allowing also for degrees in the matching of molecules; molecules having almost equally many atoms, or having atoms whose atomic numbers or atomic weights are almost equal, could be reckoned as matching better than others. At any rate a lusty chemical similarity concept is assured.

From it, moreover, an equally acceptable concept of kinds is derivable, by the paradigm-and-foil definition noted earlier in this paper. For it is a question now only of distilling purely chemical kinds from purely chemical similarity; no admixture of other respects of similarity interferes. We thus exonerate water-solubility, which, the last time around, we had reduced no farther than to an unexplained notion of kind. Therewith also the associated subjunctive conditional, 'If this were in water, it would dissolve,' gets its bill of health.

The same scientific advances that have thus provided a solid underpinning for the definition of solubility in terms of kinds, have also, ironically enough, made that line of definition pointless by providing a full understanding of the mechanism of solution. One can redefine water-solubility by simply describing the structural conditions of that mechanism. This embarrassment of riches is, I suspect, a characteristic outcome. That is, once we can legitimize a disposition term by defining the relevant similarity standard, we are apt to know the mechanism of the disposition, and so by-pass the similarity. Not but that the similarity standard is worth clarifying too, for its own sake or for other purposes.

Philosophical or broadly scientific motives can impel us to seek still a basic and absolute concept of similarity, along with such fragmentary similarity concepts as suit special branches of science. This drive for a cosmic similarity concept is perhaps identifiable with the age-old drive to reduce things to their elements. It epitomizes the scientific spirit, though dating back to the Pre-Socratics: to Empedocles with his theory of four elements, and above all to Democritus with his atoms. The modern physics of elementary particles, or of hills in space-time, is a more notable effort in this direction.

This idea of rationalizing a single notion of relative similarity, throughout its cosmic sweep, has its metaphysical attractions. But there would still remain need also to rationalize the similarity notion more locally and superficially, so as to capture only such similarity as is relevant to some special science. Our chemistry example is already a case of this, since it stops short of full analysis into neutrons, electrons, and the other elementary particles.

A more striking example of superficiality, in this good sense, is afforded by taxonomy, say in zoology. Since learning about the evolution of species, we are in a position to define comparative similarity suitably for this science by consideration of family trees. For a theoretical measure of the degree of similarity of two individual animals we can devise some suitable function that depends on proximity and frequency of their common ancestors. Or a more significant concept of degree of similarity might be devised in terms of genes. When kind is construed in terms of any such similarity concept, 'fishes' in the corrected, whale-free sense of the word qualify as a kind while 'fishes' in the more inclusive sense do not.

Different similarity measures, or relative similarity notions, best suit different branches of science; for there are wasteful complications in providing for finer gradations of relative similarity than matter for the phenomena with which the particular science is concerned. Perhaps the branches of science could be revealingly classified by looking to the relative similarity notion that is appropriate to each. Such a plan is reminiscent of Felix Klein's so-called *Erlangerprogramm* in geometry, which involved characterizing the various branches of geometry by what transformations were immaterial to each. But a branch of science would qualify for recognition and classification at all, under such a plan, only when it had matured to the point of clearing up its similarity standards. Such branches of science would qualify further as unified, or integrated into our inclusive systematization of nature, only insofar as their several similarity concepts were *compatible;* capable of meshing, that is, and differing only in the fineness of their discriminations.

Disposition terms and subjunctive conditionals in these areas, where suitable senses of similarity and kind are forthcoming, suddenly turn respectable; respectable and, in principle, superfluous. In other domains they remain disreputable and practically indispensable. They may be seen perhaps as unredeemed notes; the theory that would clear up the unanalyzed underlying similarity notion in such cases is still to come. An example is the disposition called intelligence—the ability, vaguely speaking, to learn quickly and to solve problems. Sometime, whether in terms of proteins, colloids, nerve nets, or overt behavior, the relevant branch of science may reach the stage where a similarity notion can be constructed capable of making even the notion of intelligence respectable—and superfluous.

In general we can take it as a very special mark of the maturity of a branch of science that it no longer needs an irreducible notion of similarity and kind. It is that final stage where the animal vestige is wholly absorbed into the theory. In this career of the similarity notion, starting in its innate phase, developing over the years in the light of accumulated experience, passing then from the intuitive phase into theoretical similarity, and finally disappearing altogether, we have a paradigm of the evolution of unreason into science.[15]

Harvard University

NOTES

1. C. G. Hempel, *Aspects of Scientific Explanation and Other Essays,* (New York: Free Press, 1965), 15.

2. Nelson Goodman, *Fact, Fiction and Forecast* (London: University of London Press, 1955), 74.

3. *Ibid.,* 82ff.

4. *Ibid.*, 95ff.

5. I mean this only as a sufficient condition of lawlikeness. See Donald Davidson, 'Emeroses by Other Names,' *J. Philosophy 63* (1966), 778–780.

6. This relevance of kind is noted by Goodman, 1st ed., 119 ff.; 2nd ed., 121 ff.

7. Nelson Goodman, *The Structure of Appearance,* 2nd ed. (New York: Bobbs-Merrill, 1966), 163 ff.

8. Rudolf Carnap, *The Logical Structure of the World* (Berkeley, Calif.: University of California Press, 1967), 141–147. (German ed., 1928.)

9. See my *Word and Object* (Cambridge, Mass.: M.I.T. Press, 1960), 83 ff. for further discussion and references.

10. See *ibid.*, 90–95.

11. This was noted by S. Watanabe on the second page of his paper 'Une explication mathématique du classement d'objets,' in *Information and Prediction in Science,* ed. S. Dockx and P. Bernays (New York: Academic Press, 1965).

12. J. J. C. Smart, *Philosophy and Scientific Realism* (London: Routledge and Kegan-Paul, 1963), 68–72.

13. *Fact, Fiction and Forecast, op. cit.,* 95 ff.

14. R. Carnap, 'Testability and Meaning,' *Philosophy of Science 3* (1936), 419–471; *4* (1937), 1–40.

15. I am indebted to Burton Dreben and Nelson Goodman for helpful criticisms of earlier drafts.

Concerning a Fiction About How Facts Are Forecast[*]

Andrzej Zabludowski

Nelson Goodman's *theory of projection*[†] is an attempt to answer the following query: What distinguishes credible from incredible inductive generalizations?

The answer it provides is, roughly, this: (1) any supported and unviolated generalization can be given credence unless there is a rival supported and unviolated generalization that wins or at least withstands the competition; (2) among alternative supported and unviolated generalizations, we favor those whose predicates appear *better entrenched*. And a predicate is at a given time better entrenched than another if it has previously been longer and more often used in inductions; or more exactly—for it is not words as such that matter, but the classes they select—a predicate is better entrenched than another if the class it selects has previously been longer and more often mentioned in inductions than the class selected by the other.[1]

But one should not suppose that if, among alternative inductive generalizations, we favor those whose predicates prevail in entrenchment— if, to recall Goodman's favorite example, we credit the hypothesis 'All emeralds are green' rather than an alternative to it such as 'All emeralds are grue [i.e., either thus far observed and green or not as yet observed and blue]'—it is because those predicates become better entrenched which, by themselves, are better fitted for formulating plausible inductions. On the contrary, it is just by becoming better entrenched that a predicate becomes better fitted. A choice, initially made by chance, is subsequently perpetuated by habit (cf. *PP,* 357/8; *FFF,* 98).

I, for one, am not persuaded by Goodman's insight into the roots of our inductive choices. To say that it is just by habit that we project past regularities in greenness rather than those in grueness seems to me as

From *The Journal of Philosophy,* Vol. LXXI, No. 4 (February 28, 1974): 97–112. Reprinted by permission of *The Journal of Philosophy* and the author. The present version of the paper includes a few additions to (and a few minor revisions of) the version originally published.

unconvincing as to say that it is just by habit that we use legs for walking instead of walking upside down. For just as, given our bodily structure, it is simpler to make use of legs for walking than to walk upside down, so it is simpler, given our sensory equipment, to depict the world in green, blue, etc., than to depict it in grue, bleen, and so on. But I shall not dwell on the causal aspect of the entrenchment theory of induction and argue that it is not the plausibility of certain inductions that derives from the entrenchment of certain predicates, but rather the entrenchment of certain predicates that derives from the plausibility of certain inductions. What I want to show is that there is no interesting connection at all between which predicates are, or appear, well or ill entrenched and which inductions sound plausible or implausible. As indicated by Goodman (cf. 'grue' or other illustrations of the 'new riddle,' offered in *FFF*), for any inductive generalization one can formulate another inductive generalization that is incompatible with the former; this observation will be supplemented: if "to speak of the entrenchment of a predicate is to speak elliptically of the entrenchment of [its] extension" (*FFF*, 95), then, for any inductive generalization (and thus for any credible one, in particular), one can formulate another inductive generalization that is incompatible with the former and whose predicates appear at least as well entrenched. 'All emeralds are green' outstrips in entrenchment its Goodmanesque alternatives, such as 'All emeralds are grue,' but has no advantage in this respect over a host of other rivals, as fanciful as the latter.

I shall use, throughout the paper, the vocabulary of the theory under discussion. Let me note down the relevant definitions (following "An Improvement . . . ," *PP*, 389–393).

Hypotheses[2] in a given language are said to divide, relative to a time, into projectible, unprojectible, and others, the division being dependent upon two factors: the total evidence available at the time in question[3] and the relations of comparative entrenchment obtaining at that time between particular predicates of the language.[4] A hypothesis is *projectible* at a given time iff it is then supported, unviolated, and unexhausted[5] and all conflicting hypotheses are unprojectible at that time. A hypothesis is *unprojectible* at a given time iff it is then unsupported or violated or exhausted or overridden by another. A hypothesis h is *overridden* at a time t by a hypothesis h' iff both are then supported, unviolated, and unexhausted, conflict with each other, and h' outstrips h in entrenchment at t (i.e., the antecedent-predicate or consequent-predicate of h' is then much[6] better entrenched[7]—and neither is much less well entrenched—than the corresponding predicate of h), and h' is not itself overridden at t.[8]

This criterion of projectibility is offered as an answer to the question "What hypotheses are confirmed by their positive instances?" (*FFF*, 81).[9] And a hypothesis is confirmed by its positive instances if they impart to it "some credibility that is conveyed to other instances" (*FFF*, 69)[10] or, according to another explanation, if they make it credible (*PP*, 392) or "sufficiently more credible than alternative hypotheses" (*FFF*, 88). ". . . confirmation is a guide to acceptance . . ." (*PP*, 362).

From now on, not to confuse projectibility in the pretheoretic sense (being confirmed by positive instances) with projectibility as defined by Goodman's criterion, I will italicize the word 'projectible' whenever it is used in the latter sense.

The theory can, presumably, be briefly stated as follows. Our intuitive inductive choices correspond to our virtual judgments of *projectibility;*[11] if to *adopt* (*reject*) a generalization is to consider it more credible than all (less credible than some) conflicting generalizations, we proceed as if we followed, in particular, these two rules: (*i*) reject a generalization (supported, etc.) if you judge it to be *unprojectible;* (*ii*) adopt a generalization if you judge it to be *projectible.*[12]

In sections I and II below, it will be argued (1) that no hypotheses are ever *projectible,* so that one can't apply rule (*ii*) without relying on false premises; and (2) that all hypotheses whose antecedents or consequents are at a given time less than best entrenched are at that time *unprojectible,* so that one can't consistently apply rule (*i*) without banishing a host of inductive hypotheses that in fact are commonly entertained. In section III, an effort will be made to show that these results do not depend on any secondary details (possible inaccuracies) of the definitions involved. In section IV, Goodman's theory of "comparative projectibility" will be examined; the outcome will be no more encouraging than those obtained in the preceding sections.

But first I want to express a certain doubt concerning not so much *projectibility* or related concepts as the very question to which these are supposed to provide an answer. Goodman seeks to explain "what decides between two hypotheses that conflict" ("An Improvement . . . ," 605; *PP,* 389). One might suppose that the term 'conflict' is employed here simply as another name for incompatibility; that two hypotheses *conflict* if one cannot consistently believe that both are true; or, more exactly, that they *conflict at a given time* if one cannot consistently believe that both are true, given the evidence available at that time. But Goodman defines the term differently: "Two hypotheses conflict only if neither follows from the other and they ascribe to something different predicates such that only one actually applies. 'All emeralds are green' conflicts with 'All emeralds are nongreen' if there are any emeralds, conflicts with 'All emeralds are grue' if there are any emeralds not examined before *t* [and either green or blue], and incidentally even conflicts with 'All emeralds are hard' if there is an emerald that is either green or hard but not both.[13] While our particular judgments as to whether two given hypotheses conflict may, like any other judgments, be right or wrong, we apply the rule [i.e., the projectibility criterion] for the resolution whenever we judge conflict to obtain."[14] The concept is clear; what is not clear, however, is why this concept is to be of any special interest. Let us call two hypotheses *colliding* if neither follows from the other and they ascribe the same predicate to two different things such that the predicate actually applies either to one thing or to the other but not to both. Why should the question, What decides between two hypotheses believed to *conflict?*, be of any greater moment than the question, What decides between two hypotheses believed to *collide?* And, besides, can this question be plausibly answered by reference to projectibility defined in terms of "conflict"? Cannot the competition between two conflicting hypotheses be resolved by the intervention of a third that neither conflicts nor is believed to conflict with either of the two but is incompatible with one (or both) of them? Because of these doubts, and also because Goodman himself treats his special concept without much piety,[15] I shall interpret conflict in two ways: (a) in accordance with the definition quoted above, but also (b) as incompatibility on evidence.

I. Projectibility

As an initial exercise, let us check whether there are any hypotheses that might be both *projectible* at some time and true.

(I shall first assume that 'conflicting,' in the definition of *projectibility,* means 'incompatible on the evidence,' and then switch to the other reading.)

Let h be a hypothesis of one's choice that is, at a given time t, unviolated and unexhausted (it would not be *projectible* if it were violated or exhausted), and suppose that 'Ax' and 'Bx' are a pair of predicates belonging to the best entrenched at t ('Ax' as antecedent, 'Bx' as consequent) and such that some objects are known at t to fall under both of them and some others are known to fall only under the first, so that the hypothesis h_0: $(x)(Ax \rightarrow Bx)$, is both supported and violated at t. Now, let us confront h with the following good companion of Goodman's 'grue-like' generalizations:

$$(h^*) \quad (x)(Ax \rightarrow (Bx \lor \sim Hx))$$

where 'Hx' is an abbreviation for the conjunction of h and a tautology like '$x = x$' or, if one likes, for 'x is such that . . . ,' where ' . . . ' is identical with h.[16]

Now, h^* is supported at t (since h_0 is supported), unexhausted (since h_0 is violated and h unviolated), unviolated (since h is unexhausted), and incompatible with h (since h_0 is violated).[17] So, for h to be *projectible* at t, h^* must be at that time overridden.

Suppose that h^* is overridden at t. It follows that either its antecedent or its consequent is much less well entrenched at t than the corresponding predicate of some rival hypothesis. Since "Ax" is one of the best entrenched predicates, it is "$Bx \lor \sim Hx$" that must be the culprit. But if the latter yields in entrenchment to some other predicate, it is not coextensive with "Bx," and, therefore, h is false. Briefly, if h is *projectible* at t, h is false.

Thus, if there is a pair of predicates such that both belong to the best entrenched at t—one as antecedent, the other as consequent—and such that some objects are known at t to fall under both and some are known to fall only under the first, then no hypothesis *projectible* at t is true. And since, obviously, there always is a pair of predicates of the requisite sort, no hypotheses ever *projectible* are true.

But let us check whether this result is not perhaps due to our unauthorized substitution of the familiar concept of incompatibility for Goodman's special concept of conflict.

Suppose that the 'Ax' and 'Bx' occurring in h^* satisfy one more condition: some objects that fall under the antecedent of h also fall under 'Ax' and either fall under the consequent of h but not under 'Bx' or conversely. Then, if h does not conflict with h^*, h is false.[18] And, as we have seen, if h^* is overridden, h is false. But, as h^* is supported, unexhausted and unviolated at t—for h to be *projectible* at t, h^* must either be overridden or be in no conflict with h. Hence, if h is *projectible* at t, h is false.

Thus, if h is, e.g., the hypothesis that all iron melts at $1535°$ C, and such predicates as, say, 'metallic' and 'yellow' are not much less well entrenched (as antecedent and consequent, respectively) than any others, h is not both *projectible* and true—in view of h^*, where 'Ax' stands for 'x is metallic,' 'Bx' for 'x is yellow,' and 'Hx' for 'x is such that all iron melts at $1535°$ C.' If h says that all horses are maned and such predicates as, say, 'horse' and 'white' are not much less well entrenched than any others, h is not both *projectible* and true—in view of h^*, where 'Ax' stands for 'x is a horse,' 'Bx' for 'x is white,' etc. If h says that all emeralds are green and such predicates as, say, 'stone' and 'round' are not much less well entrenched than any others, h is not both *projectible* and true—in view of h^*, where 'Ax' stands for 'x is a stone,' 'Bx' for 'x is round,' etc. And since, presumably, for any (supported) hypothesis there always is a pair of predicates of the requisite sort, one can hardly avoid concluding, again, that no hypotheses ever *projectible* are true.

So the formula, 'adopt a generalization if you judge it to be *projectible*,' is not the most appealing among the rules that we may have allowed to govern our inductive choices. Its contrary, 'reject a generalization if you judge it to be *projectible*,' may seem much more recommendable. In fact, however, there is nothing to choose between them; for, just as no hypotheses ever *projectible* are true, so no hypotheses ever *projectible* are false. Briefly, no hypotheses are ever *projectible*. Let s be a sentence of one's choice such that our hypothesis h follows, on the information accepted at t, neither from s nor from its denial. (h being unexhausted, such sentences cannot be in short supply.) And let us confront h with the following two cognates of h^*:

(h^*_1) $\quad (x)(Ax \rightarrow (Bx \vee (\sim Hx \,\&\, Sx)))$

(h^*_2) $\quad (x)(Ax \rightarrow (Bx \vee (\sim Hx \,\&\, \sim Sx)))$

where 'Sx' is an abbreviation for the conjunction of '$x = x$' and s. Both h^*_1 and h^*_2 are supported at t (since h_0 is supported), unexhausted (since h_0 is violated and h unviolated), unviolated (since the denial of h is not incompatible at t with s or with its denial), and incompatible with h (since h_0 is violated). And since either the consequent of h^*_1 or that of h^*_2 is coextensive with 'Bx,' at least one of the two hypotheses is not overridden at t (and also conflicts with h, given that 'Ax' and 'Bx' satisfy the additional condition mentioned above), and so h is not *projectible* at t.

II. Unprojectibility

An immediate corollary to what was established above is that all those hypotheses whose antecedents or consequents are at a given time less than best entrenched are at that time *unprojectible*. (If one or the other predicate of h is, unlike 'Ax' and 'Bx,' less than best entrenched, h not only has a nonoverridden rival—h^*_1 or h^*_2—but is itself overridden by the latter.)

Under the criterion we are supposed to follow, all those hypotheses (supported, etc.) that would be judged *unprojectible* should be rejected. Accordingly, all those hypotheses (supported, etc.) should be rejected whose antecedents or consequents would be judged less than best entrenched.

One may, of course, draw the bottom limit of the 'best entrenchment' as low as one likes (as emphasized in *FFF*, 96, 105, only gross differences of entrenchment are relevant to projectibility). The trouble is, however, that (as also emphasized in *FFF*, 97) a host of predicates occurring in generalizations we in fact find credible do not seem to be better entrenched than any predicates whatever. For, obviously, new generalizations often involve new predicates, not previously 'projected' and not supposed to be equivalent to any previously 'projected' predicates. As mentioned by Goodman, even such predicates can be entrenched: they may 'inherit' some entrenchment from their "parents."[19] But such new predicates as 'grue' also have some entrenched "parents" to inherit from: for instance, 'mixed in color.'[20]

Thus, either we constantly adopt, in contravention of Professor Goodman's rule, thousands of inductive generalizations that are plainly *unprojectible* or, if one likes, no predicates are ever less than "best entrenched" and no hypotheses (supported, etc.) are ever *unprojectible*.

III. Projectibility and Unprojectibility Again

But all this merely shows, so one might reply, that the intended concepts of *projectibility* and *unprojectibility* have been defined somewhat inaccurately. Presumably, the *unprojectibility* criterion for elimination is not intended to rule out any inductive generalization unless in favor of a specified alternative inductive generalization, so that the rule 'Reject a given generalization (supported, etc.) if you find it *unprojectible*' should perhaps be interpreted as telling us to throw away a generalization not when we merely find it to be overridden—i.e., not when we merely *find that there is another* that overrides it—but rather when *there is another that we find* to override it. Correspondingly, one should perhaps say that *unprojectible* hypotheses are not all those which can be shown to have overriding rivals, but rather those only which have rivals that can be shown to override them.[21] Now, given this plausible correction, the argument offered above is no longer effective, since it merely shows that every hypothesis (supported, etc.) whose antecedent or consequent is judged less than best entrenched must be judged to have some overriding rivals, not that for every such hypothesis there is a particular rival that must be judged as overriding.[22]

One might also suggest a similar redefinition of *projectibility*: instead of saying that a hypothesis (supported, etc.) is *projectible* if it has no rivals (supported, etc.) that are not overridden, one would say that a hypothesis (supported, etc.) is *projectible* if it has no rivals (supported, etc.) to be judged as not overridden. Given this change, the argument offered in the end of section I is no longer effective, since it merely shows that any (unviolated and unexhausted) hypothesis must be judged to have some rivals (supported, etc.) that are not overridden, not that for any such hypothesis there is a particular rival (supported, etc.) to be judged as not overridden. Also our initial argument (*h* vs. *h**) is ineffective on the modified definition.[23]

But though the particular arguments offered before are thus rendered harmless, the trouble is not removed.

Let *h* be a hypothesis of one's choice that is, at a given time *t*, supported, unviolated, and unexhausted, and let '*Hx*' be, as before, short for the conjunction of *h* and a tautology like '*x* = *x*.' Suppose that '*Ax*,' '*Bx*,' and '*Cx*' are a triplet of predicates reckoned at *t* among the best entrenched ('*Ax*' as antecedent, the two others as consequents) and such that (a) some objects are known at *t* to fall under all three; (b) some objects known at *t* to fall under '*Ax*' are also known at *t* not to fall under '*Bx*'; and (c) it is not excluded on the information accepted at *t*, that '$(x)(Ax \rightarrow Cx)$' is true and *h* false. Now let us consider the following generalization:

$$(h^{**}) \quad (x)(Ax \rightarrow ((Bx \ \& \ Hx) \lor (Cx \ \& \ \sim Hx))).$$

This generalization is supported at t, as follows from (a); unviolated, as follows from (c); unexhausted, as follows from (b) and the assumption that h is unviolated; and it is incompatible with h, as follows from (b).[24] But it must be reckoned at t as not overridden: its antecedent is ranked among the best entrenched and also its consequent must be ranked among the best entrenched, since, obviously, it is coextensive with either 'B' or 'C.'

So h is not *projectible* at t; and if one or the other predicate of h is then ranked as less than best entrenched, h must count as overridden by h^{**} and hence as *unprojectible* at t.

Thus, if such predicates as 'metallic,' 'yellow,' 'conductive,' are ranked among the best entrenched (the first as antecedent, the two others as consequents) and if h is a hypothesis that does not follow from 'Whatever is metallic is conductive,' h is not *projectible,* or even is *unprojectible,* because of incompatibility with h^{**}, where 'Ax' stands for 'x is metallic,' 'Bx' for 'x is yellow,' 'Cx' for 'x is conductive.' If such predicates as 'horse,' 'white,' 'heavier than water' are ranked among the best entrenched and if h is a hypothesis that does not follow from 'All horses are heavier than water,' h is not *projectible,* or even is *unprojectible,* because of incompatibility with h^{**}, where 'Ax' stands for 'x is a horse,' 'Bx' for 'x is white,' 'Cx' for 'x is heavier than water.' And so forth.

But, again, let us check whether the trouble is not removed when we substitute for incompatibility Goodman's special concept of conflict.

Let h be, again, a hypothesis of one's choice that is, at a time t, supported, etc., and suppose that 'Ax,' 'Bx,' and 'Cx' are a triplet of predicates ranked at t among the best entrenched and such that: (a) some objects are known at t to fall under all three; (b) some objects known at t to fall under both predicates of h are also known at t to fall under 'Ax' and known not to fall under 'Bx'; and (c) it is not excluded, on the information accepted at t, that the hypothesis h': (x) $(Ax \rightarrow Cx)$, is true and conflicts with h.

Now let us consider the following generalization:

$$(h^{***}) \quad (x)(Ax \rightarrow ((Bx \ \& \sim Kx) \lor (Cx \ \& \ Kx))),$$

where 'Kx' is short for 'x is such that h' conflicts with h.'

The generalization h^{***} is supported at t, as follows from (a); unviolated, as follows from (c); and unexhausted, as follows from (b) and the assumption that h is unviolated at t. And h^{***} must be admitted at t not to be then overridden: its antecedent is ranked at t among the best entrenched; and also its consequent must be ranked among the best entrenched, since it is, obviously, coextensive either with 'Bx' or with 'Cx.' Finally, h^{***} not only is incompatible with h,[25] but also must be admitted at t to conflict with it. For either h' happens to conflict with h or it does not; if it does, the consequent of h^{***} is coextensive with that of h' and, hence, h^{***} also conflicts with h;[26] and if h' does not conflict with h, the consequent of h^{***} is coextensive with 'Bx,' but in that case, as follows from what is accepted at t—cf. (b)—h^{***}, again, conflicts with h.

So h is not *projectible* at t: there is a hypothesis—e.g., h^{***}—that is supported, etc., at t and that must be admitted at t to be at that time a nonoverridden rival of h. And if one or the other predicate of h is ranked at t as less than best entrenched, h is *unprojectible* at t: there is a hypothesis—e.g., h^{***}—that admittedly overrides it.

Thus, if h says that all iron melts at 1535°C, and such predicates as 'metallic,' 'yellow,' 'conductive' are ranked among the best entrenched, h is not *projectible*, or even is *unprojectible*, because of conflict with h^{***}, where 'Ax' stands for 'x is metallic,' 'Bx' for 'x is yellow,' 'Cx' for 'x is conductive,' and 'Kx' for 'x is such that some iron either melts at 1535°C and is not conductive or is conductive and does not melt at 1535°C.' If h says that all horses are maned, and such predicates as 'horse,' 'white,' 'heavier than water' are ranked among the best entrenched, h is not *projectible*, or even is *unprojectible*, because of conflict with h^{***}, where 'Ax' stands for 'x is a horse,' 'Bx' for 'x is white,' 'Cx' for 'x is heavier than water,' and 'Kx' for 'x is such that some horses are either maned and not heavier than water or heavier than water and not maned.' If h says that all emeralds are green, and such predicates as 'stone,' 'round,' 'hard' count among the best entrenched, h is not *projectible*, or even is *unprojectible*, because of conflict with h^{***}, where 'Ax' stands for 'x is a stone,' 'Bx' for 'x is round,' 'Cx' for 'x is hard,' and 'Kx' for 'x is such that some emeralds are either green but not hard or hard but not green.' And so on.

But *projectibility* and *unprojectibility* are not the only resources of Goodman's theory.

IV. Overhypotheses and Comparative Projectibility

Another criterion for choosing between rival generalizations is provided by their *comparative* projectibility. Some hypotheses (among those supported, etc.) are said to be *more projectible* than others, and the degree of *projectibility* of each is to depend upon two factors: the entrenchment of its predicates and the evidence for suitable higher-order generalizations, *overhypotheses* of the hypothesis in question.

(This theory was offered as a supplement, rather than an alternative, to the theory we dealt with in the preceding sections; it was to apply only to those generalizations which would qualify as "presumptively projectible," i.e., "nonoverridden"; cf. *FFF*, p. 106. But, not to get discouraged, see a contrary suggestion in *FFF*, p. 118.)

To follow an explanatory example given in *FFF* (109): let *B* be a bag full of marbles, one in a certain stack *S* of such bags; suppose a number of marbles from that bag have been examined and all of those examined have been found to be red, so that one is inclined to venture the hypothesis that all the marbles in bag *B* are red. Now, the projectibility of this hypothesis— the credibility transmitted from its determined to its undetermined instances—would be enhanced if we examined a few other bags from stack *S* and found, in each case, that the marbles contained in the same bag were of the same color. And, conversely, the projectibility of our hypothesis would be reduced if each of the examined bags turned out to contain marbles varied in color.

In the first case, Goodman explains, the projectibility of the hypothesis in question would be affected by information in support of its, unviolated in that case, *positive overhypothesis:* 'Every bagful in stack *S* is uniform in color'; and in the second case, by information in support of its, unviolated in that case, *negative overhypothesis:* 'Every bagful in stack *S* is mixed in color.'[27] A hypothesis *h'* is a positive overhypothesis of a hypothesis *h* if the antecedent and consequent of *h'* are parents of, respectively, the antecedent and consequent of *h* (*FFF*, 110); *h'* is a negative overhypothesis of *h* if the antecedent of *h'* is a parent of the antecedent of *h*, while the consequent of *h'* is a predicate complementary to a parent of the consequent of *h* (*FFF*, 115); and a predicate is a *parent* of another if the extension of the latter is a member of the extension of the former (*FFF*, 106).

But it is not of course maintained that *every* overhypothesis of a given hypothesis is, if supported and unviolated, relevant to the projectibility of the latter. If, to mention a counterexample offered in *FFF* (111), some naval fleets are known to be uniform in color and none is known not to be so, and if 'bagleet' is a predicate applying just to naval fleets and to bagful *B* of marbles, then the hypothesis that every bagleet is uniform in color is of course a supported and unviolated positive overhypothesis of our hypothesis that all the marbles in bag *B* are red; yet one is not to conclude that the information concerning naval fleets contributes, via the hypothesis about bagleets, to the projectibility of the hypothesis about the marbles. Overhypotheses, Goodman explains, depend, for their effect, upon their own *projectibility,* i.e., upon the entrenchment of their own predicates and the impact of their own overhypotheses.

After this brief report, a few brief comments. The theory implies, in particular, these two troublesome results:

1. The projectibility of a hypothesis turns out to be affected, through various higher-order hypotheses, by information that would normally be regarded as confirming these but quite irrelevant to the hypothesis in question. For, to give a few examples:[28] since iron is a metal and since objects that are heavier than water are not all equal in conductivity, 'Every

metal is uniform in conductivity' is a (negative) overhypothesis of 'All iron is heavier than water'; since russet is a variety of apple, and round objects are not all equal in size, 'Every variety of apple is varied in size' is a (positive) overhypothesis of 'All russets are round'; and so forth.

2. The *projectibility* of a hypothesis turns out to be negatively affected by information that would normally be said to confirm that hypothesis. For, since iron is a metal and objects heavier than water are not all equal in density, 'Every metal is uniform in density' is a *negative* overhypothesis of 'All iron is heavier than water'; and so forth.

But these are rather minor troubles. They merely show that the intended concept of overhypothesis has been defined inaccurately. Presumably, the following correction, which seems sufficient to remove the unwanted results at issue, would fit Goodman's intentions:

h' is a negative overhypothesis of h iff the antecedent of h' is a parent of the antecedent of h and the consequent of h' denotes a class of classes none of which is included in the class denoted by the consequent of h.

h' is a positive overhypothesis of h iff the antecedent of h' is a parent of the antecedent of h' and the consequent of h' denotes a class of classes some of which are included in—and all of which are either included in or disjoint with—the class denoted by the consequent of h.[29]

The real trouble is different: the generalizations we in fact find plausible seem to have no advantage in *comparative projectibility*[30] over many of their most implausible rivals. To take again one of our previous examples: since the hypothesis *h:* "All horses are maned," can hardly be attributed any advantage in entrenchment over its queer rival h^{***} (see above, pp. 64–65), therefore, if h is to be judged *more projectible* than the other, this superiority must be accounted for by reference to some effective, that is, appreciably *projectible* overhypotheses. Perhaps, one could find some appreciably *projectible* positive overhypotheses of h;[31] the trouble is that it is much easier to find some such overhypotheses of h^{***}, for instance:

$$(H^{***}) \quad (y)(Py \rightarrow ((Qy \ \& \sim Ky) \lor (Ry \ \& \ Ky))),$$

where 'Py' stands for, say, 'y is a species of mammals,' 'Qy' for 'y is uniform in color,' 'Ry' for 'y is uniform in density,' and 'Ky' for 'y is such that some horses are either maned but not heavier than water or heavier than water but not maned.' (If the consequent of h^{***} is coextensive with 'heavier than water,' that of H^{***} is coextensive with 'uniform in density'; and if the consequent of h^{***} is coextensive with 'white,' that of H^{***} is coextensive with 'uniform in color.')

Although the predicates of H^{***} seem well entrenched, one might still try to question its *projectibility* and, thus, its effectiveness by looking for an appreciably *projectible* negative overhypothesis for it. But (to say the least), since any hypothesis that could be identified as an overhypothesis of H^{***} could only be as bizarre as H^{***} itself,[32] the argument would amount to denying the projectibility of one implausible hypothesis by ascribing projectibility to another. Finally, one might try to question the *projectibility* of h^{***} by looking for an appreciably *projectible* negative overhypothesis for it, which might be said to outweigh the effect of H^{***}. But again, since any hypothesis that can be identified as an overhypothesis of h^{***} can only be as queer as h^{***} itself,[33] this argument would, like the former, amount to denying the *projectibility* of one implausible generalization by ascribing *projectibility* to another.

V. Projectibility and Extension

The paradoxical results displayed above would of course be avoided if the foundation of Goodman's edifice were not designed according to the canons of his extensionalist engineering. But I don't think that redesigning the foundation (redefining entrenchment as a property attaching to concepts, rather than classes) would make the whole construction more secure. The claim that "in the case of our main stock of well-worn predicates . . . the judgment of projectibility has derived from the habitual projection" (*FFF*, 98), rather than vice versa—as if our initial choices of predicates to project were random ("matters of chance"; *PP*, 358), rather than constrained by innate standards of similarity and deep-seated theoretical beliefs—strikes me as a sheer fancy.[34]

Now and then Goodman declares that he is "not much concerned with whether the entrenchment or the projectibility comes first" (*FFF*, 98), that what he is "primarily suggesting is that the superior entrenchment of the predicate projected is . . . a sufficient even if not necessary indication of projectibility" (*ibid.*), and that if "psychological grounds for our decisions as to what predicates or hypotheses to project" were found, "such an explanation . . . would not conflict with [his] treatment of projectibility in terms of entrenchment of predicates" (*PP*, 357–8), for it "would merely make the initial choices psychologically determinate rather than matters of chance" (*PP*, 358).

The trouble is that while the claim that "in the case of our main stock of well-worn predicates . . . the judgment of projectibility has derived from the habitual projection," rather than vice versa (*FFF*, 98), is too extravagant to merit belief, the claim that "the superior entrenchment of the predicate projected is . . . a sufficient even if not necessary indication of projectibility" (*FFF*, 98) is[35] too modest to merit attention.

But this was a digression. The main point to note is that the paradoxical results of Goodman's theory do not depend on its appeal to predicates' entrenchment. They totally depend on its assumption that a predicate is well-fitted for projection if it has—or, more exactly, is recognized as having—the "right" sort of extension (if it is recognized as denoting a "natural kind," rather than an artificial collection; cf. *FFF*, 121). This assumption—reiterated by Quine[36]—does not withstand scrutiny. For, whatever the criterion for dividing classes into natural and unnatural or grading them as more or less natural—whether it be entrenchment or whatever else—one can always contrive perfectly implausible generalizations using predicates known to denote perfectly "natural" classes. If '*B*' and '*C*' in h^{**} are predicates that are to count as denoting natural classes, then the queer consequent of h^{**} must also count as denoting a natural class; and so must the queer consequent-predicate of H^{***} if '*A*' and '*R*' do. If such predicates are unfit for projection, it is not because of what they denote, but because of 'how' they denote, i.e., what they mean.

Postscript (1992)

I wish to comment briefly on two solutions to Goodman's problem that have been offered in the intervening years.

Ralph Kennedy and Charles Chihara[37] have proposed a simple modification of Goodman's theory, which delivers it from troublemakers such as h^{**} or h^{***}. While according to Goodman, "the entrenchment of a predicate results from the actual projection not merely of that predicate but also of all predicates coextensive with it" (*FFF*, 95), Kennedy and Chihara replace here 'coextensive' by 'believed to be coextensive.' Thus while according to Goodman, "in a sense, not the word itself but the class it selects is what becomes entrenched, and to speak of the entrenchment of a predicate is to speak elliptically of the entrenchment of [its] extension" (*ibid.*)—which implies that a predicate known to have a well-entrenched extensional equivalent is to be reckoned as just as well entrenched—on the Kennedy–Chihara proposal, a predicate *P* that has not itself been often projected is to count as well entrenched only if there is some predicate *Q* that has often been projected and that is believed to be coextensive with *P* (or a family of predicates whose aggregate record of projections is sizeable and which are all believed to be coextensive with *P*).[38] The queer consequent-predicate of h^{**} (or of h^{***}) does not satisfy this stronger condition, since—although known to be either coextensive with '*B*' or coextensive with '*C*'—it is neither believed to be coextensive with '*B*' nor believed to be coextensive with '*C*' (as long as the truth value of *h* is in question).

The paradoxical result that no generalizations are ever projectible (and any generalization whose antecedent-predicate or consequent-predicate is less than best entrenched is overridden) is thereby avoided. Yet the proposed amendment does not, I think, make Goodman's theory much more plausible.

Suppose that (*i*) 'All *A* are *B*' and its converse are inductive generalizations, both believed to be true, and (*ii*) '*A*' is a predicate that has often been projected (say, as consequent predicate), while the 'inductive history' of '*B*' amounts to its presence in the two generalizations just mentioned.[39] Let 'All *C* are *B*' be a newly advanced hypothesis rendered credible by its supporting instances.[40] On the Kennedy–Chihara account, what explains our projecting 'All *C* are *B*'—and ignoring alternatives such as 'All *C* are *B**,' where '*B**' is a Goodmanesque counterpart of '*B*'—is our belief that '*B*' is coextensive with the well-entrenched predicate '*A*.' That latter belief, however, remains unexplained: since '*B*' was not well entrenched before we came to believe that it is coextensive with '*A*,' the theory offers no answer to the question why we chose to project 'All *A* are *B*,' rather than 'All *A* are *B**.' But, if our choice of 'All *A* are *B*' over 'All *A* are *B**' had nothing to do with entrenchment, it is hard to see why our later choice of 'All *C* are *B*' over 'All *C* are *B**' should have anything to do with entrenchment. Whatever would account for the first choice should account just as well for the second.

The problem is of course quite independent of the question whether entrenchment, defined one way or another, is a right clue. The statement that if a predicate *P* is well fitted for projection and a predicate *Q* is believed to be coextensive with *P* then *Q* is equally well fitted—even if true—cannot be part of a good answer to the question what makes some predicates better fitted than others. For suppose we are told that what matters is not entrenchment, but a certain characteristic *F*: some predicates are highly *F*-ish, others less *F*-ish, and still others not *F*-ish at all; some *F*-ish predicates are, in a sense, intrinsically *F*-ish (are *F*-ish, and recognizable as such, independently of their relations to other predicates), while a predicate that does not belong to that group is *F*-ish iff, for some predicate *P* that does, it is believed to be coextensive with *P*. Let us rewrite clause (*ii*) in the preceding description of '*A*' and '*B*' thus: '*A*' is one of those predicates that are intrinsically *F*-ish, while '*B*' is not; '*B*' became *F*-ish when we came to believe that all *A* are *B* and vice versa. On the present account, our projecting 'All *C* are *B*,' rather than 'All *C* are *B**,' has to do with the fact that '*B*' is *F*-ish, by virtue of our belief that it is coextensive with '*A*.' As before, the latter belief is left unexplained; and one can only wonder why our choice of 'All *C* are *B*' over 'All *C* are *B**' should depend on the *F*-ness of '*B*,' if our earlier choice of 'All *A* are *B*' over 'All *A* are *B**' had nothing to do with that.

Let me add a few comments[41] on the idea, propounded by Sydney Shoemaker, George Bealer, and several other authors[42], that the key to the solution to Goodman's riddle lies in the distinction between genuine properties (or genuine relations) and pseudo-properties (or pseudo-relations); that what distinguishes, among supported, unexhausted, and unviolated generalizations, projectible ones from unprojectible ones is essentially this: in a projectible generalization, the antecedent-predicate and the consequent-predicate designate genuine properties (or genuine relations).

Genuine properties and relations are to be those which "endow objects with their active and passive causal powers" (Shoemaker, *op. cit.*, p. 295); those which "determine the . . . causal and phenomenal order of the world" (Bealer, *op. cit.*, p. 179). Greenness is such a property; grueness is not.

What I want to show here is that Goodman's problem is no more solvable in terms of that distinction than it is solvable in terms of the distinction between 'natural' and 'unnatural' classes—for, just as one can contrive unviolated and amply supported, yet utterly incredible generalizations using predicates that denote perfectly 'natural' classes (whatever one's criterion of that 'naturalness'), so also one can contrive unviolated and amply supported generalizations using predicates that designate perfectly 'genuine' properties (whatever one's criterion of that 'genuineness').

I cannot challenge the Shoemaker–Bealer criterion of projectibility by arguing that queer generalizations of the sort invoked in my paper satisfy that criterion. Let 'roundhard' be short for 'either both round and such that all emeralds are green or both hard and such that some emeralds are not green'; I cannot show that the hypothesis

h':   All emeralds are roundhard,

which is supported, unviolated, and utterly incredible (in view of its conflict with h: 'All emeralds are green'), satisfies the criterion at issue. For (*i*) though 'roundhard' is either coextensive with 'round' or coextensive with 'hard,' I don't see how to argue that it designates either roundness or hardness; and (*ii*) I see no way of making plausible the claim that if this predicate designates neither roundness nor hardness, then it designates some third property, as 'genuine' as the two others. Let me, then, replace h' by another rival of h:

h'':   'All emeralds are hardround.'

The predicate 'hardround' is introduced by the following stipulation:

(*S*) If all emeralds are green, 'hardround' designates roundness; and if some emeralds are not green, 'hardround' designates hardness.

(Or: If all emeralds are green, hardroundness = roundness; otherwise hardroundness = hardness.)

h'' is, like h', supported, unviolated, and utterly incredible (the two are obviously identical in truth value); and its queer consequent-predicate designates a genuine property.

It might appear that stipulation S makes no more sense than this one:

(S') If all emeralds are green, 'hardround' is to mean the same as 'round'; otherwise it is to mean the same as 'hard.'

S' makes no sense, indeed. It legislates that 'hardround' is either synonymous with 'round' or else synonymous with 'hard.' But so introduced, 'hardround' is not synonymous with either; for a 'synonymy' that one cannot detect without relying on extralinguistic information is no synonymy.

But S, so one might argue, makes no more sense than S' does, because (let us agree that predicates that are not necessarily coextensive do not designate the same property; and let us assume that neither h nor its denial is a necessary truth) S in effect stipulates that 'hardround' is either necessarily coextensive with 'round' or necessarily coextensive with 'hard,' depending on a contingent fact (the truth or falsity of h), and thus implies that either 'All and only round things are hardround' or 'All and only hard things are hardround' is a contingently necessary truth.

Although it is less than obvious that stipulating contingent necessities makes as little sense as stipulating synonymies not detectable without appeal to extra-linguistic information, I need not dwell on this; for the objection at issue is unwarranted: S does not stipulate any contingent necessity. The objector alleges that S commits one to asserting, in particular, 'It is possible that necessarily all and only round (hard) things are hardround' (A). But it doesn't. A is not entailed by 'It is possible that all (not all) emeralds are green' (B) and 'If all (not all) emeralds are green then necessarily all and only round (hard) things are hardround' (C). Nor can one validly infer A from B and 'That all (not all) emeralds are green entails that necessarily all and only round (hard) things are hardround' (i.e., from B and the analyticity of C.[43] The objection at issue rests on confusing implication or entailment with necessitation; or on confusing it being possible that so-and-so with it not being certain that not so-and-so; or on confusing stipulation S with what results from S when 'if' is replaced by 'in those possible worlds in which.'[44]

Stipulation S *is* in a way peculiar. But not because it involves referring to properties. (Nominalistic qualms aside, there is no interesting difference between saying 'Let "dred" designate the property of being dark-red' (S^* and saying 'Let "dred" be short for "dark-red"' or saying: 'Definition: x is dred iff x is dark-red'; whatever is said explicitly in one of those formulations is said implicitly in the other two.) S is peculiar in that (unlike S^*) it cannot be transcribed into an explicit definition—'x is hardround iff . . . x

. . . '—unless properties are to be equated, *à la* Lewis,[45] with sets of possible objects.[46] But, assuming realism with respect to properties (as the proposed solution to Goodman's problem requires), I don't see why this aspect of *S* should make such a stipulation objectionable (even if properties are not to be equated with any sets of possibilia).

To reiterate the conclusion: the distinction between projectible and unprojectible generalizations is not reducible to that between 'good' and 'bad' properties, any more than it is reducible to a distinction between 'good' and 'bad' classes; what matters is not just whether a predicate denotes a right kind of class or designates a right kind of property, but, so to speak, *how* it denotes or designates what it denotes or designates, i.e., what it *means*.

Albuquerque, New Mexico

NOTES

* I wish to thank Professors Nelson Goodman and Israel Scheffler for their stimulating criticisms of an earlier draft of this paper.

† See Nelson Goodman, *Fact, Fiction and Forecast*, 2nd ed. (Indianapolis: Bobbs-Merrill, 1965) (hereafter abbreviated as *FFF*); *Problems and Projects* (Indianapolis: Bobbs-Merrill, 1972) (hereafter abbreviated as *PP*); and Goodman, R. Schwartz, and I. Scheffler, "An Improvement in the Theory of Projectibility," *J. Philosophy* LXVII, 18 (Sept. 17, 1970), 605–608, reprinted in *PP*, 389–393.

1. "In a sense, not the word itself but the class it selects is what becomes entrenched, and to speak of the entrenchment of a predicate is to speak elliptically of the entrenchment of the extension of that predicate" (*FFF*, 95).

2. This term is used in *FFF* as a designation for statements of the type 'All *P* are *Q*.'

3. As far as I understand, *evidence* is to be information of whatever sort which is taken at the relevant time for granted. Cf., e.g., *FFF*, 109n.

4. Besides, hypotheses that are not unprojectible at a given time are to differ from one another in *degree of projectibility* at that time, according to the entrenchment of their predicates and the evidence for their *overhypotheses*. This portion of the theory will be discussed separately in section IV.

5. I will assume the following definitions: a hypothesis is unexhausted iff it is not implied by the evidence; unviolated iff its negation is not implied by the evidence; supported iff at least one instance of it (or at least an existential generalization of an instance) is implied by the evidence. (Instances of a hypothesis '$(x) (Px \rightarrow Qx)$' are sentences of the type 'Pa & Qa'.) This differs slightly from the definitions given in *FFF* (90); if I depart from them, it is because they have some obviously unwanted consequences—such as that a hypothesis '$(x)(Px \rightarrow Qx)$' may

be "unviolated" (and hence—if it meets the remaining conditions—"projectible") even if the evidence implies its denial (as long as the evidence implies no specific counterinstance to it, i.e., no sentence of the type 'Pa & $\sim Qa$'). But the conclusions to be reached do not depend on this departure.

6. Only gross differences of entrenchment are to be relevant; cf. *FFF,* 96, 105.

7. As antecedent or consequent, respectively; and a predicate is the better entrenched as, respectively, antecedent or consequent, the longer and more often this predicate or predicates coextensive with it have previously occurred in inductive generalizations as antecedents or consequents. Cf. *FFF,* 191–192n.

8. Here I am departing from the formula explicitly stated in "An Improvement . . ." and adopting the definition that one finds there between the lines. The authors start with the stipulation that h is overridden by h' if both are supported etc., conflict with each other, and h' is the better entrenched and conflicts with no still better entrenched hypothesis (606; *PP,* 390); then they add that this formulation is somewhat deficient, for it "covers only hierarchies of at most three supported, unviolated, unexhausted, and successively better entrenched and conflicting hypotheses" (*loc cit.,* fn 1), and offer a corrected variant, according to which "a hypothesis is overridden if it is the bottom member of a hierarchy [of supported etc. and successively better entrenched and conflicting hypotheses] that cannot be extended upward and has an even number of members" (*ibid.*). But this definition no doubt misses their intentions. The bottom member of a hierarchy of the sort at issue is supposed to be overridden by the next-to-the-bottom member of it, and the clause that the hierarchy should have an even number of members and not be extendable upward is supposed to ensure that a hypothesis not be overridden by a given other hypothesis if the latter is itself overridden. But, obviously, the next-to-the-bottom member of a hierarchy of the sort at issue (say, some hierarchy (h_1, h_2, h_3, h_4) may well be the bottom member of another such hierarchy (say, some hierarchy (h_2, h_5) and thus be itself overridden according to the proposed definition.

Needless to say, no vicious circle is created in the formula adopted in the text above, by the reappearance of the definiendum in the definiens; just as no vicious circle is involved in, say, the following definition: 'n is A iff, for some positive integer m, $m = n - 1$ and m is not A,' which unambiguously defines A as the class of even positive numbers.

9. Confirmation is circumscribed by Goodman as a relation that holds, when it holds, between a generalization and its supporting instances alone, but of course not (cf. the projectibility criterion reported above) as a relation that holds, when it holds, independently of what other evidence is available.

10. "Consider the heterogenous conjunction: *8497 is a prime number and the other side of the moon is flat and Elizabeth the First was crowned on a Tuesday.* To show that any one of the three component statements is true is to support the conjunction by reducing the net undetermined claim. But support of this kind is not confirmation; for establishment of one component endows the whole statement with no credibility that is transmitted to other component statements." (*FFF,* 69)

11. Though not always to the actual projectibility or unprojectibility of particular hypotheses. Which hypotheses are in fact projectible depends, in particular, upon the actual comparative entrenchment of individual predicates and thus, partly, upon which predicates happen to be coextensive. But that a given new predicate, not suspected to be coextensive with a given well-worn predicate, actually selects the same class of objects as the other and is thereby as well entrenched, does not of course make generalizations with this predicate more plausible. Unsuspected equivalences between predicates cannot be built into our inductive intuitions. Cf. *PP*, 360, 411–412.

12. If I have inserted here the phrase 'in particular,' it is because the theory is not meant to imply that a generalization (supported, etc.) must satisfy Goodman's projectibility criterion in order to be credible or more credible than its rivals. 'All nonblack things are nonravens' is eminently credible, even if not confirmed by its instances, i.e., not projectible: its credibility rests on the projectibility of its contrapositive (cf. *FFF*, 70–71).

13. Goodness knows why it is required, for two hypotheses to "conflict," that they ascribe to something different predicates of which exactly one applies, rather than merely: of which *at most one* applies. So fashioned, the definition hardly fits even Goodman's favorite examples. To dismiss both h_1; 'All emeralds are grue' and h_2: 'All emeralds are gred' as overridden by the better entrenched hypothesis h_3: 'All emeralds are green,' we must assume that both of the former do indeed conflict with the latter. But, obviously, for h_1 to conflict in the required sense with h_3, h_2 must be false; and for h_2 to conflict with h_3, h_1 must be false; so, when we assume that h_1 and h_2 conflict with h_3, we already assume that h_1 and h_2 are false and, thus, reject both without any reference to entrenchment.

14. "On Kahane's Confusions," *J. Philosophy* LXIX, 3 (Feb. 10, 1972): 83/4.

15. For instance, when he says ("An Improvement . . . ," 607; *PP*, 391) that all consequences of projectible hypotheses—except those consequences which are exhausted or unsupported—are also projectible, for they are unviolated and conflict with no hypotheses other than overridden. This statement is no doubt based on the assumption that consequences of a given hypothesis conflict with no hypotheses with which the latter does not conflict—which is patently true if conflict is understood as incompatibility, but patently false if conflict is defined as above.

16. Incidentally, there is nothing extraordinary in the definiens for 'Hx' containing a closed sentence. To be the color of copper is to match some copper in color and be such that specimens of copper match each other in color; to be twice as heavy as water is to be twice as heavy as some water and such that water is uniform in density; to be one meter long is to have the length of so-and-so many wavelengths of the orange-red radiation of krypton 86 and be such that all those waves are equal in length, etc.

17. h^* is equivalent, on the information accepted at t, to the denial of h.

18. For, if h is true, the consequent of h^* is coextensive with 'Bx,' and so h and h^* ascribe to something two different predicates of which only one actually applies.

(And neither of h^* and h follows from the other, as is deducible from the assumption that h is unviolated and unexhausted and that h_o is violated.)

19. Although "comparison of the inherited entrenchment of two predicates is in point only if neither has much greater earned entrenchment than the other" (*FFF*, 105). The definition of 'parent' is quoted on page 66.

20. And many others, since, as clearly follows from Goodman's definition, for any predicate P of the nth order and any predicate Q of the $(n + 1)$st order, either Q or any predicate complementary to Q is a 'parent' of P.

21. A hypothesis h (supported etc. at t) is unprojectible at t—so the definition would run—iff, for some h', it follows from the information accepted at t that h is overridden at t by h'.

22. One might also suggest another similar move: to redefine 'overridden' so that a hypothesis is overridden by another only when the latter must be *judged* to outstrip the former in entrenchment. h is overridden at t by h', so the definition would run, iff both are supported etc. at t but are incompatible at t (or, if one likes: . . . but conflict; or rather: . . . conflict according to the information accepted at t) and are such that (i) h' outstrips h in entrenchment at t, according to the information accepted at t, and (ii) h' is not overridden at t. But this correction would be of no avail: here again a host of plausible hypotheses would fall victims of such rivals as h^*_1, h^*_2, h^*; though not, as previously, all those whose antecedents or consequents would be judged less than best entrenched, yet all those whose antecedents would be judged less than best entrenched and consequents, ill-entrenched. If 'Ax' occurring in h^* is a predicate ranked at t among the best entrenched, while the antecedent of h is ranked at t as less than best entrenched and its consequent as ill-entrenched, then, according to what is assumed at t, h yields in entrenchment at t to h^*; and if also 'Bx' occurring in h^* is a predicate ranked at t among the best entrenched, then, obviously, h^* is not overridden at t on the present definition: for it does not follow from the information accepted at t that the consequent of h^* is *not* coextensive with 'Bx' (otherwise h would be exhausted at t), and hence, for any h', it does not follow from what is accepted at t that h^* yields in entrenchment at t to h'.

23. For h^* to be overridden at t, h must be false; but, on the present definition, for h to be projectible at t, h^* need not then be overridden; what is required instead is that it not follow from what is granted at t that h^* is not at that time overridden; and this does not of course require that h be false; what it requires instead (if 'Ax' and 'Bx' are a pair of predicates reckoned at t among the best entrenched) is that the truth of h not follow from what is granted at t (in other words, that h be unexhausted at t).

24. h^{**} is equivalent, on the information accepted at t, to the conjunction of '$(x)(Ax \rightarrow Cx)$' and the denial of h.

25. h^{***} is equivalent, on the information accepted at t, to the conjunction of h' and the statement that h' conflicts with h.

26. Unless (cf. the definition of 'conflict') h^{***} follows from h or h from h^{***}.

But neither does h^{***} follow from h (as is deducible from (b) and the assumption that h is unviolated) nor does h follow from h^{***} (as is deducible from (c)).

27. And if some bags turned out to be uniform and some mixed, the projectibility of the hypothesis in question might be affected through a statistical overhypothesis—a concept mentioned, though not elaborated in *FFF*, 115.

28. Overhypotheses like those mentioned below are not of course to be dismissed as ineffective.

29. These definitions have the following, presumably desired, consequences: if h' is a positive overhypothesis of h and h' is true, then, if some instances of h are true, h is true; and if h' is a negative overhypothesis of h and is true, then h is false. (Or, to put it differently: if h' is a positive overhypothesis of h and h' is true, then, if the determined instances of h are true, its undetermined instances are also true; and if h' is a negative overhypothesis of h and is true, then, if the determined instances of h are true, at least some of its undetermined instances are false.)

30. I italicize 'projectible,' 'more projectible,' etc., whenever I use them as defined by Goodman's criterion.

31. Incidentally, *projectibility* as defined by Goodman aside, *plausible* overhypotheses are often unavailable; it is hard to think of a plausible positive overhypothesis for 'All zebras have dark stripes on a whitish background' (that every species of the genus *Equus* is uniform in color is patently false, after all).

32. We do not know whether the consequent of H^{***} refers to those classes which are uniform in density or rather to those which are uniform in color.

33. We do not know whether the consequent of h^{***} refers to those objects which are heavier than water or rather to those which are white.

34. Quine remarks that through science we "rise above" our innate "quality space," revising "our innate standards of similarity . . . on the strength . . . of second-order inductions. New groupings, hypothetically adopted at the suggestion of a growing theory, prove favorable to inductions and so become 'entrenched'. We newly establish the projectibility of some predicate, to our satisfaction, by successfully trying to project it." (W. V. Quine, *Ontological Relativity and Other Essays*, New York: Columbia, 1969, 128–9.) These remarks sound to me quite plausible. But Quine's account departs significantly from Goodman's. Not just in what Quine affirms (what Goodman attributes to *habit*, Quine attributes to *success*, the record of past projections that remain unrefuted) but, more importantly, in what he refrains from affirming. Quine does not hold that the projectibility of an entrenched predicate derives from nothing but its entrenchment (for he does not maintain that the scientist tries new groupings at random, so that *any* new grouping has a chance to be tried); nor does he suggest that his remarks on the role of entrenchment in the evolving language of science apply just as well to the "main stock of well-worn predicates" (*FFF*, 98) which we employ in generalizing about the world of everyday experience.

35. When divorced from the unhappy idea that "to speak of the entrenchment

of a predicate is to speak elliptically of the entrenchment of [its] extension" (*FFF*, 95).

36. ". . . not all sets are kinds." "A projectible predicate is one that is true of all and only the things of a kind." (W. V. Quine, *op. cit.*, 118, 116.)

37. "Beyond Zabludowskian Competitors: A New Theory of Projectibility," *Philosophical Studies 33* (1978), 229–253.

38. *Ibid.*, 245–6.

39. Examples of predicates that would fit this description should not be difficult to find (among dispositional predicates in particular).

40. Whether we have additional evidence in its favor, such as independently verified instances of 'All *C* are *A*,' is immaterial.

41. Excerpted from "On Induction and Properties," *Pacific Philosophical Quarterly 72* (1991), 78–85.

42. See S. Shoemaker, "Properties, Causation, and Projectibility," in L. J. Cohen and M. Hesse, eds., *Applications of Inductive Logic* (1980); G. Bealer, *Quality and Concept* (1982), 179 ff.; D. M. Armstrong, *What Is a Law of Nature?* (1983). Cf. also R. Harré and E. H. Madden, *Causal Powers* (1975).

43. Just as—let 'meter' be defined as the length stick *S* in fact has—'$\diamond \square 2 + 2 = 5$' (*D*) cannot be validly inferred from '$\diamond$ stick *S* is not one meter long' (*E*) and 'If stick *S* is not one meter long then $\square 2 + 2 = 5$' (*F*); or from *E* and 'That stick *S* is not one meter long entails that $\square 2 + 2 = 5$' (*F'*) *E* is true; so are *F* and *F'* (since 'Stick *S* is not one meter long' is analytically false): yet *D* is false.

44. To maintain that *S* commits one to asserting both '$\diamond \square$ (all and only round things are hardround)' and '$\diamond \sim \square$ (all and only round things are hardround)' one would have to claim that *S* stipulates in effect that the conditional 'If all emeralds are green then, necessarily, all and only round things are hardround' (C_1) and the conditional 'If not all emeralds are green then, necessarily, all and only hard things are hardround' (C_2)—are to count as necessary truths. But that claim is unwarranted. If all (not all) emeralds are green, then *S* does not render C_2 (or C_1 resp.) a necessary truth; for *S* does not stipulate that if, *contrary to fact*, not all (or, resp., all) emeralds were green then "hardround" would designate hardness (or, resp., roundness).

45. Cf. his "New Work for a Theory of Universals," *Australasian Journal of Philosophy* 1983, 346.

46. If one is ready to equate properties with sets of possible objects (or at least allow quantifying over possibilia), one can accept the following explicit definition as a transcription of (or a replacement for) *S:* "A possible object *x* is hardround iff (i) *x* is round and all actual emeralds are green or (ii) *x* is hard and some actual emeralds are not green." Or: "For any possible world *W* and any object *x* in *W*, *x* is hardround in W iff (i) *x* is round in *W* and in the actual world all emeralds are green or (ii) *x* is hard in *W* and in the actual world some emeralds are not green."

Grue[*]

Frank Jackson

5

This paper is concerned with an aspect of the problem of describing or specifying those inductive practices we take to be rational.

At the level of description, there is no doubt that one common inductive practice we take to be rational is to project common properties from samples to populations, to argue from certain Fs being G to certain other Fs being G. There are many ways we can try to spell out this practice in semi-formal terms: by saying 'Fa & Ga' confirms '$\forall x[Fx \supset Gx]$,' or 'All examined As are B' supports 'All unexamined As are B,' or 'Fa_1 & . . . & Fa_n' gives a good reason for 'Fa_{n+1},' and so on. The precise way chosen will not particularly concern us, and I will simply refer to the kind of inductive argument pattern reflected in the various formalizations as the *straight rule* (SR). The discussion will be restricted to the simplest case where everything in a sample, not merely a percentage, has the property we are concerned with.

To say that the SR is one common inductive argument pattern we all acknowledge as rational, is not to say that it is the most fundamental inductive argument pattern, or the most important in science, or the pattern that must be justified if induction is to be justified; it is simply to say what is undeniable—that we all use it on occasion and take it as rational to do so. This paper is not concerned with how important or fundamental the SR is—for example, vis-à-vis hypothetico-deduction—it is concerned with the *description* of those applications of the SR which we regard as rational.

Since Nelson Goodman's 1946 paper[1] and the development of it in *Fact, Fiction and Forecast*,[2] it has been very widely supposed that the rough description of the SR given above—as certain Fs being G supporting certain other Fs being G—requires the insertion of a substantial proviso to the effect that the properties or predicates (or, in an alternative terminology, the hypotheses) involved be projectible.[3] The notion is that, though there are certain values of 'F' and 'G' for which it is manifestly true that the SR applies, there are other values for which it is manifestly false that the SR applies.

This gives rise to a new problem (Goodman's new riddle) in inductive logic—that of demarcating the projectible predicates from the

From *The Journal of Philosophy*, Vol. LXXII, No. 5 (March 13, 1975): 113–131. Reprinted by permission of *The Journal of Philosophy* and the author.

nonprojectible. The extensional aspect of this problem has not been so controversial as the intensional. There has been reasonable agreement about which predicates go into which class: 'green,' 'blue,' 'round,' etc., into the projectible; 'grue,' 'bleen,' 'sampled,' into the nonprojectible. But there has been enormous controversy over the *rationale* for this division; over what makes, for example, 'grue' nonprojectible and 'green' projectible. It has, to say the least, proved difficult to give a plausible, *nonarbitrary* account of the projectible/nonprojectible distinction other than the circular, useless one that a predicate is projectible just if the SR applies with respect to it.

I believe we can resolve the apparently interminable conflict over what it is about nonprojectible predicates that makes them so, by challenging its very foundation. I will argue in this paper that there is no "new riddle of induction," by arguing that *all* (consistent) predicates are projectible and that there is no paradox resulting from 'grue' and like predicates.

The almost universal view that we need a distinction between projectible and nonprojectible predicates and hypotheses has had, I believe, three sources: one, a tendency to conflate three different ways of defining 'grue'; two, a lack of precision about just how, in detail, the 'grue' paradox or new riddle of induction is supposed to arise; and, three, a failure to note a counterfactual condition that governs the vast majority of our applications of the SR. I will consider these matters in turn.

I. The Three Ways of Defining 'Grue'

In this section I will consider the three common kinds of ways of defining 'grue' by considering typical instances of each. I will argue that the first two ways do not pose even a prima facie problem for the SR, leaving us with the third way to consider in later sections.

A typical example of the first way is:

D_1. *x* is grue iff *x* is green before *T* and blue thereafter.

where *T* is a chosen time in the future.[4]

On D_1, 'grue' is atemporal—an object is grue or not once and for all, it cannot be grue at one time and not grue at another—and in this respect differs from 'green.'

There seems no case for regarding 'grue' as nonprojectible if it is defined in this way. An emerald is grue[5] just if it is green up to *T* and blue thereafter, and if we discovered that all the emeralds so far examined had this property, then, other things being equal, we would probably accept that all emeralds, both examined and unexamined, have this property of being green to a certain time and then turning blue; or, at least, would regard this hypothesis as supported.

We would in this case be regarding emeralds as like tomatoes and oranges, one of those things which change color dramatically during their life cycles. No doubt we would seek an explanation for the fact that the change in emeralds occurs at a fixed time, T; but there would in principle be no impossibility about finding a satisfactory explanation. For example, we might discover that emeralds contain a radioactive element the radiation of which makes them green instead of blue, and that the level of this radiation is due to drop below a crucial figure at T.

[A puzzling feature of the discussions of the new riddle of induction by those who employ a D_1-type definition is that they take it as not in dispute that all emeralds observed to date are grue, as well as green. For example, Stephen Barker simply asserts as if it were an evident truth that "all the numerous emeralds that we have observed have been grue" (*op. cit.*, p. 189)—but what is an evident truth is that these emeralds were green at the time of observation; what we all believe is that they are always green; and what none of us believe is that they are grue, for none of us believe they will change to blue in the year 2000 (Barker's choice for T).[6]]

A typical example of the second way[7] of defining 'grue' is:

D_2. x is grue at t iff (x is green at t & $t < T$)
or (x is blue at t & $t \geq T$).

'Grue' on this definition is like 'green' in being temporal: an object may be $grue_2$ at one time and not at another.

It sometimes seems to be thought that D_2 really amounts to $D_{2.1}$: 'x is grue' means 'x is green' before T and 'x is blue' after T, which is an explicit case of ambiguity; and, consequently, that it raises no problem for the SR.[8] When we read the SR as licensing the projection of a common predicate, it is understood that the predicate has the same meaning throughout.

The two definitions are not, however, equivalent. The appearance of equivalence arises from a failure to be explicit about time in $D_{2.1}$, and if we write in a time variable to give: 'x is grue at t' means 'x is green at t' before T, and 'x is blue at t' after T, the disparity becomes obvious. Consider a time t_1 before T, and whether a green emerald is grue at t_1. According to D_2, the answer is an unequivocal yes; but, according to $D_{2.1}$, the answer depends on the time at which the question is being asked. If the question is asked before T, the answer is yes; because before T, 'x is $grue_{2.1}$ at t' means 'x is green at t,' and the emerald is green at t_1: if asked after T, the answer is no; because after T, 'x is $grue_{2.1}$ at t' means 'x is blue at t,' and the emerald is not blue at t_1. In short, D_2 and $D_{2.1}$ are not equivalent because the time at which we consider the question of an object's grueness is relevant on $D_{2.1}$ and not relevant on D_2—on D_2, the time at which the object is green or blue is relevant, but not the time at which we consider the matter.

There is, I believe, no getting away from the fact that D_2 is a perfectly proper, intelligible definition. Nevertheless, D_2 does not give rise to a paradox or "new riddle" when conjoined with the SR, and so does not give grounds for supposing that there are nonprojectible predicates of which 'grue$_2$' is the best-known example.

The contrary view has arisen from confusion over whether we are considering the SR in conjunction with 'grue$_2$' as applied to objects that endure through time, that is, four-dimensional objects, or as applied to three-dimensional objects *at* times, that is, time-slices of the four-dimensional objects.

If we are considering the SR as applied to enduring objects like tables and emeralds, if we take the members of the samples and populations we discuss to endure through time, then we must read a temporal factor into the predicates with which the SR is concerned. Enduring objects aren't red, or green, or square, *simpliciter:* they are red at t_1, green at t_2, and so on. A tomato isn't both red and green; it is green early in its life history and red later.

From this it follows that when we read the SR (applied to enduring objects) as licensing the projection of common predicates from samples to populations, we must incorporate a temporal factor into these predicates. What we project must be understood as at a time; not just being green but being green at t. Only when this is overlooked does the appearance of paradox arise from applying SR with D_2, because the apparently paradoxical result only comes about with projections across T. To illustrate with the usual emerald case, suppose we have a sample of emeralds that are green at t_1, where t_1 is before T, then they will also be grue$_2$ at t_1; and, hence, the SR will equally lead to 'All emeralds are green at t_1' and 'All emeralds are grue$_2$ at t_1.' And these two universals are in no way incompatible. Whereas for time t_2 after T, it is impossible that a sample of emeralds be both green at t_2 and grue$_2$ at t_2, and so we cannot be led by the SR to hold together the incompatible universals: 'All emeralds are green at t_2' and 'All emeralds are grue$_2$ at t_2.'

It is only if we slide illegitimately from t_1 to t_2 that an appearance of paradox arises. Only if we start from the fact that the sampled emeralds are both green at t_1 and grue at t_1, and then, by conflating being green (grue) at t_1 with being green (grue) at t_2, wrongly take the SR to provide support equally for the incompatible 'All emeralds are green at t_2' and 'All emeralds are grue at t_2,' do we obtain an apparent paradox.

It may be objected that my insistence on the distinction between the predicates 'x is grue (green) at t_1' and 'x is grue (green) at t_2,' forces an unwelcome restriction on the role of the SR: sometimes we use the SR to argue from certain examined emeralds being green *now* to others being green *now;* sometimes from certain emeralds being green at one time, now, say, to certain others being green at a different time, in the future, say; and it may be thought that the second kind of use—when we go from the present to the future—requires ignoring the distinction between being F at t_1 and being F at t_2.

But this is to overlook the application of the SR to time-slices of objects as distinct from enduring objects. When we argue from the greenness of present emeralds to the greenness of future emeralds, we do best to view this as an application of the SR to temporal parts of emeralds, and so as an application involving, not being green at t true of an enduring emerald, but rather being green *simpliciter* true of the temporal part at t of an emerald. When we wish to explicate our intuitive feeling that emeralds being green now supports their being green in the future by reference to the SR, by reference to the projection of common properties, we ought not fudge the clear distinction between being green now and being green in the future; rather we should regard the projected property, being green, as a tenseless characteristic of present emerald temporal parts which is being projected to future temporal parts in accord with the SR.

(A question that might well be asked now is what happens to D_2 if we recast it as a predicate on temporal parts instead of enduring objects. What happens, as can easily be seen, is that D_2 becomes like D_3, below, in all respects essential to whether there is a 'grue' paradox; and hence does not call for separate treatment.)

Although D_1 and D_2 figure prominently in the 'grue' literature, they are not the kind of predicate with which Goodman launched it.[9] Goodman's predicates are of the kind, '$(x$ is green & $\emptyset x) \lor (x$ is blue & $\sim\emptyset x)$,' where '$\emptyset x$' is chosen so that its extension includes all the sampled (observed, examined, etc.) emeralds, that is, the emeralds from which we are imagined to be projecting, and so that the extension of '$\sim\emptyset x$' includes the other emeralds, those to which we are projecting. A simple way of doing this is to introduce a temporal factor into '$\emptyset x$,' which is Goodman's usual but not invariable practice; in particular, the following definition is close to that he uses in *Fact, Fiction and Forecast:*

> D_3. x is grue at t iff (x is examined by T and x is green at t) or (x is not examined by T and x is blue at t).

As indicated by the 'at t' in D_3, this definition is for enduring objects. To avoid tedious repetition of the 'at t,' we will conduct our discussion in the editorial present. Likewise, we will commonly drop the 'at T' by taking T to be a moment in the near future such that 'examined by T' just amounts to 'examined (to date),' and 'not examined by T' amounts to 'unexamined (to date).' Both these procedures are implicitly adopted by Goodman, so that being grue$_3$ can be simply characterized as being green and examined, or being blue and unexamined. The paradox D_3 appears to lead to, as we will see, is not essentially time-linked. It is not essential that we consider the sampled emeralds at one time, the remaining at another, to get an apparently paradoxical result; so that, with D_3, by contrast with D_2, there is no objection to making things simpler by fudging a bit with respect to time.

D_3—the correct definition in the sense that it gives rise to more trouble than D_1 and D_2, as well as being Goodman's—will be the only definition we will be concerned with in the following sections, and when I refer to 'grue' and the alleged associated paradox or new riddle, I will mean 'grue' as defined in D_3.

II

Just what is the 'grue' paradox supposed to be; just what objectionable result is obtainable? In outline, the picture is clear enough. The idea is that, by suitable choice of predicates, the SR can be deployed to reach two incompatible conclusions starting from the same evidence. In particular, it is argued that a certain fact about emeralds when expressed in terms of 'green' leads to one projection about other emeralds when we apply the SR, and the same fact expressed in terms of 'grue' leads to another, incompatible projection when we apply the SR.

Though the picture is clear enough in outline, it starts to get murky as soon as we try to fill in the details. If, to fix our discussion, we consider a series of emeralds, $a_1, \ldots, a_n, a_{n+1}$, such that $a_1, \ldots, a_n$ are known to be green and examined, while a_{n+1} is known to be unexamined and is the emerald whose color we are concerned to predict; precisely how does the SR lead to incompatible projections about a_{n+1} from equivalent evidential bases?

Well, if we use 'Grx' for 'x is green,' 'Ex' for 'x is examined,' 'Bx' for 'x is blue,' and 'Gux' for 'x is grue' = '$(Grx\ \&\ Ex) \lor (Bx\ \&\ \sim Ex)$,' we are given

$$(1) \quad Gra_1\ \&\ \ldots\ \&\ Gra_n$$

and

$$(2) \quad Gua_1\ \&\ \ldots\ \&\ Gua_n$$

But, first, (1) and (2) are not equivalent (neither entails the other), so there is no objection to the SR leading to different predictions ('Gra_{n+1}' and 'Gua_{n+1},' respectively) regarding a_{n+1}; second, the predictions are not inconsistent (neither entails the denial of the other); and, finally, neither (1) nor (2) embodies our total evidence.[10]

Our total evidence (or near enough for present purposes) is rather expressed by

(3) Gra_1 & Ea_1 & . . . & Gra_n & Ea_n

which is, of course, equivalent to

(4) Gua_1 & Ea_1 & . . . & Gua_n & Ea_n

But what (3) and (4) support by the SR is

(5) Gra_{n+1} & Ea_{n+1}

and

(6) Gua_{n+1} & Ea_{n+1}

respectively; which, far from being incompatible, are equivalent.

Perhaps it will be argued that (5) entails (as it does)

(7) $\sim Ea_{n+1} \supset Gra_{n+1}$

and that (6) entails (as it does)

(8) $\sim Ea_{n+1} \supset Gua_{n+1}$

which is equivalent to

(9) $\sim Ea_{n+1} \supset Ba_{n+1}$

And that (7) expresses the prediction that, if a_{n+1} is not examined, it is green, whereas (9) expresses the incompatible prediction that, if a_{n+1} is not examined, it is blue. So we have derived opposite, incompatible predictions from equivalent bases, (3) and (4).[11]

But this is like arguing that our observations of black ravens support white ravens being black, as follows: our observations support Joey, an as-yet unobserved raven, being black. But 'Joey is black' entails 'Joey is white $\supset$ Joey is black' so that our observations support the prediction that if Joey is white, then he is black.

The fallacy here is obvious. We do have support for 'Joey is white $\supset$ Joey is black,' but only because we have support for the falsity of the antecedent. Likewise, we do have support on the basis of (3) and (4) for (7) and (9), but only because we have support for the falsity of their antecedents. It may be replied here that we do not have support for the falsity of their antecedents, that is, for a_{n+1} being examined, because being examined or '*Ex*' is not projectible. But this is to *assume* that there are nonprojectible properties, in the course of an argument designed to show that there are; moreover, we will be giving reason later for allowing that being examined is projectible (in sec. IV).

III. The Counterfactual Condition

So far I have not used the fact that we are given that a_{n+1} is not examined. And in Goodman's view our knowledge that there are unexamined emeralds is essential to deriving a paradox. He says, for instance,

> If the hypothesis that all emeralds are green is also projected [i.e., in addition to 'All emeralds are grue'], then the two projections disagree for unexamined emeralds. In saying these projections thus conflict, we are indeed *assuming that there is some unexamined emerald* to which only one of the two consequent-predicates applies, but it is upon just this assumption that the problem arises at all (*FFF*, 2nd ed., p. 94; my emphasis).

But just how can we use the fact that a_{n+1} is not examined? It sometimes seems to be thought that it is proper to add in this additional information in a more or less mechanical fashion, somewhat as follows:

> Our evidence supports a_{n+1} is green and examined. We know independently that a_{n+1} is not examined, hence our over-all evidence supports a_{n+1} is green and not examined. Equally, as far as the SR goes, our evidence supports a_{n+1} is grue and examined, and so, via the same line of argument, we arrive at our over-all evidence supporting a_{n+1} is grue and not examined, which entails that a_{n+1} is not green.

There is no question that we have here genuinely incompatible predictions about the color of a_{n+1}, for we have categoricals, not material implications. But we also have a pattern of argument that is quite certainly fallacious.

The pattern is: If a proposition, p, which we know to be true, supports a conjunction, q & r, one conjunct, r, of which we know independently to be false; we have, over-all, support for q & $\sim r$, and so, for anything it entails.

Once this pattern is explicitly set out, I doubt if anyone would assent to it; for it leads easily to an inconsistency, as follows: p supports $(q$ & $r)$ if and only if p supports $[(q$ & $r) \lor (\sim q$ & $\sim r)]$ & r, for the latter is truth-functionally equivalent to $(q$ & $r)$. Hence, by the argument pattern just displayed, when I know r to be false on independent grounds, I have, over-all, support equally for $(q$ & $\sim r)$ and for $[(q$ & $r) \lor (\sim q$ & $\sim r)]$ & $\sim r$, which are truth-functionally inconsistent [the latter is equivalent to ($\sim q$ & $\sim r$)].

It is equally clear from actual examples that this argument pattern is fallacious. Suppose a reliable friend tells me that Hyperion won the cup by five lengths, then I have support for the conjunction, 'Hyperion won the cup and Hyperion won by five lengths.' Further suppose I have quite decisive, independent evidence that the winning margin in the cup was only three lengths, but that this evidence is neutral as to who won by that margin. Do I have, over-all, evidence for Hyperion winning, though not by five lengths? If the argument pattern in question were valid, the answer would be an invariable yes; but in fact the answer is that it all depends on the circumstances. In some it will be most rational for me to take the error as to winning margin as indicating that my normally reliable friend is having one of his few off days and so is not to be trusted concerning the identity of the winner either; in other circumstances it will be most rational for me to take it that my friend regarded the winning margin as a relatively unimportant detail compared to the identity of the winner, and was his usual reliable self concerning the latter.

What we have here is, of course, just an aspect of the universally acknowledged fact that inductive support is defeasible; and it is strange how often this defeasibility is overlooked in the context of discussions of 'grue.' For example, it is common to find it suggested that by means of a 'grue'-type maneuver it is easy to show that an unrestricted SR leads to the unacceptable consequence that *any n* objects support some $(n + 1)$st object being G, for *any* 'G,'[12] as follows: For any $(n + 1)$ objects, there will be an 'Fx' such that it is true of the first n, but not the $(n + 1)$st. But if 'Fx' is true of the first n, so is '$Fx \lor Gx$,' for any 'Gx'; therefore, runs the argument, the (unrestricted) SR supports the $(n + 1)$st being F or G. But it is given as not being F; so it is concluded that we are led to the absurdity that we have support for the $(n + 1)$st object being G, for any 'G.' Now if something like: 'If p supports q, then $(p$ & $r)$ supports $(q$ & $r)$' were valid, all would be well with this argument; *but we all know that nothing like this is valid,* and so, that the information that the $(n + 1)$st object is not F cannot be incorporated in so simple a fashion.

We must, therefore, proceed *very* carefully when attempting to incorporate the additional information that a_{n+1} is unexamined, and, in particular, we must, I think, see the matter in context.

The general context is this: we have a sample, $a_1, \ldots, a_n$, each of which has a property, being examined, in addition to the particular properties we are interested in (being green and being grue) and which is given as not being possessed by a_{n+1}. This kind of situation arises virtually whenever we use the straight rule. When we use the SR to project common properties from a sample to members of the population from which the sample comes, there are nearly always features common to every member of the sample which we know are not features of all (or any) members of the population outside the sample. Some of these common sample features are normally disregarded as being unimportant, indeed trivial, like being sampled, being one of $a_1, a_2, \ldots$, and being examined (before . . .); while others clearly cannot be disregarded, as, for instance, in the following cases: Every diamond I have observed has glinted in the light. Does this support the contention that the next diamond I observe will glint in the light? Clearly, yes. But suppose we add a detail to the story, namely, that the next diamond that I observe is unpolished. Now all the diamonds I have observed so far have been polished, and, moreover, I know that they glint *because* they have been polished—that is, if the diamonds had not been polished, then they would not have glinted. It is clear that once we add this detail, it is no longer reasonable for me to regard it as likely that the next diamond I observe will glint in the light. The fact that all the diamonds I have observed glint in the light supports the next diamond I observe will glint; but the fact that all the polished diamonds I have observed glint when taken in conjunction with my knowledge that they would not have glinted if unpolished, does *not* support an unpolished one glinting.

A similar example is afforded by lobsters. Every lobster I have observed has been red. This supports that the next lobster I observe will be red, and no doubt it will be. But every lobster I have observed has been cooked, and I know that it is the cooking that makes them red—that is, that the lobsters I have observed would not have been red if they had not been cooked. Hence I do not regard myself as having good evidence that the next uncooked lobster I observe will be red.

We have here two cases where certain Fs being G supports, by the SR, other Fs being G, but certain Fs which are H being G does not support other Fs which are not H being G; in each case the reason being that it is known that the Fs that form the evidence class would not have been G if they had not been H. The condition: that certain Fs which are H being G does not support other Fs which are not H being G if it is known that the Fs in the evidence class would not have been G if they had not been H, will be referred to as *the counterfactual condition*. I cannot think of any way of proving it, as opposed to illustrating it as I just have, but also I cannot think that anyone will seriously deny it. (For ease of reading, I have expressed the condition in a conditional form. Strictly, it should be expressed as that the *conjunction* of certain Fs which are H being G *with* these Fs being such that if they had not been H, they would not have been G, does not support other non-H Fs being G.)

We are now in a position to discuss the incorporation of the additional information that a_{n+1} is unexamined. When we argue from examined emeralds $a_1, \ldots, a_n$ being green to the unexamined a_{n+1} being green, we are arguing from certain Fs which are H being G to an F which is not H being G, in the special case got by replacing 'F' by 'emerald,' 'G' by 'green,' and 'H' by 'examined.' Hence the counterfactual condition is that the emeralds $a_1, \ldots, a_n$ would still have been green even if they had not been examined; and, in the world as we know it, this condition is satisfied. The emeralds we have examined are green not because they have been examined but because of their chemical composition and crystalline structure, and so, like most objects in our world, they would have had the color they do have whether or not they had been examined.

Precisely the opposite is the case with 'grue.' We know that an emerald that is grue and examined would *not* have been grue if it had not been examined; for if it is grue and examined, it is green and examined, and, as noted already, if it had not been examined would still have been green; but then it would have been green and unexamined, and so, not grue. In other words, a green, examined emerald would have been a green, unexamined emerald if it had not been examined, and so $a_1, \ldots, a_n$ would not have been grue if they had not been examined. Therefore, to use the SR to yield the prediction that a_{n+1} is grue (and unexamined) is to violate the counterfactual condition.

In sum, the position is this. If we use the SR with the evidence that $a_1, \ldots, a_n$ are green and examined, and grue and examined, ignoring the fact that a_{n+1} is unexamined, we get support for 'a_{n+1} is green and examined' and for 'a_{n+1} is grue and examined'; which, far from being inconsistent, are equivalent. If we bring in the fact that a_{n+1} is unexamined, we no longer are dealing with a case of certain Fs being G supporting other Fs being G, but of certain Fs which are H being G supporting certain other Fs which are not H being G; and, hence, must take note of the counterfactual condition. But if we take note of this condition, we do not get an inconsistency because— although $a_1, \ldots, a_n$ would still have been green if they had not been examined—they would not have been grue if they had not been examined. Moreover, not only don't we get an inconsistency, we *cannot* get one, because it cannot be the case both that if X had not been H, it would not have been G, and if X had not been H, it would have been G—at least, on standard views about the logic of counterfactuals.

Our discussion of the SR has been couched in terms of constants, 'a_1,' $\ldots$, 'a_{n+1},' taken to designate emeralds. It is common to discuss the SR in terms of universals. The counterfactual condition shows, I think, that it can be misleading to characterize the SR as 'All examined As are B' supports 'All unexamined As are B.'

There are cases where it is absurd to take 'All examined As are B' as supporting 'All unexamined As are B.' Some properties of the elementary particles of physics are known to be affected by examination of the particles (hence the indeterminacy principle). It would be absurd to argue, for such a property, that, since all examined particles have it, so do all unexamined particles; just because we know that if the particles in question had not been examined, they would not have had the property.

Moreover, we do not have to turn to recondite entities like submicroscopic particles for examples of properties such that something would not have them if they had not been examined. Examined emeralds have a property of just this kind, namely, being grue. Take an emerald that is green and examined, and so, grue. If it had not been examined, it would still have been green, because examining emeralds (and indeed examining most things) doesn't alter their color; therefore, if the emerald had not been examined, it would have been green and unexamined, and so, not grue. Hence, it is a mistake to argue from 'All examined emeralds are grue' to 'All unexamined emeralds are grue,' not because 'grue' is intrinsically nonprojectible, but simply because the counterfactual condition is violated.

Parallel remarks apply to functor expressions of the SR such as: 'All examined As are B' supports 'The first unexamined A is a B.' We get an apparently simple and decisive development of the 'grue' paradox by noting that: 'All examined emeralds are green' and 'All examined emeralds are grue' are equivalent, and that: 'The first unexamined emerald is green' and 'The first unexamined emerald is grue' are inconsistent.[13] But, evidently, it is reasonable to use this kind of version of the SR only when being B is appropriately independent of being examined, and this is not the case when being B is being grue.

It is, perhaps, unfortunate that being examined (observed, sampled, etc.) appears so frequently in statements of the SR. The SR is intended as an essentially *relational* principle of inductive support concerning whether p supports q, quite independently of whether p is known. Examining, observing, sampling, and so on, are how we—human beings—come to know that certain As are B; but our knowing this is separate from these As being B supporting certain other As being B. *What* we come to know does the supporting (if any), not our coming to know it.

Though it is a fact about our world that the emeralds we have examined would still have been green if they had not been examined, it might not have been a fact. We might have lived in a world in which they would not have been green if they had not been examined. For example, we might have lived in a world in which all examined emeralds were green and in which investigation of the crystalline structure of these emeralds reveals that they are naturally blue; this structure being affected by the light necessarily involved in examining them in such a way that emeralds turn green instantaneously on being examined.[14] In this world, all emeralds we have direct observational evidence concerning are green and examined and grue. What ought we believe about those not examined? Obviously, that they are blue, and, hence, that all emeralds are grue. Our counterfactual condition explains this. In this world, examined emeralds are both green and grue, as in our world, but, as not in our world, if they had not been examined, they would have been grue, not green.

IV. The Projectibility of Being Sampled

Our counterfactual condition also bears on the question of the projectibility of such properties as being sampled, being examined, and being one of $a_1, \ldots, a_n$. Richard Jeffrey holds that—whereas it may just be doubted that 'grue' is nonprojectible—it is beyond doubt that such properties as these are nonprojectible.[15]

Why is he so certain? No doubt the kind of case he has in mind is where I am drawing marbles from a barrel and noting that each marble is red. Normally we suppose this to support that the remaining marbles are red. But, equally, each marble drawn will have the property of being sampled, and we do not normally regard the proposition that the remaining marbles are sampled as being supported by this.

But it would be too hasty to infer from this point that being sampled is not projectible. Suppose my reason for thinking that all the marbles drawn out have been sampled is that they each have Jones's fingerprints on them, and so must have been sampled (in the past, by Jones). Then it is clear that I will be entitled to increase my degree of belief that the remaining marbles have been sampled.

What is the explanation for the dramatic change whereby it is evidently absurd to increase one's expectation that the remaining marbles are sampled in the first case, and evidently not absurd in the second? I think it would be a mistake to explain this change in terms of the projectible/nonprojectible distinction by saying that *being sampled by me now* is nonprojectible, whereas *being sampled by Jones in the past* is projectible. For suppose that in the first case I am Jones and that after drawing the red marbles I go out for a cup of coffee; on my return I am confronted by a group of marbles all of which have the property of being sampled by Jones in the past. Do I now increase my expectation that the remaining marbles have this, allegedly projectible, property? Quite obviously no. The projectible/nonprojectible property distinction cannot explain the divergence in our inductive behavior in the two cases—and, surely, this is just the kind of case that the distinction, if it is worth making, ought to help us with.

What does explain the divergence is our counterfactual condition. In the first case, we have certain marbles, all of which are sampled and all of which have just been drawn from the barrel, and are concerned with whether we have support for certain other marbles, not drawn from the barrel, being sampled. We do not, because we know how it is that the sampled marbles came to be sampled, namely, by being drawn out. Hence, if the marbles had not been drawn out, they would not have been sampled; and our counterfactual condition is violated. On the other hand, in the second case (where I discover that the marbles have been sampled by observing Jones's fingerprints on them), the marbles drawn out would still have been sampled (by Jones, in the past) even if they had not been drawn out by me. The counterfactual condition is not violated, and we, therefore, have in the second case support for the marbles not drawn out being sampled.

There is nothing intrinsically nonprojectible about being sampled. In some cases, it is perfectly reasonable to project it, and, in those cases where it is not, the explanation does not have to do with the nature of the property or the meaning of the corresponding predicate, that is, does not relate to a feature of being sampled that calls for a label such as 'nonprojectible,' but is rather that the counterfactual condition is violated. Exactly similar remarks apply to being examined and to being one of $a_1, \ldots, a_n$. I will look briefly at the latter.

Despite the frequency and confidence with which it is said that properties of the being one of $a_1, \ldots$ kind are not projectible, it is easy to describe the counter cases. Suppose I am a policeman investigating a series of cat burglaries, and I discover that in each case the person responsible is one of Tom, Dick, and Harry; then I will be entitled to regard 'The person responsible for the next cat burglary will be Tom, Dick, or Harry' as supported. Again, if I am drawing marbles from a barrel and find each one stamped with a name, and the name is always one of 'a_1,' 'a_2,' $\ldots$, 'a_n' I will have increasing support for the next marble being one of $a_1, \ldots, a_n$. (Of course, after I have drawn out all of $a_1, \ldots, a_n$ marbles *and if* I am drawing without replacement, I won't expect the next marble to be one of $a_1, \ldots, a_n$; but this is because I am acquainted with the necessary truth that n things cannot be identical with $n + 1$ things, and shows, not nonprojectibility, but the role of additional negative evidence.)[16]

By way of contrast, if I don't find the names already stamped on the marbles, but *give* the names to the marbles as they are drawn out, I won't expect marbles not drawn out to be identical with one of $a_1, \ldots, a_n$; because the counterfactual condition is violated. I know that the marbles drawn out would not have the names they do if they had not been drawn out.

Whenever we apply the SR, we know, as it were, too much. I am drawing marbles from the ubiquitous barrel, and, in consequence, the drawn marbles are in my hand, recently exposed to light, and observed. These are all things I know about the marbles which I would not dream of projecting to the marbles remaining in the barrel: not because these properties are intrinsically nonprojectible—there are obviously many cases where we would project, for instance, being recently exposed to light—but because I know how the drawn marbles came to be recently exposed to light (to single this property out for discussion), namely, as a result of being sampled. Therefore, if they had not been drawn out, they would not have been recently exposed to light, and so, the argument from the drawn marbles being recently exposed to light to the undrawn marbles being so exposed, violates the counterfactual condition.

I expect that two objections will be generated by the prominent role of the counterfactual condition in the above discussion. The first is the general objection that counterfactuals raise some of the most difficult problems in philosophy. This is true, but the fact remains that we do, on occasion, know with certainty that certain counterfactuals are true, despite the difficulties in analyzing just what it is that we know on such occasions and how we know it. Perhaps one day we will have a good theory of counterfactuals, or a way of eliminating the need for them; until then we must put up with them.

The second objection is the more particular one that, by appealing to the counterfactuals that I appeal to, I am introducing a kind of circularity. Take, for example, my reason for saying that the SR favors unexamined emeralds being green rather than grue: that the emeralds we have in fact examined would have been green, not grue, if they had not been examined. There is no disputing the fact that we do know this—it is as certain as any knowledge of the form: if a had not been X, it would have been Y, is—but it might be objected that we know this only because we know unexamined emeralds are green. Hence, on pain of circularity, we cannot appeal to this fact to explain why the SR leads to the prediction that unexamined emeralds are green.

However, our knowledge that the examined emeralds would still have been green if they had not been examined is knowledge about the *examined* emeralds, not about the unexamined ones. It is knowledge we might have had even if there were no unexamined emeralds to be green or not green. If it turned out that there were very many fewer emeralds than we at first thought, and that in fact every emerald has been discovered and examined, this would not alter the fact that if the examined emeralds had not been examined they would have been green. Moreover, this fact is quite consistent with the unexamined emeralds turning out to be, to our great surprise, red; the result, say, of the emeralds so far examined all coming from regions in the world where certain minerals that make things green abound, and those not so far examined coming from regions containing minerals that make things red. This surprising discovery would not undermine our belief that the *so-far examined* emeralds would have been green even if not examined.

It follows that our knowledge that the examined emeralds would be green even if not examined does not tacitly rest on our knowledge that unexamined emeralds are green. It is knowledge we might have had even if unexamined emeralds were not green or, indeed, were nonexistent, and so, is knowledge we may appeal to without circularity in describing our application of the straight rule in a way that makes clear why we have support for unexamined emeralds being green rather than grue.

The point is more obvious in the marble-barrel case. I may know that each of the three red marbles that I drew out of the barrel would still have been red even if it had not been drawn out, without knowing the color of the remaining marbles—indeed, I commonly will know the former without knowing the latter. To know the former is to know something about the lack of connection between the color of an object and whether or not it is examined in the given case, whatever that color may be; and is not dependent on knowledge of the particular color of a particular object or objects, be they drawn out or not. Similar remarks apply in the converse case where I discover that the red marbles are painted with a special paint that turns red immediately on contact with a human hand (due, say, to the warmth). In this case, the marbles would not have been red if not drawn out (by hand), and we would not increase our expectation that the remaining marbles are red for just this reason. It is quite obvious that I may know the relevant facts about the paint without knowing or having any idea of the color of the remaining marbles. There is, thus, no circularity. (Likewise, Goodman's appeal to the entrenchment of predicates isn't circular, though it also involves appeal to inductively gained knowledge. The objection to entrenchment is rather that it is excessively anthropocentric.)

V. Summary

The over-all position is this. The SR: certain Fs being G supporting other Fs being G, does not lead to incompatible predictions when combined with 'grue' and like predicates.

When we apply the SR in practice, we commonly argue on the modified pattern: certain Fs which are H being G supports Fs which are not H being G ('H' often being 'examined,' 'sampled,' etc.). When we argue on this modified pattern, we take it that it is not the case that the Fs which are H would not have been G if they had not been H. This guarantees that we can never be led from the same evidence to opposite predictions concerning whether the non-H Fs are G. For, though Fs are H and G if and only if they are H and G^{*}, where '$G^{*}x$' = '$(Hx \, \& \, Gx) \lor (\sim Hx \, \& \sim Gx)$', we cannot be led both to the non-H Fs being G and to their being G^{*}, and so—as a non-H F is G^{*} just if $\sim G$—to opposite predictions. This is because we know from the logic of counterfactuals that it cannot both be the case that the Fs which are H and G would have been G if they had not been H, and that they would have been G^{*} if they had not been H; for this amounts to '$p \, \square \rightarrow q$' and '$p \, \square \rightarrow \sim q$' being true together, since a non-H is G^{*} only if $\sim G$.

To arrive at counterfactuals of the required form, we must, of course, draw on our knowledge of the world. Just which knowledge is as controversial as counterfactuals—that is, very. But it is clear that the knowledge required is *not* the knowledge at issue in the particular application of the SR in question, and so it is not circular to appeal to it. And, of course, it is not controversial that *applying* the straight rule in a particular case requires reference, *inter alia,* to knowledge gained inductively from *other* applications of the SR. Even knowing that certain *F*s are *G* requires trusting one's senses, memory, the reliability of reference books, and so on. This may well raise fundamental problems at the level of justification, in the context of the "old problem of induction," but this has not been our concern here. Our concern here at the level of description has been to urge that the SR can be specified without invoking a partition of predicates, properties, or hypotheses into the projectible and the nonprojectible.

The Australian National University

NOTES

*This paper has benefited considerably from discussions with colleagues, particularly with Robert Pargetter.

1. "A Query on Confirmation," *J. Philosophy* XLIII, 14 (July 4, 1946), 383–385.

2. Cambridge, Mass.: Harvard, 1955; Indianapolis: Bobbs-Merrill, 1965; ch. 3.

3. I will talk primarily in terms of the projectibility or otherwise of properties, predicates, or open sentences (the differences among these three not being relevant to the arguments that follow), rather than hypotheses; that is, I will follow Goodman's usage in "A Query" rather than in *FFF*.

4. D_1-type definitions appear in the discussions of projectibility by: H. Kyburg, *Probability and Inductive Logic* (Toronto: Macmillan, 1970); I. Hacking, *The Logic of Statistical Inference* (New York: Cambridge, 1965); S. Barker, *Induction and Hypothesis* (Ithaca, N.Y.: Cornell, 1957).

5. When it is not clear from the context, 'grue$_i$' is used for: 'grue' defined according to D_i.

6. I have kept my discussion of D_1 brief, since similar points have been well made by S. Blackburn, "Goodman's Paradox," *American Philosophical Quarterly,* Monograph no. 3, 1969; and M. Kelley, "Predicates and Projectibility," *Canadian Journal of Philosophy* I, 2 (December 1971), 189–206.

7. This kind of definition appears in W. Salmon, "On Vindicating Induction," in H. Kyburg and E. Nagel, eds., *Induction: Some Current Issues* (Middletown, Conn.: Wesleyan, 1963); P. Achinstein and S. Barker, "On the New Riddle of

Induction," *Philosophical Review* LXIX, 4 (October 1960), 511–522; B. Skyrms, *Choice and Chance* (Belmont, Calif: Dickenson, 1966). The tendency (e.g., by Barker and Kyburg) to slip between D_1 and D_2 may be due to the fact that 'x is grue$_1$ $\equiv \forall t(x$ is grue$_2$ at $t)$' is true.

8. See, e.g., Kelley, *op. cit.,* §III.

9. As Goodman points out in *Problems and Projects* (Indianapolis: Bobbs-Merrill, 1972); see p. 359.

10. As, in effect, R. Carnap points out in "On the Application of Inductive Logic," *Philosophy and Phenomenological Research* VIII, 1 (September 1947), 133–147; see §3.

11. I take this to be essentially the argument in H. Leblanc, "That Positive Instances Are No Help," *J. Philosophy* LX, 16 (Aug. 1, 1963), 452–462.

12. For just one, typical example, see Skyrms, *op. cit.,* 61, 62.

13. As in W. V. Quine, "Natural Kinds," in *Ontological Relativity* (New York: Columbia, 1969).

14. And we could bring in the time factor by, for instance, supposing the method of examining changes at T.

15. R. C. Jeffrey, "Goodman's Query," *J. Philosophy* LXIII, 11 (May 26, 1966), 281–288; see p. 288. He actually has 'bleen' for 'grue' in the relevant passage.

16. Cf. Kelley, *op. cit.,* 196.

Concepts of Projectibility and the Problems of Induction

6

John Earman

Projectibility is most often discussed in connection with the distinction between "genuine" and "Goodmanized" predicates. But questions about projectibility arise for the most mundane of hypotheses and predicates where not the slightest hint of Goodmanian trickery is present. And there are a number of different concepts of projectibility, each corresponding to a different problem of induction. Some of these problems are not only solvable but have actually been solved, solved in the sense that interesting sets of sufficient and/or necessary conditions for projectibility have been found. In some cases the conditions are so mild that a coherent inductive skepticism is hard to maintain, whereas in other cases the conditions are so demanding that skepticism seems to be the only attractive alternative. Again, in some of the cases Goodmanian considerations are the key; in others they are irrelevant.

The purpose of this note is to provide a classification scheme for the various senses of projectibility that will reveal what is at stake in the corresponding problems of induction. A useful beginning can be made by recalling the twofold classification Russell offered in *Human Knowledge:*

> Induction by simple enumeration is the following principle: "given any number of α's which have been found to be β's, and no α which has been found to be not a β, then the two statements: (a) 'the next α will be a β,' (b) 'all α's are β's,' both have a probability which increases as n increases and approaches certainty as a limit as n approaches infinity." I shall call (a) "particular induction" and (b) "general induction."[1]

Each of Russell's categories needs to be refined. Under particular or instance induction I will recommend a fourfold partition, first distinguishing weak

From *Noûs,* Vol. 19, No. 4 (December, 1985): pp. 521–535. Reprinted by permission from Blackwell Publishers and the author.

and strong senses according as the induction is on the next instance or the next m instances, and second distinguishing two ways of taking the limit as the number n of instances increases toward infinity according as we march into the future with the accumulating instances or stand pat in the present and reach further and further back into the past for more instances. Under general or hypothesis induction I will recommend a twofold partition depending on whether the hypothesis is a simple generalization on observed instances or a theoretical hypothesis that outruns the data. The upshot is a collection of six problems of induction with six rather different solutions.

1. Instance Induction: Marching into the Future

Only nonstatistical hypotheses will be considered. Further, it is assumed that the "instances" E_i, $i = 1, 2, 3, \ldots$, of the hypothesis H are deductive consequences of H and the "background evidence" B (i.e., $H, B \vdash E_i$). If you want H to be a universal conditional, e.g., $(\forall x)(Px \supset Qx)$, take instances to be $(Pa \supset Qa)$ and the like; or else let B state that all the objects examined are P's and take instances to be $(Pa \& Qa)$ and the like.

> DEFINITION 1. Relative to B, H is *weakly projectible in the future-moving-instance sense* for the instances $E_1, E_2, \ldots$ *iff*
> $$\lim_{n \to \infty} Pr(E_{n+1}/E_1 \& \ldots \& E_n \& B) = 1.$$
> DEFINITION 2. Relative to B, H is *strongly projectible in the future-moving instance sense* for the instances $E_1, E_2, \ldots$ *iff*
> $$\lim_{m, \, n \to \infty} Pr(E_{n+1} \& \ldots E_{n+m}/E_1 \& \ldots \& E_n \& B) = 1.$$
> *Claim:* A sufficient condition for both weak and strong future-moving-instance projectibility is that $Pr(H/B) > 0$.
> *Proof:* (a) Weak projectibility (Jeffreys).[2] By Bayes's theorem and the assumption that $H, B \vdash E_i$,
> $$(1) \quad Pr(H/E_1 \& \ldots \& E_{n+1} \& B) = $$
> $$\frac{Pr(H/B)}{Pr(E_1/B) x Pr(E_2/E_1 \& B) x \ldots x Pr(E_{n+1}/E_1 \& \ldots \& E_n \& B)}$$

If $Pr(H/B) > 0$, the denominator on the right-hand side of (1) will eventually become smaller than the numerator, contradicting an axiom of probability, unless $Pr(E_{n+1}/E_1 \& \ldots \& E_n \& B) \to 1$ as $n \to \infty$. (b) Strong projectibility (Huzurbazar).[3] Rearrange Bayes's theorem to read

$$(2) \quad Pr(E_1 \& \ldots \& E_n/B) = \frac{Pr(H/B)}{Pr(H/E_1 \& \ldots \& E_n \& B)}$$

Setting $u_n \equiv Pr(E_1 \& \ldots \& E_n/B)$, (2) shows that $u_n \geq Pr(H/B) > 0$. Since $u_{n+1} = u_n Pr(E_{n+1}/E_1 \& \ldots \& E_n \& B)$, $u_1, u_2, \ldots$, is a monotone decreasing sequence that tends to limit $L \geq Pr(H/B) > 0$. So

$$(3) \quad \lim_{m, n \to \infty} \frac{u_{n+m}}{u_n} = \frac{L}{L} = 1$$

There is an immediate application to the projectibility of predicates.[4]

DEFINITION 3. Relative to B, the predicate "P" is *weakly projectible in the future-moving sense* over the sequence of individuals a_1, $a_2, \ldots$ iff
$\lim_{n \to \infty} Pr(Pa_{n+1}/Pa_1 \& \ldots \& Pa_n \& B) = 1$.

DEFINITION 4. Relative to B, the predicate "P" is *strongly projectible in the future-moving sense* over the sequence of individuals a_1, $a_2, \ldots$ iff
$\lim_{m, n \to \infty} Pr(Pa_{n+1} \& \ldots \& Pa_{n+m}/Pa_1 \& \ldots \& Pa_n \& B) = 1$.

From the previous results we know that a sufficient condition for both weak and strong projectibility of "P" in the future-moving sense is that

$$(C) \quad Pr((\forall i)Pa_i/B) > 0.$$

Thus, contrary to what is sometimes suggested, definitions 3 and 4 do not serve to separate "grue" from "green,"[5] except on what I take to be the wholly implausible assumption that the universal generalization of the one but not the other receives a zero prior.

When is (C) necessary as well as sufficient for future-moving instance induction? The limit of $Pr(Pa_1 \& \ldots \& Pa_n/B)$ as n goes to infinity exists and is independent of the order in which the instances are taken. Further, we know that

$$(4) \quad \lim_{n \to \infty} Pr(Pa_1 \& \ldots \& Pa_n/B) \geq Pr((\forall i)Pa_i/B)$$

But to assure that

$$(A) \quad \lim_{n \to \infty} Pr(Pa_1 \& \ldots \& Pa_n/B) = Pr((\forall i)Pa_i/B)$$

we need to assume what Kolmogorov calls an axiom of continuity.[6] Then (C) is a necessary condition for strong projectibility of "P" in the future-moving sense; for

$$(5) \quad \lim_{m, n \to \infty} Pr(Pa_{n+1} \& \ldots \& Pa_{n+m}/Pa_1 \& \ldots \& Pa_n \& B) =$$
$$\lim_{m, n \to \infty} [Pr(Pa_1 \& \ldots \& Pa_{n+m}/B)/Pr(Pa_1 \& \ldots \& Pa_n/B)],$$

and if (A) but ¬(C), this limit is not 1 independently of how m and n go to infinity; e.g., first taking the limit as $m \to \infty$ gives 0.

(C) is not a necessary condition for weak future-moving projectibility of "P." Carnap's systems of inductive logic provide examples where (C) and strong future-moving projectibility fail but weak future-moving projectibility holds. However, the point can be illustrated in a more general way, independently of Carnap's c-function apparatus.[7] Suppose that Pr is *exchangeable* for "P" over the a_is, i.e., for every m

(E) $Pr(\pm Pa_1 \& \ldots \& \pm Pa_m/B) = Pr(\pm Pa_{1'} \& \ldots \& \pm Pa_{m'}/B)$

where $\pm P$ indicates that either P or $\neg P$ may be chosen and $\{a_{i'}\}$ is any permutation of the a_is in which all but a finite number are left fixed. If (E) holds, De Finetti's representation theorem gives

(D) $Pr(Pa_1 \& \ldots \& Pa_n/B) = \int_0^1 \Theta^n \, d\mu(\Theta)$

where μ is a normed probability measure on the unit interval $0 \leq \Theta \leq 1$.[8] Choosing μ to be the uniform measure gives

(6) $Pr(Pa_1 \& \ldots \& Pa_n/B) = 1/n + 1$.

Thus, (C) fails. But

(7) $Pr(Pa_{n+1}/Pa_1 \& \ldots \& Pa_n \& B) = (n + 1)/(n + 2)$,

which is Laplace's rule of succession, so that "P" is weakly projectible in the future-moving sense. Under (E) the necessary and sufficient condition for the failure of weak future-moving projectibility is that

(CM) $\lim\limits_{n \to \infty} \dfrac{\int_0^1 \Theta^{n+1} \, d\mu(\Theta)}{\int_0^1 \Theta^n \, d\mu(\Theta)} \neq 1$.

The label (CM) is supposed to indicate a closed-minded attitude, for (CM) is equivalent to the condition that $\mu([0, \Theta^*]) = 1$ for some $\Theta^* < 1$, ruling out the possibility that an instance of "P" can have a probability greater than Θ^*. The extreme case of closed-mindedness is represented by a μ concentrated on a point; for example, if $\mu(\{1/2\}) = 1$, then each instance of "P" is assigned a probability of $1/2$ independently of all other instances, so that the user of the resulting Pr function is certain (in the sense of second order probability) of the probability of an instance of "P," so certain that no number of other instances of "P" will ever change her mind. The probability measure in Wittgenstein's *Tractatus* had this character.[9]

To summarize: Suppose that you give a nonzero prior probability to the hypothesis that the sun always rises. Then the rising of the sun is strongly future-moving projectible over the series of days. On the other hand, suppose that you are absolutely certain that the sun won't always rise. It is still possible for your belief that the sun will rise tomorrow to approach certainty as your experience of new dawns increases without bound. But, assuming (A), it is not possible for your belief that the sun will rise on any number of tomorrows to approach certainty as your experience of new dawns increases without bound.

Another sense of projectibility for predicates sometimes used in the literature[10] is codified in

> DEFINITION 5. Relative to B, "P" is *somewhat future-moving projectible* over the sequence of individuals $a_1, a_2, \ldots$ *iff* for each $n > 0$, $Pr(Pa_{n+1}/Pa_1 \& \ldots \& Pa_n \& B) > Pr(Pa_n/Pa_1 \& \ldots \& Pa_{n-1} \& B)$.

Under exchangeability (E), "P" is somewhat future-moving projectible unless the measure $\mu(\theta)$ is completely concentrated on some value of Θ, as can be seen by applying the Cauchy–Schwartz inequality. Thus, the case of a closed-minded μ which is not completely closed-minded provides an example where "P" is somewhat but not weakly future-moving projectible. And in general there is no guarantee that projectibility in the sense of definition 5 will have the limiting properties postulated in definitions 3 and 4.

Humean skepticism with respect to future-moving instance induction, weak or strong, stands on unstable ground. If $Pr((\forall i)Pa_i/B)$ is any positive real number, no matter how small, future-moving instance induction must take place, like it or not. Setting $Pr((\forall i)Pa_i/B) = 0$ avoids strong future-moving instance induction, but if past experience, as codified in B, does not record a negative instance, then $Pr((\exists i)\neg Pa_i/B) = 1$ says that there is absolute certainty that the future will produce a negative instance, a not very Humean result.

Humeans can escape between the horns of this dilemma either by refusing to conform their degrees of belief to the axioms of probability or else by refusing to assign degrees of belief at all. The first tack is unattractive in view of the 'Dutch book' and other arguments that promote the axioms of probability as rationality constraints on degrees of belief.[11] The second tack seems to lead to something closer to catatonia than to active skepticism.

2. Instance Induction: Standing Pat in the Present While Reaching into the Past

There is a second way of taking the limit as the number of instances accumulates without bound, a way that is, perhaps, more directly relevant to Hume's classic problem of induction. To explain it, suppose as before that

$H, B \vdash E_i$, but now let i range over all the integers so that we have a doubly infinite sequence of instances . . . $E_{-2}, E_{-1}, E_0, E_1, E_2, \ldots$.

> DEFINITION 6. Relative to B, H is *weakly projectible in the past-reaching instance sense* for the sequence $\{E_i\}$ *iff* $\forall n$
> $$\lim_{j \to +\infty} Pr(E_{n+1}/E_n \& E_{n-1} \& \ldots \& E_{n-j} \& B) = 1.$$
> DEFINITION 7. Relative to B, H is *strongly projectible in the past-reaching instance sense* for the sequence $\{E_i\}$ *iff* $\forall n$
> $$\lim_{m, j \to +\infty} Pr(E_{n+1} \& \ldots \& E_{n+m}/E_n \& E_{n-1} \& \ldots \& E_{n-j} \& B) = 1.$$

Corresponding senses of projectibility apply to predicates. (Of course, the future versus the past direction of time is not the issue here; rather the point concerns whether the "next instance" lies in the direction in which the limit of accumulating evidence is taken.)

For the future-moving sense of instance induction to be valid, it was sufficient that the prior probability of the universal generalization be nonzero. But not so for past-reaching instance induction. Consider the predicates "P" and "P^*," where the latter is defined by

$$P^*a_i \equiv (Pa_i \& i \leq 1990) \lor (\neg Pa_i \& i > 1990).$$

We can assign nonzero priors to both $H:$ $(\forall i)Pa_i$ and to $H^*:$ $(\forall i)P^*a_i$ but obviously not even weak past-reaching projectibility is possible for both "P" and "P^*." For P^*a_n is logically equivalent to Pa_n for $n \leq 1990$ and to $\neg Pa_n$ for $n > 1990$, so that if

$$(8) \quad \lim_{j \to +\infty} Pr(Pa_{1991}/Pa_{1990} \& \ldots \& Pa_{1990-j} \& B) = 1$$

then

$$(9) \quad \lim_{j \to +\infty} Pr(P^*a_{1991}/P^*a_{1990} \& \ldots \& P^*a_{1990-j} \& B) = 0.$$

Thus, unlike definitions 3 and 4, definitions 6 and 7 do distinguish between "grue" and "green" in the sense that both cannot be projectible in the past-reaching sense. But the cut between past-reaching nonprojectible versus projectible predicates does not necessarily correspond to the cut between Goodmanlike versus non-Goodmanlike predicates (see sec. 5 below).

If exchangeability (E) holds for "P," then past-reaching projectibility for "P" is equivalent to future-moving projectibility. Thus, if we assign nonzero priors to both $(\forall i)Pa_i$ and $(\forall i)P^*a_i$, exchangeability cannot hold for both "P" and for "P^*." Or if exchangeability does hold for both, then for at least one of them the measure μ in De Finetti's representation must be closed-minded.

This is more or less what one would have expected since in the present setting exchangeability functions as one expression of the principle of the uniformity of nature.[12] What is interesting is that there is a principle of induction—weak and strong future-moving instance induction—whose validity does not depend on a uniformity of nature postulate. Furthermore, uniformity of nature in the guise of exchangeability is precisely what one does *not* want in order to make true some of the truisms of confirmation theory, such as that variety of evidence can be more important than sheer amount of evidence. Return to formula (1) used to prove Jeffreys's theorem and note that the more slowly for given n the factor $Pr(E_{n+1}/E_1\& \ldots \&E_n\&B)$ goes to 1, the smaller the denominator on the right-hand side of (1) and, thus, the larger the posterior probability of H. Intuitively, the more various (and nonexchangeable) the $E_i s$, the slower the approach to 1 is. Perhaps this intuition can be turned round to yield an analysis of variety of evidence, but I will not pursue the matter here.

Crudely put, the problem of future-moving instance induction concerns whether the future will resemble the future, while the problem of past-reaching instance induction concerns whether the future will resemble the past. The former problem can be posed and solved without much attention to the form the resemblance is supposed to take; for *any* predicate, "genuine" or "Goodmanized," will, irresistibly, lend itself to future-moving projectibility as long as a nonzero prior is assigned to the universal generalization on the predicate, and there is no danger of being led into inconsistency as long as the initial probability assignments are coherent. But the latter problem, as Goodman's examples have taught us, requires scrupulous attention to the form of resemblance if inconsistencies are to be avoided. Future-moving instance induction leaves only narrow and unstable ground for the skeptic to stand on. By contrast, past-reaching instance induction provides the grounds for but does not require a blanket skepticism, while the strongest form of general induction virtually begs for skepticism. It is to general induction that I now turn.

3. General Induction

Still assuming that $H, B \vdash E_i, i = 1, 2, 3, \ldots$, we can say that

> DEFINITION 8. Relative to B, the hypothesis H is *weakly projectible* on the basis of instances $E_1, E_2, \ldots$ *iff* the probability of H is increased by each new instance, i.e.,
> $Pr(H/E_1\& \ldots E_{n+1}\&B) > Pr(H/E_1\& \ldots \&E_n\&B)$ for each $n > 0$.
> *Claim:* The necessary and sufficient conditions for H to be weakly projectible are that $Pr(H/B) > 0$ and that $Pr(E_{n+1}/E_1\& \ldots \&E_n\&B) < 1$.
> *Proof:* Write out Bayes's theorem.

The price for weak projectibility of H is low; but what we buy may be unexciting since there is no guarantee that the increases that come with increasing instances will boost the probability toward 1. Thus, we also formulate

> DEFINITION 9. Relative to B, the hypothesis H is *strongly projectible* on the basis of the instance E_1, E_2, . . . *iff*
> $$\lim_{n \to \infty} Pr(H/E_1 \& \ldots \& E_n \& B) = 1.$$
>
> *Claim:* H is *not* strongly projectible if there is an alternative hypothesis H' such that (i) $B \vdash \neg(H \& H')$, (ii)H', $B \vdash E_i$ for all i and (iii) $Pr(H'/B) > 0$.
>
> *Proof:* Assume that H is strongly projectible and assume that there is an H' satisfying (i) and (ii) and show that (iii) is violated. By Bayes's theorem and *(ii)*,

$$(10) \quad \frac{Pr(H/E_1 \& \ldots \& E_n \& B)}{Pr(H'/E_1 \& \ldots \& E_n \& B)} = \frac{Pr(H/B)}{Pr(H'/B)}$$

By (i), $Pr(H/X \& B) + Pr(H'/X \& B) \leq 1$. So if H is strongly projectible, the limit as $n \to \infty$ of $Pr(H'/E_1 \& \ldots \& E_n \& B)$ is 0. Thus, taking the limit in (10) gives

$$(11) \quad +\infty = \frac{Pr(H/B)}{Pr(H'/B)} \to Pr(H'/B) = 0.$$

Philosophers of science routinely claim that any amount of data can be covered by many, possibly an infinite, number of hypotheses. Strictly speaking, this is not so if it means that there are many H's satisfying (i) and (ii) above. Take the E_i to be Pa_i and take H to be $(\forall i)Pa_i$. Then H admits of no logically consistent alternatives satisfying (i) and (ii) and, hence, no alternatives satisfying (i)–(iii). Such lowly empirical generalizations escape the above negative result, and if (A) and (C) hold, so does strong projectibility. For if (A) and (C), then

$$(12) \quad \lim_{n \to \infty} Pr((\forall i)Pa_i/Pa_1 \& \ldots \& P_n \& B) =$$
$$\lim_{n \to \infty} [Pr((\forall i)Pa_i/B)/Pr(Pa_1 \& \ldots \& Pa_n/B)] = 1.$$

We can also consider a doubly infinite sequence of individuals . . . a_{-2}, a_{-1}, a_0, a_1, a_2, . . . and demand strong projectibility in the past-reaching sense, i.e.,

> DEFINITION 10. Relative to B, $(\forall i)Pa_i$ is *strongly projectible in the past-reaching sense iff* for all n
> $$\lim_{j \to +\infty} Pr((\forall i)Pa_i/Pa_n \& Pa_{n-1} \& \ldots \& Pa_{n-j} \& B) = 1.$$

If (C) holds along with exchangeability and the natural generalization of (A), viz., for all n

$$(A') \quad \lim_{j \to +\infty} Pr(Pa_{n+j}\&Pa_{n+j-1}\& \ldots \&Pa_n\&Pa_{n-1}\& \ldots \&Pa_{n-j}/B) =$$
$$Pr((\forall i)Pa_i/B),$$

then definition 10 is satisfied. In effect, exchangeability has the flavor of "If you've seen an infinite number of them, you've seen them all."

Once we move beyond direct observational generalizations to theories that outrun the data, it is surely true that there are many rival theories that cover the same data. For such a theory strong projectibility on the basis of its instances is impossible unless the dice have been completely loaded against all the alternatives.

We might then hope for a more modest form of projectibility, as given in

> DEFINITION 11. Relative to B, H is (r, s) *projectible* on the basis of its instances $E_1, E_2, \ldots$ iff $Pr(H/B) = r < .5$, but there is a sufficiently large N such that $Pr(H/E_1\& \ldots \&E_N\&B) = s > .5$.
>
> *Claim.* H is *not* (r, s) projectible for any r and s if there is an H' such that (i) $B \vdash \neg (H\&H')$, (ii) $H', B \vdash \neg E_i$ for all i, and (iii) $Pr(H'/B) \geq Pr(H/B)$.
>
> *Proof.* Use (10) with $n = N$. If H is (r, s) projectible and there is an H' satisfying (i) and (ii), the left side of (10) is greater than 1. But if (iii) holds, the right-hand side is less than or equal to 1.

For this more modest form of general induction to work we don't have to load the dice completely against all rivals covering the same instances, but we still need to load them.

Although the Bayesian apparatus has shown itself to be very useful in clarifying issues about confirmation and induction, it proves to be idle machinery when it comes to testing nonstatistical scientific theories. Such a theory can have its probability boosted above .5 and toward 1 by finding evidence that falsifies rival theories. But in such cases simple eliminative induction suffices; and when eliminative induction does not work, then neither does Bayesianism, unless the dice have been loaded against all rival theories.

4. Russell on Induction

Having begun with Russell's formulation of the problem of induction, I now want to return to *Human Knowledge* to see what progress Russell made on the problem. Given that the book is the product of one of the great minds of Western philosophy, the results are more than a little disappointing. Here are four interrelated reasons for disappointment.

First, Russell did not distinguish between the past-reaching and future-moving senses of instance induction. When he gets specific about what instance induction means he tends to make it sound like the future-moving variety, as in "Let $a_1, a_2, \ldots, a_n$ be the hitherto observed members of α, all of which have been found to be β, and let a_{n+1} be the next member of α."[13] This is the easiest and most neatly "solvable" case, but Russell makes little progress toward its "solution," despite the fact that some of his reasoning is close to that later used by Jeffreys[14] to prove that the probability of the next instance approaches 1 (see the third comment below). One can speculate that Russell, having already decided that the validity of induction requires an extralogical principle not justified by experience, was not on the lookout for the kind of result provided by Jeffreys and Huzurbazar.

Second, Russell recognized Goodman's "new problem" of induction; and then again he didn't. He did because he used examples of Goodmanized hypotheses (see the fourth comment) and because he says that β

> must not be what might be called a "manufactured" class, i.e., one defined partly by extension. In the sort of cases contemplated in inductive inference, β is always a class known by intension, but not in extension except as regards observed members . . . and such other members of β, not members of α as may happen to have been observed.[15]

But then again he didn't because he didn't recognize that there is a distinction to be drawn between past-reaching and future-moving instance induction and that it is only for the former that Goodman's "new problem" arises.[16]

Third, Russell formulated the problem of induction in part V. Part VI discusses Keynes's attack on general induction. Assuming as before that $H, B \vdash E_i$, we can apply a result from Keynes's *Treatise on Probability*[17] to conclude that

$$(13) \quad Pr(H/E_1 \& \ldots \& E_n \& B) = \frac{1}{1 + [Pr(\neg H/B)/Pr(H/B)] \times [Pr(E_1/B \& \neg H)x \ldots xPr(E_n/E_1 \& \ldots \& E_{n-1} \& B \& \neg H)]}$$

Set $Q_n \equiv Pr(E_n/E_1 \& \ldots \& E_{n-1} \& B \& \neg H)$ and $q_n \equiv Q_1 x \ldots x Q_n$. Then if $Pr(H/B) \neq 0$, the posterior probability of H will go to 1 in the limit as $n \to \infty$ if $q_n \to 0$. Russell comments:

> If there is any number less than 1 such that all the Q's are less than this number, then the product of n Q's is less than the nth power of this number, and therefore tends to zero as n increases.[18]

The reasoning here is similar to that used to prove Jeffreys's theorem on future-moving instance induction, but Russell does not make the connection. When H is a simple empirical generalization, e.g., $(\forall i)Pa_i$, and the E_i's are Pa_i, Russell says that "it is difficult to see how this condition [as quoted above] can fail for empirical material."[19] When i runs from 1 to $+\infty$ and the continuity axiom (A) holds, the factor $Pr(Pa_1\& \ldots \&Pa_n/B\&\neg(\forall i)Pa_1)$ in the denominator of the Keynes formula (13) must go to 0. But when i ranges from $-\infty$ to $+\infty$ and the instances accumulate in the past-reaching sense, this factor cannot be shown to go to 1, unless by "empirical material" Russell means material for which exchangeability or the like holds.

Fourth, the difficulty with general induction to theoretical hypotheses can be seen from a simplified version of Keynes's formula, viz.,

$$(14)\quad Pr(H/E\&B) = \frac{1}{1 + [Pr(\neg H/B)/Pr(H/B)] \times Pr(E/\neg H\&B)}.$$

Suppose that $Pr(H/B)$ is nonzero but small. Then in order for $Pr(H/E\&B)$ to be large, E must be such that it would be improbable if H were false ($Pr(E/\neg H\&B)$ small). But as Russell notes, it may be hard to find such evidence. Take, for sake of illustration, H to be Newton's theory of gravitation and E to be the discovery of Neptune. Then there are many alternatives to H "which would lead to the expectation of Neptune being where it was"; for example, take H' to be the hypothesis that Newton's law of gravitation holds up to the time of discovery of Neptune but not afterward.[20] Russell scores a point with his Goodmanian illustration, but the point obscures the fact that the general problem arises even when Goodmanian alternatives are not at issue.

5. Prospects for a Theory of Projectibility

From the perspective of the preceding approach some philosophical theories of projectibility appear to be confused as to purpose, or false, or both. Consider the most ambitious and widely discussed philosophical theory of projectibility, Goodman's entrenchment theory.[21] Conditions couched in terms of relative entrenchment of predicates seem irrelevant to some of the questions of projectibility distinguished here and inadequate to others. For example, any hypothesis, no matter how ill entrenched its predicates, is weakly projectible on the basis of its positive instances if it has a nonzero prior—that is a theorem of probability. To claim that H gets a zero prior if it conflicts with an H' that is supported, unviolated, and unexhausted, that uses better-entrenched predicates than those of H, and that conflicts with no still better entrenched hypothesis, is to make a claim that is constantly belied by actual scientific practice where new hypotheses using new predicates are given a "fighting chance" of a nonnegligible prior. On the other hand, strong projectibility of a hypothesis, even if all of its predicates are supremely well entrenched, may be provably impossible if rival hypotheses are given a fighting chance, even when the rivals use ill-entrenched predicates. The most obvious application of the entrenchment notion is to what I called the problem of past-reaching instance induction. Of course, the general problem is independent of the direction of time and, more importantly, of the time dimension, for parallel problems arise for projecting from one side of a division of the range of a nontemporal parameter into the other side (say, from cases where $(v/c) < 1$ to cases where v is near c). But as Rosenkrantz[22] has emphasized, there are numerous cases in the history of science where scientists project predicates that are unentrenched and that, from the perspective of entrenched theory, appear to be Goodmanized because they agree with the old entrenched predicates to a good degree of approximation in the well-sampled side of the division but diverge on the other side.

It is time to pause to ask what can be expected from a "theory of projectibility." A minimalist theory would be established by finding sharp and interesting necessary and sufficient conditions for the various notions of projectibility. The results reported here take us only part of the way toward this minimalist goal. But once the goal is reached, what more remains to be done? A more grandiose theory of projectibility would, presumably, consist of descriptive and/or normative rules for determining when the conditions developed in the minimalist theory are or ought to be met. The prospects for constructing such a theory with the tools of analytic philosophy seem to me dim.

To make this skeptical conclusion plausible, it suffices to focus on cases where we found that projectibility turns largely on prior probability considerations. Objectivist accounts of prior probability assignments have been offered by Reichenbach,[23] in terms of frequency counts, by Jaynes,[24] in terms of maximum entropy calculations, and by others. But in every instance there are serious if not crippling difficulties with the proposed method of assignment.[25] Without assigning specific prior probabilities we could seek a theory to justify assigning some nonzero priors to a class of favored hypotheses. Keynes's "principle of limited variety" was designed for just this purpose. In *Human Knowledge* Russell attacks Keynes's theory (and rightly so, I think). But Russell's own five 'postulates of induction,' designed he says to "provide the antecedent probabilities required to justify induction,"[26] are just as unattractive. Separability and continuity of causal lines, common causes for similar structures ranged around a center, etc., have a certain intuitive appeal, but they involve contingent assumptions that may not hold in the actual world if it is anything like what the quantum theory says it is like. For the subjectivist school of probability, as represented by De Finetti and followers, the envisioned theory of projectibility would consist of a psychological account of how people in fact distribute initial degrees of belief consistent (hopefully) with the axioms of probability. This is a task for cognitive psychology, not armchair philosophy. Of course, I expect that psychology will find that entrenchment and other considerations suggested by philosophers will play some role in the account, but I do not expect that the account will consist of a neat set of rules of the type envisioned in the philosophical literature.

Goodman has charged that the problem of induction and its solution have been misconceived. I agree, but I think the misconception extends further than Goodman would allow. In any case, it is curious that philosophers have reached for more grandiose theories of projectibility before getting a firm grip on minimalist theories. In addition to filling in the gaps in the results reported here, it would be nice to have results based on alternatives to exchangeability.[27] One would also like to have information about how fast the posterior probability increases and whether, as Keynes worried, we are all dead before the value gets anywhere near 1.[28]

Postscript (July 1992)

Nelson Goodman's projectibility puzzle was first stated in print in his article "A Query on Confirmation," *Journal of Philosophy* 43 (1946): 383–385. Starting before the publication of the Query and continuing for some years thereafter, there was an intense series of three-way conversations among Goodman, Carnap, and Hempel regarding the issues raised in Goodman's Query. Some fascinating glimpses of these conversations are preserved in documents in the Carnap *Nachlass,* which is part of the University of Pittsburgh Archives of Scientific Philosophy. One of the documents is entitled "Survey of comments and objections made by Nelson Goodman concerning Carnap and the H_2O theories of degree of confirmation."[29] It is dated 1/27/46, and consists of eight handwritten pages, numbered 3 through 10. At the top of the first page (numbered 3), Carnap has written in red a large "H," his indication that the author is Hempel. "H_2O" evidently refers to the confirmation theories of Hempel, "Studies in the Logic of Confirmation," *Mind* 54 (1945): 1–26, 97–121, and of Helmer and Oppenheim, "A Syntactical Definition of Probability and Degree of Confirmation," *Journal of Symbolic Logic* 10 (1945): 25–60. Characteristically Carnap underlined what he took to be important passages, and in the margins and between lines he scrawled comments in his barely decipherable shorthand notation. I will quote from what I take to be the most interesting part of Hempel's missive.

"Question: How if at all are we to distinguish between permissible and non-permissible predicates?"[30] Answering in the third person, Hempel responded to his question as follows:

> The difficulty here indicated is closely related to the one which struck Hempel many years ago in connection with certain descriptions of the basic idea of inductive procedures; the latter is sometimes characterized thus: Induction consists in assuming that those regularities which have been found to be satisfied in all cases [of] past experience will continue to be satisfied by future experiences.[31] But this 'assumption' is contradictory: Any given finite evidence always satisfies several incompatible general regularities, which lead to different predictions for future cases. This is illustrated by . . . the fact that any finite set of points (results of measurements of 2 magnitudes) lies on many different curves (representing different laws of ??? for the two magnitudes) which determine incompatible predictions for new values still to be measured.[32]

There are two and possibly three morals to be drawn from 'grue.' Writing before the term 'grue' was coined, Hempel had one of the morals right in advance: in part, 'grue' is an illustration of the familiar point that any given finite evidence always satisfies several incompatible hypotheses that lead to inconsistent predictions about new instances. The inductive machinery Carnap was developing was in no way idled by this commonplace since it was not designed to say which one of the competing hypotheses was confirmed (period) but rather to specify the degree to which each is confirmed by the evidence.

Why then did 'grue' become so controversial? In part the answer lies with the other (alleged) morals I will discuss below. But a significant segment of the controversy was an artifactual result of the constrained setting in which the inductive logicians of the 1940s were working. For example, Hempel's account of qualitative confirmation was designed for hypotheses formulated in first order predicate logic. In this setting it is not so easy to concoct examples of a consistent evidence set, consisting of atomic observation sentences or negations of such sentences, that simultaneously satisfies two or more general hypotheses which are also couched in observational vocabulary and which make incompatible predictions about new cases. Indeed—and this helps to explain why 'grue' generated controversy—to produce such examples in this constrained setting, it is necessary to resort to what many interpret as logical sleight of hand. And thus has arisen the impression that what is needed to resolve the grue problem is some clever bit of countermaneuvering. Perhaps 'grue' can be squashed by some clever philosophical tap dancing. But if the fundamental problem to which 'grue' averts is the one identified in Hempel's missive, a solution is not to be had by squashing of Goodmanized predicates.

To understand the second moral, recall that the inductive logicians of the 1940s took the 'logic' of inductive logic seriously in that they saw their task as one of creating an inductive logic that complements but lies parallel to deductive logic, and they took the parallelism to mean that they should produce a purely syntactical definition of confirmation. 'Grue' and related examples showed that this goal had to be abandoned.

Here it is interesting to trace Carnap's own evolving reactions to 'grue' and company. His first response was to deny that Goodman's objections affected Carnapian inductive logic as it was then conceived. All of Goodman's examples, as reported to Carnap by Hempel, seemed to involve an appeal to temporally or spatially ordered individuals. This allowed Carnap to write on March 9, 1946, that such examples are "outside my theory, because my theory applies only to a simple language with a non-ordered universe."[33] But even in a relatively simple language gruelike predicates can be defined, a point made by Goodman on March 13, 1946, in a document humorously entitled, "Notes on Notes on Carnap's Notes on Hempel's Notes on my Notes."[34] Goodman noted that the evidence that all marbles observed so far are red confirms not only the hypothesis that other marbles are red but also $(x)Tx$, where 'Tx' is a predicate that ascribes redness to observed marbles and nonredness to other marbles. So, for example, if the observed marbles were placed on desk D and other marbles are to be placed on shelf S, one could take 'Tx' to mean that x is on D and is red or x is on S and is green. Carnap acknowledged the point in correspondence and in his published reply to Goodman ("On the Application of Inductive Logic," *Philosophy and Phenomenological Research 8* (1947): 133–147) by placing restrictions on the primitive predicates of the system—in particular, requirements of simplicity and completeness. Hempel was skeptical of this approach, essentially for Carnapian reasons! His reservations were expressed in a letter to Carnap dated January 29, 1947:

> I share Nelson's [Goodman's] skepticism concerning the concept of absolute simplicity and the idea of a non-relativized analysis of attributes. Would you not have characterized these ideas some years ago, as reflecting—at least!— the material mode of speech, and as requiring a restatement which would make them relative to the language under consideration and to the logical means of analysis available in it?[35]

Carnap's response showed just how far he had moved from his position of the Vienna Circle days:

> I do not myself like at all this absoluteness of simplicity and completeness, but at the present moment I do not see a way of avoiding it. It is not meaningless, I believe. I do not condemn the material mode as strongly as earlier, but would merely warn against its possible dangers. . . . Semantics has removed some of the earlier fears of speaking about the world and the properties in it. Once we admit property variables in the metalanguage (which it is true, involves serious problems, but is anyway necessary for certain purposes of science), then we can say that *all* properties (in the universe in question) are expressible in the language. This is 'ontological' only in the new Quine sense, not in the traditional, metaphysical sense.[36]

I turn finally to the third and most controversial moral which Goodman wanted to draw from 'grue'; namely, that projectibility turns not only on matters of syntax and semantics but also on practical criteria, such as what predicates have in fact been successfully projected in past practice. The Carnap of the 1940s would have found this moral quite uncongenial. Once the appropriate restrictions on the primitive predicates (simplicity, completeness, or whatever) were in place, questions of degree of confirmation and, thus, of projectibility were for Carnap just a matter of calculation, a matter of applying *the* correct c-function, c^* being his then favorite candidate for that role.

In his later years Carnap tended towards, without ever quite reaching, the point of view of Bayesian personalism. Here talk of *the* degree of confirmation of H and E is replaced by talk of a person's degree of belief in H on E, the only synchronic constraints on such degrees of belief being the axioms of probability and the only diachronic constraint being the rule of conditionalization. From this perspective the ultimate moral of Goodman's grue problem—the descriptive nature of the problem of induction—returns with a such a vengeance that even the Goodman of the Query might have flinched. Goodman assumed that as a matter of actual fact we do largely agree on matters of projectibility and that the remaining task of induction is to describe how the agreement is manifested in rules of projectibility. By contrast the Bayesian personalist is prepared to find that such rules are a shimmering mirage. There will, of course, be rules in the sense of truisms of confirmation consisting of theorems of probability. But it is dubious that simple and general substantive rules about what degrees of belief to assign to new instances on the basis of already observed ones can be extracted from the set of degree of belief functions of all actually existing people. Perhaps such rules can be extracted from the more circumscribed set of belief functions of the members of a scientific community, the idea being that the community would not remain a community for long unless the members experience rapid merger of opinion on the relevant range of hypotheses. This idea is in danger of turning into a tautology unless communities can be identified independently of merger of opinion behavior. We have arrived at an interesting set of issues. But they are a far cry from what most of the literature takes the grue problem to be about.[37]

University of Pittsburgh

NOTES

1. Bertrand Russell, *Human Knowledge: Its Scope and Limits* (New York: Simon and Schuster, 1948), p. 401. See also Russell's *A History of Western Philosophy* (New York: Simon and Schuster, 1945), chapter 17 ("Hume"), and *Problems of Philosophy* (Oxford: Oxford University Press, 1956), chapter 6 ("On Induction").

2. H. Jeffreys, *Scientific Inference,* 2nd ed. (Cambridge: Cambridge University Press, 1957).

3. V. S. Huzurbazar, "On the Certainty of Inductive Inference," *Proceedings of the Cambridge Philosophical Society* 51 (1955), 761–62.

4. Paul Horwich, *Probability and Evidence* (Cambridge: Cambridge University Press, 1982), gives an interpretation of Russell's principle of particular induction that corresponds to our definition 3. However, since Russell's discussion was directed toward Hume's problem, definition 6 (given later) may provide a better interpretation.

5. Or "goy" from "boy" as in R. C. Jeffrey, *The Logic of Decision* (New York: McGraw-Hill, 1965), 175–77. But see Jeffrey's later discussion in the second edition of *The Logic of Decision* (Chicago: University of Chicago Press, 1983), 188–90. See also sec. 2 below. And compare with the confused discussion in K. Popper, *The Logic of Discovery* (New York: Scientific Editions, 1961), appendix vii.

6. A. Kolmogorov, *Foundations of Probability* (New York: Chelsea, 1956). In measure-theoretic terms, continuity requires that if $A_1 \supseteq A_2 \supseteq \ldots$ is a sequence of μ-measurable sets and $A = \bigcap_{n=1}^{\infty} A_n$, then $\mu(A) = \lim_{n \to \infty} \mu(A_n)$. In the presence of finite additivity, continuity is equivalent to countable additivity, requiring that if $\{B_i\}$ is a sequence of pairwise disjoint sets, then

$$\mu\left(\bigcup_{i=1}^{\infty} B_i\right) = \sum_{i=1}^{\infty} \mu(B_i).$$

7. R. Carnap, *Logical Foundations of Probability* (Chicago: University of Chicago Press, 1950), and *The Continuum of Inductive Methods* (Chicago: University of Chicago Press, 1952).

8. B. De Finetti, "Foresight: Its Logical Laws, Its Subjective Sources," in H. Kyburg and H. Smokler, eds., *Studies in Subjective Probability* (New York: Wiley, 1964). μ is uniquely determined by the *Pr* values if, as we are assuming, there are an

infinite number of individuals. Instead of exchangeability, Carnap speaks of "symmetric *c*-functions."

9. L. Wittgenstein, *Tractatus Logico-Philosophicus,* trans. D. F. Pears and B. F. McGuiness (London: Routledge & Kegan Paul, 1961), 5.15–5.152.

10. See Horwich, *Probability and Evidence,* and Jeffrey, *The Logic of Decision.*

11. See De Finetti, "Foresight," and A. Shimony, "Scientific Inference," in R. G. Colodny, ed., *The Nature and Function of Scientific Theories* (Pittsburgh, University of Pittsburgh Press, 1970). These Dutch book arguments are based on a finite series of bets and do not suffice to justify countable additivity or continuity. Extensions to an infinite series of bets are studied in E. Adams, "On Rational Betting Systems," *Archiv für mathematische Logik und Grundlagenforschung* 6(1961), 7–29, 112–28.

12. Carnap did not interpret exchangeability (or symmetry of *c*-functions) in this way since he specified that the subscripts on the individuals are to have no spatiotemporal significance.

13. Russell, *Human Knowledge,* 404.

14. Jeffreys's result was not available when Russell was writing *Human Knowledge.* Or at least the result did not appear in the first edition (1931) of *Scientific Inference* or the 1937 reissue; it is in the 1948 second edition.

15. Russell, *Human Knowledge,* 404.

16. In fairness to Russell it should be noted that it is not clear that Goodman himself passed this test.

17. J. M. Keynes, *A Treatise on Probability* (New York: Harper & Row, 1962), 235–37.

18. Russell, *Human Knowledge,* 424.

19. *Ibid.*

20. *Ibid.,* 411.

21. N. Goodman, *Fact, Fiction and Forecast,* 3rd ed. (Indianapolis: Hackett, 1979).

22. R. Rosenkrantz, "Why Glymour Is a Bayesian," in J. Earman, ed., *Minnesota Studies in the Philosophy of Science,* vol. X (Minneapolis: University of Minnesota Press, 1983), 69–97.

23. H. Reichenbach, *Theory of Probability* (Berkeley: University of California Press, 1971).

24. E. T. Jaynes, "Prior Probabilities," *IEEE Transactions on Systems Science and Cybernetics,* SSC-4, no. 3 (1968), 227–41.

25. Difficulties with Reichenbach's approach are well known. For criticisms of Jaynes's approach, see K. Friedman and A. Shimony, "Jaynes' Maximum Entropy Prescription and Probability Theory," *Journal of Statistical Physics* 3 (1971), 381–84, and T. Seidenfeld, "Why I Am Not an Objective Bayesian: Some Reflections Prompted by Rosenkrantz," *Theory and Decision* 11 (1979), 413–40.

26. Russell, *Human Knowledge,* 487.

27. Generalizations of De Finetti's representation theorem are discussed in B.

Skyrms, *Pragmatics and Empiricism* (New Haven, Conn.: Yale University Press, 1984), and J. von Plato, "The Significance of the Ergodic Decomposition of Stationary Measures for the Interpretation of Probability," *Synthese* 53 (1982), 419–32.

28. I am grateful to C. A. Anderson, G. Hellman, P. Kitcher, B. Skyrms, and W. Sudderth for helpful comments on an earlier draft of this paper.

29. Doc. # 084–19–34, Archives of Scientific Philosophy, University of Pittsburgh.

30. Here Carnap has jotted: "Nicht klar. Bezieht sich dies auf das *vorangehende* Beispiel oder auf das folgende ('projectible')" [Not clear. Does this refer to the *preceding* example or to the following ("projectible") following?]. The "preceding example" refers to the following case. Consider 99 individuals, denoted by a_1, $a_2, \ldots, a_{99}$. Let the evidence concerning them be E: $\neg Pa_1 \& \neg Pa_2 \& Pa_3 \& \neg Pa_4 \& \neg Pa_5 \& Pa_6 \& \text{etc} \& \neg Pa_{98} \& \neg P_{99}$, where '$P$' is a monadic predicate (say, is red). And let the hypothesis be H: Pa_{99}. Then we get $dc(H, E) = 1/3$ (Helmer and Oppenheim) and $c^*(H, E) \approx 1/3$ (Carnap). Now let a_1 refer to the first triple, a_2 to the second triple, etc., and let 'P' now denote the property of trios that exhibit green, green, red. With E': $Pa_1 \& Pa_2 \& \ldots \& Pa_{32}$ and H': Pa_{33} we get $dc(H', E') = 1$ and $c^*(H', E') \approx 1/3$. I am indebted to Gerald Heverly for deciphering Carnap's shorthand and to Pirmin Steckler-Weithofer for the English translation. The passage is quoted by permission of Prof. C.G. Hempel and the University of Pittsburgh. All rights reserved.

31. Carnap underlined "will continue," and above the line he jotted: "Das is eine ungenugende Formulierung; Sie wird ersetzt durch *Def* fur *dc* bzw. *c**. Dann ist keine Inkompatibilitat mehr da. [This is an unsatisfactory formulation; it is replaced by [the] *Def* for *dc* respectively *c**. Then there is no longer any inconsistency.]

32. Carnap has underlined "lies on many different curves," and above the line he has written: "Ja, das ist grosse Schwierigkeit; aber erst zu losen spater, *für quantitative Sprache!* (Ich habe einige Ideen [?], in Anschlus an Jeffreys [?] aber noch keine Losung.)" [Yes, this is a great difficulty; but only to be resolved later *for a quantitative language!* (I have some ideas in connection with a proposal of Jeffreys, but not yet a solution.)] Presumably the reference here is to work of Harold Jeffreys.

33. Doc. # 084–19–31. Quoted by permission of the University of Pittsburgh. All rights reserved.

34. Doc. # 084–19–30.

35. Doc. # 084–19–20. Quoted by permission of Prof. C.G. Hempel and the University of Pittsburgh. All rights reserved.

36. Doc. # 084–19–06. Quoted by permission of the University of Pittsburgh. All rights reserved.

37. I am grateful for helpful comments from Carl Hempel, Richard Jeffrey, and Wesley Salmon.

Induction, Conceptual Spaces, and AI

Peter Gärdenfors[†]

1. AI and the Problem of Induction

Humans do not live by deductive logic alone. We also frequently, perhaps predominantly, make successful inductive inferences. How can we hope to construct computer programs that, even in a limited way, mirror the human inductive capacity? I shall argue that this problem, like so many other problem areas of AI, essentially is a question of finding an appropriate *knowledge representation*.

Humans do not perform inductive inferences in an arbitrary manner, but are *constrained* in various ways. As C. S. Peirce puts it: "[I]f men had not come to it with special aptitudes for guessing right, it may well be doubted whether in the ten or twenty thousand years that they may have existed their greatest mind would have attained the amount of knowledge which is actually possessed by the lowest idiot" (1931, p. 476). In this paper I will focus on one particular constraint, namely the problem of *projectibility*. This is the problem of deciding which predicates can be used in inductive inferences and which cannot. (On the general issue of constraints, see Holland et al. 1986, pp. 4–5.)

My argument will have one critical part and a further part that is more constructive. The main thesis of the critical part is that if the representation of knowledge is based on narrowly *linguistic* or *propositional* formulations which treat all predicates symmetrically, then there is no way of generating appropriate inductive inferences. I shall support this thesis by an analysis of some of the problems that have plagued the logical positivists' approach to induction; in particular I shall focus on Hempel's paradox of confirmation and Goodman's riddle of induction. The conclusion will be that, in order to separate projectible predicates from nonprojectible ones, we need a way of representing knowledge that goes beyond logic and language.

The constructive part of the article consists in an outline of a theory of

From *Philosophy of Science* 57 (1990), pp. 78–95. Reprinted by permission of the Philosophy of Science Association and the author.

conceptual spaces. I shall argue that by representing knowledge in terms of conceptual spaces one can rather easily identify the projectible properties. One thereby avoids some of the old problems of induction and in this way obtains better foundations for generating inductive inferences by artificial methods.

2. Induction and Logical Positivism

For the logical positivists, the basic objects of study were sentences in some more or less regimented language. Ideally, the language was a version of first order logic where the atomic predicates represented observational properties. These observational predicates were taken as *primitive,* unanalysable notions. The main tool used when studying the linguistic expressions was logical analysis. In its most pure form, logical positivism allowed only this tool. A consequence of this methodology, which will be important here, was that all observational predicates were treated in the same way since there were no logical reasons to differentiate between them. For example, Carnap (1950, Section 18B) requires that the primitive predicates of a language be logically independent of each other.

Inductive inferences were important for the logical positivists, since such inferences were necessary for their verificationist aims. However, it became apparent that their methodology led to serious problems. The most famous ones are Hempel's (1965) "paradox of confirmation" and Goodman's (1955) "riddle of induction." To see the problems for logical positivism, I will give brief recapitulations of these paradoxes.

Hempel's paradox of confirmation deals with the problem of what observations would count as inductive support for a general law. Suppose we are interested in a law of the form $\forall x(Rx \rightarrow Bx)$ ("all ravens are black"). The most obvious confirming instances are sentences of the form Ra & Ba (black ravens). However, the general law is logically equivalent to $\forall x(\neg Bx \rightarrow \neg Rx)$. For symmetry reasons the observations confirming this law are of the form $\neg Ba$ & $\neg Ra$ (nonblack nonravens). But if this is true, we can confirm the law that all ravens are black by finding green apples, blue suede shoes, and red herrings. This is obviously counterintuitive.

Goodman's puzzle starts from the fact that all emeralds examined up to now, having been identified by some criterion other than color, have been found to be green. Let us now call anything "grue" that is green before the year 2000 and blue after the beginning of year 2000. Similarly, "bleen" means blue before 2000 and green thereafter. (These are not exactly Goodman's predicates since he complicates matters by only discussing objects that are observed. However, for the present discussion, this difference will not be of any importance.) This means that all emeralds examined up to now have been grue. So, why should we not expect that the inductive inference that all emeralds are grue is *as valid* as the seemingly more natural inference that all emeralds are green?

Note that it does not help to say that "green" is a *simpler* predicate than "grue" because it does not involve any reference to a particular point of time: It is true that "grue" can be defined in terms of "green" and "blue" and a time reference, but it is equally true that "green" can be defined as "grue before the year 2000 and bleen thereafter." So, from a purely logical point of view, "green" and "grue" are perfectly symmetrical as predicates. And the logical point of view is the only one that counts within the methodology of the pure logical positivist.

We do not expect "grue" and "bleen" to be successful in inductive inferences. However, it should be noted that even if we have a Goodman-type predicate that succeeds in some inductive generalization, we do not count it as projectible. This point can be illustrated by the predicate "whack" which is defined as "white in Europe or black in Australia." The inductive generalization "All swans are white" is false, but the generalization "All swans are whack" is much more successful. The predicate "whack" may even be used in further successful generalizations like "all aboriginals are whack." Still, at the present state of knowledge, we would hesitate to include "whack" among the projectible predicates. (However, were we to find some underlying reason why things should be black in Australia while white in Europe, the situation may change.)

Apart from these problems, there are some others of a closely related nature: first, imagine that we have examined a large number of Fs (brown bears, say) and found all to be Gs (for example hibernating). We then tend to form the inductive conclusion that all Fs are Gs. But suppose that all the examined Fs are also Hs (for example, found outside the Abisko national park in Lapland). Then the inference that all things that are F and H are G has at least as strong support as the original inference (compare Goodman 1961).

Again there is no logical reason to differentiate between the predicates in the antecedent, saying for example that "F" is a "simpler" predicate than "F and H": We may as well start from a predicate "K" meaning "F and H" and a predicate "L" meaning "F and not H" and then define "F" as "K or L."

Second, suppose again that a large number of Fs have been found to be Gs. If none of the objects examined have been an H (a lemming, say), then the observations support the general sentence "All things that are Fs or Hs are Gs" (all bears and lemmings are hibernating) as well as "All Fs are Gs." For similar reasons as above, logic alone is not sufficient to distinguish between these generalizations.

Finally, imagine that all examined instances of F have been found to be G and all instances of H have been found to be K. Why do we find "All Fs are Gs" and "All Hs are Ks" to be better generalizations than "All Fs or Hs are Gs or Ks," which has a larger class of support than the two separate generalizations?

The upshot of all these troublesome cases is that if we use *logical* relations alone to determine which inductions are valid, the fact that all predicates are treated on a par induces symmetries which are not preserved by our understanding of the inductions: "Raven" is treated on a par with "nonraven," "green" with "grue," "F" with "$F \lor H$" etc. What we need is a nonlogical way of distinguishing these predicates that may be used in inductive inferences from those that may not.

There are several suggestions for such a distinction in the literature. Goodman calls the predicates which may be used in inductions "projectible." This is only a name of the problem, not a solution. Goodman's step towards a solution is his notion of "entrenchment": a new predicate in a developing theory may be found successful in inductions and in this way become entrenched. This is a kind of "second-order" induction. As Quine (1969, p. 129) puts it: "We newly establish the projectibility of some predicate, to our satisfaction, by successfully trying to project it. In induction nothing succeeds like success."

Another idea is that some predicates denote "natural kinds" or "natural properties" while others don't, and it is only the former that may be used in inductions. Natural kinds are normally interpreted realistically and thus assumed to represent something that exists in reality independently of human cognition.

A third notion is that of "similarity." Quine (1969) discusses this notion and its relation to that of a natural kind. He notes that similarity "is immediately definable in terms of kind; for things are similar when they are two of a kind" (p. 117). Furthermore, he says about similarity that we "cannot easily imagine a more familiar or fundamental notion than this, or a notion more ubiquitous in its application. On this score it is like the notions of logic: like identity, negation, alternation, and the rest. And yet, strangely, there is something logically repugnant about it. For we are baffled when we try to relate the general notion of similarity significantly to logical terms" (Quine 1969, p. 117). To substantiate this claim he discusses and rejects several attempts to define similarity or natural kinds in logical or set-theoretical terms.

For instance, let us look at an attempt, adapted from Carnap, which says that a set is a natural kind if all its members are more similar to one another than to any one thing outside the set. Goodman (1966, pp. 162–164) has shown, however, that this construction does not work. To use Quine's example (1969, pp. 120–121), consider the set of all red round things, red wooden things, and round wooden things. This set is thus determined by the things that are similar at least in respect to two of the three properties red, round, and wooden. The set then meets the proposed definition of a natural kind. However, it is not what anyone means by a kind, since it includes yellow croquet balls and red rubber balls while excluding yellow rubber balls.

Quine concludes that the notions of similarity and natural kind are fundamental to our thinking, while they are completely alien to logic and set theory. Thus the strict methodology of logical positivism succumbs to the problem of characterizing notions like "projectible," "natural kind," or "similarity." As the paradoxes outlined above show, this problem is central for the task of distinguishing acceptable inductive inferences from unacceptable ones. It should also be obvious that the problem of defining "projectible" is intimately related to the problem of identifying lawlike sentences (compare Stegmüller 1973, pp. 507–508).

3. Induction as a Problem of Knowledge Representation

In the previous section we have seen that logical tools alone are not sufficient for the analysis of inductive inferences. The main reason is that logic treats all predicates of the language on a par and thus induces symmetries that are not preserved by inductions. Quine's negative conclusions concerning the possibilities of defining "natural kind" or the corresponding notion "similarity" indicate that we have to go beyond language to find a solution to this problem.

What is needed is a way of tapping our sources of knowledge which would enable us to distinguish the projectible predicates from the nonprojectible ones. Furthermore, the information obtained should be amenable for computational handling if we strive at constructing programs that perform successful inductive inferences. These desiderata suggest that the problem of projectible inductions, like so many other problems within AI, is basically a problem of knowledge representation.

However, the most common type of knowledge representation within the AI tradition is "propositional" in the sense that it is based on a set of rules or axioms together with a set of facts or a data base. These constituents are then combined with the aid of some inference mechanism to produce new rules or facts, which then form the basis for the planning or problem-solving tasks of the program. A typical example is the definition of a *concept-formation problem* in Genesereth and Nilsson (1987), pp. 165–166. This definition consists of a quadruple (P,N,C,Λ), where P is a set of positive instances of a concept, N is a set of negative instances, C is a set of concepts to be used in defining the concept, and Λ is a language to use in phrasing the definition. Thus, the inductive reasoning based on a concept-formation problem of this kind presumes a fixed language and a given set of basic concepts from which the inductive concepts are to be defined. Since the inductions performed by inference mechanisms of this and related kinds will preserve the logical symmetries discussed in the previous section, they will be open to the same type of criticism. Unfortunately, the current approach to knowledge representation within AI leaves us with bad prospects for mechanised induction.

Another problem of a different kind, but still a problem about knowledge representation, is that there is a strong tendency among philosophers to give the notion of "natural kind" a realistic interpretation, that is, natural kinds are claimed to exist in the external world independently of anyone thinking about them. ("Similarity" is given a realistic interpretation too, as exemplified by Lewis's writings, for example his (1973).) Now, if we want a computer program to perform inductions based on natural kinds, it is not sufficient that they exist out there somewhere, but we need some way of specifying them in computational expressions. In other words, a "conceptual" or "computational" analysis of natural kinds would be much more handy for AI than a realistic one.

The previous section raised a number of philosophical problems for an analysis of inductive inferences and the present section has introduced some further demands on such an analysis that are generated by an AI perspective. It is now time to enter a more constructive mood.

4. Conceptual Spaces

The knowledge representation to be presented here is nonlinguistic in the sense that the objects of the representation no longer form a language or even a propositional structure. (This does, of course, not exclude that the representation can be *embedded* in some linguistic structure as for example a programming language.) The representation is a cognitive or conceptual structure which I view as ontologically prior to any form of language. The "framework" of the representation, or its Kantian *"Anschauungsformen,"* consists of what I call a conceptual space. This notion can be seen as a development of the "quality spaces" in Quine (1960), the "attribute spaces" in Carnap (1971), and the "logical spaces" in Stalnaker (1979). For other presentations of conceptual spaces, although with a slightly different emphasis, see Gärdenfors (1988; 1990).

A conceptual space, which is a cognitive entity, consists of a number of *quality dimensions.* Some examples of quality dimensions are color, weight, the three dimensions of ordinary space (length, width, and height), temperature, time, and mass. When we talk about the qualities of objects it is in relation to these dimensions. The dimensions are prelinguistic in the sense that we (and other animals) can think about the qualities of objects, for example, when planning an action, without presuming a language in which these thoughts can be expressed.

I want to take the notion of a *space* seriously. It is assumed that each of the quality dimensions is endowed with a certain *topological* or *metrical* structure. For example, we normally think of ordinary space as a three-dimensional Euclidean space. It was only a century ago that we became aware of other (non-Euclidean) ways of representing this space. The weight dimension is measured on a quotient scale and is thus isomorphic with the positive real numbers, and the temperature dimension is measured on an interval scale and thus is less structured than the weight dimension.

It should be noted that some "dimensions" only have a *discrete* structure, that is, they merely divide objects into disjoint classes. Two examples are classifications of biological species and kinship relations in a human society. However, even for these dimensions we can distinguish a simple topological structure. For example, in the phylogenetic classification of animals, it is meaningful to say that birds and reptiles are more closely related than reptiles and crocodiles.

At this point it is necessary to make a distinction between a *psychological* and a *scientific* (theoretical) interpretation of the quality dimensions. For example, our psychological visual space is not a perfect three-dimensional Euclidean space. For one thing, our perception of the vertical dimension (height) is distorted in comparison with our perception of the horizontal dimensions. However, the theoretical representation of visual space as a 3-D Euclidean space is an idealization that is mathematically amenable (there is no preferred direction, "Galilean transformations" preserve the structure, etc.). Similarly, our perception of the weight of objects is not fine enough to justify its representation by the full structure of the positive real numbers, but this theoretical representation is also motivated by the fact that the mathematics of this structure is well known.

The difference between the psychological and the theoretical representation is particularly drastic for the color dimension. In scientific applications the theoretical representation of color is primarily in terms of the wavelengths of different kinds of light. This is a one-dimensional structure, isomorphic to an interval of real numbers. On the other hand, the psychological dimension of a hue is represented by the so-called color *circle:* from yellow, through red, blue, green, and back to yellow again.

This representation, being a circle, has indeed other topological properties than the theoretical wavelength representation. For instance, we can talk about psychologically complementary colors, that is, colors that lie *opposite* to each other on the circle. The theoretical representation of color, having the topology of a straight line, does not allow us to talk about "opposite" colors.

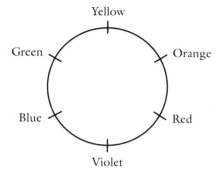

Figure 1. The color circle.

Apart from hue, there are two further psychological dimensions of color, namely brightness and saturation. The brightness dimension goes from white to black and is thus a linear dimension with end points. The saturation dimension goes from gray (zero color intensity) to greater and greater intensities. This dimension is thus isomorphic to an interval on the real line. In summary, color is represented psychologically by three dimensions, one with circular structure and two with linear.

In more abstract terms, a conceptual space S consists of a class $D_1, \ldots,$ D_n of quality dimensions. A point in S is represented by a vector $\bar{s} = (d_1, \ldots, d_n)$ with one index for each dimension. In relation to a given conceptual space, a complete description of the properties of an individual would consist in assigning it a point in the space. In this way each individual gets a specific color, spatial position, weight, temperature, and so forth. If an individual is assigned a partial vector, this means that not all the properties of the individual are known or have been determined.

As an example of a theoretical conceptual space used in science, we may take the conceptual space presumed in Newtonian particle mechanics. The quality dimensions are ordinary space (3-D Euclidean), time (isomorphic to the real numbers), mass (isomorphic to the nonnegative real numbers), and force (3-D Euclidean vector space). Once a particle has been assigned a value for each of these dimensions it is fully described as far as Newtonian mechanics goes.

The most fundamental reason for separating a cognitive structure into "dimensions" is that this separation expresses the assumption that an individual can be assigned some properties *independently* of other properties when the properties belong to different "dimensions." An individual can be assigned the weight "one kilo" independently of its temperature or color, but an individual cannot be assigned the property "green" independently of

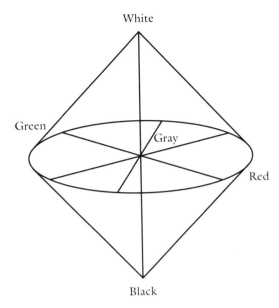

Figure 2.   The full color space.

being assigned the property "red" since these properties belong to the same dimension. In other words, different quality dimensions are *incommensurable* in the proper sense of the word (compare Johnson 1921, p. 175). A consequence of this is that each point (vector) in a conceptual space represents a "possible individual," that is, a possible assignment of properties to an individual. Within the AI tradition we find a similar distinction on p. 172 in Genesereth and Nilsson (1987) where it is said that "A version space U and a version space V are *independent* if and only if, for every u in U and every v in V, there is an object that satisfies both u and v." Within the philosophy tradition, a forerunner is Johnson's (1921, Chapter XI) distinction between "determinables" (corresponding to our dimensions) and "determinates" (corresponding to regions of dimensions). For a discussion of Johnson's theory, compare Pizzi (1983).

If we assume that the meanings of the predicates, among other things in a language, are determined in relation to a given conceptual space S, it follows from the topological structure of the different dimensions that certain statements will become true "a priori" (independent of empirical considerations). For example, the fact that comparative relations like "earlier than" are transitive follows from the linear structure of the length dimension and is thus an a priori feature of this relation (a-priori-in-*S,* that is). Similarly, it is a priori that everything that is green is colored (since "green" refers to a segment of the color circle) and that nothing is both red and green. A-priori-in-*S* is thus defined on the basis of the topological and metric structure of the conceptual space *S.* However, different conceptual spaces will yield different notions of "a priori."

As a short digression it can be noted that, in his last years, Carnap seems to have left the pure positivist methodology and was willing to introduce "metaphysical" assumptions regulating which probability functions are appropriate to use in inductive reasoning. In particular, in his (1971) he abandons the symmetry principle which treats all atomic predicates as logically independent, in favor of "attribute spaces" which induce "similarity relations" between atomic predicates (compare Stegmüller 1973, pp. 460–461). These attribute spaces, which are further developed in his (1980), show close similarities to the conceptual spaces introduced here.

5. Natural Kinds and Similarity

I now want to show how the notions of "natural kind" and "similarity" can be introduced quite easily once we have the idea of a conceptual space. Let us assume that a conceptual space *S* has been defined. The general notion of a property can then be defined as a *region* of that space. For example, the point in the time dimension representing "now" divides this dimension, and thus the space of vectors, into two regions, corresponding to the properties "past" and "future." In contrast to the definitions of properties that are used in standard semantic theories, this definition presumes neither the concept of an individual nor the concept of a possible world.

The topological properties of the dimensions now allow us to introduce the notion of a *natural property,* which we have seen to be a central task for a theory of induction. The definition is simply that a property, that is, a region of a conceptual space, is natural only if the region is *convex.* A convex region is characterized by the criterion that for every pair s_1, s_2 of points in the region all points between s_1 and s_2 are also in the region. This definition presumes that the notion of "between" is meaningful for the relevant dimensions. This is, however, a rather weak assumption which demands very little of the underlying topological structure. (In relation to this proposal it should be noted that Carnap (1980, p. 21) finds it "useful" to consider only *connected* regions of attribute spaces when looking for rules of inductive logic. This is a weaker requirement than that of convexity. However, he does not associate this proposal with the problem of projectibility.)

Most properties expressed by simple words in natural languages are natural properties in the sense specified above. For instance, I conjecture that all color terms in natural languages express natural properties with respect to the psychological representation of the three color dimensions. In other words, the conjecture predicts that if some object o_1 is described by the color term C in a given language and another object o_2 is also said to have the color C, then any object o_3 with a color which lies between the color of o_1 and the color of o_2 will also be described by the color term C. It is well known that different languages carve up the color circle in different ways, but all carvings seem to be done in terms of convex sets. Strong support for this conjecture can be gained from Berlin and Kay (1969), although they do not treat color terms in general but concentrate on basic color terms.

The notion of a natural property can be extended also to some discrete dimensions. For example, in a graph structure with nodes and arcs, we have a notion of betweenness, and thus we can identify the convex subsets of the graph (compare Johnson's notion of "adjectival betweenness" (1921, pp. 181–183)). This means that in a biological classification, which can be represented by a tree structure, a property is "natural" if it applies to all and only those parts of the classificatory tree that lie below one particular node in the tree. For example, the properties "marsupial" and "vertebrate" will be natural properties in the phylogenetic classification, while "featherless" and "biped" will not.

Now, given our standard representation of colors, "green" and "blue" are natural properties, while "grue" and "bleen" as defined above are not. "Grue" presumes two dimensions, color and time, for its description. But even if we consider the cylindrical space that would be generated by taking the "Cartesian product" of the time and hue dimensions, "grue" would not represent a convex region, but rather be discontinuous at the point on the time dimension representing the year 2000 (see Figure 4). Carnap (1971, pp. 70–76) excludes Goodman-type predicates by distinguishing between "locational" and "non-locational" attributes. "Grue" denotes a locational attribute since it refers to a particular temporal location. However, Carnap's solution seems rather *ad hoc* and it does not explain, for example, why we do not regard a nonlocational predicate like "green or orange" as projectible.

Similarly, the property "nonraven" which occurs in Hempel's paradox of confirmation would not count as a natural property. As seen in Figure 3, the complement of a convex set in a classificatory structure is normally not convex. However, "nonblack" corresponds to a convex region of the color space (any color "between" two nonblack colors is also nonblack). This indicates that convexity is a necessary but maybe not sufficient condition for a region to represent a natural property. (I have no firm intuition as to whether "nonblack" is projectible or not. "All nonblack bodies reflect some light" seems to be an acceptable generalization.)

In relation to the other problems discussed in section 2, it can be noted

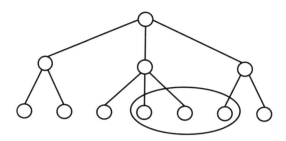

Figure 3.   A nonconvex subset of a classificatory space.

that even if both "*F*" and "*H*" denote natural properties, the disjunction "*F ∨ H*" need not denote a natural property; and if "*F*" is a natural property but "*H*" is not, then "*F&H*" need not be a natural property. However, if both "*F*" and "*H*" are natural properties, that is, correspond to convex regions in an underlying conceptual space, the conjunction "*F&H*" will also correspond to a convex region and thus represent a natural property.

Even if predicates like "grue" and its ilk do not correspond to natural properties in our standard conceptual space, it is conceivable that such predicates would correspond to natural properties in another conceptual space where, consequently, our predicates "green" and "blue" would denote nonnatural properties. Or in other words, what counts as a natural property is *dependent* on the underlying conceptual space. We will return to this form of relativism in the next section. As an example of a "nonnatural" classification, let me borrow a passage from Jorge Luis Borges where he

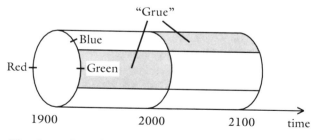

Figure 4.   The time color cylinder used to represent the nonconvexity of "grue."

writes that according to a "certain Chinese encyclopedia," animals are divided into "(a) belonging to the Emperor, (b) embalmed, (c) tame, (d) sucking pigs, (e) sirens, (f) fabulous, (g) stray dogs, (h) included in the present classification, (i) frenzied, (j) innumerable, (k) drawn with a very fine camelhair brush, (l) *et cetera,* (m) having just broken the water pitcher, (n) that from a long way off look like flies" (quoted from Foucault (1970), p. *xv*).

Thus I submit that with the aid of the topological and metric structure of a given conceptual space it is possible to define the notion of a natural property. And as regards inductive inferences, we now demand that only predicates denoting natural properties are allowed in the inferences; in other words, *only* such predicates are projectible (compare Stegmüller's *"Arbeitshypotesen"* in his (1973), p. 481). As is easily seen, this move will block all the paradoxes and logical problems of section 2. Consequently, the feature of a conceptual space that is the most essential for a theory of induction is its topological and metric properties, while the logical structure of the language that "lives on" the conceptual space is secondary for the applicability of the inductive process.

As I have already pointed out, this analysis of natural properties is based on a conceptual structure in contrast to the realistic interpretation of natural kinds that has been dominating in philosophy. However, it should be noted that the conceptual analysis given here is compatible with, though it does not require, strong metaphysical realism. On the contrary, it seems to me that adding a metaphysical component (the natural kinds *an sich*) to the conceptual spaces does not improve our understanding of natural kinds.

In relation to a given conceptual space it is also easy to introduce a relation of *similarity.* Two objects are more similar to each other the closer their set of properties is located in the underlying conceptual space. (Similarity is thus introduced as a comparative notion, not as a classificatory one.) Since the quality dimensions are independent, comparisons of similarity go primarily dimensionwise. Thus a red and an orange object are more similar to each other in our standard perceptual space than a red and a yellow because red and orange are *closer* to each other on the color circle than red and yellow. This definition of "similarity" also shows its intimate relation to "natural property": a natural property determines a class of objects that are similar to each other on some quality dimension.

We find some related ideas in Carnap's later writings. He introduces (1971, pp. 78–80) "phenomenological" assumptions for the "attribute spaces," among which we find some assumptions concerning similarity. However, even if he notes that the similarity comparisons sometimes can be expressed in terms of a metric (p. 79), he never takes such a metric as a fundamental notion. On the contrary, he assumes that the phenomenological assumptions ("B-principles") that cannot be formulated in the object language L are expressed in the metalanguage which is used to talk about the models and propositions of L and the inductive functions defined on L. This means that he never leaves the ideal that all knowledge should be expressed linguistically, although he relegates some of the information to a metalanguage.

In two other articles on conceptual spaces (Gärdenfors 1988; 1990) I have outlined an analysis of *analogies* and *metaphors* in terms of similarities of the structure of the quality dimensions. Analogical and metaphorical thinking is another way of establishing the similarity of objects. An analysis of these faculties in terms of conceptual spaces may also be helpful in explaining how inductive inferences can *transfer information* from one domain of qualities to another.

6. On the Relativism of Inductive Inferences

Natural properties have here been defined in relation to a given conceptual space. But isn't the choice of a conceptual space *arbitrary*? Since a conceptual space may seem like a Kuhnian paradigm, aren't we thereby stuck with an unescapable *relativism*? After all, anyone can pick his own conceptual space and in this way make his favorite properties come out natural in that space. For example, it is not difficult to construct a conceptual space where "grue" would correspond to a convex region and thus be a natural property in that space.

The purpose of this section is to argue that the relativism inherent in the selection of a conceptual space as a basis for identifying natural properties is not as problematic as it may first seem. The first thing to note is that human beings, to a remarkable extent, agree on which properties are projectible: these are the properties that get a foothold in language (compare Quine 1969, p. 123). For instance, identifying and naming species of animals and plants would not work unless these showed projectible regularities. This far-reaching agreement suggests that the psychological conceptual spaces of humans are, at least in their fundamental dimensions, close to identical. But even if this psychological agreement exists, we must answer the question of why our way of identifying natural properties accords so well with the external world as to make our inductions tend to come out right. As Quine (1969, p. 126) puts it: "Why should our subjective spacing of qualities have a special purchase on nature and a lien on the future?"

The answer, it seems to me, comes from evolutionary theory. Natural selection has made us all develop a conceptual space that results in inductions that are valid most of the time and thus promote survival. To quote Quine again: "Creatures inveterately wrong in their inductions have a pathetic but praise-worthy tendency to die before reproducing their kind" (p. 126).

Some of the quality dimensions of our conceptual space seem to be innate, as for example ordinary space and color (unless one is color blind). These dimensions are obviously very helpful for finding food and for getting around in the environment. Other dimensions, like volume, are probably learned (compare Piaget's "conservation" experiments with five year old children), and still others, like time, may be culturally dependent. A sophisticated time dimension is needed for advanced forms of planning and coordination with other individuals, but is not necessary for the most basic activities of an organism.

This evolutionary story of the origin of psychological forms of human conceptual spaces explains why our intuitions as to which properties are projectible are so similar. Peirce puts it as follows: "But, in point of fact, not man merely, but all animals derive by inheritance (presumably by natural selection) two classes of ideas which adapt them to their environment. In the first place, they all have from birth some notions, however crude and concrete, of force, matter, space, and time; and in the next place, they have some notion of what sort of objects their fellow-beings are and how they will act on given occasions" (1932, p. 476). The upshot is that there will be rather limited freedom for humans in choosing a conceptual space as a basis for inductive inferences, and the relativism that will occur will only apply to the more advanced, learned, and culturally dependent quality dimensions: Goodman-type predicates will in no case count as natural.

However, a far-reaching consequence of the evolutionary story is that our inductive capacities will be *dependent on the ecological circumstances under which they have evolved*. Human conceptual spaces are attuned to the environment of thousands of years of hunting and gathering. Consequently, we cannot expect our intuitions about which properties are projectible to be successful in environments that wildly diverge from those present during our evolutionary history.

This is where *science* enters on the scene. By introducing theoretically precise, nonpsychological quality dimensions, a scientific theory may help us find new inductive inferences that would not be possible on the basis of our subjective conceptual spaces alone. Witness, for example, Newton's distinction between weight and mass, which is of crucial importance for the development of his celestial mechanics, but which has no correspondence in human psychology. Or witness the distinction between temperature and amount of heat, which is central for thermodynamics: human perception of heat is basically determined by the amount of heat transferred from an object to the skin (or vice versa) rather than by the temperature of the object. The quality dimensions of scientific theories, and their associated measurement procedures, help us in producing new successful inductive conclusions in environments which are completely different from that of our evolutionary cradle.

Furthermore, the precise metrics of the scientific quality dimensions make it possible to formulate *functional laws* (Galileo's laws of free fall have set the standard) which enable us to compute more sophisticated predictions. Once a scientific conceptual space has been established, the formulation of such laws is a kind of inductive inference. Clearly, such laws supersede inductions of the form "All *F*s are *G*s" which are the only possible inductive inferences on quality dimensions which have only a crude or rudimentary metric.

7. Conclusion

Induction has been called "the scandal of philosophy." Unless more consideration is given to the question of which form of knowledge representation is appropriate for mechanized inductive inferences, I am afraid that induction may become a scandal of AI as well. I have argued that the traditional problems for the positivists' analyses of induction have arisen because they confined themselves to narrowly linguistic representations of knowledge and to logical tools for analyzing the knowledge. To the extent that AI programs for induction use the same type of representation they will succumb to similar problems. We must go deeper than language, if we want to discover the sources of successful inductions.

I do not claim that the outlined theory of conceptual spaces will solve all, or even most, of the problems of induction. I have tried to show that, in simple cases, it may help us understand why certain predicates are never used in inductions. A more extended reason for introducing the theory is to present an *alternative* to linguistic representations of knowledge which may help us see the drawbacks of such representations. But hopefully, the notion of a conceptual space and, more generally, "topological" representations of knowledge should be computationally much more efficient than traditional linguistic representations when trying to write programs that perform inductive inferences.

The relativism of conceptual spaces becomes more troublesome here, because AI practitioners cannot wait for evolution to select the appropriate quality dimensions. My analysis thus leads to a *metaproblem* of inductive inferences: What criteria can be used to choose between competing conceptual spaces? I have no general solution to this problem, but I believe that it is closely related to the metascientific project of evaluating competing scientific theories. If this is correct, it entails that an AI programmer who attempts to generate automated inductive inferences in some application domain should use the "best" scientific theory of that domain (leaving it to the scientific community to make the choice). Mature theories are generally based on clearly identifiable conceptual spaces which can be used as a basis for the program.

Finally, it can be noted that representing knowledge using conceptual spaces is an example of what Sloman (1971) would classify as an "analogical" representation. In contrast, what has here been called linguistic representation corresponds to his "Fregean" representation. From a computational point of view, these two kinds of representation call for different programming techniques. Linguistic or Fregean representations basically use formula manipulation, for example in applying logical inference rules. On the other hand, analogical representations use more directly "mathematical" operations. An implementation of the theory of conceptual spaces, for instance, would rely heavily on vector calculations. In speculations about how our brains process information, the symbol manipulation paradigm has been predominant (most typically in the writings of Fodor and Pylyshyn). However, the issues discussed in this paper suggest, if I am correct, that much more emphasis should be given to programs based on analogical representations.

Lund University

NOTES AND REFERENCES

† An earlier version of this article was presented at a conference on the Philosophy of Science, Dubrovnik, April 1987, and at an AI-workshop on Inductive Reasoning, Roskilde, April 1987. I wish to thank the participants of these meetings as well as Johan van Benthem, Jens Erik Fenstad, Lars Löfgren, David Makinson, Ilkka Niiniluoto, Claudio Pizzi, and two anonymous referees for helpful comments.

Berlin, B., and Kay. P. (1969), *Basic Color Terms: Their Universality and Evolution.* Berkeley: University of California Press.

Carnap, R. (1950), *Logical Foundations of Probability.* Chicago: Chicago University Press.

———. (1971), "A Basic System of Inductive Logic, Part II," in R. Carnap and R. C. Jeffrey (eds.), *Studies in Inductive Logic and Probability.* Berkeley: University of California Press, 35–165.

———. (1980), "A Basic System of Inductive Logic, Part II," in R. Carnap and R. C. Jeffrey (eds.), *Studies in Inductive Logic and Probability, Vol. II.* Berkeley: University of California Press, 7–156.

Foucault, M. (1970), *The Order of Things, An Archeology of the Human Sciences.* New York: Random House.

Gärdenfors, P. (1988), "Semantics, Conceptual Spaces and the Dimensions of Music," to appear in V. Rantala, L. Rowell and E. Tarasti (eds.), *Philosophy of Music.* Helsinki: Acta Philosophica Fennica, 9–27.

————. (1990), "Mental Representation, Conceptual Spaces, and Metaphors," to appear in *Synthese*.

Genesereth, M. and Nilsson, N. J. (1987), *Logical Foundations of Artificial Intelligence*. Los Altos: Morgan Kaufmann.

Goodman, N. (1955), *Fact, Fiction and Forecast*. Cambridge, Mass.: Harvard University Press.

————. (1961), "Saftey, Strength, Simplicity," *Philosophy of Science* 28: 150–151.

————. (1966), *The Structure of Appearance*, 2nd ed. New York: Bobbs-Merrill.

Hempel, C. G. (1965), *Aspects of Scientific Explanation, and Other Essays in the Philosophy of Science*. New York: Free Press.

Holland, J. H., Holyoak, K. J., Nisbett, R. E., and Thagard, P. R. (1986), *Induction: Processes of Inference, Learning, and Discovery*. Cambridge, Mass.: The MIT Press.

Johnson, W. E. (1921), *Logic. Part I*. Cambridge: Cambridge University Press.

Lewis, D. K. (1973), *Counterfactuals*. Oxford: Blackwell.

Peirce, C. S. (1931), *Collected Papers, Vol. II*, ed. Hartshorne and Weiss. Cambridge, Mass.: Belknap Press.

Pizzi, C. (1983), "Il problema dei determinabili nella logica del '900,'" *Atti del Convegno Internazionale di Storia della Logica*. Bologna: Clueb, 353–358.

Quine, W. V. O. (1960), *Word and Object*. Cambridge, Mass.: MIT Press.

————. (1969), "Natural Kinds," in *Ontological Relativity and Other Essays*. New York: Columbia University Press, 114–138.

Sloman, A. (1971), "Interactions between Philosophy and A.I.—the Role of Intuition and Non-logical Reasoning in Intelligence," *Proceedings 2nd IJCAI*. London, reprinted in *Artificial Intelligence, Vol. 2*, 1971.

Stalnaker, R. (1979), "Anti-Essentialism," *Midwest Studies of Philosophy IV*: 343–355.

Stegmüller, W. (1973), *Personelle und Statistische Wahrscheinlichkeit, Erster Halbband: Personelle Wahrscheinlichkeit und Rationale Entscheidung*. Berlin: Springer-Verlag.

Postscript (July 1992)

After writing this paper, I have continued working on the problem of induction in relation to conceptual spaces. Here are the relevant references:

"Frameworks for Properties: Possible Worlds vs. Conceptual Spaces," in *Language, Knowledge, and Intentionality*, ed. L. Haaparanta, M. Kusch, and I. Niiniluoto (Helsinki: Acta Philosophica Fennica. 49, 1990), 383–407.

"Induction and the Evolution of Conceptual Spaces," to appear in *Charles Peirce and the Philosophy of Science: Papers from the 1989 Harvard Conference*, ed. E.C. Moore (University of Alabama Press).

"Three Levels of Inductive Inference," to appear in the *Proceedings of the 9th International Congress of Logic, Methodology, and Philosophy of Science*, ed. D. Prawitz, B. Skyrms, and D. Westerståhl.

The Projectibility Constraint

8

John L. Pollock

1. Introduction

Logical inference rules are *universal* in the sense that they apply equally to all concepts. For instance, ⌜(Ax & Bx)⌝ implies ⌜Ax⌝, regardless of what *A* and *B* are. Goodman (1955) astonished the philosophical world by demonstrating that the same is not true of induction. He showed that reasoning inductively with the contrived concepts *grue* and *bleen* leads to absurd results. He recorded this observation by saying that *grue* and *bleen* are not *projectible,* and that there must be a constraint on principles of induction to the effect that the concepts involved are projectible.

Goodman's observation can be formulated more precisely in terms of the *Nicod principle,* which is as follows:

(1.1) ⌜*X* is a set of *A*'s all of which are *B*'s⌝ is a prima facie reason for believing ⌜All *A*'s are *B*'s⌝.

I have formulated the Nicod principle in terms of prima facie reasons. The general framework of defeasible reasoning based upon prima facie reasons and defeaters is, by now, a reasonably familiar one in epistemology, but I will say just a few words about it here to help orient the reader who is not familiar with this literature.[1] Defeasible reasoning has been the subject of much discussion in recent epistemology. As recently as the 1960s it was often supposed that in order for *P* to be a reason for believing *Q*, *P* must logically entail *Q*. But such a view of reasons leads inexorably to skepticism. Our knowledge of the world cannot be reconstructed in terms of logically conclusive reasons. It is now generally granted in epistemology that there are two kinds of reasons—defeasible and nondefeasible. Nondefeasible reasons are always conclusive—they logically entail what they are reasons for. Defeasible reasons are what I have called "prima facie

Includes material from *Nomic Probability and the Foundations of Induction* by John L. Pollock. New York: Oxford University Press, 1990. This material is used with the permission of Oxford University Press.

reasons." These are reasons providing justification only when unaccompanied by defeaters. For example, something's looking red to me is a reason for me to think that it is red. This is a defeasible reason. Despite the fact that an object looks red to me, I may have reasons for believing that the object is not red. For instance, I may be assured of this by someone I regard as reliable, or I may know that it was orange just a minute ago when I examined it in better light and it is unlikely to have changed color in the interim.

In general, if P is a prima facie reason for Q, there can be two kinds of defeaters for P. *Rebutting defeaters* are reasons for denying Q in the face of P. To be contrasted with rebutting defeaters are *undercutting defeaters*, which attack the connection between the prima facie reason and its conclusion rather than attacking the conclusion itself. For example, if I know that x is illuminated by red lights and such illumination often makes things look red when they are not, then I cannot be justified in believing that x is red on the basis of its looking red to me. What I know about the illumination constitutes an undercutting defeater for my prima facie reason. An undercutting defeater for P as a prima facie reason for believing Q is a reason for denying that P would not be true unless Q were true. To illustrate, knowing about the peculiar illumination gives me a reason for denying that x would not look red to me unless it were red.

Returning to projectibility, Goodman's observation was that the Nicod principle is incorrect as formulated. To make it correct, there must be a constraint to the effect that B is projectible with respect to A. We can take this as a definition of projectibility, defining:

> (1.2) B is projectible with respect to A iff $\ulcorner X$ is a set of A's all of which are B's$\urcorner$ is a prima facie reason for believing $\ulcorner$All A's are B's$\urcorner$.

We then face the task of providing an informative criterion for projectibility. Goodman proposed such a criterion in terms of entrenchment, but for reasons that will emerge below, I do not think that this criterion should be endorsed.

Goodman's discussion left many philosophers with the impression that most concepts are projectible with respect to one another, and it is really only "funny" concepts like *grue* and *bleen* for which projectibility fails. But, as I will urge below, this impression is inaccurate. Perhaps most concepts fail to be projectible with respect to one another. Projectibility is the exception rather than the rule. One of the two main points of this paper will be to establish this. The second main point will be to show that projectibility plays a more pervasive role in reasoning than has generally been appreciated. Projectibility constraints recur in a number of places throughout epistemology, and the role of projectibility in induction cannot be regarded as its most fundamental occurrence. These observations are drawn from my (1990).[2]

2. The Logic of Projectibility

The first thing to be shown is that there are objective logical principles that play a role in determining which concepts are projectible with respect to each other, and these principles imply that nonprojectibility is common. These logical principles concern closure conditions for projectibility. Closure conditions tell us that if certain concepts are projectible with respect to one another, then so are some related concepts. The simplest and most obvious closure condition is the following:

> (2.1)   If A and B are both projectible with respect to C, so is $(A$ & $B)$.

I will express this by saying that projectibility is closed under conjunction. Principle (2.1) follows fairly directly from the definition of projectibility. Suppose we know that X is a set of C's all of which are $(A$ & $B)$'s. Then X is also a set of C's all of which are A's and a set of C's all of which are B's. This gives us a prima facie reason for thinking that all C's are A's, and also a prima facie reason for thinking that all C's are B's. But the latter two conclusions jointly entail that all C's are $(A$ & $B)$'s, so it would seem that we have a prima facie reason for believing this as well.

(2.1) is a closure condition on the projectibility of the consequent in inductive reasoning. Although we cannot establish it quite so conclusively, there is a fairly compelling reason for thinking there is a similar closure condition on the antecedent:

> (2.2)   If A is projectible with respect to both B and C, then A is projectible with respect to $(B$ & $C)$.

Principle (2.2) can be defended by looking at standard scientific methodology. Suppose A is projectible with respect to B. Then a scientist may set about trying to confirm $(\forall x)(Bx \supset Ax)$. If her investigations reveal a counterexample to this generalization, she need not give up the investigation. Rather, she may try to confirm a less adventurous generalization. She may restrict the antecedent and try to confirm a weaker generalization of the form $(\forall x)[(Bx$ & $Cx) \supset Ax]$. If this is to be legitimate, A must be projectible with respect to $(B$ & $C)$.

The preceding principles will probably surprise no one. But what is surprising is that projectibility is not also closed under disjunction. In other words, the following principle fails:

(2.3)   If A and B are both projectible with respect to C, so is $(A \lor B)$.

The intuitive failure of (2.3) can be illustrated quite easily. For instance, it seems clear that *has a liver* and *has a kidney* are both projectible with respect to *is an animal having endorphins in its blood*. Suppose now that we set about trying to confirm that any animal with endorphins in its blood has either a liver or a kidney. We observe a sample of animals with endorphins in their blood, and we note that many of them have livers, and many do not. We also observe that many have kidneys and many do not. But we never check whether any of those that fail to have livers have kidneys, or whether any of those that fail to have kidneys have livers. Obviously, these observations give us no reason at all to believe that every animal with endorphins in its blood has either a liver or a kidney. But notice that we have observed a sample of animals with endorphins in their blood that have either livers or kidneys (i.e., the sample consists of all of those that we ascertained either to have livers or to have kidneys), and we have not observed any that have neither. The latter is because when we found an animal in our sample to lack a kidney, we did not go on to check whether it lacked a liver, and vice versa. Thus if *has a liver or a kidney* were projectible with respect to *is an animal with endorphins in its blood,* this sample would have to confirm that any animal with endorphins in its blood has either a liver or a kidney. As it does not, (2.3) is false.

This example provides an intuitive illustration of the failure of (2.3), but it does not explain the reason for this failure. The reason is actually a simple one. If we were allowed to make free use of disjunctions in induction then every sample would give us prima facie reasons for mutually inconsistent generalizations, with the result that we would not be justified in believing either of the generalizations on the basis of the sample. This would have the consequence that induction could never give us an undefeated reason for believing a generalization. This results as follows. Suppose (2.3) were true, and suppose we are presented with a set X of C's all of which are A's. It will turn out that projectibility is not closed under negation, but at least in many cases both A and $\sim A$ will be projectible with respect to C, so let us assume that here.[3] For any finite sample X, there will typically be some other concept B such that (1) all members of X are B's, (2) both B and $\sim B$ are projectible with respect to C, and (3) we know that there are A's that are not B's. By (2.1), the conjunctions $(A \ \& \ B)$ and $(\sim A \ \& \ \sim B)$ are each projectible with respect to C. Suppose that, in accordance with (2.3), the disjunction $[(A \ \& \ B) \lor (\sim A \ \& \ \sim B)]$ were also projectible with respect to C. The sample X consists of objects all of which satisfy this disjunction, so this would have to give us a reason for thinking that all C's satisfy it. However, $(\forall x)\{Cx \supset [(Ax \ \& \ Bx) \lor (\sim Ax \ \& \ \sim Bx)]\}$ together with $(\exists x)(Cx \ \& \ \sim Bx)$ logically entails $\sim(\forall x)(Cx \supset Ax)$. Consequently, the very same sample that provided a prima facie reason for believing $(\forall x)(Cx \supset Ax)$ also gives us a reason for denying it. If this were always the case, induction would be useless. Accordingly, (2.3) must be false.[4]

The following is also false:

> (2.4) If C is projectible with respect to both A and B, then C is projectible with respect to $(A \lor B)$.

It is quite easy to see that (2.4) cannot be true in general. For example, *having whiskers* is projectible with respect to both *cat* and *elephant*. That is, we could confirm that all cats have whiskers by observing whiskered cats, and we could confirm that all elephants have whiskers by observing whiskered elephants. But we cannot automatically confirm that anything that is either a cat or an elephant would have whiskers by observing a sample of things having the property of being either a cat or an elephant and seeing that all of its members are whiskered. A sample of things having that disjunctive property could consist entirely of cats, but observing a sample consisting of whiskered cats can give us no reason at all for thinking that any elephant would be whiskered, and the latter is entailed by the proposition that anything that is either a cat or an elephant would be whiskered. It is, of course, possible to confirm in a more complicated way that anything that is either a cat or an elephant would be whiskered, but this cannot be done just by observing a sample of cats-or-elephants and seeing that all of its members are whiskered. Instead, we must observe separate samples of cats and elephants (or a composite sample consisting of each), confirm the separate generalizations that any cat would be whiskered and that any elephant would be whiskered, and then infer deductively that anything that is either a cat or an elephant would be whiskered.

Although generalizations involving disjunctions of projectible concepts cannot usually be confirmed directly by enumerative induction, they can be confirmed indirectly. For example, how, intuitively, would we confirm that any animal with endorphins in its blood has either a liver or a kidney? We might examine a number of such animals, look to see whether they have livers, and those that lack livers would be examined to see whether they have kidneys. If they do, that confirms the generalization. Similarly, we might examine a number of animals with endorphins in their blood to see whether they have kidneys, and then further examine those lacking kidneys to see whether they have livers. What we are doing here is obtaining direct inductive confirmation for the projectible generalizations "Any animal with endorphins in its blood but lacking a liver has a kidney" and "Any animal with endorphins in its blood but lacking a kidney has a liver," each of which is equivalent to "Any animal with endorphins in its blood has either a liver or a kidney."

If projectibility were closed under both conjunction and negation, it would be closed under disjunction, so the following are also false:

(2.5)   If A is projectible with respect to B then $\sim A$ is projectible with respect to B.

(2.6)   If A is projectible with respect to B then A is projectible with respect to $\sim B$.

It follows in similar ways that projectibility fails to be closed under most logical operators. Of course, from the fact that projectibility is not closed under a logical operation like disjunction, it does not follow that no disjunctions are projectible. Such a conclusion would be too strong, because every concept is logically equivalent to a disjunction, and presumably a concept is projectible if it is equivalent to a projectible concept. However, as the examples make apparent, *most* disjunctions will fail to be projectible. The only way a disjunction can be projectible is by being equivalent to a nondisjunction that is already projectible for some other reason. And the same point applies to most logically complex concepts. This is what I meant by saying that most concepts fail to be projectible with respect to one another.

Notice that *grue* and *bleen* are defined as disjunctions. I suggest that this is the source of their nonprojectibility. They fall within a large class of nonprojectible concepts (namely, disjunctions), most of which are perfectly ordinary and noncontrived. It also deserves emphasis that the arguments establishing that projectibility is not closed under disjunction or negation turn upon objective logical relationships. Projectibility *must* work this way, as a matter of logic. Thus nonprojectibility cannot arise out of anything so ephemeral as entrenchment.

3. Statistical Induction

Projectibility was introduced as a constraint on enumerative induction, but there are other forms of induction as well, and it should not be surprising that they too are subject to projectibility constraints. The simplest is statistical induction, which is normally supposed to operate in terms of a principle of the following sort:

(3.1) $\ulcorner X$ is a set of n A's m of which are B's $\urcorner$ is a prima facie reason for believing $\ulcorner$ The probability of an A's being a B is approximately $m/n \urcorner$.

It is natural to suppose that this should be qualified by a projectibility constraint requiring that B be projectible with respect to A. However, as I pointed out in my (1990), the constraint that is actually required is a bit stronger, namely, that both B and $\sim B$ be projectible with respect to A. This requirement is easily illustrated by an example related to that illustrating the failure of (2.3). Suppose B is the conjunction $(C \& D)$, where C and D are projectible with respect to A but $(\sim C \lor \sim D)$ is not. Suppose we are testing samples of a substance for the properties C and D. We find some samples of the substance to have the property C and some to lack it, and we find some samples to have the property D and some to lack it. But when we find a sample to possess one of these properties, we never go on to test it for the other property. As a result, we know of many samples of the substance lacking the property B (i.e., all of those we know to lack one or the other of C and D), but we do not know of any possessing the property B. Thus taking X to consist of all samples of the substance regarding which we know whether they possess the property B, the observed relative frequency of B in the sample X is 0. But it would clearly be unreasonable for us to conclude that the probability of an A's being a B is approximately 0.

Apparently, statistical induction should be formulated using the following strong projectibility constraint:

(3.2)   If both B and $\sim B$ are projectible with respect to A, then $\ulcorner X$ is a set of n A's m of which are B's $\urcorner$ is a prima facie reason for believing $\ulcorner$The probability of an A's being a B is approximately $m/n \urcorner$.[5]

As far as I know, the need for this strong projectibility constraint has gone entirely overlooked in the literature on statistical induction and statistical inference. It seems likely that this same strong projectibility constraint should be imposed upon all familiar patterns of statistical inference. The need for such a constraint appears to have been ignored in statistics.

4. Direct Inference

What is perhaps more surprising is that projectibility constraints arise in other kinds of probabilistic reasoning, and not just in induction. First, consider direct inference. Direct inference arises out of the distinction between "definite" probabilities and "indefinite" probabilities. A definite probability is the probability that a particular proposition is true. Indefinite probabilities, on the other hand, concern properties rather than propositions. For example, the probability of a smoker getting cancer is not about any particular smoker. Rather, it relates the property of being a smoker and the property of getting cancer. Any probabilities derived by induction from relative frequencies are automatically indefinite probabilities, because relative frequencies relate properties. But for many practical purposes, the probabilities in which we are really interested are definite probabilities. We want to know how probable it is that it will rain today, that Bluenose will win the third race, that Sally will have a heart attack, etc. It is probabilities of this sort that are involved in practical reasoning. I will write indefinite probabilities using the lowercase "prob" and definite probabilities using the smallcaps "PROB."

Although definite and indefinite probabilities are logically distinct, we assess the former in terms of the latter, using what is called "direct inference." We judge that there is a 20 percent probability of rain today, because the indefinite probability of its raining in similar circumstances is believed to be about 0.2. We think it unlikely that Bluenose will win the third race because he has never finished above seventh in his life. We judge that Sally is more likely than her sister to have a heart attack because Sally smokes like a furnace and drinks like a fish, while her sister is a nun who jogs and lifts weights. We take these facts about Sally and her sister to be relevant because we know that they affect the indefinite probability of a person having a heart attack. That is, the indefinite probability of a person who smokes and drinks having a heart attack is much greater than the indefinite probability for a person who does not smoke or drink and is in good physical condition.

The basic idea underlying classical direct inference was first articulated by Hans Reichenbach (1949): in determining the probability that an individual c has a property F, we find the narrowest reference class X for which we have reliable statistics and then infer that $\text{PROB}(Fc) = \text{prob}(Fx/x\epsilon X)$. For example, insurance rates are calculated in this way. There is almost universal agreement that direct inference is based upon some such principle as this, although there is little agreement about the precise form the theory should take. In my (1983), (1984), and (1990), I argued that direct inference should be regarded as proceeding in accordance with the following two epistemic rules (where $\ulcorner W\phi\urcorner$ abbreviates $\ulcorner \phi$ is warranted$\urcorner$, i.e., $\ulcorner \phi$ is a conclusion that it would be reasonable to believe on the basis of the currently available evidence$\urcorner$):

(4.1)   If F is projectible with respect to G then $\ulcorner \text{prob}(F/G) = r \,\&\, W(Gc) \,\&\, W(P \equiv Fc)\urcorner$ is a prima facie reason for $\ulcorner \text{PROB}(P) = r\urcorner$.

(4.2)   If F is projectible with respect to H then $\ulcorner \text{prob}(F/H) \neq \text{prob}(F/G) \,\&\, W(Hc) \,\&\, \Box(\forall x)(Hx \supset Gx)\urcorner$ is an undercutting defeater for (4.1).

Principle (4.2) is called "the principle of subproperty defeat," because it says that probabilities based upon more specific information take precedence over those based upon less specific information.

To illustrate this account of direct inference, suppose we know that Herman is a 40-year-old resident of the United States who smokes. Suppose we also know that the probability of a 40-year-old resident of the United States having lung cancer is 0.1, but the probability of a 40-year-old smoker who resides in the United States having lung cancer is 0.3. If we know nothing else that is relevant, we will infer that the probability of Herman having lung cancer is 0.3. Principle (4.1) provides us with one prima facie reason for inferring that the probability is 0.1 and a second prima facie reason for inferring that the probability is 0.3. However, the latter prima facie reason is based upon more specific information, and so by (4.2) it takes precedence, defeating the first prima facie reason and leaving us justified in inferring that the probability is 0.3.

What is of particular interest in the present context is the projectibility constraints in (4.1) and (4.2).[6] The need for the projectibility constraints arises from the fact that, without them, direct inferences would almost invariably be defeated. The difficulty is that without the projectibility constraint it is almost always possible to construct prima facie reasons in accordance with (4.1) that conflict with and hence either rebut or undercut any given prima facie reason of that form. For example, consider a coin of some description D such that the probability of a toss landing heads is 0.5: $\text{prob}(H/T) = 0.5$ (where T is the property of being a toss of a coin of description D). Suppose we know that c is a toss of this coin, and we do not know anything else that is relevant to whether c lands heads. It is then reasonable to infer that $\text{PROB}(Hc) = 0.5$. $\text{prob}(H/T) = 0.5$ & $\mathbf{W}(Tc)$ provides a prima facie reason for this direct inference. But now let F be any predicate for which we are justified in believing that $\text{prob}(F/T\&{\sim}H) \neq 1$ and $\mathbf{W}(Fc)$. It follows from the probability calculus that

(4.3)   If $\text{prob}(F/T\&{\sim}H) \neq 1$ then $\text{prob}(H/(F \lor H)\&T) \neq$ $\text{prob}(H/T)$,

and this provides a subproperty defeater for the direct inference to the conclusion that $\text{PROB}(Hc) = \text{prob}(H/T)$.

The projectibility constraint has the effect of imposing constraints on both the consequent property and the reference property. The constraint on the reference property eliminates the problem case involving (4.3). To illustrate the effect of the projectibility constraint on the consequent property, consider a case in which, contrary to the constraint, we appear to make a direct inference regarding a disjunctive consequent property. For example, suppose we have a shipment of variously colored and shaped counters, and we know that 25 percent of them are either red squares or blue triangles. If we know only that c is one of the counters in the shipment, we will judge that $\text{PROB}((Rc \,\&\, Sc) \lor (Bc \,\&\, Tc)) = 0.25$. This appears to be a direct inference with regard to the disjunctive (and hence nonprojectible) concept $((R \,\&\, S) \lor (B \,\&\, T))$. It is explicable, however, in terms of direct inferences concerning projectible concepts. I contend that what we are doing here is making a direct inference to the conclusions that $\text{PROB}(Rc \,\&\, Sc) = \text{prob}(R \,\&\, S/C)$ and that $\text{PROB}(Bc \,\&\, Tc) = \text{prob}(B \,\&\, T/C)$ (where C is the concept of being a counter in the shipment), and then computing:

$$\text{PROB}((Rc \,\&\, Sc) \lor (Bc \,\&\, Tc))$$
$$= \text{PROB}(Rc \,\&\, Sc) + \text{PROB}(Bc \,\&\, Tc)$$
$$= \text{prob}(R \,\&\, S/C) + \text{prob}(B \,\&\, T/C)$$
$$= \text{prob}((R \,\&\, S) \lor (B \,\&\, T)/C)$$
$$= 0.25.$$

That this is the correct description of the inference can be seen as follows. Suppose we know c to be in a particular crate in the shipment, and we know that the proportion of red squares in the crate is 0.2, while the proportion of red squares in the entire shipment is only 0.1. We would take that to defeat the disjunctive inference. But for all we know, the proportion of counters in the entire shipment that are either red squares or blue triangles is the same as the proportion in that crate, so we do not have a subset defeater for the direct inference regarding the disjunction. What we do have is a subset defeater for the direct inference to the conclusion that $\text{PROB}(Rc \,\&\, Sc) = \text{prob}(R \,\&\, S/C)$. This inference is blocked, which in turn blocks the entire calculation and that prevents our concluding that $\text{PROB}((Rc \,\&\, Sc) \lor (Bc \,\&\, Tc)) = 0.25$. This is readily explicable on the supposition that the putative direct inference regarding the disjunction is parasitic on the direct inferences regarding the projectible disjuncts and is not really a direct inference in the same sense.

5. The Statistical Syllogism

Perhaps the most important projectibility constraint is that pertaining to the *statistical syllogism,* whose traditional formulation is something like the following:

> Most A's are B's.
> This is an A.
> _____
> Therefore, this is a B.

It seems clear that we often reason in roughly this way. For instance, on what basis do I believe what I read in the newspaper? Certainly not that everything printed in the newspaper is true. No one believes that. But I do believe that *most* of what is published in the newspaper is true, and that justifies me in believing individual newspaper reports. Similarly, I do not believe that every time a piece of chalk is dropped, it falls to the ground.

Various circumstances can prevent that. It might be snatched in midair by a wayward hawk, or suspended in air by Brownian movement, or hoisted aloft by a sudden wind. None of these are at all likely, but they are possible. Consequently, all I can be confident of is that chalk, when dropped, will almost always fall to the ground. Nevertheless, when I drop a particular piece of chalk, I expect it to fall to the ground.

⌜Most *A*'s are *B*'s⌝ can have different interpretations. It may mean simply that most actual *A*'s are *B*'s. But at least sometimes, "most" statements can be cashed out as statements of nomic probability. On that construal, ⌜Most *A*'s are *B*'s⌝ means ⌜prob(*B*/*A*) is high⌝. This suggests the following epistemic rule, which can be regarded as a more precise version of the statistical syllogism:

(5.1)   If $r > 0.5$ then ⌜*Ac* and prob(*B*/*A*) $\geq r$⌝ is a prima facie reason for ⌜*Bc*⌝, the strength of the reason depending upon the value of *r*.

It is illuminating to consider how this rule handles the lottery paradox. Suppose you hold one ticket in a fair lottery consisting of one million tickets, and suppose it is known that one and only one ticket will win. Observing that the probability is only 0.000001 of a ticket being drawn given that it is a ticket in the lottery, it seems reasonable to accept the conclusion that your ticket will not win. But by the same reasoning, it will be reasonable to believe, for each ticket, that it will not win. However, these conclusions conflict jointly with something else we are justified in believing, namely, that some ticket will win. Assuming that we cannot be justified in believing each member of an explicitly contradictory set of propositions, it follows that we are not warranted in believing of each ticket that it will not win. But this is no problem for principle (5.1) because it provides only a prima facie reason for its conclusion. What is happening in the lottery paradox is that the prima facie reason is defeated.

The lottery paradox is a case in which we have prima facie reasons for a number of conclusions but they collectively defeat one another. This illustrates the *principle of collective defeat*. Suppose we are warranted in believing some proposition *R* and we have equally good prima facie reasons for each of $P_1, \ldots, P_n$, where $\{P_1, \ldots, P_n\}$ is a minimal set of propositions deductively inconsistent with *R* (i.e., it is a set deductively inconsistent with *R* and has no proper subset that is deductively inconsistent with *R*). Then for each *i*, the conjunction ⌜*R* & P_1 & . . . & P_{i-1} & P_{i+1} & . . . & P_n⌝ entails ~P_i. Thus by combining this entailment with the arguments for *R* and $P_1, \ldots, P_{i-1}, P_{i+1}, \ldots, P_n$ we obtain an argument for ~P_i that is as good as the argument for P_i. Thus we have equally strong support for both P_i and ~P_i, and hence we could not reasonably believe either on this basis, i.e., neither is warranted. This holds for each *i*, so none of the P_i is warranted. They collectively defeat one another. Thus the simplest version of the principle of collective defeat can be formulated as follows:

> (5.2)   If we are warranted in believing R and we have equally good independent prima facie reasons for each member of a minimal set of propositions deductively inconsistent with R, and none of these prima facie reasons is defeated in any other way, then none of the propositions in the set is warranted on the basis of these prima facie reasons.

Although the principle of collective defeat allows principle (5.1) to escape the lottery paradox, it turns out that the very fact that (5.1) can handle the lottery paradox in this way shows that it cannot be correct. The difficulty is that every case of high probability can be recast in a form that makes it similar to the lottery paradox. We need only assume that $\mathrm{prob}(B/A) < 1$. Pick the smallest integer n such that $\mathrm{prob}(B/A) < 1 - 1/2^n$. Now consider n fair coins, unrelated to each other and unrelated to c's being A or B. Let T_i be $\ulcorner$ is a toss of coin $i \urcorner$ and let H be $\ulcorner$ is a toss that lands heads $\urcorner$. There are 2^n *Boolean conjunctions* of the form $\ulcorner(\sim)Hx_1 \ \& \ \dots \ \& \ (\sim)Hx_n\urcorner$ where each tilde in parentheses can be either present or absent. For each Boolean conjunction $\beta_j x_1, \dots, x_n$,

$$\mathrm{prob}(\beta_j x_1, \dots, x_n / T_1 x_1 \ \& \ \dots \ \& \ T_n x_n) = 2^{-n}.$$

Consequently, because the coins were chosen to be unrelated to A and B,

$$\mathrm{prob}(\sim \beta_j x_1, \dots, x_n / Ax \ \& \ T_1 x_1 \ \& \ \dots \ \& \ T_n x_n) = 1 - 2^{-n}.$$

By the probability calculus, a disjunction is at least as probable as its disjuncts, so

$$\mathrm{prob}(\sim Bx \vee \sim \beta_j x_1, \dots, x_n / Ax \ \& \ T_1 x_1 \ \& \ \dots \ \& \ T_n x_n) \geq 1 - 2^{-n} > \mathrm{prob}(Bx/Ax).$$

Let $t_1, \dots, t_n$ be a sequence consisting of one toss of each coin. As we know $\ulcorner Ac \ \& \ T_1 t_1 \ \& \ \dots \ \& \ T_n t_n \urcorner$, (5.1) gives us a prima facie reason for believing each disjunction of the form

$$\sim Bc \vee \sim \beta_j t_1, \dots, t_n.$$

By the propositional calculus, the set of all these disjunctions is equivalent to, and hence entails, $\ulcorner \sim Bc \urcorner$. Thus we can construct an argument for $\ulcorner \sim Bc \urcorner$ in which the only defeasible steps involve the use of (5.1) in connection with probabilities at least as great as that used in defending $\ulcorner Bc \urcorner$. Hence, we have a situation formally identical to the lottery paradox. Therefore, the principle of collective defeat has the consequence that if $\mathrm{prob}(B/A)$ has any probability less than 1, we cannot use (5.1) to draw any warranted conclusion from this high probability.

The difficulty can be traced to the assumption that A and B in (5.1) can be arbitrary formulas. Basically, we need a constraint which, when applied to the above argument, precludes applying (5.1) to the disjunctions $\ulcorner{\sim}Bc \vee {\sim}\beta_f t_1, \ldots, t_n\urcorner$. Disjunctions are generally problematic in (5.1). For instance, it is a theorem of the probability calculus that $\text{prob}(F/G \vee H) \geq \text{prob}(F/G)\,\text{prob}(G/G \vee H)$. Consequently, if $\text{prob}(F/G)$ and $\text{prob}(G/G \vee H)$ are sufficiently large, it follows that $\text{prob}(F/G \vee H) \geq r$. For example, because the vast majority of birds can fly and because there are many more birds than giant sea tortoises, it follows that most things that are either birds or giant sea tortoises can fly. If Herman is a giant sea tortoise, (5.1) would give us a reason for thinking that Herman can fly, but notice that this is based simply on the fact that most birds can fly, which should be irrelevant to whether Herman can fly. This indicates that arbitrary disjunctions cannot be substituted for B in (5.1).

Nor can arbitrary disjunctions be substituted for A in (5.1). By the probability calculus, $\text{prob}(F \vee G/H) \geq \text{prob}(F/H)$. Therefore, if $\text{prob}(F/H)$ is high, so is $\text{prob}(F \vee G/H)$. Thus, because most birds can fly, it is also true that most birds can either fly or swim the English Channel. By (5.1), this should be a reason for thinking that a starling with a broken wing can swim the English Channel, but obviously it is not.

There must be restrictions on the properties A and B in (5.1). It seems clear that the requisite constraint is one of projectibility. Accordingly, the statistical syllogism should be formulated as follows:

(A1) If F is projectible with respect to G and $r > 0.5$, then $\ulcorner Gc\ \&$ $\text{prob}(F/G) \geq r\urcorner$ is a prima facie reason for believing $\ulcorner Fc\urcorner$, the strength of the reason depending upon the value of r.

The reason provided by (A1) is only a prima facie reason, and as such it is defeasible. As with any prima facie reason, it can be defeated by having a reason for denying the conclusion. The reason for denying the conclusion constitutes a rebutting defeater. But there is also an important kind of undercutting defeater for (A1). In (A1), we infer the truth of $\ulcorner Fc\urcorner$ on the basis of probabilities conditional on a limited set of facts about c (i.e., the facts expressed by $\ulcorner Gc\urcorner$). But if we know additional facts about c that alter the probability, that defeats the prima facie reason:

(D1) If F is projectible with respect to H then $\ulcorner Hc\ \&\ \text{prob}(F/G\ \&$ $H) \neq \text{prob}(F/G)\urcorner$ is an undercutting defeater for (A1).

I will refer to these as *subproperty defeaters*. (D1) amounts to a kind of "total evidence requirement." It requires us to make our inference on the basis of the most comprehensive facts regarding which we know the requisite probabilities.

6. Unifying the Constraints

At this point, we have encountered three seemingly unelated projectibility constraints (or four if we count those concerning enumerative induction and statistical induction as two separate constraints). This is extremely puzzling. Why should the same rather abstruse constraint occur in three different places? It was this puzzle that originally motivated the search for the theory of probability propounded in my (1990). At this point, I will just report the main result. First, I argued that (A1) and (D1) should be generalized as follows:

(A3)   If F is projectible with respect to G then $\ulcorner \text{prob}(F/G) \geq r \urcorner$ is a prima facie reason for the conditional $\ulcorner Gc \supset Fc \urcorner$, the strength of the reason depending upon the value of r.

(D3)   If F is projectible with respect to $(G \mathbin{\&} H)$ then $\ulcorner Hc \mathbin{\&} \text{prob}(F/G \mathbin{\&} H) \neq \text{prob}(F/G) \urcorner$ is an undercutting defeater for (A3).

I take it that (A3) is quite an intuitive acceptance rule. It amounts to a rule saying that, when F is projectible with respect to G, if we know that most G's are F, that gives us a reason for thinking of any particular object that it is an F if it is a G. The only unexpected feature of this rule is the projectibility constraint.

The main conclusion of my (1990) was the rather surprising one that by starting with (A3), (D3), and a strong probability calculus, we can derive as theorems an entire theory of direct inference, including principles (4.1) and (4.2), and a theory of statistical and enumerative induction, including principles (1.2) and (3.2). This has the consequence that the projectibility constraints that occur in direct inference and induction are actually derived from the projectibility constraint on the statistical syllogism. On this account, the latter is the fundamental one. We do not really have three separate projectibility constraints, but a single basic constraint that implies related constraints in some derived epistemic rules.

It would be very nice if we could regard this as settling the matter of where projectibility constraints come from. Unfortunately, there is at least one additional place in which a projectibility constraint occurs, and it does not seem to be reducible to the constraint on the statistical syllogism. As I have pointed out elsewhere, all prima facie reasons are subject to "reliability defeaters."[7] For example, something's looking red to me gives me a prima facie reason for thinking that it is red, but if I know that color vision is unreliable under the present circumstances, this constitutes an undercutting defeater. To formulate reliability defeaters precisely, let us symbolize $\ulcorner x$(the epistemic agent) is in circumstances of type $R \urcorner$ as $\ulcorner Rx \urcorner$. Suppose $\ulcorner Px \urcorner$ is a prima facie reason for $\ulcorner Qx \urcorner$. Then as a first approximation it seems that for an agent s, $\ulcorner Rs$ and prob$(Q/P$ & $R)$ is low $\urcorner$ should be a reliability defeater for this prima facie reason. But arguments having what should now be familiar-looking structures show that we must impose restrictions on R. For example, suppose $R = \ulcorner (S \lor T) \urcorner$, where prob$(S/S \lor T)$ is high, prob$(Q/P$ & $S)$ is low, prob$(Q/P$ & $T)$ is unknown, and we know that $\ulcorner Ts$ & $\sim Ss \urcorner$ is true. Then we can conclude $\ulcorner Rs$ and prob$(Q/P$ & $R)$ is low $\urcorner$, but intuitively this should not be a defeater. For example, let $\ulcorner Px \urcorner$ be $\ulcorner x$ is appeared to redly $\urcorner$ and let $\ulcorner Qx \urcorner$ be $\ulcorner$ there is something red before $x \urcorner$. So $\ulcorner Px \urcorner$ is a prima facie reason for $\ulcorner Qx \urcorner$. Pick some highly improbable property T possessed by the epistemic agent, for instance, the property of having been born in the first second of the first minute of the first hour of the first year of the twentieth century, and let S be the considerably more probable property (not actually possessed by the agent) of wearing rose-colored glasses. Then prob$(Q/P$ & $(S \lor T))$ is low, and the agent has the property $(S \lor T)$, but this should not constitute a defeater because the agent has the property $(S \lor T)$ only by virtue of having the property T, and by hypothesis we do not know whether prob$(Q/P$ & $T)$ is low.

It seems reasonably clear that we need a projectibility constraint here. In order for $\ulcorner Rs$ and prob$(Q/P$ & $R)$ is low $\urcorner$ to be a reliability defeater for $\ulcorner Px \urcorner$ as a prima facie reason for $\ulcorner Qx \urcorner$ it is required that Q be projectible with respect to $\ulcorner (P$ & $R) \urcorner$. This is puzzling, however. There is no obvious connection between this projectibility constraint and the one in our acceptance rules. On the other hand, it also seems unlikely that there should be two separate sources of constraints in epistemology both appealing to the same concept of projectibility. I am unsure what to make of this except to suggest that the problem of projectibility is an even deeper one than we realized before.

7. Conclusions

The first main conclusion of this paper is that projectibility constraints recur throughout epistemology, and not just in inductive reasoning. Perhaps the most fundamental projectibility constraint is that on the statistical syllogism. However, this does not provide a complete account of the source of projectibility constraints, because there remains at least one such constraint (that on reliability defeaters) that does not seem to be traceable to the constraint on the statistical syllogism. There must be more to the story.

Even if we had an account that unified all of the different projectibility constraints that occur throughout epistemology, we would not be finished. At this point, "projectible" is little more than a label for an unanalyzed class of concept pairs. We need an account of what makes one pair of concepts projectible and another nonprojectible. The need for projectibility constraints is dictated by purely logical difficulties that arise for various kinds of defeasible reasoning. Many of these difficulties concern disjunctions. But this is still only a partial account of projectibility. What is required is a general criterion that tells us precisely which concepts are projectible with respect to one another.

When Goodman first called our attention to projectibility, a spate of proposals followed regarding the analysis of projectibility. Goodman himself proposed to analyze the concept in terms of entrenchment. Most other authors favored analyses in terms of "positionality." The latter analyses ruled out as unprojectible those concepts that made reference to particular individuals or particular places and times. All of these theories labored under the misapprehension that most concepts are projectible and that it is only a few peculiar ones that have to be ruled out. But as I have shown, projectibility is the exception rather than the rule. In addition, projectibility has a rich logical structure—conjunctions of projectible concepts are projectible, but disjunctions are not generally projectible, and so forth. Any adequate theory of projectibility must explain this, but no extant theory does.

In my (1974), I alleged that the problem of projectibility had a simple solution—the projectibility of a concept is part of its conceptual role. My general position is that the conceptual role of a concept is constitutive of that concept and not derivable from anything deeper, and so including projectibility as part of the conceptual role of a concept should be the end of the matter. There would be nothing more to be said about which concepts are projectible. Some have projectibility built into their conceptual roles and others do not. The trouble with this account is that it overlooks the "logic" of projectibility. The projectibility of a logically simple concept could be an irreducible feature of its conceptual role, but logically complex concepts (disjunctions, conjunctions, etc.) are characterized by the way they are constructed out of simpler concepts, and their conceptual roles are derivative from that. Thus their projectibility or nonprojectibility would have to follow somehow from the way in which they are constructed out of simpler projectible or nonprojectible concepts. The kind of account of projectibility proposed in my (1974) might conceivably be right for logically simple concepts, but an adequate account of projectibility must also determine what closure conditions hold and explain why they hold. No account of projectibility that talks only about logically simple concepts can do that. At this point, I have no idea what a correct theory of projectibility is going to look like.

University of Arizona

NOTES

1. More details can be found in my (1986), (1987), (1990), (1990a), and (1992).

2. The theory adumbrated in my (1990) is summarized in my (1992a).

3. This argument can be made to work with the weaker assumption that A entails some D such that $\sim D$ is projectible with respect to C. It would seem that this is always true.

4. I first pointed this out in my (1972).

5. One of the main objectives of my (1990) was to present a more precise formulation of this principle.

6. Kyburg (1974) appears to have been the first to observe that something like a projectibility constraint is required for direct inference.

7. Originally in Pollock (1984b).

REFERENCES

Goodman, Nelson
  1955 *Fact, Fiction and Forecast.* Cambridge: Harvard University Press.
Kyburg, Henry, Jr.
  1974 *The Logical Foundations of Statistical Inference.* Dordrecht: Reidel.
Pollock, John L.
  1972 "The logic of projectibility." *Philosophy of Science 39,* 303–314.
  1974 *Knowledge and Justification.* Princeton: Princeton University Press.
  1983 "A theory of direct inference." *Theory and Decision 16,* 29–96.
  1984 "Foundations for direct inference." *Theory and Decision 17,* 221–256.
  1984b "Reliability and justified belief." *Canadian Journal of Philosophy 14,* 103–114.
  1986 *Contemporary Theories of Knowledge.* Totowa, NJ: Rowman and Littlefield.
  1987 "Defeasible reasoning." *Cognitive Science 11,* 481–518.
  1990 *Nomic Probability and the Foundations of Induction.* New York: Oxford University Press.
  1990a "A theory of defeasible reasoning." *International Journal of Intelligent Systems 6,* 33–54.
  1992 "How to reason defeasibly." *Artificial Intelligence, 57,* 1–42.
  1992a "The theory of nomic probability." *Synthese 90,* 263–300.
Reichenbach, Hans
  1949 *A Theory of Probability.* Berkeley: University of California Press. (Original German ed., 1935.)

Simplicity as a Pragmatic Criterion for Deciding What Hypotheses to Take Seriously

Gilbert Harman

9

The most basic form of Goodman's (1965) "new riddle of induction" arises from the fact that, when scientists take certain data to support a hypothesis, there will almost always be infinitely many other, less simple, hypotheses that fit the data as well. All, or almost all, of these less simple hypotheses are not even considered by scientists and would not be taken seriously if suggested. Goodman's riddle can be interpreted as asking how to characterize the relevant sort of simplicity.

For example, given two variables P and V, suppose that the data are generally consistent with the principle $V = K \times P$. Suppose also that there are no data for $P = 16$. Then the data are also consistent with the following complicated principle: If $P \neq 16$ then $V = K \times P$ and if $P = 16$ then $V = K^2 \times P$. But, no scientist would even consider the more complicated principle and no scientist would take seriously the more complicated principle if his or her attention were called to it, unless there was some special reason to consider the more complicated principle, a reason deriving from other evidence.

A similar point holds for most inductive inferences made by almost anyone, scientist or not. When a person reaches almost any sort of conclusion at all, there are almost always infinitely many complicated alternative hypotheses equally compatible with the evidence. Almost all of these hypotheses will not be considered and would be taken to be absurd if someone were to suggest that they be considered.

For example, if a speaker says, "I went to the bank," a hearer might not be sure whether the speaker means a financial institution or the edge of a body of water. No normal hearer will consider the possibility that the speaker means that he went to the circus because on this occasion the speaker uses the word *bank* to mean *ciank,* where a ciank at time *t* is a financial institution unless *t* is today, in which case a ciank is a circus!

This interpretation of *bank* is logically possible, since a speaker could use the word with that meaning and because the past practice of this and other speakers is compatible with *bank* having that meaning. But this is an abstract possibility that it would be absurd to take seriously, so absurd that you may wonder why I bring it up at all!

Why do philosophers always think about such absurd possibilities? Because it is interesting that such possibilities are absurd. Why is it interesting? Because the data available to a hearer are as compatible with any of the infinitely many absurd hypotheses as with one of the normal, unabsurd hypotheses (edge of water, financial institution). The absurd hypotheses are not absurd because they conflict with the data. They are absurd because they are too complicated when compared with more normal unabsurd hypotheses.

Different Uses of Different Kinds of Simplicity

In this paper I am concerned with the use that scientists and ordinary people make of simplicity in order to decide what hypotheses to take seriously and what hypotheses to treat as absurd and not worth taking seriously.

This is not the only use that scientists make of simplicity. Sometimes scientists make an explicit appeal to one or another sort of simplicity or "parsimony" in order to argue for one out of several hypotheses that are worth being taken seriously. One theory is supposed to be better than another because it appeals to fewer kinds of entities: it is more parsimonious in its ontological assumptions. Or one theory is supposed to be better because it requires fewer accidents, or coincidences.

As Sober (1988, 1990) points out, using examples from evolutionary biology, the success of such explicit appeals to simplicity or parsimony can depend on what it is reasonable to believe about the domain in question. Robins and sparrows have wings; iguanas do not. It is in one respect simpler to suppose that wings evolved once in *W,* a descendant of *A* and ancestor of robins and sparrows, rather than that twice, in one descendant *X* of *A* that was an ancestor of robins and in a separate descendant *Y* of *A* that was an ancestor of sparrows. The simpler hypothesis would reduce coincidence. But it is controversial whether this particular kind of appeal to simplicity is reasonable in the context of evolutionary theory. Sober argues persuasively that the success of this particular kind of appeal to simplicity depends on special assumptions about the frequency of certain sorts of evolutionary events. Under certain assumptions about evolution, such coincidences are more likely than the one-time evolution of wings.

Sober goes on to question whether there is any useful domain independent notion of simplicity that always makes one hypothesis more reasonable than another hypothesis that accounts equally well for the data. And Sober may be right when it comes to explicit appeals to simplicity.

But I am not concerned with explicit appeals to simplicity to decide among hypotheses that are already being taken seriously. I am concerned with the sort of relative simplicity that distinguishes those hypotheses that are taken seriously from other hypotheses that account equally well for the data that are not taken seriously.

Basic Issues

By simplicity, I will mean whatever distinguishes the hypotheses people take seriously from those other hypotheses they (normally) do not take seriously even though the other hypotheses account equally well for the data.[1]

With this understanding, then, one task for the philosophy of science is to specify what makes one hypothesis simpler than another in the relevant sense. A second task is to indicate in what respects simpler hypotheses in this respect are worth taking seriously in a way that sufficiently less simple hypotheses are not.

There are two ways to approach these issues. One can begin by looking at how scientists and others actually distinguish hypotheses worth taking seriously from others. If one determines what criterion scientists use, one can next consider what is desirable about limiting consideration to simpler hypotheses as picked out by that criterion.

Alternatively, one can think more abstractly about why it might be desirable to limit consideration to hypotheses with certain features and one might then ask how to determine what theories have the desirable features.

The two tasks are related, of course. For example, if simpler theories are to be preferred because they are easier to use for certain scientific purposes, then it would seem that ease of use ought to be the relevant criterion for distinguishing those hypotheses to be taken seriously from others that account equally well for the data.

One important issue about simplicity is whether the fact that one theory is simpler than another is ever a reason to think that the first theory is more likely to be true than the second is. If simplicity has to do with ease of use, the question becomes whether a theory's being easier to use than another can make the first theory more likely to be true than the second theory.

The philosophical outlook called "instrumentalism" holds that the goal of science is not to come up with true theories but rather to come up with theories that are observationally adequate. For example, van Fraassen (1980, 1989) argues that scientists do not qua scientists believe that the theories they accept are true; as scientists they believe at most that the theories they accept are observationally adequate (or more observationally adequate than their current competitors). Scientists may actually believe that (some of) their theories are true, but they do it on their own time, so to speak, just as they may have various (other) religious and philosophical beliefs that are not implicated in their science, qua science. The fact that one theory may be simpler than another may permit that theory to give a better explanation of the evidence, but, according to van Fraassen, that cannot make the theory any more likely to be true. Indeed, van Fraassen (1989) argues that to allow simplicity or any other pragmatic advantage of a theory to affect one's view of its probability would leave one open to a temporal "Dutch book" argument.

I propose to develop a pragmatic theory of simplicity that rejects this sort of instrumentalism. I believe that instrumentalism is itself an example of a parasitical theory of a sort that is less simple than the theory on which it is parasitical. If I am right, there are pragmatic reasons not to be an instrumentalist! I will also defend the use of simplicity as one indicator of the relative likelihood of truth against objections by van Fraassen and others.

The main goal of my project, then, is to indicate what makes one theory simpler than another and to say why simplicity is a desirable feature in an hypothesis, where simplicity is identified with whatever it is that leads us to distinguish the hypotheses to take seriously from other hypotheses that account equally well for the data.

Lessons of Curve Fitting

Simplicity plays an important role in fitting curves to data points (Glymour, 1980). Suppose, for example, that we measure the relation between two variables, P and C, and obtain the following limited data, rounded to the nearest whole number (and, for the moment, ignoring what the units of measurement are).

$$P = 1, C = 2$$
$$P = 3, C = 6$$
$$P = 4, C = 8$$
$$P = 8, C = 16$$

Various hypotheses fit these data equally well. Consider, in particular,

HYPOTHESIS 1:

$$C = 2 \times P$$

HYPOTHESIS 2:

$$C = 2 \times P + (P - 1) \times (P - 3) \times (P - 4) \times (P - 8)$$

Given this evidence a scientist would normally on grounds of simplicity take hypothesis 1 seriously and would not take hypothesis 2 seriously.[2]

Notice that the two hypotheses make quite different predictions for other values of P. To take one example, for $P = 6$, hypothesis 1 predicts $C = 12$ and hypothesis 2 predicts $C = -48$. Do data of this sort make one of these predictions more likely than the other? A scientist would normally suppose that the answer is "Yes" and would suppose that the first prediction is much more likely to be true than the second.

Notice, furthermore, that there are many other hypotheses equally compatible with the data that make different predictions about the value of C when $P = 6$. Indeed, for any value N at all there are many hypotheses compatible with the data that entail that $C = N$ when $P = 6$, for example,

$$C = 2 \times P - \frac{(N - 12) \times (P - 1) \times (P - 3) \times (P - 4) \times (P - 8)}{60}$$

A scientist will on grounds of simplicity prefer to make further predictions using hypothesis 1 rather than hypothesis 2 or any of the other hypotheses just considered. Our questions, then, are (a) "what makes hypothesis 1 simpler than these other hypotheses?" and (b) "is this difference between the hypotheses a reason for a scientist to prefer using hypothesis 1 to make predictions?"

Simplicity as Simplicity of Representation

Consider the suggestion that the relevant type of simplicity of a hypothesis consists in the simplicity of its representation. One version of this suggestion would measure the complexity of a hypothesis by the number of symbols used to express the hypothesis. Hypothesis 1 uses five symbols: "$C = 2 \times P$." Hypothesis 2 uses 29 symbols:

$$C = 2 \times P + (P - 1) \times (P - 3) \times (P - 4) \times (P - 8)$$

So, by this criterion, Hypothesis 1 is simpler and more inferable.

Another version of the same suggestion applies to hypotheses that can be graphed. In such a case the simpler hypothesis is the one that has the simpler graph. Now, the graph of hypothesis 1 is a straight line whereas the graph of hypothesis 2 is a complex curve that swoops down and up and down and up. So, by this criterion also, hypothesis 1 is simpler than hypothesis 2.

But there is a possible problem. Simplicity of representation is obviously dependent on the system of representation. One hypothesis can have a simpler representation than a second given one way of representing the hypotheses and a more complex representation given a second system.

Putting the point in another way: any hypothesis can be given an arbitrarily simple representation, because any hypothesis can be represented by a single symbol, e.g. "*H*."

Similarly, the simplicity of the shape of a graph depends on the coordinate scales used.[3] In comparing the graph of hypothesis 1 with the graph of hypothesis 2, we might use coordinate scales uniform in standard units for measuring P and C. But we can use other scales also: log, loglog, and more complex scales. A change in coordinate scale can change a straight line into a curve and vice versa. There will always be a scale that gives a selected function a simple graph, at the cost of giving other functions more complex graphs. For example, if the X axis is a measure of standard units of P and the Y axis is a measure of $\dfrac{\text{value of } C}{\text{value of } C \text{ according to hypothesis 2}}$, then hypothesis 2 will be graphed by a horizontal straight line, and hypothesis 1 will be represented by a very complicated curve.

So, if simplicity is to be measured by representational simplicity, restrictions must be placed on allowable kinds of representation. But it is unclear what restrictions would do the trick and also unclear whether it would be desirable all things considered to restrict representations in this way.

For example, it might be suggested that abbreviations are not allowed, so that we cannot use an arbitrary symbol, like "*H*" to stand for a longer hypothesis. At least, we cannot do this when we are assessing the simplicity of the hypothesis. For that purpose, we must consider the hypothesis as stated in "primitive notation." Similarly, it might be suggested that in graphs we must use "natural scales" and not, e.g., $\dfrac{\text{value of } C}{\text{value of } C \text{ according to hypothesis 2}}$.

But it is doubtful that there is any way to restrict the relevant representations in a reasonable way. Any reasonable restrictions would allow new scientific concepts to be introduced, and there is no real difference between introducing an abbreviation and introducing a new concept and then using this concept to state an equivalence as a new theoretical postulate (Quine, 1936; Goodman, 1965; Harman, 1973).

A Semantic Theory of Simplicity

The theory that identifies the simplicity of a hypothesis with the simplicity of its representation might be thought of as a syntactic theory of simplicity, if syntax is concerned with the symbols used to represent something. A semantic theory of simplicity is concerned with the meaning or information contained in a hypothesis, apart from how that information is represented. For example, in Sober's early (1975) theory, one hypothesis is simpler than another if less information is needed in conjunction with the first hypothesis in order to answer certain questions.

As I mentioned earlier, Sober (1990) repudiates his earlier theory and now doubts that scientists ever appeal to a domain-independent kind of simplicity. But I am not now concerned with explicit appeals to simplicity to decide among hypotheses under active consideration. I am instead concerned with the sort of relative simplicity that distinguishes those hypotheses that will be taken seriously from those that are automatically ruled out. So, I want for a moment to see whether Sober's earlier (1975) theory provides an account of this sort of simplicity.

In this view, the hypothesis that a particular function $F(x)$ is constant, e.g., $F(x) = 7$, is simpler than the hypothesis that the function is linear, e.g., $F(x) = 7 \times x$, because the first hypothesis allows one to determine the value of the function for a given value of x without any information at all about the given value of x, whereas the second hypothesis allows one to determine the value of the function only when one is given as information what the numerical value of x is.

"All emeralds are green" is simpler by this measure than "all emeralds are either green, if first observed before A.D. 2000, or are blue, if not first observed before A.D. 2000." With the first hypothesis, the information that a given stone is an emerald is sufficient to determine that the emerald is green. With the second hypothesis, it is also necessary to have information as to whether the emerald has been observed before A.D. 2000.[4]

The semantic theory has something to say about why simplicity is scientifically desirable. It is desirable because scientists want to use hypotheses to answer certain questions. Scientists prefer hypotheses that make it easier to answer these questions. Simpler hypotheses make it easier to answer these questions in the sense that they require less information in order to answer the questions.

The semantic theory is not sensitive to the syntactic form of a hypothesis, so it is not affected by changes in the system of representation, e.g., abbreviations, or changes in the scales of graphs. However the measure is intended to be sensitive to the questions in which one might be interested. "All emeralds are green" counts as simpler if one tends to be interested in whether emeralds are green. "All emeralds are green if first observed before

A.D. 2000 and are blue if not first observed before A.D. 2000" counts as simpler if one tends instead to be interested in whether particular emeralds are grue, in other words, if one is interested in whether particular emeralds are green if first observed before A.D. 2000 and are blue if not first observed before A.D. 2000.

According to Sober (1975), people normally take the first hypothesis to be simpler than the second because people are normally interested in color, not in the sort of complex property represented by "green if first observed before A.D. 2000 and blue if not first observed before A.D. 2000."

But now consider hypotheses 1 and 2 concerning the relation between C and P. If science had only an interest in answering questions about the value of C for various values of P, the hypotheses would have to count as equally simple by Sober's measure. In both cases, to answer this sort of question information is needed about the relevant value of P and that is all the information needed.

Sober (1975) suggests somewhat surprisingly that the relative simplicity of the first hypothesis as compared with the second in a case like this arises because of an interest a scientist would have in answering questions about the derivative of C with respect to P, i.e., the slope of the curve for various values of P. Since this slope is constant for hypothesis 1 and not constant for hypothesis 2, hypothesis 1 allows one to answer this question without any further information about P, unlike hypothesis 2. So hypothesis 1 is simpler than hypothesis 2 with respect to answering such a question.

One reason that this is a surprising suggestion is that there would seem to be a clear difference in simplicity between hypothesis 1 and hypothesis 2 quite apart from any interest one would have in the derivatives of these functions. I will come back to this point in a moment.

A second reason that this is a surprising answer is that it makes simplicity indirectly relative to how hypotheses are represented after all. The slope of a line in a graph depends on the coordinate scale used. As I have already observed, there is a coordinate scale that graphs hypothesis 2 as a straight line with zero slope and graphs hypothesis 1 as a complex curve with a slope that changes in a complex way. To be interested in the derivative of a function is in part to be interested in a particular way in which that function is represented.

A Computational or Pragmatic Theory of Simplicity

I now want to consider a third theory of simplicity. This theory, like the semantic theory, takes simpler theories to be those that are easier to use to answer questions. But this third theory measures ease of use computationally rather than semantically and the theory does not require an interest in derivatives in order to account for the difference between hypotheses 1 and 2.

Suppose there is a reason to know what the value of C is when $P = 6$, and consider how this value might be deduced from hypothesis 1 and hypothesis 2 respectively.

HYPOTHESIS 1:

$$C = 2 \times P$$
$$= 2 \times 6$$
$$= 12$$

HYPOTHESIS 2:

$$C = 2 \times P + (P - 1) \times (P - 3) \times (P - 4) \times (P - 8)$$
$$= 2 \times P + (6 - 1) \times (6 - 3) \times (6 - 4) \times (6 - 8)$$
$$= 12 + 5 \times 3 \times 2 \times (-2)$$
$$= 12 + 15 \times 2 \times (-2)$$
$$= 12 + 30 \times (-2)$$
$$= 12 - 60 = -(60 - 12) = -48$$

In an obvious sense it is easier to use hypothesis 1 to get the answer in this case, because the calculation involved is less complex. So, it is this that makes hypothesis 1 simpler, according to the third theory of simplicity, which is a computational, pragmatic theory of simplicity.

The computational theory, like the semantic theory takes it to be relevant what questions scientists are interested in: Simpler theories are easier to use in getting results in which scientists are interested even though more complex theories might be easier to use in getting other results.

Consider the calculations involved using hypotheses 1 and 2 to obtain the value of

$$R = \frac{(\text{value of } C)}{(H2 \text{ value of } C)}$$

when P = 6.

HYPOTHESIS 1:

$$R = \frac{(2 \times P)}{(2 \times P) + (P - 1) \times (P - 3) \times (P - 4) \times (P - 8)}$$
$$= \frac{(2 \times 6)}{(2 \times 6) + (6 - 1) \times (6 - 3) \times (6 - 4) \times (6 - 8)}$$
$$= \frac{12}{12 + 5 \times 3 \times 2 \times (-2)}$$
$$= \frac{12}{12 + 15 \times 2 \times (-2)} = \frac{12}{-48} = -\frac{1}{4}$$

HYPOTHESIS 2:

R = 1

In this case, hypothesis 2 is much easier to use. Whether a hypothesis is easier or harder to use depends on what it is to be used for.

One advantage of the computational theory over Sober's semantic theory is that hypothesis 1 counts as simpler than hypothesis 2 in relation to an interest in the value of *C* for given values of *P*. There is no need for a further interest in what the derivative of the function is relating *C* and *P*.

The computational theory shares with the semantic theory the advantage that the measure of simplicity cannot normally be trivialized by introducing abbreviations. Adding abbreviations will not automatically make derivations easier. For suppose a complex hypothesis is abbreviated as *"H."* That makes the hypothesis very simple, according to the syntactic theory of simplicity, but it does not normally make the hypothesis any simpler according to the computational theory. If, in order to use that hypothesis to derive data from it, a scientist must first expand it to its complex formulation, nothing is gained. In fact, derivations from the abbreviated hypothesis will be more complex than derivations from the original unabbreviated hypothesis, because of the need for the expansion step.

Objections

Now we must consider certain objections to a computational theory of simplicity of this sort. First, why should this sort of ease of use matter to scientists who have calculators and computers? The function of hypothesis 2 can easily be programmed into a calculator in such a way that entering a given value of *P* will result in the immediate calculation of the corresponding value of *C*. So, why is it relevant that, if a scientist had to do the calculation "by hand," it might be more difficult to get answers using hypothesis 1 than using hypothesis 2. Since a scientist does not have to do the calculation by hand, and since no more effort is involved in the one case than the other if a calculator with the relevant function programmed in is used, what is the relevance of the difference in difficulty in doing the calculation by hand?

Second, suppose that we use a table of values or graph to represent a hypothesis like hypothesis 2. Then we can get the value of *C* when *P* = 6 from hypothesis 2 in a single step simply by looking it up. So, it would seem that, as in the case of the initial syntactic theory of simplicity, the computational theory is heavily dependent on the system of representation used. It would seem that the computational theory cannot allow hypotheses to be represented with tables or graphs. But that is absurd. We cannot rule out using graphs and tables, since scientists need to use them all the time.

Using Tables and Graphs as Hypotheses

A possible reply to the second objection is that the use of a table or graph as the hypothesis itself will make the derivation very big even though there is only one step to the derivation. The derivation will be very big because the hypothesis from which the step is made is very big. Consider how this would work for hypothesis 2.

H = (if $P=1$, $C=2$) & (if $P = 2$, $C=-8$) & (if $P=3$, $C=6$) &
. . . . . . & (if $P=6$, $C =-48$) & . . .

so, in one step

if $P=6$, $C=-48$.

So, we can meet the objection if we consider the complexity or size of entire derivations, including the size of initial assumptions (and intermediate conclusions), not just the number of steps. A derivation including a table is huge and therefore complex in at least one respect. By this measure, replacing the table with the formula in our initial statement of hypothesis 2 is a simplification of the derivation in this case even though more steps are involved in the derivation.

Instead of including a table or graph as part of a derivation, a scientist includes the results of looking things up. Contrast

$x = \sin 45$ deg

[Huge Table of Sines]

$\sin 45$ deg $= 0.70710678$

$x = 0.70710678$

with

$x = \sin 45$ deg

The sine table says: $\sin 45$ deg $= 0.70710678$

$\sin 45$ deg $= 0.70710678$

$x = 0.70710678$

A hypothesis or intermediate assumption that literally *included* a table or complex graph would be impossible to grasp, impossible to understand, impossible to remember. So, a computational account of simplicity might suppose that a scientist's interest in simplicity is an interest in having answers to scientific questions that are relatively easy to grasp.

Why? Perhaps because when a scientist accepts a hypothesis, he or she accepts it as an explanation of the certain data. So, the scientist is really accepting a collection of explanations, not just a single proposition. What is at issue, then, is the complexity of that collection of explanations. Complexity can arise either because of the number of steps involved in the explanations or because of the complexity of one of the statements from which (or to which) a step is made. Either kind of complexity can make explanations harder to use, especially explanations involved in explaining new data.

The usefulness in question is usefulness in obtaining scientific understanding, not just usefulness in predicting new data, although that is a good thing too!

Using Calculators or Tables

This suggests that, if a scientist uses a calculator or table to help with a calculation, then the resulting explanation or derivation should be taken to be something like this:

$P = 6$

$C = 2 \times P + (P - 1) \times (P - 3) \times (P - 4) \times (P - 8)$

$C = 2 \times 6 + (6 - 1) \times (6 - 3) \times (6 - 4) \times (6 - 8)$

According to the calculator, that $= -48$.

So, $C = -48$

If the calculator is preprogrammed with the relevant function for hypothesis 2, we might have this:

$P = 6$

$C = H(P)$

$C = H(6)$

According to the calculator, $H(6) = -48$

So, $C = -48$

Clearly, this is not going to be sensitive to the complexity of hypothesis H. At the same time, it provides little understanding of why the result is what it is. To get more understanding, it is necessary to have a better idea of why the calculation comes out as it does. In the computational view, the relevant complexity of various hypotheses only emerges from what is needed for this further understanding.

The Computational Theory versus the Semantic Theory

Recall that Sober's semantic theory of simplicity can treat a linear function as simpler than a quadratic function only by considering answers to such questions as "What is the derivative of $f(x)$?" (We do not need to know the value of x to answer that question if $f(x)$ is a linear function, but we do have to know the value of x if $f(x)$ is a quadratic function.) A computational theory takes the linear function to be simpler without having to consider questions about derivatives, since it is less difficult to calculate the value of $f(x)$ if it is a linear function than if it is a quadratic function.

Perhaps there is a testable difference between a semantic and a computational account. The semantic account may predict that a linear function will seem simpler than a quadratic equation only to someone who knows about derivatives, whereas the computational account predicts that the linear function will seem simpler even to someone who does not know about derivatives. An informal survey among eighth grade students (who had not had calculus) supports the prediction of the computational theory on this point. The eighth graders all considered the linear function simpler, despite not knowing anything about derivatives.

Simplicity as an Indicator of Verisimilitude

Newton-Smith (1981, pp. 230–231) expresses a widespread view when he says:

> Many scientists and philosophers of science would include simplicity as a good-making feature of a theory. This is, however, problematic for a number of reasons. . . . The case for simplicity is pragmatic. It simply is easier to calculate with simpler theories. But there is no reason to see greater relative simplicity of this sort as an indicator of greater verisimilitude.

Is simplicity "an indicator of greater verisimilitude" according to the computational theory of simplicity? We must distinguish two senses of the word "indicator."

1. X is an indicator of Y if the presence of X is in fact correlated with the presence of Y.
2. X is an indicator of Y if the presence of X gives a reason to believe Y.

According to the computational theory of simplicity, simplicity is an "indicator" of verisimilitude in the second sense. Simplicity provides a reason to believe something, a practical reason.

But can a practical reason to believe something be an "indicator" in any relevant sense? Some philosophers (e.g. Foley, 1983) would distinguish such pragmatic reasons from what they take to be more properly "epistemic" reasons to believe something.

Pragmatic reasons include such things as believing something because people will despise you for not believing it and believing in a friend's innocence because that is what loyalty requires.

Here, it may seem natural to object, "Is your friendship any reason to think it is true that your friend is innocent?" But there is no difference between believing that your friend is innocent and believing that it is true your friend is innocent. So, a reason to believe your friend is innocent is automatically a reason to believe it is true that your friend is innocent. There is no difference between a reason to believe something and a reason to believe that something is true.

There has always been a controversy as to whether pragmatic reasons to believe something are somehow to be distinguished from more properly epistemic reasons to believe something. Pragmatism, of course, denies that there is any such distinction.

The issue comes up, for example, between Rudolf Carnap and W. V. Quine. Carnap (1950) famously distinguishes "internal" from "external" questions. "Are there numbers?" is an external question, which asks whether we should adopt a linguistic framework in which we refer to numbers. "Is there a prime number between 11 and 17?" is an internal question which makes sense only after we have selected such a framework. Carnap argues that external questions call for practical pragmatic decisions: which system of representation will serve our purposes better? Internal questions are then answered in ways that are determined by the system of representation that has been chosen.

In this instance, pragmatism is defended by W. V. Quine (1960),

> I grant that one's hypothesis as to what there is, e.g., as to there being universals, is at bottom just as arbitrary or pragmatic a matter as one's adoption of a new brand of set theory or even a new system of bookkeeping.
> . . . But what impresses me more than it does Carnap is how well this whole attitude is suited also to the theoretical hypotheses of natural science itself, and how little basis there is for a distinction.

Harman (forthcoming) shows how pragmatism can allow for a distinction between epistemic and nonepistemic reasons that captures our ordinary views but also allows pragmatic considerations to be relevant to epistemic reasons.

Objections to Explanatory Inference

Replies can be given to a couple objections that may be raised against a principle of explanatory inference that would make use of simplicity as a principle of theory choice in certain cases.

First, it may be argued that no intuitively appealing rule of inference to the best explanation has ever been given an explicit statement of the sort that can be given for deductive rules.

In reply, it will be said that it is important to distinguish rules of implication from rules of inference (Harman, 1986). Plausible rules of implication have been given explicit statement in deductive logic, but they are not rules of inference. It might be said that no intuitively appealing rules of inference of any sort have ever been given an explicit statement of the sort that can be given for deductive rules. If this is an objection to inference to the best explanation, it is an objection to inference in general.

Second, Bas van Fraassen (1989) argues that allowing considerations of best explanation to modify probabilities leads to a kind of irrationality over time that permits Dutch book arguments against someone who does this.

This is a complex issue, but one possible reply is that, in as much as considerations of best explanation are treated as affecting probabilities, they should be treated as affecting (or as reflected in) the initial "a priori" probability distribution, at least in a Bayesian framework, in which case the Dutch book problems envisioned will not arise (Harman, forthcoming).

Parasitical Theories

One theory is parasitical on a second if the first theory says that the phenomena are "as if" the second theory were true. For example, in one version of creation science, God is supposed to have created the fossil record as if there had been an age of dinosaurs. Similarly, Descartes worried about the possibility that his experiences were created by an evil demon who made things appear as if there were a world of objects that in fact does not really exist. Closer to real science, there are linguistic theories that do not themselves lead to interesting new discoveries about language and that instead merely offer reanalyses of discoveries made within other approaches.[5]

Parasitical theories will normally count as less simple than the theories on which they are parasites, according to the computational theory of simplicity. A derivation of data within the parasitical theory will go like this:

> It is as if Theory T were true. Theory T provides the following derivation of data D. (This is spelled out.) So, D would be true if T were true. So D is true.

The parasitical derivation will contain as a part the derivation that is provided by the nonderivative theory. So, the parasitical derivation will necessarily be longer and more complex than the nonparasitical derivation. The nonparasitical theory will therefore provide simpler derivations of the data than will the parasitical theory.

A particular instance of this result is that instrumentalist versions of theories often provide less simple derivations of the data than their noninstrumentalist counterparts.

Idealizations and Arcane Data

If simplicity is one of our guides to truth, can we account for the natural view that certain idealizations are useful in arriving at good predictions even though the truth is more complex (Cartwright, 1983)? A natural reply is that we accept the more complex theory as true in this case because there are data that the more complex theory can account for better than the idealization.

But this raises a problem for pragmatic and instrumental approaches which say we accept theories because they help us answer questions in which we are interested. It would seem that the data that we are interested in are the data that can be handled by the idealization, not the more complex theory. So, shouldn't a pragmatic or instrumentalist approach tell us to accept the idealization rather than the more complex theory?

But then what about arcane data? If we are not really interested in such data, doesn't the pragmatic account imply we should not use the data to decide among theories? The answer is that we *are* interested in the data. However: we are interested in data because it helps us decide between theories in which we are interested!

This is where (one form of) instrumentalism goes wrong. Our interest in theory is not completely derivative from our interest in the predictions of the theory. We acquire an interest in whether the theory itself is true. That is why we are interested in certain arcane data.

An adequate pragmatism has to be against foundationalism in two different respects. There are no absolutely privileged evidential statements and no absolutely privileged interests. At any point, one has certain beliefs and intentions, and one has certain interests and desires. These all get modified as time goes on. One can acquire new intrinsic desires, including desires to know whether certain theories are true.

Conclusion

More needs to be said about all of these issues, but this paper has become too long. What I have tried to do is to formulate Goodman's New Riddle as an issue about simplicity, suggest a pragmatic account of simplicity, discuss possible objections, and indicate how the resulting theory might have something to say about parasitic theories and idealizations.

Princeton University

NOTES

1. The parenthetical "(normally)" is meant to allow for philosophers and others in a sceptical mood who might take almost any hypotheses seriously that account for the data.

2. If the data here seem too limited, notice that essentially the same point can be made with any amount of data. Given any data that support hypothesis 1, there will always be a corresponding hypothesis like hypothesis 2 that accounts just as well for the same data. Although the following discussion will continue to consider this simple case in which there are only four data points, what is said also applies to cases in which there are as many data points as one likes.

3. The same point applies to various computational approaches to induction and simplicity (Angluin & Smith, 1983; Blum & Blum, 1975; Blum, 1967; Gold, 1967; Kugel, 1977; Solomonoff, 1964; Turney, 1988, and Valiant, 1979). I explain below how a different computational theory might handle it.

4. This test case comes from Goodman, 1965.

5. In retrospect, I think Harman, 1963, exemplifies the parasitical approach in linguistics in defending phrase structure grammar. Compare Gazdar et al. (1985) who offer a similar theory that is somewhat less parasitical. Linguistic and other parasitical theories are discussed briefly in Harman, 1978.

REFERENCES

Angluin, D. C. & Smith, C. H. (1983). "Inductive inference: theory and methods," *Computing Surveys 15*, 237–269.

Blum, L. & Blum, M. (1975). "Toward a mathematical theory of inductive inference," *Information and Control 28,* 125–155.

Blum, M. (1967). "A machine-independent theory of the complexity of recursive functions," *Journal of the Association for Computing Machinery 14,* 322–336.

Carnap, R. (1950). "Empiricism, semantics, and ontology," *Revue Internationale de Philosophie 4,* 20–40.

Cartwright, N. (1983). *How the Laws of Physics Lie* (Oxford: The Clarendon Press).

Foley, R. (1983). "Epistemic conservatism," *Philosophical Studies 43,* 165–182.

van Fraassen, B. (1980). *The Scientific Image* (Oxford and New York: Oxford University Press).

van Fraassen, B. (1989). *Laws and Symmetry* (Oxford and New York: Oxford University Press).

Gazdar, G., Klein, E., Pullum, G., & Sag, I. (1985). *Generalized Phrase Structure Grammar* (Cambridge, Massachusetts: Harvard University Press).

Glymour, C. (1980). *Theory and Evidence* (Princeton, N.J.: Princeton University Press).

Gold, E. M. (1967). "Language identification in the limit," *Information and Control 10,* pp. 447–474.

Goodman, Nelson (1965). *Fact, Fiction and Forecast,* 2nd ed. (Indianapolis: Bobbs-Merrill).

Harman, G. (1963). "Generative grammars without transformation rules: a defense of phrase structure," *Language 39,* 597–616 [reprinted in Walter J. Savitch, Emmon Bach, William Marsh, and Gila Safran-Naveh, eds., *The Formal Complexity of Natural Language* (Dordrecht, Holland: D. Reidel, 1987), 87–116].

Harman, G. (1973). *Thought* (Princeton, New Jersey: Princeton University Press), viii, 199; paperback edition, 1974.

Harman, G. (1978). "Meaning and theory," *Southwestern Journal of Philosophy 9,* 9–19 [reprinted in Robert W. Shahan and Chris Swoyer, *Essays on the Philosophy of W. V. Quine* (Norman, Oklahoma: University of Oklahoma Press, 1979), 9–20].

Harman, G. (1986). *Change in View: Principles of Reasoning* (Cambridge, Massachusetts: M.I.T./Bradford Books).

Harman, G. (forthcoming). "Realism, antirealism and reasons for belief."

Kugel, P. (1977). "Induction, pure and simple," *Information and Control 35,* 276–336.

Newton-Smith, W. H. (1981). *The Rationality of Science* (Boston: Routledge & Kegan Paul).

Quine, W. V. (1936). "Truth by convention," in *Philosophical Essays for A. N. Whitehead,* ed. O. H. Lee (New York: Longmans), 90–124.

Quine, W. V. (1960). "Carnap and logical truth," *Synthese 12,* 350–374.

Sober, Elliott (1975). *Simplicity* (Oxford: Oxford University Press).

Sober, Elliott (1988). *Reconstructing the Past* (Cambridge, Massachusetts: MIT Press).

Sober, Elliott (1990). "Let's razor Ockham's razor," *Explanation and Its Limits,* ed. D. Knowles (Cambridge, England: Cambridge University Press).

Solomonoff, R. J. (1964). "A formal theory of inductive inference," *Information and Control 7,* 1–22, 224–254.

Turney, P. D. (1988). *Inductive Inference and Stability.* Ph. D. Dissertation, Department of Philosophy, University of Toronto.

Valiant, L. G. (1979). "The complexity of enumeration and reliability problems," *SIAM Journal of Computing 8,* 410–421.

A Grue Thought in a Bleen Shade: 'Grue' as a Disjunctive Predicate

David H. Sanford

Nelson Goodman's discussion of 'grue' raises the question I attempt to answer in this essay. It also raises other questions, exactly how many I cannot say, that I do not attempt to answer here. One such question I have mentioned elsewhere I want to mention again. Before doing that, I want to ditch the emeralds.

'All emeralds are green' is a good example of an analytic sentence that is not a logical truth. Thomson (1966) makes this fact of mineralogy accessible to philosophers. Emeralds are, by definition, green beryls. Since our confidence in the truth of 'All green beryls are green' can be, and should be, independent of inductive support, examples that deal with green emeralds are not ideal for illustrating puzzles about inductive support. The reasons the emerald examples are so attractive, whatever they may be, are irrelevant. The following inductive inference has a nonanalytic conclusion and concerns common garden objects that are neither scarce, expensive, refractive, durable, nor harder than iron:

> All the very young tomatoes we have observed have been green. Therefore, all very young tomatoes are green.

Given that the premise is true, one draws the inference only if one accepts each of the following claims:[1]

(1) There is a reason why all (or most of) the very young tomatoes we have observed have been green.
(2) This reason applies to very young tomatoes generally, not just to those we have observed.

This distinction we can adapt to inductive inferences of various forms. When we transpose Goodman's *grue emeralds* example to an example of *grue very young tomatoes,* we see that the New Riddle of Induction concerns step (2) rather than step (1). Something is *grue* if and only if it is green and first examined for color before time t (T), or it is blue and not T. Time t is later than this book's publication date. Let it be August 7, 2006, the one hundredth birthday of Nelson Goodman. Since it is now earlier than t, everything green first examined for color before *t* is grue. Therefore, if there is a reason why all (or nearly all) the very young tomatoes we have observed have been green, there is also a reason why the same tomatoes are grue. The puzzle arises at step (2): the reason why all or nearly all very young tomatoes we have observed have been grue does not apply to very young tomatoes generally. We want to know why. Most examples of New Riddle puzzles concern step (2) although it is possible to construct New Riddle puzzles also about questions of the step (1) type.

What information do we use to decide whether a step (1) or a step (2) claim is acceptable?[2] There has been little progress in answering these questions, so far as I know. In inductive inference, as in many other cognitive processes, our awareness of relevant information is often inexplicit; and sometimes the nature of the information is inaccessible to consciousness. Discriminating between inductive inferences, like discriminating visually between different degrees of slant, is more easily done than explained. Although I regard an explanation from the standpoint of cognitive psychology as highly desirable, my essay here does little to advance this project.

The reason I provide no connected story about the information processing that underlies inductive inference is that I have been unable to find or make up such a story. The reason I offer no explanation why 'grue' is unprojectible, in contrast, is that it is not unprojectible.[3] Those who discuss the New Riddle often assert, or deny, that a predicate is projectible. Goodman's theory of projection, however, directly concerns hypotheses rather than predicates:

> A hypothesis is *projectible* if and only if it is supported, unviolated, and unexhausted, and all such hypotheses that conflict with it are overridden.
> A hypothesis is *unprojectible* if and only if it is unsupported or violated or exhausted or overridden.
> A hypothesis is *nonprojectible* if it and a conflicting hypothesis are supported, unviolated, unexhausted, and not overridden. (Goodman (1972), p. 393)

We are confident that as the twenty-first century draws to a close, the hypothesis "All very young tomatoes are green" will be violated much less often, if at all, than the hypothesis "All very young tomatoes are grue." But it is not difficult to conceive how this confidence might be misplaced, how future evidence might violate the *green* hypothesis and not the *grue* hypothesis about young tomatoes. I do not hold that the anomalous character of "All very young tomatoes are grue" shows that the predicates 'is a very young tomato' and 'is grue' are not suited to one another: that grueness is not an inductive property of tomatoes.[4] It is not tomatoes, but our evidence about tomatoes, to which the *grue* hypothesis about tomatoes is unsuited; for the conflicting *green* hypothesis, that is also supported, unviolated, and unexhausted by evidence, overrides it. Once something violates the *green* hypothesis while nothing violates the *grue* hypothesis— the unlikely possibility just contemplated—the *green* hypothesis drops out of the running to override the *grue* hypothesis. If no other qualified overrider appears on the field, the *grue* hypothesis carries the day; it is projectible.

Goodman, if he cares to, can claim that he defines the technical term *override* in terms of entrenchment. I prefer taking the theory of entrenchment as one theory about overriding, one theory to account for our preference of one over another conflicting hypothesis when both are supported, unviolated, and unexhausted. I offer my treatment of disjunctive and independent predicates as another theory of overriding.

Although we define the predicate 'grue' disjunctively—'green and *T*, or blue and not *T*'—it is misguided to count 'grue' as disjunctive for this reason. Goodman's main purpose in introducing 'bleen' is to show how we can also define 'green' disjunctively: 'grue and *T*, or bleen and not *T*.' Goodman has the syntactic similarity of these definitions in mind when he writes:

> We may by now confidently conclude that no general distinction between projectible and non-projectible predicates can be drawn on syntactic or even on semantic grounds. (Goodman (1972), p. 357)

I appeal to semantic grounds in the following treatment of 'grue'; and to draw certain distinctions, I use syntactic techniques. Some of the tools I use are not in the standard toolbox. It makes little difference whether we classify them as syntactic or as semantic or as something else if they get the job done.

First, I want to see how far we get using only the standard tools of propositional, predicate, and modal logic. Although the disjunctiveness of 'grue' is a more complicated story, disjunctiveness of one kind is understood by reference to a strong sense of independence. A disjunctive predicate is equivalent to a disjunction of independent predicates. A nondisjunctive predicate is not equivalent to a disjunction of independent predicates.

These definitions require a notion of independence that counts some but not all predicates as independent and that coincides pretty well with our prior judgments of independence. Should we succeed in capturing a notion of independence with this character, other successes fall within our reach. A conjunctive predicate, for example, is one equivalent to a conjunction of independent predicates. A nonconjunctive predicate is one that is not so equivalent.

The ordinary notion of logical independence does not provide a notion of independence that is adequate for defining *disjunctive* and *conjunctive*.

Before saying why, I shall spell out this useful and familiar concept of logical independence (*L*-independence). This definition is modal, but I let the modal operators be unwritten and understood. Two predicates '*F*' and '*G*' and *L*-independent if and only if each conjunction on the following list is possibly true:

$(\exists x)\ (Fx\ \&\ Gx),$
$(\exists x)\ (Fx\ \&\ {\sim}Gx),$
$(\exists x)\ ({\sim}Fx\ \&\ Gx),$
$(\exists x)\ ({\sim}Fx\ \&\ {\sim}Gx).$[5]

Whatever is actual is possible, so this definition is satisfied whenever each of the four relevant possibilities is realized. 'Badly rusted' and 'sports car' are *L*-independent because there are badly rusted sports cars, sports cars that are not badly rusted, badly rusted things that are not sports cars, and (most common of all) things that are neither sports cars nor badly rusted. Sometimes when a relevant possibility is unrealized, we are confident that it could be. No full-size sports car, I suppose, has a pewter body. But it is possible for a sports car to have a pewter body. The other three possibilities are actual, so 'has a pewter body' and 'sports car' are another pair of *L*-independent predicates.

The notion of *L*-independence is too broad to use in definitions of 'disjunctive predicate' or 'conjunctive predicate.' Any predicate[6] is equivalent to a disjunction of two *L*-independent predicates and is also equivalent to a conjunction of two *L*-independent predicates. I illustrate these claims with the help of some new made-up names:

grilk: green, and either silk or felt.
nafeleen: green and not felt.
grelt: green, or both circular and felt.
nofelg: green or not felt.

Something is green if and only if it is either grilk or nafeleen. 'Grilk' and 'nafeleen' are *L*-independent, as are 'grelt' and 'nofelg.' Something is green if and only if it is both grelt and nofelg. These equivalences are merely predicate-logic instances of the following tautologies of propositional logic:

$A \leftrightarrow [(A\ \&\ (B \lor C)) \lor (A\ \&\ {\sim}C)].$
$A \leftrightarrow [(A \lor (B\ \&\ C))\ \&\ (A \lor {\sim}C)].$

To spell out the *L*-equivalence of 'grilk' and 'nafeleen,' I list some relevant possibilities (that happen also all to be actualities) in familiar terms:

green & silk & not felt: grilk & nafeleen.
green & felt: grilk & not nafeleen.
green & not silk & not felt: not grilk & nafeleen.
not green: not grilk & not nafeleen.

Spelling out the L-independence of 'grelt' and 'nofelg' is a similar exercise.

I will define a sense of independence, *minimal* or *M*-independence, such that 'grilk' and 'nafeleen' are not *M*-independent, while 'green' and 'silk' are *M*-independent. By way of preparation, I will first define *disjoint* and *disconnected* predicates that comprise together two kinds of *exclusively disjunctive* predicates. This involves using the notion of the boundary of a predicate and diagraming the boundaries of predicates.

Finding an equivalence, for the first time, between a given predicate and a disjunction of *L*-independent predicates, requires a little ingenuity. It is much easier to find an equivalence between a given predicate and a disjunction of incompatible predicates. 'Square' is equivalent to 'square and cool, or square and not cool'; 'green' is equivalent to 'green and *F*, or green and not-*F*'; and so on. Compare 'square,' though, with 'square or circular,' which wears on its sleeve its equivalence to a disjunction of incompatible predicates. 'Square or circular' is surely somehow more genuinely disjunctive than 'square.'

One explanation of this perceived difference is correct as far as it goes but is nevertheless unhelpful: any two squares resemble each other with respect to shape more than every two items that are either square or circular. Squares are more like squares than circles. Quite so: green is also more like green than blue. I shall not review the literature here about difficulties in using similarity or resemblance to distinguish 'green' from 'grue.' Briefly, similarity is with respect to something. When we define queer (or 'gruesome') predicates, we can also define gruesome respects of resemblance. Squares and circles may not resemble each other so much as squares and squares with respect to shape, but with respect to *shoop*—now that's a different matter entirely. The attempt to deal by an appeal to similarity with the disjunctive predicate 'square or circular' requires dealing with a second disjunctive predicate 'shoop.' No theoretical advance appears to occur. Puzzles about 'grue' are too close to puzzles about similarity for us to solve by appealing to similarity. I do not regard similarity as a corrupt or delusive notion. Rather than use similarity to define disjunctiveness, however, I hope in the end to use the notion of disjunctiveness to provide some objective grounds for many of our judgments of similarity.

Some of the forthcoming diagrams represent quantities, such as weight and height, that we measure on a ratio scale. A two-hundred pound man weighs twice as much as a one-hundred pound sack of peat moss, and a six-foot-tall woman is three times taller than a two-foot-tall rose bush. (Temperature, in contrast, is not a ratio scale. One hundred degrees in the shade is not five times warmer than twenty degrees in the shade.) The properties of some predicate diagrams, such as ratios, have a significance that some other predicate diagrams lack. These differences will not affect the points I illustrate with predicate diagrams. It is important, however, that the diagram has some scale so that any difference in location in the diagram corresponds to some difference in what the diagram represents.[7]

Consider two height predicates, 'tall' and 'either very tall or very short.' The second is explicitly equivalent to a disjunction of incompatible predicates. There are many pairs of incompatible predicates that disjoined are equivalent to 'tall,' for example the pair 'tall but not very tall' and 'very tall.' 'Tall' is highly relative. Tall lighthouses, tall dogwood trees, and tall stacks of pancakes are not the same height. Neither are tall professional jockeys and tall professional basketball players. Such relativity does not bear on my main point. Also, the forthcoming examples are numerical and are thus comparatively nonrelative. Any uniform specification of 'tall for . . . ' will do for now. The following two diagrams represent the two predicates 'tall' and 'very short or very tall.' The vertical axis represents height. The horizontal axis represents nothing at present; soon it will represent another physical dimension. Shading corresponds to the extension of the predicate represented.

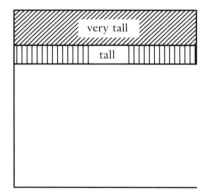

Figure 1

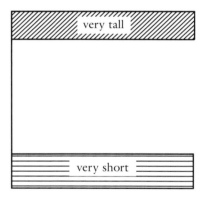

Figure 2

In each of the diagrams above (Figures 1 and 2), shading of different kinds corresponds to different incompatible predicates. Notice that the regions for 'very short' and 'very tall' are separated by an unshaded region, while the regions for 'very tall' and 'tall but not very tall' are contiguous, not separated by anything. This difference is not an artifact, and it does not rest on a comparative judgment of similarity.

'Tall,' 'very tall,' and 'very short' are all pretty vague whether or not context determines the range of their application, lighthouses or tulips or Olympic woman gymnasts. For each predicate *F* in these examples, there are borderline cases of *F*, things that are neither definitely *F* nor definitely not *F*. For now, I shall let '*BFx*' stand for '*x* is a borderline case of *F*.'[8] Using this notation, we can rewrite "Nothing is both a borderline case of 'very short' and a borderline case of 'very tall' " as:

($\forall x$) (B(x is very short) $\rightarrow$ ~B(x is very tall)).

On the other hand, something is both a borderline case of 'tall but not very tall' and a borderline case of 'very tall':

($\exists x$) (B(x is tall but not very tall) & B(x is very tall)).

We use the diagrams to represent these two facts by taking the edges of a region to stand for the borderline cases of the predicate whose extension the region represents. The borderline cases of 'very short,' for example, are located on the upper horizontal edge of the region that corresponds to 'very short.' In the diagrams, the boundaries of 'very short' and 'very tall' are distinct, while one boundary of 'tall but not very tall' is in common with the boundary of 'very tall.'

This feature of the diagrams persists when we replace the relatively vague predicates 'tall,' 'very tall,' and 'very short' with relatively precise or exact counterparts. In the following two sets of such counterparts, my selection of an exact cutoff point is, of course, somewhat arbitrary:

'over six feet tall,' 'over six feet, four inches, tall,' 'less than four feet tall.'

'six feet tall or taller,' 'not shorter than six feet, four inches,' 'not taller than four feet tall.'

Predicates in the first group map open intervals, while those in the second group map closed intervals. Differences between the extensions of corresponding predicates are limited to limiting cases. Someone exactly six feet tall is such a limiting case: she is six feet tall or taller, but she is not over six feet tall. If someone A is not exactly six feet tall, on the other hand, is not a limiting case, A is six feet tall or taller if and only if A is over six feet tall. No matter how fine-grained the scale we use, and how exact our printing techniques should be, it is impossible accurately to represent the difference between closed and open intervals diagrammatically. We can label the diagrams differently, but we cannot draw shaded areas that discriminate between including and excluding limiting cases. The boundaries of the diagramed regions are the same; and for my purposes, I regard the boundaries of the two predicates to be the same.

I intend the above elementary discussion of the open and closed intervals to support the claim that relatively exact predicates, whether open or closed, have boundaries that are very similar to the borderlines of inexact predicates. I propose to use the term 'boundary' and to use the 'B' operator generally, whether the predicates in question are pretty vague, quite precise, or intermediate with respect to exactness. If something A is on the boundary of a predicate, then the extension of the predicate both definitely includes something that is slightly different in a relevant respect from A and definitely excludes something else that is also slightly different in that respect from *A*. Another way of looking at the boundaries of an exact predicate *F* is to consider the borderline cases of an inexact predicate *F'* of which the extension is quite close to the extension of *F*. Given a relatively exact predicate such as 'over six feet tall,' we should not expect to find some one predicate that uniquely satisfies the above condition. Neither should we expect, given a relatively inexact predicate such as 'tall,' some one way uniquely to fix its boundaries.

Interpreting 'B' to be a *boundary* operator that covers borderline and limiting cases, we can notate "Nothing is both on the boundary of 'less than four feet tall' and on the boundary of 'over six feet, four inches, tall' " as:

($\forall x$) (B(x is less than four feet tall) → ~B(x is over six feet, four inches, tall)).

When a predicate '*F*' is equivalent to a disjunction of incompatible, nonempty predicates '*G*' and '*H*', '*F*' is a *disjoint* predicate when the boundary of '*G*' is completely distinct from the boundary of '*H*':

($\forall x$) (BGx → ~BHx).

When only the last condition is unsatisfied, '*F*' is a *disconnected* predicate when everything on the boundary of '*G*' or '*H*' is also on the boundary of '*F*':

($\forall x$) ((BGx ∨ BHx) → BFx).

Figure 3 represents this relation between boundaries of predicates.

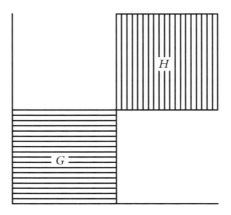

Figure 3

By twice reinterpreting the predicate letter variables as abbreviations, we can use this diagram to represent two disconnected predicates. In each case, '*F*' is the disjunction of '*G*' and '*H*.'

G: not over six feet tall, and does not weigh more than 150 pounds.
H: over six feet tall, and weighs more than 150 pounds.

Persons, and other objects that have both height and weight, that are six feet tall and weigh 150 pounds are on the boundaries of *G* and of *H* and of their disjunction *F.* Nothing else is both on the boundary of *G* and on the boundary of *H.*

G: green, and first examined for color before August 7, 2006.
H: blue, and not first examined for color before August 7, 2006.

The disjunction of *'G'* and *'H'* is our 'grue.' 'Grue' is a disconnected predicate. Something blue-green (greenish-blue, or bluish-green) that is first examined for color around midnight, August 6, 2006, is on the boundary of *'G'* and of *'H'* and of 'grue.'[9] I hope this is a persuasive illustration. It does not, by itself, offer a satisfactory response to the New Riddle of Induction; for it is too easy to define a predicate very similar to 'grue' in its inductive troublesomeness yet very dissimilar to 'grue' in its exclusively disjunctiveness. Let us define 'supergrue' as the disjunction of *'G,'* as defined above, and *'H*,'* defined as follows (the date is the one hundredth birthday of Peter Hempel):

H*: blue or bluish-green (blue-green, greenish-blue), and not first examined for color before January 8, 2005.

In Figure 4, the vertical axis represents change in hue from green to blue. (There is not room to represent every hue.) The horizontal axis represents the time something is first examined for color. Solid lines enclose the region that represents the extension of *'G,'* while dotted lines enclose the region that represents the extension of *'H*.'*

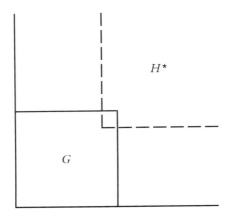

Figure 4

The extension of 'H*' is larger than the extension of 'H' in two dimensions, although enlargement along one dimension would be enough to make the point. 'Supergrue' is neither disjoint nor disconnected. For objects first examined for color by the end of the twentieth century, however, something is grue, or green, if and only if it is supergrue. As the twenty-first century works through its Edwardian period, objects first examined for color are supergrue if and only if they are blue or greenish-blue. Given that all very young tomatoes examined for color before the end of the twentieth century are green, we regard the hypothesis that all very young tomatoes in the next century are supergrue as very little if at all more acceptable than the hypothesis that all these tomatoes are grue.

The treatment of exclusively disjunctive predicates does not dispose of all the disjunctiveness that appears in New Riddles of Induction. It illustrates, rather, notions of predicate boundaries and predicate diagrams that I will use to deal with inclusively disjunctive predicates.

The problem of defining 'inclusively disjunctive,' as I said earlier, is basically the problem of defining 'independent.' An inclusively disjunctive predicate is one that is equivalent to a disjunction of independent predicates. A conjunctive predicate, similarly, is one that is equivalent to a conjunction of independent predicates. We have seen that the familiar and useful notion of L-independence is inadequate for the task at hand. Reference to relations between predicate boundaries allows us to formulate requirements that supplement the notion of L-independence.

Figure 5 represents the extensions of two schematic predicates 'G' and 'H.' The perpendicular axes represent their boundaries which cross or intersect.

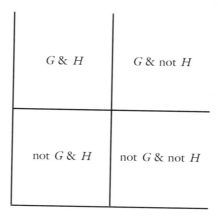

Figure 5

Let 'G' stand for 'tall' and 'H' stand for 'slender.' Then someone at a point of intersection is on the boundary of 'tall' and 'not tall' and 'slender' and 'not slender.'

It is important to distinguish "Something is on the boundary of the predicate 'G and H',"

$$(\exists x)\ (B(G\ \&\ H)x),$$

from "Something is both on the boundary of 'G' and on the boundary of 'H',"

$$(\exists x)\ (BGx\ \&\ BHx).$$

Something on the boundary of 'tall,' for example, is also on the boundary of 'not tall.' It is not thereby on the boundary of the inconsistent predicate 'tall and not tall.'

The following is a formal definition of "predicates 'G' and 'H' *intersect*":

$$(\exists x)\ (B(G\ \&\ H)\ x\ \&\ B(G\ \&\ \sim H)x\ \&\ B(\sim G\ \&\ H)x\ \&\ B(\sim G\ \&\ \sim H)x).$$

Predicates 'G' and 'H' *completely intersect* when the boundaries of the predicates intersect wherever they have a point in common:

$$(\forall x)\ ((BGx\ \&\ BHx) \rightarrow (B(G\ \&\ H)x\ \&\ B(G\ \&\ \sim H)x\ \&\ B(\sim G\ \&\ H)x \\ \&\ B(\sim G\ \&\ \sim H)x)).$$

Two predicates are *minimally independent* (M-independent) if and only if they are L-independent, they intersect, and they completely intersect.

The definition of intersection, like the definition of L-independence, uses patterns of combinations familiar from standard semantics. There are exactly four ways that two predicates and their negations combine to form exclusive and exhaustive conjunctions: G & H, G & ~H, ~G & H, ~G & ~H. When there are n predicates, there are 2^n such combinations. Three predicates are L-independent when there are (or could be) instances of each of eight combinations. A diagram of a point of intersection between three predicates shows a point on the boundaries of eight different regions. There is no upper limit to the size of an n-tuple of predicates that can fall under these variably polyadic notions of independence. In this paper, however, I shall continue to treat examples only of pairs of predicates.

Figure 6 (next page) illustrates a pair of M-independent predicates. The vertical axis represents height, and the horizontal axis represents weight. One predicate ('J') is 'more than four feet but less than six feet tall,' and the other ('K') is 'weighs more than ninety but less than one hundred forty pounds.' The vertically hatched region corresponds to the extension of 'J,' and the horizontally hatched region corresponds to the extension of 'K.' The cross-hatched region of intersection represents the conjunctive predicate 'J & K.' The whole cross-shaped region, shaded in one way or another, represents the disjunction. Four points on the diagram are on a boundary of

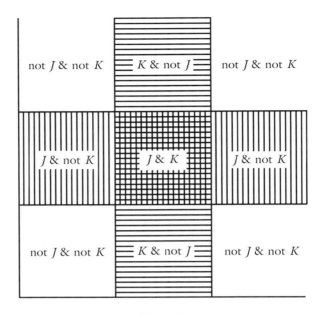

Figure 6

each predicate, and each of these is a point of intersection. The two *L*-independent predicates are also *M*-independent.

Figure 7 (facing page) represents two *L*-independent predicates that intersect but that are not minimally independent.

The horizontally hatched region represents the extension of 'K' as before. The vertically hatched region represents the extension of 'J*,' a limitation of 'J.' Something is J* if and only if it is J and also weighs more than ninety pounds. Someone (or something) that weighs ninety pounds and that is between four feet and six feet tall is on the boundary of both 'J*' and 'K' yet is not on a point of intersection. It is not on the boundaries of regions that correspond to each of the four combinations: J* & K, J* & ~K, ~J* & K, and ~J* & ~ K.

One hopes that a notion of independence adequate to deal with gruesome predicates requires nothing more complicated than the definition of *M*-independence. Slight extensions of our diagramming techniques dash this hope. A well-behaved predicate such as 'K,' 'weighs more than ninety but less than one hundred forty pounds,' is equivalent to a disjunction of *M*-independent predicates and is also equivalent to a conjunction of *M*-independent predicates.

The ordinates and abscissae of the height/weight diagrams above are not calibrated. Exact numerical values are irrelevant to the relationships between boundaries that these diagrams illustrate. All the predicate bound-

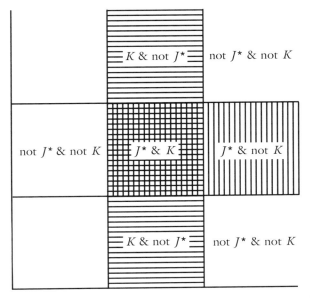

Figure 7

aries depicted so far are parallel to one coordinate and perpendicular to the other. In beginning algebra, one learns to diagram equations. Not all the resulting lines are straight, and some of the straight lines are diagonal. In this context, a diagonal straight line would represent the predicate 'when x is n feet tall, $30n$ is x's weight in pounds.' Supplement or replace equalities in this formula with inequalities and the diagram of the resulting predicate is a region with positive area, as in the earlier predicate diagrams. Figure 8 is

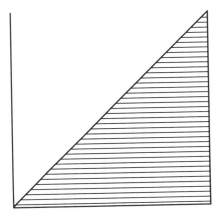

Figure 8

the diagram of the predicate 'when *x* is *n* feet tall or less, **30***n* or less is *x*'s weight in pounds.'

The shaded region corresponds to the extension of the predicate. Figure 9 contains not one but four diagonal boundaries. It also contains two boundaries perpendicular to the horizontal axis. These are the boundaries of '*K*,' 'weighs more than ninety but less than one hundred forty pounds,' that Figures 6 and 7 both represent. '*K*' is the intersection of two strange predicates '*B*' and '*C*.' Unshaded regions correspond to 'neither *B* nor *C*'. Two kinds of parallel shaded regions correspond to '*B* but not *C*' and to '*C* but not *B*.' The cross-hatched region corresponds to '*B* and *C*,' that is, to '*K*.' Exactly which algebraic formulae about relations between height and weight (or age and weight, or salary and weight, and so forth) determine the slant of the diagonal boundaries does not matter. What matters is the spatial relations between the boundaries. I have contrived the predicates '*B*' and '*C*' so that their conjunction corresponds precisely to '*K*' and so that they are *M*-independent. The two boundary points that *B* and *C* have in common are both points of intersection. These diagrams are slightly asymmetric to show that several easily produced symmetries are irrelevant to the topic at hand.

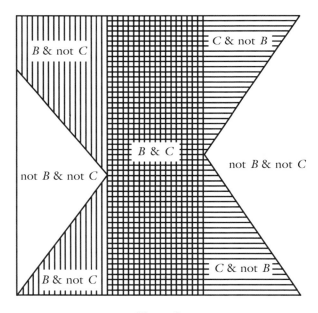

Figure 9

Figure 10, using the same conventions, shows two *M*-independent predicates '*D*' and '*E*' whose disjunction is equivalent to '*K*.' As before, every boundary point in common is a point of intersection, that is, under the current conventions of representation, on a boundary of a region of each of the four possible kinds: unshaded ('not D and not E'), parallel shaded one way ('D and not E'), parallel shaded the other way ('not D and E'), and cross-hatched ('D and E').

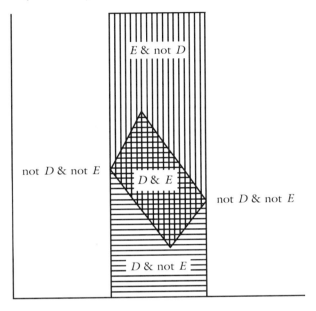

Figure 10

Supplemented only by each other, the notions of L-independence and M-independence are inadequate to distinguish intuitively disjunctive or conjunctive predicates on the one hand from intuitively simple predicates on the other. Yet the examples that Figures 9 and 10 depict both have a peculiarity with respect to the relations between two predicate boundaries. Describing this peculiarity requires a notion of a *distinct boundary*.

In the diagrams above, lines represent predicate boundaries. The predicate 'K' has two distinct boundaries, 'weighs ninety pounds' and 'weighs one hundred forty pounds.' The lines representing these two boundaries are not connected. To trace the lines that represent the boundaries of 'K' with a pencil, touching the pencil point to every position on the lines, and not touching the pencil point anywhere on the diagram that is not a boundary line, one has to lift the pencil off the paper. A predicate diagrammed in the fashion of Figures 6–10 has n distinct boundaries if such pencil tracing of its boundaries requires $n - 1$ lifts from the paper surface.

Another way to explain the notion of distinct boundary involves regarding an expression like 'BK,' "on a boundary of 'K,'" as itself a predicate with boundaries.[10] 'BK' is a disjoint predicate equivalent to the disjunction of two incompatible predicates, 'weighs ninety pounds' and 'weighs one hundred forty pounds,' that have no boundary points in common. Neither of these two predicates, on the other hand, is disjoint. There is no pair of incompatible predicates sharing no boundary points to which one or the other is equivalent. 'K' has exactly two distinct boundaries. Any predicate that applies to something but not to everything has at least one distinct boundary. There is no upper limit to the number of distinct boundaries a predicate can have.[11]

In addition to the notion of a distinct boundary, we need the notion of a *distinct intersection.* Diagrams represent intersections as distinct if and only if they represent them at different locations. Another way to explain the notion of a distinct intersection involves regarding a specification of an intersection as a predicate. Such a predicate is not disjoint when and only when there is exactly one distinct intersection of that kind. When such a predicate is disjoint and equivalent to a disjunction of n mutually incompatible nonintersecting predicates, there are $n - 1$ distinct intersections of that kind.[12]

Looking back at Figures 9 and 10 that are designed to show the limitation of M-independence, we see the peculiarities earlier referred to. In Figure 9, predicates 'B' and 'C' each have two distinct boundaries. (One distinct boundary of 'B' coincides with one of the distinct boundaries of 'K,' and one distinct boundary of 'C' coincides with the other of the distinct boundaries of 'K.') Although the boundaries of 'B' and 'C' intersect wherever they have a point in common, each has a distinct boundary that has no point in common, and thus no point of intersection, with the other. This is a mark of nonindependence. Two predicates are *genuinely independent* (G-independent) only if each distinct boundary of one intersects each distinct boundary of the other.

In Figure 10 each distinct boundary of 'D' intersects with each distinct boundary of 'E.' Indeed these predicates each have but a single distinct boundary. The peculiarity in this example, the mark of nonindependence, is that there is more than one distinct intersection of distinct boundaries. Two predicates are G-independent if and only if they are L-independent, M-independent, and each distinct boundary of one intersects each distinct boundary of the other in exactly one distinct intersection.

Is 'grue' a disjunctive predicate? As often defined, it is an exclusively disjunctive predicate. As the discussion above of 'supergrue' shows, however, a basic puzzle of the New Riddle of Induction does not require an exclusively disjunctive predicate. Although it is possible to stipulate extended meanings of 'disjunctive' such that 'grue' and 'supergrue' are disjunctive while 'green' is not, I do not see that there is a single neatest and most natural way to do this. The New Riddle challenges us to locate an objective relevant asymmetry between 'green' and other "natural" predicates on the one hand, and 'grue' and other "perverse" predicates on the other. In developing the notion of G-independence, I intend to provide a distinction, independent versus nonindependent, that is useful in explaining asymmetries of this kind.

To explain an asymmetry between 'green' and 'grue,' let us consider four different predicates that are syntactically disjunctions of two conjunctive predicates in which a conjunct of one is the complement of a conjunct of the other ('T' still abbreviates 'is first examined for color before August 7, 2006'):

(1) 'green and T, or green and not T,'
(2) 'grue and T, or bleen and not T,'
(3) 'grue and T, or grue and not T,'
(4) 'green and T, or blue and not T.'

Both (1) and (2) are equivalent to 'green'; both (3) and (4) are equivalent to 'grue.' (1) to (4) all share the following logical form (among others):

'A and C, or B and not C.'

One significant feature (feature "WHOLE"), that (1) and (3) share, and (2) and (4) do not share, is the identity of 'A' and 'B.' 'Green' appears in both disjuncts of (1), and 'grue' appears in both disjuncts of (3). The feature WHOLE has little intrinsic importance. Its importance derives from its relation to another feature (feature "SOME"): 'A' and 'C,' and also 'B' and 'not C,' are G-independent. Since 'grue' and 'T' are not G-independent, (3) does not have feature SOME. Only (1) on this list has both features WHOLE and SOME; it is WHOLESOME. (I capitalize this technical term to indicate that I do not depend in a theoretically serious way on the meaning of the real word "wholesome.")

It is easy to find a predicate such as 'S,' 'has been purchased from Sears,' that permits the construction of a WHOLESOME predicate that is equivalent to 'grue':

'grue and S, or grue and not S.'

The parallel construction equivalent to 'green' is also WHOLESOME:

'green and S, or green and not S.'

So in the case of 'green' and 'grue,' the predicate 'S' reveals no asymmetry. The predicate 'T,' on the other hand, does reveal an asymmetry. There is a

WHOLESOME construction for 'green' that uses '*T*,' but no such construction for 'grue.' Is there some predicate '*X*' that reverses this asymmetry, that allows for a WHOLESOME construction of 'grue' but not of 'green'? If so, my recent attempt to define an asymmetry is a failure. A proof that my attempt succeeds would include a proof that there is no such predicate '*X*.' I believe, but cannot prove, that there is no such predicate.

I defined 'supergrue' so that it is not an exclusively disjunctive predicate. One way to reveal its asymmetry with 'green' is to consider the following three-disjunct disjunction ('*T**' abbreviates 'is first examined for color before January 8, 2005'):

> 'green and *T**, or green and *T* and not *T**, or green and not *T*.'

Although the predicates '*T*', and '*T**' are not independent of each other ('*T**' and 'not *T*' are incompatible), both predicates are *G*-independent of 'green.' By a natural extension of the technical term 'WHOLESOME,' this three-disjunct predicate, that is equivalent to 'green,' is WHOLESOME. There is no way of constructing a similar WHOLESOME three-disjunct disjunction with '*T*' and '*T**' that is equivalent to 'supergrue.' The following predicate is WHOLE but not SOME:

> 'supergrue and *T**, or supergrue and *T* and not *T**, or supergrue and not *T*.'

Neither '*T*' nor '*T**' is *G*-independent of 'supergrue.' There is no other pair of predicates, so far as I can see, that allow the construction of a WHOLESOME equivalent to 'supergrue' but not to 'green.'

There may be asymmetries between 'grue' and 'green,' and between 'supergrue' and 'green' that are simpler, more general, or more elegant than my sketch of WHOLESOMEness above. If so, I hope that the notion of *G*-independence, or some successor to it, assists the formulation of these asymmetries.

Why might there be a successor to *G*-independence? There is no specific objection to my definition of *G*-independence that I have up my sleeve. So of course I also have no remedy in reserve. Should objections eventually come forth, I or someone can decide what kind and how much revision they require. My current conviction, deep but fallible, is that the notion of relations between predicate boundaries helps explain an objective difference we detect between a wholesome predicate like 'green' and a perverse predicate like 'grue.'

Duke University

NOTES

1. I draw this distinction in Sanford (1988), section IX, "Two-step Induction," 528–531.

2. See Morton (1977), 46–7, for some background to this question. I quote and discuss Morton in Sanford (1988), 531.

3. This point is neither new nor original with me. I heard Sara Ruddick report this as someone's view, if memory serves, in the early 1960s.

4. Compare Davidson (1980), 218.

5. I lift this sentence nearly verbatim from Sanford (1981), and I mean in this note to serve general notice that I derive much of the present article from Sanford (1981) and (1970). I will not acknowledge further borrowings, whether more or less verbatim or (more frequently) paraphrased or restated. Neither Sanford (1970) nor Sanford (1981) contain diagrams. I hope that diagrams here make crucial definitions of Sanford (1981) easier to comprehend. Sanford (1981) is itself an attempt to improve on Sanford (1970), an attempt I would not have made without Joseph Ullian's understanding and encouragement.

6. If we choose to use the nonmodal version of the definition of *L*-independence, we should add this qualification: any predicate whose extension includes at least two things.

7. Venn diagrams and other logic diagrams do not satisfy this requirement. In a two-circle Venn diagram, the two circles intersect twice; but no interpretation supplies meaning to the spatial difference of these two intersections. Moreover, there is no point in a three-circle diagram that represents the mutual intersection of the three circles.

8. See Sanford (1975) for a further treatment of the B operator, especially in sections VII to XIII (34–39) which is largely independent of the eccentric semantics for propositional logic that appears in sections II to VI.

9. I hesitated to make this assertion in Sanford (1970), 165–6. In that discussion, I claimed that logical truths of predicate logic can lose their status as logical truths once we allow the possibility of borderline cases. This is a view that I reject, with some reasons for the rejection, in Sanford (1975). Another reason why I now hesitate less about claiming that 'grue' is disconnected is that I have come to regard this as a helpful illustration rather than as a final result.

10. When a predicate is vague, objects on its boundaries are borderline cases, and objects on the boundaries of its boundaries are higher-order borderline cases. See Sanford (1975), section XI, for a treatment of higher-order borderline cases. When a predicate is not vague, objects on its boundaries ideally have an exact value. Although the determination that an empirical concept has an exact value, for example, *exactly* ninety pounds, not a wisp or a glimmer more or less, is impossible, this inescapable vagueness is not essentially involved in the notion of higher-order boundaries. The boundary points of 'BK' need not be different from the boundary points of 'K'; that is, they can be the same as the extension of 'BK.'

11. A reader with qualms about these two explanations of *distinct boundary* can consult Sanford (1981), 174, for a third style of explanation provided in the familiar notation of predicate logic.

12. A reader who follows the reference of the last footnote will find another explanation of *distinct intersection* in Sanford (1981), 174.

REFERENCES

Davidson, Donald. 1980. *Essays on Actions and Events.* Oxford: Oxford.

Goodman, Nelson. 1972. *Problems and Projects.* Indianapolis: Bobbs-Merrill.

Mellor, D. H. 1992. "There are no Conjunctive Universals." *Analysis 52,* 97–103.

Morton, Adam. 1977. *A Guide Through the Theory of Knowledge.* Encino: Dickenson.

Oliver, Alex. 1992. "Could there be Conjunctive Universals?" *Analysis 52,* 88–97.

Sanford, David H. 1970. "Disjunctive Predicates." *American Philosophical Quarterly 7,* 162–70.

Sanford, David H. 1975. "Borderline Logic." *American Philosophical Quarterly 12,* 29–39.

Sanford, David H. 1981. "Independent Predicates." *American Philosophical Quarterly 18,* 171–4.

Sanford, David H. 1988. "Epistemology Meets Cognitive Psychology." *Inquiry 31,* 519–33.

Thomson, Judith Jarvis. 1966. "Grue." *Journal of Philosophy 63,* 289–309.

Entrenchment

Ian Hacking

1 Introduction

To use a name for any kind is (among other things) to be willing to make generalizations and form expectations about individuals of that kind. Goodman's artificial predicate "grue" confirms this fundamental relation between naming, predicting, and generalizing.[1] It teaches an overarching lesson about our usage of names for what Goodman calls relevant kinds— not just natural kinds, but any kind of thing, person, action, activity, behavior, substance, composition, manufacture, quality, relation, etc. The lesson extends far beyond kinds that we are tempted to characterize by similarity or "something in common," for it persists into kinds that are connected only by family resemblances. Conversely, we learn also that one of the ways in which things come to be seen as similar, of a kind, and deserving of a name of their own, is by way of expectations that we put into practice and inferences or arguments that we are prepared to make.

Our culture of prediction and control emphasizes lawlike statements, universalizable predicates, and counterfactual conditionals. But Goodman's lesson is not only about the kinds that we who live in an industrialized part of the world use to describe nature, society, and our companions. It seems to apply to classifications and their use in any readily imaginable or actually studied civilization whose versions of the world are very different from our own.

These ideas are not novel. They rephrase Goodman's own doctrines about similarity, projectibility, entrenchment, and world-versions. If I modify his views, it is chiefly by making a certain symmetry more explicit. He wrote that

> without the organization, the selection of relevant kinds, effected by evolving tradition, there is no rightness or wrongness of categorization, no validity or invalidity of inductive inference, no fair or unfair sampling, and no uniformity or disparity among samples.[2]

Such statements encourage a picture—not Goodman's—of *first* selecting kinds and *then* categorizing, inducing, sampling. That picture, or at any rate that manner of speaking, may be a residue of the Carnapian programme: "first select your language—the one you think will prove most useful—and then use it." We need a more symmetric image. To oversimplify too much, there is not much selection before use, although there is almost always some evolving selection in use. To use names for kinds is to be engaged in expecting and generalizing, and to generalize is to reinforce any selection that has evolved.

Aside from a few of Goodman's close associates such as Catherine Elgin, Israel Scheffler, and Joseph Ullian, most people who have written in detail about his new riddle have aimed at refuting him, correcting him, or co-opting him into a comparatively narrow and technical enterprise of little general interest to philosophy. Nevertheless, I hold that his solution in terms of entrenchment is the right way to go. Agreement with Goodman requires a larger view of his projects than is common among his commentators. Douglas Stalker's amazing bibliography at the end of this book shows that consensus is not easily reached. Here I mostly reposition his problem after forty years of debate. Yet my approach will prove to be unexpected in several respects.

First, I discount the details of Goodman's examples about colors and minerals, for although there are numerous little objections specific to them, they do not matter much. The statements that he mentions, the ones about emeralds, for example, express more fiction than fact, but I don't mind. We might think of his discussion of "grue" as the sketch of a recipe for setting problems. In the same spirit I discount Goodman's focus on induction by simple enumeration. We should not limit the scope of his work in that way. Induction is no more than a crisp way to pose a general difficulty. Thus, unlike many readers, I take Goodman to have posed a quite general problem for metaphysics and epistemology (sections 2–8).

Next, we require a stronger thesis than the assertion that predicates in use are projectible. A converse statement is called for. There is a sense in which some predicates cannot be projected. No amount of mental self-deception allows me to use the predicate "grue." Here I discount the historical, conservative aspect of entrenchment—something agreeably objective and almost measurable. Instead I would emphasize an obscure but philosophically central notion of being a predicate in use. And being used need not imply a long history of usage. Entrenchment had the nominalist virtue that one could measure it by counting instances of past usage. Goodman determined entrenchment longitudinally, by observing past usage. We need what might be called a latitudinal indicator of usage, of how readily a predicate can be used now. This can be done so as to preserve the profoundly nominalist aspect of Goodman's doctrine.

I conclude by urging that Goodman's riddle arose, in part, because we so sharply distinguish classifying from generalizing. That creates a space for his problem. I enumerate three distinct forces that have driven us to the chasm between classification and generalization: a priori learning theory, natural history, and a play between the older ideas of extension and intension. All three are embedded in a larger cultural matrix that leads us to picture classification as collection, accumulation, piling up, fencing in, all acquisitive activities that leave out the other uses of predicates.

2 Scope and Significance

Goodman's riddle has had a curious reception. On the one hand a number of analytically oriented philosophers have examined the riddle in detail as a minor technical problem, without reflecting on its wider implications. On the other hand Goodman is much read outside the narrow confines of analytic philosophy—I venture that he has a far wider readership than his contemporary Quine, for example. Thinkers who swim in from deep waters find the riddle an embarrassingly small trick of a logician, hardly worthy of a powerful intellect. After all, Goodman himself called it, in self-deprecatory mood, a mere riddle! Is it not to be ignored, as the wider readership suggests, or defeated by definitions and distinctions, as some logicians propose?

No. I do not regret having written, a very long time ago, that the riddle combines "precision of statement, generality of application, and difficulty of solution to a degree greater than any other philosophic problem broached in this century."[3] Russell's paradox would be an example of a problem with greater precision of statement but less generality of application than Goodman's. Conversely one may suggest that matters arising from the private language argument are more general than Goodman's, but are not readily encapsulated with comparable precision.

Goodman's riddle goes hand in hand with his lifelong repugnance to the very idea of similarity as a raw material of thought or logic. It is integral to *Ways of Worldmaking*. Thinkers moved by other aspects of Goodman's thought ignore his riddle at their peril. I do nevertheless sympathize with the desire to forget about "grue." It is petty and unseemly. Anyone who has studied it at length knows how easy it is to make mistakes. In writing about "grue" perhaps only Goodman himself managed to steer a steady course between facile error and boring pedantry. And, arguably, the triviality of "grue" deflects attention from the deeper points that it serves to illustrate.

I nevertheless take the mindlessness of "grue" to have the virtue of sharp focus. For the same reasons I will retain Goodman's emphasis on induction by simple enumeration. That is the most banal type of inference about matters of fact. It was called "puerile" by Sir Francis Bacon and has been derided by Sir Karl Popper. Despite their animadversions, its elementary character makes it a sturdy vehicle for formulating global facts about kinds, names for kinds, and generality. I follow Goodman in discussing induction, neither because of its intrinsic interest nor because it matters much in daily life or science, but because it is handy for a brief exposition.

The same is true for predicates such as "grue" or "emeruby." We should always beware of philosophy that uses the colors as examples. If the color green mattered to the riddle, we would be well advised to learn some color science. Goodman used "green" and "emerald" only as representatives for many or most kind-terms, with "grue" and "emeruby" intended to suggest an open-ended class of artificial terms associated with them. He was operating in the hallowed tradition of philosophical fictions. Here it serves him well, for it is precisely the imaginary character of Goodman's example that is wanted here. And of course no one is in doubt as to whether to prefer "grue" over "green" when making inductions. That is not what William James called a live question.

There have been attempts to find living predicates that somehow resemble "grue." David Hull has recently urged that the concept "species" really has been a bit like "grue," although in so doing he is advancing his own doctrine on the species concept.[4] With more limited ambition F. M. Ackroyd shows that an economic concept (the relation between percentage unemployment rate and percentage change of money wage) is grue-like, entering into lawlike generalizations up to 1969 and irregular thereafter.[5] These examples may be seen as possibility-proofs or consistency-proofs (in the sense of Leibniz): they show that scientists have used predicates or concepts that have been in certain respects grue-like. Otherwise they are irrelevant. Ackroyd writes that his economic example "is a stronger example [than 'grue'] since entities in the real world started to behave in an extremely unpredictable fashion." On the contrary it is a weaker example because it is not generalizable, and so is of no global philosophical interest.

What Hull says about species is also not generalizable, but, if he is right, it may be relevant to another interest of Goodman's, namely the way in which we revise our categories as we introduce "novel organizations that make, or take account of, newly important connections and distinctions."[6] Goodman has said all too little about how we construct versions that seem right. In my opinion that is inevitable: there is no *general* story to tell. We must proceed by example. There are now detailed studies of the modification, modulation, and mutation of thick concepts.[7] Such studies, like that of David Hull's work on species, are too specific to be relevant to Goodman's riddle. His problem lives in fictions, while kind-modification can be studied only contextually, in the rich density of historical fact.

3 Induction

Induction has been described in various ways. People often think of inference from the past to the future, founded on true-in-spirit slogans such as "the future resembles the past" or the uniformity of nature. We induce to particulars as well as to generals, and backwards as well as forwards— inferring not only that my letter will probably reach you if posted today, but also that the one I wrote a fortnight ago has been in your possession for some time.

There are two forms of induction by simple enumeration: inferences (i) from particulars to particulars, and (ii) from instances to a generalization in the absence of counterexamples. Mill and Carnap, for very different reasons, thought that (i) is what matters. Goodman's own bland but celebrated shorthand example is an inference of type (ii), from the assertion that all known emeralds are green, to the conclusion that all emeralds are green. In daily life we seem to use (i) as the form that matters. Fortunes are staked on this or that future product of the emerald mine, not on all emeralds. But only with conclusions as in (ii) do we have the generality required for testability, explanation, and the adumbration of theories. Throughout my discussion I intend Goodman's ideas to apply to both (i) and (ii).

Philosophers have from time to time undertaken to justify induction. That has not been the dominant theme: witness Mill, who was so little interested in justifying induction that he justified deduction inductively. The justification-in-general of induction tends to appeal to cowardly minds and feeble intellects, so it is good that I need not resort to a straw man for an example of a justifier. The classic, and certainly most witty and intelligent, attempt to justify induction is Bertrand Russell's.[8] He had to conclude with a classic justificatory cop-out: the principle of inductive inference is synthetic a priori.

Russell presented his task in two parts. First formulate a rule for induction by simple enumeration and then provide a justification for using it. Many, including Russell at the time he wrote *Problems,* thought that the second task was the hard one. His simple and unguarded abstract rule was, in essentials, this:

From the premises that,
    $a, b, c, \ldots$ are both f and g, and nothing is known that is f but not g,
To infer,
    (probably) (i) z, which is f is g, or
    (probably) (ii) all f are g.

Russell added the rider that the more the positive instances the greater the probability. He must have known from Mill that the number of instances is not enough for stating a sensible inductive rule:

> Why is a single instance, in some cases, sufficient for a complete induction, while in others, myriads of concurring instances, without a single exception known or presumed, go such a very little way towards establishing an universal proposition? Whoever can answer this question knows more of the philosophy of logic than the wisest of the ancients, and has solved the problem of induction.[9]

It would of course be quite wrong to take Goodman's riddle as the limiting case of this question (myriads of concurring instances going zero distance towards establishing anything). Mill was making a distinction among "healthy" attributes.

Philosophical discussions of induction often use an odd convention. Despite Mill, we pretend that we have been able to capture the essence of induction in a rule. Then we ask whether the rule can be justified. It seems to have been left to Goodman to notice that nothing like Russell's principle can be right. It is inconsistent.

From this point of view (and only this one) the problem is eerily reminiscent of Russell's own paradox. That paradox shows that not every expressible predicate defines a healthy set. Goodman's riddle shows that not every expressible predicate defines a healthy kind. We can follow Quine: "Kinds can be seen as sets, determined by their members."[10] Then we ask, which (healthy) sets are (healthy) kinds? Goodmanic issues nevertheless remain entirely different from Russellian ones. Whatever set-theoretic school of foundations of mathematics we favor, Russell's paradox is avoided by constraints on set-formation. These constraints can be stated formally, because they are internal to the subject matter of set theory. The constraints that determine which kinds are relevant seem not to be internal to inductive reasoning. Hence they are not susceptible of formal statement within inductive logic or the foundations of statistical inference.

In what L. J. Savage calls a personalist version of the Bayesian approach to probable inference, a person's assignment of probabilities to a range of beliefs will imply that person's commitment to healthy as opposed to grue-like predicates. So it might seem as if anti-grue choices can be formalized after all. That is an illusion. There is in principle no formal theory about the choice of personal probabilities; there is only a logic of what F.P. Ramsey called consistency or what Bruno de Finetti called coherence. For example, to hold that certain possible outcomes of an experiment are what de Finetti called exchangeable is to be committed (presumably) to healthy predicates, but there is no theory, internal to personalism, about preference for healthy predicates. Thus in his contribution to the present volume, Brian Skyrms shows how a man may formalize for himself the fact that in his system of beliefs, he presupposes an anti-grue stance. This technique, using Bruno de Finetti's exchangeability, does not formalize entrenchment. Entrenchment is an ethnographic and linguistic concept that involves communal practice, as opposed to private and purely personal expectations. It is as intimately linked to the social and the public as Wittgenstein's private language argument, although the linkages are different.[11]

4 The Inconsistency

We took the rule of induction by simple enumeration to be inadequate, inexact, or boring: Goodman observed that it is virtually inconsistent. I say virtually because a formal inconsistency follows only when the evidence is not exhaustive, that is, if there are more f's in the world than are enumerated in the premises. I shall tacitly ignore this condition in what follows.

Given any premises of forms (i) or (ii), you can always invent predicates h, contrary to g, such that the premises are exactly as true with h replacing g as they were with g itself. Hence the rule tells you to infer that all f are h. So you can infer that all f are g and, to the contrary, that all f are h.

Goodman's familiar example uses "grue" (a predicate that becomes specific when the reader assigns a definite future time to the free time parameter t). Definition: x is *grue* = x is examined before time t and is found to be green, or x is not examined before time t and is blue.[12] Taking f = emeralds, g = green, and h = grue, and $a, b, c, \ldots$, to be examined emeralds, rule (ii) enables us to infer that all emeralds are green and that all emeralds are grue. This conclusion is impossible, for it implies that any unexamined emerald is green, and also, that it is blue. That is a contradiction (unless all emeralds in the universe are examined before t). Rule (i) is equally troubling, for using it one concludes that an emerald z not examined before t—if there is one—is blue.

There are many variants on "grue." The differences among them show up when we consider future expectations. What would happen if all emeralds were grue, and not green? Emeralds would not change color. An emerald recently found to be green would stay green; an emerald first examined after t would be blue, and, we suppose, would always have been blue. But consider another predicate (against which Goodman has not protested).[13] Definition: x is *grue** at a time before t if and only if it is green; at t or later, x is *grue** if and only if it is blue. If all emeralds were grue*, some, the ones we have examined and found to be green, would change color at time *t*. Some authors prefer "grue'" to "grue," perhaps because the definition of "grue" alludes to examiners or observers. That somehow seems inappropriate, improperly subjective. "Grue'" can make a point without an observer, but it invites us to think of green things changing color at *t*.

"Grue" and "grue'" provide counterexamples to the rules of inference (i) and (ii). It is not to the immediate point that the unqualified premise, "all examined emeralds are green," is false. The example is intended to establish the invalidity of an argument form; the truth or falsehood of the premises is irrelevant. With equal irrelevance one could urge the opposite point, that when restricted so as to be true, it is analytic that all emeralds are green. So what? We are concerned with the derivability of a conclusion, not with its modality. In fact, Chinese uses the same characters, *lu (se)*, for green and for emerald. The analyticity, in Chinese, of the translation of "emeralds are green" never gave a moment's pause to my students at Wuhan University.

5 Rejections of the Riddle

The Russellian rule is inconsistent. Two strategies present themselves: either modify the rule into a consistent version, or conclude that rules of this type are fundamentally mistaken. Paul Feyerabend took the second route, urging that Goodman's riddle is a stark way to prove that induction is invalid.[14] That reinforced Popper's opinion that we should not, but luckily do not, make inductions by simple enumeration. Unfortunately the riddle is contagious. Feyerabend thought that it is a problem only for induction. Not so. For every physics conjecture Popper may wish to test, there are endless incompatible Goodmanic conjectures consistent with known facts and with corroborated physical theory—and which are just as testable as Popper's hypothesis. Of course they are not serious. They are positively disrespectful. That's part of what is so annoying.

Goodman's route appears to be the exact opposite of Feyerabend's. Find a consistent rule of induction by modifying the inconsistent one. The result will not be a justification of induction but a rule that we hope is consistent. The only viable modification, he believed, relies on our previous usage of predicates. That was far too nominalist a conclusion for his readers. Hence, publication of Goodman's riddle launched a sort of anti-man hunt, that is, an attempt to find some ahistorical, nonanthropological basis for distinguishing healthy predicates like "green" from sick ones like "grue." Most proposed solutions to Goodman's riddle aimed at vindicating the so-called intuition that "green" is a qualitative or observational predicate whereas "grue" is somehow positional (or that green is a good and natural attribute whereas grue is a positional one). Goodman did not deny that. He denied that restricting an inductive rule to nonpositional predicates was plausible, statable, or sufficient. Much has been written about positional predicates. I shall not add to that literature. Putnam's introduction to the current (fourth) edition of *Fact, Fiction and Forecast* rebuts, with precision, many of the ideas used in attempts to evade Goodman's riddle.

6 How "Projectibility" Acquired Its Meaning

Goodman introduced two neologisms. One of them, *projectible,* is almost too good a coinage, for we seem to know what it means without explanation—and that entails that people can understand it in various ways. Anyone starting with the first page of the present edition of *Fact, Fiction and Forecast* will read Hilary Putnam writing of "Goodman's celebrated argument to show that all predicates are not equally projectible."[15] Like Putnam and many recent writers I too shall take "projectible" to be a predicate of predicates. But I should record Goodman's original usage. He first used "project" metaphorically and then gradually assigned to it a family of explained uses. He began this trek using "projected" as a predicate of hypotheses. He called an hypothesis *"actually projected* when it is adopted after some of its instances have been examined and determined to be true, and before the rest have been examined."[16] He then said,

> obviously, not all the hypotheses that are projected are lawlike or legitimately projectible; and not all legitimately projectible hypotheses are actually projected. Hence we come to the task of defining projectibility—or projecting the predicate "projected" to the predicate "projectible."[17]

Readers less nimble with words than Goodman may well balk. In a footnote we get: "A predicate 'Q' is said to be projected when a hypothesis such as 'All P's are Q's' is projected."[18] When Goodman wrote, he tied his exposition all too closely to induction. A Popperian, who held that people never make inductions by simple enumeration, might polemically maintain that no hypothesis is actually projected, and hence that no predicate was ever projected.

Forty years later, and much philosophical usage under the bridge, it seems safe to start with the idea of a predicate being projectible. The idea is that some and only some predicates can, prima facie, be legitimately substituted into a rule of inductive inference—or used for any purpose of generality, say for stating Popperian conjectures. "Projectibility" becomes the name of an as yet unanalyzed feature of predicates, namely that they are and can be used inductively. Then the new riddle of induction achieves a succinct formulation, "Which predicates are projectible?"

7 Entrenchment

Goodman's answer is radical. A predicate is *entrenched* if in fact it is in use among us. In use for what? Because of his focus on induction, Goodman explains entrenchment, or rather earned entrenchment, in terms of the extent to which predicates have been previously used in making predictions and generalizations that have thus far panned out. He adds suitable supplementary clauses for synonyms, and for translations into other languages in our language group, thus conveying the idea of inherited entrenchment. He allows for the introduction of predicates whose intended extension is genuinely novel. Those are niceties compared to the central thesis, that projectible predicates differ from nonprojectible ones only to the extent that they are entrenched. If there is anything like a sound inductive rule it must begin, "For any two entrenched predicates f, g . . . ." That does not mean that the only lawlike propositions we can establish must employ entrenched predicates. In an exchange about Donald Davidson's example, "all emerubies are gred," it was made clear that some generalizations using grue-like predicates can be derived indirectly, by deduction from other inductions.[19]

Entrenchment is not a reason for projecting a predicate. It does not justify the use of a predicate. It does not justify induction. It is used in stating a consistent rule, to which, it is hoped, there are neither patent nor latent counterexamples. Although it is very well known, Goodman's famous statement about justifying rules is worth repeating. No matter whether a rule is deductive, inductive, aesthetic, or moral, we need not necessarily seek higher level principles of unquestioned certainty. Instead we are to consider both the rule and its consequences. We are to bring our judgments about them into harmony. If a rule has plainly false consequences, revise the rule; if a specific conviction of ours violates an otherwise viable rule, revise that conviction.

> This looks flagrantly circular. . . . But this circle is a virtuous one. The point is that rules and particular inferences alike are justified by being brought into agreement with each other. *A rule is amended if it yields an inference we are unwilling to accept; an inference is rejected if it violates a rule we are unwilling to amend.*[20]

Russell's rules yield an inference that we are unwilling to accept (all emeralds are grue). So the rule is revised. It must be restricted to entrenched predicates.

Entrenchment has seemed to most readers to be all too superficial a restriction on Russell's principles of induction. "Grue" should be excluded on grounds that are more stringent than our past history of communal speech and practice. The objection is not that Goodman's restricted rules of induction—Russell for entrenched predicates only—is inconsistent. The objection is that entrenchment does not go to the heart of the matter.

In my opinion entrenchment does go near the heart of the matter. There are fine details to be sorted out, but in large, the emphasis on use is right. The emphasis on prolonged use is more questionable. The more used, the longer used, the more entrenched, and so (it seemed) the higher on some scale of projectibility. This measure of degree of entrenchment is happily extensional—just count the number of past uses of a word. That has a strong appeal for the nominalist. But it makes entrenchment smell of conceptual conservativism. I claim that to use a predicate is (usually) to be willing to project it—even if the predicate has never been used before. To use a predicate, however, is to try to say something, and that demands usage. That does bring in usage—at least the people I talk to must be willing to try to understand me and to see why I want to use the predicate now or in the future. But mere counting of past occurrences of use seems too indelicate a way of picking out the projectible predicates. Goodman and Elgin know well that new terms are introduced: " 'quark' had no history of projection, and hence no earned entrenchment. Still, from the outset the term had some measure of entrenchment—entrenchment it inherited from terms like 'subatomic particle'."[21] This does not cater to more revolutionary change in which an entire framework of concepts replaces an old one.

Conversely, I have some sympathy with those who feel entrenchment to be too superficial a concept. "Grue" lacks earned or inherited entrenchment. We don't use it. But that seems not to exhaust the matter. Somehow, we can't use it. I don't mean that we would be wrong to use it and to make projections accordingly. I mean that we can't bring ourselves to use it. I shall take up such unprojectibility in sections 9–14, and revolutionary change in 14–15. We should first briefly consider a quite unusual ground for dismissing Goodman's problem, for if his problem does not arise, we have no need to discuss the niceties of entrenchment at all.

8 Ramifications

The most important published objection to Goodman's riddle is due to Mary Hesse.[22] Like virtually every other objector, she begins by narrowly construing the problem as about one predicate, "grue," and one mode of reasoning, induction, but she has something very important to say. Hesse has been holistic. She considers the ramifications of "grue" within a larger body of scientific theorizing and experimental manipulation. Thus, within the sciences she takes us beyond the narrow confines of induction. She takes us away from mindless generalization using only a couple of predicates. I believe that rather than refuting Goodman she leads us to understand the force of his thinking when it is extended to larger bodies of knowledge. This is not surprising, for Goodman is notoriously holistic about his world-versions.

Let us say that Goodman gruified "green" with the predicate "grue"; there is also the gruestarification with "grue*." These are among the innumerable ways of Goodmanizing predicates. Any one predicate can be Goodmanized at will—and in endless directions, to "grue" or to "grue*" or whatever. Hesse insists that our knowledge does not stop at "all emeralds are green." That belief is part of a larger account of the world, including for example the fact that green light is from a particular band in the spectrum. We know not only that emeralds are green, but also that they reflect light around the 550-nanometer wave band. We can't consistently maintain that belief, the belief that green light is around 550 nm, and also project "grue." So either we have found a way to block the projection of "grue," or else we have to Goodmanize more predicates. Perhaps there are several ways to go here.

Suppose we could Goodmanize many predicates, so that we expect emeralds not examined before t to reflect light with a wave length around 475 nm, to have the kind of crystalline structure that reflects light of that wave length, and so on. Then there arises a real question as to whether we are talking about emeralds. I do not maintain that the common noun "emerald" is a rigid designator of a natural kind, or that it denotes an essence. But if one were to say that emeralds not examined after t have none of the salient features of emeralds examined before t, one would have little warrant for calling them emeralds. Emerires, perhaps, that is, emeralds examined before t or sapphires not examined before t. Someone who believes that all emerires (by any name) are grue has exactly the same expectations as the rest of us. A Goodman paradox requires what Shoemaker calls the "agreement after-t principle," namely that the situation is such that after t, those who project "grue" should agree that one had been making a right prediction, one a wrong one.[23]

This objection—he's talking about emerires, no problem—takes for granted that the properties of emeralds are mostly connected by underlying physics. Secondary qualities, we like to suppose, derive from primary ones and a nexus of law. If we are moved by this objection we might try a different tack. We could try to Goodmanize physical law. At that juncture we had better switch to gruestarification, for a great many quantities that occur in physical laws are not subject to examination, and so a grue-style definition makes little sense.

The trouble with Goodmanizing laws is that many laws of nature are interconnected. Let us be systematic. To simplify, suppose light reflected by emeralds is exactly 550 nm. How do we grustarify? Do we make a predicate *el*, so that *el* is a crypto*-wave-length (C^*WL)? Before *t* light whose C^*WL is *el* is of wave length 550 nm, after *t*, light whose C^*WL is *el* is of wave length 475 nm. A person who projects grue* and C^*WL will coherently hold that emeralds are grue* and that all emeralds reflect light whose C^*WL is *el*. We could even be systematic, defining C^*WL as the quantity that equals a length of *wl* nm before *t* and a length of *wl* − 75 nm after *t*. This won't readily do because not all our knowledge is linear with respect to wave lengths. Wave lengths are related to velocities as *velocity = frequency × wave length*. Shall we gruestarify velocities to get crypto*velocities? (The C^*V if *frequency* × C^*WL.) Velocities enter as squared terms, starting with $E = mc^2$. Better gruestarify frequencies. But then we have nonlinear laws about phase differences for interference of light. Then there are the supposed structural laws about wave length of light reflected or transmitted by crystals. Gruestarification of these becomes unmanageable. Hesse's point is not that a body of physical knowledge using the predicate "green" will be simpler than one using "grue." Goodman would at once retort by challenging the very idea of simplicity. Her point is that in practice there is no intelligible step-by-step gruification of physics.

One response is to limit Goodman's problem to situations where people don't know much and are forced to that most menial type of inference, namely induction by simple enumeration. That would be contrary to my claim about the scope of the problem. Another is to say that any local body of knowledge can be gruified holistically, not step by step, but as a totality. Local needn't be little; astrophysics and cosmology are local in that they are nowhere near the neighborhood of, say, theories about multiple personality disorder or the causes of famine in the Sahel. A local theory of some domain can be gruified by projecting into the future a Goodmanized variant, said to hold after time *t*. So-called exotic cosmological theories are slightly (but only slightly) like that: they hold that the fundamental laws of nature (or less dramatically, the constants of nature) change in time. The result of holistic gruestarification is, say, the Grewtonian theory of navitation, in which the world is Newtonian before *t*, but where, after *t*, the gravitational law has the gravitational force varying as the inverse cube of the distance. Unlike exotic cosmology, the result is not a sensible physical theory—any more than "grue" is a sensible predicate.

This second, totalizing, response is more useful than restricting Goodman's riddle to puerile inductions. As Goodman made plain in his later work, it is characteristically systems of predicates that are projected. Kind terms get their place within a version of the world—and the version that is in use by us contains the predicates that we project. We do require of a totalizing gruification of T that it should not result in just another way of expressing T itself. That is, there must remain future states of affairs in which someone who maintains T ought to be surprised, while someone who maintains gruified-T ought not to be—or vice-versa. Hesse made this requirement plain in her paper. It is a variant of what Shoemaker later called the agreement-after-t principle. After t, assuming that observations are possible at all, one party has to agree that its theory is in trouble, not necessarily by admitting defeat, but at least by sending out a postcard to the group members, "Emergency tea meeting to save theory."

9 On Projecting the Unprojectible

I take this heading from the title of Sidney Shoemaker's classic paper. What makes some predicates projectible and others not? Nothing. Goodman's approach stops the demand for explanation. It reminds us of Wittgenstein's dream of philosophy as description, not explanation. Or even of the Mill who wrote that the best proof that something is desirable is that it is desired. The best proof that something is projectible is that is projected. There is no other proof. The evidence for projectibility is the history of usage, what Goodman calls entrenchment.

What about unprojectibility? Are we to say that a predicate is unprojectible if it is not in use? That is plainly false. If the best description of the projectible is some qualified form of entrenchment, how shall we describe the unprojectible? It cannot simply be the unentrenched. Entrenched implies projectible, perhaps, but unentrenched should not imply unprojectible.

The relevant fact is not just that "grue" is not in use, and so plays no role in predicting and generalizing. A stronger fact than that is to hand: no amount of mental self-deception or public pretence allows us seriously to use the word "grue" in our lives. What can this mean? Here are five candidates, of which the first is Goodman's. I would like to go a little further than Goodman, but not much.

Extensional. "Green" but not "grue" is used in making predictions and generalizations. It may for example be used for induction by simple enumeration. That is as far as Goodman wants to go.

Ethnographic. We—the author and readers of this paper, for example—

are at present unable to project "grue." Mention it as we will, we are unable even to intend to use this predicate. Certainly we can translate many elementary sentences in which "green" is used into sentences in which "grue" and "bleen" occur, but we understand these sentences as we understand code.

Cognitive. Our inability to project "grue" or "emeruby," except in some sort of parasitic way, is a consequence of some facts of neurology, or about "processing." It is to be understood literally as a fact about the actual brain, or metaphorically as about some functional equivalent of the brain, about parallel neural networks or whatever.

Translational. Any terms in use in any human language, if they are to be understood at all, must be translatable by us into terms that are projectible in English. Thus "grue" is not only not in use among us, but could not be used by any people in such a way that we could translate it.

Transcendental. The question whether "grue" is projectible presupposes beliefs about nature and its laws that are incompatible with projecting "grue." The question of projectibility can be posed only if it has in effect been answered already.

These five appeal to distinct philosophical interests. Goodman stops at the first. Many critics resent that. Perhaps this is because the extensional account of unprojectibility does not go to the heart of the matter. It is somehow repugnant to distinguish valid rules of induction in terms of our past usage of words! We have come to live with Hume's talk of custom and habit, but at least Hume did not speak of merely verbal practices. This antagonism to the seeming triviality of Goodman's approach is perhaps the underlying psychological reason that so many authors write as if they resented it. Entrenchment demeans reason and insults philosophy.

Instead of throwing up our hands we should attempt a more modest reaction. The problem is that Goodman tries to describe our habits without saying how ingrained they are. Not only don't we project "grue," but we find ourselves unable to do anything of the sort. Hence I should like to develop the ethnographic idea which is, unfortunately, the most difficult of the five to explain. But I won't go further than that, for the following reasons.

10 Cognition

The ethnographic idea is a gray area. The cognitive one is a gleaming white—but because in respect of "grue" nothing has yet been written on it. There is a lot of cognitive science, but no ground in cognition or neurology for supposing that "grue" is unprojectible by human beings. We can build into a model of cognition a preference for healthy predicates—analogous to the personalist form of Bayesian statistics, incorporating such a preference into personal probabilities and exchangeability judgment. But that is to take a sensible distinction for granted, not to help us understand its nature. Nevertheless cognitive science may well be the way to go.

It is important here not to confuse the projection of predicates with their acquisition. It may well be a fact about human sensory apparatus, or neurology, or about "processing," that people are able to acquire grue-like concepts only parasitically. That does not seem to show very much. The predicate "conducts electricity" must also depend upon the possession of other concepts, yet we project that and not its gruified form. Even the recognition of emeralds is facilitated by possession of other ideas.

Aside from that, there is no evident connection between how we acquire concepts and their projectibility—except the one that I emphasize in my conclusion, that to acquire a classificatory concept is to acquire a projectible one. Could there be a deep connection between learnability and projectibility to be revealed by the cognitive sciences? Perhaps we are so made that we willingly project whatever we learn ostensively. Perhaps we are so made that to acquire a concept ostensively is to be prepared to project it. It would be a triumph to establish something like that. But that result would not imply that "grue" is unprojectible. Ostensive learnability cannot be a necessary condition for projectibility. At best we could infer that whereas some cognitive fact engenders a prima facie inclination to project "green," there is none to incline us to project "grue."

Goodman is silent on such matters, but one can usefully adapt a remark he made in a quite different context. Judith Jarvis Thomson had argued that a rule of induction should apply to observational predicates but not to what might be called their rivals ("green" but not "grue").[24] Goodman doubted that when made precise the condition of observability was either necessary or sufficient. More importantly, if Thomson could show that her "distinctions are rooted in some essential features of the human organism"—which would involve several "very large orders indeed"—that would not be "incompatible with a definition of projectibility in terms of entrenchment; rather we would have a psychological explanation of entrenchment."[25] The same could be said of Hesse's implication that we are unable in practice to gruify the theories that we do in fact project, because we are unable to keep track of the ramifications. If that claim were filled out—a very large order—we might expect some sort of neural explanation of the facts of entrenchment for theories. That would not be inconsistent with Goodman's doctrine of entrenchment.

Thus Goodman does not preclude a cognitive or neurological account of our habit of projecting "green" and not "grue." He says only that there is none.

11 Translation

The translation argument does not bear on the question of why you and I cannot seriously intend to project "grue." It is an argument to the effect that other people can't be understood as using a predicate that means grue. Sidney Shoemaker put the argument very cautiously:

> The fact that a term is entrenched [in another language] will be an important indication as to how it is to be understood—that is, how it is to be translated into one's own idiolect; it is evidence that if it is translatable at all it must be translated by a term that one regards as projectible.[26]

I believe we should make a slightly stronger argument. It derives to some extent from Quine arguing that it is always most charitable to translate foreigners as if they use classical logic. It owes much to Davidson. It would be all too uncharitable to translate a foreign term as meaning "grue," because that would be to imply that the foreigners have what we think of as quite mad expectations.

The point is that if some people really did use "grue" or "green" or some other predicate to mean grue, then they would use it to form expectations and make generalizations. That is what it is to use a predicate. These people will expect emeralds first examined in the future to be grue. Why should we attribute such weird beliefs to them? We invoke not only the principle of charity but what Richard Grandy called the principle of humanity. That abjures us to not attribute beliefs to others that imply they are in some way outside the human condition.[27] The argument requires Shoemaker's agreement after-*t* principle. I shall not pursue the matter here, as I provide a more detailed examination elsewhere.[28] In fact, the issue does not matter to my present concerns. I am not addressing the outer-directed question of why I can't sensibly conjecture that other people use a predicate ("green," say) that means grue. I am asking what makes it impossible for me to mean grue.

12 A Transcendental Argument

In the two final sentences of the same essay, Shoemaker contrasted himself with Goodman:

> For [Goodman], apparently, whatever it is that endows particular words with the extensions they have (and about this he says virtually nothing) is independent of what makes certain words, and not others, projectible

(namely, their being employed in actual projections). For me, the crucial point is that the fact that words are used, meant, and understood in such a way as to have particular extensions is part of "how the world is" (if you like, a fact about the natural history of human beings), and consists in lawlike, or causal, truths which cannot be stated in a way that is non-committal as to what terms are projectible and what terms are not.

This is a very rich passage to which I shall return. Here I attend to the concluding clauses. They invite a transcendental argument.

Taking just the case of the word "green," I can read Shoemaker's final sentence as follows (the star [*] marks a break in the argument). It is a fact that the word "green" is used, meant, and understood in a certain way, as denoting a class, i.e., the class of things colored green. This fact is part of how the world is. The fact consists in lawlike or causal truths. There is no way to state these truths without committing oneself to the projectibility of some terms, including "green." [*] Thus we could not use the word "green" to classify objects as green or nongreen, without being committed to the projectibility of the predicate "green" itself. Use of "green" presupposes its projectibility. If a question presupposes its answer, it is illicit and should not be posed.

I do agree that to use, mean, and understand "green" is not just to use it to make classifications but also to make predictions and form expectations. I query only the transcendental presupposition alleged in this argument. I have two distinguishable problems. One is about an implied premise. I am unable to state the causal or lawlike truths to which Shoemaker alludes, for I do not know what they are. I don't know what facts about "how the world is" underpin our use of "green." I do not even know what kind of facts they might be. My second, closely related problem is about an implied inference, which occurs around the starred break [*] in the argument. Even if the statement—a statement that since I do not know it I cannot make—of the underlying truths that make possible my use of "green" is not noncommittal about the projectibility of "green," it does not follow that I, in using "green," am committed to what makes its use possible.

Shoemaker, as he brought his paper to a close, may not have intended anything like the transcendental argument. I have painfully set it forth because although it is an interesting idea, it does not seem to work. There is a much milder version of Shoemaker's conclusion which seems right. To use the word "green" is to be willing to project it (and in that sense to be committed to projecting it). But there is nothing stronger to be said. There is no truth, whose statement is committed to the projectibility of "green," and which somehow underlies or is presupposed by our use of "green." We should go no further than the merely ethnographic observation, that we are unable to project "grue."

13 Ethnography

I call this notion ethnographic rather than anthropological because, in philosophy, the latter word may refer to philosophical anthropology, making claims or observations about *anthropos,* about the human condition. Here I refer only to something about our condition. Speaking for myself, I can't seriously use "grue" and I daresay you can't either. We are not here concerned with what Wittgenstein called "the natural history of mankind," which would state general truths about the human condition. I do think there is a place for this phrase of Wittgenstein's, and the correlated one of philosophical anthropology. Wittgenstein was very selective in his usage of these expressions (as he was of other subsequently trendified phrases such as "form of life"). I am not ruling these expressions out of court. I gladly employ the phrases "philosophical anthropology" and "natural history of mankind" elsewhere.[29] It is possible that Shoemaker was being ironic in his parenthetical "if you like, 'the natural history of mankind'." I can see it being a true claim about human cognition that no one could pick up "grue" ostensively, but we are here concerned with projection, not language acquisition. I don't know what humans are able to project. I know that you and I can't seriously intend to project "grue." That is why I speak of a merely ethnographic fact. But what fact is it, if it is to be more than a qualified version of Goodman's entrenchment?

14 Groofy Predicates

Grue-like predicates are unprojectible. But what's like grue? At whimsy's beckon there arise before the mind a host of artificial predicates, more or less like either "grue" or "grue*," and which could painlessly be put to use not only for classification but also for projection. I interject these here to avoid misunderstanding. It is all too easy solemnly to state that nothing grue-like is projectible, and in riposte to say that anything goes. I want to pause to see what does go.

The most plausible grue-like predicates involving that indexical parameter t will have a strong social component. How about "elegamp"? "Elegamp" is of the "grue*" type (changes at t). It applies to something before t if and only if it is elegant, and it applies to something after t if and only if it is camp. You choose the t: Many is the elegamp gown, tie, brooch, or suite of furniture.

Lawlike generalizations will be harder to come by. Everything by Worth is elegamp? We can get closer to nature than that. I suppose that when running before a force 6 wind, any ketch is (ceteris paribus) faster than any yawl. But with the new rigging for yawls that will be introduced soon, the situation will be reversed. So our generalization is: when running before a force 6 wind, any kawl is as fast as any ketch or yawl (c.p.). Much remains ungoodmanic and familiar: every kawl is a two-masted sailing vessel with a tall mainmast and a stepped mizzen.

Words like "kawl" surely cannot be learned directly, ostensively? Well, yes and no. I think you will readily grasp the meaning of "clotty" from this example. Iris Murdoch describes how when she first read *Language, Truth and Logic* in the 1940s she was "together with so many others, impressed by its wonderful clarity and simplicity." Ayer's book will nevertheless "now seem to us brilliant and ingenious, but also unsophisticated and dotty."[30] The reader will have no difficulty in designating more recent clotty philosophy books, in which the *t* lies not between the '40s and the '90s but somewhere close to hand. But of course what we are really playing with here is, as with "elegamp," not a fixed *t,* but a characteristic of a thing-as-perceived where the perceptions change with time.

The point of these examples is to defuse the objection that we can use all sorts of odd predicates in all sorts of odd ways. Yes we can, but no such examples are anywhere close to Goodman's paradigm. Anyone familiar with the slang of yesteryear will have known at once what I meant by "groofy." Something is groofy if it is groovy before *t or* goofy thereafter. "Heterological" is groofy, but is "groofy" heterological?[31]

15 Incommensurability

I can think of no circumstances in which I could use the word "grue" for classifying and predicting. But there are predicates that lie between the groofy and "grue." We can't project them, but people have done so, and we can even understand how they could have done so. These are suggested by the Kuhnian idea of incommensurability. It provides a partial model for unprojectibility. Kuhn is now completing a work in which a philosophy of language will provide an analysis of and foundation for some of the insights of *The Structure of Scientific Revolutions.* A theory of kinds will play a major part in it.[32] It will be a theory of what Goodman calls relevant kinds, not just natural kinds or the kinds distinguished in the natural sciences. Projectibility will have to loom large in this work. Here, however, I am concerned not with Kuhn's novel and perhaps still not completely worked-out ideas but rather with the idea that all readers take away from *Structure:* incommensurability. It is an idea older than Kuhn's, well developed in cultural anthropology and given its classical philosophical statement in Peter Winch's *The Idea of a Social Science.*[33] Winch made it inevitable for a generation of philosophers, looking for a cultural example, to invoke

Evans-Pritchard's investigations of witchcraft among the Zande and the Nuer.

The standard rebuttal of incommensurability is conveniently formulated by Hilary Putnam.[34] Here is Kuhn or Winch (Evans-Pritchard) saying that certain ideas are incommensurable with ours. That means that they cannot be translated into our language, that they cannot be expressed in English. Yet Kuhn and his colleagues, or Evans-Pritchard and his colleagues, do a wonderful job of conveying in English just the system of ideas that they contend is alien and incommensurable. "To tell us that Galileo had 'incommensurable' notions [to ours] *and then to go on to describe them at length* is totally incoherent."[35] The best short reply to Putnam is by Paul Feyerabend: the incommensurability brigade never said you can't learn the alien. What the brigade does in English is to give you a partial introduction to another way of thinking, and convey at least the feeling of understanding, albeit an imperfect one.[36]

To reduce this debate to the barren language of kinds, Feyerabend is saying that he and others can teach strange methods of classification. But no one, until perhaps Kuhn in his current work, has sufficiently emphasized projectibility. You can learn how to classify, but that does not mean that you can use the sorting that you have acquired. I can effortlessly pick up the classifications of modern degenerate homeopathic medicine. I can easily learn what caloric is. I can readily learn what phlogiston is. I can with much pain acquire the conceptions of Paracelsus. In every case I can add lots of new (or obsolete) words to my vocabulary, and thereby express my newly won classifications, or I can use familiar words in odd ways. I happen to find it easier to do this than pass the mineral identification test in first-year geology, let alone learn the names for little brown birds. But (speaking for myself) I cannot use those newly acquired predicates. I cannot form expectations according to them. I cannot organize my life, make my choices, or act under descriptions that are invited by these predicates. Perhaps I could decide to do so, but it would mean a lot of changes in my life. I would need (Pascal-like) to adopt a lot of practices until they had become part of me and I felt differently about that aspect of my life. There is something of a continuum. It is not so hard to get into modern (degenerate) homeopathic medicine while also consorting with topnotch consultants from the medical school—especially for those of us who have a knowledgeable skepticism about the entrenched beliefs of modern medicine. I could, furthering my study of experimental science, get into the practice of thinking phlogistonistically. Nothing would induce me to become a Paracelsan; even to get close would require that I become infected with that madness.

In short, incommensurability has been too much presented in terms of translation and understanding, and too little in terms of using and doing. To understand a classification, to know exactly how to apply a kind word, is not to be able to use it. The most important aspect of using is not the sorting but the forming of expectations, the guessing of generalizations, the making of inductions, the testing of hypotheses. Putnam's right. The incommensurability brigade can tell us, painfully, what Paracelsus meant. But they can't get us to use Paracelsus's predicates. *That* is part of what it is for his predicates and his ideas to be incommensurable with ours.

I would not leave this topic with the implication that projectibility exhausts incommensurability. Generalizing is only the beginning of reasoning. A thoroughly alien way of thinking will involve styles of reasoning different from our own—a topic of great interest, but involving issues of a quite different sort from the present paper.[37] Here I have used the idea of incommensurability to recall one way in which it may be in fact impossible to use a predicate. No logical, transcendental, or cognitive impossibility is in question. We just can't use those dead predicates to think about the world and interact with it.

16 Length and Width

These reflections return us to the worry that entrenchment, as originally described by Goodman, is too conservative a notion. If we took Kuhn's excessively sharp gestalt-switch, religious-conversion, vision of scientific revolution, the born-again can't use the old prerevolutionary predicates even though those predicates have been vastly better entrenched than the new postrevolutionary ones. Goodman certainly welcomes conceptual evolution. He conveys a picture of gradual change. He surely ought to be more generous, and allow at least for the possibility of scientific revolutions in the style of Kuhn—not to mention those more frequent events, revolutions in taste. That would force us to qualify the conservationist aspect of early accounts of entrenchment.

It should be possible to do this while keeping the spirit of Goodman's nominalism. A kind term that is projected is not merely entrenched, but part of a larger way of talking. Right categories, as Goodman later put it, are part of world versions. But world versions are not *Weltanschauungen*, all-encompassing life visions. As is made clear in later work, Goodman's world versions may be as local as the disciplinary matrices of which Kuhn wrote. Entrenchment should involve not just being used, but being used in one or more world versions. That means being used with many more predicates. Perhaps we need a two-dimensional view of entrenchment. It should be longitudinal in going back in time. That was Goodman's original idea. It should also be latitudinal. A predicate may be projectible when, with a number of other predicates, it shares in a way of describing some aspect of the world. New families of descriptions, especially the sort envisaged by Kuhn, may need no past so long as they have willing users, now. Yet even here one may argue that revolution cannot be total. No matter how radical a scientific shift within a community, it must always be calibrated, as Nicholas Jardine puts it, to previous world versions that still remain.[38] Likewise, as Peter Gallison has insisted, there are many layers in scientific work. Instrumental practice may remain fairly unchanged during radical theoretical shift; theories may be unmoved by change in phenomenology.[39] Perhaps the idea of inherited entrenchment could be enriched to include such real life aspects of science.

17 A False Dichotomy

We may nibble at entrenchment around the edges. We may be unable to express, in any clear way, the sheer experienced impossibility of thinking "grue." But Goodman's lesson is plain and definite. I stated it in my opening sentence. To use a name for any kind is to be willing to make generalizations and form expectations about individuals of that kind. To use a name for any kind is also, of course, to be prepared to distinguish, to sort, to classify according as things are, or are not, of that kind. Goodman's riddle arises in full force when we separate classifying from generalizing, and think of classifying first, and inducing later. Goodman showed how to build artificial predicates that classify with exactly as much precision as the familiar predicates on which they are based. Goodman's own words sometimes lend themselves to a picture of first classifying and then generalizing. His own riddle undermines that very picture.

Human beings do both classify and generalize. Those do look like two distinct mental operations. Traditionally they were held to be distinct parts of "logic." In modern times logic became the science of inference, therefore taking generalization under its wing but pushing classification and the theory of attributes elsewhere. Goodman's 1940 doctoral dissertation *A Study of Qualities* had already set him to rectifying this: "without some techniques for applying symbolic logic to extra-logical subject matter, problems that require symbolic logic will never yield clear and precise solutions."[40] Perhaps cognitive science will effect a reunion of classification and generalization.

I don't deny that the subtle problems of generalization have become a science in their own right, or rather several sciences. Open problems about quanitification in deductive and generalization in inductive logic have nothing to do with classification. On the other hand we have become increasingly aware of technical problems about taxonomies, to the extent that there are now entire journals dedicated to the pure theory of classification. Kind-making, classification, and generalization are nevertheless of a piece. I shall conclude by noticing three factors that hinder us from seeing this clearly.

18 A Priori Psychology

We have a long tradition of speculating on the origin and formation of ideas. Locke's *Essay* can be read as a treatise on exactly that topic, with many of its philosophical conclusions based upon the way in which our ideas originate. Those ideas are largely ideas of what he called sorts or what we call kinds. That was a theory of how the Human Understanding forms ideas. During the nineteenth century the idea of Human Nature was replaced by that of Normal People. As the ideas of the child, and of child-development, swung into place late in that century, philosopher-psychologists turned their attention to the way in which Normal Children acquire ideas.

Despite the prodigal growth of experimental techniques, there is still a good deal of the Lockian a priori style in developmental psychology and psycholinguistics. I shall, however, restrain comment to the a priori psychology of philosophers. It is well illustrated in Quine's wonderful paper "Natural Kinds" (surely the richest essay on that topic ever written). Quine, like so many others, but more clearly than most, supposes that there is one problem, namely, what enables babies to acquire kind-concepts in the first place? There is a second problem, why is it reasonable to generalize with the kind-concepts that we acquire in infancy? The third problem is, why are our kind-concepts so well adapted to forecasting events?

Quine thinks that in the beginning children are equipped with an inherited quality space that enables them to make distinctions. Then he notes that in acquiring words, children make inductions "in a favorable environment." Adult human beings have already made the distinctions, and it is not surprising that children, who have roughly the same mental or cranial equipment as adults, should be born so as to catch on, inducing which sounds are words. More surprising is the fact that kinds picked out by humans should be good for making predictions. The innate ones have perhaps been selected by evolution. As for more sophisticated kinds that have no evident survival value, Quine reflects that we constantly modify the kinds of interest to us, retaining those that have proved useful: "In induction, nothing succeeds like success." Intuitive, inherited kinds— including green—become less and less important, vanishing on the "cosmic" scale.

All of that is sensible, and much of it is wise. I have some reservations, especially about Quine's starting point, an innate all purpose quality space.[41] But now I wish to express a doubt that begins even earlier than that. I question the idea of pure classifying, grouping. When we look at Quine's suggestion of how to investigate the groupings made by children, we can notice a quite profound cultural prejudice. It pervades not only armchair psychology but also much experimental work on language acquisition. Quine has a picture of children being asked to pile things up, of where to put the yellow rag, on top of the yellow ball and the yellow block, or elsewhere. When the piles are right, the child has mastered the kind. Concept acquisition is modelled on acquisitive practices, on accumulation. Why should not a child show its mastery of "yellow" by spreading the yellows around? Why not by sharing the wealth, or by potlatching, rather than making a little pile of its very own? The child learns early that collecting is what is wanted—learns that from family and experimenter.

I don't mean to imply that classification is not something in its own right, and I don't mean to imply that accumulation is peculiar to bourgeois societies and their historico-geographic predecessors. Everyone outside Eden collects necessities against hard times, as squirrels store nuts for winter (but even squirrels don't store all their nuts in one place!). Power is represented almost everywhere by accumulating some kind of material thing. It is nevertheless peculiar that we should think that distinguishing *any* kind of thing is piling it up. How many civilizations have been so obsessed with collecting that they drew figures around the stars to collect them into constellations? For in our picture of classification, the next best thing to heaping up is to draw a circle around, to fence in. I would not press this observation too far. I want only to guard against very deep-seated pictures of what classification has to be. As soon as you think of kind-forming as fencing, you will find it natural to think that generalizing and the forming of expectations is something quite other than, and after, classification. Perhaps "the doctrine of natural kinds"—as it was called by generations of writers—was destined to contain the metaphor of fencing. If we think of classes as fenced in, most of us will at once have a picture of Venn diagrams. And who was the first philosopher to publish the actual phrase, "natural kind"? John Venn.[42]

19 Natural History

There is another, apparently quite unrelated, cause of our thinking of classification on its own, as prior to generalization. It has to do with the species. It is now almost fashionable to say that the biological species are not natural kinds. That denial has two forms. There are the theories originating with Michael Ghiselin, that species are individuals, not kinds—a fortiori, not natural kinds. But even those who think of species as set-like argue that they are not natural kinds.[43] This fashion is, however, quite recent. At least since the Enlightenment, philosophical discussions of what we now call natural kinds have been inextricably connected with natural history and systematics. Many of Locke's most forceful observations were jointly about sorts and species. Whewell and Mill restored the word "kind" to technical philosophy in the few years around 1840, just at the height of debates about right species, right genera, and right families. Historically, natural history and natural kinds have been all too closely connected, and that has fostered a vision of classifying separate from expecting and generalizing. The task of the classifier has been to lay down a scheme of things, a table laid out on a table (to use Michel Foucault's astute observation[44]). By natural history I don't mean any old custom of sorting the species. I mean the specific cultural activity that emerged during the Renaissance and flourished most fully during the last great wave of colonial expansion, exploration, and collection.

It is possible that intrinsically human relationships with plants, animals, and other living things contributed to the concept of natural kinds with essential characteristics. Perhaps an inbred attitude of human beings to respond to ecosystems in which they find themselves leads inexorably to some such conception. So argues Scott Atran, who uses innatist cognitive science to make sense of cross-cultural uniformities of classification.[45] Atran also recounts how natural history, far from confirming some human predilection for purposive natural kinds, systematically led us to attend to classification for its own sake. Inquisitive and acquisitive Westerners tried to accommodate, into their own local scheme of things, the vast variety of living beings found upon the face of the earth.

Plants and fishes, reptiles and birds, but above all insects flowed into the taxonomic centers of Paris or London, Berlin or Washington, too fast to be sorted. Men in the field bemoaned the fact there were not enough classifiers at home to do the work. Natural history, from its Renaissance beginnings to its nineteenth century dominance, strongly reinforced our inclination to distinguish classifying from generalizing. Classification became a practice and indeed a profession in its own right. During the nineteenth century, classification, no matter how much debated for its principles, was confirmed as an autonomous practice. Perhaps this story of natural history is not quite so different from my conjectured roots of Western a priori psychology. Certainly the standard museums vied with each other to have the master accumulation, the collection of collected kinds which serve as the standard for all others, the home of the paradigm specimens against which the whole world of living things would be classified.

20 Extension and Intension

There are distinctions based on practices older than Enlightenment a priori psychology (continued in our day by cognitive science) or natural history (continued in our day by the warring schools of systematics and taxonomy). We have the scholastic distinction of extension and intension. As it is carried into modern times, we have, with Mill, denotation and connotation, where the denotation of a common name is a class. Nowadays the extension of a predicate is equally a class. Or we have Frege's *Sinn* and *Bedeutung*. The *Bedeutung* of a proper name is an individual; the *Bedeutung* of a common noun is a class.

One version of the great battle, between nominalists and realists, is this. Realism: Intensions (*Sinnen,* meanings) are given, and they enable us to pick out classes of individuals. Nominalism: Only extensions are given, and they are no more than the individuals of which they are comprised. That is a caricature of a central issue in Western metaphysics. Insofar as it has merit, it displays the autonomy of questions about classification as opposed to generalization. So long as we worry which comes first, intension or extension, we shall think of classification as autonomous, as something that must be in place before there is projection.

It is very striking how those of a more or less nominalist persuasion would like extensions to be *there*. And of course the individuals are there, but we would like the fences to be there too, without our having to invoke intensions to draw the fences. I quoted Shoemaker above, "whatever it is that endows particular words with the extensions they have (and about this [Goodman] says virtually nothing)." But suppose *nothing* endows words with their extensions?

Shoemaker suggests that the endowment comes from "lawlike, or causal, truths." That was certainly the idea of Hilary Putnam's famous paper, "The Meaning of 'Meaning'." Meaning was a sort of vector that starts pretty much like a dictionary definition: syntactic marker, semantic marker, stereotype. It ends not just with a list of examples or a picture, such as one finds in illustrated dictionaries, but with the "extension" of the term. But of course we can't say what the extension is, so we are left with what I have elsewhere called "dots of extension."[46] That is, some examples of the kind, followed by dot dot dot (carry on). In that theory, which Putnam seems to have jettisoned, nature and its laws did the carrying on. For if we did succeed in referring to a natural kind, that kind would be constituted by a set of laws about things of that kind. This could not be a complete explication of Shoemaker's suggestion, for most of the names for kinds of things do not name what we might, following Quine, call the cosmic kinds, the real natural law-governed kinds of the theory of Putnam or Kripke. Most kinds that we distinguish, such as head and foot, wind and mountain, sand

and sea, vegetable and mineral, or flesh, blood, and bone, are what I call mundane kinds.[47] There are no Putnamian laws of nature that circumscribe these highly relevant kinds. Locke's famous assault on essence comes to this: for all we know, all the kinds that we distinguish are mundane kinds.

Shoemaker speaks of words being "endowed" with extensions. Putnam may provide an explication of the endowment of real natural kind terms, that is, those terms that really do denote (cosmic) natural kinds. Such talk invites an ironist's picture. There is this extension, this accumulation of goods, piled up, fenced in, with which the word is endowed. The theories of Kripke and Putnam further ritualize this relation. We owe a great debt to their theories, especially to Putnam's having used his to demolish the idea that when a theory changes, the technical terms of the theory necessarily change meaning. (The "experimental realism" of my *Representing and Intervening* does not require their approach, but that kind of realism does take for granted the way that their work liberated readers from an older account of the meaning of theoretical terms.) Nevertheless, their curious emphasis on certain rites should be noticed. Kripke speaks of *baptism* in connection with names of individuals. Names of natural kinds are rigid designators too, and perhaps the ritual of baptism is extended to kinds. If a word does in fact refer to a real natural kind, then nature itself puts items into that kind. Nature has its extensions. We may from time to time be fortunate enough to discern a kind sufficiently well to have given it a name, to have baptized it. That is how a word can become endowed with an extension.

The endowment is there, nature's gift, and a rite confirmed in practice hooks up the word and the gift. Perhaps the baptism metaphor was not intended for names of kinds, but Putnam speaks of *dubbing*. I dub thee Sir Green? The green knight to the dark tower came. We should escape this dark tower altogether. I of course do not know what Wittgenstein meant when he said, don't ask for the meaning (*Bedeutung*), ask for the use, but we can certainly apply that maxim here. Don't ask what endows extensions. If we like, we can use Kripke's turn of phrase. There is no fact of the matter, about what the extension of "green" is—that is, no fact that can be stated without using the word "green" itself. We can say things like "green" means green. But that is not because the intension, green, can be used to say what "green" means. Shoemaker notes that Goodman says "virtually nothing" about what endows words with the extensions they have. Goodman was right. There is nothing to say. As the first public linguist, Georg Friedrich Hamann, put it in 1784, our words have "no other credentials than tradition and usage."[48]

One of the reasons we so gladly separate classification and generalization is that we think there is some nontautologous, statable, fact of the matter about how words get their extensions. Goodman explicitly demolished one attempt to state such a fact—that things are of a kind and in a class *because* they resemble each other. They do resemble each other, but that is not *why* they are of a kind. That is a particular and well-known plank in his philosophy. Here I have been articulating a feature shared by many of his planks, and which is displayed in his new riddle of induction. Classification and generalization must be rejoined. To use a name for any kind is to be willing to make generalizations and form expectations about individuals of that kind. To use a common noun to classify is to use it, and to use it is to be willing to project it.[49]

University of Toronto

NOTES

1. Nelson Goodman, *Fact, Fiction and Forecast* (1954), chapters 3 and 4. Page references are to the 4th edition, Cambridge, Mass.: Harvard University Press, 1983, henceforth *FFF*.

2. *Ways of Worldmaking* (Indianapolis: Hackett, 1978), 138. Henceforth *WW*.

3. Ian Hacking, *Logic of Statistical Inference* (Cambridge: Cambridge University Press, 1965), 41.

4. David Hull, "Biological Species: An Inductivist's Nightmare," in *How Classification Works: Nelson Goodman among the Social Sciences,* Mary Douglas and David Hull, eds. (Edinburgh: Edinburgh University Press, 1992), 42–68.

5. F. M. Ackroyd, "A Practical Example of Grue," *British Journal for the Philosophy of Science 42* (1991), 535–539.

6. *WW,* 128.

7. One of my own is "World-Making by Kind-Making: Child Abuse as an Example" in Douglas and Hull, *How Classification Works,* 180–238, and "The Making and Molding of Child Abuse," *Critical Inquiry 17* (1991), 253–288.

8. Bertrand Russell, *The Problems of Philosophy* (Oxford: Oxford University Press, 1912), ch. vi.

9. J. S. Mill, *A System of Logic* (1843), III. 111.2, at the end of the section called "The Question of Induction Stated," *The Collected Works of John Stuart Mill,* J. M. Robson, ed. (Toronto: University of Toronto Press, 1973), 7, 314.

10. "Natural Kinds," in *Ontological Relativity and Other Essays* (New York: Columbia University Press, 1969), 114–38, on p. 118.

11. See Ian Hacking, "On Kripke's and Goodman's Uses of 'Grue'," *Philosophy 68* (1993) 269–295.

12. Nelson Goodman and Catherine Z. Elgin, *Reconceptions in Philosophy and Other Arts and Sciences* (Indianapolis: Hackett, 1988), 14.

13. First given wide currency in S. F. Barker and P. Achinstein, "On the New Riddle of Induction," *Philosophical Review 69* (1960), 511–522.

14. Paul Feyerabend, "A Note on Two 'Problems' of Induction," *British Journal for the Philosophy of Science 19* (1968), 251–253.

15. Hilary Putnam, "Foreword to the Fourth Edition," *FFF*, vii.

16. *FFF*, 87.

17. *FFF*, 92.

18. *FFF*, 94.

19. Donald Davidson, "Emeroses by Other Names," *Journal of Philosophy 63* (1966), 778–80. Goodman, *Problems and Projects* (Indianapolis and New York: Bobbs-Merrill, 1972), 410f.

20. *FFF*, 64.

21. *Reconceptions in Philosophy*, 15.

22. "Ramifications of 'Grue'." *British Journal for the Philosophy of Science 20* (1969), 13–25.

23. Shoemaker, "On Projecting the Unprojectible," *Philosophical Review 84* (1975), 178–219, on p. 185.

24. Judith Jarvis Thomson, "Grue," *Journal of Philosophy 63* (1966), 289–309.

25. *Problems and Projects*, 409.

26. Shoemaker, "On Projecting the Unprojectible," 218.

27. Richard Grandy, "Reference, Meaning and Belief," *Journal of Philosophy 70* (1973), 443.

28. In "On Kripke's and Goodman's Uses of 'Grue'."

29. " 'Style' for Historians and Philosophers," *Studies in History and Philosophy of Science 23* (1992), 1–20.

30. *Metaphysics as a Guide to Morals* (London: Chatto & Windus, 1992), 42–43.

31. A predicate is heterological if it does not truly apply to itself. Kurt Grelling and Leonard Nelson, "Bemerkungen über den Paradoxien von Russell und Burali-Forti," *Abhandlungen der Fries'schen Schule N.S. 2* (1908), 301–334.

32. For my version of his work in progress, as of April 1990, see "Working in a New World: The Taxonomic Solution," in Paul Horwich, ed., *World Changes: Thomas Kuhn and the Nature of Science* (Cambridge, Mass.: MIT Press, 1993), 275–310. For some indication of Kuhn's developing views on the topic, and a statement of how my version is not now his, see his "Reflections on the Occasion," *Ibid.*

33. *The Idea of a Social Science and its Relation to Philosophy* (London: Routledge & Kegan Paul, 1958).

34. *Reason, Truth and History* (Cambridge: Cambridge University Press), 1981.

35. *Ibid.*, 114.

36. "Putnam on Incommensurability," in *Farewell to Reason* (London: Verso, 1987), 265–272.

37. See my " 'Style' for Historians and Philosophers."

38. *The Fortunes of Inquiry* (Oxford: Clarendon Press, 1986) passes from the

calibration of instruments to the calibration of ways of assessing theories, an idea that is further generalized in *The Scenes of Inquiry* (Oxford: Clarendon Press, 1991).

39. *How Experiments End* (Chicago: Chicago University Press, 1987).

40. *A Study of Qualities* (Garland Publishing, New York, 1990)

41. See my "Natural Kinds," *Perspectives on Quine,* R. Gibson, ed. (Blackwell, Oxford, 1989), 129–42.

42. In the first edition of *The Logic of Chance* (London: Macmillan, 1866). The more readily available 2nd edition is completely rewritten.

43. For example, John Dupré, "Natural Kinds and Biological Taxa," *Philosophical Review 90* (1981), 66–90. The best statement of the position that species are to the contrary (very real) natural kinds is to be found in Richard Boyd's theory of homeostatic cluster kinds.

44. *The Order of Things.* The collector lays out the species in his cabinet, on a plane surface, and arranges them on that surface according to the table of the species.

45. *Cognitive Foundations of Natural History: Towards an Anthropology of Science* (Cambridge: Cambridge University Press, 1990).

46. Ian Hacking, *Representing and Intervening* (Cambridge: Cambridge University Press, 1983), 80.

47. See my "Working in a New World."

48. See Ian Hacking, "How, Why, When and Where did Language go Public?" *Common Knowledge 1* (1992), no. 2, 89.

49. I am grateful to Rupert Read for his long and careful criticism of previous versions of this essay. It resulted in countless clarifications and improvements.

No Model, No Inference: A Bayesian Primer on the Grue Problem[1]

Elliott Sober

1. Introduction

Stripped to its bare quintessence, the grue problem reduces to two issues. The first concerns the relationship between *generalizations* and their *instances*. If I've observed a number of emeralds before now and have found each to be green, what epistemic difference is there between the following two generalizations?

> (ALLGREEN) All emeralds are green.
> (ALLGRUE) All emeralds are grue.[2]

The second problem concerns the relationship between *predictions* and their *precedents*. If I've observed a number of emeralds before now and have found each to be green, what epistemic difference is there between the following two predictions?

> (NEXTGREEN) The next emerald I examine will be green.
> (NEXTGRUE) The next emerald I examine will be grue.

The phrase "epistemic difference" is vague and requires clarification. However it is understood, it is meant to rule out some obvious differences between the two hypotheses. The GREEN hypotheses are stated in a familiar vocabulary, whereas the GRUE hypotheses make use of a made-up word. Unless one is prepared to regard this difference between the hypotheses as *epistemically* relevant—as somehow relevant to what we ought to believe—this obvious difference makes no difference as far as the grue problem is concerned.[3] Beyond this, it falls to any solution of the problem to make the concept of epistemic difference precise.

I have tried to state a minimum formulation of the grue problem because the *problem* is too often conflated with some of the ideas that figured in

Goodman's proposed *solution.* Goodman held that ALLGREEN is confirmed by its instances, whereas ALLGRUE is not. This goes beyond my minimal formulation of the problem, in that instance confirmation is just one concept of epistemic relevance. We should not assume at the outset that this is where the relevant difference between the GREEN and GRUE hypotheses is to be found. Goodman also asserted that the two problems I've sketched bear an important connection to each other; he maintained that ALLGREEN is confirmed by its instances only if NEXTGREEN is too. Again, the grue problem should not be burdened with this assumption; rather, this is a thesis that needs to be argued for explicitly. And finally, Goodman claimed that these evidential issues bear an important connection to the problem of distinguishing lawlike from accidental generalizations. Goodman believed that lawlike generalizations (like ALLGREEN) are confirmed by their instances, whereas accidental generalizations (like ALLGRUE) are not.[4] Having separated these Goodmanian theses from the problem they are meant to address, I will argue that each is incorrect and can be seen to be so by giving the grue problem a probabilistic representation.

During the time that Goodman wrote about the grue problem, philosophers often focused on the problem of *qualitative confirmation.* Just as Goodman had his emeralds, Hempel (1965) had his ravens. Hempel's problem was not to measure *the degree of confirmation* that observing red shoes provides for the generalization "all ravens are black." Rather, he wanted to say whether such observations provide any confirmation at all. Now, quite apart from the merits of what Goodman and Hempel said about emeralds and ravens, it seems undeniable that a theory of qualitative confirmation should be embeddable in a theory of *quantitative* confirmation. We need the notion of *degree of confirmation,* not just the dichotomous division of *confirmed* versus *not confirmed.* The scientific community employs probability concepts in its understanding of this quantitative notion. So a natural place to begin discussion of the grue problem is with the concept of probability.

2. Bayesianism—The Basics

Those who agree that probability is a useful concept for explicating epistemic concepts nonetheless disagree about how it should be deployed. Bayesianism constitutes an influential school in this debate, but it is not the only game in town.[5] I'll mention later on a standard criticism of Bayesianism. But for now, Bayesianism is a perfectly sensible place to begin. For many inference problems, the Bayesian solution is not at all controversial, in that it happens to coincide with the verdicts, if not the exact reasoning, of other approaches. In addition, the broad lessons I will draw from my Bayesian analysis are *robust;* they are very much in harmony with the conclusions that would be generated by non-Bayesian positions.

Bayesians think that observations confer probabilities on hypotheses and that the mathematical idea of probability is the right way to measure the epistemic property of plausibility. Bayes's theorem describes how the *posterior probability* of hypothesis H—the probability it has in the light of the observation O—is a function of three other quantities:

$$P(H/O) = P(O/H)P(H)/P(O).$$

$P(O/H)$ is called the likelihood of H. It describes the probability that the hypothesis H confers on the observations. Don't confuse $P(O/H)$ with $P(H/O)$; the likelihood of H and the probability of H are different. $P(H)$ is termed the *prior* probability of H, meaning the probability the hypothesis has *before* the observation O is made.

The grue problem, whether it is understood in terms of generalizations or in terms of predictions, involves *comparing* two hypotheses in the light of a body of observations. By bringing together two applications of Bayes's theorem, we can derive a comparative principle of the kind required:

(S) $P(H_1/O) > P(H_2/O)$ if and only if $P(O/H_1)P(H_1) >$ $P(O/H_2)P(H_2)$.

If H_1 is to have a higher posterior probability than H_2, this must be because H_1 has the higher likelihood or the higher prior probability (or both). So if we are to find a difference between the GREEN and the GRUE hypotheses in this Bayesian format, we know that there are exactly two places to look.

Principle (S) is a *synchronic* principle. It does not describe how much *change* the observation O engenders in the probabilities of the hypotheses; it simply describes what it takes for the one to have a higher value than the other, after the observations are obtained. However, the *diachronic* issue is also worth considering. If $P(H/O)$ represents the plausibility that H has *after* O is found to be true, and $P(H)$ is the plausibility that H possesses *before* that event, then it is natural to describe the *change* in plausibility that H experiences across this change as follows:

O confirms H if and only if $P(H/O) > P(H)$.
O disconfirms H if and only if $P(H/O) < P(H)$.

Notice that O can confirm H even though $P(H/O)$ is quite low; merely let $P(H) = 0.0000001$ and $P(H/O) = 0.01$. And O can disconfirm H even though H remains quite probable in the light of O; merely let $P(H) = 0.95$ and $P(H/O) = 0.94$.

Two applications of these definitions yield the following diachronic principle:

(D) O confirms H_1 more than O confirms H_2 if and only if $P(H_1/O) - P(H_1) > P(H_2/O) - P(H_2)$.

I take the *difference* between the posterior and prior probabilities, rather than the *ratio* between them, to represent degree of confirmation. Ellery Eells has suggested to me the following argument for this choice. Suppose that

$$P(H_2/O) = 0.9 \qquad\qquad P(H_1) = 0.1$$

and that

$$P(H_2/O) = 0.001 \qquad\qquad P(H_2) = 0.0001.$$

If degree of confirmation is measured by taking differences, H_1 is confirmed by O more than H_2 is. But if degree of confirmation is measured by the ratio of posterior to prior, the reverse is true. Surely a jump from 0.1 to 0.9 reflects a larger change in plausibility than a jump from 0.0001 to 0.001. In any event the main conclusions I will argue for in what follows do not turn on my choice of measure.

Although Goodman formulated his puzzle as one about *confirmation*, there is no reason to restrict our attention to the diachronic issue. We want to know if observing green emeralds raises the probabilities of the GREEN hypotheses more than such observations raise the probabilities of the GRUE hypotheses. But we also would like to know whether the GREEN hypotheses are more probable, in the light of these observations, than the GRUE hypotheses are. So there are four cases to consider—the generalization and the prediction problems each need to be considered both diachronically and synchronically.

Even though the ideal of minimalism has guided me in my description of the grue problem, I have to admit that I introduced a substantive choice in my formulation. This involves the way I have described the evidence. I imagine that our evidence was obtained by examining some emeralds and finding out what color they exhibit. This search strategy differs from that of sampling the universe at random and noting whether the things we come up with are emeralds and what their colors are. With fairly modest assumptions, it turns out that sampling the emeralds is a better strategy than sampling the world at random (if the goal is to test either of the two generalizations described above).[6] I assume in what follows that this is how our evidence was obtained. But once again, many of the broad lessons I will draw from my analysis do not turn on the details of this assumption.

3. Generalization—The Diachronic Question

Let's begin with a simple point about Bayesianism. If *H* deductively entails *O* and if *O* was not certain to be true before the observation was made, then *O* confirms *H*. This is true because Bayes's theorem can be rewritten as follows:

$$P(H/O)/P(H) = P(O/H)/P(O).$$

O confirms *H* precisely when the left-hand side is greater than 1, which must be so, if $P(O/H) = 1$ and $P(O) < 1$.

What does this mean about the grue problem? Here we must tread carefully. Let us begin with the formulation that focuses on generalizations. Notice that ALLGREEN and ALLGRUE both deductively imply that the emeralds examined before now are green.[7] If it was not a certainty beforehand that those emeralds should have turned out to be green, we must conclude that both hypotheses are confirmed by the past observations. Where the proposition *E* says that the sampled past emeralds are green, the relevant facts are

$$P(ALLGREEN/E)/P(ALLGREEN) = P(E/ALLGREEN)/P(E) > 1$$

and

$$P(ALLGRUE/E)/P(ALLGRUE) = P(E/ALLGRUE)/P(E) > 1.$$

Both generalizations are confirmed by their instances if this simply means that each has its probability increased by the past observations.

But now let us consider the degree of confirmation that each generalization experiences. I begin by noting that

$$P(ALLGREEN/E) - P(ALLGREEN) > P(ALLGRUE/E) - P(ALLGRUE)$$

if and only if

$$P(E/ALLGREEN)P(ALLGREEN)/P(E) - P(ALLGREEN) > P(E/ALLGRUE)P(ALLGRUE)/P(E) - P(ALLGRUE).$$

This latter inequality is true precisely when

$$P(ALLGREEN)(1/P(E) - 1) > P(ALLGRUE)(1/P(E) - 1),$$

which simplifies to P(ALLGREEN) > P(ALLGRUE), if $P(E) < 1$. In other words, if we assume that the observations were not certain beforehand and that each generalization implies the observations, then ALLGREEN is confirmed more than ALLGRUE if and only if the former has the higher prior probability.

What would make it plausible to assign ALLGREEN the higher prior probability? Rather than addressing that question here, I postpone it until the next section.

4. Generalization—The Synchronic Question

As noted before, if we are sampling from the population of emeralds, then the generalizations ALLGREEN and ALLGRUE each deductively entail that the items sampled before now were green. Since the two hypotheses both have likelihoods of unity, principle (S) entails that a difference in posterior probability must be due entirely to a difference in prior:

If $P(O/H_1) = P(O/H_2)$, then $P(H_1/O) > P(H_2/O)$ if and only if $P(H_1) > P(H_2)$.

So ALLGREEN is more probable than ALLGRUE, given the evidence E, precisely when the former hypothesis has the higher prior.

What could justify the belief that ALLGREEN has a higher prior probability than ALLGRUE? It is at this point in the story that I must confess my anti-Bayesian sympathies. If prior probabilities are to be objective, I do not see how they can be assigned a priori. And if they are merely subjective—simply indicating the degree of belief of some agent—then I don't see that they have any epistemic relevance to this problem. One does not show that ALLGREEN is more plausible than ALLGRUE simply by giving voice to the autobiographical remark that one finds the former more plausible a priori than the latter.

Furthermore, I do not see how these hypotheses can have (objective) probabilities unless they describe possible outcomes of a chance process (Edwards 1972). I do not know what it means to say that Newton's law of gravitation or Darwin's theory of evolution has an objective probability. They were not made true by God's reaching into an urn that contained slips of paper on which candidate laws were inscribed. So if we can't specify a chance process that produces a coloration pattern for emeralds, I don't know what it means to assign ALLGREEN and ALLGRUE objective prior probabilities.

Having said that I find both objective and subjective Bayesianism unattractive as general doctrines, I do not think we must concede that the problems at hand are insoluble. If we find ALLGREEN more plausible than ALLGRUE, this is because we hold various substantive, if hard to articulate, theories about the world. Perhaps we expect emeralds to be alike in color because we think that they are alike in physical structure, and we believe that color supervenes on physical structure. Of course, these convictions involve assumptions about the future. But there is no escaping such commitments; based solely on our experience of the past, the generalizations cannot be shown to differ in their probabilities.

5. Prediction—The Diachronic Question

Let us now shift from the issue of generalization to the issue of prediction. NEXTGREEN does *not* deductively imply that the emeralds examined before now have been green, and neither does NEXTGRUE. So the arguments that solve the problems associated with the generalizations do not apply to the problems about prediction. Is there some other argument that forces the same conclusion? Or are generalizations and predictions not as tightly coupled epistemologically as Goodman and many others have thought?

To answer this question, let us leave the strange and wonderful world of grue behind for a moment, and consider a rather more mundane inductive problem. Imagine an urn that is filled with a thousand balls by drawing from a source whose composition is known. Suppose the source contains 50 percent red balls and 50 percent green balls. By random sampling from the source, the urn is filled with a thousand balls. The problem is to sample from the urn (with replacement) and to draw two inferences based on the sample obtained. The first inference is to be a generalization concerning the composition of the whole urn. The second is to be a prediction concerning the color of balls that will be sampled in the future.

Since we know that the urn was composed by draws from the source, we can assign prior probabilities to each of the possible compositions, from 1000 red and 0 green to 0 red and 1000 green. When we sample from the urn, we can use Bayes's theorem to compute the posterior probability of the various hypotheses about the urn's composition. Suppose I take 250 draws from the urn and find that each ball I sample is green. These observations make the hypothesis that all the balls in the urn are green more probable than it was initially. Just as was true for ALLGREEN and ALL-GRUE, the generalization is confirmed when a prediction deduced from the generalization comes true, provided that the prediction was not certain beforehand.

But now let us consider the problem of predicting what the next ball will be like, given information about the character of the sample. In this case, the probability that the next ball will be green is 0.5, regardless of what the previously sampled balls were like. Observing 250 green balls does *not* raise the probability that the next ball drawn from the urn will be green, even though the observations do raise the probability that all the balls are green. How can we make sense of the fact that generalization and prediction part ways in this example?

We can grasp the general point by considering the simple case in which we make just two draws (with replacement) from the urn. There now are four equiprobable sequences of green (*G*) and red (*R*) draws—*GG, GR, RG,* and *RR*. If the first ball sampled is green, then the probability of *GG* increases from 0.25 to 0.5. However, after this first observation, the probability that the second draw will be green is still 0.5, just as it was before any ball was drawn. I conclude that confirming a generalization and confirming a claim about the next instance are not always as intimately connected as Goodman suggests.

This example illustrates another defect in what Goodman said about the grue problem. He claimed that a generalization is confirmable by its instances only if it is lawlike. This latter concept, whatever else it might mean, entails that the generalization "supports" a counterfactual. If "All *X*s are *Y*s" is lawlike, then if it is true, so is the statement "If *a* were an *X*, then *a* would be a *Y*." In the example just given, the generalization "All balls in the urn are green" is confirmed by its instances. Yet knowledge of the process whereby the contents of the urn were assembled guarantees that this generalization, if true, is only accidentally so. It is a mere fluke if all the balls in the urn happen to be green. There is nothing about being a ball in this urn that makes something green, nor is it true that a ball would not have been put into the urn unless it were green. "If this tennis ball were in the urn, then it would be green" is as false as any counterfactual can get.[8]

When questions of lawlikeness are considered, it makes all the difference in the world whether the mechanism whereby the population is assembled is known in advance or is inferred in the process of sampling. If I sample balls from the urn and find that all are green, and I have no idea how the urn was formed, the suspicion naturally arises that the homogeneous character of my sample is not an accident. However, the fact that nomological connections are reasonably suspected in such cases does not show that lawlikeness is a presupposition of instance confirmation. Simply replace prior ignorance of process with a substantive process assumption (of the kind just sketched for the urn problem), and the composition of a population known to be fortuitously assembled can be confirmed by random sampling.[9]

The urn example establishes that confirming a generalization does not require that one confirm a prediction about the next instance. Sampling from the population of emeralds, it is inevitable (given the modest assumption that it was not a certainty that the sampled emeralds would turn out to be green) that observing green emeralds before now should raise the probability that all emeralds are green (ditto for grue). But no such inevitability attaches to the prediction that the next emerald examined will be green (or grue). Having separated these two problems, let us now explore the prediction problem on its own.

We have observed emeralds before now and found each to be green. What does it take for that body of observation (E) to raise the probability that the next emerald I examine will be green? A useful representation of when this is true is provided by the following:

P(NEXTGREEN/E) > P(NEXTGREEN) if and only if
P(NEXTGREEN & E) > P(NEXTGREEN)P(E).

The right-hand side of this biconditional says that the *covariance* of NEXTGREEN and E is positive. The covariance of A and B is defined as Cov(A, B) = P(A&B) − P(A)P(B). When A and B are independent of each other, Cov(A,B) = 0. Positive covariance means positive association.

So the GREEN prediction is confirmed by the evidence only if the prediction and the evidence exhibit positive covariance. The 2 × 2 table below represents this constraint on the confirmation of NEXTGREEN.

In Table 1, P(E) = p and P(NEXTGREEN) = q. A positive covariance means that $c > 0$.

As noted earlier in connection with the urn example, it is not inevitable that past precedents should confirm a prediction. The information presented in that example concerning how the urn was filled made all the difference. I suggest that a similar answer be given in connection with this problem about NEXTGREEN. If NEXTGREEN is confirmed by E, this is because some sort of process induced a correlation (a positive covariance)

		(q) NEXTGREEN	($1-q$) NOT-NEXTGREEN
(p)	E	$pq + c$	$p(1-q) - c$
($1-p$)	NOT-E	$(1-p)\,q - c$	$(1-p)(1-q) + c$

Table 1

between past and future emeralds with respect to their color.

What sort of process might this be? In this respect Goodman's example is a bit unfortunate, since emeralds, I gather, are standardly said to be green *by definition*. But ignoring this wrinkle in Goodman's example, a natural suggestion is that the relevant process assumption is that emeralds had their color determined *as a group*. If emeralds share the same microstructure, and if microstructure determines color, then one has the basis for expecting, before even one emerald is examined, that emeralds will be alike in color.

But suppose that no such process assumption is available. If we know nothing about the process by which emeralds receive their colors (or grulers), how are we to decide whether past precedents confirm a prediction? The answer, I think, is that *we cannot*. As Hume argued, a description of the past, in and of itself, offers no guidance whatever as to what the future will be like. Here I don't mean just that we can't *deduce* what the future will be like from a description that is solely about the past. The Humean point is more profound: we can't even infer what the future will *probably* be like, based solely on a description of the past. Nor can we say whether past precedents confirm a prediction about the future unless we are willing to make assumptions concerning how past and future are related (Sober 1988b).

I so far have explored what it takes for the prediction NEXTGREEN to be confirmed by the observation *E*. What can be said of the relationship of NEXTGRUE to the same observation? If "grue" just meant *green before or not green after*, then we could conclude that NEXTGREEN is confirmed just in case NEXTGRUE is disconfirmed. But the usual definitions of "grue" do not permit this simple conclusion to be drawn. It is possible for *E* to confirm both NEXTGREEN *and* NEXTGRUE. No first principle rules out the assumption that the past observations raise the probability of both predictions (even though they are incompatible with each other).

Nonetheless, we have obtained a *necessary* (but not a sufficient) condition for NEXTGREEN to be confirmed more than NEXTGRUE; for this to be so, NEXTGREEN must be confirmed, which requires that $c > 0$. And if we assume that the next emerald will be either green or blue, then $c > 0$ is both necessary and sufficient for NEXTGREEN to be confirmed and NEXTGRUE to be disconfirmed.

6. Prediction—The Synchronic Question

Given that the emeralds observed before now have all been green, is it more probable that the next emerald will be green or that it will be grue? If we reformulate this question a little, we can use the 2×2 table described before to identify an assumption on which this difference in probabilities depends:

P(NEXTGREEN/E) > P(NOT-NEXTGREEN/E)
if and only if $[pq + c]/p > [p(1 - q) - c]/p$
if and only if $c > p(1 - 2q)/2$.

Here we have shifted the problem to asking whether past observations make it more probable that the next emerald will be green or that it will be *not* green. Since the probability of NOT-NEXTGREEN cannot be less than the probability of NEXTGRUE, the biconditional describes a necessary condition for P(NEXTGREEN/E) > P(NEXTGRUE/E). And as before, if we assume that the next emerald will either be green or blue, then the condition cited is both necessary and sufficient.

I noted in connection with the diachronic prediction problem that we can't assume *a priori* that $c > 0$. The point of interest here is that this assumption does not *suffice* for the GREEN prediction to be more probable than the GRUE prediction. Here we see a difference between the synchronic and the diachronic versions of the prediction problem.

7. Summary

Let's take stock. Inferring the color of the next emerald and inferring what all emeralds are like are different inference problems. Prediction and generalization present different issues. Likewise how much an observation boosts the probability of a hypothesis is a different question from how high that probability actually becomes. The diachronic and synchronic issues need to be separated. The results obtained from applying this pair of dichotomies to the grue problem are summarized in Table 2. In each case, we can assert that an epistemic asymmetry obtains between the GREEN and the GRUE hypothesis only if we are prepared to make a substantive assumption about the way the world is. What is more, the assumptions change as we shift from problem to problem.

8. Concluding Comments

With these results in hand, it is worth stepping back for a moment to reflect on the nature of the grue problem and on what kind of solution we can hope to attain.

Once again, a comparison with Hempel's raven problem is instructive. In a paper of breathtaking brevity, Good (1967) showed that observing a black raven (sampled at random from the world at large) can actually *dis*confirm the generalization that all ravens are black, provided one adopts a few simple (if implausible) empirical assumptions about the inference problem. Hempel (1968) replied that Good's argument misconstrued

Diachronic   Synchronic

	Diachronic	Synchronic
Generalization	P(ALLGREEN/E) − P(ALLGREEN) > P(ALLGRUE/E) − P(ALLGRUE) if and only if P(ALLGREEN) > P(ALLGRUE) and P(E) < 1.	P(ALLGREEN/E) > P(ALLGRUE/E) if and only if P(ALLGREEN) > P(ALLGRUE).
Prediction	If the next emerald will be either green or blue, then P(NEXTGREEN/E) − P(NEXTGREEN) > P(NEXTGRUE/E) − P(NEXTGRUE) if and only if $c > 0$.	If the next emerald will be either green or blue, then P(NEXTGREEN/E) > P(NEXTGRUE/E) if and only if $c > p(1 − 2q)/2$.

Table 2

the problem that he, Hempel, had wanted to pose. Hempel (1965) had indicated that he was interested in exploring the relationship of observation to hypothesis within a "theoretically barren" background context. Assuming nothing at all about the world, the question is whether black ravens and red shoes both confirm the generalization that all ravens are black.

Good took the view, and so do I, that almost nothing can be said about confirmation in a background context of this sort. In all four of the problems surveyed above, an epistemic asymmetry between the GREEN hypothesis and the GRUE hypothesis is possible. But notice what the asymmetries in these cases depend upon: for GREEN to be more probable than GRUE, or for GREEN to receive a greater boost in probability than GRUE does, *empirical assumptions must be made that go beyond the testimony of past observation.* It isn't reason alone (or "the scientific method") that induces an asymmetry here, but substantive assumptions about the way the world is.

I therefore think it is misleading, at best, to claim that the GREEN hypothesis is preferable to the GRUE hypothesis on the ground that the former is "simpler." This appeal to simplicity gives the impression that the simplicity of a hypothesis is a reason to think that it is true. Although many philosophers believe that appeal to such "extra-empirical" virtues is part of what it means to do science, I do not. The austere framework of Bayesianism, and of other probabilistic epistemologies, accords no irreducible role to simplicity, unification, non-*ad hocness,* and so on.[10] What this means is that simplicity never provides an irreducible justification of any hypothesis. To be sure, it is sometimes true that the simpler theory is more probable, or more likely, or more strongly confirmed by a body of data; however, the simpler theory never has these properties *because* it is simpler (Sober 1988b, 1990). In the present context, it does no harm to admit that the GREEN hypothesis is "simpler" than the GRUE hypothesis. But if this difference is to count as epistemically relevant, it will be necessary to appeal to empirical matters of fact of the sort described in the above table. Once these empirical assumptions are made explicit, any further mention of simplicity will be quite unnecessary.

For me, the fundamental lesson of the grue problem is that empirical assumptions that go beyond the content of past observations are needed to establish an epistemic asymmetry between GREEN and GRUE. Whereas philosophers often formulate this point by appealing to the need for "auxiliary assumptions," scientists of a statistical bent often stress the importance of specifying a "model" of the relation of data to the various hypotheses under test. Without assumptions of this sort, the data cannot be interpreted. The slogan for scientists is: *NO MODEL, NO INFERENCE.* This entirely familiar point from the practice of science should not be forgotten when we investigate the theory of that practice.

If this is the right lesson to draw from the grue problem, we can reach an assessment of the solution to the problem that Goodman proposed—his theory of entrenchment. A predicate becomes entrenched when people use it to formulate predictions and generalizations. It has always been a mystery to me why the fact that people use a predicate should have any epistemic relevance. Why should our use of a predicate be evidence that this or that hypothesis is true? This naive question is sometimes answered with the response that the "new" riddle of induction involves describing our inductive practices, not trying to justify them. I have my doubts about this descriptive claim as well. Is it really so obvious that human inference makers think a hypothesis with unentrenched predicates is less plausible than a hypothesis with entrenched predicates, all else being equal? But this reply to one side, I hope it is clear why Goodman's theory is the wrong *kind* of theory, at least if one is interested in normative questions of evidence and confirmation. To describe how well entrenched a predicate *now* is involves describing *past* events only. No such description can suffice to establish an epistemic asymmetry between a GREEN hypothesis and a GRUE hypothesis.

I suspect that many philosophers who may have been skeptical of the details of Goodman's entrenchment theory nonetheless thought that Goodman was at least looking for the right *kind* of asymmetry; they implicitly assumed that a solution to the problem could be found in some fact established solely by past experience and a priori reasoning, without recourse to induction itself. To rest an asymmetry between GREEN and GRUE on an assumption about the future was standardly said to "beg the question." But what question are we thereby begging? It is the following ill-formed question: *Which beliefs based just on past experience and on a priori reasoning suffice to show that the GREEN hypothesis is more reasonable than the GRUE hypothesis?* To me, this question resembles another: *Which types of butter are capable of cutting a diamond?*

University of Wisconsin, Madison

NOTES

1. I thank Ellery Eells, Malcolm Forster, and Douglas Stalker for helpful comments on an earlier draft of this paper. I also am grateful to the editors of the *Philosophical Review* for granting me permission to reprint here a few paragraphs from my article (Sober 1988a).

2. Since the year 2000 is fast approaching, I will define "grue" so that the grue problem retains its timeless immediacy: An object is said to be grue at a given time precisely when it is either green and the time is before now, or it is blue and the time is not before now. As has become somewhat customary, I delete the concept of "being examined" from Goodman's original definition.

3. Vocabulary differences between the two hypotheses cannot make any epistemic difference, if a *principle of logical equivalence* is correct. As Goodman pointed out in his exchange with Carnap, once "bleen" is defined in tandem with grue (bleen = blue before or green after), the GRUE hypotheses can be reformulated in familiar vocabulary and the GREEN hypotheses can be expressed by using the made-up words.

4. Here is a passage from Goodman (1965, 73) in which these three theses are asserted:

> That a given piece of copper conducts electricity increases the credibility of statements asserting that other pieces of copper conduct electricity, and thus confirms the hypothesis that all copper conducts electricity. But the fact that a given man now in this room is a third son does not increase the credibility of statements asserting that other men now in this room are third sons, and so does not confirm the hypothesis that all men now in this room are third sons . . . The difference is that in the former case the hypothesis is a *lawlike* statement; while in the latter case, the hypothesis is a merely contingent or accidental generality.

Only a statement that is *lawlike*—regardless of its truth or falsity or its scientific importance—is capable of receiving confirmation from an instance of it; accidental statements are not.

5. Two alternatives should be mentioned here. First, there is likelihoodism, according to which hypotheses are evaluated solely in terms of the probabilities they confer on observations (Edwards 1972). Second, there is the approach of Akaike (1973) and his school; see Forster and Sober (forthcoming) for discussion.

6. Discussion of the raven problem from a Bayesian point of view has made it abundantly clear why looking at ravens and seeing whether they are black is a better strategy for testing "All ravens are black" than the strategy of looking at nonblack things and seeing if they are nonravens (or, for that matter, the strategy of looking at objects drawn from the whole universe and seeing if they are consistent with the hypothesis). See, for example, Chihara (1981), Horwich (1982), Eells (1982), Howson and Urbach (1989), and Earman (1992).

7. Of course, ALLGREEN does not deductively imply that an object sampled at random from the whole universe will be both an emerald and green. Recall that I am assuming that the sampling takes place within a restricted universe; it is part of the sampling problem that the population of objects from which the sample is drawn is composed entirely of emeralds. The relevant fact here is that for each object a sampled before now from this population, P(a is green / ALLGREEN & a is an emerald) = P(a is green / ALLGRUE & a is an emerald) = 1.

8. I discuss what other philosophers have said about Goodman's proposed connection between confirmation and lawlikeness in Sober (1988a).

9. Many sciences (e.g., population biology) test generalizations by drawing samples from populations that are known to be fortuitously assembled. This undertaking would be impossible if only lawlike statements could be confirmed by their instances. It is worth remembering that Goodman's proposal was advanced during a period in which philosophers often equated science with physics and physics with the search for physical laws.

10. Of course, one might take this fact to be a *reductio* of such probabilistic epistemologies; one might argue that they are mistaken precisely because they fail to accord an irreducible importance to these "epistemic virtues." An assessment of this suggestion can be developed only by attending closely to the dialectics of theory choice in a variety of scientific controversies.

REFERENCES

Akaike, H. (1973). "Information theory and an extension of the maximum likelihood principle." In B. Petrov and F. Csaki, eds., *Second International Symposium on Information Theory,* Akademiai Kiado, 267–81.

Chihara, C. (1981). "Quine and the confirmational paradoxes." In P. French, H.

Wettstein, and T. Uehling, eds., *Midwest Studies in Philosophy,* vol. 6, University of Minnesota Press, 425–452.

Earman, J. (1992). *Bayes or Bust.* MIT Press.

Edwards, A. (1972). *Likelihood.* Cambridge University Press.

Eells, E. (1982). *Rational Decision and Causality.* Cambridge University Press.

Forster, M. and Sober, E. (forthcoming). "How to tell when simpler, more unified, or less *ad hoc* theories will provide more accurate predictions."

Good, I. (1967). "The white shoe is a red herring." *British Journal for the Philosophy of Science 17,* 322.

Goodman, N. (1965). *Fact, Fiction and Forecast.* Bobbs-Merrill.

Hempel, C. (1965). "Studies in the logic of confirmation." In *Aspects of Scientific Explanation and Other Essays in the Philosophy of Science.* Free Press.

Hempel, C. (1968). "The white shoe—no red herring." *British Journal for the Philosophy of Science 18,* 239–40.

Horwich, P. (1982). *Probability and Evidence.* Cambridge University Press.

Howson, C. and Urbach, P. (1989). *Scientific Reasoning: The Bayesian Approach.* Open Court.

Sober, E. (1988a). "Confirmation and law-likeness." *Philosophical Review 97,* 93–98.

Sober, E. (1988b). *Reconstructing the Past: Parsimony, Evolution, and Inference.* MIT Press.

Sober, E. (1990). "Let's razor Ockham's razor." In D. Knowles, ed., *Explanation and Its Limits.* Cambridge University Press. 73–94.

Bayesian Projectibility

Brian Skyrms

> *Undoubtedly we do make predictions by projecting the patterns of the past into the future, but in selecting the patterns we project from among all those that the past exhibits, we use practical criteria that so far seem to have escaped discovery and formulation.*
>
> Nelson Goodman, "A Query on Confirmation" (1946)

1. Introduction

In 1946 Nelson Goodman raised the problem of the projectibility of hypotheses in a note addressing the confirmation theory of Rudolf Carnap. He later gave a sensational illustration: the hypothesis "All emeralds are grue," which came to be discussed as the Goodman Paradox. The predicate "grue" was so manifestly pathological many were led into thinking that the problem was to find some criterion which would exclude similar pathology from inductive reasoning.

Goodman sees clearly that the problem of projectibility is much more general, and that judgments of projectibility must be central to any adequate theory of confirmation. He believes that a theory of projectibility should be a pragmatic theory, and sketches the beginnings of such a theory in the last chapter of *Fact, Fiction and Forecast*.

I believe that the broad outlines of Goodman's approach to a theory of projectibility are just right. The theory will not attempt to tell one in a vacuum which predicates are projectible. Rather it will explain how present judgments of projectibility should be based on past judgments of projectibility together with the results of past projections. The circularity involved in such a theory is not to be viewed as vicious. The theory can still inform our understanding of projectibility. And a theory with this sort of "virtuous circularity" is really the best that can be expected. However, the implementation of Goodman's program for a theory of projectibility does not seem very far advanced. There is, however, a preexisting pragmatic framework which offers precise tools for addressing the question: the theory of personal probability. How is projectibility represented within this framework? This question leads straight to central concepts of Bayesian statistics.

2. Goodman on Projectibility

Goodman sees the problem of projection as of a piece with the problem of counterfactual conditionals and the related problem of lawlikeness. Counterfactuals—at least the kind that underlie disposition terms in science—are supported by laws. Not every true generalization is a law. Goodman gives "All coins in my pocket on VE day were silver" as an example of an accidentally true generalization. One mark of its accidental nature is that it is not projectible: it would not be well confirmed *via* its instances unless all of them were surveyed. Goodman parses the problem as: (1) A law is a true lawlike statement. (2) "A statement is lawlike if its determination does not depend on any given instance."[2]

In *Fact, Fiction and Forecast* Goodman concocts the "grue" hypothesis to show both the ubiquity of the problem of projectibility, and the hopelessness of syntactical theories of confirmation. The predicate "grue" applies to all things examined before *t* just in case they are green and to all other things just in case they are blue. At time *t* our evidence is that all previously examined emeralds have been green. Then, providing we know what time it is, our evidence is also to the effect that all previously examined emeralds have been grue. We do not take the two hypotheses "All emeralds are green" and "All emeralds are grue" to be equally well confirmed on the evidence, but syntactically the relation between generalization and evidence seems to be the same.[3]

He concludes that by similar tricks a theory which uncritically assumes that any generalization is confirmed by its instances can be made to predict anything. This remark is amplified in a footnote:

> For instance, we shall have equal confirmation, by our present definition, for the prediction that roses subsequently examined will be blue. Let "emerose" apply just to emeralds examined before time *t*, and to roses examined later. Then all emeroses so far examined are grue, and this confirms the hypothesis that all emeroses are grue and hence the prediction that roses subsequently examined will be blue. The problem raised by such antecedents has been little noticed, but is no easier to meet than that raised by similarly perverse consequents.[4]

Donald Davidson used the technique of gerrymandering predicates in both the antecedent and the consequent to show that the lawlikeness or projectibility of a hypothesis is not simply a function of the projectibility of its constituent predicates "taken one by one," but must take into account their relation to one another.[5] An *emerose* is something which is an emerald examined before *t* or a rose not examined before *t*. It is *gred* if green and examined before *t* or red and not examined before *t*. Davidson invites us to consider:

H1: All emeroses are gred

which he takes to be lawlike. Goodman replies that *H1* is not confirmed by its instances[6] in the proper way. Instances of *H1* observed before *t* do not increase the probability of instances of *H1* after *t*: green emeralds do not increase the probability of roses observed after *t* being red. This reply derives from the conception of confirmation set forth in *Fact, Fiction and Forecast:* "Confirmation of a hypothesis occurs only when an instance imparts to the hypothesis some credibility which is conveyed to other instances."[7] Thus, despite the plausibility of Davidson's conclusion, his example does not make his point on Goodman's own terms.

This is not to say that Davidson is wrong, but rather that he is working with a different notion of confirmation than Goodman. If confirmation means *increase in probability of the hypothesis,* then Davidson is right. But, as we have seen, Goodman wants to build more into the notion of confirming a universal generalization. (This distinction will take on added significance in the light of the upcoming discussion in section 3.)

Goodman established the pervasiveness of the problem of projection by an elementary logical construction. He saw the problem of projection as the real problem of induction which has been neglected while philosophers have debated the empty schema of confirmation of a generalization by its instances. Thus, in "A Query on Confirmation":

Undoubtedly we do make predictions by projecting the patterns of the past into the future, but in selecting the patterns we project from among all those that the past exhibits, we use practical criteria that so far seem to have escaped discovery and formulation.

And in *Fact, Fiction and Forecast:*

To say that valid predictions are those based on past regularities, without being able to say *which* regularities, is quite pointless. Regularities are where you find them and you can find them anywhere. As we have seen, Hume's failure to recognize and deal with this problem has been shared by even his most recent successors.[8]

Goodman's remarks here are, I believe, quite accurate except, perhaps, for the parting shot. It seems to me that this is not quite fair to Hume. Hume's famous passage about eggs indicates that some resemblances seem to be more projectible than others: *"Nothing is so alike as eggs; yet no one on account of this appearing similarity, expects the same taste and relish in all of them."*

Furthermore, looking at the problem of projectibility in the most general terms, let us suppose that we do not have to construct hypotheses by elementary means, but rather take hypotheses in a free swinging way as sets of possible world scenarios. Then the analogue of the grue problem is the multiplicity of incompatible hypotheses which are compatible with a given history up to now, and it is exactly true that confirmation by positive instances can be made to predict *anything*. But this most general formulation of the new riddle of induction is precisely the most general formulation of Hume's problem.[9]

On the other hand, Hume did not have such abstract general formulations in mind; they represent a more modern point of view. His general theory is that induction is based on habit, and this leaves open questions as to the possibility and plausibility of habits. Even if Hume did show some awareness of the problem, we must agree with Goodman that Hume does not make any real contribution to the development of the logic of projectibility.

As for "Hume's most recent successors," I suppose that here Goodman had in mind Carnap and Hempel. But there was another—more Humean—successor who did recognize the problem, and who made major advances in dealing with it. That was Bruno de Finetti.

3. Exchangeability

De Finetti is at least as radical as Goodman in questioning the basis of the received categories:

> What are sometimes called repetitions or trials of the same event are for us so many distinct events. In general they will have common or symmetric characteristics which make it natural to attribute equal probabilities to them, but there is no a priori reason which prevents us in principle from attributing to the events $E_1 \ldots E_n$ distinct and absolutely arbitrary probabilities $p_1 \ldots p_n$. In principle there is no difference for us between this case and that of n events which exhibit no similarities; the similarity which suggests the name "trials of the same event" (we would say "of the same phenomenon") is not intrinsic: at the very most, its importance lies in the influence it may have on our psychological judgement. . . .[10]

Judgments of similarity are, for de Finetti, subjective and they are embodied in one's subjective probabilities. How?

Suppose that we have an infinite sequence of random variables which may or may not be thought of as trials "of the same phenomenon." For simplicity, we suppose them to be dichotomous—a sequence of yes or no answers to unspecified questions. (Perhaps it is a sequence of observation reports of the color of observed emeralds or emeroses; answers to the question "Is it green?" or "Is it grue?") Our prior degrees of belief over possible outcome sequences determine our inductive behavior as the data comes in and we condition on it.

According to de Finetti, we treat the trials as maximally analogous when our degrees of belief are *exchangeable*, that is, invariant under finite permutations of trials. Another way of saying this is to say that relative frequency is a sufficient statistic: that is, that all initial segments of the same length, with the same numbers of Yeses and Nos, are equally probable. De Finetti showed that such exchangeable probabilities have a unique representation as expectations of probabilities which make the trials independent and identically distributed. That means that if your beliefs are exchangeable here, your inductive behavior is the same as if you believed that the trial were generated by flipping a coin with unknown bias, you had a prior distribution over the possible biases, and you updated by using Bayes's theorem and conditioning.

Bayesian inductive behavior for the biased coin is well known. Suppose that the prior over the possible bias is *open-minded* in that for each possible value of the bias every open interval containing that point receives positive prior probability. Then with chance[11] equal to one, induction will converge to a probability of the next instance being heads equal to the limiting relative frequency of heads in the outcome sequence.[12] (Absolute inductive skepticism is not an option for this Bayesian observer.) Should nature serve up a sequence of all heads, the probability that the next trial will yield heads goes up as each piece of data comes in, just as Goodman says that it should in the case of projectibility, and converges to one.

This is not quite enough to guarantee inductive inference to the universal generalization that every trial is a head, however. For the stated conditions could hold when the prior probability of the sequence consisting of all heads was zero. And in that case it would remain zero on any finite data. One could, with Ramsey, Carnap, and many earlier probabilists, take the position that prediction of future instances is all we should care about in confirming a generalization. But if it is desired that the universal generalization be well confirmed by positive instances as well, we might impose in addition to the foregoing *UG open-mindedness:*[13] that is that the two outcome sequences consisting of all heads and of all tails each receive positive prior probability. Then, indeed, the probability of "All heads" goes up with each head, and converges to one if it is true that every trial gives heads; likewise for tails.

Brian Skyrms

De Finetti showed that we can use this analysis without any assumptions about unknown chances. The exchangeability of our degrees-of-belief over outcome sequences gives us the de Finetti representation, and the open-mindedness conditions on priors on Bernoulli trials become conditions on virtual priors which are artifacts of the representation. The restriction to dichotomous variables was for purely expository reasons. If the exchangeable sequence of random variables take on a finite sequence of values, the de Finetti representation gives a mixture of multinomial probabilities and inductive behavior is like sampling from "the great urn of nature." The representation theorem has been generalized to exchangeable sequences of random variables taking values in more general spaces.[14]

Suppose a coin of unknown bias is about to be flipped, and you are to be presented with the results in an unusual way. For the first 100 trials there is a random variable that takes the value 1 if heads, 0 otherwise. For the subsequent trials there are random variables which take the value 0 if heads, 1 otherwise. If you have ordinary beliefs about coin flipping, this "Goodmanized" sequence of random variables will not be exchangeable for you. It seems that much of the intuitive concept of projectibility is captured in a subjective Bayesian setting by *exchangeability,* or *open-minded exchangeability,* or *exchangeability that is both open-minded and UG open-minded.* With the latter condition a universal generalization is confirmed by an incomplete survey of its positive instances both in the sense that they raise its probability and in the sense that in the limit they raise it to one. And that confirmation transfers to unexamined instances in the way Goodman supposed in his interchange with Davidson.[15] This cannot, however, be a complete account of projectibility in a probabilistic setting because it makes nonsense of the passage from Goodman that I have taken as epigraph; exchangeable subjective probabilities do not project *patterns*[16] in the data.

5. Markov Exchangeability

The simplest sort of patterns in the data stream that we might want to project are those in which the outcome of a trial tends to depend on that of the preceding trial. Exchangeable degrees of belief cannot project such patterns because exchangeability is essentially the property that order makes no difference. The probability of heads on the eleventh toss conditional on the first ten tosses being HTHTHTHTHT must be the same as that conditional on the first ten tosses being HHTHTTTHTH since the relative frequencies are the same. In terms of the de Finetti representation, having exchangeable degrees of belief is tantamount to concentrating one's beliefs on the hypothesis that the true chances—whatever they are—make the trials independent, and thus on the hypothesis that nature does not follow a pattern in the phenomenon under consideration.

Already in 1938 de Finetti suggested that exchangeability needed to be extended to a more general notion of partial exchangeability. The idea was that where full exchangeability fails, we might still have some version of conditional exchangeability. With respect to the kind of pattern just considered, the relevant condition would consist of the outcome of the preceding trial. The notion desired here is that of *Markov exchangeability*. It did not receive precise formulation, and the appropriate forms of the de Finetti representation theorem were not proved until the work of Freedman (1962) and Diaconis and Freedman (1980).

We are considering a loosening of the assumption of patternlessness in the data stream to one where the simplest types of patterns can occur; that is, those where the probability of an outcome can depend on the probability of the previous outcome. One way to say this is that we loosen the assumption that the true chances make the trials independent to the assumption that the true chances make the trials *Markov dependent*. Here we can replace the iconic example of the coin flip with that of the Markov thumbtack of Diaconis and Freedman (1980). A thumb tack is repeatedly flicked as it lays. It can come to rest in either of two positions: point up or point down. The chance of the next state may well depend on the previous one. Thus there are unknown transition probabilities:

	PU	PD
PU	Pr(PU|PU)	Pr(PD|PU)
PD	Pr(PU|PD)	Pr(PD|PD)

which an adequate inductive logic should allow us to learn. More generally, for a physical system with states $S_1 \ldots S_k$, a Markov Chain (with stationary transition probabilities) consists of a k-place probability vector for the initial state[17] together with a k-by-k square matrix of transition probabilities.

The formulation of exchangeability that generalizes most smoothly to this case is the one based on sufficient statistics. A stochastic process is *Markov exchangeable* if the vector of initial state and transition counts is a sufficient statistic for all finite sequences of given length generated by the process. That is to say that sequences of the same length having the same transition counts and the same initial state, are equiprobable.[18] A state of such a stochastic process is called *recurrent* if the probability that it is visited an infinite number of times is 1. Freedman (1962) showed that any stationary Markov exchangeable process is representable as a mixture of stationary Markov chains. Diaconis and Freedman (1980) show that

recurrent Markov exchangeable stochastic processes have a unique representation as a mixture of Markov chains. These are two forms of de Finetti's
theorem for Markov chains. In this setting, we could investigate *recurrent
Markov exchangeable beliefs with various forms of open-mindedness* as further
varieties of projectibility.[19]

It is of some interest to note here that the sort of sequences of 0's and 1's
gotten by "Goodmanization" in the last section can arise naturally in the
mathematics of representation theorems for Markov-exchangeable stochastic processes. Consider the class of 0–1-valued stochastic processes which
are Markov exchangeable. This is a convex set, any member of which has a
representation as a mixture of its extreme points. But the extreme points
now contain more than Markov chains. The extreme points now consist of:

(1) The recurrent Markov chains starting at 0.
(2) The recurrent Markov chains starting at 1.
(3) The "Goodman $0,k$" processes starting deterministically with k
    zeros and then continuing with all ones.
(4) The "Goodman $1,k$" processes starting deterministically with k
    ones and then continuing with all zeros.

These "Goodman processes" are Markov exchangeable in a rather degenerate way. Thus the process that puts probability one on the sample path
001111 . . . is Markov exchangeable because this is the unique sample path
having this initial point and transition counts. Agents who put degree of
belief one on the "Goodman processes" have both inductive and
counterinductive aspects to their beliefs, and are worthy of some philosophical attention.[20] "Goodman processes" are neither stationary not recurrent,
and so do not appear in the representation for stationary or recurrent
Markov exchangeable beliefs. (End of digression: for more details see
Diaconis and Freedman (1980) section 3.)

It should be clear that the sort of analysis that I have sketched here can be
applied to higher-order Markov chains, where the probability of an outcome
depends on 2, 3, or N previous outcomes. And there is no reason why the
random variables with which we are concerned have to only be ordered in
one dimension. All sorts of orderings or partial orderings are possibilities.
For example, we could consider the case of ordering in three or more
dimensions. Possible instantiations would be Ising spin models of
ferromagnets, lattice gases, or stochastic cellular automata. Some extensions
of de Finetti's theorem to such domains exist in the literature[21] and provide
the framework for extension of the foregoing analysis of projectibility.
Investigation of the logic of the projectibility of patterns is a rich and
flourishing enterprise.

6. Partial Exchangeability and Sufficient Statistics

De Finetti also had other sorts of cases of partial exchangeability in mind in 1938. He conceptualizes the question of partial exchangeability in general as modeling degree of *analogy* between events:

> But the case of exchangeability can only be considered as a limiting case: the case in which this "analogy" is, in a certain sense, *absolute* for all the events under consideration. . . . To get from the case of exchangeability to other cases which are more general but still tractable, we must take up the case where we still encounter "analogies" among the events under consideration, but without attaining the limiting case of exchangeability.[22]

For his simplest example, he takes the case in which two odd-looking coins are flipped. If the coins look exactly alike, we may take a sequence consisting of tosses of both to be exchangeable. If they look quite different, we may take the trials of one to be subjectively independent of trials of the other. If they look almost alike, we will want an appropriate form of partial exchangeability where a toss of coin A may give us some information about coin B, but not as much as we would get from a toss of coin B. Later, he discusses a more interesting, but essentially similar, case in which animal trials of a new drug are partially exchangeable with human trials.

Here, the trials of coin one are exchangeable as those are of coin two, but they are not exchangeable with each other. One way to say this is to say that for a mixed sequence of trials of both coins, initial segments of the same length that have both the same numbers of heads on coin one and the same number of heads on coin two are equiprobable. In other words, the vector $\langle f1, f2 \rangle$ whose components are respectively those frequency counts is a sufficient statistic.

This case, that of Markov exchangeability and many others can be brought under a general theory of partial exchangeability in which the concept of a sufficient statistic plays a key role. For simple coin tossing the statistic is the frequency of heads; for tossing several coins it is the vector of frequencies of heads of the respective coins; for the Markov case it is the vector of initial state and transition counts. In each case, under appropriate conditions we have (1) *a deFinetti type representation* of degrees of belief as mixtures of the extreme points of the convex set probabilities for which that is a sufficient statistic and (2) *a projectibility result* to the effect that learning from experience will almost surely converge to one of these extreme points. For some more detail on this theory see Diaconis and Freedman (1980)(1981) and Dynkin (1978).

7. Invariance and Projectibility

Projectibility can also be studied from a different (though related) mathematical viewpoint: that of ergodic theory.[23] From this perspective, the key concept for understanding projectibility is that of an *invariant measure*. If an agent has degrees of belief that are invariant with respect to a transformation, then that agent—in a sense to be made precise—believes in induction with respect to the notion of repetition of an experiment given by that transformation. But two agents whose degrees of belief are invariant with respect to different transformations differ in their judgments of projectibility. The philosophical analysis of inductive skepticism, therefore, should focus on questions of the existence and nature of invariant degrees of belief. It is regrettable that this central concept is so little discussed in the philosophical literature on induction.

In order to set the foregoing remarks in context, I will give a thumbnail sketch of the early evolution of ergodic theory. Ergodic theory had its origin in statistical mechanics. Consider the dynamics of an idealized system of gas as it evolves in continuous time. We assume here that time is infinite in both directions. The state of the gas at any moment of time is given by a point in phase space. The laws of classical mechanics specify the time evolution of the system. Thus for a time interval—for example, 2—the dynamical laws specify for each point in phase space what point it would evolve into in two units of time. This gives a transformation of phase space into itself, T_2. Likewise for any other real number, r, there is an associated transformation. By the law of conservation of energy, the system will always be in the same region of phase space with the same energy; this region is called a constant energy (hyper)surface.

Boltzmann wanted to prove the equality of time averages and phase space averages for such a system; that is to say that for some reasonable quantity[24] on the constant energy surface, and for any point on the surface, the limiting time average of the quantity as the system evolves from that point onwards is equal to the phase space average of that quantity over the surface where the weighting of the average is taken with respect to the natural measure on the surface.[25] As a basis for this program he advanced the *ergodic*[26] *hypothesis* approximately to the effect that for every point on the surface, its trajectory through phase space passes through every point on the surface. Notice that this hypothesis can be reformulated as saying that there is no proper subset of the surface such that the trajectory of every point in the subset remains within it. That is, there is no proper subset that is strictly invariant in that the dynamics maps it into itself. Viewed this way, we can call Boltzmann's ergodic hypothesis a hypothesis of *strict dynamic transitivity*. It soon became apparent to Boltzmann himself and others that, stated strictly, the ergodic hypothesis could not be satisfied. Boltzmann knew that the "approximately" in the foregoing statement of the ergodic hypothesis must somehow be taken seriously and made precise, but he did not know how to do it.[27] Despite considerable discussion of this problem, no satisfactory solution was put forward until the ergodic theorems of von Neumann and Birkhoff.

Von Neumann replaced Boltzmann's ergodic hypothesis with the hypothesis of *metric transitivity*. This uses the natural measure on the constant energy hypersurface to relax the assumption of strict dynamic transitivity. Metric transitivity says that there is no measurable invariant subset of the surface other than one of measure zero or one whose complement is of measure zero. A measure zero subset is negligible from a measure theoretic point of view, and a subset whose complement is of measure zero is hardly proper from a measure theoretic point of view. This weakening turns out to be just the right reformulation of Boltzmann's ergodic hypothesis, and "ergodicity" in current usage just means metrical transitivity in the sense of von Neumann.

Metrical transitivity was a strong enough property to allow von Neumann and Birkhoff to prove equality of time averages and phase averages almost everywhere. And it is weak enough so that the physical systems under consideration might conceivably have it. But there was no proof that boxes of gas, or anything like them, are ergodic. It was known however that the natural measure is invariant under the transformations given by the dynamics.[28] von Neumann showed that an invariant measure has a (unique) representation as a mixture of ergodic measures—measures such that if one of them is used in the formulation of metrical transitivity, metrical transitivity obtains. This is called the *ergodic decomposition of invariant measures*.[29]

von Neumann established a convergence result[30], which really gave what was required for Boltzmann's purposes, but Birkhoff proved convergence in an even stronger sense. Birkhoff showed that except for a set of points of measure zero in the invariant measure, the limiting time average over the orbit of a point exists and coincides with the phase space average according to one of the ergodic measures. This is the *Birkhoff pointwise ergodic theorem*. If the natural invariant phase space measure is ergodic, then we have equality of time and phase space average almost everywhere.

But the immediate importance of Birkhoff's ergodic theorem was not so much for physics—where the ergodicity of the natural physical measure proved remarkably difficult to demonstrate for any physical system of any complexity[31]—but rather for probability theory—and for the theory of induction. The connection with the theory of stationary stochastic processes was explicitly made three years after Birkhoff's proof[32] by Doob, Hopf, and Kintchine. The pointwise ergodic theorem and the theorem on the ergodic decomposition of stationary measures hold for dynamical systems with discrete time. Consider a stochastic process as a sequence of random variables (for example, coin flips) infinite in both directions. Define the shift transformation as that which maps an infinite outcome sequence to one shifted forward one unit of discrete time. Then the stochastic process is *stationary* just in case the probability measure on the underlying space is *invariant with respect to the shift transformation*. The ergodic decomposition still applies. The invariant measure has an essentially unique representation as a mixture of ergodic measures. *If the invariant measure is ergodic, then Birkhoff's pointwise ergodic theorem gives a generalization of the strong law of large numbers from independent and identically distributed random variables to ergodic stationary stochastic processes.*

To recover the strong law of large numbers for coin flipping, consider a stationary stochastic process with independent, identically distributed 0–1-valued random variables. The shift transformation is ergodic with respect to the product measure on the product space. Then application of the Birkhoff ergodic theorem gives the strong law of large numbers for Bernoulli sequences.

Suppose an invariant measure is not ergodic. Then, as Freedman (1962)(1963) shows, the ergodic decomposition of invariant measures gives a far-reaching generalization of the de Finetti representation theorem. In this case, the Birkhoff ergodic theorem still says that time averages exist almost everywhere, but they will not in general be equal to the phase space averages corresponding to the invariant measure. Rather, for almost all points, the time average corresponding to it will be equal to the phase space average of one or another of the ergodic measures of which the invariant measure is a mixture according to the ergodic decomposition of invariant measures. For example, consider again a stationary stochastic process with 0–1-valued random variables, but instead of independence assume invariance under finite permutations of trials. The ergodic measures in this class are the independent ones, so the ergodic decomposition gives the de Finetti representation of exchangeable measures as mixtures of independent and identically distributed ones. The Birkhoff ergodic theorem then says that for almost every point, the time average along its orbit is equal to one of the independent and identically distributed ones. Freedman uses the ergodic representation to establish a general result that stationary stochastic processes characterized by a kind of sufficient statistic are mixtures of ergodic measures characterized by that statistic. He applies this to show, in particular, that stationary Markov-exchangeable stochastic processes are mixtures of stationary Markov chains.

It should be born in mind that the ergodic theory is even more general than the foregoing application. The ergodic decomposition and convergence results do not depend on taking the points in our probability space to be sequences and the relevant transformation being the shift transformation. For example, consider again a space whose outcome sequences are generated by sequences of coin flips, but suppose that up to and including time 0, "Heads" is coded by a 1 and "Tails" by a 0 while after time 0 the coding is reversed with "Tails" being coded by a 1 and "Heads" by a 0. Then if your degrees of belief would be invariant with respect to the shift transformation on the space of sequences of heads and tails, they will not be invariant with respect to the shift transformation on this "Goodmanized" space. Rather they will be invariant under a more complicated transformation, T^*, which is most intuitively described as (1) decode the Goodmanized sequence as the equivalent outcome sequence in the space of sequences of H and T, (2) do the shift transformation on the space of sequences of H and T, (3) code the result into the space of Goodmanized sequences. Consider two agents, one sane and the other crazy, who have degrees of belief over the Goodmanized space of outcome sequences: the sane agent has degrees of belief that are invariant under T^*; the crazy agent has degrees of belief that are invariant under the shift transformation. In a sense both will believe in induction: the sane agent with respect to T^* and the crazy agent with respect to the shift transformation. Although they both believe in the form of inductive reasoning, they differ in their application of it.

What is the significance of ergodic theory for the philosophy of induction? We can see it as providing the mathematical backing for a very general implementation of de Finetti's point of view. The invariant probability measure can be interpreted as degree-of-belief of a scientist. The transformation under which it is invariant can be taken, as Billingsley (1965) suggests, as defining a subjective notion of repetition of the same chance experiment—as providing a subjective individuation of the chance setup. The ergodic decomposition gives a representation in the form of an expectation of chance, with the ergodic measures being subjective surrogates for objective chances. The Birkhoff ergodic theorem shows that the scientist must expect—with degree-of-belief 1—that repetition of the experiment will converge to the true chances. Thus, in a certain sense, inductive skepticism is impossible for a scientist having invariant degrees-of-belief.

In this framework one can *settle* precise forms of various questions regarding inductive skepticism. For instance, we know that an agent with invariant degrees of belief cannot be an absolute inductive skeptic. Thus we may be led to ask whether it is true that for *any* transformation someone could have beliefs which would be invariant under that transformation? This question has been studied under various conditions. Here—under some topological regularity conditions—is an affirmative answer, due to Krylov and Bogoliubov:

Theorem: Suppose that the probability space on which your degrees-of-belief are to be defined is a compact topological space and the transformation with respect to which invariance is to be evaluated is continuous. Then an invariant degree-of-belief measure exists.[33]

This theorem establishes one precise version of Goodman's dictum:[34]

Regularities are where you find them, and you can find them anywhere.

8. Symmetry

All the foregoing varieties of projectibility are, in various ways, manifestations of probabilistic symmetries. Van Fraassen (1989) has argued persuasively that symmetries play a fundamental role in guiding the development of scientific theory. He believes that symmetry—rather than the old metaphysical notion of law—should be taken as basic in the analysis of science.[35] As van Fraassen points out, this perspective on laws seems natural to many scientists (for example, Wigner (1967)), but seems to have been somewhat neglected by philosophers.

I have advocated a closely related Humean view of the supposed natural necessity of laws. In a nutshell the position is that the apparent nomic force of statements taken as laws of nature derives not from any metaphysical necessity but rather from invariances—sometimes approximate invariances —in our scientifically informed degrees-of-belief. This is discussed in terms of the concept of *resiliency* in Skyrms (1980) (1984) (1991b). These invariances are symmetries in degrees-of-belief. We have seen in the foregoing discussion that symmetries in the probabilities on which induction is based are the fundamental determinants of varieties of projectibility. One of Goodman's fundamental insights—the association between projectibility and lawlikeness[36]—closes the circle. Another of Goodman's basic insights connects statements treated as laws and associated counterfactual conditionals. In a pragmatic Bayesian theory of subjunctive conditionals (Skyrms (1984)) symmetries of degrees-of-belief again play a key role.

With these ideas in mind, it may be useful to set the foregoing in a general theory of probabilistic symmetry. I will begin in this section with a brief introduction to our most general notion of symmetry and then proceed to its application to probability.

Consider the symmetry of the equilateral triangle pictured in Figure 1. One symmetry is indicated by the fact that if we rotate each point 120 degrees about the midpoint of the triangle, we get the same figure. Another is that if we reflect each point on the triangle about the dotted midline shown, we get the same figure. Each of these operations can be viewed as a

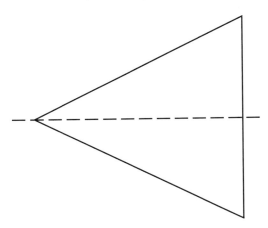

one-to-one transformation of the plane into itself which preserves the structure of the triangle. (Think of the points on the original triangle as black and the other points on the plane as white. That the transformation preserves the same structure means that black points get mapped to black and white points to white.) Obviously if we compose symmetry transformations, we get another[37]. Thus if we first rotate through 120 degrees and then reflect, we again get the same figure. Or if we rotate through 120 degrees and then do it again (giving a total rotation through 240 degrees), we preserve the figure. If we rotate through 240 degrees and then rotate through 120 degrees, we map each point onto itself. This is the identity transformation, *I,* which obviously preserves structure. Notice that the 360-degree rotation can be described equally well as "First two 120 degree rotations, then another" or as "First one 120 degree rotation, then two others." Note also that since our transformations preserve structure, we can run them backwards (the inverse transformation) and still preserve structure. If rotation through 120 degrees gives the same structure then rotation through −120 degrees (= rotation through 240 degrees) also preserves structure. Of course running a transformation forwards and then running it backwards, or running it backwards and then running it forwards, give no net change—i.e., the composition of a transformation with its inverse gives the identity transformation.

What has been illustrated in the last paragraph is that if we have a notion of same structure, then the symmetry transformations—those that preserve structure—form a group under composition. This can be taken as a characterization of symmetry in the abstract—*symmetry is invariance under a group of transformations which preserve structure.* A more detailed exposition of this point of view is contained in Weyl's classic book, *Symmetry.*

For our purposes, the structure to be preserved is probabilistic structure. This makes it clear why exchangeability is a symmetry: it is invariance of probability under the group of finite permutations of trials. We can also see how the partial exchangeability with respect to a statistic discussed in the last section is a symmetry. Just consider the group of transformations of the probability space into itself which leave the sufficient statistic unchanged. And in the discussion of invariance in the last section, we have already been dealing with groups of transformations of the probability space. In the examples of stochastic processes with discrete time we iterate the shift transformation, so we have $T(w)$, $T2(w) = T(T(w))$. We are dealing with an infinite set of transformations:. . . . $T-2$, $T-1$, $T0$, $T1$, $T2$ . . . which inherits the group structure of the integers under addition. Likewise, the continuous time dynamical systems deal with a group of transformations which inherit the group structure of the real line under addition. There is no reason why attention should be limited to these particular groups.[38]

9. Probability-Symmetry Structures

Definition 1: A *probability-symmetry structure* as an ordered quadruple, $<W,F,m,G>$ where W is set, F is the sigma-field of subsets of W, m is a countably additive probability measure on F, and G is a group of invertible, measurable, measure-preserving transformations on $<W,F,m>$. (Thus, by definition, the measure, m, is invariant with respect to every transformation, T, in G, that is for all A in F and all T in G, $m(A) = m(T^{-1}(A))$.)

Definition 2: A measurable set, A, in F, is *an invariant set with respect to G* if it is invariant with respect to every member of G, that is, if for all T in G, $A = T^1(A)$. (Since complements and countable unions and intersections of invariant sets are invariant, the invariant sets form a Boolean σ-algebra.)

Definition 3: A measure, m, of a probability-symmetry structure is *ergodic* if for every invariant set, A, $m(a) = 0$ or $m(A) = 1$.

Under mild topological regularity conditions, an analogue of the de Finetti representation theorem holds for probability-symmetry structures. Suppose that W is a standard Borel space (a complete separable metric space) and F is its Borel δ-field. Assume further that G is countable. *Then* m *has a unique representation as a mixture of measures on $<W,F>$ which are ergodic with respect to G.* Furthermore, the ergodic measures are the regular conditional probabilities with respect to the σ-field of sets invariant with respect to G.[39]

There are relevant generalizations of the Birkhoff ergodic theorem as well, although the picture here is less complete. For example, suppose that instead of a one-dimensional temporal sequence of coin flips, we have a three-dimensional array of coin flips, indexed by the set of triples of integers.

The points in the associated probability space are infinite three-dimensional outcome arrays of zeros and ones. The natural generalization of stationarity to this case is invariance under the n-dimensional shift group of transformations. Suppose that we have a probability measure, m, that is invariant in this sense—i.e., our probabilities are spatially homogeneous. We want to think of the limiting relative frequencies of heads starting at a point in space, as gotten by taking the relative frequencies over bigger and bigger cubes centered at that point—that is, we are interested in the limit as n goes to infinity of (# of heads)$/(n^3 + 1)$ over cubes centered at our initial point. What guarantee is there that this limit exists? In the one dimensional case the Birkhoff ergodic theorem guarantees its existence for almost every (with respect to m) point. The n-dimensional ergodic theorem which establishes the analogous result for n-dimensional space was proved by Norbert Wiener in 1939.[40] There are applications in the theory of the thermodynamic limit for lattice gases.[41]

From our philosophical point of view, the n-dimensional ergodic theorems show that in a certain sense, spatial homogeneity of our degrees-of-belief is incompatible with general inductive skepticism. General inductive skepticism, in the sense of Reichenbach, is giving weight to the possibility that limiting relative frequencies might not exist. If our weights (= degrees-of-belief) are spatially homogeneous in the foregoing sense, and the relative frequencies are to be taken in the foregoing way, then we simply cannot be general inductive skeptics.

The foregoing analysis generalizes. Exactly how far it generalizes is a matter of ongoing mathematical research. The sequence of cubes in the random field example above is called a *universal averaging sequence*. The notion has been extended to more general probability-symmetry structures and in many cases such universal averaging sequences have been found.[42] These provide refutations of general inductive skepticism in very general contexts. However it should also be emphasized that the refutations are not universal. There are always some regularity assumptions involved on the topology of the space of possibilities and on the symmetry group. Some potential inductive skeptics might be skeptical about these assumptions; others might not.

We see that—at increasingly general levels of abstraction—projectibility is a reflection of probabilistic symmetries. The logic of projectibility[43] is probability logic. At the most abstract and general level, it is the mathematics of probability-symmetry structures. Much of this logic is known as the result of the efforts of statisticians, mathematicians, and physicists. The scandal of philosophy is not that the logic of induction does not exist, but rather that philosophy has paid so little attention to it.

University of California, Irvine

NOTES

1. This essay grew out of two philosophical talks given in October 1991 to a conference on "Recent Developments of Exchangeable Random Processes" in Cortona, Italy, sponsored by the *Instituto Nazionale di Alta Matematica*. I would like to thank the organizers for inviting me, and the participants—especially Persi Diaconis and Colin Mallows—for helpful discussions. I would also like to thank Ermanno Bencivenga, Donald Davidson, Persi Diaconis, Ian Hacking, Richard Jeffrey, Hugh Mellor, Peter Woodruff, Jim Woodward, and Sandy Zabell for useful comments on earlier versions of this work.

2. *Fact, Fiction and Forecast,* 23.

3. To Carnap's complaint that "grue" was positional—i.e., has an explicit time in its definition—Goodman replied that if grue and bleen were taken as primitive, then "green" and "blue" would be positional.

4. This is footnote 9 to ch III, "The New Riddle of Induction," *Fact, Fiction and Forecast,* 1st ed., 85–86.

5. Davidson's example [originally "All emerires are grue"] had circulated by word of mouth for years and was reported in Jeffrey (1966) and Wallace (1966) and addressed in Goodman's "Comments" (1966). Davidson's (1966) "Emeroses by Other Names" is his rejoinder to Goodman's "Comments."

6. The concept of an instance is left somewhat ambiguous here and in much of the related literature. Properly, the instance of a universal generalization, "All *F*s are *G*s" is not the conjunction "This is an *F* and a *G,*" but rather the material conditional "This is either no *F* or a *G.*" But if we suppose that we are sampling *F*s, then this background knowledge collapses the potentially pernicious ambiguity.

7. 69.

8. 82.

9. John Earman has discovered some unpublished correspondence in which Hempel makes just this point. See Earman's contribution to this volume.

10. "On the Condition of Partial Exchangeability."

11. With "chance" replaced by "degree of belief," the statement is true without the assumption of open-mindedness.

12. With degree-of-belief one this limiting relative frequency exists.

13. For some early history of UG-openmindedness, see Zabell (1989) and the 1919 article of Jeffreys and Wrinch to which he refers. For later developments, from somewhat different points of view, see Shimony (1967) and Hintikka and Niiniluoto (1980).

14. See, for example, Hewett and Savage (1955).

15. For further discussion of exchangeability and projectibility, see John Earman (1992) and his contribution to this volume. This paper and Earman's essays are in much the same spirit, and the discussions are complementary in coverage. Earman treats the case of exchangeability in more detail, while I concentrate on generalizations of exchangeability.

16. If "pattern" is construed so broadly that any regularity or stable relative frequency qualifies as a pattern, then exchangeability can be said to be compatible with patterns. But, as will be shown in the following discussion, this leaves out many important cases where there are patterns of probabilistic dependency.

17. So to make the Markov thumbtack example into a full Markov chain we can imagine flipping a (possibly biased) coin to determine the initial position of the thumbtack.

18. Markov exchangeability, like ordinary exchangeability, can also be given an equivalent formulation in terms of invariance. [Diaconis and Freedman (1980)]. A primitive block-switch transformation of a sequence takes two disjoint blocks of the sequence with the same starting and ending states and switches them. A block-switch transformation is the composition of a finite number of primitive block-switch transformations. A probability is then Markov exchangeable just in case it is invariant under all block-switch transformations.

19. Open-mindedness is related to Bayesian consistency. See Diaconis and Freedman (1986) for a discussion of Bayesian consistency.

20. For example, suppose someone puts a prior probability of .9 on HTTT . . . , .09 on HHTTT . . . , .009 on HHHTTT . . . , etc., gets an outcome sequence consisting of all heads, and updates by conditioning. Such an agent is coherent but her prior is not Bayesian consistent in the sense of footnote 19.

21. Preston (1976), Georgii (1979).

22. 197.

23. See von Plato (1982) and Skyrms (1984). Also see Jeffrey's remarks on stationarity as a generalization of exchangeability in Jeffrey (1971).

24. Bounded continuous real-valued function.

25. The Liouville measure.

26. Boltzmann's coinage from *ergon* = work for the constant energy hypersurface and *odos* = path for the trajectory of a point.

27. The development of Boltzmann's thought in this area is a complex story. For a sympathetic discussion of Boltzmann's ideas, see von Plato (forthcoming).

28. Liouville's Theorem.

29. Other versions of this result are proved by Kryloff and Bogoliouboff (1937) and Oxtoby (1952). All the results require some regularity conditions. More will be said in this regard in the last section of this paper.

30. von Neumann proved convergence in the L^2 norm.

31. Birkhoff put forward the "Hypothesis of Metrical Transitivity" according to which it is generally true for Hamiltonian systems that the Liouville measure restricted to a constant energy hypersurface is ergodic. In the 1950s, Kolmogoroff, Arnold, and Moser showed that this hypothesis fails. Ergodicity is not generic for Hamiltonian systems, although there are some important special cases for which ergodicity has been established.

32. In 1934.

33. See Sinai (1976), 12–13.

34. *Fact, Fiction and Forecast*, 82.

35. See van Fraassen (1989), III.

36. This is not to endorse the exact form of the association proposed by Goodman—that lawlike sentences are just those which can be confirmed by an incomplete survey of their instances.

37. For the transitivity of "same structure."

38. For instance, physicists have studied what are essentially stochastic processes in three-dimensional time. See Preston (1976) and Georgii (1979).

39. See Farrell (1962). This holds even if G is only a semigroup (Th. 5). It can be extended to separable locally compact groups (Cor. 4), and continuous groups (Th. 6).

40. Cubes and spheres also work for continuous n-dimensional space.

41. In this respect see Mackey (1974).

42. See Tempel'man (1972) and Krengel (1985), especially ch. 5.

43. Ermanno Bencivanga and Hugh Mellor have complained that this paper neglects the "external" question of the justification of induction in favor of "internal" questions connected with the logic of projectibility. This is not because I think that nothing at all sensible can be said about "external" questions of reliability, but rather because the subject of this paper is Bayesian projectibility. I approach the "external" questions in terms of Bayesian consistency, where something precise can be said about reliability—but only relative to assumptions about the operative chance model. From this perspective internal questions are not irrelevant to external ones. See footnotes 19 and 20 and Skyrms (1991a), (1993), (forthcoming). For his approach to external justification, see Mellor (1988).

REFERENCES

Billingsley, P. (1965). *Ergodic Theory and Information* (New York: Wiley).

Davidson, D. (1966). "Emeroses by Other Names," *J. Philosophy 64*, 1778–1790.

de Finetti, B. (1937). "La Prévision: ses lois logiques, ses sources subjectives," *Annales de l'Institut Henri Poincaré 7*:1–68. Translated as "Foresight: its logical laws, its subjective sources," in *Studies in Subjective Probability*, ed. H.E. Kyburg, Jr., and H. Smokler (Huntington, N.Y.: Kreiger, 1980).

de Finetti, B. (1938). "Sur la condition d'équivalence partielle," *Actualités scientifiques et Industrielles 739*, Hermann & Cie. Translated as "On the Condition of Partial Exchangeability" by P. Benacerraf and R. Jeffrey in *Studies in Inductive Logic and Probability II*, ed. R. Jeffrey (Berkeley: University of California Press, 1980), 193–205.

Diaconis, P. and Freedman, D. (1980). "de Finetti's Theorem for Markov Chains," *Annals of Probability 8*, 115–130.

Diaconis, P. and Freedman, D. (1980). "de Finetti's Generalizations of Exchangeability," in *Studies in Inductive Logic and Probability II*, ed. R. Jeffrey (Berkeley: University of California Press).

Diaconis, P. and Freedman, D. (1981). "Partial Exchangeability and Sufficiency," in *Statistics: Applications and New Directions* (Calcutta: Indian Statistical Institute), 205–236.

Diaconis, P. and Freedman, D. (1986). "On the Consistency of Bayes Estimates," *Annals of Statistics 14*, 1–26.

Dynkin, E. (1978). "Sufficient Statistics and Extreme Points," *Annals of Probability 6*, 705–730.

Earman, J. (1992). *Bayes or Bust?* (Cambridge, Mass.: MIT Press:) [Sec. 4.7, "Goodman's New Problem of Induction"].

Farrell, R. H. (1962). "Representation of Invariant Measures," *Illinois Journal of Mathematics 6*, 447–467.

Freedman, D. (1962). "Mixtures of Markov Processes," *Annals of Mathematical Statistics 33*, 114–118.

Freedman, D. (1962). "Invariants under Mixing which Generalize de Finetti's Theorem," *Annals of Mathematical Statistics 33*, 916–933.

Freedman, D. (1963). "Invariants under Mixing which Generalize de Finetti's theorem: Continuous Time Parameter," *Annals of Mathematical Statistics 34*, 1194–1216.

Georgii, H. O. (1979). *Canonical Gibbs Measures* (Lecture Notes in Mathematics 760) (Berlin: Springer).

Goodman, N. (1946). "A Query on Confirmation," *J. Philosophy 43*, 383–385.

Goodman, N. (1955). *Fact, Fiction and Forecast* (Cambridge, Massachusetts: Harvard University Press).

Goodman, N. (1966). "Comments," *Journal of Philosophy 63*, 328–331.

Hewitt, E. and Savage, L. J. (1955) "Symmetric measures on Cartesian Products," *Transactions of the American Mathematical Society 80*, 470–501.

Hintikka, J. and Niiniluoto, I. (1980). "An Axiomatic Foundation for the Logic of Inductive Generalization," in *Studies in Inductive Logic and Probability, Volume II*, ed. R. Jeffrey, 157–181.

Jeffrey, R. (1966). "Goodman's Query," *Journal of Philosophy 63*, 281–288.

Jeffrey, R. (1971). "Probability Measures and Integrals," in *Studies in Inductive Logic and Probability, Volume I*, ed. R. Carnap and R. Jeffrey (Berkeley: University of California Press), 169–221.

Krengel, U. (1985). *Ergodic Theorems* (Berlin: Walter de Gruyter).

Kryloff, N. and Bogoliouboff, N. (1937). "La théorie générale de la mesure dans son application à l'étude des systèmes de la mécanique non linéaire," *Annals of Mathematics 38*, 65–113.

Mackey, G. W. (1974). "Ergodic Theory and its Significance for Statistical Mechanics and Probability Theory," *Advances in Mathematics 12*, 178–278.

Mellor, D. H. (1988). *The Warrant of Induction; an inaugural lecture* (Cambridge: Cambridge University Press).

Oxtoby, J. C. (1952). "Ergodic Sets," *Bulletin of the American Mathematical Society 58*, 116–136.

Preston, C. (1976). *Random Fields* (Springer Lecture Notes in Mathematics 534) (Berlin: Springer).

Shimony, A. (1967). "Amplifying Personal Probability," *Philosophy of Science 34*, 326–332.

Sinai, Y. (1976). *Introduction to Ergodic Theory* (Princeton: Princeton University Press).

Sinai, Y. (1989). *Dynamical Systems II* (Berlin: Springer).

Skyrms, B. (1980). *Causal Necessity* (New Haven: Yale University Press).

Skyrms, B. (1984). *Pragmatics and Empiricism* (New Haven: Yale University Press) [Ch. 3 "Learning from Experience"].

Skyrms, B. (1991a). "Carnapian Inductive Logic for Markov Chains," *Erkenntnis 35*, 439–460.

Skyrms, B. (1991b) "Stability and Chance," in *Existence and Explanation: Essays Presented in Honor of Karel Lambert* (Dordrecht: Kluwer), 149–163.

Skyrms, B. (1993). "Analogy by Similarity in HyperCarnapian Inductive Logic," in *Philosophical Problems of the Internal and External Worlds,* ed. J. Earman et al. (Pittsburgh: University of Pittsburgh Press), 273–282.

Skyrms, B. (forthcoming). "Carnapian Inductive Logic for a Value Continuum," in *The Philosophy of Science* (Midwest Studies in Philosophy Volume 18), ed. H. Wettstein (South Bend, Indiana: University of Notre Dame Press).

Tempel'man, A. A. (1972). "Ergodic Theorems for General Dynamical Systems," *Transactions of the Moscow Mathematical Society 26*, 94–132.

van Fraassen, B. (1989). *Laws and Symmetry* (Oxford: Clarendon).

von Plato, J. (1982). "The Significance of the Ergodic Decomposition of Stationary Measures for the Interpretation of Probability," *Synthese 53*, 419–432.

von Plato, J. (1994). *Creating Modern Probability* (Cambridge: Cambridge University Press).

Wallace, J. (1966). "Goodman, Logic and Induction," *Journal of Philosophy 63*, 328–331.

Weyl, H. (1952). *Symmetry* (Princeton: Princeton University Press).

Wiener, N. (1939). "The Ergodic Theorem," *Duke Mathematical Journal 5*, 1–18.

Wigner, E. (1967). *Symmetries and Reflections,* ed. W. Moore and M. Scriven (Bloomington, Indiana: Indiana University Press).

Zabell, S. L. (1988). "Symmetry and Its Discontents," in *Causation, Chance and Credence,* ed. W. Harper and B. Skyrms (Dordrecht: Kluwer), 155–190.

Zabell, S. L. (1989). "The Rule of Succession," *Erkenntnis 31*, 283–321.

Learning and Projectibility

Patrick Suppes

It is surprising, and perhaps a reflection of a certain provincialism in philosophy, that the problem of induction is so seldom linked to learning. On the face of it, an animal in a changing environment faces problems no different in general principle from those that we as ordinary humans or as specialized scientists face in trying to make predictions about the future. But requests for a solution to the problem of induction, I would very much agree with Goodman, are usually formulated in ways that are inappropriate. A purely deductive justification is surely out of the question. We might as well ask for a logical solution to the problem of surviving forever.

The two basic ideas I will explore here are these. First, much of learning is nonverbal, and consequently a statement-type formulation of inductive problems is inappropriate. Second, scientists are no different from other mammals trying to survive in the wilderness in terms of the basic problems of projectibility, or put in another standard way, prediction. I do not mean to say that scientists do not have better methodologies in many cases, but that the fundamental problem is little changed when we confront such troublesome problems as prediction of the weather, of earthquakes, of ozone depletion, and the like, compared to what must have been a relatively stationary environment from the standpoint of dinosaurs, for instance, for many millions of years. I am not suggesting that dinosaurs were better predictors, but that the enormous advantage of a relatively stationary environment, from the standpoint of the features in which one is interested, is much more important than scientific methodology. If one is interested in predicting and using features of the world that are highly nonstationary then more than methodology, mainly a lot of good luck, is needed to do very well at prediction. In the worse kind of environment, no significant event, good or bad, has a high probability, and the best we can do is try to optimize, on the basis of fallible ideas of projectibility, prediction of the most likely, even if improbable, occurrence. That induction should deal with the probable is one of the most common mistakes of philosophical discussion. For a hungry animal finding a delectable prey may be the most improbable of events and there may be no prey, delectable or not, that has a high probability of being caught. Animals in such an environment learn to be persistent, patient, and attentive to very subtle perceptual cues if they are to survive. Stationarity, exchangeability, and many other assumptions of much modern statistics do not hold for environments of this kind.

I have organized my analysis into four sections: animal learning, human learning, experimental science, and induction revisited.

1. Animal Learning

I include in animal learning much human learning because at all levels of animal behavior, nonverbal learning is central. It is the only kind of learning for almost all animals, but its essential presence in human learning cannot be emphasized too strongly. For the child learning to walk downstairs, to recognize familiar faces, or to engage in a thousand other developmental projects of learning, it is evident enough, but later the adult walking, running, lifting, grasping, etc., also requires a range of nonverbal skills. It is nonverbal skills that we are very poor at verbalizing at all. Try describing with any physical accuracy how you write your name, hit a backhand in tennis, or walk into a room without falling over chairs.

Artificial predicates like *grue* and *grund* are no problems for animals, because they are not considered, but projectibility is. Much learning occurs in relation to features of the environment that are partly stationary, and those stationary features have nice properties of projection. What is important about learning, however, is dynamic adaptability. Animals that can only survive in a rigidly stationary world will not make it long in most places. The adaptability of learning is in the sharpest possible contrast to most conceptions of scientific experimentation under sharply defined circumstances. Examples of this adaptability are to be seen in every aspect of behavior, of course in hunting prey or avoiding becoming prey, but also in just the mundane task of getting around in the world. An animal that is raised initially in an environment of physical objects in fixed positions, as for example in a cage or a maze, can have considerable difficulty initially adapting to what we would call a wilderness environment.

For animals that want to survive, there is a problem of projectibility, but it is not exactly Goodman's problem. Can what they have learned in the past be flexible enough to permit them to adapt to a changing environment in the future? The answer is, of course, sometimes *yes* and sometimes *no*. Moreover, at the heart of the problems of projectibility for animals in a natural environment is the shortage of the pretty symmetries dear to the hearts of statisticians. For example, the symmetry of exchangeability pressed into such good service by de Finetti and other Bayesians is one that will not work well in a natural environment. In fact, it is generally a criticism of learning models if they satisfy a strong exchangeability assumption because they are not sensitive to new developments. One way of putting the matter is they do not adapt to the current moving average. Another is that the learning operators are commutative.

2. Human Learning

Much of what I have said about animal learning applies to nonverbal human learning. Philosophers through the ages have been beguiled by our ability to talk and reason with words and have not recognized how much of human behavior is inaccessible to accurate verbal description in ordinary circumstances. It is of the greatest importance to recognize that walking, talking, etc., cannot be adequately described by ordinary verbal concepts, and even with the best scientific apparatus only partially. There is an absence of symmetries, an absence of explicit theory to guide experiment, and a paucity of adequate scientific knowledge even now. In the meantime, learning rolls along, robust and dynamic, providing us like other animals with a host of ways of dealing with the world as long as it is not too radically changed. Moreover, this absence of anything like accurate verbal description excludes the artificial problems of *grue* and *grund,* as in the case of other animals, from even arising for this whole domain of experience.

The absence of symmetries of a serious kind in our dealings with the ordinary world is evident in our ordinary descriptions of spatial and temporal phenomena (for more extended discussion of this point see Suppes 1991). It is empty space, not space filled with the bric-a-brac of ordinary existence, that exhibits the symmetries so important in the history of modern geometry. Abstraction and simplification in other areas of experience are similarly required to move from the framework of ordinary language from which symmetries are mainly lacking to obtain any of the symmetries fundamental to modern science.

3. Experimental Science

The ideal environment for projectibility, as has already been emphasized, is one that is stationary. This same ideal, and for closely connected reasons, holds for the design and execution of experiments in any domain of science. The Bayesian who wants to apply exchangeability in the spirit of de Finetti's fundamental theorem can only do so if he is persuaded that the experimental environment is one of stationarity. De Finetti's well-known lectures (1937/1964) are aimed at prevision, or what we could term in the present context, a form of projectibility. Just as exchangeability is an assumption stronger than stationarity—for example, stationary Markov chains can exhibit partial exchangeability, but not exchangeability—so the Bayesian, operating with conditioning as a form of learning with commuting operator properties based on the assumption of exchangeability, does not adapt well to changing environments.

It is important, however, to emphasize that the methodology implied by stationarity assumptions is not necessary for good experimental work. It is, for example, exactly the study of nonstationary processes that is characteristic of learning and of problems of control and adaptability. Moreover, there are a variety of standard statistical methods for analyzing the fit of a given learning model to given experimental data.

On the other hand, it should be emphasized that in many learning situations, but not all, one expects the learning and the associated learning models or theories to be ergodic in the following sense. The stochastic process that embodies the learning model has a unique stationary distribution, and it is the asymptotic distribution of the process under any initial distribution. Put another way, we expect most learning models to have the property that the initial probabilities of responding are not the same as the final ones, but the asymptotic stationary distribution of responses is independent of whatever distribution of responses we may start with. To achieve the ergodicity expected, the learning process need not be a finite Markov process, but it should have a distance-diminishing property that corresponds, roughly speaking, to a geometric fading away of the influence of the past (for technical details of such conditions and how they lead to a proof of ergodicity I just defined, see Lamperti and Suppes 1959). An important class of learning models that do not have such an ergodic property is studied in Karlin (1953). Organisms that for one reason or another have a genetic disposition or an environment that makes them behave in a way to satisfy nonergodic constraints will inevitably have a limited range of adaptability.

A wide class of phenomena, much studied experimentally but ordinarily not under the heading of learning, is the biological development of species and the modification of that development by various traditional and modern methods of changing the genetic structure. However, in a broader context and certainly in the context of modern theories of learning, the Darwinian model of survival is not only a kind of learning associated with species but has also been converted into a standard class of models of learning in artificial intelligence. These models, like other learning models, are not stationary processes except in very special cases.

Two fundamental aspects of learning, present in everyday experience and much studied experimentally, are transfer and generalization. Learning one task and then another can in many cases lead to positive or negative transfer. A well-known anecdote illustrating negative transfer is that of the Southern mules who, having been taught to plow up the weeds growing between the rows of young corn or cotton plants, could not then be taught to plow up the plants as required after World War I by government measures to deal with an agricultural surplus. Transfer is negative when prior learning gets in the way of new learning. There is truth in the adage that you cannot teach an old dog new tricks.

Similar problems arise for generalization. An intense focus on a narrow range of problems can make subsequent generalization of the same skills to new problems difficult. But without generalization reasonable behavior in a natural environment would be nearly impossible. Positive generalization and transfer are forms of projectibility required for survival.

More important than asymptotic stationarity for a learner, or a mathematical model of the learner, is adaptability, which is the essence of transfer and represents a further move from stationarity. It is why learning models that one way or another use estimators of parameters that are like good statistical estimators for stationary environments often do poorly in fitting transfer data. For example, the maximum-likelihood estimate of a numerical parameter for stationary processes is just the mean of the number of observations, little changing after a large number of observations. But this ever slower rate of change over time can be disastrous for adaptability. Learning models aimed at experiments to study initial learning but not transfer often exhibit this failure, probably much more often than the animals they are meant to model.

The experimenter as learner.

What I have said earlier about experimentation sounds much too formal and theoretical. We run carefully designed experiments and then apply carefully thought-out statistical analysis to see what the quality of the learning is, and especially to see how well the actual data of learning fit our theoretical model. But there is another sense in which learning is fundamental to experimentation and is of quite another sort. This is the learning that takes place on the part of the experimenter. For any experiments of any complexity, there are a number of technical things that must be done, ranging from extremely elaborate technological preparation in the case of modern physics experiments, to learning experiments with humans that involve carefully thought-out instructions and psychological settings. Whether it is a matter of physics or psychology, the activities of the experimenter cannot be described with any completeness and corresponding accuracy in ordinary language. Moreover, the detailed execution of the physical actions required of the experimenter are to a large extent not under conscious control. The physicist handling delicate equipment cannot describe the subtle manner in which his perceptual and motor control systems operate to do just what he wants them to. The psychologist instructing subjects does not have under his own explicit conscious command the variety of cognitive and emotional cues that surround the handling of experimental subjects. The most unmanageable and most unruly part of experimental science is the fact that the learning of experimenters is not itself an easy subject for experimental study.

Scientific reports of experiments are like sports reporting, unintelligible to the uninitiated and sketchy and incomplete in description. Moreover, much of this understood background knowledge is not codified or written down somewhere else that can be looked up as occasion demands. It is rather like looking up the rules of chess and being disappointed that they tell you very little about how to play the game. No philosopher who holds some strong propositional theory of knowledge or is much caught up with the content of thought has yet had anything very interesting or subtle to say about complex scientific experiments and how experimenters learn to conduct them. I claim to understand why this is so. Too much of the experimenter's essential behavior cannot be accurately described with verbal concepts currently in use.

4. Induction Revisited

Much that Goodman (1955) has to say about induction and his new riddle continues to seem eminently sensible and pertinent. I especially agree with him that the traditional view has been that the central problem of induction is justification. He says, for instance,

> The typical writer begins by insisting that some way of justifying predictions must be found; proceeds to argue that for this purpose we need some resounding universal law of the Uniformity of Nature, and then inquires how this universal principle itself can be justified (p. 65).

(The ghost of John Stuart Mill is rightly stalked in this passage.)

Validity.

Goodman goes on to ask what we mean by a valid prediction. He says:

> predictions are justified if they conform to valid canons of induction; and the canons are valid if they accurately codify accepted inductive practice (p. 67).

In spite of my sympathy for much that Goodman has to say in expanding on the passage just quoted, I am skeptical that we can hope to find a unique sense of validity applicable to all environments in which we or others make predictions. First, as already stressed, I take the case of animal behavior to be important, but I find it very awkward to talk about valid animal predictions. Certainly it is uncontroversial to talk about animals making *correct* predictions when hunting prey or being hunted, but correctness, unlike validity, is in this context purely result, not rule, oriented.

Second, there is the Bayesian answer that there can in general be no universal criterion of validity, for inductive inferences or behavior are for a good Bayesian first of all a subjective matter, and we can hope for intersubjective convergence of belief or inference only in certain restricted classes of cases about which I have more to say below. Although I am also skeptical of the range of the positive Bayesian program, which I consider below, I am wholly sympathetic with this negative point. Third, Goodman himself gives a good argument for skepticism when he later stresses the importance of the background and context within which predictions are made.

Role of language.

I am also skeptical of the central role Goodman assigns to language and his claim that inductive validity arises from regularities which are a function of our linguistic practice (p. 117). Why I find this idea hard to accept is clear from what I have already said. Too much learning even by humans is utterly nonverbal in character and yet in much of our ordinary getting about in the world it is inductively highly successful.

Bayesian projectibility.

In another article in this volume, Brian Skyrms sets forth a clear and persuasive case for a Bayesian concept of projectibility. As might be expected, he stresses stationarity and the symmetries of various kinds of exchangeability. In the final paragraph, he has this to say:

> We see that—at increasingly general levels of abstraction—projectibility is a reflection of probabilistic symmetries. The logic of projectibility is probability logic. At the most abstract and general level, it is the mathematics of probability-symmetry structures.

I applaud such symmetries when they can be found or, more likely, be imposed by experiment. But such a regime of experimentation occupies a very special place in the world, not even satisfied by many experiments in physics, and certainly not at all in important nonexperimental sciences such as astrophysics, geology, and meteorology. (Skyrms rightly points out the great difficulty of proving the ergodicity of any natural physical systems.)

If animals of any species had had to count on such symmetries to develop workable projectible concepts, evolution would in all likelihood have never gotten off the ground. It is the development of robust learning mechanisms and ever better evolutionary features, which work well enough in environments without such symmetries, above all without stationarity, that lead to projectible concepts good enough to facilitate survival.

Learning and lawlikeness.

Much philosophical talk about induction has been aimed at characterizing genuine as opposed to not so genuine laws, but it seems to me there is good reason to be skeptical of the outcome of this effort—if only because of the negative results thus far. Goodman gives Hume his due for suggesting a mechanism, that of custom or habit, for making predictions. What Hume has to say in Book I of the *Treatise* (1739/1951), especially in Part III, is a brilliant early contribution to the theory of learning. His sketches of how the mind works are directed toward the acquisition of knowledge. No doubt he assumes an environment that is too stationary, but that is hardly surprising.

The central point I want to make by invoking Hume is that he was even more on the right track than Goodman. Hume replaced the necessary connections often thought essential for knowledge by psychological mechanisms of learning. As Hume emphasizes, learning is mostly unconscious and unreflective. We do not think before we walk or talk. We think while we are walking or talking, but ordinarily not about the walking or talking.

So what I urge is to change the focus of projectibility from concepts and laws to the more fundamental mechanisms of learning. I turn to the informal description of some results along the line suggested for various learning models.

Measuring projectibility.

There is no direct way to determine an optimal measure of projectibility of a given learning model relative to a set of tasks and a set of possible environments, also possibly changing from time to time. There is, in principle, a Bayesian approach to the problem of choosing an optimal measure, but it is too intricate to consider at this preliminary stage. Some Bayesian aspects of the problem are mentioned below. What is important is that for nonstationary environments and problems or tasks involving transfer it is inappropriate to use as a measure of success the cumulative relative frequency of success, a measure that accommodates badly to change, as already emphasized.

Let L be a finite nonempty set of learning models whose performance on a finite sequence of prediction tasks $\tau_1, \ldots, \tau_N$ we evaluate for projectibility using the following recursive linear model. For every model i in L, let the projectibility measure $p_{i,1}$, i.e., at the beginning of trial 1 be 0.5 — this choice of a particular number between 0 and 1 is a parameter that can be changed. Then for any learning model i in L the recursive rule is:

$$pi, n + 1 = \begin{cases} (1-\Theta)\, p_{i,n} + \Theta & \text{if a correct prediction was made on trial } n, \\ (1-\Theta)\, p_{i,n} & \text{otherwise.} \end{cases}$$

Again, the particular number Θ is a projectibility parameter which may be changed as long as it lies between 0 and 1. (A good Bayesian problem is to derive optimal estimates of $p_{i,1}$, and Θ.)

As in good horse races, we do not expect one learning model to have the largest projectibility measure for all trials. In extensive but as yet unpublished studies of a variety of neural net learning models, Lin Liang and I have found that a multivariate normal learning model, i.e., a model which recursively estimates a multivariate normal classification model on each trial, does very well on a variety of classification tasks, but only after a substantial number of trials. At the beginning and in the short run several other models formulated only in terms of individual feature inputs or a few combinations often do better, i.e., have a higher projectibility measure for an initial segment of trials. Something similar happens after a large number of trials on a given classification task. Transfer to a new task is often poor because of the relative frequency estimates of feature means relative to each class of the classification scheme.

Note that $p_{i,n}$ is meant to give a reasonable estimate of the probability that the prediction of model i on trial n is correct. We can obviously refine the measure to correctness for a given response. For example, a model may have little difficulty in predicting when an observed "object" belongs to class α, but great difficulty discriminating between objects in classes β and γ.

It may seem to some that I have, inadvertently or not, abandoned the problem of giving a principled account of projectibility for the weak solution of a purely phenomenological quantitative measure. It has been a deliberate advertent choice. A measure just of the blind success of predictions is limited, but here the measure is tied to individual mechanisms of learning. Beyond such mechanisms there is no meaningful concept of validity of predictions or deeper concepts of justification of induction. As Hume rightly said most learning in ordinary experience is unconscious and unreflective. There can be no logical or transcendental justification of the inherited biological mechanisms of learning beyond some measure of their success. Exactly which measure is a good topic for constructive academic dispute.

Furthermore, I would argue that the same is to be said for the systematic methods of statisticians, Bayesians or otherwise. The contribution of these methods to the design and evaluation of experiments in many scientific domains is one of the signal methodological achievements of this century, but their ultimate justification is at bottom very similar. The pragmatism of success is not replaceable by a religion of justification, not even by theistic invocations of the uniformity of nature.

Stanford University

REFERENCES

De Finetti, B. (1937/1964). "Foresight: Its Logical Laws, Its Subjective Sources," in *Studies in Subjective Probability,* ed. Henry E. Kyburg and Howard E. Smokler (New York: J. Wiley).

Goodman, Nelson. (1955). *Fact, Fiction and Forecast.* (Cambridge, Massachusetts: Harvard University Press).

Hume, D. (1739/1951). *A Treatise of Human Nature,* ed. L. A. Selby-Bigge (Oxford and New York: Oxford University Press).

Karlin, S. (1953). "Some Random Walks Arising in Learning Models I." *Pacific Journal of Mathematics 3:* 725–756.

Lamperti, J. and Suppes, P. (1959). "Chains of Infinite Order and their Application to Learning Theory." *Pacific Journal of Mathematics 9:* 739–754

Skyrms, Brian. "Bayesian Projectibility." This volume.

Suppes, P. (1991). "The Principle of Invariance with Special Reference to Perception," in J. Doignon and J. Falmagne, eds., *Mathematical Psychology: Current Developments* (New York: Springer), 35–53.

Selecting Variables and Getting to the Truth

Clark Glymour and Peter Spirtes

Goodman's grue example suggests many questions it does not pose. We will discuss this one in particular: are there contexts of inquiry in which, if one set of variables is used to form hypotheses, some method or other will lead from observations to conjectures that converge to the truth, but if another set of variables, definable from the first, is used, then no method will converge to the truth? If there are such contexts, what confidence can we have that the variables we choose are the right ones? Our examples concern inquiries into causal processes. First, however, consider the relation of such questions to the "new riddle of induction."

Goodman introduced "grue" as a startling objection to syntactic accounts of how evidence confirms hypotheses. Goodman showed that without a further account of how to select the predicates used in hypotheses, there are languages for which a class of syntactic accounts of confirmation yield unintuitive claims about confirmation, although not strict contradictions. The accounts of confirmation Goodman criticized were informally connected with recommendations about prediction, and Goodman's examples did show that the natural use of syntactic confirmation relations for prediction could indeed generate contradictory predictions. The important point was not the contradictory predictions themselves, but how one might know which forecast is correct. Goodman's "new riddle of induction" therefore has two aspects. One, partly psychological and social, is a challenge to explain how we do in fact select from all possible properties those we use in generalizations about the world. The other, not psychological or social at all, is to show how to select properties that can be used for reliable inference and prediction. This second aspect was in most respects very old hat; the essential point is found in Plato's *Meno* and in Sextus Empiricus. From a contemporary perspective it amounts to a throwaway line, an aside, within any of several mathematical accounts of inductive inference.[1] The introduction of grue predicates or bleen predicates is a way of emphasizing that no method will reliably yield true universal hypotheses in the short run, but the use of grue and bleen predicates of itself does not prohibit reliable inference in the long run. On this score Goodman's originality was only in formulating the problems of reliable inference and prediction as problems in the selection of predicates to use in generalizations or, since predicates are binary valued variables, problems about the selection of variables. Goodman's own view of his riddle, which he called "pragmatic," seems to have been that in addressing the first aspect one would thereby resolve the problems of the second. We think confusing the two issues does nothing to advance understanding.

Goodman's puzzle has been a wonderful source of motivation. Charmed by the elegance of the example, philosophers have since made liberal use of analogy to discuss any number of issues about inductive inference as aspects of Goodman's grue puzzle, including questions of the role of simplicity principles and curve-fitting practices. In that spirit, we will make some observations about the role of the selection of variables in reliable inductive inference and in prediction where the aim is to identify causal structure.

We require some preliminaries about causal inference. Details of definitions and descriptions and proofs of results we claim in passing will be found in Spirtes, Glymour, and Scheines (1993). We will assume that the causal relations to be inferred are among variables, which may take an array of values. Causal relations among variables can be defined in terms of causal relations among appropriate events, but we will not bother here. We will say a set V of variables is *causally sufficient* if every cause of two or more variables in V is in V. We will represent hypotheses about causal relations among a causally sufficient set V of variables by a directed acyclic graph, where a directed edge $Y \to Y$ signifies that some variation in X produces a variation in Y even if all other variables in V are held constant.

For a population of systems with the same causal structure over a set V, we assume that variation in the values of the variables in V that have no causes in V, and variation of variables omitted from V that, however, influence some variable in V, generates a joint probability distribution over V. We assume any such distribution is related to a causal graph by a Markov condition:

> **Causal Markov Condition:** Let G be a causal graph with vertex set V and let P be a probability distribution over the vertices in V generated by the causal structure represented by G. G and P satisfy the Causal Markov Condition if and only if for every W in V, W is independent of $V\backslash(\text{Descendants}(W) \cup \text{Parents}(W))$ given $\text{Parents}(W)$.[2]

The Markov condition says that a causal graph determines a collection of conditional independence relations among the variables. We further assume that all conditional independence relations among variables in V arise from causal structure, an assumption we call Faithfulness:

Faithfulness Condition: Let *G* be a causal graph and *P* a probability distribution generated by *G*. <*G, P*> satisfies the Faithfulness Condition if and only if every conditional independence relation true in *P* is entailed by the Causal Markov Condition applied to *G*.

Not every distribution satisfying the Markov condition for a directed acyclic graph *G* also satisfies the Faithfulness condition, but in a natural sense *almost* every such distribution does. The distributions that violate the Faithfulness condition have measure zero in a measure on the parameters that characterize the distributions satisfying the Markov condition for the graph.

Now the inference problem we consider is to discover whatever one can about a causal graph *G* from samples drawn from a probability distribution *P* generated by *G*, where *G* and *P* satisfy the Markov and Faithfulness conditions. Of course it may be that two graphs *G* and *G'* are indistinguishable in the sense that any distribution meeting the Markov and Faithfulness conditions for one also satisfies those conditions for the other. For any directed acyclic graph *G*, we call the set of graphs that admit the same set of faithful distributions as does *G* the *faithful indistinguishability class* of *G*.

Assuming the Markov and Faithfulness conditions, the most that can be required of a procedure for identifying causal structure from probabilities is that the procedure identify the faithful indistinguishability class with probability approaching 1 as the sample size increases without bound, or that it identify the faithful indistinguishability class with certainty given an oracle for conditional independence facts in a distribution.

When *V* is casually sufficient and all variables in *V* are measured, there are many such algorithms. But in certain cases all such algorithms can be defeated by a gruesome procedure.

Consider the graph:

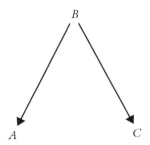

Figure 1

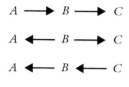

Figure 2

Its indistinguishability class is shown in Figure 2. All three graphs require that A and C be statistically independent conditional on B, and that no other conditional independence relations hold among the three variables. Given these facts about independence as input, reliable procedures for causal inference return the three graphs in Figure 2 as output.

In contrast, the indistinguishability class of the graph shown in Figure 3 contains only that graph itself. Given the facts that A is independent of C and that no other conditional independence relations obtain, the same methods will return the graph in Figure 3, as must any reliable, fully informative method for causal inference from probabilities.

New random variables can always be defined from a given set of variables by taking linear or Boolean or other combinations. For any specified apparatus of definitions and any axioms connecting graphs with distributions, questions about indistinguishability classes arise parallel to those we have just considered for fixed sets of variables. A distribution P over variable set V may correspond to a graph G, and a distribution P' over variable set V' may correspond to a different graph G' (with P' and V' obtained from P and V by defining new variables, ignoring old ones, and marginalizing). The differences between G and G' may in some cases be unimportant, and one may simply want to say that each graph correctly describes causal relations among its respective set of variables. That is not so, however, when the

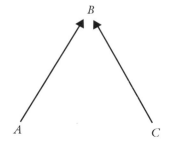

Figure 3

original variables are ordered by time, and redefinition of variables results in a distribution whose corresponding graphs have later variables (or events) causing earlier variables (or events). Consider the pair of graphs in Figure 4. In directed acyclic graph (i), where A and C are effects of B, suppose that B occurs prior to A and C. By the procedure of definition and marginalization, a distribution faithful to graph (i) can be transformed into a distribution faithful to graph (ii). First, standardize A and C to form variables A' and C' with unit variance and zero mean. Then consider the variables $(A' - C')$ and $(A' + C')$.

Their covariance is equal to the expected value of $A'^2 - C'^2$ which is zero. Simple algebra shows that the partial correlation of $(A' - C')$ and $(A' + C')$ given B does not vanish. The marginal of the original distribution is therefore faithful to (ii) if the original distribution is normal.

Suppose now Figure 1 describes the causal relations among A, B, and C, and a causal inference is made from a distribution faithful to Figure 1 but using the variables B, $(A' - C')$, and $(A' + C')$. Then the graph in Figure 3 will be output and will of course be false.

Note that the transformation just illustrated is unstable; if the variances of A' and C' are unequal in the slightest, or if the transformation gives $(xA'\ Y\ zC')$ and $(yA' + wC')$ for any values of x, y, z, and w such that $xy + wz + \rho A'C'(zy + xw) \neq 0$ (where $\rho A'C'$ is the correlation of A' and C'), then the marginal on the transformed distribution will be faithful, not to (ii), but to all acyclic orientations of the complete graph on the three variables, a hypothesis that is not inconsistent with the time order.

Viewed from another perspective, a transformation of variables that produces a "coincidental" vanishing partial correlation is just a violation of the Faithfulness condition. Consider the linear model in Figure 5.

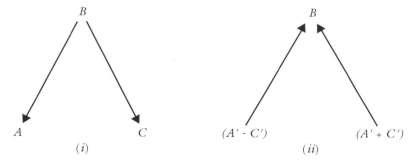

Figure 4

Let $A' = rB + \epsilon_{A'}$, $C' = sB + \epsilon_C$, $D = xA' + zC' + \epsilon_D$, and $E = yA' + wC' + \epsilon_E$. If the variables are standardized, ρ_{DE} is equal to $xy + zw + rysz + rxsw = xy + zw + rs(yz + xw)$, which, since $rs = \rho_{A'C'}$, is the formula of the previous paragraph. If $\rho_{DE} = 0$, the Faithfulness condition is violated. We get the example of Figure 3 when $D = A' + C'$(i.e., $x = z = 1$), and $E = A' - C'$ (i.e., $y = -w = 1$) where the variances and unity and means of the error terms have been set to zero. Since the set of parameter values that violate Faithfulness in this example has measure zero, so does the set of linear transformations of A and C that produce a "coincidental" zero correlation.

The upshot is that if variables are improperly (or better: unfortunately) selected, gruesome examples can arise in the sort of causal inference that goes on all the time in social science, epidemiology, and other subjects that rely on empirical data. But such variables are infinitely rare under a natural measure. Put subjectively, in any empirical case, we are nearly certain our variables are not gruesome. That is not a great reason for optimism. If the transformations of the previous paragraph are taken to define a family of variables, then the set of variables from which the causal structure in graph (*i*) of Figure 4 can be recovered is *also* of measure zero. In between are most sets of variables compounded of A and C, variables that remain correlated and whose conditional probability relations determine an indistinguishability class of six complete graphs. The problem for empirical, nonexperimental science is not gruesome variables but variables that are neither greensome nor gruesome, variables whose statistical dependencies provide little information about causal structure.[3]

Carnegie Mellon University

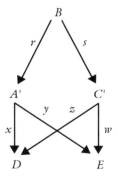

Figure 5

NOTES

1. Before you is an endless array of black boxes, their mechanisms forever sealed from your knowledge, except in one respect, soon to be described. Now and then each box pushes out a marble, colored either green or blue. What you know is this: For each box the color of the marbles emitted from that box will change at most once. A box may give green marbles for a while, then blue, but not then green again; a box may give blue marbles for a while then green, but not then blue again. Or a box may ever give the green marbles, another always the blue. Say any particular box is grue(N) just if the first N marbles emitted by the box are green and the remainder blue; say a box is bleen(N) if the first N marbles emitted by the box are blue and the remainder green. Among the array of boxes every such possibility is realized, in every consistent way, but which boxes will realize which possibility is unknown to you. Now consider the following questions:

1. Is there a method to predict for any box, for all N, from the colors of its first N marbles, the color of its $N + 1$st marble?
2. Is there a method to provide for each box and all K, from K observed marbles a number $N > K$ and to predict, for all $M > N$, from the colors of the first M marbles emitted by the box, the color of the $M + 1$st marble?
3. Is there a method that for each box, for some M correctly predicts the colors of all marbles after the Mth?
4. Is there a method that for each box, from observations of marble colors emitted by the box, for all N, conjectures whether the box is green, blue, grue(N), or bleen(N), and such that every conjecture produced by the method is correct?
5. Is there a method that for each box, from observations of marble colors emitted by the box, for all N, conjectures whether the box is green, blue, grue(N), or bleen (N), and such that the method makes no more than two conjectures, and such that the final conjecture made is always correct?

No method as required in 1 exists; no method as required in 2 exists. There is a simple method as required in 3. No method as required in 4 exists; there is a simple method as required in 5. And that is almost all there is to say about grue and getting to the truth.

2. $X\backslash Y$ denotes the members of X that are not members of Y. Descendants (W) is the set including W and all X in V such that there is a directed path from W to X. Parents (W) is the set of members of V that have directed paths to W.

3. We thank Judea Pearl, who brought to our attention the possibility of redefinitions of the kind noted in this paper.

REFERENCE

P. Spirtes, C. Glymour, and R. Scheines, *Causation, Prediction and Search* (Springer Lecture Notes in Statistics 81) (New York: Springer-Verlag, 1993).

ANNOTATED BIBLIOGRAPHY

Achinstein, Peter. "Confirmation Theory, Order, and Periodicity." *Philosophy of Science* 30 (1963): 17–35. Examines adequacy conditions for a confirmation function in a Carnapian coordinate language that can express elementary number theory. Notes how various adequacy conditions become inappropriate because a coordinate language recognizes periodicities in the evidence and periodicities can influence degrees of confirmation. Concentrates on two specific conditions that seem justified by the fundamental principle that "the greater the number of positive instances of an hypothesis, and the fewer its negative instances, the higher its degree of confirmation." Formulates one condition with respect to a hypothesis that an individual in the ordering has a certain property; says the hypothesis receives more support from r previous individuals in the ordering having the property than from all but one of r previous individuals having the property. Formulates the other condition with respect to two hypotheses about individuals having a certain property, one on the evidence that r previous individuals have the property, the other on the evidence that s previous individuals have the property; says that where r is greater than s, the former hypothesis is confirmed to a greater degree than the latter. Argues against these conditions (and subsequent modifications of them) by introducing two positional predicates: "M" applies to a red object just in case "the ordinal number which designates the position of the object in the ordering is not a power of 10," and "N" applies to a red object just in case it "does not occupy a position in the ordering immediately following the second object in the ordering." Considers modifying the fundamental principle (as Carnap does in response to Goodman's questions about projectible predicates) so that it holds for hypotheses "that contain only qualitative predicates and their truth-functional compounds." Points out that the two adequacy conditions then have to be restricted to hypotheses with qualitative predicates, and this overcomes the difficulties produced by predicates "M" and "N" because they are positional predicates. Claims this modification has the "extremely undesirable effect of preventing a confirmation function from recognizing simple periodicities" because periodicity predicates are defined in terms of arithmetic predicates and this makes them positional predicates. Notes that the two adequacy conditions involve an assumption about what counts as a positive instance of a hypothesis. Replaces this assumption by one providing sufficient conditions for being an instance of a hypothesis without positional predicates, and for being an instance of a periodicity hypothesis with positional predicates, where sets of individuals can be instances of periodicity hypotheses. Reformulates the two adequacy conditions in line with adopting this assumption and taking the fundamental principle to hold for all predicates. Argues that the adequacy conditions now avoid difficulties produced by positional predicates. Points out how these conditions require enriching the formal language with predicates and quantifiers for sets. See the reply by Carnap (1963).

Achinstein, Peter. "On the Choice of Functional Hypotheses." In *The Business of Reason*, edited by J.J. Macintosh and S. Coval, 1–25. London: Routledge & Kegan Paul, 1969. Examines criteria for choosing a functional hypothesis describing the relationship between several physical quantities based on a set of observed values for them. Starts from an example of a linear hypothesis corresponding to a straight line drawn through all of the data points ("the smoothest curve which fits the data"). Considers and rejects a simple inductivist criterion that looks for the hypothesis with the most positive instances and no negative ones, an unqualified simplicity criterion that looks for "the simplest hypothesis compatible with the data," a Carnapian criterion that looks for the degree of confirmation in terms of relative frequency of a property in observed pairs of data points, a Reichenbach straight rule criterion and then Reichenbach's own inductive justification for a simplest curve criterion, Popper's (1959) simplicity criterion that looks for the most (or more) falsifiable hypothesis, Barker's (1957) logical measure criterion that takes into account "the entire system of propositions to which the hypothesis and evidence belong," and a rational decision theory criterion that looks at the estimated utility of adopting a hypothesis. Proposes that a confirmation theory's basic rules should satisfy a principle about only the simplest hypothesis receiving positive inductive support (other things equal, the more observed instances the more support) in a curve-fitting situation with mutually exclusive hypotheses fitting the data. Argues that this principle "reflects the actual scientific practice of accepting the simplest functional hypothesis and maintaining furthermore that this hypothesis is indeed supported by the evidence, whereas other hypotheses, though compatible with the evidence, are not." Notes that, on this proposal, only certain positive instances provide support for a hypothesis and only certain observed regularities can be projected, and that for functional hypotheses, "only the simplest observed regularity can legitimately be projected." Discusses changing an inductive theory of confirmation so that it satisfies his proposed principle; considers defining a confirmation function for a language that can express scientific functional hypotheses and states a condition on a function so that a hypothesis receives a considerable degree of confirmation if and only if there are many data points and the hypothesis is the simplest one compatible with them.

Achinstein, Peter. *The Concept of Evidence.* Oxford: Oxford University Press, 1983. Edited collection of readings (eight selections) with an introduction and selected bibliography with comments. Includes Hempel (1945) and pages 84–108 from chapter IV, "Prospects for a Theory of Projection," *FFF.* Also has selections by Braithwaite, Hanson, Carnap ("The Concept of Confirming Evidence"), Salmon, Glymour, and Achinstein.

Ackermann, Robert. "Inductive Simplicity." *Philosophy of Science* 28 (1961): 152–161. Critically examines proposals for simplicity rules to solve the curve-fitting problem, especially those by Jeffreys (1957), Popper (1959), and Kemeny (1953). Thinks these simplicity ordering proposals do not solve the problem because the orderings are not well defined and are not practical. Thinks that laboratory handbooks (for practical data analysis) do not help solve the problem because they do not deal with inductive simplicity. Claims that most proposals involve three unwarranted assumptions: continuity of functions, adequacy of measurement, and nonstatistical data. Argues that most proposals gratuitously impose "an *a priori* limit on scientific hypotheses to the set of equations representing continuous functions"; that any proposal resulting "in the notion that a hypothesis must fit the data is not sufficient to explain why certain hypotheses with real numbers in their expressions are an integral part of science"; and that most proposals do not cover conflicting sets of data from more than one experiment and the practice of interpreting and juggling data points. Maintains there are two serious problems even if we discover a well-ordering of hypotheses as, for example, some authors propose for polynomials in terms of the number of their parameters. Wonders if "any clear notion of simplicity can be invoked to justify the ordering as a simplicity ordering." Also wonders how adequately the well-ordering proposals explicate actual scientific practice in view of the fact that "scientists are able to work efficiently while only considering some small number of hypotheses." Claims that the inductive approach to curve-fitting "minimizes or ignores the important way in which previously considered theories and hypotheses determine experiment, and experimental interpretations in science." Ends by discussing another problem with these proposals: viz., the idea that scientists accept hypotheses.

Ackermann, Robert J. "Projecting Unprojectibles." *Philosophy of Science* 33 (1966): 70–75. A reply to Kahane (1965). Notes that the third elimination rule is now (in the second edition of *FFF*) the second rule. Thinks that Kahane's examples all "trade on intuitively *ad hoc* enlargements of suitable evidence classes" and these make the second rule fail because the evidence class for the unprojectible hypothesis is not contained in, or identical to, the evidence class for the presumptively projectible hypothesis. Suggests eliminating Kahane's examples by adding a third rule to cover times when two thinkable hypotheses have identical projective classes and they make the same predictions over this class: then one hypothesis is presumptively projectible if and only if the other is. Notes that Goodman may simplify the second rule in a way that, in effect, omits the condition about the relation between the two evidence classes. Claims this would also eliminate Kahane's examples. Discusses a difference between these two proposals that appears with the introduction of a genus predicate as "an *explication* of examined species classes which extend them to previously unconsidered individuals as a result of theoretical considerations." Points out we need to assume an observation of an emerald that is not in the current evidence class to have a conflict between the grue and green hypotheses. Characterizes the situation in terms of a consistent set of sentences comprised of the pair of hypotheses and the definition relating their predicates, producing an inconsistency in this set by adding a sentence reporting an observation as per the assumption, but not producing an inconsistency in a subset created by deleting the grue hypothesis or a subset created by deleting the green hypothesis. Cites Leblanc (1963) for a formal treatment. Claims that Kahane is wrong to think conflict depends on the analytic-synthetic distinction. Contends that some of his examples are wrong because he does not "compare fixed pairs of hypotheses against a fixed evidence class." With respect to entrenchment and introducing new scientific terms, points out that the examples typically introduce a theoretical term in a single hypothesis, and that "the introduction of theories depends upon a great many other considerations than the projectibility indices of its constituent hypotheses in terms of current evidence classes." Considers it "misdirected" to test Goodman's theory of projectibility as the only criterion for judging the future projectibility of hypotheses with new theoretical terms. See the response by Kahane (1967).

Ackermann, Robert J. "Conflict and Decision." *Philosophy of Science* 34 (1967): 188–193. A reply to Kahane (1967). Attempts to clarify the notion of conflict between hypotheses and explain why the proposed revisions of the second elimination rule (his addition and Goodman's omission) are not too strong. Informally describes conflict between the green and grue hypotheses as a matter of their consequent predicates being dependent "in a manner which entails that if any new evidence constitutes an instance of one hypothesis, it cannot also be an instance of the other." More formally describes conflict by specifying how a pair of nonindependent hypotheses can strongly conflict given certain evidence, identifying "the strongest legitimate existential claim" involved in these hypotheses, and finally giving an account of conflict in terms of the set of all possible individuals that may be recorded as instances of both nonindependent hypotheses P and Q, where this set has at least one member, neither P nor Q is exhausted after all of the members are recorded as instances of P and Q, an additional individual is assumed to exist, and trying to record this individual as an instance of either P or Q makes for inconsistency in the set comprised of P, Q, and the definitions or entailments relating their predicates. Believes this account shows all of Kahane's examples are misdirected, even the one about eliminating "All emeralds are G-grue." Discusses Goodman's unrevised second elimination rule, how it does not eliminate Kahane's "All A-emerubies are green" example, how our knowledge about the color of emeralds and rubies might be influencing our judgments here, and how we cannot revise the second rule on the basis of the obvious difficulty produced by introducing a few *ad hoc* individuals. Describes Goodman's revision and maintains it does eliminate Kahane's counterexample. Reviews his own example of finding that some members of two classes have a property in common, and claims that "Kahane's discussion of my example involves a misconception of what I mean by a genus." Views introducing genera as conceptual revision that "may provide better ways of understanding or treating familiar cases as well as suggesting new cases." Contends that typically a genus hypothesis is not equivalent to the simple conjunction of separate hypotheses about its species: "the significance of a natural genus is not exhausted by listing the species known to belong to it." Emphasizes that his proposed third elimination rule is applied after the first two rules, that it eliminates by comparing hypotheses to ones eliminated by the first two rules, and that the first two rules can be blocked from eliminating a hypothesis under certain conditions.

Akeroyd, F.M. "A Practical Example of Grue." *British Journal for the Philosophy of Science* 42 (1991): 535–539. Claims it is more convincing to introduce the new riddle with the predicate "regulatic," which refers to phenomena that "exhibit regularities before time t and erratic behaviour thereafter." Presents an economic example, the Phillips curve, relating changes in wage rates to the level of unemployment; the data conform to the Phillips hypothesis before 1969 and do not thereafter. Also introduces the predicate "tralse" to mean "true before time t and false thereafter." Presents the hypothesis "Gold is immutable" as tralse because it was true until approximately 1300 and false thereafter. Distinguishes between tralse hypotheses and hypotheses "falsely believed to be true"— such as "Noble gases are inert." Recommends this terminology for real-world grue examples and falsified scientific theories, respectively.

Alder, Michael D. "On Theories." *Philosophy of Science* 40 (1973): 213–226. Formalizes, with an axiom set, the notion of a theory "involving results of a general measuring process," develops a measure of simplicity for such theories in terms of their abstract pretheories, and considers the confirmation and refutation of pretheories by a datum. Discusses confirmation in connection with "grue-blite theories." Maintains that "it does not follow that because a datum confirms an infinite collection of theories that we must fail to prefer one of them." Characterizes the situation as one in which "we find a more complex theory than some given theory and restrain the admissible data so as to prevent a 'crucial experiment' which will distinguish between them." Thinks we view these theory comparisons as paradoxical only because we are not familiar with them, and we are not familiar with them because "we reject the complex theory out of hand." Emphasizes that, with respect to all the theories confirmed by a datum, we might find the simplest theory but not one theory confirmed more than any of the others.

Allen, Barry. "Gruesome Arithmetic: Kripke's Sceptic Replies." *Dialogue* 28 (1989): 257–264. Discussion of a skeptical argument in Kripke (1982) about saying "plus" and meaning addition as opposed to something like qaddition. Notes that Kripke's argument is similar to Goodman's new riddle of induction, and that Kripke himself points this out. Contends that Kripke's argument "simply *is* Goodman's riddle of induction, tailored to field linguistics rather than mineralogy." Claims there is a "precise analogy" between the "idea that there could be evidence to confirm the greenness (but not the grueness) of emeralds and evidence that events are intentional under the description 'adding' (but not under the description 'qadding')." Goes on to contend that the skeptical argument is a variation on Quine's arguments about radical translation and that it attacks "the idea of something whose presence makes a sound or graphic token full of meaning." Also see Mulhall (1989).

Altham, J.E.J. "A Note on Goodman's Paradox." *British Journal for the Philosophy of Science* 19 (1968): 257. Argues that neither the qualitative/nonqualitative nor the observational/nonobservational distinctions provide the basis for a solution to the new riddle of induction. Introduces the predicate 'gracet' as a qualitative, observational predicate and claims it is similar to 'grue' in six relevant ways.

Armstrong, D. M. *Universals and Scientific Realism,* Volume II of *A Theory of Universals.* Cambridge: Cambridge University Press, 1978. See chapter 15, "Acceptance of Conjunctive Universals," for a discussion of Grossman (1973) and his position on grue being a property. Contends that "grue" is not a property-predicate. Introduces property-predicates and relation-predicates as the two types of strictly universal predicates. Characterizes these predicates as applying "in virtue of a single universal alone, monadic or polyadic, a property or a relation." Notes that he cannot give an uncontroversial example of a strictly universal predicate because "total science" decides what universals exist. Suggests that "weighs one kilogram exactly" is a plausible example of a strictly universal predicate. Thinks that "grue" is not a property-predicate because, with the predicate applying to an object *a* prior to time *t* and also after *t,* "we are not *forced* to say that the predicate applies at the two times in virtue of something about the object *a* which is identical." Adds that "what we know of the world makes it fairly clear that in fact no such identical property is involved."

Armstrong, D.M. *What is a Law of Nature?* Cambridge: Cambridge University Press, 1983. Criticizes the regularity theory and develops a theory of laws as relations between universals. Brings up grue (p. 16) in connection with distinguishing between uniformities and pseudo-uniformities, especially a pseudo-uniformity based on a disjunctive predicate. Notes (p. 60) that "grue" poses a problem for regularity theories (especially naive ones) with regard to specifying what counts as a uniformity because gruelike predicates can appear in universal generalizations and yet pick out "a heterogeneous miscellany." Considers how a more sophisticated version of the regularity theory, the Ramsey–Lewis or systematic version, makes the distinction between laws and accidental generalizations. Presents (pp. 68–69) an objection to this version by introducing gruelike predicates into a strong and simple system. Maintains that, in order to meet this objection, a systematic theorist "cannot treat the classes of things linked together in uniformities as *mere* classes, or classes unified only by the application of the same (!) predicate to each member of the class." Claims you must "carve nature at the joints" and either appeal to certain objective resemblances or objective universals such as properties. Says (p. 99) his theory (laws as relations between universals) deals with pseudo-uniformities produced by predicates like "grue." Claims "on the basis of total science, that 'grue' is a predicate to which no genuine, that is, unitary, universal corresponds," and so there is no relation between universals in these strange uniformities. Says (p. 138) the grue problem dissolves (at least for naive regularity theories) with stipulating that both antecedent and consequent predicates in universally quantified generalizations must name distinct universals. Also see Armstrong (1978).

Aune, Bruce. "The Paradox of Empiricism." *Metaphilosophy* 1 (1970): 128–138. Attempts to demonstrate that empiricists "have actually rested their case on the flimsiest foundations and have been no less critical on matters of basic principle than their avowed enemies the rationalists." Considers Hume's view that there is no a priori knowledge of matters of fact and existence, and that "acceptable knowledge of such matters must have a secure basis in observation, memory, or experimental inference." Regards experimental inference as inductive generalization or enumerative induction. Points to Goodman as showing that enumerative induction is "highly questionable," and cites Russell as first stating the new riddle in *Human Knowledge: Its Scope and Limits*. Maintains that "not all of the needed limitations are covered by the theory of entrenchment": e.g., claims Goodman's rules do not eliminate the false but well-supported hypothesis that all ravens are observed, but that Russell's postulate of Quasi-Permanence does eliminate it.

Ayer, A. J. *Bertrand Russell*. New York: The Viking Press, 1972a. See pages 92–102. Discusses Russell's principle of induction from *The Problems of Philosophy* and notes that Russell later saw it was "insufficient." Cites Russell's (1948) discussion of probability in *Human Knowledge: Its Scope and Limits*, pages 413–414, where Russell points out that in a next-case induction from all observed *A*s are *B*s, *A* and *B* cannot stand for any classes we like if the induction is to even have a chance of being valid. Comments that "it is the selection of these favored classes that constitutes what Nelson Goodman has called the new riddle of induction" and contends that "no single principle of uniformity will do this work, just because it will be too general." See Sainsbury (1979) and Salmon (1974 and 1975).

Ayer, A. J. *Probability and Evidence*. New York: Columbia University Press, 1972b. Discusses Goodman's paradox on pages 82–88. Considers Goodman's paradox to be a qualitative example of the fact that "in every case in which a set of instances exemplifies a hypothesis *H*, it is possible to find another hypothesis *H'*, incompatible with *H*, which they equally exemplify." Notes how much of the dispute has been about positional predicates; thinks this misses the main point. Sees Goodman as framing "a hypothesis which we should naturally express by saying that some *A* is *B* and some *A* is not-*B* into a universal form." Points out that the grue hypothesis does this by referring to when the instances are examined, and that there are other ways to do this. Goes along with deciding which predicates are projectible, but thinks "it is to some extent arbitrary." Also thinks there is more to the problem than this; claims that "even if we are operating only with the most respectable, the most firmly entrenched predicates, a given body of evidence is still going to be consistent with mutually incompatible hypotheses." Claims neither Goodman nor Hempel have given any reason for restricting attention to universal generalizations, and so if we have ten emeralds, have examined five of them, and found all five to be green, then this is equally consistent with all of the emeralds being green or various other proportions from 50 percent to 90 percent. Discusses whether Popper's approach avoids the Goodman paradox. Presents two conditions as necessary and sufficient for a statement being evidence for another; notes five consequences of the conditions. Concludes that we need to "legislate" that only some types of predicates and some types of hypotheses are projectible, that this legislating "takes account of extra-logical considerations, such as simplicity," and that this is the only way to "make it rational to accept any given hypothesis rather than any one of the others that can be devised to accord with our existing information." Also mentions Goodman's paradox on page 109 in discussing Harrod's postulate.

Barker, S.F. *Induction and Hypothesis: A Study of the Logic of Confirmation*. Ithaca, N.Y.: Cornell University Press, 1957. Argues for a criterion of confirmation that combines the method of hypothesis and the notion of logical simplicity; develops the criterion in connection with competing systems of empirical hypotheses and their logical measures as determined by the number of models per system. Considers the new riddle as an objection to the criterion on pages 188–191. Maintains that 'green' is an observational predicate, 'grue' is not; concludes there is no reason for introducing 'grue' into the language we use for empirical statements. Claims that if the term were introduced, then "the simplest and preferable system of hypotheses will be one which includes a hypothesis that will serve to prevent 'grue' from adding to the number of models that the system has." Supposes this hypothesis will make the predicate true of nothing, and thus 'All emeralds are grue' will be "trivial and uninteresting" compared to 'All emeralds are green.' Claims the green hypothesis can produce "an interesting and nontrivial simplification in the system" because it has, unlike the grue hypothesis, an observational predicate.

Barker, S.F. and Achinstein, Peter. "On the New Riddle of Induction." *Philosophical Review* 69 (1960): 511–522. Define "grue" so it applies to something at a given time if and only if "the thing is then green and the time is prior to time *t*, or the thing is then blue and the time is not prior to *t*." Note the Carnapian response to the new riddle based on the distinction between predicates that refer to time and ones that do not. Also note Goodman's reply based on a symmetry between the grue-bleen language and the green-blue language: predicates are relatively, not inherently, temporal or nontemporal, as can be seen by defining "green" in terms of "grue" and "bleen" and a temporal term. Believe this reply involves two claims: viz., that grue speakers apply "grue" to all and only objects that green speakers apply "green" to if it is before 2000 or apply "blue" to if it is 2000 or after, where this includes applying the term to fictional objects, imaginary objects, or objects in pictures; and that grue speakers do not have to "ascertain the date of an object before being able to tell whether the object is grue or not." Ask what it would be like for there to be grue speakers who could do this. Consider how Mr. Grue and Mr. Green think of the color of objects in representational pictures. Note that Mr. Green will call an object in a picture green if and only if it is represented with green pigment. Argue that Mr. Grue must call an object in a picture grue if and only if the pigment in question is green and "the date in the picture" is before 2000 or the pigment is blue and "the date in the picture" is 2000 or after. Describe a case about choosing the paint to make the grass in two pictures grue—one picture of Harvard Yard in 1958, the other of the Yard in 2000, and both pictures screened off except for identical black-and-white plots of grass. Claim that if Mr. Grue can choose the right paints here, then he "must possess a faculty of extrasensory perception not possessed by people such as ourselves who are speakers of the green-blue language." Ask Mr. Grue what color of paint he would use to color the tympanum of a chapel bleen in 1959 and again in 2001, and presume he will choose our blue for 1959 and our green for 2001. Believe this shows "grue" and "bleen" are temporal predicates for Mr. Grue because he needs to know the date of an object in order to apply the predicates correctly. Consider Mr. Grue's claim that, for him, "green" and "blue" are also temporal predicates. Believe this is wrong because Mr. Grue can tell whether an object in a picture is green without determining the date of the scene in the picture: e.g., we can inform him that whenever he sees grue paint, the object is green and whenever he sees bleen paint, the object is blue. Consider a reply that claims, from Mr. Grue's point of view, Mr. Green will have extrasensory perception and use "green" as a temporal predicate. Describe two experiments that do not show Mr. Grue has an occult power. Maintain it "seems impossible to demonstrate that Mr. Green possesses any faculty of extrasensory perception." Also maintain that knowing the date of a scene is irrelevant to Mr. Green coloring objects in a picture blue or green as per our instructions. Consider another reply: while Mr. Grue can't choose the right color of paint to use in a picture, he can tell when an object in a picture is grue or not. Note how the reply makes it hard to view "grue" as a color predicate. Maintain the examples (e.g., the grass in Harvard Yard pictures, the color of a chapel's tympanum in a picture) can be changed from choosing colors to identifying the color of objects in the pictures, and they will still show that Mr. Grue has extrasensory powers and that he is using "grue" as a temporal predicate. Conclude that there is a "logically important difference" between "grue" and "green" in that the former is a temporal predicate, the latter is not. Maintain this point applies to other Goodmanized predicates such as "condulates electricity," which is true of something that conducts electricity before 2000 or something that is an electrical insulator at or after 2000. Claim we can tell if an ammeter in a picture is a conductor without knowing the date in the picture and with the rest of the picture hidden from our view, but that it will take extrasensory powers to tell whether the object is a condulator because the temporal clues are hidden from ordinary view. See the replies by Goodman (1960), Ullian (1961), Sollazzo (1972), and Shirley (1981).

Bartley, W. W. III. "Goodman's Paradox: A Simple-Minded Solution." *Philosophical Studies* 19 (1968): 85–88. Argues that we do not take seriously the hypothesis "All emeralds are grue" because it is not presented in response to a problem in mineralogy. See the reply by Hullett (1970).

Bealer, George. *Quality and Concept.* Oxford: Oxford University Press, 1982. See chapter 8, "Qualities and Concepts," for his position on grue and the new riddle. Distinguishes between properties that are genuine qualities and properties that are Cambridge properties. Considers grue to be "the most notorious Cambridge property in recent philosophical literature." Maintains that qualities, not Cambridge properties, play a special role in descriptions of experiences and in theories. Claims that we can experience genuine qualities, not Cambridge properties, that changes in the world mainly are changes in qualities and connections, not Cambridge properties and relations, and that identification and categorization of objects is a matter of genuine qualities and connections, not Cambridge ones. Takes the view that "qualities and connections are determinants of the phenomenal, causal, and logical order of the world whereas Cambridge properties and relations are idle in these respects." Uses this distinction to solve the new riddle: viz., inductive generalizations on genuine properties receive, *ceteris paribus,* a high degree of justification and inductive generalizations on Cambridge properties receive, *ceteris paribus,* a low degree of justification. Argues that "the ideal inductive generalization begins with an observed order and projects it into a general order," and yet "the very concept of orderliness is one that pertains to qualities and connections." Goes on to consider what a Cambridge property, like grue, amounts to. Maintains it is not a phenomenal property, is not causally efficacious, is not a basic logical property; concludes that a Cambridge property is a mere concept and that its "primary role is in thinking, and that role is often playful." See Shoemaker (1982) and Zabludowski (1991 and this volume).

Bernadette, Jose A. "Induction and Infinity." *Ratio* 13 (1971): 139–149. Formulates the problem of induction as inferring the sun will rise tomorrow from its rising every day of an infinite past. Views this as an instance of a general argument form that generates an ordered, infinite class K of particular arguments belonging to one of three subclasses (good, bad, irrelevant) with respect to determining the validity of the argument form. Claims "it is logically impossible for more than one argument in K to be a bad case." Maintains the general argument form is valid in a restricted sense ("infinity valid").

Considers a problem in using this argument form effectively: viz., the infinitely many good cases are in the past while the bad case is in the future. Posits a sempiternal god in order to describe conditions under which the inductive schema can be used effectively. Argues that it is a rational inductive rule for the god to follow. Considers an objection based on Goodman's puzzle about grue. Regards this as more of a "clarification of precisely how much may and how much may not be expected of the inductive schema even allowing for utopian conditions." Posits another sempiternal god who follows a deviant grue schema about emeralds compared to the previous god who follows a standard green schema. Considers the deviant schema to be "logically on a par with" the standard schema. Posits infinitely many gods, each following a deviant schema from a sequence so that each day we have predictions conflicting with those of our first, standard god. Wonders if the first god is irrational in following the standard schema because "he cannot defend his predictions against those of his rivals." Claims the god is irrational only to some extent: while the standard schema is no better than any of the deviant ones, the deviant ones are "so powerful that the standard schema cannot suffer by being placed on their level."

Bertolet, R. J. "On the Merits of Entrenchment." *Analysis* 37 (1976): 29–31. Argues that on Goodman's view we do not know whether "green" and "grue" are coextensive and so equally well entrenched, and thus we cannot conclude that "All emeralds are green" is projectible while "All emeralds are grue" is not.

Blackburn, Simon. "Goodman's Paradox." In *Studies in the Philosophy of Science,* American Philosophical Quarterly Monograph Series, No. 3, edited by Nicholas Rescher, pp. 128–142. Oxford: Basil Blackwell, 1969. States three properties of a paradoxical predicate; introduces "grue" as a truth-functional disjunction that involves the notion of being examined. Argues that there is an epistemological asymmetry between the property grue and the property green: viz., "to know that something is grue entails knowing not only what it looks like, but also what time it is, or at what time it was first examined." Claims this asymmetry is not relative to any particular language or contingent upon any particular sensory ability. Maintains that grue predictions are irrational because we expect the future to be like the past and grue predictions do not give us a reason to expect otherwise: they do no more than postulate a difference on the basis of an arbitrary time feature. Takes this as showing that the new riddle "reduces" to the old problem of justifying induction. Examines three other definitions of "grue" in the literature (Kyburg 1964, Hacking 1965, Barker and Achinstein 1960); considers whether they make the term into a paradoxical predicate. Discusses the relation between Goodman's argument and passages from the later Wittgenstein.

Blackburn, Simon. *Reason and Prediction.* Cambridge: Cambridge University Press, 1973. See chapter 4, "Goodman's Paradox," pp. 61–96. Presents and expounds on most of the points from Blackburn (1969); more detailed but also more precise. Adds a section on inductive predictions about "the continued possession of a property by one object"; omits his critical discussion of other definitions of "grue" from (1969). Argues the asymmetry between grue and green involves a logical truth; maintains that Goodman's paradox does not involve "some issue concerned with our perception of change"; discusses Altham (1969) on page 82. Ends with a long section attempting "to demonstrate the way in which a correct apprehension of Goodman's problem clarifies the inadequacy of certain theories of rational expectation:" viz., Bayesian confirmation theory, Popperian falsification views, and vindication approaches like that of Salmon (1963).

Bokhorst, Frank D. "Intelligence and Nonentrenchment: A Replication." *Journal of General Psychology* 113 (1986): 127–137. Reports a replication of Sternberg's (1982) experiments that make use of the nonentrenched (i.e., new and unconventional) terms "bleen" and "grue" in a color-naming task. Compares "the analysis of response latencies into information processing components with the model originally proposed for this task" and tests "the results of this analysis for discriminant validity using tests of fluid and crystallized ability." Claims to show that "latencies in a nonentrenched reasoning task are related to fluid ability," thereby opposing criticisms about the theoretical validity of Sternberg's componential analysis of intelligence.

Bunch, B.L. "Rescher on the Goodman Paradox." *Philosophy of Science* 47 (1980): 119–123. A reply to Rescher (1976). Claims Rescher is inconsistent in taking a color taxonomy to be time dependent relative to a perspective and yet not taking it to be economical relative to a perspective. Also claims he does not consider the role of other factors in deciding on a taxonomy—e.g., that an unacceptable taxonomy might be economical to operate with. Nor does he consider that a taxonomy might be economical because it is entrenched and not the other way around. Regards the Goodman paradox as showing that something is wrong with treating sentences and predicates as tenseless; maintains that an adequate solution involves viewing predicates "as relating to an ostensive reality that can change over time."

Butler, R.J. "Messrs. Goodman, Green, and Grue." In *Analytical Philosophy*, Second Series, edited by R.J. Butler, pp. 181–193. Oxford: Basil Blackwell & Mott Ltd., 1965. Examines a disjunctive and a conjunctive definition of 'grue.' Considers the disjunctive definition irrelevant to the new riddle because it will not license subjunctive conditionals and thus will not license any predictions. Considers the conjunctive definition relevant; claims this definition refers to a time when a change will take place, indeed "a change without process"; argues that in consequence there is a systematic "lack of symmetry" between the green-blue language and the grue-bleen language. Maintains that the new riddle is "a species of Hempel's First Paradox" (see Hempel, 1945) because the grue hypothesis is actually a "heterogeneous coupling" of two hypotheses, and that both require direct inductive support before we can regard 'grue' as meeting a basic principle of inductive inference, viz., that it must use class concepts.

Cargile, James. "On Goodman's Riddle of Induction." *Ratio* 12 (1970): 144–147. Argues that the grue hypothesis is ridiculous because 'grue' is a predicate we must apply by referring to a cut-off number and 'grue'-type predicates with earlier cut-off numbers have not projected well.

Carnap, Rudolf. "On the Application of Inductive Logic." *Philosophy and Phenomenological Research* 8 (1947): 133–148. In part a reply to Goodman (1946). Distinguishes between problems within a system of inductive logic and problems in the application of that system to certain situations; regards projectibility questions as questions about applications. Argues (in section 3) that Goodman violates the principle of total evidence in setting up his two examples because he omits the temporal order of the events. Distinguishes (in section 6) purely qualitative, purely positional, and mixed properties; tentatively maintains that all purely qualitative properties are inductively projectible, no purely positional properties are, and probably no mixed properties are. Claims that Goodman's property *S* is a mixed property.

Carnap, Rudolf. "Reply to Nelson Goodman." *Philosophy and Phenomenological Research* 8 (1948): 461–462. A response to Goodman's "On Infirmities of Confirmation-Theory"

(1947), which is a response to Carnap's "On the Application of Inductive Logic" (1947). Does not see whether he can avoid, or how he can avoid, "the concepts of absolute simplicity and absolute completeness." Does not think they are meaningless and does not wish to forbid completely the material mode of speech. Remarks that it is the job of deductive logic to provide both positive and negative answers about sentences being logically true or logically implying one another; adds that "it is with respect to these negative results that the requirement of simplicity becomes relevant." Maintains it is important that a system of inductive logic be intuitively adequate. Suggests two cases worth examining for intuitive adequacy: the degree of confirmation for a hypothesis about a single unobserved individual, and the estimated relative frequency of a property M in an unobserved sample or the estimated frequency of M in a population based on its frequency in an observed sample. Claims "these results can then also be used for an examination of projectibility." Takes Goodman's position (on the projectibility problem) to be that "the construction of an adequate system of inductive logic *pre-supposes* a solution of the problem and involves an explicit formulation of a criterion of projectibility." Considers this possible but needlessly complicated. Prefers to define degree of confirmation based on "the concepts of state-description and isomorphism" and "not containing an explicit reference to projectibility." Believes the problem of projectibility is relevant in reviewing a definition for adequacy.

Carnap, Rudolf. "Variety, Analogy, and Periodicity in Inductive Logic." *Philosophy of Science* 30 (1963): 222–227. A reply, in part, to Achinstein (1963). Comments on inductive methods for coordinate languages in the last section. Does not "require that only qualitative predicates occur in a law or other hypothesis." Allows any sentence (of a coordinate language) to be a hypothesis. Does require qualitative predicates in "certain axioms and theorems referring to predicates." Doubts that Achinstein's fundamental principle is valid in a coordinate language, even for hypotheses with qualitative predicates. Describes a counterexample that involves the proximity influence: viz., the number of instances having less influence than their proximity to the position specified by the hypothesis. Illustrates his approach with an example about five predicates for colors. Introduces Q-predicates for the possible properties of a series of m consecutive positions. Claims these predicates allow us to formulate many kinds of regularities in the order of the colors: e.g., if the fourth color is followed by the third, then the first always follows, followed next by either the third or fifth color. Maintains these predicates allow us to deal with "all laws with finite span, whether periodical or not." Notes that he takes a law of periodicity to be a law describing "a regular recurrence with a fixed period length *n*."

Carnap, Rudolf. "A Basic System of Inductive Logic, Part I." In *Studies in Inductive Logic and Probability,* Volume I, edited by Rudolf Carnap and Richard C. Jeffrey, pp. 33–166. Berkeley: University of California Press, 1971. See section 4. "Pure and Applied Inductive Logic." Claims the relation between pure and applied inductive logic is like the relation between mathematical and physical geometry. Maintains that pure inductive logic describes a language system in the abstract and does not interpret the nonlogical individual and predicate constants, while applied inductive logic interprets the language system. Thinks applied inductive logic should set the requirements for admitting primitive attributes and relations as primitive concepts in the object language (here an observational one) of an inductive logic. Intends to make his previous (1947) requirement more specific: viz., that the primitive concepts should be purely qualitative concepts as opposed to positional concepts. Considers families of attributes and classifies them by modality: spatial, temporal, or qualitative. Points out that "spatial and temporal *location* attributes may serve for the *identification* of an object or event," while "spatial and temporal nonlocational attributes serve for the *description of an identified* object." Distinguishes between absolute and relative spatial or temporal coordinate systems, and regards absolute systems as locational. States a rule for selecting primitive attributes: the primitive predicates designate descriptional attributes, where spatial-nonlocational, temporal-nonlocational, and qualitative attributes are descriptional. Describes qualitative attributes as including "all modalities that are neither spatial nor temporal." Cites "grue" and "bleen" as examples of concepts that do not meet the rule because they combine two modalities instead of being purely one, and the temporal modality is locational. Considers whether a native grue-bleen speaker would view "grue" as regular and "green" as irregular; feels the speaker would discover the "irregular character" of "grue" after learning about logic and semantics. Views this as "only a psychological question." Compares his notion of a modality with W. E. Johnson's notion of a determinable. Compares locational and descriptional concepts to space coordinates and state variables in the description of a physical system. Emphasizes that his rule applies to primitive concepts, and so it does not restrict introducing predicates by definition. Considers defining "grue" in a formal language with individual constants for slices of things and the temporal, nonlocational predicate "earlier." Uses this predicate and an individual constant denoting the first A.D. 2000 slice of a calendar clock. Discusses how to restrict principles that are valid for descriptional attributes but not for attributes like grue. Illustrates the point with the principle of instantial relevance. Notes that the restriction must be general and must be stated with terms from pure inductive logic, not applied. Suggests the phrase: for any attribute in this language which is either primitive or defined by a definition free of individual constants. Claims this is an adequate restriction because all primitive attributes are descriptional, and so "any attribute or relation defined by a definition free of individual constants is likewise descriptional."

Chao-Tien, Lin. "Solutions to the Paradoxes of Confirmation, Goodman's Paradox, and Two New Theories of Confirmation." *Philosophy of Science* 45 (1978): 415–419. Presents two confirmation theories, each consisting of the same six basic concepts from Hempel (1945) and differing in their underlying three-valued quantificational logic. Maintains the second confirmation theory is better than the first as well as Hempel's confirmation theory, one reason being that it avoids Goodman's paradox. Claims that in order to derive Goodman's paradox a certain biconditional must be true and it is not true in the underlying logic of his second theory.

Chihara, Charles. "Quine and the Confirmational Paradoxes." In *Midwest Studies in Philosophy: The Foundations of Analytic Philosophy,* Vol. VI, edited by Peter A. French, Theodore E. Uehling, Jr., and Howard K. Wettstein, pp. 425–452. Minneapolis: University of Minnesota Press, 1981. Section 1: "Quine's Solution." Describes how Quine (1970 and this volume) solves both the raven paradox and the grue puzzle by distinguishing between projectible and nonprojectible predicates. Notes that Quine explains projectibility in terms of natural kinds, simplicity, similarity, and traits we notice. Also refers to Quine and Ullian (1970). Presents a counterexample to the claim that the predicate "is prior to time t" is nonprojectible, and a counterexample to the claim that "green" is projectible and "grue" is not. Section 2: "Jackson's Counterfactual Condition." Considers how Jackson (1975 and this volume) solves the grue puzzle in terms of grue inferences failing to satisfy the counterfactual condition: viz., if the emeralds in our evidence set had not been examined prior to t, they would not have been grue. Introduces "hepeven" to mean having hepatitis and receiving a physical examination or having an even-numbered social security number and not receiving the physical examination. Describes a case in which soldiers in a specific camp are randomly examined and every one examined has hepatitis, but the counterfactual condition does not block a next-case inference—that Smith has hepeven, where Smith is a soldier in the camp who is not examined—because we do not have the right information (viz., the social security numbers) about the members of the evidence set. Section 3: "Do Positive Instances Always Confirm?" Presents I.J. Good's counterexample to Nicod's principle. See "The White Shoe is a Red Herring," *British Journal for the Philosophy of Science* 17 (1967): 322. Considers a box with either (a) one hundred black glass balls and one million plastic ones, or (b) one thousand black glass balls, one white glass ball, and one million plastic ones. Supposes we select just one ball at random and obtain a black glass ball, and so a positive instance of "All glass balls in the box are black." Points out, however, that "the glass ball constitutes good evidence that the box is correctly described by (b) and hence is one in which not all glass balls are black." Notes that while Hempel thinks this counterexample illicitly uses background information, Jackson and Quine really could not; also notes that there are real "problems involved in determining what background information one is allowed to use in intuitively testing Nicod's principle." Section 4: "A Bayesian Analysis of the Grue Puzzle." Does not believe that some predicates are "intrinsically unfit for inductive inferences." Presents his analysis "within the framework of an orthodox Personalist version of Bayesian confirmation theory." Notes that in Quine's analysis "there is no place given to gradations of belief," while the Bayesian approach takes "probability to be equated with the relevant agent's degrees of belief." Also notes that a Bayesian approach deals efficiently with background information and theories by systematically summarizing them in the form of a subjective prior probability distribution. Emphasizes that background information and theories play an important role in a Bayesian approach, but not in Quine's analyses. Maintains that we have "in the Grue situation much background information and beliefs that are relevant to the question of which of the competing hypotheses is confirmed by the evidence given." Believes that given such information and beliefs, virtually everyone would view the following conjunction as impossible: "Many emeralds have been examined and all those examined prior to *t* are green, whereas all emeralds not examined prior to *t* are blue." Asks why—given what we know about the number, distribution, mining, and value of emeralds—only green emeralds have been observed prior to *t,* and why none will be left on earth after *t.* Formulates the grue puzzle as a question about which probability is greater: the probability of the green hypothesis and the green evidence, or the probability of the grue hypothesis and the grue evidence, where the prior probabilities are assumed to be equal. Claims we can see how the latter probability ought to be very small from the implausible conjunction case. Considers the symmetry reply that the green hypothesis and the green emeralds evidence imply an implausible conjunction about all the emeralds examined prior to *t* being grue and those not examined prior to *t* being bleen. Claims this conjunction is not implausible because even if the examined emeralds had not been examined before *t,* they would have been green. Believes this reply is not circular because it appeals to a counterfactual that is based on things we know about the examined emeralds, not the unexamined emeralds. Considers whether grue speakers could appeal to their background theories to argue that the grue-bleen conjunction is implausible. Does not believe we need to consider this fictional case because he is not saying one of the conjunctions would be more plausible "no matter what one's background theories happen to be." Examines Hullett and Schwartz's (1967) infinite regress objection: viz., we cannot explain why we prefer the green hypothesis to the grue hypothesis until we explain why we prefer these regular background beliefs to gruified alternatives, and if we try to explain this by appealing to other background beliefs, we could be involved in an infinite regress. Notes that he is concerned with the grue puzzle and not the new riddle of induction. Describes the grue puzzle as explaining why we—"who always come to our experiences with an encompassing complex web of beliefs"—see the emerald evidence as supporting the green hypothesis over the grue one. Discusses the principle of maximizing expected utility as an example of a principle of rationality that does not require "ultimate foundations." Argues that we do not have to "stop the regress at some point" in order to explain specific scientific inferences. Thinks there is a burden of proof on proponents of the infinite regress objection; wants them to show "why the potentially infinite regress has the dire consequences presupposed by the argument." Notes how Quine uses the principle of conservatism and appeals to evolutionary theory to explain inductive success. Considers the role of counterfactuals in his analysis. Says they merely "facilitate bringing home" some obvious facts and so his analysis does "not also need a logical analysis of counterfactuals." Goes on to give a Bayesian analysis of the hepeven case that uses "what we know about how social security numbers are assigned and about how people get hepatitis." Shows that the evidence set—examined soldiers with hepatitis—does not confirm "Smith has hepeven" because the fact that some soldiers contracted hepatitis "would not be probabilistically relevant to whether Smith's Social Security number is odd or even." Section 5: "Another Bayesian Analysis of the Raven." Presents a more or less standard Bayesian analysis that starts from the fact that the prior probability "of finding a black raven is much smaller than that of finding a non-black non-raven." Considers three objections to this analysis—Hempel (1945), Scheffler (1963), and Black (see his *Margins of Precision*)—and develops his own view in the process. Shows that a black object confirms "All ravens are black" more than a nonraven does, given that the black object is randomly selected from the class of ravens and the nonraven is randomly selected from the class of nonblack objects. Using "the crudest of estimations of probability based mostly on very rough estimations of cardinality," shows that this hypothesis receives an insignificant degree of confirmation from a nonraven: "less than one over ten to the ten billion—a number too small to be used in calculations of probabilities we can expect to make in any real situation, given the kind of accuracies we can obtain or use." Argues that his analysis does not imply that a white shoe confirms the raven hypothesis to any degree, nor that we can only confirm the raven hypothesis by randomly selecting a black object from the class of ravens, nor that if a contrapositive instance does not confirm a hypothesis, then this is because of "cardinality considerations of the sort given." Section 6: "Concluding Remarks." Emphasizes that there are many Bayesian solutions to the raven paradox, that he really hasn't provided final and generally adequate solutions to the confirmation paradoxes, and that he hasn't provided "a general method for dealing with every grue-type puzzle that someone may think up." Does claim his analysis is "more realistic and scientifically satisfying" than Quine's. Believes this indicates that Bayesian confirmation is superior to Quinian. See the reply by Quine (1981) in the same volume.

Clendinnen, F. John. "Induction and Objectivity." *Philosophy of Science* 33 (1966): 215–229. Attempts to vindicate induction by arguing that it is "the only possible way of predicting that is objective" and that only objective methods are concordant, where a method is concordant if "there are no contradictory conclusions drawn from it." Considers Goodman's paradox as an objection to his claim about the objectivity of induction because it seems to present "in the same set of facts two or more patterns which are inconsistent with each other." Claims that "grue" is a more complicated predicate than "green," agrees that "all emeralds have been observed to be grue" is consistent with the observations to date, but denies that it describes or represents the observed pattern or regularity because "grue" is the less simple predicate here. Goes on to present a version of the principle of induction telling us to conclude, in a Goodman paradox situation, the simplest of our universal generalizations is true. Maintains that "green" is plainly simpler than "grue" because "any ostensive predicate is simpler than a predicate which is not ostensive and must be introduced via the former." Notes that his vindication must be for this version of the principle of induction because "only in this form is induction free of arbitrary decision."

Cohen, L. Jonathan. *The Implications of Induction*. London: Methuen & Co., Ltd., 1970. See chapter III, "Problems and Paradoxes about Experimental Support," section 11, "The elimination of Hempel's and Goodman's paradoxes." Claims that Goodman's paradox dissolves if we "spell out" the grue hypothesis with the definition of grue so that we have the generalization "All emeralds are green if and only if examined before moment *m* and blue if and only if not examined before moment *m*." Notes that this is equivalent to the conjunction "All green emeralds are examined before moment *m* and all emeralds examined before moment *m* are green and all blue emeralds are not examined before moment *m* and all emeralds not examined before moment *m* are blue." Maintains that the grue hypothesis has "the same grade of support on given evidence as the least well-supported conjunct" in this conjunction, that the green emeralds examined before *m* "could not give any support at all to the third and fourth conjunct," and so the conjunction "has no support at all." Believes that Goodman's entrenchment solution is unacceptable because "it would block the path of enquiry, if ever a weakly entrenched predicate like 'grue' were really needed as a rival to some strongly entrenched one like 'green'." Adds that "a philosopher of science is not entitled to solve his logical problems by proposing criteria of confirmability that would, in effect, anticipate the future of science." Maintains that there is no paradox even if we do not have a conjunctive equivalent to the grue hypothesis because "no evidence is capable of giving positive inductive support to a hypothesis unless it is constituted by favourable test-results under manipulation of at least the most relevant variable" and "no variable can be more relevant to a hypothesis about a discontinuity or dividing-line than the variable that includes both sides of the line." Points out that evidence obtained before moment *m* "cannot give even 1st grade support to 'All emeralds are grue' because it cannot have been obtained with concurrent manipulation of the most relevant variable or under insulation from its effects." Also claims that "All emeralds are grue" is a qualitative correlational hypothesis (emerald examined before/emerald examined after *m* correlated with green/blue) and "this one too must always be tested over suitable variations in its antecedent variable." Presents another solution in chapter IV, "Induction and Probability," section 12, "Induction by simple enumeration." Treats enumerative induction as "concerned with estimates of probabilities" instead of support for generalizations. Believes this avoids the grue paradox because "the probabilities we estimate do not license predictions in the way that generalisations do." Notes that, on the examined-before-moment *m* sample of emeralds, we cannot predict that a specific emerald is green—even if we know that the probability of something being green, given it is an emerald, "is within a very small interval indeed of 1"—because the emerald might have another characteristic such that the probability of having that characteristic, given the object is an emerald, is also high and having that characteristic is incompatible with being green; likewise "the very same object about which we are tempted to predict, because it is emerald, that it will be grue and therefore blue after *m*, may also be a member of the class of green or red objects that do not change their colour at *m*; and members of that class have quite a different probability of being blue after *m*." Notes that we can estimate "the probability of the predicted characteristic for the subset of these features that the object in question possesses"—but it will take "very much more evidence" than we have in our sample of emeralds (green and grue) examined before moment *m*. Also see Cohen (1989).

Cohen, L. Jonathan. *An Introduction to the Philosophy of Induction and Probability*. Oxford: Oxford University Press, 1989. See chapter VI, "Four Paradoxes about Induction," section 25, "The Grue Paradox," pp. 197–203. Believes two assumptions produce the grue paradox: viz., that something both *A* and *B* confirms "All *A* are *B*" and that a predicate like "grue" can be the predicate of a well-confirmed hypothesis. Considers limiting the predicates in (well) confirmable hypotheses to purely qualitative ones. Rejects this because we can state the paradox with a disjunction of complex descriptions that use only purely qualitative terms applying to just the emeralds examined before time *t*. Notes how Goodman argues that predicates are not absolutely qualitative, just relatively qualitative. Considers whether the relevant difference between "green" and "grue" is comparative simplicity. Rejects this because we could take "grue" and "bleen" as basic expressions and then define "green" and "blue" in terms of them, which would make "green" and "blue" into the comparatively more complex expressions. Maintains that Goodman's entrenchment solution "makes far too drastic an inroad on our terminological open-mindedness, and forces science into an excessively conservative posture." Believes we can resolve the grue paradox by using factual background knowledge with either Bayes's law or Cohen's method of relevant variables (explained in chapter V, "The Baconian Gradation of Ampliative Induction"). Takes the prior probability of the green hypothesis to be much more than the prior of the grue hypothesis because "in the past hypotheses about objects' changing their colour if not already examined have all proved false." Maintains that, on Bayes's law, the green hypothesis must be more probable than the grue hypothesis given the evidence because the evidence is the same for both hypotheses and so is the probability of the evidence on each hypothesis. Claims the Bayesian solution does not beg the question by assuming gruelike hypotheses are always falsified; argues that we would assign a low prior probability to the notion of gruelike hypotheses always being falsivered—propounded before *t* and falsified or not propounded before *t* and verified. Points out that, on his relevant variables method, a gruelike hypothesis will first be given a canonical test manipulating the before *t*/after *t* variable, and this will never produce confirmatory evidence "unless the hypothesis under examination does indeed describe, for a specified value of '*t*', a genuine turning-point in Nature." Sees the grue paradox as resulting from a concept of confirmation that "is neither graduated nor variative and is therefore insufficiently sensitive to background knowledge about locally relevant factors." Also see Cohen (1970).

Collins, H.M. *Changing Order: Replication and Induction in Scientific Practice*. Chicago: University of Chicago Press, 1992. Author is a well-known British relativist sociologist of science. Discusses the new riddle in chapter 1 and claims to provide a "sociological resolution." Claims that Goodman's entrenchment solution does not solve the "sociological puzzle" because it does not tell us "how we first came by these particular orderly ways of seeing, how we maintain them and how we develop new ones." Speaks about following the correct rules for describing emeralds and seeing their color as green; views this in terms of "members of a social group which is at one with these rules." Introduces the notion of joint entrenchment of concepts; claims that "the joint entrenchment of the concepts of green and emerald reinforce each other"; extends joint entrenchment to multiple entrenchment and a network of interrelated concepts or, from a sociological point of view, "networks of social institutions that comprise forms of life." Claims this explains the stability of entrenched inductive generalizations: viz., "it is the stability of cultures and their social institutions." Views their development as cultural development. Chapter 6 also discusses the "sociological resolution to the problem of inductive inference" and the new riddle, especially pages 145–148.

Cooley, John C. "Professor Goodman's *Fact, Fiction & Forecast.*" *Journal of Philosophy* 54 (1957): 293–311. Sketches the main points of the book. Objects to the cotenability requirement in Goodman's solution to the counterfactual problem; claims Goodman only needs this requirement because he ignores time relations in his analysis. Wonders if the positional/qualitative distinction is very important because there do not seem to be predicates that are positional in one natural language and not in another, and so a Hempelian could accept a relativized definition. Notes that Goodman himself uses some relativized definitions. Thinks there is very little chance of defining dispositional predicates in terms of certain manifest ones. Doubts that "projectible" is a typical disposition term; views it as a methodological term that specifies certain conditions in order to classify sentences as, e.g., evidence for other sentences. Claims that chapter IV of *FFF* actually reads like "an ordinary explication without reference to the supposedly dispositional character of the term," and that while Goodman speaks of hypotheses being projected without being projectible, it makes no sense to speak of something dissolving without being soluble. Favors dropping Goodman's three elimination rules and entrenchment, and retaining comparative projectibility along with "the practice of operating only on hypotheses for which there is supporting evidence and which are neither exhausted nor violated." Claims the concept of comparative projectibility resembles the concept of degree of confirmation "when this is handled (as was once customary) by way of the amount and kind of supporting evidence." Feels that Goodman, in discussing various cases, is looking for natural kinds. Maintains that, with more practice-based screening prior to applying criteria for comparative projectibility, Goodman's theory can handle "the problem of lawlikeness and, in contrast to the rigid exclusion of positional predicates, it has much to recommend it on intuitive grounds." Ends by discussing how counterfactuals can be construed as prediction schema. See the reply by Goodman (1957) and Cooley's response (1958).

Cooley, J.C. "A Somewhat Adverse Reply to Professor Goodman." *Journal of Philosophy* 55 (1958): 159–166. A response to Goodman (1957), which is a reply to Cooley (1957). Argues that Goodman's example of a cotenability problem (about a black, iron bolt) "can't be stated nontemporally." With regard to defining disposition terms, emphasizes that Goodman has not provided even one example of an adequate definition with manifest predicates. Claims Goodman seems to be defining "projectible" with the manifest predicate "properly projected." Maintains that we do not have a prior understanding of this manifest predicate like we have of "dissolves" before considering issues about "soluble." Discusses in detail Goodman's example (about diamonds and mushrooms) that supposedly shows we need initial indices of projectibility connected with extent of entrenchment. Distinguishes between uniform and nonuniform classes with respect to a given characteristic, cites time-divided classes as nonuniform with respect to physical characteristics, and claims this helps to solve Goodman's problematic example in terms of generalizations that usually break down compared to ones that usually do not. Discusses how he believes Goodman would solve this problem and claims that Goodman's "intricate machinery works after a fashion." Contends that we can bypass it by distinguishing between types of classes (or kinds of things) and then making direct judgments about the probability of inductive success. Considers the objection that he is appealing to entrenchment when he appeals to kinds of things; maintains that "any inductive procedure is superimposed on a language which is already in operation."

Creath, Richard. "A Query on Entrenchment." *Philosophy of Science* 45 (1978): 474–477. Argues that in crucial cases (e.g., with 'green' and 'grue') we cannot determine in fact or in principle whether a predicate is entrenched, and so whether it is more entrenched than another predicate and thereby should be projected. Maintains the problem comes from having to tell which class a word selects when that word is projected. Claims this obstacle does not show Goodman's theory of projectibility is wrong; rather, that we cannot use Goodman's theory in deciding which inductive inferences to make.

Creath, Richard. "Mowing the Grass that's Grue: What Carnap Should Have Said to Goodman." In *Scientific Inquiry in Philosophical Perspective,* edited by Nichola Rescher, pp. 281–294. Lanham: University Press of America, 1987. Explains how Carnap tried to answer the new riddle in terms of three categories of logically simple and independent predicates. Argues that Carnap should not have assumed some predicates are absolutely simple; rather, he should have viewed projectibility as relative to a language system, made a predicate purely qualitative relative to a language system, and required all basic predicates within a system to be qualitative with respect to each other—therein avoiding the problem of incompatible projections by agreeing to a certain level of arbitrariness.

Davidson, Donald. "Emeroses By Other Names." *Journal of Philosophy* 63 (1966): 778–780. A reply to Goodman (1966). Considers whether the hypothesis "All emeroses are gred" is lawlike and so a counterexample to Goodman's views on projectibility. Goodman maintains that it is not lawlike because its positive instances do not in general add to its credibility; they do not because "emeralds found before t to be green do not confirm" the hypothesis. Questions how this reason supports his claim about the status of the hypothesis. Considers whether it might be because green emeralds examined before t have nothing to do with the color of roses examined after t; rejects this because it would also mean that the hypothesis "All emeralds are green" is not lawlike. Argues that Goodman's reasoning here "seems to be a non sequitur" when seen along with his notion of a positive instance; it goes from the fact that green emeralds examined before t do not confirm the hypothesis to the conclusion that the hypothesis is not confirmed by statements about objects being gred emeroses. Considers whether being lawlike is connected with the positive instances being examined before t, and so "the observer determines that an instance is positive by noting the time and observing that the object is a green emerald." Maintains that this is not essential and may be false because there are circumstances in which it seems one can know that an object is gred or an emerose without knowing the time. See the reply by Goodman (1967), also comments on page 106 of *FFF,* current edition.

Deledalle, Gerard. "The Actuality of Peirce: Abduction, Induction, Deduction." *Semiotica* 45 (1983): 307–313. Article in French. Discusses the new riddle in connection with Harris and Hoover (1980).

De Sousa, Ronald. "The Natural Shiftiness of Natural Kinds." *Canadian Journal of Philosophy* 14 (1984): 561–580. Claims there are no ontological categories independent of our interests and so "virtually any kind can be termed 'natural' relative to some set of interests and epistemic priorities." Thinks the grue-bleen problem "has a bearing on the topic of natural kinds which has not been generally noted." Reviews Goodman's entrenchment answer. Thinks it needs "some deeper level of explanation." Presents a naturalistic explanation: viz., our "neural apparatus tends to frame" natural properties that are the result of "evolutionary success," and these properties "tend to correspond to useful properties in the world." Maintains that projectible properties must be real properties, but they do not have to be specially basic or explanatory. Claims that as the sciences change, so does our view of the important properties. Argues that the projectible predicates are "the shifting set of vestigial natural kinds" and these vestiges do not have seven characteristic features of natural kinds: viz., objectivity, explanatory primacy, multiplicity, sharp boundaries, stability, equipollence, and perspicuity.

Domincy, Marc. "Falsification and Falsifiabilization from Lakatos to Goodman." *Revue Internationale de Philosophie* 37 (1983): 163–197. Claims to provide "an integrated Popperian solution" to questions about Lakatos's notion of a research program, problems with counterfactuals, and Goodman's paradox. Maintains (in section 3) that Goodman's paradox is not due to temporal variables, temporal singular terms, or nonqualitative predicates, and that all non-Popperian solutions presuppose "an advanced background knowledge" and yet do not prove that "theories put up an inner resistance to the intrusion of Goodmanian predicates." Claims that Popperians tend to view Goodman's paradox as a problem for inductivists; insists it is also a problem for Popperians because they need to explain why Goodmanian hypotheses are "not put forward" when they have the same degree of corroboration as normal hypotheses. Argues that there has not been a satisfactory Popperian solution to the paradox up to now. Proposes a solution based on a methodological principle that constrains quasirestrictive statements. Claims that quasirestrictive statements "falsifiabilize nonfalsifiable hypotheses" and that his principle "rules out vicious falsifiabilizations." Regards this as solving Goodman's paradox because "All emeralds are grue" is a quasirestrictive statement that makes falsifiable the nonfalsifiable and nonverified hypothesis "according to which some emerald is not green." Maintains there are three advantages to this solution: viz., it does not assume there is at least one emerald after time t; it helps us understand why Goodmanian predicates conceal "hidden hypotheses"; it applies to restrictive statements essential to Lakatos's notion of research programs.

Dorling, John. "Bayesian Personalism, Falsificationism, and the Problem of Induction." *Proceedings of the Aristotelian Society, Supplementary Volume* 55 (1981): 109–125. Defends a Bayesian (personalist) solution to both the practical and skeptical problem of induction. Considers Goodman's skepticism, Millenarian skepticism, Popperian rivals, and David Miller's criticisms of maximizing expected utility. (Miller's response is in the volume.) Construes Goodman's problem in terms of assigning prior probabilities to the rival hypotheses. Maintains that "only if a *prima facie* symmetry can be established between the two rival hypotheses, will there be a *prima facie* case for assigning them equal prior probabilities." Claims that, without this symmetry, Goodman's problem becomes the Millenarian problem about induction: viz., the Millenarians predict that the universe will come to an end $1/1/2000$, we predict otherwise, and the evidence supports both equally. Argues that Goodman, in order to establish symmetry between green speakers and grue speakers, "must use sensory predicates, and trade on their indefinability and on the indescribability of the sensory qualities to which they refer." Thinks this shows Goodman's problem is only a problem if we subscribe to an extremely dubious thesis about perception, and then it is only a problem in connection with certain sensory terms. Goes on to maintain that Goodman's symmetry thesis requires even more of a Bayesian: viz., that a Bayesian would have to assign a probability of 1 to this perceptual thesis as well as a probability of 1 to "a form of interactionism which will be in gross conflict with the validity of ordinary laws of physics and chemistry."

Earman, John. "Concepts of Projectibility and the Problems of Induction." *Noûs* 19 (1985): 521–535. Also in this volume with a postscript. Provides "a classification scheme for the various senses of projectibility," identifies the problem of induction corresponding to each sense, and discusses whether these problems can be solved or have been solved by finding necessary, sufficient, or necessary and sufficient conditions. Deals with nonstatistical hypotheses whose instances are deductive consequences of the hypothesis and the background evidence. Distinguishes between weak and strong projectibility "as the induction is on the next instance or the next m instances." Also distinguishes between "future moving" and "past reaching" projectibility in terms of "two ways of taking the limit as the number n of instances increases towards infinity according as we march into the future with the accumulating instances or stand pat in the present and reach further and further back into the past for more instances." Section 1: "Instance Induction: Marching into the Future." Defines "relative to background evidence B, hypothesis H is weakly projectible in the future-moving instance sense" in terms of the probability equaling 1, as n approaches infinity, that instance $n + 1$ is positive given that instances 1 through n have been and the background evidence. Defines "relative to B, H is strongly projectible in the future-moving instance sense" in terms of the probability equaling 1, as m and n approach infinity, that instances $n + 1$ through $n + m$ are positive given that instances 1 through n have been and the background evidence. Proves that $Pr(H/B) > 0$ is a sufficient condition for both of these senses. Makes "an immediate application to the projectibility of predicates" and defines weakly and strongly projectible in the future-moving sense for predicates, and notes the immediate application of the sufficient condition as well. Points out that these predicate definitions will separate "grue" from "green" only if we make "the wholly implausible assumption that the universal generalization of the one but not the other receives a zero prior." Maintains that the nonzero prior condition is also a necessary condition for the strong future-moving projectibility of predicate "P" if we "assume what Kolmogorov calls an axiom of continuity," but that the nonzero prior condition is not a necessary condition for the weak future-moving projectibility of "P." Introduces a necessary and sufficient "closed-minded attitude" condition for "P" failing to be weakly projectible in the future-moving, instance-induction sense. Also defines "relative to B, 'P' is somewhat future-moving projectible over a sequence of individuals" as the probability that individual $n + 1$ is P, given that individuals 1 through n are P and the background evidence, is greater than the probability that individual n is P, given that individuals 1 through $n - 1$ are P and the background evidence. Believes that, given these definitions and conditions, "Humean skepticism with respect to future-moving instance induction, weak or strong, stands on unstable ground." For example: if the probability that, for every individual a, a is P, given the background evidence, "is any positive real number, no matter how small, future-moving instance induction must take place, like it or not." Section 2: "Instance Induction: Standing Pat in the Present While Reaching into the Past." Introduces another way of taking the limit as the number of positive instances increases without bound, and notes that "the point concerns whether the 'next instance' lies in the direction in which the limit of accumulating evidence is taken." Supposes a doubly infinite sequence of instances indexed over all integers. Defines "relative to B, H is weakly projectible in the past-reaching instance sense" and "relative to B, H is strongly projectible in the past-reaching instance sense." Characterizes this sense of weak projectibility in terms of the probability that instance $n + 1$ is positive, given that instances n through $n - j$ are positive and the background evidence B, equaling 1 as j approaches plus infinity; characterizes this sense of strong projectibility in terms of the probability that instances $n + 1$ through $n + m$ are positive, given that instances n through $n - j$ are positive and B, equaling 1 as m and j approach plus infinity. Notes that "corresponding senses of projectibility apply to predicates." Argues that a nonzero prior probability is not a sufficient condition for past-reaching instance induction, strong or weak. Points out the these senses of projectibility "do distinguish between 'grue' and 'green' in the sense that both cannot be projectible in the past-reaching sense." Also points out that if exchangeability holds for predicate "*P*," it follows that past-reaching projectibility is equivalent to future-moving projectibility for "*P*." Characterizes the problem of past-reaching instance induction as (roughly) a problem about "whether the future will resemble the past." Believes that Goodman's examples show this problem "requires scrupulous attention to the form of resemblance if inconsistencies are to be avoided," and so this form of induction "provides the grounds for but does not require a blanket skepticism." Section 3: "General Induction." States that, relative to B, H is weakly projectible on the basis of its positive instances if and only if "the probability of H is increased by each new instance." Proves that the necessary and sufficient conditions for H being weakly projectible are that $Pr(H/B)$ is greater than 0 and that the probability instance $n + 1$ is positive, given instances 1 through n are positive and B, is less than 1. States that, relative to B, H is strongly projectible on the basis of its positive instances if and only if the probability of H, given instances 1 through n and background evidence B, equals 1 as n approaches infinity. Proves that H is not strongly projectible if there is an alternative hypothesis H' which meets the following conditions: it is a deductive consequence of B that both H and H' cannot be true at the same time, the positive instances are deductive consequences of H' and B, and $Pr(H'/B)$ is greater than or equal to 0. Shows it is not true that "any amount of data can be covered by many, possibly an infinite number of hypotheses." Defines relative to B, for all individuals i, a_i is P, being strongly projectible in the past-reaching sense. Points out that "once we move beyond direct observational generalizations to theories that outrun the data, it is surely true that there are many rival theories that cover the same data." Notes that strong projectibility, on the basis of a theory's instances, is impossible for such a theory "unless the dice have been completely loaded against all the alternatives." Defines "a more modest form of projectibility" in terms of $Pr(H/B) < .5$ and the existence of an n large enough for $Pr(H/\text{instances 1}$ through n and $B)$ to be $> .5$. Proves that H is not modestly projectible if there is an alternative hypothesis H' which meets the following conditions: it is a deductive consequence of B that H and H' can't both be true, the positive instances are a deductive consequence of H' and B', and the prior probability of H' is greater than or equal to the prior probability of H. Section 4: "Russell on Induction." Points out that Russell did not distinguish between past-reaching/future-moving instance induction; that Russell recognized the new riddle by using Goodmanized hypotheses and ruling out manufactured classes, but he didn't realize the new riddle is only a problem for past-reaching instance inductions; that Russell didn't see a connection between his reasoning about the problem of induction and Jeffreys's theorem on future-moving instance induction; and that Russell did not see how the problem with general induction to theoretical hypotheses can occur without involving Goodmanized alternative hypotheses. Section 5: "Prospects for a Theory of Projectibility." Maintains that Goodman's entrenchment theory is irrelevant to some questions about projectibility, inadequate for others. For example: if a hypothesis has a nonzero prior, it is weakly projectible (on its positive instances) irrespective of the entrenchment of its predicates; if a hypothesis has the best entrenched predicates, it may not be strongly projectible "if rival hypotheses are given a fighting chance, even when the rivals use ill-entrenched predicates." Believes a minimalist theory of projectibility will consist of precise and interesting necessary and sufficient conditions for the concepts of projectibility. Believes "a more grandiose theory" would "consist of descriptive and/or normative rules for determining when the conditions developed in the minimalist theory are or ought to be met." Doubts that "the tools of analytic philosophy" will produce such a theory. Supports this point by reviewing approaches to assigning prior probabilities. Also see Earman (1993).

Earman, John. *Bayes or Bust? : A Critical Examination of Bayesian Confirmation Theory.* Cambridge, Mass.: The MIT Press, 1992. See chapter 4, section 7, "Goodman's New Problem of Induction." Points out that it is not clear what the new problem is supposed to be. First considers the problem as describing the hypotheses that can be confirmed by their positive instances, where positive instances are deductive consequences of a hypothesis and background knowledge. Explains how this problem becomes identifying the hypotheses with nonzero prior probabilities. Points out this does not agree with Goodman's claims about positive instances failing to confirm "All men now in this room are third sons" and the grue hypothesis. Considers it "much too draconian to suppose that these and other hypotheses in the target class of unprojectible hypotheses are to be initially and forever condemned to limbo by receiving zero priors." Notes that positive instances increase the probability of the third son and grue hypotheses by cutting or exhausting their content, but they do not increase the probability of future instances being as predicted by these hypotheses. Calls a hypothesis projectible when its past instances can increase the probability about its future instances. Defines a hypothesis being, relative to certain background knowledge, weakly and strongly projectible in the future-moving sense over its instances. Proves that, for background knowledge K and hypothesis H, $Pr(H/K) > 0$ is a sufficient condition for H being weakly and strongly projectible in the future-moving sense. Defines a predicate "P" being, relative to certain background knowledge, weakly and strongly projectible in the future-moving sense over individuals. Proves that $Pr((i)Pa_i/K) > 0$ is a sufficient condition for "P" being weakly and strongly projectible in this sense. Formulates a necessary and sufficient condition (indicating a closed-minded attitude) for a predicate failing to be weakly projectible in this sense. Also defines a predicate being somewhat projectible in the future-moving sense. Emphasizes that these definitions of projectibility do not distinguish the green from the grue hypothesis without implausibly supposing the green hypothesis has a nonzero prior, the grue hypothesis a zero prior. Introduces a doubly infinite array of individuals. Defines a predicate being weakly and strongly projectible in the past-reaching sense. Maintains there is a real inductive problem with this sense of projectibility because, unlike the future-moving sense, it may not hold when $Pr((i)Pa_i/K) > 0$. Explains how, with a predicate "P" and its grue analogue "P^*" and i ranging between minus infinity and plus infinity, "the assignment of positive priors to both $(i)Pa_i$ and $(i)P^*a_i$ does not guarantee, on pain of contradiction, that 'P' and 'P^*' are both projectible in the past-reaching sense." Points out that when exchangeability holds for a predicate, past-reaching projectibility is equivalent to future-moving projectibility; that when the universal generalization over the predicate "P" and the one over its grue analogue "P^*" have nonzero priors, exchangeability does not hold for both predicates; and that exchangeability functions as a postulate about the uniformity of nature in demonstrations of projectibility. Regards Goodman's problem as one form of "the general problem of underdetermination of hypotheses by evidence." Discusses the exchange between Goodman (1946, 1947) and Carnap (1947) about projectible predicates. Agrees with Carnap on the importance of taking a probabilistic approach; agrees with Goodman on the need for evidence that qualitative predicates are the probabilistically projectible ones. Also discusses unpublished correspondence between Carnap and Hempel during 1946 and 1947. Notes how, with the restrictions of Hempel's 1945 confirmation theory, Goodman had to use a gerrymandered predicate to produce an example of evidence satisfying incompatible hypotheses. Thinks this may be responsible for the false impression that Goodman's problem is really a trick "to be solved by a clever logical maneuver." Ends by speculating on how Carnap should have replied to *FFF*. Believes he should have claimed there are no universal rules of projectibility, just Bayesian personalism constraining different inductive agents as they project various predicates to various degrees. Also see Earman (1985 and this volume).

Eells, Ellery. *Rational Decision and Causality.* Cambridge: Cambridge University Press, 1982. Presents Bayesian decision theory, defends the principle of maximizing conditional expected utility, examines causal decision theory, and attempts to deal with Newcomb's problem. Gives (pp. 52–64) a Bayesian analysis of confirmation, uses it to explicate some well-known maxims of inductive reasoning, and shows how the analysis deals with the raven paradox and the grue puzzle. Maintains that evidence *e* confirms hypothesis *h* if $P(h/e)$ is greater than $P(h)$ and that the degree of confirmation is $P(h/e) - P(h)$. Attempts to show that $P(green\ hypothesis/observed\ green\ emeralds) - P(green\ hypothesis)$ is greater than $P(grue\ hypothesis/observed\ green\ emeralds) - P(grue\ hypothesis)$ when we assume "almost anybody's (reasonable) degrees of belief." Argues that $P(green\ hypothesis/observed\ green\ emeralds)$ is greater than $P(grue\ hypothesis/observed\ green\ emeralds)$ because the latter probability involves a very improbable sample of emerald observations. Also argues that $P(green\ hypothesis/the\ negation\ of\ our\ observations)$ is about equal to $P(grue\ hypothesis/the\ negation\ of\ our\ observations)$. Uses these two relations in trying to establish the main inequality. Notes that his approach is "patterned after" Chihara (1981).

Eichner, Klaus. "The Solution of Goodman's Paradox: Goodman's Mistaken Conclusion." *Kant-Studien* 66 (1975): 500–509. Article in German.

Eichner, Klaus and Frank, Claus. "Paralogisms and Pathological Predicates." *Kant-Studien* 69 (1978):209–212. Article in German. A reply to Habermehl (1975).

Elder, Crawford L. "Goodman's 'New Riddle'—A Realist's Reprise." *Philosophical Studies* 59 (1990): 115–135. Connects realism with the thesis that natural kinds are not relative to a language, theory, or conceptual scheme. Construes natural kinds in terms of "properties answering to projectible predicates." Takes Goodman's position (his entrenchment view) to be that projectible predicates are relative to the customs or practices of a culture. Presents the new riddle in terms of our system of predicates and a rival system. Contends that "such a system of rival predicates cannot consistently be envisioned." Discusses the claim that an impeccable inductive inference can become an outlandish one by replacing the projected predicate (e.g., "green") with a foreign predicate (e.g., "grue"). Maintains that Grue-Bleen speakers must "be viewed as sharing all our second-order beliefs about colors, if the entire blame for the outlandishness of their inferences is to fall on their 'foreign' predicates." Notes how this means that our inferences will look outlandish to Grue-Bleen speakers, just as their inferences look outlandish to us. Goes on to argue that green is a genuine property because green objects have certain standard causal powers as a result of being green, while grue is not a genuine property because grue objects do not have such powers as a result of being grue. Maintains that a Grue-Bleen speaker can only associate a combination or amalgam of causal powers with grue. Examines Hesse's (1969) claim that in consequence green predictions are simpler than grue predictions when they span time *t*. Notes how this depends on whether you take our position or that of Grue-Bleen speakers. Explains the point in terms a report that blue clothing attracts mosquitoes, which might provide a test for the color of things observed after time t. Maintains that, contrary to us, a Grue-Bleen speaker will see attracting mosquitoes as a causal amalgam and regard "attracts mosquitoes" as unprojectible because it fails Jackson's (1975) counterfactual test. Attempts to determine the elements of the amalgamated causal power Grue-Bleen speakers associate with grue. Proceeds to construct, for Grue-Bleen speakers, their predicate for the power of attracting mosquitoes. States one disjunct as: x is observed prior to t and x has the power to attract mosquitoes. Formulates three requirements for the second disjunct: we must regard it as a different property from the one in the first disjunct, it must be invariant under counterfactuals about being observed prior to time t, and it must provide evidence of being bleen after t (if observed) whenever attracting mosquitoes would indicate being blue after t. Eventually formulates the second disjunct as a disjunction: x is not observed prior to t and x is one kind of blue clothing observed to date and x has the power to protect inchworms from notice by predators, or x is a sample of human sweat, or x is a sample of mosquito pheromones. Maintains that the full definition "does not uniformly look like a causal power" because the second disjunct "does not amount to a kind of *doing* at all." Claims that, when things are not observed before time t, having this amalgamated property amounts "merely to *being* one kind of object or another." Maintains that this is an inductively relevant difference between our predicate "attracts mosquitoes" and the Grue-Bleen predicate for attracting mosquitoes. Argues that Grue-Bleen speakers will have to say their amalgamated predicate is unprojectible and does not designate a causal power. Claims this holds for other causal powers the Grue-Bleen speakers might associate with being grue or bleen, and so even Grue-Bleen speakers must say that "virtually no genuine causal powers are associated with bleenness (or grueness)."

Elgin, Catherine Z. *With Reference to Reference*. Indianapolis: Hackett Publishing Company, 1983. Clarifies and extends Goodman's extensional account of reference. Chapters on denotation, fictive terms, metaphor, exemplification, structures of symbol systems, quotation, complex and indirect reference, and determining what a sentence is about. Relevant to understanding Goodman's notion of entrenchment and criticisms directed at its extensional aspects. See for example chapter 2, sections 3 and 4, for a critical discussion of determining the extension of a predicate and whether two predicates are coextensive, including remarks about nautral kinds. See chapter 5, section 7, "Learning From Experience," for a discussion of projectibility in terms of identifying the labels that a sample exemplifies, deciding whether a sample is fair, and (with fair samples) determining the class of things to project a label over. Refers to grue in chapter 6, page 111. Points out that the compliance class for "green" includes all emeralds observed so far, so does the compliance class for "grue," and the predicates are not coextensive, so "any generalization regarding the color of emeralds requires a choice between them." Maintains this is because discursive languages are not semantically disjoint.

Elgin, Catherine Z. "The Cost of Correspondence." *Philosophy and Phenomenological Research* 47 (1987): 475–480. A reply to Shalkowski (1987a). Maintains that Shalkowski is wrong about Goodman and the truth of "Emeralds are green." Claims Goodman would not admit that the statement is true, nonconventionally or otherwise, because in the green/grue emerald problem we don't know which hypothesis is true. Agrees with Shalkowski that Goodman's entrenchment solution does not refute realism about truth. Goes on to maintain that Goodman does show how "realism is neither required nor useful for resolving the paradox"; in the new riddle, "the realist does not know which sentence to be a realist about" and so the realist is on a par with the irrealist. See the response by Shalkowski (1987).

Elgin, Catherine Z. "Outstanding Problems: Replies to ZiF Critics." *Synthese* 95 (1993): 129–140. Section 2 is a reply to Rheinwald (1993). Maintains that the grue hypothesis does not require emeralds to change color, that examining emeralds does not make them one color or another, and that "Goodman's hypothesis neither makes nor is committed to any causal claims." Also maintains that gruelike predicates do not "depend on position, person, or perspective in any way." Introduces "schmessure" as an example of this, where "schmessure" is defined as force/unit area when even and twice force/unit area when odd. Notes that Goodman does not claim "a predicate is projectible *if and only if* sufficiently entrenched." Adds that, on Goodman's view, the predicate must also be in a supported, unviolated, and unexhausted hypothesis. Contends that we can learn a language without the causal relations associated with a predicate like "green" (and not associated with a predicate like "grue"). Believes we only need "a limited base of intersubjectively discernible constancies." Agrees that inductive reasoning involves background information, but denies that "belief in the hypothesis under investigation must be part of the relevant background information." Emphasizes that if a predicate is entrenched, this does not guarantee that it is projectible, that if a predicate is projectible, this does not guarantee inductive validity, and that "our beliefs about the domain and the methods for investigating it impose additional constraints."

Ellis, Brian. "A Vindication of Scientific Inductive Practices." *American Philosophical Quarterly* 2 (1965): 296–304. Argues that a pragmatic justification of induction can only justify "using certain inductive rules to make probability estimates about things that are *theoretically isolated.*" Characterizes theoretically isolated things as things we can say anything we like about "without affecting, in any way, our understanding of the rest of nature." Goes on to argue (section II) that straight inductive rules do not help us make predictions even when we are dealing with theoretically isolated things. Claims that "where there is no relevant background of scientific theory, every prediction is as good or bad as every other, and each can be justified on the basis of straight inductive rules." Notes that his argument does not involve any odd gruelike predicates. Contends that his argument shows, contrary to Goodman, that "our actual *practice* of applying straight inductive rules cannot possibly be justified by any theory of *predicate-entrenchment.*" Bases his argument on predicting ("within our present language") how a computer-generated sequence of numbers will continue; contends that nothing changes with predicting a natural sequence of events or when the case involves nonquantitative results. Emphasizes that stating the straight rule is one thing, applying it is another. Considers Salmon's claim (1963) that the rule should be restricted to purely ostensive predicates. Claims this is an *ad hoc* restriction that eliminates some normal and obviously projectible predicates and appears to work only if humans are not very good at learning sequences by ostension. Proceeds to argue that a nondemonstrative argument is rational only if it is about theoretically involved things. Takes this to be the lesson of the Goodman paradox and thinks we see the situation as a paradox "only because we vacillate in our way of regarding such terms as 'emeralds' and 'green'," sometimes disregarding theoretical commitments and other times not.

Ellis, Brian. "Solving the Problem of Induction Using a Values-Based Epistemology." *British Journal for the Philosophy of Science* 39 (1988): 141–160. Views inductive rules as means to an end: viz., strategies for maximizing the satisfaction of, or promoting, certain epistemic values. Takes showing these rules are rational to be showing that they are effective or useful strategies or means. Argues that there are four basic epistemic values: regularity, epistemic conservatism, corroboration, and connectivity. Claims that "epistemic conservatism exercises control over what inductive generalisations we may make." Maintains, as a general principle, that we value the kinds of generalizations that have proven "useful to us as language and thought evolved." Takes these to be generalizations about things belonging to our "basic ontological categories." Claims, in consequence, that we ought to prefer generalizations about recognized kinds of things to ones about unrecognized kinds of things; that is, "we should prefer generalizations which derive from conceptually and ontologically conservative descriptions of things." Takes this to rule out "Goodman inferences." Argues that we could not accept the property of grueness as part of our ontology "without doing a great deal of violence to our conceptual framework" and "abandoning much of what we think we know for a concept of no proven worth." Notes that epistemic conservatism sets up an onus of proof and so compelling reasons could make grue descriptions preferable to green ones, but in the absence of such reasons, the grue descriptions are unacceptable for inductive inferences.

Essler, Wilhelm K. "Corrupted Concepts and Empiricism." *Erkenntnis* 12 (1978): 181–187. Subtitles his paper "the philosophical relevance of the Goodman paradox." Attempts to show that the orthodox version of nonholistic empiricism is "not a sound philosophical position." Cites members of the Vienna Circle (e.g., Schlick) as proponents of nonholistic empiricism. Views two theses as defining the position: every statement in a given formal language is either analytic or empirical, and the credibility of an empirical statement about properties (of certain objects) in the future depends on observation statements about them in the past. Takes this second thesis as a statement that "learning from experience is possible" and expresses it formally with a strictly coherent, symmetric credibility function and a condition on the function specifying that observations increase credibility. Presents an abstract version of the new riddle in terms of a formal language. Introduces two predicates that can be defined disjunctively in terms of each other and an individual constant. Points out that one of the predicates is a "corrupted" predicate and one "non-corrupted," and that a strictly coherent, symmetric credibility function is inadequate for the former, adequate for the latter. Introduces a "corrupted" credibility function for the "corrupted" predicate. Notes that this function is not symmetric and violates the "learning from experience" condition on the "non-corrupted" credibility function. Claims it is impossible to determine which predicate is the "corrupted" predicate if the formal language includes only analytic rules (definitions and consequences of definitions) for predicates, and so it is impossible to determine which credibility function is adequate for either predicate. Considers a solution to be identifying which predicate is "corrupted" and which is not, and using the "non-corrupted" credibility function with the "non-corrupted" predicate. Claims we can identify the predicates by first identifying the credibility functions. Maintains that the "non-corrupted" function is simpler than the "corrupted" one because it can be characterized without using some individual constant. Remarks that it is not a simple thing to adequately characterize this notion of simplicity. Distinguishes between the simplicity of the concepts of some language and the simplicity of the empirical hypotheses "that may be formulated with these concepts." Notes how these two kinds of simplicity may conflict (e.g., the case of general relativity theory).

Fain, Haskell. "The Very Thought of Grue." *Philosophical Review* 76 (1967): 61–73. Defines "grue" as green if and only if examined before *t*. Discusses the new riddle in terms of ten marbles drawn from a bag (without replacement) before *t*, all of them green. Considers whether this information (as a list of ten sentences for green, another list for grue) is evidence the next marble will be green or not green, where the next marble will be drawn after *t*. Adds a third list of sentences about some marbles being left in the bag after *t*, notes how this disconfirms "all marbles in the bag are grue," and notes a parallel argument to the effect that we also have evidence against "all marbles in the bag are green." Maintains that the parallel argument changes the new riddle into the paradox of induction: viz., "that the *same* body of evidence both supports and undermines the *same hypothesis.*" Maintains this is a genuine paradox and therefore its basic premise must be false: viz., that the evidence equally supports both the green and the grue hypothesis. Maintains that either the three evidence lists do not confirm or disconfirm both hypotheses, or that they confirm one hypothesis more than the other. Sees Goodman's entrenchment view as the latter approach. Claims that "grue"could become entrenched in a language, and that even so there is a distinction between a disposition to project a term and confirmation. Considers whether the paradox of induction depends on introducing the definition of "grue" in the parallel argument, and argues that it does not because the predicate can be produced with a sentence extensionally equivalent to "All the marbles in the bag are grue if and only if all the marbles in the bag are examined prior to *t*." Considers whether the predicate "green" is only qualitative in a relative sense because it is extensionally equivalent to an expression containing two temporal terms. Introduces the self-contradictory predicate "dred" (red if and only if not red), notes that "*x* is red" is extensionally equivalent to "*x* is dred if and only if *x* is not red," and claims that this equivalence does not show contradictoriness is relative any more than the green-grue equivalence shows qualitativeness is relative. Considers how the total evidence might favor one hypothesis if there are eleven marbles in the bag and ten have been examined before *t* and found to be green, and "grue" is taken to mean that ten of the eleven marbles are green. Notes that if the green and grue hypotheses have the same initial probability, then on the total evidence the green hypothesis has a probability of 10/11 and the grue hypothesis has 1/11. Maintains, however, that this case involves affirming the consequent. Emphasizes how "everything depends upon what estimates we make of the initial likelihoods of two hypotheses *before* we begin to collect the evidence that is supposed to decide between them." Argues that the eleven marbles case will not help us determine the "circumstances in which one could increase the likelihood that all are green while, at the same time, *decreasing the likelihood* that all are grue." Points to the fact that the eleven-marble case uses the hypothesis that ten of the marbles are green, which is not equivalent to the grue hypothesis that the first ten to be drawn are green and marble eleven is not. Claims there is only one alternative left: viz., the green marble observations before *t* do not favor one hypothesis over the other. Maintains that if the grue and green hypotheses have the same initial probability and you think positive instances discriminate between them, then you are committing a version of the gambler's fallacy. Sees the grue example as dramatizing this. Adds that this does not present a problem when we have some reason to think our hypotheses do not have the same initial probability: i.e., "one must have some reason for believing that in the universe as a whole the ratio of green to non-green marbles is not one to one." Concludes that justifying induction depends on our reasons for thinking that "not all hypotheses are, to begin with, equally likely," and so justifying a particular induction is "outside of the particular induction itself."

Fetzer, James H. *Scientific Knowledge: Causation, Explanation, and Corroboration.* Dordrecht, Holland: D. Reidel Publishing Company, 1981. Discusses the new riddle in a section on the paradoxes of confirmation (pp. 187–192). Considers the claim that only a lawlike statement can be confirmed by its instances. Maintains that "Goodman's analysis is confused and his solution is mistaken." Argues that accidental generalizations can be confirmed by their instances (e.g., generalizations based on customs and traditions). Claims Goodman is "mistaking a semantic and ontological problem for an epistemic and pragmatic one." Takes lawlike statements to be "subjunctive generalizations, which characterize classes of possible worlds by means of their ontological structure, while accidental generalizations are extensional sentences which characterize the actual world by describing (some segment of) its history." Considers Goodman's account of projectible predicates "beside the point" because it does not recognize that "grue" is "the wrong kind of predicate." Takes "green" to be a purely dispositional predicate, but not "grue," because "pure dispositions are universals" and "purely dispositional predicates are rigid property designators." Maintains that "grue" is a historical relation because it is defined with a temporal reference to the history of a particular world.

Feyerabend, Paul K. "A Note on Two 'Problems' of Induction." *British Journal for the Philosophy of Science* 19 (1968): 251–253. Argues that only negative instances are relevant in judging a hypothesis true or probable, and in consequence there is no paradox to worry about in connection with Hempel's hypothesis about black ravens or Goodman's hypothesis about grue emeralds. Maintains that Goodman's problem actually refutes the very idea of confirming a hypothesis with positive instances or with anything else. See the replies by Foster (1969) and Settle (1969).

Fodor, Jerry A. *The Language of Thought.* New York: Thomas Y. Crowell Company, 1975. See chapter 1, the discussion of concept learning, especially pages 36–42. Maintains that concept learning involves inductive extrapolation and so it involves Goodman's situation of choosing among hypotheses that predict the very same data up to any given trial. Claims the solution to Goodman's puzzle is "to assume that candidate extrapolations of the data receive an a priori ordering under a *simplicity metric,* and that that metric prefers 'all xs are green' to 'all xs are grue' as the extrapolation of any body of data compatible with both." Maintains that a simplicity metric must take account of the syntax and vocabulary of hypotheses ("the way in which the hypotheses are expressed") in order to produce an a priori ordering of hypotheses. Claims this view of concept learning "commits one to postulating a representational system in which the relevant inductions are carried through."

Foster, Lawrence. "Feyerabend's Solution to the Goodman Paradox." *British Journal for the Philosophy of Science.* A reply to Feyerabend (1968). Argues that Feyerabend makes two mistakes. He is wrong in stating Goodman's problem as based on the view that all hypotheses are confirmed by their positive instances; also wrong in claiming there is no problem if we consider only negative instances of hypotheses—both "All ravens are black" and "All ravens are blite" do not have negative instances, they make conflicting predictions for unexamined cases, and we would choose the former hypothesis over the latter.

Foster, Lawrence. "Differential and Projectible Predicates." *Critica* 3 (1969): 101–108. A reply to Slote (1967). Assumes that Slote is trying to state necessary or sufficient conditions for a predicate being projectible when he distinguishes between differential/nondifferential predicates and between inductively vicious/nonvicious predicates. Argues that if a predicate is nondifferential, then it is not automatically nonprojectible: e.g., "arctic" and "terrestrial" are nondifferential and yet projectible. Argues that if a predicate is nonprojectible, then it does not have to be nondifferential: e.g., "emerub" is differential (either an emerald or a ruby) and yet nonprojectible. Introduces "gree" as a differential predicate and shows that "All emeralds are gree" is not projectible. Defines "gree" as being exactly like four emeralds we have examined and green, or not exactly like them and not green. Notes that Slote regards "grue" as an inductively vicious predicate and "green" as an inductively nonvicious predicate. Argues that if a predicate is nonprojectible, then it does not have to be inductively vicious: e.g., "emerub" and "gree" are nonvicious and nonprojectible. Introduces "grone" as a nonvicious predicate (green and not in Bayonne or blue and in Bayonne) and shows that "All emeralds are grone" is nonprojectible. Argues that if a predicate is inductively vicious, then it is not automatically nonprojectible. Introduces a series of numbers such that every examined member k has been $2k-1$ and so we expect the next member to be $2k-1$. Maintains we are saying "that at any future time any new kth member of the series which is found will be unlike the previous kth members": e.g., even though every kth member of the series has the property of being $2k-1$, 17 is not exactly like 15, 13, 11, 9, 7, 5, 3, or 1. Takes this as showing "some projections of unlikeness into the future are projectible." Concludes that "even if Slote's distinctions are accepted as legitimate (and no Goodmanean would accept them as legitimate) they are irrelevant to the problems of projectibility."

Foster, Lawrence. "Hempel, Scheffler, and the Ravens." *Journal of Philosophy* 68 (1971): 107–114. Examines and rejects Scheffler's (1963) argument against the equivalence condition, which is supposed to show "that it is sometimes reasonable to base a prediction on a given hypothesis formulated by a sentence S_1, but not reasonable to base the prediction on an equivalent formulation S_2." Claims that Scheffler "switches examples in mid-argument." Goes on to propose a solution to the raven paradox that depends on accepting "the view that logically equivalent hypotheses need not be equally projectible." Believes that Scheffler and Hempel are wrong in assuming "d is not black and d is not a raven" confirms "All nonblack things are nonravens." Maintains that "All ravens are black" is projectible while "All nonblack things are nonravens" is not projectible. Argues that the raven hypothesis is projectible because its selectively positive instances "in general increase the credibility of statements asserting that other ravens are black," and that its contrapositive is unprojectible because its selectively positive instances "do not in general increase the credibility of statements asserting that other nonblack things are nonravens." Maintains that his assumption—logically equivalent hypotheses do not have to be equally projectible—is compatible with Goodman's views in *FFF*. Notes that the "projectibility value" of a hypothesis depends on the entrenchment of its antecedent and consequent predicates and that the antecedent and consequent predicates of the raven hypothesis are not coextensive with those of its contrapositive. Believes it follows that the two hypotheses do not have to be equally projectible. Claims that "All nonblack things are nonravens" is unprojectible because both of its predicates are poorly entrenched. Believes we can accept the equivalence condition if we deny that "d is not black and not a raven" confirms "All nonblack things are nonravens." Points out that he is then committed to "a is a raven and a is black" confirms "All nonblack things are nonravens." Claims this is "perfectly legitimate" because "finding a black raven does increase the credibility of the hypothesis that all nonblack things are nonravens." States this more generally: "a hypothesis that is not projectible still is confirmed by the selectively positive instances of a logically equivalent hypothesis, provided that such instances confirm the hypothesis of which they are selectively positive instances." Notes how it satisfies the equivalence condition about evidence E confirming hypothesis H and so confirming all hypotheses logically equivalent to H. Proposes a definition of evidence E directly confirming H: H must be projectible, and E must be a selectively positive instance of H or a selectively positive instance of H', where H' is a projectible hypothesis and logically equivalent to H. See the replies by Scheffler and Goodman (1972) and Schwartz (1972).

Foster, Marguerite H. and Martin, Michael L. *Probability, Confirmation and Simplicity: Readings in the Philosophy of Inductive Logic.* New York: The Odyssey Press Inc., 1966. Edited collection of readings (thirty-six selections) on the meaning of probability, problems of confirmation theory, simplicity, and the justification of induction. Includes Ackermann (1961), Kemeny (1953), and Scheffler (1958). Also includes "On Inductive Logic" by Carnap, "Studies in the Logic of Confirmation" by Hempel (1945), and "A Definition of 'Degree of Confirmation'" by Hempel and Oppenheim. Goodman (1946) is in response to these papers (along with others by these three authors) which present definitions of confirmation and degree of confirmation. Goodman claims they "leave untouched one basic problem that must be solved before we can say that the proposed definitions are intuitively adequate."

Friedman, Kenneth. "Son of Grue: Simplicity vs. Entrenchment." *Nous* 7 (1973): 366–378. Criticizes Goodman's entrenchment view of projectibility; argues for his own simplicity view. Presents two counterexamples (one about a person who perceives grue but not green, the other about people with a superstitious grue belief) to show that "the better entrenched class need not be the more projectible one." Claims in addition that, on Goodman's view, we can't tell which class (green or grue) is more projectible until after time t, and that we can have good reason to believe two classes differ in projectibility when in fact they do not, which does not fit in with the connection between projectibility and "reasonableness of projecting." Maintains that "a predicate is projectible for a person on the basis of positive instances unless its projection conflicts with the projection of a simpler predicate for that person projectible on the same evidence." Notes two requirements for an adequate simplicity solution: it must be based on a theory of simplicity that solves other problems and explains the methodological importance of simplicity, and it must provide a general solution to the new riddle. Claims his theory of simplicity ("Empirical Simplicity as Testability," *British Journal for the Philosophy of Science*, 1972) satisfies the first requirement. Considers class C simpler than class D if it is more testable than D "in that it requires less relevant information to determine whether a given object is a member of C than to determine whether it is a member of D." Defines a test for C being independent of information I, information for D being dependent on class C, and information for class D being parasitic on C. Defines a test for a class D such that it is independent of all information for class D parasitic on another class C. Characterizes one class being simpler than another in terms of these tests: i.e., C is simpler than D for a person if and only if, for the set of tests this person can conduct, the set of these tests for D is a proper subset of those for C. Applies this to the class C of green things and the class D of grue things. Argues that all of these tests for grue things are also tests for green things, and the set of grue tests is a proper subset of the set of green tests. Points out this argument only depends on "the fact that more relevant information is necessary to determine whether an object is grue than to determine whether it is green." Claims his full theory of simplicity (in the above article) can deal with more complicated Goodmanesque predicates such as "diagrue" (either a diamond or grue) because it construes "is simpler than" as transitive. Makes the psychological claim that "people tend to associate the first learned, most familiar predicates with those properties (or classes) which are simplest for them." States the principal assumption behind this claim: viz., that if a person selects a class with a predicate, then there isn't a more preferable class. States two conditions for one class being preferable to another—a condition about simplicity and about the predicate in question applying to all and only members of the preferable class. Uses this assumption to show that "if a person learns the word 'green' before the word 'grue', the class C he associates with 'green' will be simpler for him than the class D he associates with 'grue'." Notes that he is not claiming green is objectively simpler than grue or simpler for all people. Maintains that simplicity explains entrenchment in that "the simplest classes (for each individual) become associated with the most commonly used and earliest learned predicates." Feels this is why his theory and the entrenchment theory give similar results for most cases. Also maintains that a society will naturally evolve from using a grue-type predicate to a green-type predicate. Describes a society in which this happens. Also see Friedman (1990).

Friedman, Kenneth S. "Another Shot at the Canons of Induction." *Mind* 84 (1975): 177–191. Maintains the new riddle is a problem for the pragmatic justification, the inductive justification, and the analytic justification (or dissolution) of induction. Discusses how Salmon (1961, 1963) restricts the straight rule to purely ostensive predicates, thereby avoiding grue-type predicates. Argues that some legitimate scientific predicates (e.g., "positron") are not purely ostensive, and that "grue" itself may not be purely ostensive because someone might be able to see ("directly perceive") the difference between grue and bleen things. Also mentions how Max Black's self-supporting inductive argument applies to both "green" and "grue," and how the new riddle is a difficulty for Strawson's dissolution approach because "in the absence of a distinction between inductive arguments and Goodmanesque counterfeits, Strawson's arguments make it analytic that it is reasonable to project Goodmanesque predicates on the basis of positive instances." Develops his own noncircular inductive justification of induction. Characterizes induction as "projection of the simplest hypothesis compatible with the data." Refers to his (1973) definition of simplicity in terms of testability and his view of "Goodmanesque predicates and hypotheses as more complex than normal ones." Argues there is evidence for the hypothesis that "true hypotheses are generally simple, so that induction is (and will be) successful most of the time." Claims "it is more probable that induction would have been generally successful in the past were true laws simple than were they generally complex." Makes use of a case involving data points for the orbit of a planet. Uses Bayes's theorem to show how the past success of induction "increases the likelihood that induction will generally work in the future." Believes the new riddle is a problem for his justification as well. Considers the hypothesis that "true hypotheses are generally simple, so that induction generally quirks." Defines "ximple" as simple before t and complex after; defines "quirk" as working before t and failing after. Thinks the orbit data points support this hypothesis as well as the one above (true hypotheses are generally simple). Maintains it would be circular to claim Goodmanesque hypotheses are not as well supported here because they are not as simple as normal ones. Believes "the answer to this problem lies in distinguishing among different levels of description of the information we have." Considers how "a coarser level of description" influences testability of hypotheses. Maintains that in general "coarse graining increases the relative testability of simple hypotheses, as opposed to more complex ones." Adopts a general methodological principle that eliminates the ximple/quirk hypothesis: viz., with two competing hypotheses, if no coarse graining makes one of the hypotheses less testable than the other, but some coarse graining (here, omitting the time reference) makes the former more testable than the latter, then the evidence only supports the former hypothesis— even if both hypotheses equally imply the evidence. See Friedman (1990).

Friedman, Kenneth S. *Predictive Simplicity: Induction Exhum'd.* Oxford: Pergamon Press,

1990. Discusses the new riddle in chapters 5, 6, and 9. Attempts to resolve the new riddle by characterizing induction in terms of simplicity. Develops an account of simplicity in chapters 7 and 8. Incorporates material from his previous articles on the topic (1973, 1975). Claims any justification of induction (Hume's problem) must include a solution to the new riddle, otherwise it will justify projecting the grue hypothesis, therefore justifying too much. Explains how the new riddle can occur with Max Black's inductive justification, Strawson's dissolution approach, and Salmon's (1961, 1963) pragmatic vindication. Discusses how Salmon restricts the straight rule to ostensive predicates. Replies that many scientific predicates are not ostensive predicates, and that "grue" might be an ostensive predicate if someone could directly perceive grue. Emphasizes how justifying induction must involve demarcating "what one wants to justify from what is unjustifiable." Introduces five necessary conditions for an adequate solution to the new riddle: the solution must identify a real asymmetry between "green" and "grue"; the asymmetry must be a general one between normal and Goodmanian predicates, not just between "green" and "grue"; the asymmetry must also be accessible in that we must be able to tell "before time T which predicate is favored by this asymmetry"; the asymmetry "must be based on prior considerations or purely descriptive differences, and must not require inductive evidence"; and the solution must also solve the curve-fitting problem. Notes that the new riddle is not simply the curve-fitting problem because the new riddle has two parts, the curve-fitting part (as it were) for "inductive extensions of the data" and the criteria part for "designating the coordinate axes." Argues that Goodman's entrenchment solution does not satisfy four of the necessary conditions. Agrees there is an asymmetry between "green" and "grue" with respect to entrenchment, but maintains there are cases "in which projectibility does not vary with entrenchment." Describes cases involving superstitious grue beliefs, two classes for newly observed birds, color-blind people who use "green" for "grue," and sinusoidal curves vs. straight lines. Characterizes a hypothesis as inductive if and only if it is "at least as simple as any competing hypothesis that receives as much evidential support." Claims the green hypothesis is inductive, the grue is not, because the green hypothesis is simpler than the grue hypothesis. Argues this point in terms of his testability account of simplicity and its notion of parasitic information, the prime consideration being, with regard to tests for applying "is grue" that do not depend on information for "is grue" parasitic on "is green," and with regard to tests for applying "is green" that do not depend on information for "is green" parasitic on "is grue," whether all of the former tests also count as tests for the latter. Maintains that his simplicity solution satisfies the five necessary conditions: i.e., simplicity is a general asymmetry, it allows us to tell that the green hypothesis is simpler than the grue hypothesis before time T, it does not involve or depend on inductive evidence, and it applies to the curve-fitting version of the new riddle. Claims this simplicity solution also solves "second-generation Goodman problems" about gred emerubies. Argues that Goodman's entrenchment solution seems to work in many cases because "there is a tendency for simplicity to determine entrenchment," not the other way around. Introduces a principle that connects using a predicate with selecting a certain class provided there is no preferable class for that person; explains a class being preferable in terms of it being simpler and having no reason to doubt the predicate in question applies to all and only its members. Uses this principle in describing cases in which there is a "natural evolution" from using grue-type predicates to green-type predicates. Claims it is "most difficult to conceive of" the reverse.

Friedman, Michael. "Truth and Confirmation." *Journal of Philosophy* 76 (1979): 361–383. Considers what theories of confirmation and truth must be like if well-confirmed theories tend to be true theories. Argues that a theory of confirmation will be an empirical theory that appeals to facts about the actual world and includes a causal theory of reference. To illustrate the view, considers (in section iv) when a generalization is confirmed by its instances. Includes information about projectible predicates in a syntactic definition of confirmation. Asks which predicates are the projectible ones; maintains that Goodman's entrenchment answer "leaves too much unexplained" because it does not tell us "why it is better to make inferences with projectible predicates rather than nonprojectible predicates." Claims that on Goodman's definition of 'projectible' "we have given no independent specification of the class of projectible predicates" and so "all the generalizations we actually accept are automatically justified." Claims this produces (along with a theory of truth without a theory of reference) a viciously circular justification of scientific method. Suggests defining 'projectible' independently of accepted generalizations by specifying projectible predicates in terms of "the history of their acquisition." Would then use a causal theory of reference (with "our theory of the world") to show the reliability of inferences to generalizations with projectible predicates. Claims this is circular but not viciously circular.

Gärdenfors, Peter. "Induction, Conceptual Spaces and AI." *Philosophy of Science* 57 (1990): 78–95. Also in this volume. Section 1: "AI and the Problem of Induction." Concerned with constructing computer programs that "mirror the human inductive capacity." Believes this is essentially a problem about "finding an appropriate *knowledge representation.*" Points out that humans make inductive inferences under certain constraints, and that he will focus on the projectibility constraint: viz., that some predicates can be used in inductive inferences, some cannot. Outlines the critical and the constructive parts of his argument. Section 2: "Induction and Logical Positivism." Presents the logical positivists as concerned with the logical analysis of sentences in a regimented language whose atomic predicates designate observational properties. Points out that the logical positivists took observational predicates to be "*primitive,* unanalysable notions" and treated all observational predicates "in the same way since there were no logical reasons to differentiate between them." Reviews Hempel's raven paradox and Goodman's new riddle. Notes that "even if we have a Goodman-type predicate that succeeds in some inductive generalizations, we do not count it as projectible." Maintains that "if we use *logical* relations alone to determine which inductions are valid, the fact that all predicates are treated on a par induces symmetries which are not preserved in our understanding of the inductions:" e.g., "green" is treated on a par with "grue," and "*F*" is treated on a par with "*F* or *H*." Believes we should find a nonlogical way of distinguishing between "green" and "grue." Mentions Goodman's notion of entrenchment, and discusses Quine's views on defining "natural kind" and the notion of similarity. Section 3: "Induction as a Problem of Knowledge Representation." Believes the problem is how to represent our knowledge about projectible predicates in a computational form. Points out that AI usually has represented knowledge in a propositional form "in the sense that it is based on a set of rules or axioms together with a set of facts or a data base." Mentions a definition of a concept-formation problem as an example and claims that inductive reasoning based on this definition "will preserve the logical symmetries" and so "will be open to the same type of criticism" as the logical positivist approach. Also points out that, for AI purposes, it is better to have a conceptual/computational analysis of natural kinds instead of a realistic one. Section 4: "Conceptual Spaces." Introduces a nonlinguistic way of representing knowledge "in the sense that the objects of the representation no longer form a language or even a propositional structure." Views this as "a cognitive or conceptual structure" that is "ontologically prior to any form of language." States that a conceptual space ("a cognitive entity") has a number of prelinguistic quality dimensions such as color, weight, temperature, mass. Views each quality dimension as "endowed with a certain *topological* or *metrical* structure": e.g., the interval scale of the temperature dimension. Distinguishes between a psychological and a scientific interpretation of quality dimensions. Emphasizes how the psychological color dimension differs from the theoretical: e.g., the psychological interpretation of hue in terms of the color wheel and the theoretical/scientific interpretation in terms of wavelengths of light with a straight line topology. Defines a conceptual space S as consisting of a class of n quality dimensions, where a point in S is a vector. Maintains that, in a conceptual space, "a complete description of the properties of an individual would consist in assigning it a point in the space." Cites the space assumed in Newtonian particle mechanics as a "theoretical conceptual space used in science." States that a conceptual space is separated into dimensions in order to represent the fact that "an individual can be assigned some properties *independently* of other properties when the properties belong to different 'dimensions' ": e.g., we can assign the weight of 1 kilo to an individual independently of its color or temperature. Notes that certain statements will be "a-priori-in-S" and that "different conceptual spaces will yield different notions of 'a priori'." Section 5: "Natural Kinds and Similarity." States that a property can be defined as a region of a conceptual space S, and that if the property is a natural property, then the region is convex: i.e., the region is such that for every pair of points in the region, every point between them is also in the region. Points out that "grue" does not represent a convex region because it uses both the color and time dimensions; also points out that "even if we consider the cylindrical space that would be generated by taking the 'Cartesian product' of the time and hue dimensions, 'grue' would not represent a convex region." Notes that "non-raven" would not correspond to a convex set in a classificatory structure, but that "non-black" would correspond to a convex region in the color space because every color between a pair of nonblack colors is also nonblack. Believes this "indicates that convexity is a necessary but maybe not sufficient condition for a region to represent a natural property." Admits that "what counts as a natural property is *dependent* on the underlying conceptual space," and so "grue" might correspond to a natural property in some other conceptual space. Contends that the projectible predicates are the predicates designating natural properties, and that only these predicates should be allowed in inductive inferences. Notes that we can define a relation of comparative similarity in terms of a conceptual space by letting two objects count as "more similar to each other the closer their set of properties is located in the underlying conceptual space." Section 6: "On the Relativism of Inductive Inferences." Considers whether "the choice of a conceptual space is *arbitrary*" and so we are "thereby stuck with an unescapable *relativism.*" Argues that this relativism "is not as problematic as it may first seem." Claims that humans generally agree on which properties are the projectible ones, and this suggests that humans have "close to identical" psychological conceptual spaces. Argues that evolutionary theory (via natural selection) explains why we agree, and it also explains why "our way of identifying natural properties accords so well with the external world as to make our inductions tend to come out right." Believes that some of our quality dimensions are innate, some learned, and some "may be culturally dependent." Concludes that there is "rather limited freedom for humans in choosing a conceptual space as a basis for inductive inferences." Believes that relativism will only appear, if it does, with "the more advanced, learned, and culturally dependent quality dimensions: Goodman-type predicates will in no case count as natural." Points out that if his evolutionary story is correct, then "our inductive capacities will be *dependent on the ecological circumstances under which they have evolved.*" Recalls that scientific theories introduce "theoretically precise, non-psychological quality dimensions," and these "help us in producing new successful inductive conclusions in environments which are completely different from that of our evolutionary cradle." Section 7: "Conclusion." Emphasizes that conceptual spaces are "an *alternative* to linguistic representations of knowledge which may help us see the drawbacks of such representations." Discusses how the conceptual space approach "leads to a *metaproblem* of inductive inferences: What criteria can be used to choose between competing conceptual spaces?" Suggests the answer is related to "the metascientific project of evaluating competing scientific theories." Believes AI programmers should use the best scientific theory of a domain when trying to produce automated inductive reasoning within that domain. Suggests that "much more emphasis should be given to programs based on analogical representations" instead of linguistic or Fregean representations.

Gemes, Ken. "The World in Itself: Neither Uniform nor Physical." *Synthese* 73 (1987): 301–318. Claims the grue problem shows two unrestricted rules are unacceptable: viz., that the future will be like the past and that we can infer "All *A*s are *B*" from "All observed *A*s are *B*." Interprets the uniformity rule to mean that by and large, or in most respects, the future will be like the past. Rejects this interpretation because the future differs from the past in at least as many respects as it is similar to the past. Considers an ontology of properties and kinds and the view that real change involves real properties or natural kinds, that a predicate like "green" names a real property (or kind) but a predicate like "grue" does not, and that the uniformity principle actually means the future will, for the most part, be like the past with regard to real properties or natural kinds. Asks how we know that the greenlike predicates name real properties and the gruelike ones do not, and whether we have any reason to believe this version of the principle "even embodies our actual expectations, for instance, our expectation that emeralds will remain green after the year 2000 A.D." Examines the claim that a real change involves an accompanying change in microstructure, and that is why changing from green to blue at A.D. 2000 counts as a real change while changing from grue to bleen does not. Notes that there are gruelike predicates for microstructure and so there will be a problem about real change at this level as well as the macro level of color changes. Introduces the gruelike microstructure predicates "gre$X$" and "bl$Y$" for grue-bleen changes. Considers the claim that a predicate like "green" refers to a real property and can be used in inductive reasoning because it can be ostensively defined. Cites Salmon (1974). Replies that any predicate (including "grue") can be ostensively defined because ostensive learning is relative to an individual and our physiological makeup is not the only one possible or perhaps even one that has "a purchase on the structure of the universe." Believes the moral of Goodman's grue problem is that we should get rid of the notion of real or absolute change and instead view change as "frame-of-reference-dependent." Believes Goodman shows that it is only "with respect to our favored frame of reference (Goodman's so-called entrenched predicates) we assume the future will be like the past." Maintains that "the universe *in itself* is neither uniform nor non-uniform," only uniform relative to some frames of reference, nonuniform relative to others. Notes that similarity and difference are therefore frame-of-reference dependent notions. Maintains this has implications for views that make use of these notions such as the physical supervenience thesis about all facts supervening on physical facts. Argues against three versions of the supervenience thesis: one about everything true of two physically identical worlds, another about no changes or differences without physical changes or differences, and a limited linquistic thesis about changes in applying color predicates and changes in applying normal physical predicates. Argues against the identical worlds and no-change views by introducing gruelike disjunctive predicates, and argues against the linguistic view by introducing other restricted linguistic supervenience theses that can be true at the same time, thus showing how these linguistic views are "as much as reflection of the nature and limits of the vocabularies in question as a reflection of the nature and limits of the world." Contends that gruelike predicates are odd because they represent *ad hoc* or nonperspicuous categories. Emphasizes that categories are "non-perspicuous or *ad hoc* to particular agents or particular types of agents." Introduces the predicate "pawberry" to mean a strawberry before A.D. 2000 or a nightshade berry after, the hypothesis that all pawberries are nutritious, and two individuals, one like us and one for whom strawberries become poisonous and nightshade berries nutritious after A.D. 2000. Claims this shows how certain predicates are useful in predicting or conducive to survival or pick out kinds that are natural only for particular agents as they experience the world, not for others. Thinks that it is futile to try and explain "what is objectively wrong with grue-like predicates."

Glymour, Clark. *Theory and Evidence.* Princeton, N.J.: Princeton University Press, 1980. Discusses the curve-fitting problem in chapter III, "Why I Am Not a Bayesian," and in chapter VIII, "The Fittest Curve." Claims that Jeffreys's Bayesian account (1957) is based on the ordering of prior probabilities of hypotheses, and yet "it is just very implausible that scientists typically have their prior degrees of belief distributed according to any plausible simplicity ordering, and still less plausible that they would be rational to do so." Maintains that Hesse's Bayesian account (1974), featuring her clustering postulate to constrain prior probabilities, seems "incoherent" because impossible probability assignments result from her postulate, the probability axioms, and a few trivial assumptions. Considers Popper's falsifiability explanation (1959) for preferring linear to quadratic hypotheses and describes a case in which, given three data points, they are equally falsifiable. Claims that Schlesinger's rule of simplicity (1974) fails to select a unique curve with measurements having uncertain but bounded error, and that many alternative objective rules also select a unique curve when the measurement error has a known probability distribution. Goes on to consider whether our curve-fitting preferences are connected with our preferences for more frequently tested hypotheses, more informative hypotheses, or more severely tested hypotheses. Concludes that, on one counting principle and with uncertain yet bounded measurement error, the number of tests does provide "a reason to prefer the intuitively less complicated parametric families to more complicated ones when both fit the data." Points out problems with this account as the number of tests becomes larger and the evidence accumulates. Concludes with regard to hypotheses being informative that "hypotheses with fewer parameters permit more precise determination of those parameter values than do more general hypotheses containing more parameters." Develops a way to compare the severity of tests in terms of the range of possible outcomes that would contradict a hypothesis, and two ways this might apply to curve-fitting cases. Attempts to explain particular cases in which we prefer a simple polynomial to a more complex one in terms of severity of tests and informativeness of hypotheses. Concludes that these ideas will not explain some of his cases. Cautions against contriving a solution or accepting one that is not supported by a plausible general principle. Draws the following moral: "there is no satisfactory rationale for curve fitting available to use yet."

Goldstick, Dan. "What are 'Purely Qualitative' Terms?" *American Philosophical Quarterly* 23 (1986): 71–81. Defines a purely qualitative expression in terms of a definitely referring expression. Definitely referring expressions have existential implications or presuppositions. The basic idea involved in the definition: it is self-contradictory to assert a statement with a definitely referring expression and then conjoin that statement with another denying the existence of whatever the referring expression commits you to.

Goldstick, D. "The Meaning of 'Grue'." *Erkenntnis* 31 (1989): 139–141. Defends Carnap's (1947) reply to the new riddle in terms of purely qualitative versus positional predicates. Goodman claims "green" can be defined in terms of "grue" and "bleen," and thus is as positional as "grue." Goldstick argues that this extensional definition does not help because "green" is not synonymous with any expression making reference to a specific time such as the present moment. Also see Goldstick (1986) on the notion of a purely qualitative term.

Good, Irving John. "Explicativity, Corroboration, and the Relative Odds of Hypotheses." *Synthese* 30 (1975): 39–73. Explicates corroboration (in section IV) in terms of the weight of evidence. Defines the weight of evidence in favor of hypothesis H provided by evidence E given background information G as "the logarithm of the factor by which the odds of H are multiplied when E is observed, given G." Generalizes the definition for the weight of evidence in favor of one hypothesis compared with another; also expresses weight of evidence in terms of the amount of information. Uses the notion to compare Goodman's grue and green hypotheses. Claims that the weight of evidence in favor of the grue compared to the green hypothesis equals 0 with our background information and all observed green emeralds. Points out that this means the posterior odds are equal to the prior odds. Maintains, however, that the grue hypothesis is "*physically* more complicated" and "it loses an enormous factor on its initial probability because of the arbitrary choice of the parameter 1990." Considers this to be an example of a situation in which "the weight of evidence is zero and a judgment of initial probabilities *must* be made." Also claims it shows how "simplicity of expression as a linguistic string does not necessarily provide high initial probability, especially in a language designed to mislead." Discusses complexity and relative odds of theories in sections II and III.

Good, I. J. "A Bayesian Approach to the Philosophy of Inference." *British Journal for the Philosophy of Science* 35 (1984): 161–173. A review article of Horwich (1982b). Emphasizes a "Bayes factor" explication of weight of evidence; regrets that Horwich ignores this explication. Comments on the new riddle. Claims that the Bayesian solution is the only solution here, and that the Bayesian solution focuses on how "the *prior* probability of gruesomeness is extremely small." Notes that Horwich points this out, and so does Good (1975).

Goodman, Nelson. "A Query on Confirmation." *Journal of Philosophy* 43 (1946): 383–385. Introduces the first grue-type predicate "*S*" in connection with drawing marbles from a certain bowl. Each has been red up to and including VE day; each has also been *S*—drawn by VE day and red, or drawn later and nonred. Intended to show problems with definitions of confirmation and degree of confirmation by Hempel (1943, 1945), Hempel and Oppenheim (1945), Oppenheim and Helmer (1945), and Carnap (1945a, 1945b). See the reply by Carnap (1947) and the discussion by Leblanc (1963).

Goodman, Nelson. "On Infirmities of Confirmation-Theory." *Philosophy and Phenomenological Research* 8 (1947a): 149–151. A reply to Carnap's "On the Application of Inductive Logic" (1947), which is a response to Goodman's "Query on Confirmation" (1946). Does not accept Carnap's assumption that "there are absolutely simple properties into which others may, and indeed for some purposes must, be analyzed." Views analyzability as relative to "a sphere of reference and a method of analysis." Does not accept

Carnap's analogy with restrictions for deductive logic; points out that we do not need to know if predicates are logically independent in order to safely make valid deductive inferences, but we need to know this in order to safely make inductive inferences in Carnap's system. Maintains Carnap has not offered any support for his claim that "either the class of purely qualitative predicates is identical with the class of intuitively projectible predicates, or that such predicates as are intuitively projectible though not purely qualitative will also prove to be projectible by his definition." Notes that some projectible predicates are not purely qualitative: e.g., "solar," "arctic," and "Sung." Considers the comparison between Carnap's system of inductive logic (no rule specifying which kind of properties are projectible) and Euclid's system of geometry (no rule specifying which kind of triangles the Pythagorean theorem holds for); insists that questions of intuitive adequacy are relevant for both systems. Attempts to clarify examples that Carnap sees as violating the principle of total evidence. Claims he was trying to show that if we must allow order predicates in our evidence statements, then we must have a criterion of projectibility as well. Also discusses how these examples involve an important fact about order that Carnap's system must take into account: viz., "that regular orders influence our expectations in a way that irregular ones do not." See the reply by Carnap (1948).

Goodman, Nelson. "The Problem of Counterfactual Conditionals." *Journal of Philosophy* 44 (1947b): 113–128. Also appears as "Predicament," chapter I of *Fact, Fiction and Forecast*. Points out that in a counterfactual "the consequent seldom follows from the antecedent by logic alone." Attempts "to specify what sentences are meant to be taken in conjunction with an antecedent as a basis for inferring the consequent." Takes these to be sentences describing relevant conditions and general sentences that we call natural or physical or causal laws. Believes the two major problems are defining relevant conditions and defining these laws. Discusses (in section III) the problem of determining whether certain general sentences ("arrived at by generalizing conditionals of a certain kind") are laws or not. Considers a law to be a true lawlike sentence, and a general sentence to be lawlike "if its acceptance does not depend upon the determination of any given instance." Turns to then current "theories of induction and confirmation to learn the distinguishing factors or circumstances that determine whether or not a sentence is acceptable without complete evidence." Claims these theories do not even see a problem about distinguishing between confirmable and nonconfirmable sentences, and that most confirmation theories are open to very "damaging counterexamples of an elementary kind." Introduces one of these counterexamples: twenty-six marbles in a sack are named with the twenty-six letters of the alphabet, we are told that twenty-five of the marbles (all except marble d) are red, and we are not told the color of marble d. Notes how this is usually taken as strong confirmation that all of the marbles are red, and so marble d is red as well. Also notes how, arguing in the same way, we seem to have strong confirmation that all of the marbles are P, and so marble d is not red. Uses "P" to mean "is in the sack and either is not d and is red, or is d and is not red." Maintains that the problem of defining confirmable statements is equivalent to the problem of defining projectible predicates. Notes that his paper "A Query on Confirmation" (1946) deals with these points in more detail.

Goodman, Nelson. "Reply to an Adverse Ally." *Journal of Philosophy* 54 (1957): 531–535. A reply to Cooley (1957). Also appears in Goodman (1972), pages 398–402. Presents an example of the cotenability problem that does not explicitly involve a causal time sequence. With regard to using relative definitions, says the real point "is simply that non-positionality is not concomitant with projectibility." On finding manifest predicates to define dispositional ones, notes that we will "have first to do a good deal of trimming and patching, refining and dividing—and often end with several definitions for more specific terms." Contends that "projectible" is a disposition term: just as some things that break are not fragile, some predicates that we project are not projectible. Maintains that comparative projectibility cannot handle all of the projectibility problems because "unless some initial differences of projectibility are admitted, no differences will result from the relation of hypotheses to their overhypotheses." Sees Cooley's review as more of an attempt to improve his theory rather than seriously disagree with it. See the response by Cooley (1958).

Goodman, Nelson. "Positionality and Pictures." *Philosophical Review* 69 (1960): 523–525. A reply to Barker and Achinstein (1960). Takes the main issue to be whether Barker and Achinstein successfully define the distinction between positional and nonpositional predicates. Sees the Barker and Achinstein attempt in terms of pictures and predicates: viz., we only need one picture to represent any example of applying a nonpositional predicate but at least two pictures for an example of applying a positional predicate. Points out that there are no obvious limitations on what can represent what. Asks what Barker and Achinstein will count as a representation. Argues that a color does not have to be represented by a sample of it, that it is only begging the question to deny that grue is a single color, and that the color of an object does not have to be represented by something with a matching color. Considers the possibility that Barker and Achinstein only mean "ordinary, everyday, realistic representation." Takes this to mean using only common, familiar, and accustomed modes of representation. Argues that if Barker and Achinstein mean this by representation, then they are not presenting a new alternative to facts about our habits—they "are making much the same appeal to entrenchment but in a more roundabout and covert way." Adds that it will not help to appeal to a distinction between natural and artificial representation here. Argues the point by considering Barker and Achinstein's representation for the predicate "conducts electricity" and describing how adding a verbal inscription would render it a representation for "condulates electricity." Reprinted in Goodman (1972).

Goodman, Nelson. "Safety, Strength, Simplicity." *Philosophy of Science* 28 (1961): 150–151. Also in Goodman (1972). Considers hypothesis choice when the hypotheses are equally supported by the evidence and vary in strength. Rejects choosing the weakest because we would then choose "a hypothesis that does not go beyond the evidence at all." Rejects choosing the strongest because "for every hypothesis strong enough to go beyond the evidence, there is an equally strong conflicting hypothesis based upon the same evidence." Argues that "neither safety nor strength is the measure of simplicity, and that simplicity takes precedence over both as a factor in the choice of hypotheses." Believes that standards of simplicity "derive from our classificatory habits as disclosed in our language, and that the relative entrenchment of predicates underlies our judgment of relative simplicity." Comments that his entrenchment criteria of projectibility (*FFF*, 1st edition) are "perhaps essentially a simplicity criterion."

Goodman, Nelson. "Faulty Formalization." *Journal of Philosophy* 50 (1963): 578–579. A criticism of Martin (1959). Argues that Martin has not provided a correct formalization of projectibility because he has relied on his particular notion of acceptance. Maintains that Martin's definition of 'actually projected' would require inconsistent behavior: viz., "accepting a hypothesis while accepting some of its instances and rejecting others." Maintains that, as Martin defines 'accept' and 'instance,' there is the following "remarkable" consequence: "a hypothesis is actually projected when it and some of its instances are accepted, the negates of none of its instances are accepted, and some instance and its negate are both rejected." Points out that projection "does not consist of accepting a hypothesis while accepting some but not others of its instances." Reprinted in Goodman (1965) on pages 404–405.

Goodman, Nelson. "Comments." *Journal of Philosophy* 63 (1966): 328–331. Replies to Jeffrey (1966), Thomson (1966), and Wallace (1966). All are in the same issue; the reply also appears in Goodman (1972), pages 405–410. Explains why "All emerubies are gred" should be regarded as unprojectible, and so why his entrenchment solution is not wrong in ruling it out. Regards Jeffrey as emphasizing how the Hempel and Carnap definitions of confirmation do not come with a general criterion for identifying projectible predicates, and instead rely on particular decisions about projectibility for each predicate. Regards Thomson as trying to define projectibility in terms of observability; maintains that it will be very hard to formulate an adequate, general definition of an observation predicate, that the difference between observation and nonobservation predicates is not the same as the difference between projectible and nonprojectible predicates, that it is not clear what Thomson is claiming about applying 'grue' after examining an object in good light, and that Thomson's views are not incompatible with defining projectibility in terms of entrenchment. See the response by Thomson (1966b). Regards Wallace as pointing to how he does not view equivalent hypotheses as identical hypotheses; maintains that Wallace's problems actually disappear when one recognizes this.

Goodman, Nelson. "Two Replies." *Journal of Philosophy* 64 (1967a): 286–287. A reply to Davidson (1966) and Wallace (1966b). Maintains that "All emeroses are gred" is not lawlike because "an emerose found before *t* to be gred does not increase our belief that emeroses examined after *t* will be gred." Claims the lawlikeness question cannot be settled by pointing to anything syntactic or semantic about these predicates, and explains how the apparent truth of "All emeroses are gred" is irrelevant. Wonders, contra Davidson, how the lawlikeness question could depend on a relation between predicates of a hypothesis. Argues that Wallace has not shown anything wrong with the entrenchment theory of projection: i.e., "to know that a given hypothesis is true if and only if lawlike does not help us decide whether or not it is true and lawlike, or whether to project it at a given time in favor of a competing hypothesis." Also appears in Goodman (1972) as "Two More Replies," pp. 410–412.

Goodman, Nelson. "Uniformity and Simplicity." *Geological Society of America, Special Paper* 89 (1967b): 93–99. Reprinted in Goodman (1972), pp. 347–354. Discusses, in the last pages, "grounds for choosing the simplest among nonequivalent theories that fit the evidence but conflict for unexamined cases." Notes that "we are always faced with making a choice among hypotheses when there is no ground for supposing any of them more likely to be true than any of the rest." Maintains that "the simplest theory is to be chosen not because it is the most likely to be true but because it is scientifically the most rewarding among equally likely alternatives."

Goodman, Nelson. "Seven Strictures on Similarity." In *Experience and Theory,* edited by Lawrence Foster and J.W. Swanson, pp. 19–29. Boston: University of Massachusetts Press, 1970. Also in Goodman (1972). The fifth stricture is about inductive inferences, especially predictive ones. Maintains that similarity does not explain "our predictive, or more generally, our inductive practice." Considers the assumption that the future will be like the past. Claims it will be true no matter what happens. Notes he is not sure how the future will be like the past. Illustrates this with a plot of data on two variables for some material (as in the curve-fitting problem). Asks if the next point will be similar to all of the observed points in falling on a straight line, or similar to all of the observed points in falling on some broken or curved line, where there are countless of these. Takes this to show that our predictions cannot be based on this bald assumption about the future resembling the past. Emphasizes that the real problem is about "*how* what is predicted is like what has already been found." Suspects that "inductive practice may provide the basis for some canons of similarity," and not the other way around. The seventh stricture is also relevant: similarity cannot be measured in terms of having common properties. Examines and rejects five common property views: at least one property in common, all properties in common, more properties in common than certain other things, some number of intensional properties in common, important properties in common. Regards similarity as "relative and variable."

Goodman, Nelson. "On Kahane's Confusions." *Journal of Philosophy* 69 (1972a): 83–84. A reply to the two objections presented in Kahane (1971). Maintains that conflict is plainly described in the revised theory of projectibility: viz., if two hypotheses conflict then "neither follows from the other and they ascribe to something different predicates such that only one actually applies." Also maintains that the new first entrenchment rule does not (as Kahane argues) eliminate all hypotheses with new predicates; claims that Kahane is "mistaking nonprojectibility for unprojectibility" in his account of the conflict between two supported, unviolated, unexhausted hypotheses with equally well-entrenched predicates.

Goodman, Nelson. *Problems and Projects.* Indianapolis: The Bobbs-Merrill Company, Inc., 1972b. Currently available from Hackett Publishing Co., Inc. Forty-four selections: "most of my previously published papers, excerpts from my three earlier books, and some half-dozen items not before published." Ten chapters/subjects: defining philosophy (its aims, methods), epistemological absolutism, aesthetics, individuals and nominalism, meaning and extension, determining what a statement is about, simplicity, induction, similarity, and a logic puzzle. Includes "Safety, Strength, Simplicity," "Science and Simplicity," "Uniformity and Simplicity," "A Query on Confirmation," "On Infirmities of Confirmation-Theory," "The New Riddle of Induction" (chapter III of *FFF*, second edition), "An Improvement in the Theory of Projectibility," "Inductive Translation" (section 9, chapter IV of *Languages of Art*), "Replies to Comments on *Fact, Fiction and Forecast*" ("Reply to an Adverse Ally," "Positionality and Pictures," "Faulty Formalization," "Three Replies" to Jeffrey, Thomson, and Wallace from *Journal of Philosophy* 1966, "Two More Replies" to Davidson and Wallace from *Journal of Philosophy* 1967), "Seven Strictures on Similarity." See the foreword to chapter VII, "Simplicity." Maintains that "whenever we make any inference beyond the evidence, we must choose among countless alternative hypotheses, and the choice must favor simplicity." Claims that "a measure of inductive simplicity must disallow the spurious gain that results from smoothing out a rough curve or hypothesis (such as 'All emeralds are examined before t and green, or not so examined and blue') by use of specially contrived coordinates or terms (such as 'grue')." Believes we must "take into account the familiarity of the predicates along with the grammatical composition of the hypotheses." Also see the foreword to chapter VIII, "Induction." Remarks that in his entrenchment solution "scientific procedure rests upon chance choices sanctified by habit." Is confident that we cannot distinguish between projectible/nonprojectible predicates "on syntactic or even on semantic grounds." Maintains that a psychological explanation (of why we choose to project certain predicates) "would not conflict with my treatment of projectibility in terms of entrenchment of predicates but would merely make the initial choices psychologically determinate rather than matters of chance."

Notes that a psychological explanation would have to show projectible predicates have a "common and independent characteristic that can be correlated with" some "non-random operation of the mind." Claims that we have the new riddle and attempt to solve it in terms of "chance and habit" because of "the unavailability of any such characteristic." Considers the view that projectibility is not a matter of entrenchment but of "past successes and failures." Points out that both the green and the grue hypothesis have "never failed us," and that if we prefer the green hypothesis because we have projected it before and it has not been discredited, then this makes projectibility a matter of entrenchment. Interprets the view to be: we reject the grue hypothesis because "kindred hypotheses have been violated in the past"—for example, the hypothesis "All emeralds are either examined before 1900 A.D. and determined to be green, or not so examined and blue." Points out that there is a parallel argument for choosing the grue hypothesis over the green hypothesis, namely that kindred green hypotheses have been violated in the past, such as "All emeralds are either examined before 1900 A.D. and determined to be grue, or not so examined and bleen." Concludes that we cannot explain why we project the green hypothesis, or why it is projectible, by appealing to survival of the fittest. Refers to Quine and Ullian (1970). Claims the green and the grue hypothesis "have been, and until 2000 A.D. will be, equally useful for survival." Also claims that past choices of some hypotheses kindred to the grue hypothesis "would have been detrimental to survival" and "so would past choice of some hypotheses kindred to" the green hypothesis. Points out that it is careless to say the new riddle is a problem in which the same evidence confirms two conflicting hypotheses because "evidence consists of statements," the statement that "emerald *a* is green" is not the same as "emerald *a* is grue," and so we actually have "exactly equal and parallel evidence for the two conflicting hypotheses." Notes that the definition of "grue" in *FFF* "does not require that a thing change from green to blue in order to remain grue, or from blue to green in order to remain bleen." Claims the grue hypothesis can be true even if some emeralds are always green and the rest are always blue. Comments on his claim that if two predicates are coextensive, then they have the same entrenchment. Emphasizes that this does not mean "we must know what predicates are coextensive before making any inductive choices," and that it does mean "whatever judgments of coextensivity we do make are relevant to our inductive choices."

Goodman, Nelson. "Science and Simplicity." Originally given in 1963 in a series of philosophy of science talks for Voice of America. Published in Goodman's collection of essays *Problems and Projects,* pp. 337–346. Indianapolis: Bobbs-Merrill, 1972b. Considers, in the last three pages, how "simplicity, in at least some respect, is a test of truth." Notes the curve-fitting problem: "no matter how many points we have plotted, infinitely many curves of different degree of jaggedness or complexity pass through all these points." Considers a botanist examining elm trees in various places and under various conditions, and finding them all to be deciduous, but not examining any tree in Smithtown. Suggests the botanist might adopt the hypothesis "All elm trees are deciduous" and hypotheses like "All other elm trees, but not those in Smithtown, are deciduous." Notes again that "for any hypothesis that does venture beyond the evidence there is an alternative hypothesis that gives conflicting results for the unexamined cases." Maintains that "simplicity is used as a test of truth" in the curve-fitting case and the botany case, and that "the pragmatic factor of linguistic habit clearly plays a fundamental role in simplicity of this kind."

Goodman, Nelson. *Languages of Art.* Second edition. Indianapolis: Hackett Publishing Company, 1976. See chapter IV, section 9., "Inductive Translation." Examines the process of message supplementation by considering how a computer might produce a curve from data points. Notes this is a version of producing a hypothesis from instances. Asks how a computer will select a curve when several are compatible with the data points. Mentions three ways a computer might proceed "independently of what has gone before, except for canceling out curves that conflict with the data." For example: the computer might choose the curve ranked highest in a linear preference ordering. Describes a computer that rejects curves incompatible with present data and then rejects curves incompatible with any set of past data having the present data as a proper subset. Maintains there still will be alternative curves left and "no prediction concerning remaining points is excluded." Finally describes a habit-acquiring computer that takes account of present data, past data from curve problems, and its record of past choices, and that proceeds by rejecting curves based on data, then selecting the most frequently used curve and continuing with it until a conflict with new data. Explains how the question is "what curves the machine can handle at all and how it chooses among them," and not the distinction between the machine's initial and generated curves. Asks when supplementation becomes induction: e.g., when it takes account of evidence, or the evidence does not produce a unique choice, or some choices are the result of a chance mechanism. Notes some obvious characteristics of human induction, such as being able to deal with any curve, and asks whether humans have a decisive preference ordering or must use chance procedures at times. Emphasizes three points about general symbols (labels, terms, hypotheses): evidence "takes effect" only by applying a general symbol having an extension with the data as a proper subset, alternatives are mainly general symbols instead of particulars, and efficient habits develop only by using general symbols.

Goodman, Nelson. "Replies." *Erkenntnis* 12 (1978a): 281–291. Includes replies to Essler (1978b) and Kutschera (1978). Agrees with Essler's paper. Maintains Essler is right to emphasize that learning from experience includes looking at data as well as choosing predicates for describing data and stating hypotheses. Notes that simplicity is an important factor in choosing predicates and a component of inductive validity. Adds that to a great extent simplicity "depends upon habit, upon entrenchment; and predicates that are of equal simplicity by any formal criterion may differ drastically in the simplicity that guides selection for inductive use." Claims this disagrees with both traditional versions of empiricism and contemporary "irrational" versions of rationalism. Points out that if one defines simplicity in terms of entrenchment ("an accident repeated over and over"), this does not prevent or demand "a further explanation of the initial accident from some empiricist or rationalist or other orientation." Disagrees with Kutschera's paper. Finds him making objections that others have made and that have been answered. Discusses three of these. Replies that there is nothing circular about how we use the notion of conflict in determining which hypothesis (of two) is projectible; we are proceeding on the assumption that the hypotheses in question conflict, and the rules we use do not depend on our assumption being correct. Replies that there is also nothing circular about comparing predicates with respect to entrenchment if this means considering other predicates that we inductively infer to be coextensive; if we make mistakes in judging comparative entrenchment, we may be wrong in judging projectibility—the rules do not guarantee their own correct application. Replies that there is nothing wrong with his entrenchment view when it comes to introducing new predicates into the sciences; points out that predicates may inherit entrenchment from parent predicates, and that overhypotheses may reinforce hypotheses. Comments on Kahane's example (1965) of "radioactive" and the gruelike "radiotractive." Claims that "radioactive" inherits entrenchment from terms like "green" and "blue" because "relative to predicates already classed as projectible, nonpositionality becomes a legitimate avenue for the inheritance of entrenchment." Maintains that Kutschera's main argument is confusing. Sees Kutschera as first rejecting his problem of defining confirmation and then later accepting it. Quotes Kutschera to show this. Repeats his view on how codifying normal behavior establishes inductive validity. Cannot see how Kutschera's view differs from this.

Goodman, Nelson. *Ways of Worldmaking*. Indianapolis: Hackett Publishing Company, 1978b. Mentions grue and relevant kinds in chapter I, section 4, under the heading "Composition and Decomposition." Notes that repetition is relative to how things are organized, and that induction "requires taking some classes to the exclusion of others as relevant kinds." Cites two reasons for saying relevant kinds instead of natural: wants to refer to artificial kinds (music, experiments, machinery) as well as biological ones (species); does not want to suggest any "absolute categorical or psychological priority" when "the kinds in question are rather habitual or traditional or devised for a new purpose." Also mentions grue and relevant kinds in chapter VI, section 4, in connection with weighting or emphasis. Considers one version of the world that regards "grue" as naming a trivial class, another that regards it as naming a natural or relevant kind, that is a kind "important for description or investigation or induction." Claims that if we project "grue" and not "green," this "would be to make, and live in, a different world." Discusses projectibility in chapter VII, section 4, "Veracity and Validity." Points out that inductive rightness requires true premises, (inductive) validity, use of all examined instances or all real evidence available, and both evidence statements and hypothesis must be in terms of projectible predicates. Notes that others would say in terms of genuine or natural kinds instead of projectible predicates. Also calls projectible predicates "inductively right categories." Maintains that rightness of categorization "attaches to categories or predicates—or systems thereof—which have no truth-value." Considers "what distinguishes right inductive categories from others" and cites *FFF*. Refers to habit as a primary factor in projectibility. Notes that inductively right categories "tend to coincide with categories that are right for science in general." Considers choosing among versions of the world that employ different schemes of categorization. Distinguishes between arguing for a scheme and proposing one. Maintains that arguing for a scheme could not be arguing for its truth ("it has no truth-value"). Emphasizes what categorial systems can do, how effective they are "in worldmaking and understanding."

Goodman, Nelson. *Fact, Fiction and Forecast*. Fourth edition. Cambridge, Mass.: Harvard University Press, 1983. First edition published in 1954 by Athlone Press, University of London. Published by Harvard University Press in 1955. Second edition published in 1965 by Bobbs-Merrill; third edition published in 1973 by Bobbs-Merrill. Fourth edition includes the introductory notes to the first, third, and fourth editions. The principal change has been in chapter IV with respect to the rules for eliminating unprojectible hypotheses: there are three rules in the first edition, two in the second edition, one in the fourth edition. The introductory notes for the third and fourth editions contain brief responses to criticisms and misunderstandings. Lists six common mistakes in the introductory notes to the third edition: e.g., failing to realize "that the projectibility status of a hypothesis varies from time to time." Warns against other "specious objections" in the introductory note to the fourth edition, notably Zabludowski's (1974) objections. Makes it clear that "one condition upon projectibility is *not* that there is an *assumption of no conflict* with any no-less-well-entrenched hypothesis but that there is *no assumption of conflict* with any such hypothesis." The new riddle is introduced and discussed in chapters III and IV. But note chapter 1, section 3. Discusses the difference between confirmable and non-confirmable general sentences such as "All butter melts at 150 degrees fahrenheit" and "Everything in my pocket is silver." Introduces the red marbles example from Goodman (1946) to show that not all general statements are confirmed by their positive instances. Also note chapter II, section 5. Points out that the problem of dispositions looks like the problem of induction, and that these two problems "are but different aspects of the general problem of proceeding from a given set of cases to a wider set." Chapter III is "The New Riddle of Induction." Section 1: "The Old Problem of Induction." Reviews "Hume's answer to the question how predictions are related to past experience." Believes that Hume's problem of justifying induction is connected with "the problem of describing how induction takes place." Section 2: "Dissolution of the Old Problem." Introduces his mutual adjustment view of justifying both deductive and inductive inferences: viz., "rules and particular inferences alike are justified by being brought into agreement with each other." Admits this is circular but maintains "this circle is a virtuous one." Does not regard the inductive problem as "a problem of demonstration but a problem of defining the difference between valid and invalid predictions." Section 3: "The Constructive Task of Confirmation Theory." Examines attempts to define confirmation in terms of the converse of the consequence relation. Especially concerned with Hempel's (1943, 1945) view of how instances confirm a general hypothesis. Points out that a positive instance confirms a lawlike hypothesis and not an accidental generalization: e.g., a piece of copper confirms "All copper conducts electricity" while a third son (now in this room) does not confirm "All men now in this room are third sons." Claims that Hempel's raven paradox depends on "tacit and illicit reference to evidence not stated" in the "All ravens are black" example. Section 4: "The New Riddle of Induction." Introduces the emeralds example: all emeralds examined before *t* are green, this confirms the green hypothesis and the prediction that if the next emerald is examined after *t*, it will be green. Introduces the predicate "grue" as applying "to all things examined before *t* just in case they are green but to other things in case they are blue." Notes that the emeralds are all grue (green and examined before *t*) and that this seems to confirm the grue hypothesis and the prediction that if the next emerald is examined after *t*, it will be blue. Points out how this generalizes "for any prediction whatever about other emeralds—or indeed about anything else." Considers the view that lawlike hypotheses are completely general and accidental hypotheses refer to a particular space, time, or individual. Examines Carnap's (1947) attempt to exclude positional or nonqualitative predicates from syntactically universal hypotheses. Claims he does not know how to determine whether a predicate is positional or not without "completely begging the question at issue." Maintains that "qualitativeness is an entirely relative matter and does not itself establish any dichotomy of predicates." Argues that if we start with "green" and "blue" as basic terms, then "grue" and "bleen" (examined before *t* and blue or not examined before *t* and green) will be explained with a temporal term; but if we start with "grue" and "bleen" as basic terms, "green" and "blue" will be explained with a temporal term—e.g., "green" will apply to grue emeralds before *t* and bleen emeralds after *t*. Section 5: "The Pervasive Problem of Projection." Believes the important (and so far unanswered) question is: "What hypotheses are confirmed by their positive instances?" Believes the new riddle shows that "any statement will confirm any statement" if we define confirmation in terms of the converse of the consequence relation. Comments on Hume's account: "to say that valid predictions are those based on past regularities, without being able to say *which* regularities, is thus quite pointless." Sees the grue case as showing that "regularities are where you find them, and you can find them anywhere." Believes the new riddle is important because it is a specific case of "the general problem of projection," and other problems (e.g., about dispositions and possibility) can be reduced to problems about projecting from one set of cases to others. Chapter IV is "Prospects for a Theory of Projection." Section 1: "A New Look at the Problem." Claims that we should use information about "past predictions actually made and their outcome" in defining the relation of confirmation between a hypothesis and any given evidence. Notes that this sort of information is available when we try to determine whether some evidence confirms a hypothesis. Maintains that if we use this information about past projections along with the evidence and the hypothesis in question, then we will be "defining valid projection—or projectibility on the basis of actual projections." Notes that this is a typical problem of dispositions: i.e., defining the dispositional predicate "projectible" in terms of the manifest predicate "projected" and other relevant information. (See chapter II, section 3, for Goodman's analysis of dispositional predicates.) Section 2: "Actual Projections." States that a hypothesis is actually projected "when it is adopted after some of its instances have been examined and determined to be true, and before the rest have been examined." Maintains that "we need here only a summary sketch of what is meant by saying that a hypothesis is actually projected." Explains positive, negative, and undetermined instances or cases of a hypothesis; the evidence class and the projective class for a hypothesis at a given time; also supported, violated, and exhausted hypotheses. Notes that if adopting a hypothesis counts as actually projecting it, then "at the time in question, the hypothesis has some undetermined cases, some positive cases, and no negative cases." Section 3: "Resolution of Conflicts." Considers "simple universal hypotheses in categorical or hypothetical form" and projectibility at a time. Asks how to eliminate unviolated, unexhausted, and yet unlawlike hypotheses such as the grue hypothesis (where we suppose it to be projected and it is just prior to time t). Points out that this sort of projection "will often *conflict* with other projections": e.g., if we project the green hypothesis, it will conflict with the grue hypothesis for unexamined emeralds. Maintains that "we must consult the record of past projections of the two predicates." Points out that the predicate "green" has been projected longer and more frequently than the predicate "grue." Describes the predicate "green" as much better entrenched than the predicate "grue." Emphasizes that we can distinguish between these predicates "only if we consider those occasions when each predicate was actually projected." Adds that a predicate becomes entrenched through its actual projections and those "of all predicates coextensive with it." Notes that "to speak of the entrenchment of a predicate is to speak elliptically of the entrenchment of the extension of that predicate." Formulates one principle that will eliminate unprojectible projections: viz., "a projection is to be ruled out if it conflicts with the projection of a much better entrenched predicate." Notes that this principle applies only when the difference in entrenchment "is great enough to be obvious." Maintains that "entrenchment and familiarity are not the same," and so his proposal does not exclude unfamiliar predicates. Points out that an unfamiliar predicate might be well entrenched because of predicates it is coextensive with; also that the elimination principle is eliminating projected hypotheses and not predicates, and not "merely upon general grounds of the youth or oddity of the predicates projected." Denies that we must explain why "the really projectible predicate happens to have been the earlier and more often projected" in these conflict cases; also denies that his proposal begs the question. Notes that he is using superior entrenchment (in these conflict cases) as a sufficient condition for projectibility and that he is not concerned with a genetic question. Nonetheless submits that we judge "our main stock of well-worn predicates" to be projectible because they have been habitually projected, not the other way around. Section 4: "Presumptive

Projectibility." Defines two hypotheses being unequal in entrenchment in terms of the entrenchment status of their antecedent and consequent predicates. Defines two hypotheses conflicting: "neither follows from the other (and the fact that both are supported, unviolated, and unexhausted) and they ascribe to something two predicates such that only one actually applies." Points out that we can appeal to hypotheses that are not actually projected but that could have been projected in the sense of being supported, unviolated, and unexhausted at the time in question. States a general rule for supported, unviolated, and unexhausted hypotheses: viz., "a hypothesis is *projectible* if all conflicting hypotheses are overridden, *unprojectible* if overridden, and *nonprojectible* if in conflict with another hypothesis and neither is overridden." Says that if hypothesis *H* conflicts with hypothesis *H'*, *H* is better entrenched than *H'*, and *H* does not conflict with an even better entrenched hypothesis, then *H* overrides *H'*. Notes that the grue hypothesis is unprojectible because the green hypothesis overrides it. Considers the hypothesis "All emeralds are grund," where "grund" applies to everything examined up to *t* and green, or everything not examined up to *t* and round. Describes a case in which the grund hypothesis is unprojectible because the hypothesis "All emeralds are square" overrides it. Describes a case in which the grund hypothesis and "All emeralds are grare" are both nonprojectible because they conflict and neither overrides the other. Introduces "grare" as applying to everything examined before *t* and green, or not examined before *t* and square. Notes that "nonprojectibility does not in general imply illegitimacy." Describes a case in which the grund hypothesis is projectible and adds that it is normally not a projectible hypothesis, but has become projectible in this case because of "evidence that neither violates nor exhausts it but overrides all conflicting hypotheses." Distinguishes between two senses of "projectible": if support normally makes the hypothesis credible, then the hypothesis is projectible; if a hypothesis is projectible, then "the actual evidence supports and makes it credible." Discusses how the general rule handles hypotheses with "troublesome antecedents," such as "All emerubies are green," where "emeruby" applies to "emeralds examined for color before *t* and to rubies not examined before *t*." Describes a case in which the emerubies hypothesis is unprojectible because the hypothesis "All rubies are red" overrides it. Describes a case in which the emerubies hypothesis is nonprojectible because it conflicts with the equally entrenched hypothesis "All sapphirubies are blue." Also describes a case in which the emerubies hypothesis is nonprojectible because it conflicts with the equally entrenched hypothesis "All Eifferubies are black." Describes a case in which the hypothesis "All things are green" is projectible and so the emerubies hypothesis "will be harmless" as one of its consequences. Discusses how the general rule handles hypotheses like "All emerubies are gred," where both the antecedent and the consequent are troublesome. Describes a case in which the emerubies-gred hypothesis is unprojectible because "All emerubies are green" overrides it. Describes a case in which the emerubies-gred hypothesis is projectible because "All rubies are red" overrides "All emerubies are green." Finally considers the hypothesis "All emerubies are grund" and describes cases in which it is not projectible and in which it is projectible. Distinguishes between earned or direct entrenchment and inherited or indirect entrenchment. Introduces the notion of a parent predicate: "*P*" is a parent predicate of "*Q*" if the extension of "*Q*" is among the classes that "*P*" applies to. For example: "army division" is a parent of "soldier in the 26th division." Points out that "a novel predicate may inherit entrenchment from a parent predicate." Stresses that in order to consider the inherited entrenchment of two predicates, neither predicate can have greater earned entrenchment than the other. Views earned entrenchment as establishing "major levels of entrenchment," and views inherited entrenchment as producing "a subsidiary grading." Concludes that if one predicate is clearly better entrenched than another or is about equally entrenched as another but clearly has more inherited entrenchment, then the former predicate is clearly better entrenched than the latter. States definitions of a projectible hypothesis, a nonprojectible hypothesis, and an unprojectible hypothesis in the form of necessary and sufficient conditions based on the general rule. For example: a hypothesis is unprojectible if and only if "it is unsupported, violated, exhausted, or overridden." Notes that these definitions are provisional and define presumptive projectibility. Section 5: "Comparative Projectibility." Considers factors involved in the ultimate index of degree of projectibility for a hypothesis. Introduces the notion of a positive overhypothesis: "a hypothesis is a positive overhypothesis of a second, if the antecedent and consequent of the first are parent predicates of, respectively, the antecedent and consequent of the second." Describes a case in which "Every bagful in stack S is uniform in color" is a positive overhypothesis of "All the marbles in bag B are red." Points out that if an overhypothesis is not presumptively projectible, it will have "no reinforcing effect, for such a hypothesis can be used to tie totally irrelevant information to a given hypothesis." Points out further that a highly projectible overhypothesis with a few positive instances can influence projectibility a lot, while a negligibly projectible overhypothesis, even with many positive instances, will influence projectibility very little. Notes that the projectibility of an overhypothesis results from its initial degree of projectibility and the influence from its overhypotheses: e.g., "Every stack of marbles in Utah is homogeneous in color variegation" is an overhypothesis of "Every bagful in stack S is uniform in color," where bag B is a bag in Utah. Argues that "the process of appraising the projectibility of a hypothesis need not run up through an endless hierarchy of overhypotheses." Maintains that if a hypothesis has a very low initial index of projectibility, then it will also have a very low ultimate index of projectibility. Goes on to discuss "how closely the evidence for an overhypothesis is allied to the hypothesis in question, or in other words, upon how specific the overhypothesis is." Maintains that "where both projectibility and amount of support are equal, the effect of overhypotheses varies inversely with their generality." Outlines how the comparative effectiveness of a presumptively or appreciably projectible overhypothesis depends on specificity, degree of projectibility, and amount of support: e.g., if two overhypotheses are equal with respect to specificity and amount of support, then their effectiveness varies with their projectibility. Considers extending his treatment of comparative projectibility to presumptively nonprojectible hypotheses in order to resolve some of these conflicts between equally entrenched hypotheses: "although neither of the hypotheses overrides the other, one may *outweigh* the other." Considers cases in which we want more evidence because both the degrees of projectibility and the initial indices are equal. Points out that "the projectibility of a hypothesis may often be decreased rather than increased by correlative information." Defines the complementary to a parent predicate and introduces the notion of a negative overhypothesis: e.g., "Every bagful in S is mixed in color" is a negative overhypothesis of "All marbles in bag B are red." Notes that even when two competing nonprojectible hypotheses are both very well entrenched, one of the hypotheses may outweigh the other because "the adverse effects of negative overhypotheses upon them may differ greatly." Notes that if we have mingled evidence—some bagfuls in S being uniform in color, some mixed in color—then we will have a statistical overhypothesis whose effectiveness depends on its projectibility. Also notes his account needs to be extended to cover statistical hypotheses. Contemplates extending his treatment of comparative projectibility to supported, unviolated, and unexhausted hypotheses that are unprojectible because they are overridden. Section 6: "Survey and Speculations." Stresses the "function of our linguistic practices" in distinguishing valid and invalid predictions. Maintains that the distinction "is drawn upon the basis of how the world is and has been described and anticipated in words."

Suggests that if we wish to interpret a counterfactual adequately, then we will have to take into account whether it conflicts with other conditionals, and we will need principles to resolve such conflicts. Discusses how his account of projectibility may provide a way to distinguish between genuine and artificial kinds in terms of entrenched classes. Expects this to answer questions about simplicity and randomness.

Goodman, Nelson. *Of Mind and Other Matters*. Cambridge, Mass.: Harvard University Press, 1984. Updates his views on a wide range of topics: e.g., cognition, irrealism, reference, and art. Mentions "grue" in two places. See chapter II, section 1, the "Truthmaking" subsection. Claims inductive validity is a matter of "certain formal relationships among the sentences in question *plus* what I shall call right categorization." Maintains that "the wrong categories will make an induction invalid no matter how true the conclusion." Introduces the grue example and claims "grue" refers to a "nonrelevant kind" in this context. Points out that "rightness of categorization, in my view, derives from rather than underlies entrenchment." Says there is a debate over why some categories become entrenched and not others, but "entrenchment, however achieved, provides the required distinction." See chapter IV, section 5. Discusses the characteristics of aesthetic predicates. Maintains one characteristic is that "they tend to cut across our entrenched scientific and everyday categories." Views this as presenting a problem "entirely parallel to that of allowing for novel categories and predicates in science while banning troublemakers like 'grue'." Considers parent predicates, inherited entrenchment, and overhypotheses relevant to the aesthetic problem.

Goodman, Nelson and Elgin, Catherine Z. *Reconceptions in Philosophy and Other Arts and Sciences*. Indianapolis: Hackett Publishing Company, 1988. Comment on grue, induction, projectibility, entrenchment, and categories at various points. See chapter 1, section 4, about adequacy requirements for symbol systems. Consider two systems of color classification, the green-blue and the grue-bleen. Claim the right system is relative to your purpose. Note that the green-blue system is right for making inductive inferences. Go on to discuss why (section 5: "Rightness of Categories"). Consider "grue" a novel predicate that "cuts across our familiar categories and would require awkward revision of our practical and scientific vocabulary and our linguistic and cognitive practice." Point out that novel predicates can be introduced into a system (e.g., the term "quark") or replace predicates in a system (e.g., relativistic categories replacing classical physics categories). Maintain that "predicates whose projection leads regularly to false conclusions are unprojectible, regardless of their history." Emphasize that entrenchment is neither necessary (e.g., in fiction) nor sufficient (e.g., in biology) for rightness of categorization. Compare realistic representations with projectible predicates, noting how both are habitual, may change over time, and may require learning to use new categories that disagree with common practice. Also see chapter 10, section 3. Introduce adoption to replace acceptance. Maintain that "as an adoption continues in effect, what is adopted earns an increasing claim to rightness." Cite entrenchment as an example of how a category may come to outrank others because of "continued or repeated use."

Goodman, Nelson and Ullian, Joseph. "The Short of It." *Journal of Philosophy* 75 (1978): 263–264. A brief, additional reply to Zabludowski's arguments (1974, 1977 especially). Make two points. First, maintain it is false that "for every otherwise qualified hypothesis *H* there is always another equally well-qualified hypothesis *K* such that our assumptions do not exclude conflict with *H*." Point out that judging a hypothesis to be projectible is betting "that there is no competitor it does not override," and so "whenever we project a hypothesis, we resolve any indecision concerning its conflict with an able competitor." Second, note that if three or more hypotheses conflict, then "they assign to something several predicates such that only one actually applies."

Gottlieb, Dale. "Rationality and the Theory of Projection." *Nous* 9 (1975): 319–328. Views Goodman's theory of projection "as an attempt to partially explicate confirmation." Points out that confirmation theory deals with rationally justifying beliefs. Interprets Goodman as saying that when positive instances confirm a hypothesis, they "help make the hypothesis worthy of rational belief." Sees the connection between projectibility and rational support as: positive instances rationally support a hypothesis if and only if the hypothesis is projectible. Argues that projectibility is not a necessary or sufficient condition for rational support by positive instances. Claims people rationally believed "All heavenly bodies revolve daily around the sun" because of its positive instances, and yet this hypothesis was never projectible because its positive instances are all false. Claims a hypothesis may be projectible because its predicate earns entrenchment from hypotheses projected in the past but currently known to be false, and in this case "the regular use of a predicate for projection in the past has no rational weight for its use in the future." Claims a hypothesis may be projectible because its predicate *A* earns entrenchment from a coextensive predicate *B* whose coextension we do not even know about, and in this case "the unsuspected co-extensiveness of *A* and *B* can have no bearing on the rationality of projecting hypotheses containing them." Claims a hypothesis may be unprojectible because another hypothesis overrides it, even one that has not been formulated, and yet in this case the overridden hypothesis "does not lose the rational support of its positive instances." Maintains these four consequences do not obtain if projectibility is made relative to a larger body of information: "it depends upon the set of data of which the positive instances are taken to be a part, and it depends upon the set of alternative hypotheses." Goes on to argue that the central thesis of the projectibility theory is false: viz., if a hypothesis is not projectible, then its positive instances do not support it. Considers it obvious that there is a point (a credibility or support point) to getting more positive instances for either of two equally well entrenched, conflicting hypotheses that override all of the other conflicting hypotheses (and so both are nonprojectible) as long as they stay unviolated. Describes this situation in the abstract and then with an example about discovering what went wrong in an attempt to introduce two mutations into a population of sterile fruit flies. Formulates a new yet weaker thesis: if one hypothesis overrides another, then it gains more rational support from its positive instances than the overridden hypothesis gains from its positive instances. Notes how this thesis explains why the grue hypothesis should not be projected. Also how it allows for degrees of projectibility between compatible and competing hypotheses. Suggests taking relative entrenchment as one factor (among many) determining relative strength of support from data. See the reply by Ullian (1975).

Graves, John C. "Uniformity and Induction." *British Journal for the Philosophy of Science* 25 (1974): 301–318. Defends Mill's principle of the uniformity of nature as a justification of induction by arguing that the principle is not based on a fallacy, hopelessly vague, unnecessary, or incapable of doing what it is supposed to. Claims Mill took an ontological and pragmatic approach to justifying induction, considered what the world must be like for induction to work most of the time, and concluded that it must have a high degree of uniformity. Tries to show it makes sense to speak of situations being more or less uniform, but says "at this point Nelson Goodman's criticism may raise its ugly head." Considers whether the notion of uniformity is vacuous because "no matter how complex and apparently non-uniform the actual world seemed to be, one could always define some artificial set of grue-like predicates such that the world would have an arbitrarily high degree of uniformity with respect to these predicates." Claims that Mill would solve Goodman's paradox "through his belief in the existence of natural kinds." Maintains that "we simply do not perceive something as a uniformity unless it appears simple to our human understanding" and so Mill's principle can be strengthened to say that nature is uniform "with respect to relatively simple human concepts." Claims that even if 'grue' and 'green' are logically symmetrical, the former term "involves changing our perceptual criteria in a way that 'green' does not."

Grossman, Reinhardt. *Ontological Reduction*. Bloomington, Ind.: Indiana University Press, 1973. See chapter 15, pages 116–122. Maintains that the principle of property abstraction is false, and so "not every well-formed propositional form represents a property." Argues (pp. 116–122) that there are no complex properties ("properties represented by complex propositional forms") such as the property of being green and round. Claims that saying *A* has the property of being both green and round is saying nothing more than *A* is green and *A* is round. Notes that we can abbreviate "*A* is green and *A* is round" with "*A* is ground," but the abbreviation "ground" does not name a complex property: if it did, it could not be an abbreviation for "*A* is green and *A* is round" because it would represent a different fact, one containing the property *ground*. Says, in a footnote (p. 200) to this discussion of "ground," that "what holds for 'ground', holds ipso facto for 'grue'." Contends that "there simply is no such property as *grue*, because there is no such property as the property of being green if examined before time *t*, and otherwise being blue." Goes on to conclude that "since there is no such property, Goodman's new riddle of induction disappears." Presents the same view in an earlier article: "Russell's Paradox and Complex Properties," *Nous* 6 (1972). This view is discussed in Armstrong (1978).

Grunstra, Bernard R. "The Plausibility of the Entrenchment Concept." In *Studies in the Philosophy of Science*, American Philosophical Quarterly Monograph Series, No. 3, edited by Nicholas Rescher, pp. 100–127. Oxford: Basil Blackwell, 1969. Compares Goodman's projection problem (stated in terms of abnormal predicates) with the problem of alternative hypotheses, especially the curve-fitting version; doubts the latter will clarify the role of entrenchment without involving abnormal predicates. Comments upon four misunderstood features of Goodman's "grue" example: reference to time *t*, applying the predicate, the word "examined," and establishing the evidence class of emeralds. Considers the "grue" example as showing how projectibility choices cannot be explained in terms of "descriptive adequacy to the data available at *t*." Points out that the entrenchment solution involves a wide conception of data, is empirically constrained, and may be compatible with other solutions. Critically examines nine alternative explanations of projectibility judgments; claims the entrenchment solution is better. Presents two arguments in support of entrenchment: one about "the way things are" being partly determined by the words we use, the other about principles based on entrenchment being special cases of "the methodological principle of insufficient reason."

Gutting, Gary. "Can Philosophical Beliefs Be Rationally Justified?" *American Philosophical Quarterly* 19 (1982): 315–330. Argues that "philosophers have not been able to establish their claims by argument." Examines examples from the work of Kripke, Plantinga, Goodman, and Rawls. Begins with Goodman's view of justifying inference rules by mutual adjustment until reaching equilibrium; views this as a best explanation approach or method for providing an "effective non-deductive justification of an adequate philosophical account of induction." Contends that the method is "not really adequate to its purpose" and we can see this in Goodman's attempt to solve the new riddle. Claims the inadequacy appears when Goodman rejects the view that projectible predicates are purely qualitative because the distinction here is a relative one. Maintains Goodman is assuming it is "just an arbitrary fact, with no basis in, say, a special epistemic status" that "green" is basic in English rather than "grue." Thinks Goodman is not using the best explanation approach here and instead rejecting the view because it goes against his prior nominalist and antifoundationalist commitments. Goes on to claim that "a successful piece of philosophizing 'makes intellectual room' for a view that has previously been rejected out of hand or perhaps not even thought of." Regards Goodman's work as making intellectual room for "a new way of thinking about inductive inferences" and as rationally establishing "the intellectual viability of an important philosophical picture."

Habermehl, Werner. "Eichner's Solution of the Goodman Paradox." *Kant-Studien* 66 (1975): 510–513. Article in German. A reply to Eichner (1975).

Habermehl, Werner. "Reply to Eichner and Frank." *Kant-Studien* 69 (1978): 213–214. Article in German. A reply to Eichner and Frank (1978).

Hacking, Ian. *Logic of Statistical Inference*. Cambridge: Cambridge University Press, 1965. Examines, in chapter IV, the notion of long-run frequencies in statistical inference, especially the long-run justification for guessing about particular cases. Discusses Goodman's riddle in an aside, pages 41–42. Introduces "blight" (black until the end of 1984, white thereafter) and "wack" (white until the end of 1984, black thereafter). Describes the new riddle in terms of drawing balls from an urn: "every shred of evidence which supports the claim that most balls in an urn are black . . . equally supports the claim that most are blight." Maintains that it is absurd to think the long-run rule is indifferent between guessing black and blight, or to think it recommends guessing black all the time and guessing blight all the time. Says that Goodman's new riddle has "precision of statement, generality of application, and difficulty of solution to a degree greater than any other philosophic problem broached in this century." Notes that one can restrict the long-run rule to projectible predicates, but prefers to "postpone the difficulty" and put the onus on the undefined phrase "shown by experiment," as in: "currently practicable experiments can show, and justly show, that black, as opposed to blight, is drawn more often in the long run." Admits that it is hard to state exactly why they show this, and adds "that is why Goodman's riddles are so pressing."

Hacking, Ian. *Why Does Language Matter to Philosophy?* Cambridge: Cambridge University Press, 1975. See chapter 6, "Noam Chomsky's Innatism." Discusses grue in connection with abstractionism, the blank slate theory of language learning, and "the fact that the environment underdetermines what is learned from it." Notes that "according to the abstractionist it is from examples of green that we abstract the idea of green," and that "I cannot today point to anything visible that exhibits the property of greenness and not that of grueness." Concludes that "the examples *underdetermine* the quality, greenness, that we are supposed to abstract from them." Later in the chapter (p. 69) remarks that Wittgenstein, in his *Remarks on the Foundations of Mathematics*, was "concurrently but independently of Goodman, drawing attention to the underdetermined character of mathematical concepts."

Hacking, Ian. "On Kripke's and Goodman's Uses of 'Grue'." *Philosophy* 68 (1993): 269–295. Discusses Kripke's (1982) analogy between Goodman's new riddle of induction and Wittgenstein's skepticism about meaning. Argues that "the analogy is inexact, and that Kripke's use of 'grue' is importantly different from Goodman's." Contrasts Kripke's version of philosophical skepticism with Goodman's version (or the version we can derive from Goodman's new riddle). Points out that Kripke defines "grue" without referring "to a subjective element, namely examination at a time," and such that if all emeralds are grue, "then emeralds would change colour at t." Notes that he will use Goodman's definition. Believes that Goodman's new riddle is an important general problem in epistemology and metaphysics, not "a merely technical difficulty" in connection with induction by simple enumeration and a foolish nonword. Points out that "we need not say anything about scepticism in drawing conclusions from Goodman's riddle," and "yet readers have always inferred some kind of scepticism." Argues that "there is some sound independent ground for treating Goodman's riddle as sceptical." Notes that Goodman's "pragmatic vision of justification as coherence" is an internal analysis of inductive reasoning. Claims it is wrong to view defining valid inductive inferences as describing ordinary inductive practices. Distinguishes between internal and external responses to a problem, and claims a skeptical solution "is about something external to the object of analysis." Maintains that "Goodman's notion of entrenchment is external to inductive inference" because "it refers to our past usage of some predicates." Regards Goodman's entrenchment view as going "outside the form and content of the queried type of inference," and so "a sceptical solution to a sceptical problem." Examines Kripke's question about "who is to say that in the past I did not mean grue by 'green', so that now I should call the sky, not the grass, 'green'." Believes this is an odd question because "what I meant in the past seldom matters to how I ought to use a word, or whether I should call something so and so." Comments on a similar question by Wittgenstein about knowing that the color you are now seeing is called "green." Notes that Goodman has never examined "the possibility that there should be grue-speakers": i.e., the possibility that some people "now use the word 'grue' (meaning grue), or are now using a more familiar word (such as 'green') to mean grue." Proceeds to argue that "gruespeak is incoherent." Says the main idea in his argument is Shoemaker's (1975) agreement after t principle: "our usage and their usage must be such that after t, both of us would agree that one of us had the wrong expectations about emeralds." Maintains we would not "attribute to anyone the weird belief that emeralds first examined after t will prove to be blue" because that would violate both the principle of charity and the principle of humanity, and so we should "conclude that people do not use a predicate that means grue." Discusses "an application of Goodman's riddle to field linguistics" and ultimately shows that we obtain a question that includes a subquestion on "who is to say that I should now call the grass, and not the sky, 'green'." First considers disunified science, where we project "grue" in field linguistics but not in mineralogy. Maintains this violates the principle of charity and the principle of humanity in our translations because "we would conclude not only that these people mean odd things by words but also that they have very different expectations from us." Next considers unified science, where we "project 'grue' in field linguistics if and only if we do so in mineralogy," and maintains "there is a certain coherence" because "after our initial, irrational, projection of 'grue', we are not also demanding that the foreigners be any more out of their minds than we are." Considers radical interpretation in connection with every conversation, and so I practice field linguistics on what my neighbors say. Notes that this involves the subquestion. Believes there is no problem because "in either coherent event—whether they mean grue by 'green' or green by 'green'—I should call the new emerald 'green'." Points out that the field linguistics questions are about other people ("outer-directed") while Kripke's question is about himself ("inner-directed"). Distinguishes between *I*-skepticism and *U*-skepticism: between worrying about yourself and being neutral about what other people mean, and "universalized worry" about what we all mean. Stresses that "Kripke's scepticism is different in kind from Hume's, or from the sceptical use of Goodman's new riddle of induction." Explains this by distinguishing (in terms of "what it would be like to experience them as living doubt") between existential and fearful skepticism. Claims that Kripke's skepticism is existential while Goodman's skepticism (or the skepticism associated with Goodman's new riddle) is fearful. Rejects the notion that Kripke's skepticism proves "there is no fact of the matter about what I may have meant by my words." Notes how both Kripke and Goodman present skeptical solutions based on "something social and communitarian." Also notes how "Goodman's sceptical solution is a far less romantic invocation of the social than Kripke's" because it is about how frequently people utter certain words. Believes that Goodman's new riddle "is directed at the actual, Kripke's at the possible" because Kripke's work is also concerned with mathematics and mathematical knowledge.

Hanen, Marsha. "Goodman, Wallace, and the Equivalence Condition." *Journal of Philosophy* 64 (1967): 271–280. A reply to Wallace (1966). Agrees with Wallace that if Goodman accepts a principle of indiscernibility of logical equivalents and a principle of indiscernibility of definitional equivalents, then his theory of projectibility "is in serious difficulty." Argues that Goodman does not accept these principles, that they are not plausible as stated, and that Wallace has failed to appreciate "the frame of reference within which Goodman is operating." Discusses only the logical equivalents principle; claims her points also apply to the definitional equivalents principle. Maintains that "Wallace's procedure is question-begging" because he assumes his principles are acceptable instead of arguing they are. Notes that the logical equivalents principle is a generalization of Hempel's equivalence condition for confirmation, and that Hempel's arguments "are not strong enough to support Wallace's principle." Believes the principle "sounds rather like an ad hoc stipulation meant to rule out the sorts of explications Goodman offers in chapter IV of *FFF*." Maintains Wallace is mistaken "in his tacitly supposing that Goodman cannot consistently accept Hempel's condition while rejecting his (Wallace's) stronger version of it." Put another way: Wallace is wrong about whether explications and predicates in Goodman's theory of induction "have the effect of rejecting accepted principles of quantificational logic." Considers whether Goodman's explication of "positive instance" violates any principle of quantificational logic. Points out that principles in deductive logic may not hold "in a straightforward way in inductive logic or when inductive and deductive inferences are combined." Maintains that it does not violate quantification theory if "some other principle that holds for deductive logic fails to hold for inductive inferences," and so "no violence is done to quantificational logic if we maintain that logically equivalent sentences cannot always replace one another in the context of inductive inferences or when inductive and deductive inferences are combined." Stresses that Goodman drops Hempel's equivalence condition (a condition weaker than Wallace's condition) when he defines the new predicates in his theory of projection, and these new predicates "are introduced precisely because even Hempel's definition of 'positive instance', without control over the predicates or hypotheses admitted, leaves confirmation theory in the sad plight of admitting that any statement confirms any other." Also stresses that for Goodman "a hypothesis does not have many formulations." That is: "a hypothesis is a statement—a particular set of utterances or inscriptions, and its equivalents are just that—equivalents —but different statements." Goes on to consider "what sort of thing a hypothesis is."

Notes that Hempel would say "All ravens are black" is the same hypothesis as "All nonblack things are nonravens," while Goodman would not, "nor would he be likely to say that they express the same content." Maintains that Goodman is not rejecting the usual quantificational logic, "but rather a pair of equivalence conditions which tacitly presuppose a sort of propositional view of things." Claims this view of hypotheses and statements (as "not something extralinguistic") is consistent with Goodman's "other writings on related subjects" such as the theory of individuals and nominalism. Notes that Scheffler (1963) also distinguishes between Hempel's abstract, invariant content view of hypotheses and Goodman's particular statement view of them. Also notes that Scheffler adopts Goodman's view and drops Hempel's equivalence condition when he discusses his notion of selective confirmation because selective confirmation involves the contrary of a hypothesis and the notion of the contrary of a hypothesis does not make any sense with Hempel's equivalence condition and his view of hypotheses. Concludes by "noting that Goodman does manage to retain for his theory much of the intuitive acceptability that adherence to an equivalence condition is meant to ensure" by making entrenchment a matter of the extension of a predicate and all predicates coextensive with it, and by overruling the elimination of a hypothesis when the hypothesis follows from another hypothesis that escapes elimination entirely.

Harris, James F. and Hoover, Kevin D. "Abduction and the New Riddle of Induction." *The Monist* 63 (1980): 329–341. View the new riddle as a problem of selecting hypotheses to test and so as a problem of abduction, theory construction, and the logic of discovery. Maintain that Goodman confuses induction with abduction because he also confuses the psychology of belief with its logic. Attempt to show that "Peirce's theory of inference anticipates Goodman's 'new riddle,' analyzes it more adequately, and resolves it more completely." Compare Goodman's theory of projectibility with Peirce's theory of abduction. Also see Deledalle (1983), Rescher (1976), and Rescher (1978) for discussions and applications of Peirce's work.

Harris, James F. *Against Relativism: A Philosophical Defense of Method*. La Salle, Ill.: Open Court Publishing Company, 1992. See chapter 3, "Goodman on Ways of Making Worlds." Discusses Hume and Goodman on induction, the grue paradox, and Goodman's theory of projectibility. Emphasizes "the fact that the theory of entrenchment ultimately resolves into matters of language." Concludes that, on Goodman's view, "both the factual claims we make about the world and the predictions we make based upon those factual claims are simply the result of linguistic practice." Views this as "the source of the relativism arising from Goodman's new riddle of induction." Believes that, on Goodman's view, "facts become language-relative and language-dependent." Considers this "reducing scientific observation and prediction to linguistic usage." Believes this makes scientific explanations and predictions depend on linguistic practices, and so "any realistic or absolute basis for science is undermined, and science does indeed become relative." Maintains that if induction depends on linguistic practices, then scientific method is also relative. Maintains that Goodman's new riddle is not a problem about induction, and so these relativistic consequences do not obtain. Introduces Peirce's distinction between abduction (forming a hypothesis) and induction (confirming a hypothesis), and his Rule of Predesignation, according to which an abduction must come before each induction. Thinks it is clear that Goodman's problem is about selecting a hypothesis, the grue or green one, and not about confirming a hypothesis. Views the problem as preinductive and metascientific. Goes on to construe Goodman's theory of projectibility as a theory of abduction and asks if it provides reasons for selecting a hypothesis. Argues that it does not because of "a strong psychological component" that is unreliable (e.g., the notion of credibility). Considers whether it would help to develop "a mechanical procedure for the selection of hypotheses based upon comparative quantitative indices for different predicates." Argues that it would not help because there are many factors involved in deciding which hypothesis to test besides the entrenchment of predicates. Believes that, using entrenchment alone, all the scientists in a particular field might end up testing a hypothesis with well-entrenched predicates even though it will take longer and cost more than testing another hypothesis with less-entrenched predicates; or a scientist might end up projecting a hypothesis that no one will ever be able to test. Advocates Peirce's pragmatic view. Also see Harris and Hoover (1980).

Hempel, Carl G. "A Purely Syntactical Definition of Confirmation." *Journal of Symbolic Logic* 8 (1943): 122–143. Classic attempt to define a "non-quantitative relation of confirmation" in "purely logical terms." Specifies the model language L and restates the problem in terms of this formal language: viz., "to lay down purely formal conditions under which a molecule M confirms a sentence S." States three groups of logical conditions of adequacy, and one material condition of adequacy, for a solution. Develops and expands upon the basic idea of an "inclusion criterion"; makes use of the recursively defined concept of the C-development of a sentence, where C is a finite class of individual constants. Presents successive approximations of the final definition, each time defining confirmation in terms of "a narrower relation of direct confirmation." Claims the final version (p. 142) satisfies the logical conditions of adequacy and passes all the tests of material adequacy discussed in connection with definitions found to be inadequate. Notes that the final definition is "analogous in various ways to the relation of consequence in its syntactical interpretation" and indeed seems to be "a generalization of the converse of the syntactical consequence relation." For a less detailed and less technical exposition of the analysis, see Hempel (1945).

Hempel, Carl G. "Studies in the Logic of Confirmation." *Mind* 54 (1945): 1–26 and 97–121. Aims to provide the elements of a general theory of confirmation. Focuses on the nonquantitative concept of confirmation. Notes that a precise definition of confirmation is a necessary condition for adequate solutions to problems about relevant evidence, instances of a hypothesis, objective criteria for a body of evidence corroborating a hypothesis, standards of rational belief, and empiricist criteria of meaning. Examines Nicod's (1930) criterion of confirmation and presents two objections to it. States the equivalence condition as a requirement for any adequate definition of confirmation. Presents the well-known paradoxes of confirmation as implications of the equivalence condition and a sufficient condition version of Nicod's criterion for universal conditional hypotheses with one variable. Contends that these are not real, logical paradoxes but "a psychological illusion." Construes confirmation as a logical relation between sentences instead of as a semantical relation between sentences and extra-linguistic objects, and as analogous to the relation of logical consequence viewed in purely syntactical terms. Examines the prediction criterion of confirmation and claims it is too narrow because only some scientific hypotheses can be construed "as asserting regular connections between observable features of the subject matter." States three logical requirements (as well as their implication and corollaries) for an adequate definition of confirmation: viz., the entailment condition, consequence condition, and consistency condition. Presents his satisfaction criterion of confirmation (for scientific languages with a simple logical structure) by introducing the concept of developing a hypothesis for a finite class of individuals (see Hempel 1943 for technical details); goes on to define the special relation of direct confirmation and then the general relation.

Calls this the satisfaction criterion because "its basic idea consists in construing a hypothesis as confirmed by a given observation report if the hypothesis is satisfied in the finite class of those individuals which are mentioned in the report." Also defines disconfirmation and neutrality. Claims that his definition meets the logical requirements and is also materially adequate. Ends by discussing the relative and absolute concepts of verification and falsification.

Hempel, Carl G. "Inductive Inconsistencies." *Synthese* 12 (1960): 439–469. Attempts to show that two familiar types of inductive inference rules are defective because they "lead into logical inconsistencies." Considers inconsistencies generated by inference rules typically used with statistical syllogisms and by elementary induction rules typically used with inductions by simple enumeration. Generates the latter inconsistencies by showing that a collection of measurements of physically associated values of two magnitudes x and y will produce infinitely many incompatible presumptive laws in which y is a certain mathematical function of x. Views this as similar to Goodman's way of generating inconsistencies in the new riddle of induction: viz., both "lead from a consistent body of total evidence to an inconsistent set of conclusions." Considers it different from Goodman's way because the grue hypothesis is not lawlike while there are many equally lawlike conflicting generalizations in the functional relationship approach, and so "none of these incompatible generalizations would be ruled out by restricting permissible inductive conclusions to lawlike statements." Discusses the Carnapian objection that these inconsistencies can be attributed to violating the requirement of total evidence because, with respect to Goodman's grue example, we are not including the information about when the emeralds were examined. Points out that a Carnapian inductive logic might avoid the new riddle because it does not "lend itself to the categorical establishment of the conclusion even if the premises are known to be, or are accepted as, true statements." Describes another way in which these problems might appear in a Carnapian inductive logic. Also see Hempel (1966) and Hempel (1981).

Hempel, Carl G. *Aspects of Scientific Explanation and Other Essays in the Philosophy of Science.* New York: The Free Press, 1965. Reprints twelve essays by a major figure in philosophy of science. Main topics are: confirmation, cognitive significance, scientific concepts, scientific theories, and scientific explanation. From the new riddle point of view, reprints "Studies in the Logic of Confirmation" (1945) and "Inductive Inconsistencies" (1960). Includes a 1964 postscript on confirmation. See the index of names for references to Goodman's views on lawlike versus accidental sentences.

Hempel, Carl G. "Recent Problems of Induction." In *Mind and Cosmos,* Volume 3, edited by Robert G. Colodny, pp. 112–134. Pittsburgh: University of Pittsburgh Press, 1966. Maintains that the classical problem of induction cannot be stated clearly until we address some new problems of induction that concern the description of, and criteria for, sound inductive reasoning in science. The new problems are the paradoxes of qualitative confirmation, Goodman's riddle, and the problem of inductive ambiguity. Emphasizes how, on Goodman's view of projectibility, basic rules of inductive inference cannot be stated in purely syntactical terms: "entrenchment is neither a syntactical nor even a semantic property of terms, but a pragmatic one." Points out that Nicod's criterion fails for relational terms as well as the Goodmanian variety of property terms. Also see Hempel (1960).

Hempel, Carl G. "On a Claim by Skyrms Concerning Lawlikeness and Confirmation." *Philosophy of Science* 35 (1968): 274–278. A reply to Skyrms (1966). Examines Skyrms's claim that some generalizations "receive no confirmatory support from their positive instances even though all the predicates they contain are well entrenched in Goodman's sense." Believes that Skyrms's argument "presupposes an unwarranted assumption which raises a problem of general importance for confirmation theory." Considers Skyrms's generalization "All blades of grass or cloths on billiard tables are green" and Skyrms's question "Does the observation of a green blade of grass lend any support to the assertion that all cloths on billiard tables are green?" Considers premise two of Skyrms's argument: viz., if the evidence statement "b is a blade of grass and b is green" supports the blade of grass/billiard table generalization, then it also has to support the generalization "All cloths on billiard tables are green." Notes that this premise assumes the consequence condition, and that Carnap has shown this condition is violated by any concept of confirmation (such as Skyrms's concept) according to which "if E confirms H, then the probability of H on E is greater than the probability of H on tautological evidence." Calls this "Carnap's condition." Claims that "in much the same way as in Skyrms's argument, the validity of the consequence condition for the concept of confirmatory support is presupposed also in Goodman's argument that the hypothesis 'All emeralds are grue' is not 'genuinely confirmed' by its positive instances established before the critical time t." Believes the assumption is plausible in Goodman's argument. Adds that "the same assumption underlies, of course, the many arguments by other writers that are patterned on Goodman's model." States the basic idea as: "whatever gives support or credibility to a given hypothesis surely does so also to any part of its content, to anything that the hypothesis asserts implicitly, i.e., by way of its logical consequences." Notes how Carnap regards confirmation as relative to the total evidence available in a situation, and emphasizes that he does not intend to relativize his concept as Carnap does. Points out Skyrms will have to restrict the consequence condition if he also adopts Carnap's condition for the special case of tautological prior evidence or the general case of total prior evidence available in the situation.

Hempel, Carl G. "Turns in the Evolution of the Problem of Induction." *Synthese* 46 (1981): 389–404. Concerned with characterizing the method of inductive acceptance "in terms of rules that specify under what conditions a given hypothesis may be inductively inferred from, or inductively accepted on the basis of, a given body of evidence." First considers a rule that licenses arguing from all examined instances of A are B to the conclusion that all A are B. Shows it is defective because it obliges us "to accept logically incompatible hypotheses on one and the same body of evidence." Makes use of a curve-fitting problem: i.e., given a plot of data points on two variables, we can draw different curves through the points, each curve representing one variable as a different function of the other, and each curve standing for a generalization incompatible with the generalizations from the other curves. Notes that Goodman's new riddle also illustrates this point. Goes on to discuss probabilistic construals of inductive reasoning, rules for determining probabilities and rules of acceptance, values attached to accepting a hypothesis or rejecting it, epistemic values and accepting hypotheses for pure or basic research, pragmatist construals of theory choice (Kuhn, Laudan), and justifying rules of acceptance. See Hempel (1960) and (1966) for more on the new riddle.

Henderson, G.P. *"Fact, Fiction and Forecast."* *Philosophical Quarterly* 6 (1956): 266–272. A review of the first edition of Goodman's book. Offers criticisms of specific points about counterfactuals, dispositions, and possibilities; emphasizes that Goodman construes possibilities and dispositions in terms of projections.

Hendry, Herbert E. and Roper, James E. "Anything Confirms Anything?" *Synthese* 45 (1980): 217–232. Present a summary of Hempel's (1943, 1945) theory of qualitative confirmation. Do not require that the E-development of a hypothesis is logically true only if the hypothesis is logically true, but do restrict the *E*-development of a hypothesis to the essentially occurring constants of an evidence sentence. Also simplify the definition of "*E* confirms *H*" by dropping the first disjunct of "either implied by *E* or directly confirmed by *E*." Note that Goodman's grue-green examples show Hempel's satisfaction criterion does not meet the material condition of adequacy. Introduce "the supremum of *E*" as "a strongest sentence confirmed by an evidence sentence *E*," where this means *E* confirms the supremum and the supremum implies every sentence confirmed by *E*. Notes that if *E* is logically true or logically false, then *E* is its own supremum. Add that they will only be concerned with formal languages with finitely many primitive predicates. Define a predicate *O* for quasi-identity that is formally indistinguishable from identity in the sense of satisfying the standard axioms for identity, but whose definition does not refer to individual constants or assume finitely many of them. Point out that *E* confirms "everything is quasi-identical with one of the objects mentioned (essentially) in the evidence sentence *E*" and that the conjunction of *E* and this claim "is a strongest sentence confirmed by *E*." Consider (in section IV) whether the grue-green examples show that Hempel's satisfaction criterion allows anything to confirm anything. Claim these examples do not generalize in this way because "the evidence sentence *Pa*, for example, does not confirm −*Pa*." Point out Goodman does have a "knockdown argument" about theories of confirmation entailing that every statement confirms every other statement when they satisfy the consequence and converse conditions. Consider interpreting the grue-green example as an implicit argument about there being a sense in which everything confirms everything because the grue and green hypotheses are, in a sense, incompatible and "incompatible hypotheses, taken together, entail every statement." Maintain the most this argument shows is "that there is a sense in which *something* confirms everything." Contend that Goodman's "anything confirms anything" remark is sometimes "repeated as gospel, sometimes it crops up as a source of confusion, sometimes it is repeated with guarded reservation, but seldom is it referred to with what we take to be appropriate bewilderment." Claim that Marsha Hanen and Richard Rudner have accepted the claim, while C.A. Hooker (1968) has been misled by it. Also cite Lambert and Brittan (1970) and Grunstra (1969) as more or less accepting the claim. Proceed to show that "there is indeed a perfectly clear sense in which" Goodman's claim "is warranted." Introduce "*E* indirectly confirms *H*" to mean *H* is a consequence of sentences "each of which is either confirmed by *E* or accepted as a background assumption." Claim that the conjunction "individual 1 is a green emerald examined before *t* and . . . individual *n* is a green emerald examined before *t*" indirectly confirms everything, where *n* emeralds have been examined to this point in time, because the conjunction directly confirms "All emeralds are green" and "All emeralds are either examined before *t* and green or not examined before *t* and blue," these two hypotheses along with the background assumptions "Anything blue is not green" and "Some emerald is not examined before *t*" form an unsatisfiable set, and with every hypothesis a consequence of this set, "every hypothesis is indirectly confirmed by the evidence." Generalize the grue-green example in terms of a condition *C* and its complement, with one hypothesis being "Everything satisfies *C*" and the other being a statement about each object satisfying condition *C* and everything indiscernible from these objects satisfying the complement of *C*. Believe "whether this formulation is good enough depends on whether *O* is a genuine identity predicate for the language in question." Go on to explain how the evidence sentence here—the conjunction showing each object satisfies condition *C*—confirms both hypotheses, and yet the "hypotheses are incompatible with an assumption that must be made if there is to be any point to further scientific inquiry": viz., that there are unexamined cases. Point out that the evidence sentence confirms the negation of this background assumption:

i.e., it "confirms a hypothesis that can be true only if there is no point to further scientific inquiry." Emphasize that this does not completely vindicate Goodman's claim because some evidence sentences have a different form than the condition C evidence sentence. Point out that "if our background assumptions are consistent, the only hypotheses confirmed by a logically true evidence sentence are those that are consequences of these background assumptions." Conclude by proving (section V) the theorem that the supremum of E is the conjunction of E and the claim "everything is quasi-identical with one of the objects mentioned (essentially) in the evidence sentence E," where E is a logically indeterminate sentence. Note that a corollary of the theorem "provides an alternative (but equivalent) definition of confirmation."

Hertzberg, Lars. "Inductive Soundness, Entrenchment, and Luck." *Ajatus* 33 (1971): 40–63. Attempts to explain why some collections of inductive evidence seem better than others. Concentrates on an unacceptable induction by enumeration: a person A has had accidents on n consecutive Fridays of 1969, so probably the person will have one on the $n + 1$ Friday. Discusses and rejects a variety of formal or syntactic explanations of why the bad luck induction is not acceptable. Goes on to consider a nonformal explanation in terms of Goodman's notion of entrenchment: viz., that the expressions "a Friday of 1969 or later" and "an accident happening to A" are poorly entrenched. Claims this explanation is inadequate because these expressions inherit entrenchment from their parent classes, and we can't prove how well entrenched they are. Construes entrenchment as varying with context: "the question whether the circumstance that an event took place on a Friday is an entrenched circumstance, must be differently answered, depending on whether the context is that of natural science, or of human affairs." Presents two necessary conditions for inductive soundness; maintains that one of them—about types of events being causally homogeneous—explains why the bad luck induction is unacceptable.

Hesse, Mary. "Ramifications of 'Grue'." *British Journal for the Philosophy of Science* 20 (1969): 13–25. States two principles "essential to any satisfactory solution to Goodman's puzzle." Principle (A): the problem must be stated in terms that "yield predictions which are both genuinely different, and different in respects which the 'green' and 'grue' speakers (who will be called 'Green' and 'Grue' respectively) can explain to each other and agree to be different." Principle (B): "the problem should be shown to be soluble in its *strongest* form, and that since the solution is to be sought by finding asymmetries in the predictions of Green and Grue, it should not be set up in such a way as to introduce needless asymmetries into the definition or interpretation of the problematic predicates." Adopts a definition of "grue" from Blackburn (1969): an object is grue at a time t, if and only if, if t is earlier than the crucial grue time T, the object is green and if t is later than T, the object is blue. Notes that in this definition "colour predicates are applied to things *at a given time*, and no assumption is built into the definition about persistence of the colour of a given object." Assumes that "both Green and Grue commit themselves in their respective predictions to 'Emeralds remain the same colour after T'." Maintains that each will expect a change in the other's reports of color experiences, and conclude that the other has misremembered what certain colors look like, misremembered the meaning of certain color terms, or changed physiologically at T so that certain objects look different in color: e.g., if Green's prediction is correct for after T, then Green will not experience a change in color, but Grue will report one because Grue has misremembered what "grue" means. Emphasizes that "the asymmetry must be found, if at all, in predictions made *before T*, although they are predictions about what is expected to happen after T." Presents a dialogue between

Green and Grue about whether their predictions really differ. Has Green maintain there must be a difference with respect to objective tests of color in which, for example, you measure the wavelength of reflected light, and in this case his prediction of no wavelength change is simpler than Grue's prediction of wavelength change. Has Grue reply that there is no asymmetry here because Green is predicting certain objective properties will change at T while Grue is not, such as the kwell-measure of an object, the number of electrons it has before T and the number of neutrons it has after T. Believes "this dialogue draws attention to two important features of the puzzle which are frequently overlooked." Claims the dialogue shows how the grue puzzle involves metric and order properties, not just qualitative ones, how it is about the objective colors of objects, not just how they look, and how the predicates to be projected "should be defined in accordance with principle (A)." Notes that accordingly principle (A) will introduce objective differences into the predictions of Green and Grue, and these differences will be "related in a network of physical laws with other objective differences," and so they will introduce asymmetries "unless wholesale modifications of Green's theory are assumed." Considers whether the grue puzzle assumes that some objective qualitative properties are not related in a network of physical laws with other objective differences. Replies that the grue puzzle cannot be stated in terms of unattached predicates (e.g., "psycho-kinetic transmitter") because we will not know how to satisfy principle (A) and what to say about rival hypotheses. Also claims the dialogue shows how symmetry cannot always be preserved "by *ad hoc* and artificial introduction of more grue-like predicates into Green's theory": i.e., when Grue predicts a change at T and Green does not, you cannot always introduce "a grue-like predicate which does not change value in Grue's prediction, but changes in Green's." Maintains that "in order at some point to satisfy principle (A), there must be an end to this process at which at least one determinate value of a predicate expressible in both languages cannot be so treated, namely that which Green and Grue agree they will agree upon when it is tested for after T." Argues that if Green expects an objective predicate will stay the same and Grue expects it will change, then Grue cannot preserve symmetry by constructing another objective predicate (from Green's predicates) such that "(i) its value remains constant for grue objects at T, (ii) Green and Grue can agree on its value before and after T, (iii) its place in Grue's and Green's systems is symmetrical with" the first objective predicate's "place in Green's and Grue's systems respectively." Believes she has shown that "our inductive expectations can be explicated by the absence of a grue-like alternative symmetrical theory," and that "Grue cannot provide this by trivial construction from Green's theory." Also believes that Goodman's puzzle shows something important about pairs of very different fundamental theories that conflict: viz., they are "confirmationally incommensurable." Changes the Green and Grue situation into a case of radical meaning-variance between the Green and Grue theories, with Grue using the same words as Green to describe examined evidence while "his predictions and his confirmation theory correspond to the grue theory." Maintains that "in so far as the puzzle about meaning variance is a puzzle about incommensurability of theories with respect to confirmation and testing, it is identical with the non-trivial form of Goodman's puzzle." Claims "that when Goodman's puzzle is genuine, it is insoluble." Adds, however, that "our inductions rarely involve such fundamentally conflicting theories, and when they do it is even rarer to find the theories perfectly symmetrical in all relevant respects." Claims that Goodman's entrenchment solution is "misleading" in a basic theory-conflict. Thinks that entrenchment "involves general assumptions about the historical sequence of theories which are not necessarily acceptable," and that "other considerations should certainly be given priority over entrenchment" in a conflict between a comprehensive Green and a comprehensive Grue theory. See the discussion by Hunt (1969) and also Hesse (1974).

Hesse, Mary. *The Structure of Scientific Inference.* Berkeley and Los Angeles: University of California Press, 1974. See chapter 3, "The Grue Paradox," pages 75–88. Virtually the same as Hesse (1969). Makes additional points in the last two paragraphs. Considers an objection: viz., that her solution "appeals to a system of *physics,* which cannot enter the intuition of nonscientific persons, and yet it is quite clear that these people would unhesitatingly opt for the green hypothesis." Maintains that she appeals to physics because physical tests are objective tests of color that do not depend on how objects look and because in physics "terms are interrelated in a network of laws and that alternative sets of tests are available for them." Goes on to maintain that this is "true in principle of *all* descriptive terms whether in science or ordinary language." Claims a layman projects green because "no alternative system of classification in which grue becomes a primitive has ever been suggested in his education." Believes that if a term (e.g., "green") is entrenched, this means it "is entrenched in a network of common expectations or low-level laws, and that there is currently no alternative network of such laws." Allows that "grue" could have been as entrenched as "green," and then we would have been uncertain about which inductive inferences to make with these terms. Claims we are uncertain about which inferences to make with the term "peace-loving." Considers whether we are uncertain because of the meaning of the term or because of facts about the world. Claims that facts "may be reflected in the case of some universals in terms of their 'meanings', that is, in terms of what dispositions to recognize the universal it has been found convenient to learn." Believes the grue example shows that "these dispositions may be present in different ways even in a language that refers to the same facts and apparently has common meanings as between speakers." Believes the grue paradox shows "the indeterminacy of truth and meaning values which infects the network model" of universals.

Hintikka, Jaakko. "Inductive Independence and the Paradoxes of Confirmation." In *Essays in Honor of Carl G. Hempel,* edited by N. Rescher et al., pp. 24–46. Dordrecht, Holland: D. Reidel, 1971. Presents a partial solution to Hempel's raven paradox. Introduces "a formal system of confirmation theory (inductive logic) in which the paradox does not arise." Presupposes familiarity with his paper "A Two-Dimensional Continuum of Inductive Methods" in *Aspects of Inductive Logic,* edited by Jaakko Hintikka and Patrick Suppes (Amsterdam: North-Holland Publishing Company, 1966), pages 175–197. Points out "the application of my methods to the problems which are usually formulated in terms of Goodman's queer predicates." Believes we must create an asymmetry among the primitive predicates in order to deal with the raven paradox. Suggests we "assume that the order of the primitive predicates somehow matters." Argues that "the usual paradox about the black ravens does not arise if we can assume that the two relevant predicates R (=raven) and B (=black) are taken in this order." Explains how, in his formal system, "our raven generalization is confirmed by ravens only" because of the ordering assumptions. Regards his solution "as a formalization of that proposed solution of the paradox according to which the gist of the situation lies in the fact that the generalization 'All ravens are black' speaks only of ravens and does not say anything of non-ravens." Emphasizes, however, that his ordering assumptions are empirical assumptions "concerning the factual situation" and that his solution "represents a step away from the purely logical treatment of induction and towards some suitable form of the Bayesian position." Also views his ordering assumptions "as assumptions concerning the inductive independence of different predicates of each other." Deals with Goodman's paradox "along the same lines as the raven paradox." Introduces his own gruelike example. Assumes a domain of individuals consisting of emerald-stages. Defines the predicate "grot" so that "an emerald-stage has the predicate grot if it either is green and occurs before 2000 A.D. or else is not green and occurs during or after 2000 A.D." Assumes that all of the observed members of the domain have the predicate "*x* is green and *x* occurs before 2000 A.D." and that there will be yet-to-be-observed emeralds during or after 2000 A.D. Notes that "all the talk of queer predicates is merely a way of dramatizing a certain problem which can be perfectly well posed and discussed without recourse to them." Believes Goodman's paradox is also "an almost direct consequence of the symmetry between the different *Q*-predicates," where the *Q*-predicates are formed from the primitive predicates. Solves Goodman's paradox by ordering the predicates "*x* is green and *x* occurs before 2000 A.D." such that "the generalization 'All emerald-stages are green' will become highly confirmed when our evidence grows while the generalization 'All emerald-stages are grot' will receive arbitrarily small degrees of confirmation when *n* grows." Discusses the fact that his solution is "based on an ordering which matches the relative degrees of entrenchment of the two predicates." Maintains that we should be able to say the same thing about the ravens paradox if it is similar in logical structure to Goodman's paradox, yet "black" seems better entrenched than "raven" and "raven" precedes "black" in the ordering. Concludes that "our ordering thus cannot be identified in general with an ordering that depends on relative degrees of entrenchment in Goodman's sense."

Hirsch, Eli. "Rules for a Good Language." *Journal of Philosophy* 85 (1988): 694–717. Considers division questions about "why the words of our language divide up reality one way rather than another." Views 'grue' as posing a division question about the justification for dividing reality in terms of green/blue as opposed to grue/bleen. Presents his own example: the Gricular language, where 'gricular' applies to things that are either green or circular. Prefers to discuss 'gricular' instead of 'grue' because it is "absurdly disjunctive without being positional." Examines five rules that might serve as "rational constraints on how our words should classify and individuate" and that should, minimally, exclude strange examples like 'grue' and the Gricular language: viz., a metaphysical rule about dividing reality at the joints, an epistemological rule about allowing correct inferences, a language-learning rule, a rule about allowing correct explanations, and a pragmatic rule about serving our practical needs. Introduces a subrule to the epistemological rule about formulating correct inferences: viz., "a general word should be projectible." Asks how it would make for an epistemological problem here if expressions, not words, were projectible in a language, or if some expressions were entrenched in a language and no words were. Considers projectibility again in connection with learning a language ostensively; argues against the claim that "only projectible words are ostensively learnable." Concludes that none of the five rules provide a serious rationale or justification.

Hirsch, Eli. *Dividing Reality*. New York: Oxford University Press, 1993. Deals with the division problem: i.e., "why it seems reasonable for us to have words that classify and individuate in ordinary ways rather than other ways." Maintains that the division problem is distinct from the problem of projectibility. Cites "the Grue language" (pp. 23–25) as a "famous example of classificatory strangeness." Explains why it may "divert attention away from the general division problem." Compares the Grue language, the Gricular (green or circular) language, and incompatibility languages. Connects the division problem (in chapter 2, "Projectibility and Strange Languages") with issues about projectibility, similarity, and ostensive definitions. See Hirsch (1988) for a similar discussion. Argues (by appealing to the evidential equivalence principle) that "the division problem must be kept distinct from the projectibility problem." Asks whether there is "any important connection between the division problem and the notion of projectibility." Introduces the Projectibility Principle as an explanation of why the strange languages are absurd: i.e., "a general word ought to be projectible." Claims that a projectible term "must not apply to two classes of objects having no special evidential relationship to each other." Assumes that English satisfies the Projectibility Principle. Wants to determine if "there is some *virtue* in having only projectible words." Criticizes the epistemological claim as a defense of the Projectibility Principle: viz., if people speak a language that violates the Projectibility Principle, then "they could not rationally make the projections in their language that are equivalent to the ones we make in ours." Criticizes an argument for the epistemological claim based on having "an ordinary sense-of-similarity." Introduces the similarity principle as another attempt to connect how people use words and a notion of similarity: "a general word ought to denote only things that form a similarity class." Asks "why should there be *any* kind of special connection between the use of words and the similarity relation?" Considers an argument for the epistemological claim based on a system of rules that "constitutes our rules of inductive logic" and in which the first rule is "words (without negative prefixes) are typically projectible." Rejects this because rules of logic cannot "depend on the contingencies of a language's lexicon." Argues that a transcendental argument will not support the epistemological claim. Considers a defense based on learning a language: i.e., if the words of a language are not projectible, then we cannot learn the language, where we must either learn a general word ostensively or define it in terms of words learned ostensively, and where we must regard a general word as projectible in order to learn it ostensively. Claims that we do not need ostensive learning for a nonpublic "language of thinking" or for "every imaginable public language." Also claims that this argument "presupposes a dubious model of ostensive learning" and that even if we assume this model is correct, we do not have to regard a general word as projectible in order to learn it. Believes that "grue" is different because, on the model of ostensive learning assumed, we would have to regard "grue" as projectible in order to project "Anything that is grue is called 'grue'." Notes, however, that this does not hold for a nonpublic Grue language of thinking or for every imaginable Grue language, and that it involves "a questionable model of ostensive learning." Goes on to argue that cases of individuative strangeness do not violate either the Projectibility Principle or the Similarity Principle. Attempts to clarify the notion of a projectible term in appendix 1, "Projectible Terms." Points out that while "grue" is not a projectible term, "many hypotheses that contain 'grue' as either the whole subject or the whole predicate are projectible." Wonders if this shows we can only view terms as projectible relativized to other terms, and so we should relativize the Projectibility Principle. Specifies that one sentence is stronger than another "if the first entails the second but not vice versa." Specifies that "*p* cannot raise the credibility of *q* except by raising the credibility of *r*" means "while the credibility of *q* given *p* is higher than the prior credibility of *q*, the credibility of *q* given both *p* and not-*r* is not higher than the credibility of *q* given only not-*r*." Specifies that terms "*F*" and "*G*" are evidentially disconnected if and only if "for any term '*H*', the truth of 'All *F* are *H*' cannot raise the credibility of 'All *G* are *H*' (nor can the truth of the latter raise the credibility of the former) except by raising the credibility of some sentence that is stronger than 'All things that are either *F* or *G* are *H*'." Then specifies that "a term '*F*' is *projectible* if and only if it is not equivalent to the disjunction of two terms that are evidentially disconnected." Points out that, on this definition, "intuitively disjunctive" terms (such as "grue") are not projectible, that many conjunctions of compatible projectible terms are projectible, that conjunctions of a projectible and a nonprojectible term "will often seem to be non-projectible," that "the complement of a projectible term will often be non-projectible," that "if the complement of some color word is projectible, then so is the complement of any other color word," and that "the complement of no color word is projectible." Does not believe there is a connection between projectible terms and projectible hypotheses because we can make assorted hypotheses projectible relative to normal evidence, not to mention hypothetical evidence. Believes, however, there is a connection between projectible terms and hypotheses projectible in the standard way. Says that "a hypothesis is projectible *in the standard way* if it can be projected on the basis of any (sufficiently large) set of positive instances, given the absence of negative instances." Argues that if a hypothesis is projectible in the standard way, then it must have a projectible subject term. Suggests that if the subject term and the predicate term are both projectible in a hypothesis, then the hypothesis is projectible in the standard way.

Hoche, Hans-Urlich. "Does Goodman's 'Grue' Serve Its Purpose?" *Ratio* 21 (1979): 162–173. Notes that "the predicate 'grue' must be defined in such a way that an object can be said to possess the property of being grue at any moment of time t_n." Asks how to translate "This emerald is grue at t_n" into our ordinary language. Considers "This emerald is green at t_n and was examined before t_0 or this emerald is blue at t_n and was not examined before t_0" as the most obvious translation. Substitutes "t_0" for time t in Goodman's definition of "grue." Asks whether t_n is before, after, or at the same time as t_0. Claims there are pragmatic reasons why t_n canot precede t_0: viz, the disjunct "This emerald is blue at t_n and was not examined before t_0" violates one of John Searle's speech act rules for asserting because we have not examined this emerald for color and so we do not have evidence about it being green. Also claims that it is a pragmatic contradiction (as in Moore's paradox) to say this emerald was blue yesterday but was not examined for color until today. Maintains that t_n must be later than or coincide with t_0, and so in principle there are counterexamples to the grue hypothesis: e.g., an emerald examined no earlier than t_0 for color and that turns out to be green at t_n. Concludes that "grue" cannot function as Goodman intends "in precisely those cases where its use does not appear, from the very outset, to be doubtful in the light of the pragmatics of our language." Discusses how his argument also applies to two other translations of "This emerald is grue at t_n," each involving the expression "t_{n+a}" where "a" denotes an arbitrarily chosen positive or negative period of time. Points out that his argument does not have to consider the time of utterance for "This emerald is grue at t_n." Nevertheless lists thirteen cases that take this time to be earlier than, later than, or coincidental with t_0. Maintains this list confirms his previous conclusion about "grue." Goes on to discuss three other gruelike predicates: Goodman's (1946) disjunctive predicate that involves numbered balls being red or not; Scheffler's (1963) definition of "grue" that enumerates all the available evidence cases; and Scheffler's (1963) definition of "grue" that involves a predicate for some nontemporal feature of just the evidence cases. Examines these predicates to show there is no justification (observational or inductive) for asserting their second disjuncts (e.g., ball 100 is not red) and so they have assertive force problems like the predicates referring to t_0. Believes all of these errors are based on using disjunctive propositions "in whose second components something is predicated of an object which it is pragmatically correct to predicate with 'assertive force' only within the framework of an observational statement but not within the framework of a prediction."

Holland, John H.; Holyoak, Keith J.; Nisbett, Richard E.; and Thagard, Paul R. *Induction: Processes of Inference, Learning, and Discovery*. Cambridge, Mass.: The MIT Press, 1986.

Develop a pragmatic approach emphasizing "the role of the system's goals and the context in which induction takes place." Regard the raven and grue paradoxes as showing "the fundamental inadequacy" of purely syntactic approaches. Maintain (in chapter 1) that inference rules should "take into account the kinds of things being reasoned about" and that grue is not "a kind of property, except in an arbitrary world irrelevant to the goals of everyday human inference." Provide a pragmatic resolution in chapter 8, "Generalization and Knowledge of Variability," where they examine instance-based generalization. Focus on "the relevance of variability and randomness" in evaluating generalizations, "the crucial role played by the selection of what statisticians call a reference class," and "the organization of concepts into default hierarchies." Maintain this approach has implications for the grue paradox: viz., that "the grue problem will never arise" in a "pragmatically reasonable inference task." Regard the concept of grue as being "of no significance to the goals of the learner" and so the concept "will never be generated and hence will not form part of the default hierarchy that is employed in making generalizations." Claim entrenchment, in their approach, depends on a concept's place in a default hierarchy and this allows variability calculations, which in turn allow us to see how much an instance confirms a hypothesis. See Thagard and Nisbett (1982).

Hooker, C. A. "Goodman, 'Grue,' and Hempel." *Philosophy of Science* 35 (1968): 232–247. Section I. Considers whether "grue" is a problem for Hempel's (1943, 1945) confirmation theory in the sense that "there exists some evidence statement, formulable within Hempel's system, and such that it confirms two incompatible hypotheses." Notes that while "M confirms H" and "It is not the case that M confirms H" are contradictory, the grue situation is different: viz., "M confirms H," "M confirms H'," and H and H' are incompatible, which does not give us a contradiction. Maintains that if we could change the grue situation to something like "M confirms H" and "M confirms not H," then (using Hempel's General Consistency condition) we might be able to derive "a contradiction between what Hempel's meta-theory asserts his system is like and what the system is in fact like." Emphasizes that this would only show there is an error in Hempel's metatheory and that his definition of confirmation is inadequate because it fails to satisfy one of his own conditions of adequacy. Section II. Notes that Hempel's system is "restricted to a language, L, which is the first order predicate calculus without identity." Introduces the relevant predicates and hypotheses for the grue situation, and lists ten hypotheses that are consequences of the hypothesis "All emeralds are grue." Describes some of the main features of Hempel's system: direct confirmation, confirmation, molecular sentences, the development of a sentence, and disconfirmation. States three features as theorems: the general consequence condition about a molecule M confirming every consequence of a class K, and two theorems about a molecule confirming a hypothesis whose development is in disjunctive form. Section III. Defines "grue" by letting "x is grue" be materially equivalent to "x is examined before t and x is green, or x is not examined before t and x is not green." Notes that "any stronger form of the equivalence would not be expressible in L." Considers whether it would be more accurate to define "grue" in terms of "x is green" and "there exists a y such that y examines x before time t." Points out that "only molecules, *which contain no quantifiers,* are admissible as evidence statements in Hempel's system." Believes the phrase "x has not been examined before time t" is ambiguous between "it is not the case that x has been examined prior to time t" and "x has been examined after time t." Chooses the first meaning for his discussion. Section IV. Attempts to introduce the appropriate evidence statements. Claims they will be consistent conjunctions of the predicates "is an emerald," "is green," and "is examined before *t*," as well as the consistent conjunctions of their negations—with the exception of "is an emerald" because we are not concerned with negative instances of emeralds. Gives ten examples of the relevant types of evidence statements (with no more than two individuals) and the confirmation relations between these statements and six relevant hypotheses: e.g., "*a* is an emerald, not examined before *t*, and not green" confirms "All emeralds are grue" and disconfirms "All emeralds are either examined before *t* and are not green, or not examined before *t* and are green." States that "what is of substance in this paper can be made on the basis of a discussion" of one particular evidence statement: "*a* is an emerald, is examined before *t*, and is green." Notes that this evidence statement confirms the ten consequences of "All emeralds are green" (listed in section II) and that if "grue" creates any logical problems for Hempel's system, "then it must be possible to show that the same evidence confirms conflicting hypotheses." Section V. Points out that "*a* is a green emerald examined before *t*" confirms "All emeralds are green" but not the contrary hypothesis "All emeralds are not green"; that it confirms "All emeralds are green" and "All emeralds examined before *t* are green," but these are compatible hypotheses; and that it confirms "All emeralds are green" and hypotheses like "All emeralds not examined before *t* are not green" and "Everything not examined before *t* is, if an emerald, not green," which are also compatible but might appear otherwise if we use colloquial versions of the hypotheses and expect "that things which are emeralds *will* be examined after time *t*." Argues, in particular, that there is no way to introduce an evidence statement into Hempel's system which will keep "All emeralds are green" confirmed while confirming "There exists an emerald not examined before *t*" and disconfirming "Everything not examined before *t* is, if an emerald, not green." Maintains that we feel "grue" creates a problem for Hempel's system "largely because of intuitive judgments made *externally* to Hempel's system and which we falsely believe either properly belong to the system or could without difficulty be incorporated into it." Also thinks we are tempted to "smuggle in extra information" because (as noted before) the predicate "has not been examined before *t*" is ambiguous. Goes on to maintain that "*a* is a green emerald examined before *t*" confirms $(x)(Ex)$ or "Everything is examined before *t*," and so it also confirms "*any and every* hypothesis of the form $(x)(\ldots x \ldots \supset Ex)$, *regardless of what is inserted in the place of* '... x ...'." Notes that "*a* is a green emerald examined before *t*" confirms every hypothesis of this form "no matter what it asserts will happen after time *t*," that this also holds for hypotheses of the form $(x)(\ldots x \ldots \supset (\ldots x \ldots \supset Ex))$, and that all grue-predicate hypotheses can be put into one of these forms. Claims this is a genuine difficulty for Hempel's system because it "will afford no way of judging among hypotheses that assert things (no matter how wild!) about tomorrow—so long, that is, as the hypotheses are carefully framed using grue-type predicates and *it is insisted that the evidence statements incorporate the times of their observations, etc.*" Claims the same holds for hypotheses with predicates that specify spatial location. Believes this is an important asymmetry between these predicates and normal ones because the normal predicates do not create this sort of problem. Section VI. Argues that the "remaining evidence statements introduce no new features of interest into the present situation." Considers (among others) the evidence statements "*a* is an emerald, is not examined before *t*, and is not green"; "*a* is an emerald, is examined before *t* and is green, and *b* is an emerald, is examined before *t* and is green"; "*a* is an emerald, is examined before *t* and is green, and *b* is an emerald, is not examined before *t* and is not green." Claims, in connection with the last evidence statement, that "the only likely candidates for intuitive conflict would be clashes between" hypotheses like "All emeralds examined before *t* are green" and "All emeralds not examined before *t* are not green." Points out that these hypotheses are both consequences of the consistent hypothesis "All emeralds are grue" and "hence could not possibly be in conflict with one another." Believes you could only forget this by reading the hypotheses colloquially and introducing background information about temporal position making "no difference to the law-like connection, if any, between such predicates as 'is green' and 'is an emerald'." Section VII. Warns about "the dangers of reading expressions of formal languages colloquially and of importing 'illicit' information into the confirmation context." Admits there is "an external, over-arching difficulty over the performance of Hempel's system under the introduction of explicitly spatio-temporally restricted evidence statements." Emphasizes that this is "a far cry from a claim that Hempel's system is inconsistent."

Horwich, Paul. "An Appraisal of Glymour's Confirmation Theory." *Journal of Philosophy* 75 (1978): 98–113. Ends by considering whether Glymour's (1975) theory helps to solve problems about relevant evidence, variety of evidence, observationally adequate but still neglected theories, and simplicity. Examines Glymour's example of six data points that fall on a line and both a linear hypothesis and a polynomial one that accounts for them. Takes Glymour to be arguing that the linear hypothesis is preferable because the data points provide more positive tests of the linear than the polynomial hypothesis. Contends that, when we look at the actual hypotheses scientists would decide between here (the ones whose coefficients are the specific numbers from the six data points), they are equally well confirmed according to Glymour's principle. Also claims that, on Glymour's view, the data confirm the actual polynomial hypothesis more than Glymour's candidate and yet the latter is a logical consequence of the former. Adds that Glymour's principle "leads to absurdity" when we suppose one scientist is determining the relation between X and Y, a second is determining the relation between Z and X, they both end up with the same data points, and the linear hypothesis of one scientist ends up (because of how the quantity Z is defined) equivalent to the polynomial hypothesis of the other, and vice versa. See Horwich (1982b) and Glymour (1980).

Horwich, Paul. "How to Choose between Empirically Indistinguishable Theories." *Journal of Philosophy* 79 (1982a): 61–77. Examines the problem of underdetermination. Views the problem in terms of incompatible theories, their testable consequences, and reasons for choosing one theory over another. Considers local conventionalism, global conventionalism, anti-foundationalism, and inductivism. Construes inductivism as the view that the problem of underdetermination is a special case of the traditional problem of induction and so, for example, we should appeal (as Putnam does) to simplicity in choosing between empirically equivalent theories. Argues that inductivism is inadequate and, more specifically, that considerations of simplicity are "both inapplicable and unnecessary" when the empirically equivalent theories are isomorphic; that is, "when their formulations are potential notational variants of one another." Discusses the grue problem because someone might think it shows that theory simplicity and inductive argument strength depend on nonsyntactic factors, and so isomorphic theories can be distinguished with regard to simplicity and inductive plausibility. Argues that there is no reason to think that the green emeralds argument has the same logical form as the grue emeralds argument (and yet differ in inductive strength) because the premises of the two arguments do not have the same logical form. Claims the premises are not "All sampled emeralds are green" and "All sampled emeralds are grue"; rather, in each case the real premise involves a set of beliefs about sampling, being green, being grue, and emeralds conjoined with each of these statements about all sampled emeralds. Maintains that this set contains a belief about being able to see whether something is green without knowing the time, and not being able to see whether something is grue without knowing the time; takes this to be a reason for thinking that the two premises do not have the same logical form. Also see Horwich (1982b).

Horwich, Paul. *Probability and Evidence.* Cambridge: Cambridge University Press, 1982b. Introduces the grue problem (pp. 5–8) with an argument schema: all sampled As have been B, therefore probably all As are B. Defines "grue" as "sampled and green or unsampled and blue." Takes the problem to be specifying "the class of predicates (so-called projectible predicates) whose substitution in the inductive schema will yield acceptable arguments." Introduces the topic of simplicity with a curve-fitting example and a graph version of the grue problem, both of which involve choosing between observationally adequate hypotheses. Sees the grue problem as "an element in this general problem of devising a description of our inductive practice." Examines the grue problem in chapter 3, "Confirmation," pages 67–72. States four Russellian principles of induction: e.g., where H is "All As are B" and "nAB" is "n known As have been found to be B," $P(H/(n + 1)AB)>P(H/nAB)$. Gives a Bayesian justification for each principle. States the grue problem in a general form: lets "Cx" mean $(Bx \ \& \ Sx) \lor (-Bx \ \& \ -Sx)$, "$Sx$" mean x is sampled, the hypothesis be "All As are C," and then points out that if our evidence is nAB, we know nAC; then using the Russellian principles, we can see this evidence confirms to an arbitrarily high degree both $(n + 1)AB$ and $(n + 1)AC$, which also confirms the prediction that the next A will be B and that it will not be B. Claims the grue problem makes it appear "that the Russellian principles of induction must be incorrect, and their Bayesian rationale invalid." Proposes an alternative resolution by locating "the source of confusion in a failure to recognize that our evidence is not simply nAB, as has been assumed, but rather $nASB$." Notes the Russellian principles are not about probabilities relative to the information that n sampled As have been found to be B. Also notes that now nAB and nAC are not equivalent, and so the Russellian principle is not inconsistent. Regenerates the problem by adopting the revised principle that, in the limit, $P(H/nASB) = 1$ and noting ASB is now equivalent to ASC. Shows this principle cannot be justified because we cannot assume the sample is unbiased in the sense "that the chances of an A turning out to be B are unaffected by its presence in the sample." Notes, in particular, that it will influence the chances A turns out to be C when there are unequal numbers of B and non-B. Maintains that green emeralds, observed before t, confirm—increase the probability of—both the green and grue hypothesis. Emphasizes that this is not to be confused with "claims about the evidence regarding unobserved cases." Distinguishes between $nASB$ raising the probability of "All As are B" and $nASB$ making "it more likely that the unsampled As are also B." Maintains that we have $P(H/nASB)>P(H)$ but not $P((n + 1)AB/nASB)> P(nAB/(n - 1)ASB)$. Calls a hypothesis projectible when "the observation of positive and no negative instances tends to confirm the conclusion that the unsampled As are B." Asks if there is a necessary and sufficient projectibility condition on the prior probability of a hypothesis. Argues that if the hypothesis H ("All sampled and unsampled As are B") is projectible, then "the product of the prior probabilities of the grue-like alternatives to H" must be less than $1/16$. Adds that "projectibility is associated with high prior probability." Points out: in most cases the probability is approximately 1 that not all sampled and not all unsampled As are B, and so if $P(H)$ is greater than the probability that all sampled and not all unsampled As are B or the probability that not all sampled and all unsampled As are B, then H is projectible. Views this as a first attempt "to express the idea of projectibility in probabilistic terms." Believes the consequence condition is false and yet "a central element of scientific methodology." Explains this by claiming the condition works with hypotheses that have high prior probabilities, but not with hypotheses that have low prior probabilities, such as the grue hypothesis, "the observation of whose positive instances we feel provides no reason to believe that they will be satisfied in the future." Summarizes the discussion (pp. 80–81) by claiming that the new riddle "reduces to the problem of describing the basis of our prior probability assignments." Notes that "the notion of prior probability is relative," and so the new riddle amounts to finding "a systematic characterisation of those combinations of" A, B, and background information K such that the degree of confirmation for (All As are B/K) is fairly high. Also mentions the green and grue hypotheses (p. 75) in connection with constraints on rationality. See the reviews by Good (1984), Spielman (1984), and Woodward (1985).

Howson, Colin and Urbach, Peter. *Scientific Reasoning: The Bayesian Approach.* La Salle, Ill.: Open Court Publishing Company, 1989. See chapter 4, section k, "Infinitely Many Theories Compatible with the Data." Introduce the problem with the example (from Jeffreys, 1931) of Galileo's law of free fall and the infinitely many conflicting alternative laws that also imply the experimental data. Point out that some noninductivist, nonprobabilistic views judge hypotheses solely in terms of evidential support, where evidential support is a function of $P(e/h)$ or $P(e)$. Maintain that such views would have to consider the alternative laws just as good as Galileo's law (on the evidence available to him). Claim Goodman makes the same point with his green and grue emeralds example because "the grue-hypothesis represents an infinite number of alternatives to the more natural hypothesis, for t can assume any value, provided it is later than now." Think these examples illustrate a general problem: infinitely many rival theories explain some data, yet scientists only take a few seriously. Describe a Bayesian approach to this kind of problem. Note this approach "does not imply that every hypothesis similarly related to the data is of equal merit." Note further that, on a Bayesian approach, "if two theories which explain the data equally well nevertheless have different posterior probabilities, then they must have had different priors too." Accordingly maintain that the grue hypotheses have lower prior probabilities than the green hypothesis. Believe the problem then becomes discovering "the criteria and rationales by which theories assume particular prior probabilities." Discuss the probabilistic reason for assigning a low prior probability to a theory about all future Prime Ministers having last names that begin with the letter "T." Cite chapter 11, "The Objections to the Subjective Bayesian Theory," as discussing factors that determine prior probabilities.

Hullett, James N. "On a Simple-Minded Solution." *Philosophy of Science* 37 (1970): 452–454. A reply to Bartley (1968). Argues that Bartley's key notion—that of a hypothesis being responsive to a problem—does not provide a way of distinguishing between hypotheses we take seriously and those we do not, such as the grue hypothesis.

Hullet, James and Schwartz, Robert. "Grue: Some Remarks." *Journal of Philosophy* 64 (1967): 259–271. Characterize the new riddle as determining which hypotheses are confirmed by their positive instances. Maintain that the curve-fitting problem is a version of the new riddle and that the grue problem is "a linguistic analogy or model of the curve-fitting situation." View "grue" as "symbolic of any predicate whose projection would result in such bizarre predictions." Claim the riddle can occur with any properties plotted along the axes "as long as there are some values that have not yet been determined." Accordingly see the temporal features of "grue" as accidental. Note that a solution is a general criterion for distinguishing projectible and nonprojectible predicates, and so "merely finding asymmetries specific to a particular pair of predicates is not enough." Regard Goodman as claiming that a general criterion will not involve syntactic or semantic asymmetries between predicates like "green" and "grue." Argue that a syntactic definition of the smoothest curve does not solve the curve-fitting version because a curve is smoothest only "with respect to some particular representation of our evidence," and so we have the additional problem of choosing "among graphs that differently represent our data." Maintain that we do not have a good criterion of positionality, we have no a priori reason for believing all positional predicates are nonprojectible, predicates like "equatorial" are positional and projectible, and positionality cannot be identified with nonprojectibility while the former is considered an absolute feature of predicates, the latter a relative feature of predicates. Examine the contention that "green" and "grue" are observationally asymmetric because we can tell that something is green by observation alone, but we also need a calendar or clock with something being grue. Also examine the contention that they are epistemically asymmetric because we can tell that something is green without knowing the time, but we must know the time for something being grue. See the first contention as an issue about the observational content of predicates, the second as an issue about the epistemic presuppositions of predicates. Claim it is obvious that "neither the class of directly observable predicates nor the class of epistemically primitive predicates will be coextensive with the class of projectible predicates." Argue that these contentions are so programmatic we simply do not know if the yet-to-be-developed principles excluding "grue" (for some observational or epistemic reason) will also exclude projectible predicates and include nonprojectible ones. Also point out that these observational and epistemic points seem to be specific to the grue version of the new riddle because the evidence in a curve-fitting version (e.g., data on pressure and volume) does not have observational or epistemic differences. Go on to reply to Thomson (1966). Consider whether Thomson's methods generally eliminate nonprojectible hypotheses with disjunctive predicates and whether they specifically show why the green hypothesis is preferable to the grue one. Claim that her methods do not eliminate the nonprojectible hypothesis "All lumps of sumond dissolve in acid P," where "sumond" means "either sugar or diamond," we have found n lumps of sugar dissolve in acid P, and no diamond has been put into acid P. Argue that Thomson does not show how the green hypothesis is preferable because she assumes there is an epistemically privileged vocabulary for evidence statements, overlooks how a machine could register whether objects are grue and in consequence we could know each emerald "presented to the machine was grue without knowing of any particular emerald that it is green and examined before t," overlooks how, on some definitions of "grue," we can apply the term without deducing it applies from the fact that "green" and "examined before t" apply, presents a circular argument purporting to show an asymmetry between "green" and "grue," and cannot show that her assumption "all emeralds contain chromium" is preferable to the gruelike hypothesis "all emeralds contain chromalum" (because we can always produce gruelike subpuzzles).

Hunt, G.M.R. "Further Ramifications of 'Grue'." *British Journal for the Philosophy of Science* 20 (1969): 257–259. Discusses Hesse (1969). Argues that "it is not necessary to identify the predicate 'green' with another observable property in order to achieve the effect of entrenchment," where entrenchment is entrenchment in a theory and "consists in the law-like relations between the predicate 'green' and other predicates in the theory." Assumes certain color-mixing laws are empirically verified for monochromatic light (e.g., mixing yellow and blue to get green) and colored objects provide light that is mixed with "half silvered mirrors; one source seen through the mirror, the other seen by reflection." Notes that color-mixing laws can be derived from the relation between color names and light frequency, and the frequency mixing relation. Notes that statements of the form "When light from objects X and Y are mixed, the resultant light is similar in color to object Z" can be derived from the relation between standard objects and color names. Claims that if the object interaction relations stay homomorphic and the Grue speaker preserves the color mixing laws after the crucial time T—when the colors of objects change—then he "will have to sacrifice a colour at one end of the spectrum and gain an unnamed colour at the other." Claims, for example, that "blue will become indigo or the colour mixing laws will be violated," which is contrary to Grue's assertions about "bleen." Also claims that "the laws of diffraction may serve to entrench colour names by specifying the angle of diffraction of the light of each colour through a particular grating or prism." Notes that if Grue preserves "the relations between diffraction angles through various prisms for pairs of colours" after time T, then there will be "no colour name change at T." Concludes that the Grue speaker's predictions are not as simple as the Green speaker's predictions because the Grue speaker "cannot permute the colour words in such a way as to preserve colour interaction relations."

Indurkhya, Bipin. "Some Remarks on the Rationality of Induction." *Synthese* 85 (1990): 95–114. Attempts to refute four arguments (from Stove, 1986) aimed at justifying inductive reasoning, one of which uses the sampling principle: viz., given a reasonably large random sample from a population, "the probability that the sample is representative of the population is very high." Maintains that the sampling principle cannot justify induction unless one introduces certain assumptions about randomness or uniform distribution (section 4) because it "is fatally vulnerable to Goodman's grue paradox." Claims the grue paradox "exposes the flaw in any argument that attempts to justify an inference spanning over all times based on a sample that is restricted over a smaller time span." Takes the key point to be that the sample is not a random sample with respect to the time span of the population. Points out that if we allow the possibility of time travel, then a sampling principle justification will be invulnerable to the grue paradox because "the sample, being random, is as likely to contain objects that are examined before the year A.D. 2000 as objects examined after the year A.D. 2000." Formulates a generalized version of the grue paradox for "any argument that tries to justify a conclusion about a whole population based on a sample that is drawn from a small section of the population." Claims the grue paradox can occur when two conditions are not satisfied: viz., that the sample is random with respect to an interval the population spans over in some dimension, and that we do know a priori that the objects which satisfy the predicates in our inductive statement are uniformly distributed in that interval. Maintains that, when these conditions are not satisfied, we can introduce a gruelike disjunctive predicate to produce the paradox. Goes on to suggest a cognitive approach that studies cognitive mechanisms and tries "to explain the characteristics of induction in terms of these mechanisms."

Jackson, Frank. "Grue." *Journal of Philosophy* 72 (1975): 113–131. Presents the straight rule informally in terms of arguing "from certain Fs being G to certain other Fs being G." Notes that the SR can be formalized in various ways: e.g., in terms of "All examined As are Bs" supporting "All unexamined As are Bs." Restricts his discussion to the simple case in which "everything in a sample, not merely a percentage, has the property we are concerned with." Concerned with "the *description* of those applications of the SR which we regard as rational." Will argue that there isn't any new riddle of induction because "*all* (consistent) predicates are projectible." Section I: "The Three Ways of Defining 'Grue'." The first way: something is grue if and only if it is green before T and blue thereafter, where T refers to some designated time in the future. Notes how "grue" is atemporal on this definition because an object is grue once and for all, or not grue once and for all. Maintains that if "grue" is defined in this way, we have no case for taking "grue" to be nonprojectible. Points out that if we determined that all the examined emeralds have this property, then we would probably "accept that all emeralds, both examined and unexamined, have this property of being green to a certain time and then turning blue." Notes that if this were so, emeralds would be like tomatoes and oranges because they "change color dramatically during their life cycles." The second way: something is grue at t if and only if it is green at t and t is before T, or it is blue at t and t is simultaneous with or is later than T. Notes that "grue" is temporal on this definition because something can be grue at one time and not grue at another. Points out how this definition is not equivalent to defining "x is grue" to mean "x is green" before T and "x is blue" after T. Maintains that we do not get the new riddle or a paradox when we use this second way of defining "grue" along with the SR. Believes the contrary view involves a confusion over the SR "as applied to objects that endure through time, that is, four-dimensional objects, or as applied to three-dimensional objects *at* times, that is, time-slices of the four-dimensional objects." Claims we must add a temporal factor to our predicates if we are applying the SR to enduring objects: i.e., "what we project must be understood as at a time; not just being green but being green at t." Believes the paradox only appears when we conflate being green (grue) at a certain time before T with being green (grue) at a certain time after T. Sees the SR as applying to temporal parts of emeralds "when we argue from the greenness of present emeralds to the greenness of future emeralds." Presents the third way of defining "grue" as something is grue at t if and only if it is examined by T and is green at t, or it is not examined by T and it is blue at t. Believes this is Goodman's definition. Will be concerned with this definition in the rest of his paper. Believes this definition "gives rise to more trouble" than the other two. Section II. Wants to know how, in detail, the grue paradox comes about. Considers an indexed series of emeralds. Supposes that we know emeralds 1 through n have been examined and are green, while we know emerald $n + 1$ has not been examined. Asks how the SR takes us to incompatible predictions about emerald $n + 1$ from equivalent evidential bases? Says we are given that emerald 1 is green, and emerald 2 is green, . . . , and emerald n is green; also that emerald 1 is grue, and emerald 2 is grue, . . . , and emerald n is grue. Claims these are not equivalent and so "there is no objection to the SR leading to different predictions" about emerald $n + 1$. Also claims the predictions (that emerald $n + 1$ is green, that emerald $n + 1$ is grue) "are not inconsistent (neither entails the denial of the other)." Points out that this does not present our total evidence. Expresses our total evidence as a conjunction about emeralds 1 through n: i.e., emerald 1 is green and examined, emerald 2 is green and examined, . . . , emerald n is green and examined. Notes that this is equivalent to a conjunction about the emeralds being grue and examined. Notes that the first conjunction supports, via the SR, the prediction that emerald $n + 1$ will be green and examined; notes that the second (grue) conjunction supports the prediction that emerald $n + 1$ will be grue and examined. Notes that these are equivalent, not incompatible. Considers the following argument (see Leblanc, 1963): the green prediction entails that if emerald $n + 1$ is not examined, then it is green; the grue prediction entails that if emerald $n + 1$ is not examined, then it is grue—and this is equivalent to: if emerald $n + 1$ is not examined, then it is blue. Sees this as a fallacy because the conjunctions support their respective conditionals here "but only because we have support for the falsity of their antecedents." Section III: "The Counterfactual Condition." Considers how to use the fact that emerald $n + 1$ is not examined. Criticizes an attempt to "add in this information in a more or less mechanical fashion" by showing it depends on a fallacious pattern of argument: viz., if we know p is true and p supports the conjunction q & r, and we independently know r is false, then we have overall support for the conjunction q & not r and therefore anything it entails. Emphasizes "the universally acknowledged fact that inductive support is defeasible." Believes we need to "see the matter in context." Takes the general context to be: each member of our sample 1 through n has a property (being examined) as well as the properties we are concerned with (being green, being grue), and the individual $n + 1$ does not have this property. Comments that "when we use the SR to project common properties from a sample to members of the population from which the sample comes, there are nearly always features common to every member of the sample which we know are not features of all (or any) members of the population outside the sample." Notes that normally we disregard these common features of the sample, but sometimes we cannot. Describes a case about glinting diamonds and a case about red lobsters. The lobster case: if every lobster you have seen has been red, this supports the next-case prediction that the next one you see will be red as well; but if every lobster you have seen has been a cooked lobster, and you know that cooking makes a lobster red, then your lobster observations do not support the next-case prediction that the next uncooked lobsters you see will be red. Stresses the point that the lobsters you have seen "would not have been red if they had not been cooked." States the counterfactual condition: "that certain Fs which are H being G does not support others Fs which are not H being G if it is known that the Fs in the evidence class would not have been G if they had not been H." Points out that the examined emeralds would have been green "whether or not they had been examined," and yet they would not have been grue if they had not been examined. Concludes that if we use the SR to predict that emerald $n + 1$ is grue (and unexamined), then we will violate the counterfactual condition. Emphasizes that we cannot get an inconsistency here because both of the following can't be true at the same time: if X had not been H, then it would not have been G; if X had not been H, then it would have been G. Notes that he has been discussing the SR in terms of constants designating emeralds. Considers the counterfactual condition with a universal statement version of the SR and a functor version. Points out that the SR is a relational principle of inductive support, and that "*what* we come to know does the supporting (if any), not our coming to know it." Admits that we might have found ourselves in a world in which emeralds would not have been green unless they were examined, and that unexamined emeralds were blue, and so we would believe (in that world) that all emeralds are blue. Believes the counterfactual condition explains this because (in this world) if the examined emeralds had not been examined, they would not have been green. Section IV: "The Projectibility Of Being Sampled." Considers the claim that being sampled, being examined, and being a member of the series of 1 through n individuals (the sample) are nonprojectible properties. Notes that Jeffrey (1966) makes this claim. Describes a case of drawing marbles from a barrel and observing each marble is red; takes this to support the conclusion that the rest of the marbles are red, and not to support the conclusion that the rest of the marbles are sampled, even though each of the marbles drawn has the property of being sampled. Changes the case: if we think all of the marbles drawn have been sampled because each has Jones's fingerprints on it, indicating that it was sampled in the past by Jones, then we have support for the conclusion that the rest of the marbles have been sampled. Maintains that the projectible/nonprojectible distinction can't explain this change, while the counterfactual condition can. Claims that in the original marbles case we have a violation of the condition: viz., "if the marbles have not been drawn out, they would not have been sampled." Claims that in the revised case we do not have a violation: viz., "the marbles drawn would still have been sampled (by Jones in the past) even if they had not been drawn out by me." Claims that the same remarks apply to being examined and to being one of the series comprising the sample; describes a "cat burglary" case to show the latter property is not nonprojectible. Goes on to consider two objections to the counterfactual condition: a general objection about using counterfactuals, and a specific objection about his use introducing a circularity. Maintains, in response to the general objection, that we know some counterfactuals are true, even though we don't have an adequate theory of counterfactuals. Maintains that he is not introducing a circularity because "our knowledge that the examined emeralds would still have been green if they had not been examined is knowledge about the *examined* emeralds, not about the unexamined ones." Notes that we might know this "even if unexamined emeralds were not green or, indeed, were nonexistent, and so, is knowledge we may appeal to without circularity." Tries to make this point obvious by discussing the point in terms of drawing marbles from a barrel. Section V: "Summary." States his general position: the SR does not produce incompatible predictions with "grue" and gruelike predicates. Notes that if we apply the SR, then we argue on a modified pattern (*F*s that are *H* being *G* supporting *F*s that are not *H* being *G*) and assume the counterfactual condition is not violated. Describes how this guarantees we will never be taken from the same evidence to incompatible predictions about *F*s that are non-*H* being *G* or not. Acknowledges that when we use the counterfactual condition, we must "draw on our knowledge of the world." Believes it is clear that this knowledge "is *not* the knowledge at issue in the particular application of the SR in question."

Jackson, Frank and Pargetter, Robert. "Confirmation and the Nomological." *Canadian Journal of Philosophy* 10 (1980): 415–428. Attempt to solve the selection problem for instantial confirmation, simple induction or the straight rule. Note that members of a sample have indefinitely many common properties, and that we must choose some of these properties to project via simple induction. Present the selection problem as stating rules about choosing the properties to project. Consider the new riddle as a special case of the selection problem: choosing "green" as the predicate to project from the examined to the unexamined emeralds, even though "grue" is also true of the examined emeralds. Introduce the term "differentiating pair" to refer to property-pairs that distinguish sample items from items being projected to: e.g., the pair being examined-being unexamined distinguishes emeralds in the sample from emeralds outside the sample. Claim there are two general difficulties with the classical approach to the selection problem, where the classical approach is any attempt to divide properties (or predicates) into the projectible and nonprojectible ones. Argue first that a predicate can be projectible in one circumstance and yet nonprojectible in another. Describe a case in which "grue" is projectible because emeralds are naturally blue and turn green when examined (because of the light); also describe the case of Caligua meeting pale-in-the-face villagers and wondering if he should project being pale in the face or being palemet, where the latter term means pale and met by Caligua, or not pale and not met by him. Argue second that "whether or not a predicate ought to be projected is *relative* to the differentiating pair in question." Explain that projecting "grue" depends on the circumstances (color changing upon examination or not) and on whether the differentiating pair is examined-unexamined or examined-examined. Claim the classical approach also does not adequately explain simple cases involving disjunctive predicates because some disjunctive predicates are projectible: e.g., the disjunctive predicate in the hypothesis "All pulsars are white dwarfs or neutron stars." Argue against the view that "confirmation is necessarily confirmation of the law-like." Discuss Goodman's example "All men in this room are third sons." Maintain that a sample of third sons does confirm this nonlawlike generalization. Emphasize that we cannot take the sample's existence "*both* to confirm and to be a fluke." Put another way: "one can have no reason to expect the purely accidental to continue." Introduce a nomological condition on a sample: e.g., for a sample of green emeralds and the differentiating pair examined-unexamined, the condition requires a nomological connection in the sample between emeralds and being green with respect to the differentiating pair, and the connection in question is that the sample members would still have been both emeralds and green even if they had been unexamined instead of examined. Apply this to resolve the new riddle by noting that we should project "green" because "in normal circumstances the sampled emeralds would still have been green even if they had been examined." Point out that we would project "grue" in the abnormal circumstances (examining the emerald changes it from blue to green). Also apply the nomological condition to a disjunctive predicate case about meeting some members of a club and finding each is in the Social Register, and so each of them is in the Register or has visited Pisa, to the Caligua and villagers case where Caligua "must decide whether the villagers he has met would have been pale in the face if they had not met him," and to the case of examined green emeralds being green emeroses, and so unexamined ones, or roses, being green as well. Note how the grue and emerose cases illustrate there are two ways to fail to meet the nomological condition. Attempt to show generally (with an assumption about counterfactuals) that the nomological condition does not lead to inconsistent simple induction results. Agree with the view that simple induction requires some sort of theoretical involvement. Remark that if simple induction does require the nomological condition, then justifying simple induction does not seem to be the same as justifying induction (the classical problem). Also see Jackson (1975 and this volume).

Jeffrey, Richard C. "Goodman's Query." *Journal of Philosophy* 63 (1966): 281–288. Compares Goodman's approach to confirmation theory with Carnap's approach. Notes differences in how they describe induction: e.g., in terms projectible properties for Goodman, degrees of confirmation (relative to a body of evidence) for Carnap. Considers the approaches independent of each other. Sees the new riddle as showing Carnapians that "credibilities depend on meanings." Maintains that Carnapians must do more than classify primitive predicates as projectible or not when choosing a confirmation function; emphasizes taking account of how some predicates are more projectible than others and how predicates fail to be projectible in different ways. Provides semantic and pragmatic definitions of a property P being projectible relative to a property Q. The semantic definition involves a function $s(P,Q,n)$ increasing toward 1 as a limit as n increases without bound; this function is "the degree of confirmation of the hypothesis that the next Q will be a P, given that a particular n objects are $P \cdot Q$'s." The pragmatic definition is an indexical analogue of this. Grue is a projectible property of emeralds on the semantic definition, but unprojectible on the pragmatic definition. Claims that projectibility questions can be handled in Carnapian confirmation theory "once it is placed squarely on the semantical footing it requires." See comments by Goodman (1966).

Jeffrey, Richard C. *The Logic of Decision.* Second edition: Chicago: University of Chicago Press, 1983. A well-known Bayesian framework for decision making. See the last chapter, "Induction and Objectification," section 12.3, for a discussion of the principle of simple induction and projectible properties. Presents his version of the new riddle with the terms "goy" and "birl." Maintains that "unless the projectible properties can be characterized in some noncircular way, the principle of simple induction is useless, being either unsound or platitudinous." Examines a psychological characterization based on the fact that natural languages have simple terms for certain properties. Considers this "misguided"; takes the projectibility of a predicate to be an anthropological fact, and regards linguistic data as only some of the data involved in determining whether a predicate is projectible. Defines projectibility in terms of a sequence of numbers increasing towards 1 as a limit, each number representing the probability that an agent attributes to a certain proposition being true, and each proposition attributing the predicate in question to a named individual.

Jeffreys, Harold. *Scientific Inference*. Cambridge: Cambridge University Press, first edition 1931, second edition 1957, third edition 1973. Considers "the nature of inference from empirical data so as to predict experiences that may occur in the future." Claims that "the actual behaviour of physicists in always choosing the simplest law that fits the observations therefore corresponds exactly to what would be expected if they regarded the probability of making correct inferences as the chief determining factor in selecting a definite law out of an infinite number that would satisfy the observations equally well or better, and if they considered the simplest law as having the greatest prior probability." Formulates the simplicity postulate: "the set of all possible forms of scientific laws is finite or enumerable, and their initial probabilities form the terms of a convergent series of sum 1." Believes that "in the absence of observational evidence, the simpler law is the more probable and the initial probabilities can be placed in an order." Identifies this with the simplicity postulate by claiming "that the order of decreasing initial probabilities is that of increasing complexity." Develops a simplicity ordering for laws (as algebraic and differential equations) in terms of the number of adjustable parameters. Also see his *Theory of Probability* (Oxford: Oxford University Press, third edition 1961; second edition 1948, first edition 1939), in which he attempts "to provide a method of drawing inferences from observational data that will be self-consistent and can also be used in practice."

Johnsen, Bredo. "Russell's New Riddle of Induction." *Philosophy* 54 (1979): 87–97. Interprets Russell's views on inductive inference from *Human Knowledge: Its Scope and Limits* (1948). Argues that Russell discovered the new riddle but did not offer a solution to it. Maintains Russell could have explicated projectibility in terms of members of a class being similar in structure according to some science. Uses Quine's approach to natural kinds (1969). For Russell's views, also see Salmon (1974) and (1975).

Johnson, David. "Induction and Modality." *Philosophical Review* 100 (1991): 399–430. Asks if there is any rational basis for preferring the green hypothesis to the grue hypothesis. Criticizes answers that appeal to the meaning of "reasonable," natural kinds or real properties, and entities like universals. Construes the problem as a practical one about choosing a course of action (e.g., put your hand in the fire or not) in order to show that inductive inference involves counterfactuals. Argues that universal generalizations alone cannot provide us with compelling reasons for performing one action instead of its opposite. Maintains that we must consider what would be the case if we had performed one act or the other. Regards inductive inference as indirect in that "we infer from the way the world was to the way the world would be, and then from the way the world would be to the way the world will be." Distinguishes between active and passive counterfactuals: whether an active counterfactual is true or false depends on what the dynamic processes in nature, or the laws of nature, are; whether a passive counterfactual is true or false "is independent of what the dynamic processes in nature are." Thinks active counterfactuals reduce to "facts about what is so in certain relevantly similar worlds," passive counterfactuals do not. Maintains that passive counterfactuals are a priori truths or falsehoods. Considers a dispute over which passive counterfactual is an a priori truth, one about a blue sapphire in a box always being blue and staying blue if you were to open the box and opening the box does not causally interfere with the color, the other about the sapphire always being grue and staying grue if you were to open the box and opening the box again does not interfere with the color. Argues (by appealing to our a priori knowledge) that the blue passive counterfactual is an a priori truth, and that, since passive counterfactuals constrain our choice of active ones, we should also believe the corresponding active blue counterfactuals about the sapphire. Claims this shows "that a reliance on grue-like predicates inevitably produces a flawed modal picture of reality *and is therefore irrational.*" Maintains that we can solve the original problem about grue and green hypotheses by noting "the intimate association of active counterfactuals with the laws of nature." Gives a modal argument to show that the law-candidate "All emeralds are green" is rationally preferable to the law-candidate "All emeralds are grue." Discusses why "All emeralds are green" has, for all practical purposes, only gruesome competing law-candidates. Considers the situation in which all of the nongruesome law-candidates have been refuted and we must choose between competing gruesome law-candidates. Illustrates a general method for proving one gruesome law-candidate is rationally preferable to another. Uses the hypotheses that all water is soliqueous and that all water is suddenlysoleous. Points out that gruesome hypotheses are equivalent to conjunctions of nongruesome hypotheses. Appeals to these nongruesome hypotheses in arguing for the rational preferability of one gruesome law-candidate over another. Ends by claiming that we care about finding laws of nature because they, unlike true accidental generalizations, "are uniquely suited to carry us from the second step to the third" in inductive reasoning: from *would* to *will.*

Kahane, Howard. "Nelson Goodman's Entrenchment Theory." *Philosophy of Science* 32 (1965): 377–383. Critically examines Goodman's three entrenchment rules and makes two general objections to the entrenchment theory. (N.B., the first edition of *FFF* has three rules, the second has two, the third has one; the second edition appeared in 1965.) Points out that the third entrenchment rule is supposed to eliminate hypotheses that have gruelike antecedent terms. Introduces two hypotheses with the antecedent terms "*A*-emeruby" and "*B*-roseby." Claims the third rule does not eliminate these hypotheses, and we can infer from these hypotheses that all rubies examined in the future will be green and not green. Maintains that "in general, we can prove in the same way that *anything* not already examined for a particular property both does, and does not have, that property." Considers whether these hypotheses can be eliminated because they conflict with background hypotheses available on a higher level. Argues that higher level hypotheses are not always available, and when they are, "*grue-like* background hypotheses are also available to counteract their force." Claims that just as rule three fails to eliminate gruelike projections on lower levels, it fails to eliminate them on higher levels, and so on a higher level we have unwanted hypotheses with gruelike antecedent terms. Goes on to note a necessary condition on how the two other rules operate: the hypotheses must conflict. Argues that "there seems to be no reasonable way to interpret the notion of conflict so that entrenchment rules one and two eliminate the projection of all and only those hypotheses they were designed to eliminate." Maintains that we do not arrive at a satisfactory criterion of conflict by looking at purely logical reasons, information from other inductive inferences, or the meanings of the consequent terms. Concludes with general objections to Goodman's theory with regard to introducing terms in new fields of science, and with regard to determining how much difference in entrenchment we need for the rules to operate. Describes a case about all radium being radioactive or radiotractive when radioactivity was first discovered. Maintains that entrenchment does not eliminate either hypothesis (both having a zero rating then) even though, even then, the radiotractive hypothesis is unacceptable. Points out that Goodman says it takes an obvious difference in entrenchment for the rules to operate.

Contends this is unsatisfactory because the rules will then eliminate projecting hypotheses with the term "turquoise" when they conflict with hypotheses containing a color term like "green."

Kahane, Howard. "Reply to Ackermann." *Philosophy of Science* 34 (1967): 184–187. A response to Ackermann (1966), which is a response to Kahane (1966). Maintains that Ackermann's additional third elimination rule is too strong because it eliminates "many legitimate projections over poorly entrenched classes wider than some well entrenched class," including Ackermann's example of "All rubies and precious garnets are red." Notes that Goodman's suggestion (omitting a condition in the second rule) also eliminates many legitimate hypotheses. Provides three interpretations of Ackermann's criterion for when hypotheses conflict. Argues that, interpreted in these ways, the criterion is either too strong or too weak, eliminating (via rule one) hypotheses such as "All emeralds are E-green" or failing to eliminate hypotheses such as "All emeralds are G-grue" or even "All emeralds are grue." Makes two points about introducing new theoretical terms in areas where there are no well-entrenched predicates, and whether the entrenchment theory rejects gruelike hypotheses in those areas. On his example of radium being radioactive and being radiotractive, claims this cannot be handled in terms of comparative projectibility because there is no reason to think that the relevant parent predicates differ in entrenchment. On theoretical criteria applying in these cases and not entrenchment rules, considers this simply giving up the game because it is equivalent to saying that the entrenchment theory does not eliminate an illegitimate hypothesis like "All radium is radiotractive." Adds that, as far as he knows, current theories of simplicity will not eliminate it either. See the response by Ackermann (1967).

Kahane, Howard. "A Difficulty on Conflict and Confirmation." *Journal of Philosophy* 68 (1971a): 488–489. Makes two criticisms of Goodman, Schwartz, and Scheffler (1970), which presents a revised version of Goodman's entrenchment solution to the new riddle. Maintains that the revised version needs a satisfactory criterion of conflict between hypotheses. Argues that the revised version introduces a new problem: viz., the new version of Goodman's first entrenchment rule "eliminates not only the unwanted grue-like projections, but also any and every projection containing a newly introduced predicate."

Kahane, Howard. "Pathological Predicates and Projection." *American Philosophical Quarterly* 8 (1971b): 171–178. Introduces the notion of a temporal individual; uses it to define the notion of a temporal predicate; goes on to define the notions of a temporal class, temporal subclass, and temporal span. Points to "the unevenness of the temporal span of grue-like predicates with respect to the span of other dimensions of those predicates." States a rule to the effect that a temporal predicate is not projectible if its temporal span is not uniform throughout any given dimension of the predicate. Claims this rule "eliminates all of the grue-like predicates heretofore mentioned in the literature." States another rule (sufficient condition) to eliminate temporal predicates similar to cyclic predicates: e.g., the predicate "black$_6$," defined to mean black and not examined at time t_6. Maintains that nontemporal gruelike predicates can be eliminated by appealing to background information and overhypotheses. Emphasizes that temporal pathological predicates "have a projectibility rating of zero, no matter what empirical evidence we obtain, no matter what the world in fact turns out to be like," while nontemporal pathological predicates "have only a very low projectibility rating, calculated via already obtained empirical information, subject to revision upward in the future." Considers four kinds of objections to his solution: viz., that gruelike predicates are not a priori unprojectible (see Hullett and Schwartz 1967, Stenner 1967), that temporal predicates can be replaced by nontemporal predicates (see Scheffler 1963), that all temporal predicates are unprojectible and so the two rules are superfluous, and that the correct solution to the new riddle is in terms of natural kinds.

Kelley, Michael H. "Predicates and Projectibility." *Canadian Journal of Philosophy* 1 (1971): 189–206. Doubts there are any nonprojectible predicates; argues that 'third son,' 'observed by VE day,' and 'being one of a hundred particular objects' are not examples of nonprojectible predicates. Claims that only some definitions of 'grue' produce a paradox; argues that Barker's (1957) definition does not. Goes on to examine four other definitions, the last being Goodman's own definition; argues that Goodman's definition makes the term equivocal and in consequence the new riddle appears to commit the fallacy of equivocation—the term "means something entirely different when applied to the projective class than it means when applied to the evidence class."

Kemeny, John G. "The Use of Simplicity in Induction." *Philosophical Review* 62 (1952): 391–408. A well-known analysis of simplicity; often discussed in connection with the curve-fitting problem. Considers selecting a hypothesis from a set of alternative hypotheses given the results of the first n experiments designed to eliminate incorrect hypotheses. Describes two examples: selecting a hypothesis about the fraction of white balls in an urn after n draws, and selecting a polynomial hypothesis about the relationship between two independently measurable quantities after n measurements. Proposes a simplicity rule: "select the simplest hypothesis compatible with the observed values." Explicates "compatible" in terms of 99 percent of the observations falling within a certain level of deviation from the observations predicted by the hypothesis. Maintains that his simplicity rule is justified because "if the true hypothesis is one of the hypotheses under consideration, then—given enough experiments—we are 99 percent sure of selecting it." Explicates "simplicity" in terms of a class of possible orders of hypotheses relative to an inductive problem. States four necessary conditions for ordering hypotheses according to simplicity. Claims the fundamental property is that "for each hypothesis we can find an integer such that for n at least as great as this we are assured that, if the hypothesis is compatible with the observations, no other hypothesis as simple is compatible." Applies his method to the problem of planetary motion for Copernicus and going from Special to General Relativity for Einstein. Discusses the relation between his rule and Reichenbach's posits as well as Carnap's work on degrees of confirmation. Emphasizes the need to make his fourth condition (about the number of hypotheses being as low as possible) more precise in order to reach the 99 percent level with a minimum of experiments.

Kennedy, Ralph C. "On the Projection of Novel Predicates." *Southern Journal of Philosophy* 15 (1977): 487–492. Maintains that in many cases Goodman's theory of projectibility does not handle novel predicates correctly. Believes the theory has been modified in Ullian (1975) and Ullian and Goodman (1975). Emphasizes that now we may rationally take a hypothesis to be confirmed by its instances relative to a corpus of beliefs when, and only when, the corpus gives rise to the judgment that the hypothesis is projectible on the basis of plausible inferences from admissible, and only admissible, premises. Contends that the modified theory does not correctly judge hypotheses with novel predicates "when the belief corpus in question does not already include the belief that the hypothesis being assessed is confirmed by its positive instances." Claims this sort of corpus may not enable us to judge a hypothesis to be projectible, and yet relative to this corpus it would be rational to regard the hypothesis as confirmed by its positive instances. Maintains that (circa 1896) the Curies would have taken "All chunks of pitchblende are radioactive" to be confirmed by its instances, and that they would have been rational to do so. Imagines that they doubt whether this hypothesis is confirmed by its instances, and so this belief is not in their corpus. Asks if Goodman's theory would have resolved their doubts. Claims that the radioactive hypothesis conflicts with "All chunks of pitchblende are radiotractive" and that both pitchblende hypotheses have equally ill-entrenched consequent predicates—one a novel scientific predicate, the other a novel gruelike predicate. Maintains the conflict can be resolved by inferring, from admissible premises, that some hypothesis overrides the radiotractive one. Argues that "not even the best candidates for overriders" work. Considers the hypothesis "All chunks of pitchblende darken photographic plates" and claims the Curies would have to assume it conflicted with the radiotractive hypothesis if they took it to override that hypothesis. Argues (with a distinction between early and late pitchblende) that they would have no reason to believe there was a conflict here unless they believed the radioactive hypothesis was confirmed by its instances. Maintains that if they simply believed there was a conflict for no reason and went on to plausibly conclude the photographic plate hypothesis overrides the radiotractive one, they "would have had no more reason to believe this conclusion than they had to believe that" the two hypotheses conflicted. Also argues that Goodman's theory does no better in the actual situation with Curies believing the radioactive hypothesis is confirmed by its instances. Says Goodman's theory would have told them that the radioactive hypothesis was projectible and thus it would be rational to consider confirmed by its instances. Asserts that "a more trivial and useless result is hardly conceivable" because their belief corpus already included the belief about this hypothesis being confirmed by its instances.

Kennedy, Ralph and Chihara, Charles. "An Improvement on Zabludowski's Critique of Goodman's Theory of Projection." *Journal of Philosophy* 72 (1975): 137–141. A response to Zabludowski (1974; revised version in this volume). Believe that Zabludowski's criticisms "demolish" Goodman's theory of projectibility. Claim there are, however, "serious and rather obvious discrepancies between his and Goodman's definition of certain key terms (most importantly 'violated' and 'exhausted') which on the face of it undermine most, if not all, of Zabludowski's arguments." Examine Zabludowski's argument that, on Goodman's view, projectible hypotheses cannot be true and show that if "violated" and "exhausted" have Goodman's sense, then two "cornerstones of an imposing argument" are false. Introduce the idea of a sentence *s* being *determinably true* if and only if "there is a set *S* of sentences such that *s* is deducible from *S* and, for each sentence *t* in *S*: either (i) *t* has been determined to be true or (ii) the negation of *t* has been determined to be false or (iii) *t* is the negation of a sentence that has been determined to be false." Also introduce the idea of a sentence being determinably false: "either it is the negation of a determinably true sentence or its negation is determinably true." Present an argument that parallels Zabludowski's argument and that shows "the only hypotheses ever projectible are either false or determinably true." Note that this is a weaker conclusion but claim it is still "extremely damaging" because if we follow this parallel argument, we will have no use for projectibility: i.e., we will not adopt a hypothesis that we believe to be projectible without also believing that it is deducible from our evidence—and if we believe the hypothesis is deducible from our evidence, then "the question of its projectibility will be considered irrelevant to the question of whether it should be adopted." See the discussion by Ullian and Goodman (1972, same issue). Also footnote 9 of Zabludowski (1975) and footnote 1 of Kennedy and Chihara (1978).

Kennedy, Ralph and Chihara, Charles. "The Principle of Wanton Embedding." *Journal of Philosophy* 74 (1977): 539–540. Attempt to show that "All emeralds are green" wantonly embeds "All emeralds are grue," as Zabludowski (1975) maintains. Believe that Zabludowski's argument for this claim is defective, as Ullian and Goodman show (1976). Have U = "the set of emeralds that have been neither determined to be grue nor determined not to be grue," U^* = $U - \{x\}$, and rho = a conjunction of pertinent information and assumptions. Claim one conjunct of rho will be the sentence "All members of U^* are emeralds," and another will be "For every x and y, if x has the same color as y, then, if y is green, x is green." Proceed to show that "'x is green' adds to the U^*-information in the conjunction of rho with 'x is an emerald' and hence that 'all emeralds are green' wantonly embeds 'all emeralds are grue'." Introduce the sentence T: if (y)(if y is an emerald then either y is grue or y has the same color as x), then (y)(if y is a member of U^* then either y is grue or y is green). Note that T follows from the conjunction of rho with "x is green & x is an emerald," but it does not follow from "x is green" or from the conjunction of rho with "x is an emerald." Argue that T is a unitary consequence of the conjunction of rho with "x is green & x is an emerald," and that it also follows differentially with respect to U^* from this conjunction. Conclude this justifies Zabludowski's thesis about the green hypothesis wantonly embedding the grue hypothesis. See the reply by Ullian (1980).

Kennedy, Ralph and Chihara, Charles. "Beyond Zabludowskian Competitors: A New Theory of Projectibility." *Philosophical Studies* 33 (1978): 229–253. Section I. Note that Ullian and Goodman (1975) reply to Zabludowski (1974) by appealing to a principle of admissible information. Claim that "Ullian and Goodman have simply developed a new theory of projectibility in order to meet Zabludowski's objections." Test the new theory by seeing whether it tells us to choose the green hypothesis over the grue one, and whether it tells us the former hypothesis is projectible, the latter unprojectible. Argue that if we follow the principle of admissible information, then "neither of these conclusions is forthcoming." For example: the grue hypothesis is unprojectible if the green hypothesis overrides it, and the green hypothesis overrides it only if the green hypothesis does not conflict with a better entrenched supported, unviolated, unexhausted hypothesis—and "the information or assumption that this is true is, however, inadmissible." Analyze "the reasoning according to which Ullian and Goodman hoped to eliminate the troublesome Zabludowskian competitors" such as "All stones are either round or not such that all emeralds are green and $x = x$." Believe this reasoning shows that the admissible information principle "is not meant to apply to explicit assumptions only: those *implicit* assumptions involved in any application of the rule of projectibility must conform as well." Believe it is wrong to extend the principle to implicit assumptions. For example: if we accept the extended principle, then we cannot apply the theory to the green and grue hypotheses because making the explicit assumptions in this case also involves making inadmissible implicit assumptions such as "If the grue hypothesis is true, then the green hypothesis is false." Note that if the principle is restricted to explicit assumptions, then it avoids this particular difficulty. Review Ullian and Goodman's principle of wanton embedding which "says that no sentence effectively competes with a sentence it wantonly embeds." Maintain that this principle rules out all of Zabludowski's competitors "at the cost of rendering the resulting theory of projectibility thoroughly unacceptable" because all hypotheses end up wantonly embedding "many hypotheses with which, intuitively, they have nothing to do." Present a proof that the green hypothesis wantonly embeds the grue hypothesis, and which can be converted to a proof that (e.g.) the hypothesis "All horses are maned" wantonly embeds the hypothesis "All dogs are near-sighted." Section II. Examine Zabludowski's claim that Goodman's theory of projectibility is "fundamentally wrong" because it assumes the difference between plausible/implausible inductive generalizations is a difference between the classes picked out—natural or artificial ones. Note how Zabludowski introduces hypothesis h^{***} as a counterexample to this assumption: "though not, itself, intuitively, a reasonable inductive generalization, its antecedent and consequent predicates have perfectly natural classes as extensions (and it is, furthermore, supported, unviolated, unexhausted, and not overridden)." Hypothesis h^{***} is "All stones are either round and fusible, or round and not K, or fusible and K," where "K" stands for "such that something is a stone and an emerald, and either fusible and not green or not fusible and green." Review Ullian and Goodman's argument (1976) that h^{***} poses no more of a problem than a hypothesis like "All stones are fusible," and even less for a theory extended to deal with degrees of credibility. Maintain that if we apply Goodman's theory of projectibility (with the principle of admissible information) and do not regard "All stones are fusible" as showing the green hypothesis to be nonprojectible, then we will not regard h^{***} as showing the green hypothesis to be nonprojectible. Consider this "a Pyrrhic victory" because it undermines "the ability of 'All emeralds are green' to compete with 'All emeralds are grue'" and because it seems to involve making admissible posits on the basis of inadmissible information. Point out that the extended theory (for degrees of credibility) "has no bearing on the success of Zabludowski's assaults on the *old* theory," and believe Ullian and Goodman must formulate this extended theory before we can tell if it deals with h^{***}. Go on to discuss Zabludowski's claim about Goodman's approach being fundamentally wrong. Note that his claim is a conjunction of two different propositions, and maintain that "neither of these propositions appears to express anything to which the current theory of projectibility is committed." Note that, on the current theory, an inductive generalization is plausible or not based on (in part) the apparent—not actual—extensions of its predicates. Also believe "the theory does not hold that there is any relation between the *actual* projectibility (or lack thereof) of a hypothesis and the goodness of inferring it from present evidence." Proceed to argue that "the principles on which Goodman's theory is built can be made the basis of a theory which will rule against h^{***} and in favor of such of its competitors as 'All emeralds are green'." Note three assumptions of Goodman's theory: the connection between inductive validity and actual inductive practice, the connection between inductive validity and our linguistic habits, and the connection between the "inductive viability" of a new predicate and its relationship with older predicates. Believe the third assumption is "a principal cause of the difficulties his theory has encountered." Also believe "it is so vague that it has very little content." Suggest that the correct relation between old and new predicates is "believed coextensiveness, rather than *de facto* coextensiveness." Develop an account of entrenchment in terms of predicates, times, and persons. Define "P is well-entrenched as an antecedent (consequent) for S at t" as the disjunction of: (1) "P has often been involved as an antecedent (consequent) predicate in projections made prior to t by S" and ($2'$) "there is a family $O_1, \ldots, O_n$ of coextensive predicates such that the total number of projections made prior to t by S in which some O_i has been involved as an antecedent (consequent) is fairly large, and S believes at t that each of the O_i is coextensive with P." Note that many other factors contribute to entrenchment and so their definitions are not totally correct. Begin to outline a theory of projectibility based on this notion of entrenchment. Note that the theory will tell us "whether a person S will at time t take a given hypothesis to be supported by its instances on the evidence available to him," and that it will not tell us which hypotheses it would be rational for S "to regard at t as supported by their instances on evidence available to him." Consider their theory as providing, at most, a concept of relative justification or relative rationality. Emphasize two points about the scope of their theory: viz., the theory is not supposed to provide "correct predictions for *all* persons and *all* times" and it "does not apply to hypotheses which either follow from statements believed at *t* by *S* or have negations which so follow." State definitions for a positive instance for *S* at *t*, a negative instance for *S* at *t*, a hypothesis *H* being supported for *S* at *t*, a hypothesis *H* being violated for *S* at *t*, a hypothesis *H* being exhausted for *S* at *t*, a hypothesis *H* conflicting with a hypothesis *H'* for *S* at *t*, and a hypothesis *H* overriding another hypothesis *H'* for *S* at *t*. For example: a positive instance for *S* at *t* "of a universally quantified conditional hypothesis is any sentence obtained from that hypothesis by replacing the variable (at each occurrence) by an individual constant and dropping the quantifier prefix such that the resulting sentence is believed by *S* at *t* to be true and has an antecedent which is believed by *S* at *t* to be true." Finally define their notions of a projectible and an unprojectible hypothesis for *S* at *t*: e.g., *H* is projectible for *S* at *t* if and only if it is supported, unviolated, and unexhausted for *S* at *t*, and all hypotheses that conflict with *H* for *S* at *t* are unprojectible for *S* at *t*. Point out that, on their theory, *h**** is unprojectible (in their sense) because "All emeralds are green" overrides *h****.

King, John L. "Coextensiveness and Lawlikeness." *Erkenntnis* 14 (1979): 359–363. Argues that Goodman's theory of projectibility cannot distinguish between general statements that we accept as laws and general statements that we accept as accidentally true. Bases his argument on a counterexample to a consequence of Goodman's theory: viz., that if a predicate *B* and a predicate *C* are coextensive, then the general statements "All *A* are *B*" and "All *A* are *C*" must have the same standing as far as being laws. Maintains that the problem is the theory's "extensionalistic commitment to the functional equivalence of predicates which are (or are known, judged, supposed to be) coextensive."

Konyndyk, Jr., Kenneth. "Solving Goodman's Paradox: A Reply To Stemmer." *Philosophical Studies* 37 (1980): 297–305. Maintains that Stemmer (1971, 1975, 1978) does not solve either Hempel or Goodman's paradox, nor does he justify inductive inferences by appealing to evolution. Claims Stemmer does not solve Hempel's paradox because he only states sufficient conditions for a correct and justified inference, and so he does not prevent the paradox from occurring. Notes that Stemmer's two conditions cannot be taken as necessary conditions because they would rule out correct inferences with predicates like "proton." Also notes problems with adding a condition that rules out inferences with the complements of innate generalization classes. Claims Stemmer does not solve Goodman's paradox for two reasons. One: as before, Stemmer only gives sufficient conditions and so he does not prevent the paradox from occurring. Two: Stemmer's solution is based on telling, from observed behavior, that green and not grue is being projected, but it is not clear that we can do this. Points out that Stemmer suggests we might do this by introspecting our own "expectancy feelings" and projecting them to other members of our species, given that the feelings are species specific. Replies that we cannot establish this species specificity experimentally without first ruling out Goodmanian predicates. Considers Stemmer's claim about instinctive behavior normally having survival value. Thinks the only defensible interpretation is that "some, perhaps, most, kinds of instinctive behavior have had or still have some survival value." Considers Stemmer's claim about inductive inferences being reliable. Thinks the best interpretation is that they have helped our species with reproduction, protection, and food. Sees this as justifying inductive inferences as instruments of survival, not of truth. Considers Stemmer's claim that if an inference has survival value, then it is reliable. Interprets the "if-then" in three ways, the third being as "a strong statistical correlation." Contends that discovering this correlation "would involve us in a circle of justification." Considers Stemmer's claim that evolution only justifies generalizations about the past. Argues that this claim either makes these inferences irrelevant to the evolution of a species, or makes them "prey to the sort of paradox he thought he had avoided." Introduces the predicate "groo" (green after 100,000 B.C. or blue before) to produce a counterpart of Goodman's paradox for the past. Views Stemmer's continuity postulate as an *ad hoc* proposal that begs the question.

Kripke, Saul A. *Wittgenstein on Rules and Private Language: An Elementary Exposition.* Cambridge, Mass.: Harvard University Press, 1982. Compares the new riddle with skeptical problems in Wittgenstein's later work—i.e., the private language argument in his *Philosophical Investigations* and the notion of following a mathematical rule in *Remarks on the Foundations of Mathematics*—on pages 20, 58, 62n, 82, 84n, and 98n. Believes that "serious consideration of Goodman's problem, as he formulates it, may prove impossible without consideration of Wittgenstein's." Putnam (1983) briefly compares Goodman's views with those of the later Wittgenstein; cites Kripke. Mulhall (1989) criticizes Kripke's discussion of how you know that you mean green, and not grue, when you use the word 'green.'

Kukla, Andre. "Endogenous Constraints on Inductive Reasoning." *Philosophical Psychology* 5 (1992): 411–425. Claims that a computational theory of learning "must posit the existence of *a priori* constraints on hypothesis selection." Believes the new riddle makes this point because both the green and the grue hypothesis "are maximally confirmed by the data" and yet we systematically prefer the green hypothesis, which means we must "posit non-empirical constraints on our inductive choices." Considers simplicity, minimalist, and finitistic theories "for modelling the dynamic process whereby the *a priori* constraints have their effect." Discusses Goodman's entrenchment solution in the last (fifth) section. Considers whether Goodman's "law of entrenchment" is a psychological theory. Notes that Goodman does not regard his solution as a psychological theory and that he doubts we can psychologically explain how we initially choose projectible predicates. Considers how we might select "entrenched hypotheses" when we already have some entrenched hypotheses. Proposes that "we go through a computational process of assessing the hypotheses for their degree of entrenchment, and we accept the winner." Claims, contrary to Goodman, that there are many ways to distinguish "one hypothesis from another for the purpose of formulating the rules that determine abductive order or relative simplicity." Maintains that we can add the computational proposal to the simplicity or minimalist theory and then "rely on other mechanisms for accepting hypotheses until we are able to confirm and accept hypotheses about the entrenchment of other hypotheses, whereupon entrenchment considerations begin to make their contribution." Argues that we can derive a probabilistic version of the "law of entrenchment" from the simplicity theory, and that the "law of entrenchment" follows from the minimalist theory if we assume "entrenchment causes hypotheses to rise in abductive order."

Kutschera, Franz Von. "Goodman on Induction." *Erkenntnis* 12 (1978): 189–207. Considers Hume's view on justifying inductive inferences and Goodman's descriptive approach to questions about inductive validity. Maintains that he is interested in the logical question of justification and validity, not the empirical or descriptive one. Describes the new riddle and claims it shows the impossibility of distinguishing between projectible and nonprojectible predicates with "logical or empirical criteria." Reviews four well-known responses to the new riddle and the replies to them: viz., that it violates the requirement of total evidence or that it shows we should restrict induction to qualitative or observational predicates, or predicates that result in lawlike sentences.

Presents Goodman's "pragmatical" theory of projectibility with eight definitions. Argues that Goodman's entrenchment approach is "hopeless" because his notion of conflict (between hypotheses) involves a circularity, the notion allows a correct hypothesis to end up unprojectible, and even a narrower definition of conflict (in terms of analytical incompatibility) will not work here; also argues that Goodman's appeal to coextensive predicates is circular, legitimate new scientific terms end up nonprojectible if we go on entrenchment, and there seems no way to measure entrenchment by counting how many times a hypothesis has been accepted. Gives a probabilistic interpretation of induction in terms of de Finetti's theory of subjective probability. Defines exchangeable events and maintains that "all and only predicates expressing exchangeable properties are projectible." Construes principles of inductive inference as statements about conditional belief and introduces probabilistic analogues of singular predictive inference and general predictive inference. Believes these principles are justified because "they are mathematical theorems derived from analytical postulates for the concept of rational subjective probability." Notes that the principles "tell us what we should believe given some *a priori* probability and some observations." Considers how rational these a priori probabilities might be. Maintains that "if we do not know what is true, any coherent guess is as good as another." Claims, therefore, that we cannot justify "probability distributions that mark out some predicates rather than others, for instance 'green' rather than 'grue', as exchangeable in some objective manner." Considers how to explain the fact that "our probability distributions agree to a large extent with regard to what events are exchangeable." Points out that "our more fundamental beliefs are not privately conceived but publicly imparted." Rejects the contention that his probabilistic interpretation substitutes a question about expecting future events for a question about inferring them. Concludes that his interpretation does justify inductive inferences "relative to *a priori* assumptions" and emphasizes that "there are no purely rational or empirical criteria for the correctness of such assumptions." See the reply by Goodman (1978).

Kyburg, Henry E. "Recent Work in Inductive Logic." *American Philosophical Quarterly* 4 (1964): 249–287. A good survey of issues and developments from 1951 through 1964. Discusses Goodman-type predicates on pages 263, 265–266, and 276. Sees the new riddle as a problem in "every attempt to formalize induction"; maintains it "cannot be solved by considering only ostensive predicates" (as does Salmon, 1963); concludes that the problem "has many ramifications that haven't been explored yet, and no solution even to the simple cases has gained anything like universal acceptance." Includes a bibliography with more than four hundred entries.

Kyburg, Jr., Henry E. *Probability and Inductive Logic*. London: The Macmillan Company, 1970. An introductory textbook with chapters on interpretations of probability, demonstrative induction, presuppositions of induction, statistical inference, the hypothetico-deductive method, confirmation theories, and acceptance theories. Includes an extensive bibliography. Discusses "grue" in connection with Salmon (1961) and the criterion of linguistic invariance (pp. 132–133). Presents "grue" as a problem for all inductive and noninductive confirmation theories and almost all formal theories of scientific inference; reviews various attempts to solve the problem (pp. 172–175). Mentions "grue" in connection with Hintikka's system of inductive logic and the languages it has been applied to (pp. 184–185).

Lambert, Karel and Brittan Jr., Gordon G. *An Introduction to the Philosophy of Science*. Englewood Cliffs, N.J.: Prentice-Hall, Inc., 1970. See chapter 4, section 3., "The 'Paradoxes' of Confirmation." Discuss the raven paradox and the grue paradox. Claim it is hard to identify real objections to Goodman's theory of projectibility because entrenchment is not a precise notion. Maintain that Goodman's entrenchment criterion is too weak because it is not a matter of chance that "green" has been projected; it was "clearly more projectible to begin with." Also maintain that Goodman's criterion is too strong because it does not take account of scientific changes from well-entrenched to poorly entrenched predicates, such as the change from "has a weight" to "has a mass" in the seventeenth century. Maintain that "the projectibility of predicates is in large measure a function of the type of thing of which they are predicated." Claim that "grue" is not projectible with respect to emeralds because emeralds are physical objects and can change in definite, caused ways, while grue things can stay grue (presumably through time t) and yet change. View our concepts of change and causality as "not geared to" gruelike predicates. Deny there is a general, theory-independent way to distinguish between projectible and nonprojectible predicates, or to define the notion of a positive instance. Insist both are relative to a theoretical context, and so a predicate may be projectible in one context and not in another. Note that the projectible predicates are not "determined by the primitive vocabulary of the theory." Maintain that if gruelike predicates ever become projectible with respect to emeralds, then either emeralds will have changed from being typical physical objects, or our concept of physical object will have changed.

Laudan, Larry. "Demystifying Underdetermination." In *Scientific Theories,* Minnesota Studies in the Philosophy of Science, Vol. XIV, edited by C. Wade Savage, pp. 267–297. Minneapolis: University of Minnesota Press, 1990. See the section on ampliative underdetermination for a discussion of the new riddle as "a proof that the inductive rules of scientific method underdetermine theory choice in the face of any conceivable evidence." Maintains there is a difference between having the same positive instances and being equally well confirmed. Points out that Goodman himself does not take theory choice to be underdetermined when we take into account the entrenchment of predicates. Emphasizes that the new riddle provides "scant comfort to the relativist's general repudiation of methodology." Views Goodman as examining just one rule of induction, the straight rule, and as trying to show that "there will always be a family of contrary hypotheses between which it will provide no grounds for rational choice." Notes how this differs from trying to show that the rule "will provide support for any and every hypothesis."

Leblanc, Hugues. "A Revised Version of Goodman's Confirmation Paradox." *Philosophical Studies* 14 (1963): 49–51. Restates the new riddle to avoid Carnap's (1947) objection that Goodman's two examples (1946) violate the principle of total evidence. Specifies a formal language meeting two conditions on individual constants and predicates, defines a gruelike predicate for any one-place predicate of the language, notes two theorems of the language, uses the theorems to show that projecting two such predicates will lead to a contradiction by way of conflicting predictions, and then shows how this applies to emeralds and the one place predicate "is green". See also Leblanc (1963b).

Leblanc, Hugues. "That Positive Instances Are No Help." *Journal of Philosophy* 60 (1963b): 453–462. Restates Goodman's paradox to avoid an objection—from Carnap (1947) and Hempel (1960)—that it violates the requirement of total evidence. Argues that, properly stated, the paradox shows four common rules of inductive inference to be self-contradictory: e.g., starting from the same data, a pair of contradictory predictions follow from applying the typical logic handbook rule about concluding that every A examined after time t is a B from some A's have been examined before this time and all of them have proven to be B. See also Leblanc (1963a).

Lewis, David. "New Work for a Theory of Universals." *Australasian Journal of Philosophy* 61 (1983): 343–377. Investigates adding universals to his nominalistic ontology. Examines D. M. Armstrong's theory of universals and discusses how universals help "in connection with such topics as duplication, supervenience, and divergent worlds; a minimal form of materialism; laws and causation; and the content of language and thought." Mentions grue on pages 345 and 349 in discussing two main differences between universals and properties. Says "a universal of grueness would be anathema," but there is no problem with a property of grueness. Distinguishes between natural and unnatural properties; claims an adequate theory of properties will recognize an objective difference in degree between natural and unnatural properties, and that a combined theory of properties and universals would be an adequate theory of properties. Calls a property perfectly natural "if its members are all and only those things that share some one universal." Argues that we need natural properties in order to analyze both lawhood and causation.

Mackie, J.L. "A Defence of Induction." In *Logic and Knowledge,* Volume I of his selected papers, edited by Joan Mackie and Penelope Mackie, pp. 159–177. Oxford: Oxford University Press, 1985. Focuses on induction in the form of extrapolation and inference to a deeper explanation. Describes a game of chance with ten balls in a bag, nine of them black, one white, all equal size, weight, etc. Mixes the balls thoroughly, takes hold of one of them in the bag, and claims that his "information and lack of information together probabilify the judgement 'This ball is black'." Hopes to justify these two forms of inductive reasoning "by showing that in each such inference the conclusion is probabilified by the premises or evidence in accordance with the apparently cogent sort of reasoning illustrated by the example of balls in a bag." Considers whether this approach is undermined by Goodman's new riddle (pp. 166–167) because the probability in question is logical or quasi-logical, and so based "on purely formal relations between the premises and the conclusion." Says that Goodman's grue paradox shows we cannot describe respectable temporal extrapolations "in any purely syntactical way, since rival, unwanted, extrapolations are syntactically on the same footing." Maintains that "syntactical" may be less exacting than "formal." Agrees with the commonsensical view that green things, at different times, resemble each other in a way that grue things, at different times, may not. Concludes that formal principles of probabilification "will take account of the presence or absence of real resemblances rather than the merely syntactical forms." Editors add a marginal note by Mackie: "Goodman's pseudo-problem results from over-attention to language."

Madden, Edward H. "Review of *Fact, Fiction and Forecast* and *The Philosophy of Nature.*" *Philosophy and Phenomenological Research* 16 (1955): 271–273. Spends most of the review discussing the new riddle. Construes it as finding adequate definitions for "lawlike universal statement" and "accidental universal statement." Notes that Goodman is so concerned with the notion of valid projection because he views it as "the root problem not only of confirmation theory but also of dispositions, possibility, real kinds, and (in part) counterfactual inference." Emphasizes the connection between lawlike sentences and counterfactuals, but claims that Goodman's view (lawlike sentences sustain counterfactuals) is not completely right because there is a sense in which an accidental sentence also sustains a counterfactual: viz., by "interpreting the antecedent of the counterfactual as asserting identity."

Martin, R.M. *Toward a Systematic Pragmatics.* Amsterdam: North-Holland Publishing Company, 1959. See the appendix, "On Goodman's Theory of Projectible Predicates," pages 95–103. Attempts to show that "the foundations of Goodman's theory may be formulated within a pragmatical metalanguage similar to those discussed" in the volume. Specifies a syntax and "a pragmatics of acceptance" (and eventually adds a relation of multiple denotation) in order to define actually projected (predicate and sentence), positive instance, negative instance, undetermined case, evidence class, projective class, supported, violated, or exhausted sentence, projection index, better entrenched, much better entrenched, and projectible predicate. Does not claim that "the formal definitions given here mirror adequately or with full correctness Goodman's informal ones."

Martin, Robert M. "It's Not That Easy Being Grue." *Philosophical Quarterly* 40 (1990): 299–315. Presents "a non-empirical argument for the existence of innate ideas" that is "based on Nelson Goodman's invention, the notion of *Grue*." Defines 'grue' as time-indexed because "colour-attributions are not timeless." Entertains the "Paranoid Hypothesis" that only you associate 'green' with the concept green and everyone else associates 'green' with the concept grue. Considers and rejects four attempts to show that no one has the concept grue because it is "not the sort of concept people could reasonably be supposed to have." Argues for innateness by claiming that no one has had a grue concept with a past time *t*, and claiming that the only explanation is "people had an innate predisposition against all these concepts." Notes this is a weak innateness claim in that it is about a disposition to learn one concept instead of another "from experience." Argues that there is no evolutionary explanation for this innate predisposition; regards it as a lucky fortunate coincidence. Comments on Quine and Ullian's (1978) remarks to the contrary. Considers a natural kinds argument against his innate disposition claim: viz., people didn't form those grue concepts (where *t* has passed) because color concepts result from causal interaction with objects and their natural properties, and grue is not a natural property. Criticizes the premise about concepts only coming from interaction with natural properties. Ends by discussing "the diachronic nature of concepts" and emphasizes that "the content of one's present concept is constituted not only by present facts but also by non-present—past or future—facts."

Matthew, Anthony. "Prediction and Predication." *British Journal for the Philosophy of Science* 22 (1971): 171–182. Attempts to show you cannot avoid Goodman's paradox with prediction rules that prohibit the use of "grue" and gruelike predicates. Distinguishes two aspects of the paradox: predicting emeralds will be blue when there is nothing blue in the evidence, and predicting emeralds will not be green when all emeralds in the evidence are green. Notes that while the former prediction entails the latter in Goodman's example, they do not have to. First considers the prediction that an emerald will not be green. Introduces the new predicate "O" to mean green and observed before *t* or not green and not observed before *t*, the evidence that *a* is a green emerald observed before *t*, and the selectively confirmed hypothesis "All emeralds are O." Draws the conclusion that if *b* is an emerald not observed before *t*, then *b* is not green. Draws the same conclusion, without introducing a new predicate, from the selectively confirmed hypothesis "All green things have been observed before *t*." Also maintains that "if the emeralds used in the evidence are described as having the property O, it may still be predicted that those which will be examined after *t* are green." Reaches this prediction from the selectively confirmed hypothesis "All O things have been observed before *t*." Considers next why the more reasonable prediction is that emerald *b* is green. Claims the nongreen prediction is not less reasonable because it comes from a hypothesis with a locational predicate. Produces an example of the paradox (this aspect) without locational predicates, predicting a penguin is flightless from the hypothesis that all penguins are flightless, and predicting it is not flightless from the hypothesis that all flightless birds are birds weighing more than one pound as adults. Considers whether Goodman's entrenchment rules explain why the flightless prediction is more reasonable. Claims these rules do not help because "with predicates that have not been specially invented we have very little idea how relatively well entrenched they are, and yet we have fairly clear intuitions of what predictions are reasonable on the evidence." Maintains that Goodman's rules are inadequate because "entrenchment is an absolute property of a predicate used as an antecedent (or consequent) at a given time." Views the flightless prediction as more reasonable because it comes from a hypothesis in which one predicate is relevant to the other, while the other prediction comes from a hypothesis about the weight of flightless birds and "it is irrelevant to the question asked that the objects used as evidence have the property" of weighing more than a pound as an adult. Criticizes Blackburn's (1969) attempt to solve the paradox in terms of an epistemological asymmetry. Goes on to consider the second aspect of the paradox, the prediction than an emerald will be blue. Makes the prediction in two ways: with a rule of inference and the original evidence, or with some additional evidence. Introduces the rule "that a prediction X can be made from evidence Y, provided that X could be predicted both from a conjunction of Y with some additional evidence Z, and also from a conjunction of Y with the negation of Z." Describes the additional evidence as finding either that an emerald is blue or not blue for at least one green emerald observed before t. Predicts that an emerald is blue from a hypothesis about emeralds being blue, and predicts that an emerald is not blue from a hypothesis about nonblue things being observed before t. Attempts to produce an example of the unreasonable prediction (an object having a property not included in the evidence) without a locational predicate. Uses the negative predicate "is not a sea-bird living in warm water" and evidence about flightless penguins, where at least one of them either lives in warm water or does not. Discusses how the prediction depends on finding a predicate true of all the penguins in the evidence class, but not true of the penguin in the prediction. Maintains that if there is a suitable predicate here, "there is no reason why it should not be non-locational and as well entrenched as one pleases, though quite irrelevant to the prediction." Notes there is a question about whether his treatment of the second aspect (with the additional evidence) results in a paradoxical prediction or a form of Goodman's problem.

Miller, David. "Can Science Do Without Induction?" In *Applications of Inductive Logic,* edited by L. Jonathan Cohen and Mary Hesse, pp. 109–129. Oxford: Oxford University Press, 1980. Presents the main ideas of falsificationism and defends it against "criticisms that falsificationism is ridden with inductive elements." Responds to Goodman's paradox on pages 125–127. Believes his response is "an utterly trivial one." Maintains that "there cannot be any empirical reason for expressing a preference between two hypotheses that are empirically indistinguishable." Claims that the green hypothesis "has not been tested well enough for us to justify a strictly empirical preference (that is, one that does not appeal to other, perhaps more comprehensive, hypotheses) for it over" the grue hypothesis. Claims that if we do not wish to justify a preference now, there is no harm done because "science can quite well accommodate both hypotheses until the year 2001, at which time a simple crucial test will become available." Claims that if we do wish to justify a preference now, "then we must make it possible for ourselves to do so" by accepting "methods that are not strictly empirical." Maintains, in line with the demarcation principle, that "if decisions have to be empirical then we should not allow disputes on which no empirical decision is possible." Believes that Goodman's paradox seems to be a problem "because it is mistakenly thought that it is empirical support that makes a hypothesis eligible for admission into the body of science." Discusses Goodman's paradox again in the comments and replies section, pages 144–146, when he replies to Lehrer's criticism "that if all unfalsified hypotheses are admitted into science then science is unable to offer any guidance about the future." Repeats that we must not admit the empirically indistinguishable green and grue hypotheses "unless we are prepared to delay a decision between these two hypotheses until the year 2001." Considers whether we must choose between two practical proposals, one "in accordance with our present knowledge, and one in accordance with a system currently indistinguishable from it empirically and composed entirely of gruelike hypotheses." Maintains that "there is no need to choose" because "there will be no conflict in guidance they give about what we should do now," and as for how they differ about advice for after 2001, "by then we shall know which of the systems is false."

Miller, Steven J. and Fredericks, Marcel. "Some Comments on the Projectibility of Anthropological Hypotheses: Samoa Briefly Revisited." *Erkenntnis* 30 (1989): 279–299. Introduce two general hypotheses about Samoan culture, one asserting that Margaret Mead's views are correct (with the predicate "Mead-True") and one asserting (with the gruelike predicate "Mead-Free") that Mead's views are correct before 1982 or Derek Freeman's views are correct after 1982. Claim "Mead-True" might be regarded as a positional predicate because it refers to a specific culture at a specific time, but "the methodology of Anthropology is such that its claim is to universal applicability, although applied to a given unique culture." Maintain we must distinguish between the form of a hypothesis and the methodology associated with its confirmation. Claim "Mead-Free" might be regarded as positional and yet it is projectible. Go on to formulate confirmation rules to use "as a means of 'bridging-the-gap' between Anthropological hypotheses and the projectibility issue." Attempt to show "that the notion of confirmation and hence projectibility is different in its qualitative conception." Maintain there is a limited case for epistemological equivalence of "Mead-True" and "Mead-Free." Make the general point that "the issue of projection must be ruled as inappropriate for hypotheses drawn from the social and behavioral 'sciences'."

Moreland, John. "On Projecting Grue," *Philosophy of Science* 43 (1976): 363–377. Argues that the new riddle "can be assimilated to a more general problem, the problem of determining in what ways a sample is random." Discusses the new riddle in terms of confirmation functions and a Carnapian framework. Argues that Jeffrey's (1966) notion of pragmatic projectibility is useless in testing conflicting hypotheses. Introduces a projectibility criterion (for a specific confirmation function) that lets a predicate O be projectible of P's "just in case being O given that an individual is a P is probabilistically independent of being examined." Defines a random sample (for a specific confirmation function) so that it is "random with respect to a particular property when the chance of an individual being in the sample is probabilistically independent of its having the property in question." Relates randomness and projectibility so that, with all and only the individuals in our sample having been examined, the sample of P's will be random with regard to property O for confirmation function c "just in case O is projectible of P's on c." Maintains that each adequate confirmation function will meet a randomness condition of rationality instructing you to choose, for a given sample, a confirmation function that "reflects" your beliefs about the randomness of that sample. Describes a sample of emeralds that is random with regard to 'green' but not 'grue,' and so "one ought to project 'green' of the emeralds in the population and not project 'grue' of them." Also describes a sample where one ought to project 'grue' but not 'green.' Discusses the distinction between being sampled and being examined (generally extensionally equivalent, sometimes not); also how the notion of examination is and is not essential to the new riddle. Considers how to determine the randomness of a sample when you do not know the actual composition of the universe; points to the sampling procedure, the meaning dependence of predicates, and general theoretical and empirical information. Emphasizes that he is taking a subjectivist view of projection and that, on this view, an inductive logic provides "a criterion for rational belief given what one already believes." Claims that Goodman's formulation of the new riddle "mixes questions of induction with questions of abduction"; notes that he is concerned with the grue hypothesis and projecting, not explaining.

Mormann, Thomas. "Natural Predicates and Topological Structures of Conceptual Spaces." *Synthese* 95 (1993): 219–240. A reply to Gärdenfors (1990 and this volume). Section 1: "Introduction." Claims that set theory will not help us distinguish natural/nonnatural predicates. Believes the raven and grue paradoxes demonstrate this. Notes how Gärdenfors distinguishes between natural/nonnatural predicates: viz., natural predicates "can be represented by *convex* subsets of conceptual spaces, whereas non-natural ones like 'grue' and 'bleen' cannot." Will argue that a better criterion can be formulated in terms of topological structures such as connectedness and closedness, and show a connection between the problem of distinguishing natural/nonnatural predicates and the problem of geometric conventionalism. Section 2: "Conceptual Spaces of Colour Language." Considers Gärdenfors's definition of a convex region in connection with the color circle and claims that, on this definition, the only convex region of the circle is the circle itself. Redefines a convex region in terms of points and the shortest line connecting them. Shows how the redefinition does not represent a natural change of color as natural nor complementary colors. Suggests using the notion of pathconnectedness to analyze the notion of a continuous process. Notes that connectedness "can be defined for any topological space whatever, and not just for metrical or linear spaces." Also notes that "even on this elementary level conceptual spaces yield different natural predicates." Introduces saturation of colors and points out how this shows the redefinition of convexity is unstable. Claims that even if we use Gärdenfors's original definition of convexity with a spherical instead of a standard Euclidean metric, "the criterion of connectedness scores better." Section 3: "Closure Structures and Natural Predicates." Considers "some examples of conceptual spaces for which the class of nice subsets is characterized by the topological concept of closure structures": viz., orthoframes for quantum logics, closed and open subsets for refutative and affirmative properties, and closed and nonclosed sets for natural and not-so-natural color predicates. Proves (by displaying the relevant parts of the color cylinder) that "in the colour cylinder the predicates 'grue' and 'bleen' are represented by non-closed sets, whereas 'blue' and 'green' are represented by closed sets." Defines a Goodmanian color cylinder so that, with a natural closure structure, it represents "grue" by a closed subset and "green" by a nonclosed subset. Notes that "the selection of the conceptual space seems to be arbitrary" and so it does not seem to provide a solution to the grue paradox. Argues (in sections 4 and 5) that "the shift from predicates to conceptual spaces is definitively a turn to the better." Section 4: "Structural Conventionalism." Describes geometric conventionalism as the view that "physical space is *metrically amorphous* and may be metrically structured in many different ways, and all these metrical structures have equal rights." Describes structural conventionalism as "the corresponding generalized thesis concerning the structure of conceptual spaces." Endorses Hilary Putnam's criticism of geometric conventionalism. Provides "a formal basis for a similar line of criticism of structural conventionalism, thereby resolving or at least defusing the destructive scepticism spread by Goodmanian and other non-natural predicates." Constructs a common background conceptual space and proves, in terms of set-theoretical isomorphisms, a proposition that "is essentially nothing but the assertion that the pairs (blue, green) and (grue, bleen) are interdefinable." Considers the analogue of this proposition "in the case of conceptual spaces (frames) of possible world semantics." Section 5: "Natural Predicates and Structures of Conceptual Spaces." Reformulates "the thesis that everybody can choose his own conceptual structure (to make his preferred predicates come out as natural)" as a "radical conventionalist thesis": viz., that it is a matter of convention if we choose a structure that represents a predicate as natural or another structure that represents this predicate as nonnatural. Maintains that we fix the reference of the term "natural predicate defined on the common background conceptual space" by coherence and not convention, and that "it involves large parts of scientific (and cultural) background knowledge." Discusses "a coherentist fixing of the concept of projectibility in the case of colour theories." Appeals to the neurobiological theory of color vision "based on the fact that the human eye possesses three different types of visual cells . . . adapted for the colours blue, green, and orange . . . such that every physiological colour is realized by a mixed stimulus of these three cell types." Uses bridge principles to connect this theory with the commonsensical color theories "based on conceptual spaces": e.g., something is seen as blue if and only if it preferably stimulates cells of a certain type. Notes that Goodmanian bridge principles will be "more complicated disjunctive assertions." Argues that "grue" is more complicated than "green" because "according to the neurological theory of colour vision there are no Goodmanian cells." Suggests, however, that "the problem of selecting natural predicates for a given conceptual space generally does not possess a clear-cut solution." Believes that "a kind of approximation process has to take place if we want to fix the term 'natural' with respect to a conceptual space." Maintains that projectibility "is not—so to speak—in the possession of an insulated conceptual space but is specified by the whole of our conceptual apparatus." Suggests a "structural enrichment" approach: viz., the more structure we impose on conceptual spaces, "the better we can distinguish natural from not-so-natural predicates."

Morris, John M. "Some Problems Concerning Projection." *Australasian Journal of Philosophy* 49 (1971): 38–46. Criticizes Goodman's entrenchment account of projectibility. Thinks Goodman uses "projectible" as a normative term (as in legitimately projectible) even though he calls it a dispositional term. Claims that, using Goodman's elimination rules with "All flammables readily unite with oxygen" and "All flammables contain phlogiston," we would reject the oxygen hypothesis as unprojectible in 1800. Maintains that "the practising scientist simply does not adopt or reject a predicate on the basis of the number of times that it has been used in the past: a popularity contest is no criterion of usefulness." Thinks Goodman's account has a problem with new scientific terms because it does not "deal with the epistemological question of the relation between language and the referents of language." Considers defining entrenchment in terms of the number of times a word could have been used; claims this is out of the question because it would be impossible to tell which terms are better entrenched, and because "could have been" introduces "an intolerable circularity into the system." Goes on to argue that Goodman's definition ("in terms of the sheer number of projections of a predicate") turns out to be disastrous. Claims that a computer could print out projections to make a predicate entrenched, and that Goodman's account cannot exclude this because it does not have a criterion for "appropriate usages." Introduces the predicate "swell-entrenched" for a predicate that is well entrenched prior to time *t*, and after that time "invented on the spur of the moment." Considers choosing at *t* between a well-entrenched predicate and one that is not well entrenched because it is swell-entrenched. Claims we are "equally justified in choosing either." Makes the same point with "green" and "grue." Contends that we do appeal to the history of predicates, but assuming "a concept of empirical law." Thinks that Goodman's difficulties are the result of "a thorough-going empiricism."

Mulhall, Stephen. "No Smoke Without Fire: The Meaning of Grue." *Philosophical Quarterly* 39 (1989): 166–189. Argues that two constraints must be satisfied at the same time in order to produce the Goodman paradox, the constraints are incompatible, hence there is no Goodman paradox or new riddle. Views the paradox as requiring two hypotheses that actually conflict and that are equally well supported as a result of applying the relevant principle of induction to parallel evidence statements. Claims 'grue' must be related to our color concepts in order to end up with conflicting hypotheses; claims 'grue' must not be related to our color concepts in order to end up with hypotheses that result from applying the same principle of reasoning—i.e., a principle that makes a universal, nonpositional prediction about emeralds being grue as well as about them being green. Goes on to examine three skeptical problems connected with the Goodman paradox. Maintains that skepticism about natural kinds comes from treating concepts as propositions; that skepticism about translation comes from confusing "the logical possibility of a doubt with an actual doubt"; and that Kripke's (1982) skepticism about translation comes from taking "a third-person perspective upon first-person issues."

Nelson, Alvin F. "Simplicity and the Confirmation Paradoxes." *Southwest Journal of Philosophy* 3 (1972): 99–107. Takes simplicity to be a type of efficiency associated with how a scientist pursues goals at a given time: viz., "maximizing convenience in pursuit of scientific ends." Compares his view of simplicity with the views of Goodman and Popper. Claims his view resolves Hempel's raven paradox and Goodman's grue paradox. Maintains that if a scientist wants to test the hypothesis "All emeralds are green," it would be a waste of time and effort to think about other color properties that can be connected Goodman-style to the property we have observed to date.

Nicod, Jean. *Foundations of Geometry and Induction.* London: Routledge & Kegan Paul, 1930. Contains *Geometry in the Sensible World* and *The Logical Problem of Induction.* The well-known Nicod criterion of confirmation occurs on page 219 in a section entitled "Hypothesis about the Two Relations of a Fact to a Law: Confirmation, Invalidation." Nicod thinks his "hypothesis" describes "the entire influence of particular truths or facts on the probability of universal propositions or laws." The new riddle is regarded as showing, among other things, that Nicod's criterion is not a sufficient condition for the confirmation of simple generalizations of the form "All *F* are *G.*"

Niiniluto, Ilkaa and Tuomela, Raimo. *Theoretical Concepts and Hypothetico-Inductive Inference.* Dordrecht, Holland: D. Reidel Publishing Company, 1973. See chapter 10, "Linguistic Variance in Inductive Logic," section 3, "Goodman's New Riddle of Induction." Discuss the new riddle in terms of advocates (Mr. Green, Mr. Grue) for each hypothesis. Formulate two criteria of adequacy for a solution: the paradox should be stated and solved so that (1) the post A.D. 2000 predictions should be factually different and incompatible, and Mr. Green and Mr. Grue should agree that they are (because their languages are intertranslatable); and (2) there should be no superfluous linguistic asymmetries between the two predicates. Present two solutions, the first based on estimating the degree of regularity of the world with regard to an initial vocabulary (as in Hintikka-type inductive logics). Claim that the probability of the green hypothesis (given the green emeralds) is greater than the probability of the grue hypothesis (given the grue emeralds) if and only if Mr. Green's degree of regularity estimate is less than Mr. Grue's estimate. Support these estimates (Green's less than Grue's) by pointing out that Mr. Green's language is intertranslatable with Mr. Grue's language and so the languages have principles "correlating language with the external world by similar means," especially with regard to the criteria for applying primitive descriptive predicates. Believe that "green" needs one criterion or one set of criteria, while "grue" needs two criteria or two sets, one for color and one for time. Maintain that "our conceptual system should reflect the general regularity and orderliness of the world." Conclude that the difference in criteria (one vs. two) represents a difference in the regularity estimates about the world. Go on to consider satisfying the intertranslatability requirement by adding the same auxiliary predicates to each language, and whether the resulting languages are inductively equivalent (i.e., their regularity estimates are equal) given that Mr. Green's estimate was less than Mr. Grue's in the initial languages. Maintain "this problem is strongly context-dependent." Present a second solution based on how different background assumptions might influence the probabilities of each hypothesis, even with intertranslatable languages and the same regularity estimates: e.g., the probability of the green hypothesis, given the emerald evidence and a background theory, might be greater than the probability of the grue hypothesis, given the emerald evidence and the same background theory. Introduce a background theory specifying that the objective criterion for "green" always stays the same, while the criterion for "grue" changes at A.D. 2000. State a first-order consequence of this theory: viz., a conjunction of universal generalizations about green, not green, or grue emeralds, examined or not before A.D. 2000, and the objective criterion for the color in question being the same or not being the same as prior to A.D. 2000. Present this situation in a 4 × 4 cross-classification table and note that the grue hypothesis makes one more cell empty than the green hypothesis, and so there is a probability difference favoring the green hypothesis here. View both solutions as depending on "the differences in the objective application criteria of the disputed predicates." Also see Hintikka (1970).

O'Connor, John. "Differential Properties and Goodman's Riddle." *Analysis* 28 (1967): 59. A criticism of Slote (1967). Argues that Slote does not solve the new riddle because he does not show green is a differential property and grue is not. Slote does not rule out defining "green" in terms of "grue," "bleen," and a temporal expression, and thereby making "green" into a nondifferential predicate and "grue" into a differential one. See the reply by Slote (1968).

Owens, David. "Disjunctive Laws?" *Analysis* 49 (1989): 197–202. Does not mention the new riddle but relevant because the grue hypothesis is a generalization with a disjunctive consequent. Does mention Goodman as claiming that laws support counterfactuals and predictions about unexamined instances or cases. Argues that some disjunctive generalizations follow from genuine laws, have these two features, and yet are not laws: e.g., anything that is either a rigid size *S* cube or appears yellow will either pass through a size *S* square hole or reflect wavelength *W* light. Claims this fails to be a law because it cannot be confirmed by its instances and cannot explain their occurrence. Argues the confirmation point with a relevance principle (for generalizations of the form 'All *A*s are *B*s'): "if we observe an event which satisfies both *A* and *B*, we are entitled to infer that other events which satisfy *A* will also satisfy *B*." Views confirmation as (more or less) the converse of explanation, thus considers it no surprise that the cube generalization does not explain "the occurrence of an event which instantiates its consequent." Says these disjunctive properties are unnatural properties because they do not refer to a natural kind. Adds disjunctive properties are not unnatural simply because they are disjunctive, for any property can be "represented as a disjunction of less inclusive properties." The problem here is disjoining "disparate properties" to produce "an ontological mongrel that cannot enter into laws of nature."

Pap, Arthur. *"Fact, Fiction and Forecast." The Review of Metaphysics* 9 (1955): 285–299. Long review by a well-known philosopher of science. Discusses dispositions, possibility, and the new riddle. Argues that Carnap (1947) was correct in his reply to the new riddle. Maintains that Goodman confuses the logical equivalence of terms with the analysis of terms, and thus is wrong about no predicate being purely qualitative. See the reply by Sweigart and Stewart (1959).

Plantinga, Alvin. *Warrant and Proper Function.* Oxford: Oxford University Press, 1993. See chapter 7, "Induction," pages 122–136. Discusses Hume's old riddle of induction and Goodman's new riddle. Sees the new riddle as: "what makes a property projectible?" Sees a projection as involving a reference property (e.g., *being an emerald*) and a projected property (e.g., *being green*). Considers three kinds of cases: "projecting such properties as *being observed*, projecting such properties as *being grue*, and having a disjunctive reference property where one of the disjuncts is had by all members of the sample class." Argues against Goodman's entrenchment solution by supposing a nuclear malady will make its victims project Goodmanized predicates on a regular basis for generations; claims that no matter how often the victims project these predicates, the predicates do not designate projectible properties. Argues against the view that disjunctive properties are unprojectible. Notes that any inductive inference with a universal conclusion is equivalent to a projection with a disjunctive reference property having all the evidence under its first disjunct, but that it is not a proper projection when the disjuncts are relevantly different. Points out that it is logically impossible to have a counterexample to the conclusion in the sample class in cases of projecting properties like *being observed:* i.e., from "all observed emeralds have been observed" to "probably all emeralds have been observed." Also points out that it is impossible now to have a green counterexample to the conclusion in the sample class in cases of projecting the property *being grue.* Also claims it is impossible to have a counterexample (having P) to the conclusion "everything that has C or D has P" when all members of the sample have C. Characterizes a projection as limited at time t if it is possible at t for there to be a counterexample to the conclusion but impossible for it to be in the sample class at t, and a projection as limited with respect to a property P at t as the same thing except the counterexample has property P. Does not believe the problem with the new riddle is one of limited properties because "nearly every projection is limited with respect to some property." Claims in particular that it does not follow the sample is biased because the projection is limited, while it does follow that we do not know the sample is not biased—which is true of many perfectly fine projections. Also does not believe the problem here is being limited with regard to the projected property because almost the same problem occurs in connection with any induction: viz., there will be possible kinds of counterexamples to the conclusion that can't be in the sample class. Maintains that "the crucial question is this: which properties are the ones a properly functioning adult human being in our circumstances will in fact project?" Believes that grue reasoning is defective because "properly functioning human beings (in your circumstances) would never in fact reason in that way." Claims this is because of "our design plan." Believes grue projections are literally signs of dysfunction and pathology. Points out that grue reasoning is not defective because there is another inductive inference whose conclusion is inconsistent with it—this holds for nearly any inductive inference. Takes grue emeralds to be weak evidence that all emeralds are grue, and views degree of projectibility or strength of evidence as determined by "our design plan." Considers his design plan solution to be normative in the same proper function sense as the "ought" in "an adult resting human heart ought to beat 40–80 times per minute." Thinks the design plan solution extends to Quine's radical translation issues and Kripke's Wittgensteinian rule-following issues.

Pollock, John L. "The Logic of Projectibility." *Philosophy of Science* 39 (1972): 302–314. Regards a conditional as projectible "if positive instances of it confirm its universal generalization." Points out three types of nonprojectible conditionals: most conditionals with disjunctive antecedents, conditionals with Goodmanesque predicates, and some conditionals with noncontrived predicates like "observed." Investigates "what sorts of logical operations, when applied to projectible conditionals, yield new projectible conditionals." Claims to find "that projectible conditionals are more the exception than the rule." Deals with a monadic predicate calculus and assumes that if a sentence X confirms a sentence Y and Y entails sentence Z, then X confirms Z; and that if X confirms Y and Y confirms Z, then X confirms the conjunction of Y and Z. Uses a Nicod criterion definition of positive instance, requires that confirming a projectible conditional with positive instances be direct confirmation, and defines direct confirmation as X confirms Y when this can only be defeated by a certain conjunction of conditionals in cases where any sentence Z entails X and Z does not confirm Y. Proves two equivalence principles, defines "a kind of consistency condition" requiring no automatically defeated positive instances of a conditional. Proves that right projectibility (i.e., the consistency condition holds) is almost closed under conjunction, that projectibility is not closed under contraposition, and that right projectibility "is not closed under either disjunction, negation, or the formation of conditionals." Also shows the following principles fail: if Q is projectible with respect to P, then Q is projectible with respect to $(P \& R)$; if Q is projectible with respect to P, then (if R, then Q) is projectible with respect to Q; and if Q is projectible with respect to P and R is projectible with respect to P, then (if Q, then R) is projectible with respect to P. Summarizes his results about closure conditions for right projectibility as "Nothing works." Notes that closure under conjunction has "little practical consequence" because it "in no way increases the class of sentences that can be established inductively beyond what we have using those basic projectible conditionals with which we began." Considers how to weaken basic projectible conditionals so that their universal generalizations are not mostly false. Discusses strengthening the antecedent by forming conjunctions and conjectures that if R is projectible with respect to P and R is projectible with respect to Q, then R is projectible with respect to $(P \& Q)$. Proves that if this conjecture is true, then "If Q is projectible with respect to P, then Q is projectible with respect to not P" is false. Develops a second conjecture that explains why the first conjecture is true and also explains "just how negations can enter into projectible conditionals." Claims that "whatever is projectible with respect to one predicate is projectible with respect to any other predicate which enters into basic projectible conditionals," which implies that we can begin with a class of basic predicates in order to construct basic projectible conditionals, and any conditional with both predicates from this class will be a basic conditional. Argues that "there is a clear distinction between projectibility and lawlikeness" in order to rebut the claim that projectibility is always relative. Maintains "that if a predicate A is projectible with respect to one predicate B, then it is projectible with respect to any other predicate C with respect to which anything is projectible." Permits conjoining basic predicates in order to construct the antecedents or consequents of projectible conditionals. Permits negations of basic predicates to occur in the antecedent only when the consequent is a conjunction of unnegated basic predicates; and when the consequent is a consequent of unnegated basic predicates, the antecedent can be a conjunction of both basic predicates and negations of basic predicates. Characterizes type I projectible conditionals as conditionals with antecedents that are conjunctions of basic predicates and negations of basic predicates, and with consequents that are conjunctions of basic predicates. Characterizes type II projectible conditionals as (essentially) conditionals with negations in their consequents but not in their antecedents. Argues that disjunctions cannot be allowed to occur in either antecedents or consequents of projectible conditionals. Formulates the second conjecture as: there is a class of basic predicates such that for all P and for all Q, Q is projectible with respect to P if and only if P is equivalent to the antecedent and Q is equivalent to the consequent of either a type I or type II projectible conditional. Deals inductively with nonprojectible conditionals (e.g., "All nonblack things are nonravens") in terms of indirect or derivative confirmation, and calls such conditionals pseudo-projectible conditionals because they "can be confirmed inductively although not necessarily by observing P's which are Q's." Proves that "every quantifier-free conditional in our language is pseudo-projectible." Points out that "every simple universal sentence is amenable to at least indirect inductive confirmation," and that "every sentence of our language which cannot be verified directly is subject to at least indirect inductive confirmation." Emphasizes that "it is only the exceptional hypothesis that can be confirmed simply by observing positive instances of it." Notes that the positive results (in connection with the two conjectures) have been demonstrated just for a monadic predicate calculus with basic predicates as the atomic predicates. Believes that "in languages of arbitrary complexity it will remain true that every sentence is subject to at least indirect inductive confirmation," even the sentence "All emeralds are grue."

Pollock, John L. *Knowledge and Justification.* Princeton, N.J.: Princeton University Press, 1974. See chapter 8, "Induction," section 5, "A Theory of Projectibility," and section 6, "Projectibility and Induction." Believes that a version of the Nicod principle is the correct principle of induction. Regards the fact that some conditionals are not projectible as "the most serious difficulty for the Nicod principle." Notes that Goodman has cited three classes of nonprojectible conditionals: conditionals with disjunctive antecedents, conditionals with "Goodmanesque" predicates, and certain conditionals with predicates like "has been observed." Maintains that "induction receives its validity from the fact that principles of induction are built into the justification conditions of our concepts." Sees no reason why they should be built into the conditions for all concepts, and so believes it is possible "to have concepts which cannot be handled inductively, and these are precisely the ones that generate nonprojectible conditionals." Attempts to show that "*most* conditionals fail to be projectible." Maintains that most (perhaps all) conditionals can be confirmed, but only some can be confirmed directly via the Nicod principle—the projectible conditionals, which "receive their projectibility directly from the justification conditions of certain fundamental concepts into which the Nicod principle is built." Divides the theory of projectibility into basic and nonbasic projectible conditionals. Asks where "the basic projectible conditionals come from," which logical operations produce new projectible conditionals from old ones (i.e., the logic of projectibility), and how nonprojectible conditionals (built from projectible ones) can be confirmed. Defines "*B* is projectible with respect to *A*" so that projectible conditionals are "elementarily confirmed by evidence containing their positive instances just in case that evidence directly confirms them." Does this by taking into account two kinds of defeaters. Examines closure conditions for projectibility as in Pollock (1972): notes two equivalence principles, proves that "projectibility is closed under the conjunction of consequents," that "projectibility is not closed under contraposition," that "projectibility is not closed under either the disjunction or the negation of consequents," and that "projectibility is not closed under the formation of conditionals in the consequent." Concludes that conjunction is "the only truth function we have found the consequents to be closed under" and that "closure under conjunction is of little practical importance" because it does not increase "the class of propositions that can be established inductively beyond what we have using those basic projectible conditionals with which we begin." Believes we must weaken basic conditionals in order to get useful projectible conditionals, and that we should try strengthening the antecedent. Considers strengthening the antecedent by forming conjunctions: i.e., conjectures that if C is projectible with respect to A and C is projectible with respect to B, then C is projectible with respect to the conjunction of A and B. Proves it is false that if B is projectible with respect to A, then B is projectible with respect to not A. Points out that "whatever is projectible with respect to one predicate is projectible with respect to any other predicate which enters into basic projectible conditionals." Takes this to mean that it is a class of projectible predicates which are basic, not the conditionals themselves. Calls these predicates the "class II of predicates" and claims that "we can put negations of members of II into both the antecedents and consequents" of projectible conditionals. Makes the following "all-encompassing conjecture": there is a class II of predicates such that, for all A and B, B is projectible with respect to A if and only if A and B are "each equivalent to conjunctions of members of II and negations of members of II." Discusses how to deal "inductively with nonprojectible conditionals" such as "All pulsars are either neutron stars or white dwarfs," which can be confirmed indirectly by confirming "All pulsars which are not neutron stars are white dwarfs." Defines "B is pseudoprojectible with respect to A" and characterizes pseudoprojectible conditionals as "those that can be confirmed inductively, although not necessarily by observing A's which are B's." Proves, for a monadic predicate calculus with atomic predicates from class II, that if A and B are "any quantifier-free formulas of our language which contain no individual constants," then B is pseudoprojectible with respect to A. Notes two consequences: viz.," every simple universal sentence is amenable to at least indirect inductive confirmation, and *"every* sentence of our language which cannot be verified directly is subject to at least indirect inductive confirmation." Emphasizes that basic projectible conditionals "are constructed out of a set of *projectible predicates* each of which can occupy any place in a projectible conditional that can be occupied by any other." Asks "by virtue of what does a predicate come to be projectible?" Answers that "it is built into the justification conditions of a predicate whether or not it is projectible, and hence is part of its meaning." Notes that "grue" is not projectible even though it is defined in terms of two projectible predicates, "green" and "blue." Maintains that "some modes of definition lead from projectible predicates to projectible predicates, and others do not." Says the simple reason Goodmanesque predicates are not projectible is "that their definitions do not normally force projectibility into the justification conditions of the predicates so defined." Concludes that "there are no principles of induction applicable to all concepts" and that the Nicod principle "certainly does not have the status of a general principle applicable to all concepts." See Pollock (1972), (1984), (1990), and (this volume).

Pollock, John L. "A Solution to the Problem of Induction." *Noûs* 18 (1984): 423–461. Maintains that "precise principles of induction can be derived from (and hence justified on the basis of) more basic epistemic principles." Argues that statistical induction is more fundamental than enumerative induction. Points out that "inductive reasoning is restricted to *projectible* properties." Says that *"A is projectible with respect to B* iff observation of a sample of B's all of which are A's gives us a prima facie reason for believing that any B would be an A, and this prima facie reason would not be defeated by learning that there are non-A's." Shows that projectibility is closed under conjunction but not disjunction. Emphasizes that "the precise objective arguments we can give regarding projectibility show that there is nothing fuzzy or illegitimate about the concept." Admits that the concept needs to be analyzed, and notes that he does not endorse Goodman's "ephemeral" entrenchment analysis. Derives and justifies (in detail, pp. 425–453) principles of statistical induction. Constructs "the statistical induction argument" as his "reconstruction of the reasoning underlying statistical induction." Uses "various computational principles governing nomic probability," his theory of direct inference from indefinite to definite probabilities, and a generalized acceptance rule. States direct inference rules that are restricted to projectible properties. Wonders why there should be projectibility constraints in direct inference as well as induction. Claims that "the projectibility constraint in direct inference is more fundamental than the projectibility constraint in induction, the latter being derived in part from the former." Points out that we need a projectibility constraint in a probabilistic acceptance rule (his $A1$) in order to avoid generalized versions of Lehrer's racehorse paradox. Notes that the constraint stops us from using the rule with aribtrary disjunctions. Illustrates why we need a projectibility constraint in the acceptance rule for statistical induction (his $A2$). States the statistical induction argument in two stages, the first using his theory of nonclassical direct inference and the second using his generalized acceptance rule (pp. 448–450). Believes this argument "makes precise the way in which observation of the relative frequency of A's in our sample justifies us in thinking that prob (Ax/Bx) is approximately the same as that relative frequency." Section 2.6 is entitled "Projectibility." Claims that "we now have a partial explanation for the restriction to projectibility in induction": viz., two parts of the statistical induction argument (direct inference, acceptance rules) "are restricted to projectible properties." Takes this as showing that projectibility is connected "with induction only derivatively." Observes that "the requirement that $-A$ be projectible with respect to B marks an important difference between statistical induction and enumerative induction." Does not have (at present) an explanation for projectibility restrictions in his acceptance rules. Goes on to discuss enumerative induction. Shows that "although enumerative induction is not just a special case of statistical induction, principles of enumerative induction can nevertheless be derived from our account of statistical induction." States two principles that connect nomic probability, nomic generalizations, and physical necessity. Defends the use of these principles in the enumerative induction argument. Comments that "the enumerative induction argument proceeds by adding a third stage to the statistical induction argument." Concludes by discussing the new riddle. Sees it as "a more serious problem for statistical induction than for enumerative induction" because "when we turn to statistical induction, we find that there are serious practical problems regarding its employment." Acknowledges that his theory of nomic probability does not provide a theory of projectibility. Considers this "the major lacuna of the theory in its present form." Emphasizes "just what a difficult problem it is to formulate a theory of projectibility." Claims that the account in Pollock (1974) is wrong because "it overlooks the 'logic' of projectibility." Maintains that only logically simple concepts have justification conditions that "are constitutive of them" and so Pollock (1974) could only be correct for logically simple concepts. Emphasizes that "an adequate theory of projectibility must determine what closure conditions there are and explain them." See Pollock (1990) and this volume.

Pollock, John L. *Nomic Probability and the Foundations of Induction.* Oxford: Oxford

University Press, 1990. Uses material from Pollock (1984). See chapter 3, "Acceptance Rules," section 2.3, "Projectibility," pages 81–87. Considers how to restrict the principle of statistical syllogism: viz, that if an individual *c* is a *B*, and the probability of an individual being *A*, given it is *B*, is greater than or equal to *r*, then this is a prima facie reason for concluding individual *c* is an *A*. Notes problems created by the behavior of disjunctions in probabilities. Concludes that *B* must be projectible with respect to *A* in the statistical syllogism principle. Points out that projectibility is not closed under disjunction, while it is closed under conjunction. For example: it does not hold that if *A* and *B* are projectible with respect to *C*, then (*A* or *B*) is also projectible with respect to *C*; while it does hold that if *A* is projectible with respect to both *B* and *C*, then *A* is also projectible with respect to (*B* and *C*). Notes that projectibility is also not closed under negation. Admits he does not have an account of projectibility, but believes the "conclusions about closure conditions provide a partial account." Adds that "similar considerations establish that it is not closed under the formation of conditionals or biconditionals." Is not clear about how projectibility "behaves with quantifiers." Discusses whether negations of simple projectible properties are projectible. For example: "red" and "nonred" are projectible with respect to "robin." Conjectures that there is a class of logically simple properties and that if *A* and *B* are conjunctions of members of this class and negations of members of this class, then *A* is projectible with respect to *B*. Also see chapter 4, "Direct Inference and Definite Probabilities," section 2.4, "Projectibility," pages 123–126. Considers the rule of classical direct inference and notes difficulties "reminiscent of the behavior of disjunctions in connection with acceptance rules," which suggests that we need "a restriction requiring that the consequent property in direct inference be projectible with respect to the reference property." Illustrates the effect of this projectibility constraint on the consequent property by discussing a case in which it seems we are making a direct inference with respect to a disjunctive consequent property and yet this inference actually "is parasitic on the direct inferences regarding the projectible disjuncts." Admits that it might seem puzzling to have a projectibility constraint with direct inferences, but says this constraint derives from the constraint in connection with the acceptance rule (his *A*3, which has the statistical syllogism rule as one of its consequences). Also see chapter 6, "Recapitulation," section 3, "Prospects: Other Forms of Induction," section 3.2, "Curve Fitting," pages 193–195 and section 4, "The Problem of Projectibility." Believes you can't solve the curve-fitting problem by "denying that the competing generalizations are all projectible." Also believes that "we take each curve to be confirmed only when we have acquired data ruling out all the simpler curves." Suggests explaining this "by supposing that the generalizations represented by the curves are not projectible *simpliciter*, but are only projectible with respect to the additional assumption that no simpler competing generalization is true." Is bothered by how this imposes "a very rich *a priori* structure on projectibility." Notes, in section 4, that projectibility "plays a pervasive role" in his theory of nomic probability. Believes his theory is incomplete without "an analysis of projectibility." Has "none to offer." Stresses that "most properties are unprojectible." Also that "projectibility has a rich logical structure." Discusses his "conceptual role" solution from Pollock (1974). Claims that "it overlooks the 'logic' of projectibility" and it could only be correct for logically simple concepts. Discusses how projectibility "may have an even more fundamental role to play than in acceptance rules" because "it appears to play a general role in prima facie reasons." Also see chapter 11, "Advanced Topics: Induction," section 1, "Projectibility," pages 296–303. Points out that he needs to show that "inductive projectibility is the same things as projectibility." Argues that "inductive projectibility has the same closure properties as those defended for projectibility in Chapter 3." Defines "concept *B* is inductively projectible with respect to concept *A*" and argues that inductive projectibility is closed under conjunction, but not closed under disjunction or negation. For example: it holds that if *A* and *B* are inductively projectible with respect to *C,* then the conjunction (*A* and *B*) is also inductively projectible with respect to *C;* it does not hold that if *A* and *B* are inductively projectible with respect to *C,* then the disjunction (*A* or *B*) is also inductively projectible with respect to *C.* Points out that "if we were allowed to make free use of disjunctions in induction then every sample would give us prima facie reasons for mutually inconsistent generalizations, with the result that we would not be justified in believing either of the generalizations on the basis of the sample." In sum: "induction could never give us an undefeated reason for believing a generalization." Provides a general argument to show this. Discusses how we can indirectly confirm generalizations that involve disjunctions of inductively projectible concepts—e.g., all animals with B-endorphins in their blood have either a liver or a kidney—"by making use of entailments between nomic generalizations." Points out that both projectibility and inductive projectibility are both closed under conjunction, are both not closed under disjunction, negation, and other simple logical operations; also that the principles of induction are derived from the statistical syllogism. Concludes "projectibility and inductive projectibility are one and the same thing." Emphasizes that "there is nothing fuzzy or illegitimate about the concept" of projectibility. Does not endorse Goodman's entrenchment analysis of projectibility. Ends by noting that "although the enumerative induction argument imposes the expected projectibility constraint on enumerative induction, the statistical induction argument imposes an additional projectibility constraint on statistical induction." Namely: −*A* must be projectible with respect to *B* in a statistical induction but not an enumerative induction. See Pollock (this volume) for a survey of his views on projectibility constraints.

Popper, Karl R. *Conjectures and Refutations: The Growth of Scientific Knowledge.* Originally published by Basic Books, New York, 1962. Harper Torchbook edition 1968 (Harper & Row, New York). See chapter 11, "The Demarcation Between Science and Metaphysics," section 6, "Probability and Induction," page 284. Describes a "paradox of inductive confirmation" formulated by Joseph Agassi. Introduces an Agassi-predicate as any factual predicate "so chosen as to hold for all individuals (events or perhaps things) occurring in the evidence at our disposal; but not for the majority of others." Gives as an example the predicate "*A*(*x*)" defined as "*x* has occurred (or has been observed) before 1st January 1965." Claims that, on Carnap's theory of confirmation, "with growing evidence, the degree of confirmation of '*A*(*a*)' must become indistinguishable from 1 for any individual *a* in the world (present, past, or future)." Claims the same thing "holds for the (qualified or unqualified) instance confirmation of the universal law, '(*x*)*A*(*x*)'—a law stating that all events in the world (present, past, or future) occur before 1965." Notes how this makes 1965 "an upper bound for the duration of the world," and yet this sort of highly confirmed universal law obviously will not appear in cosmology books. Adds in footnote 2a that Goodman has informed him that "he has anticipated Dr. Agassi in the discovery of this paradox" and Agassi-predicates. This chapter also appears in *The Philosophy of Rudolf Carnap* (1965, Open Court) edited by Paul Schilpp.

Popper, Karl R. *The Logic of Scientific Discovery.* New York: Harper & Row, 1965. English translation of *Logik der Forschung* (1934); first published in 1959 by Basic Books, New York, and Hutchinson & Co., London. Harper edition contains revisions. Discusses representing theories with curves in section 39, "The Dimension of a Set of Curves," in chapter VI, "Degrees of Testability." Compares a circle-hypothesis and a parabola-hypothesis by taking 'circle' and 'parabola' to each denote a set of curves, each set having the dimension d if d points are necessary and sufficient for characterizing one particular curve from the set of curves. Represents this algebraically in terms of "the number of *parameters* whose values we may freely choose." Considers this "characteristic for the degree of falsifiability (or testability) of that theory." Discusses the curve fitting problem in chapter VII, "Simplicity." Notes how the epistemological concept of simplicity plays an important role in inductive logic because "through a finite number of points we can always draw an unlimited number of curves of the most diverse form." Also notes the usual answer: choose the simplest curve. Equates simplicity with degree of falsifiability or testability: one theory (curve) is simpler than another if it is more testable, and it is more testable if it has a lower dimension (fewer parameters). Also see appendix i for an attempt to define the dimension of a theory "so as to make it agree with the dimension of the set of curves which results if the field of application of the theory is represented by a graph paper." In the "New Appendices," see appendix viii, "Content, Simplicity, and Dimension," for an attempt to show that "for a sufficiently large finite universe, the theory with the greater number of parameters will always be more probable (in the classical sense) than the theory with the smaller number of parameters." Also argues that Jeffreys's simplicity postulate (1921) "must contradict every adequate axiom system for probability."

Poundstone, William. *Labyrinths of Reason: Paradox, Puzzles, and the Frailty of Knowledge.* New York: Anchor Press, Doubleday, 1988. A popular book (in the Martin Gardner–Isaac Asimov genre) covering recent paradoxes that "deserve a place in the mental bestiary of any broadly educated person." Chapter 3, "Categories, The Grue-Bleen Paradox," discusses the new riddle as a challenge to "our thinking about categories"; claims that "to resolve the paradox, even partially, you must find a way in which the situation isn't symmetrical"; maintains that the situation is not symmetrical when it comes to learning these color words. Thinks scientists "must be wary of nonprojectible terms" and wonders if "unseen quarks may be something like the unseen blue of twenty-first-century grue emeralds."

Priest, Graham. "Gruesome Simplicity." *Philosophy of Science* 43 (1976): 432–437. Discusses the curve-fitting problem for a set of observed corresponding values of two related quantities. Notes the standard solution of choosing the simplest curve that fits the observed values, and how simplicity is often taken to be the number of parameters in equations defining a family of curves. Argues that, for a usual form of equation, the family will vary under certain natural transformations; that is, "which prediction is best depends not on the situation but on how you describe it." Presents examples to show that "equivalent descriptions do not give the same answers." Describes predicting the momentum of a particle from its velocity, and then from a correlation between its velocity and kinetic energy, both based on the same data set; concludes that the best predictions depend on what you decide to correlate velocity with here. Goes on to show how this example generalizes, then how to obtain it via an inverse function and correlating a quantity with the dependent variable. Claims simplicity will not help us in these situations because "if f is the curve from the simplest family which fits data S and if O is virtually any transformation of the cartesian plane into itself, then the image of f under O will not in general be the curve from the simplest family which fits the image of S under O." Describes a curve-plotting version of the grue paradox in terms of the frequency of emitted light rays. Maintains that it is a special case of the general problem here, and so it cannot be solved "along phenomenological lines" or by appealing to whether "grue" can be learned. Does not attempt to resolve the general problem. Suggests the issue involves quantities that have "theoretical significance for us," but notes we cannot identify those quantities as the simpler ones because simplicity seems to be nothing more than familiarity.

Putnam, Hilary. "'Degree of Confirmation' and Inductive Logic." In *The Philosophy of Rudolf Carnap*, edited by Paul Arthur Schilpp. pp. 761–783. LaSalle, Ill.: Open Court Publishing Company, 1963. Attempts to prove that there is no adequate definition of degree of confirmation, the focal notion of Carnap's system of inductive logic. Argues that his proof does not present a difficulty for all formalized systems of inductive logic. Describes one of these, inductive method M, which is based on rules of acceptance that depend on the hypotheses actually proposed and the order they have been proposed. Method M has a corrigibility feature in that it abandons a hypothesis if it is inconsistent with the data. Method M also has a tenacity feature for hypotheses that have been accepted: they are not subsequently rejected unless they become inconsistent with the data. Considers (section VII) how method M and Kemeny's (1953) method deal with the grue and green hypotheses. Notes that both hypotheses are consistent with the data, the grue hypothesis is not as simple as the green hypothesis, and if a language does not have the word "grue," then the hypothesis "all emeralds are green prior to time t; and blue subsequently" is less simple on a symbol count criterion of simplicity. Considers the three possibilities for method M: first the green hypothesis is accepted and then the grue hypothesis is proposed, first the grue hypothesis is proposed (and accepted) and then the green hypothesis is proposed, or both hypotheses are proposed at the same time. Thinks method M is defective with regard to this last possibility because it will not accept either hypothesis before time t. Thinks Kemeny's method is better than method M because it allows us to accept the green hypothesis before t even if the grue hypothesis has been proposed first or at the same time. Points out that Kemeny's method "places a premium on simplicity, as M does not." Suggests that Goodman's entrenchment order might be regarded as one of Kemeny's simplicity orders. Points out, however, that it might be desirable to keep the two measures distinct if simplicity is a formal characteristic and entrenchment a factual one, and to order hypotheses with a weighted combination of simplicity and entrenchment.

Putnam, Hilary. "On Properties." In *Mathematics, Matter and Method, Philosophical Papers,* Volume I, pp. 305–322. Cambridge: Cambridge University Press, 1975. First published in 1970 in N. Rescher et al. (eds.), *Essays in Honor of Carl G. Hempel* (Dordrecht, Holland: D. Reidel). Examines criteria for the identity of properties and considers whether properties are dispensable. Makes the following parenthetic remark about Goodman's solution to the new riddle: "Goodman's solution is, in effect, to say that a term is projectible if we do in fact project it sufficiently often. This leaves the whole problem of why we project some terms to begin with and not others up to psychology. I am inclined to believe that this, far from being a defect in Goodman's approach, is its chief virtue. It is hard to see . . . how this question could be anything but a question for psychology. But anyone who feels that there is *some further* philosophical work to be done here is welcome to do it; my feeling is that what we have here is not so much an unsolved philosophical problem as an undefined one."

Putnam, Hilary. "Foreword to the Fourth Edition." In *Fact, Fiction and Forecast,* Fourth Edition, by Nelson Goodman, pp. vii–xvi. Cambridge, Mass.: Harvard University Press, 1983. Maintains that the grue puzzle does not support positive views (e.g., Fodor or Chomsky) about innate ideas. Notes a similarity between Goodman's views and those of the later Wittgenstein with regard to practices and standards. Sees Goodman as proving that "inductive logic isn't formal in the sense that deductive logic is." Argues against some attempts to solve Goodman's problem: viz., excluding all disjunctive predicates, designating (as Carnap does) certain predicates as qualitative and primitive, and restricting induction to ostensively defined predicates (Salmon, 1974). Views the ostensive predicate solution as excluding nonobservational predicates. Argues that it is unmotivated because "grue" can be ostensively defined with a measuring instrument and so will count as ostensive unless "we rule out mechanical aids to observation altogether." Notes that some projectible predicates ("is an S-shaped bacillus") would not count as observational unless we allow measuring instruments such as microscopes. Also argues that the ostensive predicate solution is too severe because it does not have a mechanism (and blocks Goodman's overhypothesis mechanism) for transferring "projectibility from projectible observation predicates to nonobservation predicates." Discusses connections between Goodman's entrenchment solution and his metaphilosophy. Emphasizes Goodman's view on pluralism, his pragmatic approach to formalism, and his interest in construction as opposed to the defense of theses.

Putnam, Hilary. *Renewing Philosophy.* Cambridge, Mass.: Harvard University Press, 1992. See chapter 1, "The Project of Artificial Intelligence," the section entitled "Induction and Artificial Intelligence." Critically examines the attempt to simulate intelligent human abilities such as the ability to make inductive inferences. Discusses the "so-called bootstrapping methods—that is, methods which attribute a great deal to background knowledge." Thinks they emphasize background knowledge primarily because of the problem of conflicting inductions. Uses a Goodman example to illustrate the problem: after observing that no one who enters Emerson Hall speaks the Eskimo language Inuit, it would be wrong to infer that no one who enters Emerson Hall speaks Inuit. Presents Goodman's explanation of what is wrong with this inference: viz., the Emerson Hall generalization conflicts with "the 'better entrenched' inductively supported law that people do not lose their ability to speak a language upon entering a new place," where "conflict" means one of the generalizations will be shown to be false if an Inuit speaker enters Emerson Hall. Considers whether this entrenchment information is part of our background knowledge, or whether "we have an innate propensity to believe it," or perhaps conclude it from very little experience. If it is part of our background knowledge, wonders how it got there. Maintains there are two strategies for dealing with the problem of background knowledge: give a computer all the information a good human reasoner has, or make a computer that learns background information. Goes on to point out ("The Natural Language Problem") that the second strategy involves making a computer that learns and processes a natural language.

Quine, W.V. "Natural Kinds." In *Essays in Honor of Carl G. Hempel,* edited by Nicholas Rescher et al., pp. 5–23. Dordrecht-Holland: D. Reidel Publishing Company, 1970. Also in this volume and in *Ontological Relativity & Other Essays* by W. V. Quine (New York: Columbia University Press, 1969). Regards predicates "*F*" and "*G*" as projectible when all of their shared instances count as confirming "All *F* are *G.*" Assimilates Hempel's raven puzzle to Goodman's grue puzzle "by inferring from Hempel's that the complement of a projectible predicate need not be projectible." Notes that if a statement is logically equivalent to "All *F* are *G*" for some projectible "*F*" and "*G,*" then the statement is lawlike. Claims that there are no projectible predicates with projectible complements (excluding limited or relative complements). Believes we prefer the green hypothesis because of the similarity among green emeralds (all green) compared to the similarity among grue emeralds (some green, some blue)—that is, green emeralds are a kind, grue emeralds are not, and "a projectible predicate is one that is true of all and only the things of a kind." Believes the real puzzle "is the dubious scientific standing of a general notion of similarity, or of kind." Comments that these are basic notions, and that they "seem to be variants or adaptations of a single notion." Discusses how difficult it is "to relate the general notion of similarity significantly to logical terms": e.g., we can't define "*a* is more similar to *b* than to *c*" as "*a* and *b* belong jointly to more sets than do *a* and *c*" because "any two things are joint members of any number of sets." Notes that if we appeal to the number of common properties instead of sets, we will need to decide what to count as a property. Introduces a "somewhat limping definition of comparative similarity in terms of kinds" that will work for finite systems of kinds: if *a* and *b* belong jointly to more kinds than do *a* and *c*, then *a* is more similar to *b* than it is to *c*. Considers how to define the notion of kind in terms of the notion of comparative similarity. Claims that if we assume there are paradigm cases and foils "that deviate just barely too much to be counted into the desired kind at all," then we can define a kind with a paradigm *a* and a foil *b* as "the set of all the things to which *a* is more similar than *a* is to *b*." Points out that this definition "does not give us what we want as kinds" because if we take (e.g.) red things as a kind, the definition will not "distill purely chromatic kinds from mixed similarity." Notes another definition from Carnap and how Goodman has shown it wrong because of "the difficulty of imperfect community." Believes that the notion of similarity and the notion of kind "vary together" in the sense that if we believe *a* is more similar to *b* than to *c* and then change our opinion to *a* is less similar to *b* than to *c*, we will also change our belief (and correspondingly so) about the kinds *a*, *b*, and *c* belong to. Stresses how fundamental the notion of similarity is. Points to its role in language learning by ostension (e.g., learning "yellow"). Maintains that "a standard of similarity is in some sense innate" and argues this by observing that we need them for any kind of learning at all and so "these distinctive spacings cannot themselves all be learned." Stresses that he can interpret this claim about innate standards in behavioral terms, and that it "can be said equally of other animals." Characterizes induction as "animal expectation or habit formation" and regards learning a word ostensively to be a case of induction. Compares generalizing about another person's verbal behavior with generalizing about "the harsh impersonal world." Claims it is reasonable to believe "that our quality space should match our neighbor's, we being birds of a feather," but wonders about believing "that our quality space matches that of the cosmos." Put another way: "why does our innate subjective spacing of qualities accord so well with the functionally relevant groupings in nature as to make our inductions tend to come out right?" Put yet another way: construes the naturalistic problem of induction as "a problem of how we, as we now are (by our present scientific lights), in a world we never made, should stand better than random or coin-tossing chances of coming out right when we predict by inductions which are based on our innate, scientifically unjustified similarity standard." Maintains that "Darwin's natural selection is a plausible partial explanation." Notes how color is important in our innate quality space but not important in basic science, and how we have developed "modified systems of kinds, hence modified similarity standards for scientific purposes." For example: excluding whales and porpoises from the class of fish. Observes that a theoretical kind does not have to result from changing an "intuitive" kind. Believes that we have various gradations of similarity standards between the innate and the scientific standards. Stresses how the notion of similarity "permeates our thought" by discussing how a number of important notions can be defined in terms of similarity or kinds: i.e., dispositions (e.g., being soluble in water can be defined in terms of being the same kind as things that have or will dissolve in water), subjunctive conditionals (mentioned but not discussed in the current printing), and causes (singular causal statements can be defined in terms of the two events belonging to a kind "between which there is invariable succession"). Points to "a development away from the immediate, subjective, animal sense of similarity to the remoter objectivity of a similarity determined by scientific hypotheses and posits and constructs." Admits, however, that "the similarity notion even in its theoretical phase is itself a muddy notion still." Has not defined it in adequate scientific terms, though has given a behavioral criterion. Believes "it does get defined in bits: bits suited to special branches of science." For example: we can define comparative similarity in chemistry "in terms of chemical composition." Proposes that we can explain a being chemically more similar to b than to c in terms of ratios of pairs of matching and unmatching molecules, and that we can derive a concept of chemical kinds from this by the paradigm and foil approach (now adequate because we are "distilling purely chemical kinds from purely chemical similarity"). Illustrates this line of definition with solubility, and points out how advances in chemical theory have not only made it possible to pursue this line of definition but also have made it "pointless by providing a full understanding of the mechanism of solution." Discusses the attempt to find a more general similarity standard than the different ones suited to special branches of science, and the idea of classifying branches of science in terms of their relative similarity notions. Concludes that it is "a very special mark of the maturity of a branch of science that it no longer needs an irreducible notion of similarity and kind."

Quine, W.V. "Reply to Chihara." In *The Foundations of Analytic Philosophy, Midwest Studies in Philosophy,* Volume VI, edited by Peter A. French, Theodore E. Uehling, Jr., and Howard K. Wettstein, pp. 453–454. Minneapolis: University of Minnesota Press, 1981. A reply to Chihara (1981), same volume. Points out that he does not have his own theory of confirmation, but subscribes to "what is loosely described as the hypothetico-deductive method." Considers simple induction a special case of this method, and involving the psychological relation of subjective similarity in generalizing to natural kinds, where natural kinds are "kinds that are natural to us." Repeats that he considers projectibility, similarity, and simplicity to be "all of a piece." Maintains that standards of similarity, natural kind, and projectibility can change with changes in theoretical context. Also that projectibility is sensitive to the accompanying body of theory: it can help make a predicate count as projectible, or help stop one from counting as that. Remarks that one of Chihara's examples (the grueness of Neptune) does not seem to be about projectibility because it does not seem to be an example of induction.

Quine, W.V. and Ullian, J.S. *The Web of Belief.* 2d ed. New York: Random House, 1978. See chapter VII, "Induction, Analogy, and Intuition," especially pages 84–89, for an introduction to the new riddle and a discussion of projectible traits. The authors connect projectibility with similarity and simplicity: "projectible traits are felt to be simpler than others, as well as making for similarity." Posit an innate tendency to notice certain traits and therefore project them; appeal to natural selection and survival value in explaining why these traits (e.g., green) tend to succeed in predictions while others (e.g., grue) do not. Goodman (1972, p. 358) objected to this appeal in the first edition; second edition considers the objection (pp. 88–89) and replies by appealing to "theories of neural organization." Also see pages 101–102 for points about grue and lawlike general sentences; see pages 69–73 for a discussion of simplicity.

Rescher, Nicholas. "Peirce and the Economy of Research." *Philosophy of Science* 43 (1976): 71–98. Maintains that a cost-benefit analysis can resolve various issues in philosophy of science and inductive reasoning: e.g., issues about Carnap's total evidence requirement, Hempel's ravens paradox, Goodman's grue paradox, simplicity, generality, rational acceptance, and selecting hypotheses for testing. With regard to the Goodman paradox, argues that the green/blue color taxonomy is more efficient and convenient to operate with than the grue/bleen color taxonomy. Claims that the orthodox taxonomy is cheaper to use because it involves "an ostensively taught language where all that matters is the surface appearance of things," while the unorthodox taxonomy "adds to this ostensively accessible phenomenology also a layer of chronometric issues at the level of learning, teaching, explanation, and application." Emphasizes that he is not comparing one taxonomy from the perspective of the other, but determining internally what each requires in order to work out. See the criticism by Bunch (1980).

Rescher, Nicholas. *Peirce's Philosophy of Science: Critical Studies in His Theory of Induction and Scientific Method.* Notre Dame: University of Notre Dame Press, 1978. Chapter 4 is a revised version of Rescher (1976).

Rescher, Nicholas. *Cognitive Economy: The Economic Dimension of the Theory of Knowledge.* Pittsburgh: University of Pittsburgh Press, 1989. Chapter 6 includes material from Rescher (1976). Includes a version of the cost-benefit analysis of Goodman's grue paradox from Rescher (1976). Chapter synopsis maintains that "Nelson Goodman's renovated riddle of induction also loses much of its puzzlement when one adopts an economic point of view."

Rheinwald, Rosemarie. "An Epistemic Solution to Goodman's New Riddle of Induction." *Synthese* 95 (1993): 55–76. Believes some discussions of the new riddle are confusing because they define "grue" in a different way, mix actual and counterfactual epistemic situations, and view lawlikeness, confirmation, and projectibility as matters of degree. Discusses another example in order to "avoid some of the difficulties connected with 'grue' (and to be able to appeal to intuitions which are not so much influenced by philosophical discussion)." Wants to show that "the notions of 'confirmation', 'projectibility', and 'lawlikeness' are essentially epistemic." Claims we can only tell whether data confirm a hypothesis, a predicate is projectible, or a hypothesis is lawlike "relative to certain background information or background beliefs—i.e., to a certain epistemic situation." Presents an example about the color of hares. Distinguishes three epistemic situations: one actual situation in which a person has correct beliefs about the colors of field hares and alpine hares (all field hares are brown, some alpine hares are white, others brown in summer, white in winter), and two counterfactual situations in which "we know less than we actually do and where we have (what I take to be) false beliefs." Introduces the artificial predicates "brote" and "su-wi-brote," and three hypotheses: all hares are brown, are brote (either field hares and brown or alpine hares and white), are su-wi-brote (either field hares and brown or alpine hares and white or brown in summer and white in winter). Also introduces three "series of observations of hares" and asks whether they are appropriate given the background beliefs in one of the epistemic situations, and whether the observations confirm the hypotheses in that situation. Concludes that "if we address the question of appropriateness, the background information or background beliefs are relevant" and "if we address the questions of *confirmation, projectibility,* and *lawlikeness,* not only the background beliefs are relevant but also the relation between the hypothesis and the background beliefs." States necessary and sufficient conditions for an examination being appropriate for answering a question, for data to confirm a hypothesis, and for a hypothesis to be lawlike. States, for example, that data confirms a hypothesis relative to an epistemic situation and answering a certain question, the data are positive instances of the hypothesis, "the hypothesis does not contradict the background beliefs," and the examination is appropriate "for answering this question in this situation" and "takes account of all aspects or kinds that are relevant for the answer according to the hypothesis." Claims that Goodman's paradox "can be analyzed in essentially the same way as the example of hares." Defines "grue" to mean first examined before t and green then or first examined after t and blue then, or not examined and always blue. Distinguishes three epistemic situations, one actual and two counterfactual: the person in the actual situation believes all emeralds are always green and that green and blue are permanent qualities of gemstones and do not change because of time or examination; the person in one counterfactual situation believes all emeralds are grue, and green and blue are not permanent qualities of gemstones, and they can change because of time and examination; the person in the other counterfactual situation is in "a situation of ignorance" and "has no information about the colors of emeralds." Considers the data to be "the examination E of emeralds" before time t. Claims that, in the actual situation, the data confirm the green hypothesis but not the grue one "because this hypothesis contradicts the background beliefs in that situation." Claims that, in the first counterfactual situation, the data confirms the grue hypothesis if the person has "a general well-confirmed theory about the influence of examinations"; also claims that the data does not confirm the green hypothesis in this situation "because it contradicts the background beliefs (in this situation)." Claims that, in the second "total ignorance" counterfactual situation, "the data do not confirm any general hypothesis." Discusses three other definitions of "grue": something is grue if and only if it is examined before t and is green or is not examined before t and is blue; the definition in Barker and Achinstein (1960); and the definition in Shoemaker (1975). Believes the first definition is obscure because we do not know if "green," "blue," and "grue" must be relativized to time; believes her "analysis can also be defended with respect to the Barker-Achinstein definition"; and believes she can defend her analysis with respect to Shoemaker's definition by adopting "a belief in backward causation." Discusses "the relation between entrenchment, projectibility, and background beliefs." Maintains that "whether a term is entrenched, or rather can be entrenched, depends essentially on the way the world is and how we believe the world to be." More specifically: "if we believe that words have definite meanings and extensions, we also have to believe in the existence of certain causal connections, in the truth of certain causal laws, and in the projectibility of these words." Claims that entrenched terms will figure "prominently in the ordinary expression of our beliefs about the world and vice versa." States that, for the hypothesis "All As are P" and a given epistemic situation: "if the predicate P is not entrenched, but could become entrenched without a change in our background beliefs about the world—especially about the truth of the hypothesis—P is projectible in the given situation." Also states that "if the predicate P is entrenched but its entrenchment is due to epistemic situations in which the beliefs contradict the hypothesis, P is not projectible in the given situation." Claims that " 'grue' could only become entrenched if our background beliefs about the world were to change." That is, "if we came to believe that certain examinations of certain gemstones sometimes had a causal effect on the color of the stones." Believes that her epistemic solution is compatible with both a linguistic solution (such as Goodman's) and an evolutionary solution (such as Quine's). Notes that Goodman rejects an evolutionary solution because he believes "green" and "grue" have been "equally useful for survival" up until time t. Does not find this convincing because if there is a genetic basis for projecting certain predicates, then either we would have projected "green" and normal predicates or we would have projected "grue" and "a *comprehensive* gruified vocabulary," and this latter alternative would not have been as successful. Claims her epistemic solution "can also be interpreted as an attempt to explain the process of entrenchment." Stresses that "our inductive practice is the result of several factors" (mainly "nature, evolution, language, and beliefs") and that they are "interconnected." Nonetheless views beliefs, "especially beliefs about the causal structure of the world," as a more basic factor than entrenchment. See the reply by Elgin (1993).

Roper James E. "Models and Lawlikeness." *Synthese* 52 (1982): 313–323. Examines the dispute over whether analogical models in science just have a heuristic function or whether they also have some explanatory and confirmatory function. Construes explanation in terms of deducing statements from a general law and confirmation in terms of the positive and negative instances of a general law. Introduces the new riddle as a problem about distinguishing the lawlike and nonlawlike statements. Describes Goodman's theory of projectibility, especially how it deals with new scientific predicates in terms of parent predicates and inherited entrenchment. Distinguishes between natural and foster parent predicates, and proposes that entrenchment can be inherited by adoption when "a novel predicate *shares the same structure* with comfortably entrenched predicates." Analyzes similarity of structure in terms of Hempel's view (1965) of analogical models in the sciences: viz., that they establish a syntactic isomorphism between specific laws of two physical systems. Regards a predicate *P* as a foster parent of a predicate *Q* if *P* is much better entrenched, they occur in corresponding positions in specific laws in a syntactic isomorphism, predicate *Q*'s law has actually been projected at a prior time, and at that time scientists presented and explained this law using the nomic isomorphism in question. Claims his proposal explains why, given two theories about "a newly observed phenomenon which cannot be explained in terms of any of our stock of entrenched predicates," scientists prefer (other things being equal) the theory with a well-established, familiar theory as its analogical model, why they expend so much energy trying to discover such models, and why new theories (with infrequently projected hypotheses) are sometimes accepted on little evidence. Also claims his proposal provides a rational explanation for the quick acceptance of Kuhnian-style revolutionary hypotheses when this involves an analogical model. Emphasizes that his proposal also shows how models may have explanatory and confirmatory functions: e.g., if a law must have entrenched predicates and models can entrench predicates, then "the discovery of a model may be one of the things that makes a particular explanation possible." Considers whether his proposal is circular in that his characterization of a foster parent predicate involves actual projections, and whether, after dropping the circular parts, it is open to a gruelike problem in that "we could always create a *grue-like* variant of the new theory which would also stand in the appropriate modeling relation with the older, more entrenched theory." Maintains this criticism is based on confusing the old problem of justifying principles of inductive reasoning with the new problem of explicating principles of inductive reasoning and thereby avoiding the new riddle. Notes that Hempel analyzes models in terms of a formal analogy, while others analyze models in terms of a formal and a material analogy. Uses Hempel's analysis because Hempel has argued that models just have a heuristic function. Regards his proposal as "very programmatic in nature." Believes it can be adjusted for other analyses of analogical models.

Rosenkrantz, R.D. "Probabilistic Confirmation Theory and the Goodman Paradox." *American Philosophical Quarterly* 10 (1973): 157–162. Uses probabilistic confirmation theory to resolve the Goodman paradox. Notes that probabilistic confirmation theory is based on measuring the degree of confirmation (dc) an observation x gives to a hypothesis H in terms of the increment $P(H/x) - P(H)$. Section I. Shows, from a probabilistic view, that confirmation is symmetric and nontransitive, that x confirms H more than hypothesis K when the relevant likelihood ratio is greater than 1, that dc is inversely proportional to $P(x)$, and that the consequences of H will confirm H but "what confirms (resp. disconfirms) a consequence of H need not confirm (resp. disconfirm) H." Explains the reasoning behind the fact that evidence E may confirm H & K but fail to confirm the extraneous conjunct K. Section II. Shows how a non-AB can disconfirm the hypothesis "All A are B" under certain conditions. Notes that an AB can also disconfirm the hypothesis under certain conditions. Discusses the positive and negative parts of the Nicod criterion: AB confirms and A non-B disconfirms "All A are B," while non-AB and non-A non-B are irrelevant. Points out that Hempel "accepts the consequences of the positive Nicod criterion and the equivalence condition: it admits everything as relevant." Emphasizes that Hempel's view of confirmation produces the raven and Goodman paradoxes because, in his view, if an observation is consistent with a hypothesis, then it confirms the hypothesis: "finding green emeralds prior to time t is consistent with the finding of blue emeralds after t, and therefore 'confirms' that prediction." Section III. Derives two equations from Bayes's theorem—one about $P(H/AB)$: $P(H)$, the other about $P(H/\text{non-}A \text{ non-}B)$: $P(H)$—and considers their implications: e.g., if $P(\text{non-}A \text{ non-}B)$ is less than $P(AB)$, then non-A non-B confirms "All A are B" more than AB. Discusses I.J. Good's case in which a black raven confirms the hypothesis that the world has 1,000 black ravens, 1 white, and 1 million other birds, while disconfirming the hypothesis that the world has 100 black ravens and 1 million other birds. Considers Hempel's objection that "this example illegitimately exploits background knowledge," and suggests the positive Nicod criterion might hold "only when the lumpen hypothesis not-H is taken as the alternative to H." Describes a case in which a non-A, non-B disconfirms "All A are B" without depending on background knowledge; lets the hypothesis be "Every rhinoceros can mate with some hippopotamus" and notes that on Hempel's definition "every hippo who can't mate with a rhino should add to our confidence in" this hypothesis. Describes another case in which N hats are randomly distributed among their N owners, the hypothesis is "No person receives their own hat," the first two people receive each other's hat, and this disconfirms the hypothesis. Claims the important feature in these examples is "that probabilities do vary with the *description* of the experimental results." Maintains that the positive Nicod criterion holds with stoogian observations (observations reported as consistent or not with the H), but cannot be assumed to hold with nonstoogian observations. Sees the raven paradox as a non sequitur: it does not follow, from the Nicod criterion and the equivalence condition, that a red pencil confirms the raven hypothesis. Section IV. Maintains that we should not "feel any temptation to argue that because green emeralds examined prior to time t are grue, they *therefore* confirm the grue hypothesis." Acknowledges that the green emeralds do slightly confirm the grue hypothesis, not because of the positive Nicod criterion but because "the dc which a consequence E of H affords the conjunction of H with a consistent K is the fraction $P(K/H)$ of the dc which E affords H." Notes that the grue hypothesis is actually a conjunction, that the probability all emeralds not examined before t are blue, given all examined before t are green, is minute, and that in consequence "the dc which finding green emeralds prior to t accords the grue hypothesis is likewise minute." Points out that if this dc is supposed to be transmitted to the conjunct predicting emeralds will be blue after t, this will require a principle that does not hold in probabilistic confirmation theory, the direct consequence condition. Notes that when E is a consequence of hypothesis H and consistent with K, E may disconfirm K. Section V. Considers Goodman's entrenchment account of lawlike generalizations. Claims we can combine well-entrenched predicates to produce "scientific monstrosities" like "All obsessive-compulsives are color-blind," which "is ruled out because it connects a non-heritable to a heritable trait." Emphasizes how "subject-matter-specific considerations," and not entrenched predicates, show "All alkaline-earth metals combine with chlorine to form colorless salts that crystallize in cubes" has a higher prior plausibility than "All alkaline-earth metals are poisonous." Claims it is important that a predicate "be projectible over the subject class of the hypothesis considered," as chemical properties (predicates) are projectible over samples of a chemical element. Points to "grue-like hypotheses which, under the right circumstances, are better entrenched than their greenlike counterparts." Describes an urn that contains green or blue spheres and cubes, and whose composition confirms "All spheres are green" less than "All elements are grue," where "grue" applies to a green sphere or a blue cube. Describes a mathematically similar case about flipping a coin one hundred times and the hypotheses "All flips are heads" and "All flips are hails," where "hails" applies to heads in the first fifty flips or tails in the second fifty flips. Also see Rosenkrantz (1977) and (1982).

Rosenkrantz, Roger D. *Inference, Method and Decision: Towards a Bayesian Philosophy of Science*. Dordrecht, Holland: D. Reidel Publishing Company, 1977. See chapter 2, "The Paradoxes of Confirmation," pages 33–41. Believes there is at least one major lesson to learn from the paradoxes: viz., that "general laws are not necessarily confirmed by their positive cases." Describes two examples from I.J. Good's "The White Shoe Is A Red Herring," *British Journal for the Philosophy of Science* 17 (1967): 322. Presents his own example about randomly distributing N hats among their N owners, where our hypothesis is "No one receives their own hat" and we consider subevents of the event that neither of the first two owners received their own hat. Claims that "when we fill out our description of a grue emerald to include its being green and examined prior to time t, we single out a subevent, and no inference to the confirmation of the grue hypothesis can be drawn." Also claims that we cannot "infer confirmation of the grue hypothesis by observation of grue emeralds" because, as Good shows, we can't conclude that AB's or non-AB's necessarily confirm "All A are B." Maintains that when we use a probabilistic analysis of confirmation and allow background information, the grue problem is stopped dead in its tracks. Notes the sense in which stoogian observations confirm a hypothesis in the sense of being consistent with it. Goes on to consider Goodman's entrenchment view of confirmability and lawlikeness. Believes that if a hypothesis is lawlike, then there are "theoretically grounded relations between the predicates which the hypothesis links," which amounts to saying that "the residual background theory provides some prior presumption in favor of the hypothesis." Claims one can easily think up cases in which a gruelike hypothesis is more confirmable and has a higher prior presumption than its nonpathological counterpart. Describes a case in which we randomly sample chips from an urn, the chips are black or white circles and squares, and our hypotheses are "All circular chips are black" and "All chips are blite," where "blite" means a black square or a white circle. Believes that "industrial melanism" provides an example of this situation, with the hypotheses "All British moths except rare mutants are white" and "All British moths except rare mutants are blite." Points out that Goodman's puzzle seems to require a transitivity principle because if we find green emeralds before t, this is supposed to increase "the probability of finding blue emeralds after t." Maintains "it is child's play to find examples where X increases the probability of H & K but decreases the probability of K, or where X confirms H while disconfirming a consequence of H." Adds that, in his view, confirmability also depends on the simplicity of a hypothesis. Emphasizes that a major thesis of his book is "that simpler theories are more confirmable." Ends the chapter by examining Hempel's context restriction on the satisfaction definition of confirmation: viz., that Hempel's satisfaction concept "applies only to 'theoretically barren contexts' where background knowledge is lacking." Doubts whether there is a context like this, whether "inductive inference in a theoretical vacuum" has any clear meaning, and whether we could draw any conclusions about confirmation even if we understood what induction meant in such a vacuum. Also see Rosenkrantz (1973) and (1982).

Rosenkrantz, R. D. *Foundations and Applications of Inductive Probability.* Atascadero, Calif.: Ridgeview Publishing Company, 1981. Discusses Goodman's paradox in chapter 1, section 4 and in chapter 7, section 1. Presents the new riddle (in chapter 1) as a challenge to the predictivist criterion of confirmation: viz., "hypotheses are confirmed by (verification of) their consequences." Notes that one could view the new riddle as a *reductio* of Hempel's criterion of confirmation and the notion of induction by enumeration. Maintains that the problem does not depend on using odd predicates, and that it is a variant of Hempel's raven paradox. Points out that a green emerald examined prior to *t* is a Hempelian positive instance of the hypothesis that all emeralds examined after that time are blue. Takes a Bayesian position (chapter 7) on the paradoxes of confirmation and maintains "it doesn't follow that any outcome consistent with a hypothesis confirms it." Claims this stops the Goodman and Hempel paradoxes in their tracks. Argues that Goodman's entrenchment solution is wrong because it excludes "all bent hypotheses in blanket fashion as non-starters." Discusses Newton's second law as a straight hypothesis and its relativistic modification as a bent hypothesis with novel predicates such as "relativistic mass" and "mass-energy." Claims that when Einstein introduced his relativistic hypothesis, it would have been (on Goodman's account) unprojectible because the Newtonian hypothesis had a better entrenched consequent predicate (Newtonian momentum vs. relativistic momentum). Sees the grue hypothesis as a radically bent hypothesis because "it posits a temporal discontinuity of behavior." Regards bent hypotheses as scientifically respectable and often connected with scientific revolutions. Views confirmation as a matter of degree, with "no sharp break between the confirmable and the unconfirmable." Considers "simplicity and theoretical assimilability" as two of the most important factors in determining whether a hypothesis is lawlike. Also see Rosenkrantz (1973, 1977, 1982).

Rosenkrantz, R.D. "Does the Philosophy of Induction Rest on a Mistake?" *Journal of Philosophy* 79 (1982): 78–97. Section I: "The Current Impasse" Claims that Goodman's paradox "does not really turn on the introduction of bizarre predicates like 'grue'." Notes that if white crows confirm Hempel's raven hypothesis, then green emeralds confirm "All emeralds not examined before *t* are blue." Regards "the Goodman paradox as a *reductio ad absurdum* of the Nicod criterion and the enumerative conception of induction." Section II: "Bayesian Analysis of the Paradoxes." Discusses how the Hempelian and Bayesian views differ with respect to the inverse condition, how the Bayesian view involves specifying alternative hypotheses, and how it substantiates certain Popperian ideas about confirmation and the risk of falsification. Shows that, "on a Bayesian analysis, observation of non-*F* non-*G*s and even of *FG*s can disconfirm 'All *F* are *G*'." Notes how this happens when we have "(a) a very large number of *FG*s with some rare *F* non-*G*s, or (b) a modest number of *FG*s without any *F* non-*G*s." Believes that in these cases we are changing the relevant conditional probabilities "by picking out a subevent of the observation of an *FG* or a non-*F* non-*G*." Illustrates this with a quantitative example about randomly distributing *N* hats to their *N* owners, where the hypothesis is that no person gets their own hat and the evidence is that the first two owners get the other's hat. Claims this is "a very clear-cut case in which a Hempelian positive instance is, in Bayesian terms, disconfirming." Concludes that if an observation conforms to a hypothesis, it does not follow that it confirms the hypothesis. Accordingly sees a non sequitur in the paradoxes of confirmation: i.e., if you find green emeralds prior to t—and so you find grue emeralds—it does not follow that they confirm "All emeralds are grue." Section III: "A Distinguishing Feature of Goodman's Paradox." Points out that the grue hypothesis is a conjunction of (H) all emeralds examined before t are green and (K) all emeralds not examined before t are blue. Measures degree of confirmation (dc) by the increment $P(H/E) - P(H)$. Notes that when E follows from H, $dc(E, HK)=P(K/H)dc(E,H)$, and that the $dc(E,HK)$ is the fraction $P(K/H)$ of $dc(E,H)$. Claims that "given our knowledge of the color constancy of emeralds, the probability $P(K/H)$ that emeralds unexamined before t are blue given that those examined before t are green, is minute," while the degree of confirmation E accords the green hypothesis—all emeralds are green—"will be much higher than the degree of confirmation E accords the grue hypothesis HK." Believes this is an important asymmetry. Acknowledges that "it depends heavily on the assumed background knowledge that emeralds as a class are likely to be color-homogeneous and do not, at any rate, change color all at once." Claims the asymmetry is still present when we reformulate all of this with "grue" and "bleen." Points out that $P(K/H)$ becomes the probability that all emeralds not examined before t are bleen, given that all of them examined before t are grue—and this is "the probability that emeralds unexamined before t are green given that those examined before t are green, and this probability is large." Section IV: "The Bent and the Straight." Notes that a Bayesian analysis also blocks the anti-inductive inference because it does not "transfer the confirmation that E accords HK (or H alone) to the consequence K of HK." Believes Goodman is wrong in trying to stop E from confirming HK. Discusses how overhypotheses influence the confirmability of hypotheses, how Goodmanized overhypotheses can also influence confirmability, and how Goodman deals with this problem by excluding hypotheses "*at any level* which project 'unprojectible' (gruelike) predicates." Describes Goodman's entrenchment solution and how it determines whether a hypothesis can be confirmed and, if so, the degree to which it can be confirmed. Notes that the green hypothesis overrides the grue hypothesis, thereby showing it is unprojectible (or not confirmed by its instances). Emphasizes that an overriding hypothesis can be a supported, unviolated, and unexhausted hypothesis that could have been projected. Asks "why require that predicates (any more than hypotheses) be *actually* projected to acquire entrenchment?" Argues that if we allow possible projections of predicates, then "grue" seems to be as entrenched as "green" because it "could have been projected on all those past occasions when 'green' was actually projected." Goes on to describe a problem that occurs whenever a bent or crooked hypothesis "posits small deviations from a 'straight' hypothesis at extreme ranges of the relevant variables." Considers the grue hypothesis to be an extreme and atypical example of a bent hypothesis. Claims that "a theory of induction that would exclude all bent hypotheses as nonstarters in blanket fashion cannot be taken very seriously." Explains how Goodman's entrenchment view does that because it only uses background knowledge about entrenchment to determine whether a hypothesis is presumptively projectible. Illustrates this with two examples that involve unfamiliar predicates: one example about all moths being white or blite (white inhabitants of rural areas or black inhabitants of industrial areas), the other about Newton's second law and its relativistic modification. Section V: "Goodmanizing the Background Knowledge." Considers the problem about poorly entrenched overhypotheses connecting irrelevant evidence to hypotheses, as with Goodman's bagleet hypothesis. Argues (among other things) that the problem comes from taking a Hempelian positive-instance view of support and that on a Bayesian view the bagleet hypothesis does not transfer any confirmation. Believes the problem about

Goodmanizing overhypotheses also comes from taking the Hempelian view: e.g., a hypothesis like "All elements are homogeneous" is supported by quantum theory, not an enumeration of instances. Claims it is unclear how to appropriately Goodmanize the theory behind his bent relativistic hypothesis, and believes there is a burden of proof on proponents of Goodmanizing to show how it would be done in scientifically interesting cases and "to show, further, that these overhypotheses are well supported in a Bayesian sense." Section VI: "What Survives?" Considers inductive inferences "from a sample proportion to a population proportion." States, as a rule of thumb, that if we do not have other information, then we should consider the population proportion to be near the sample proportion. Points out that this rule follows from a fundamental principle: viz., "that it is reasonable to adopt a diffuse or 'relatively uninformative' prior where pertinent data are lacking." Discusses Carnap's lambda-continuum methods, Reichenbach's straight rule and pragmatic approach, and justifying inductive methods such as the principle about uninformative priors "by looking at the *rate* at which different inductive methods converge to the truth." Section VII: "Confirming Generalizations." Points out that if we examines Fs and find them to be G, this is a consequence of "All F are G" and confirms this generalization, but this is not a consequence of a next-case prediction (the next F will be G) and may not confirm it. Argues for the "thesis that Bayesian conditionalization can account quite adequately for the confirmation of generalizations without resort to additional assumptions." Uses the Goldbach conjecture as a test case. See Rosenkrantz (1973) and (1977).

Russell, Bertrand. "On the Notion of Cause." *Proceedings of the Aristotelian Society, New Series* 13 (1912–1913): 1–26. In discussing whether the material universe is subject to laws, notes that "given some formula which fits the facts hitherto–say the law of gravitation–there will be an infinite number of other formulae, not empirically distinguishable from it in the past, but diverging from it more and more in the future." Emphasizes that "we cannot say that *every* law which has held hitherto must hold in the future, because past facts which obey one law will also obey others, hitherto indistinguishable but diverging in the future." Claims the sciences deal with this situation by selecting the simplest formula that fits the facts. Views this as following a "methodological precept, not a law of Nature." Thinks we might avoid the problem by following "the principle that the *time* must not enter explicitly into our formulae." Maintains that time is irrelevant to all scientific laws and that the uniformity of nature means time is not an argument of any scientific law unless "it is given in an integrated form." See Sainsbury (1979).

Russell, Bertrand. *Human Knowledge: Its Scope and Limits.* New York: Simon and Schuster, 1948. See chapter VII, "Probability and Induction," especially pages 404 and 413–414. Considered a predecessor of the new riddle. Takes up the problem of induction by simple enumeration. Asks: "Given that a number of instances of a class *x* have all been found to belong to a class *B*, does this make it probable (a) that the next instance of *x* will be a *B*, or (b) that all *x*'s are *B*'s?" On page 404, maintains that induction is invalid as a logical principle; says "it is obvious that if we are allowed to select our class *B* as we choose, we can easily make sure that our induction shall fail." Describes three cases in which the next-case induction will fail because of the class *B*. Claims that *B* cannot be a manufactured class, i.e., a class "defined partly by extension," and that for induction we must have a class "known in intension." Says on page 414 that both *x* and *B* "must be defined by intension, not by mention of their membership." Holds the general position that "whatever relation justifies induction must be a relation of *concepts*." For comments on Russell's position, see Ayer (1972), Sainsbury (1979), and Salmon (1974 and 1975).

Sagal, Paul T. "Paradox, Confirmation and Inquiry." *Philosophy* 51 (1976): 467–470. Discussion of how philosophers attempt to resolve paradoxes; emphasis on Quine's attempt to resolve Goodman's puzzle of the grue emeralds. See Quine (1970).

Sainsbury, R.M. *Russell.* London: Routledge & Kegan Paul, 1979. See chapter VI, "Knowledge," for a discussion of Russell's views on induction, especially pages 163–168 for Russell's views on the characteristics of strong inductive arguments. Claims Russell deserves credit for discovering Goodman's point forty-three years before *FFF;* cites Russell's 1912 essay "On The Notion of Cause" and notes that Russell sees the problem as letting time enter explicitly into a predicate. States the problem in a way that does not involve time by slightly modifying Russell's (1948) class names version. Claims that Russell did not regard his 1948 solution, restricting induction to intensionally defined classes, as adequate and yet he did not say why. Offers two reasons why this restriction is not adequate, one about coextensive primitive predicates and one about replacing class names by definitions, and considers how Russell might reply. Considers how his interpretation differs from that of Salmon (1974) in the footnote on page 168. Also see Salmon (1975) and Ayer (1972).

Salmon, Wesley. "Vindication of Induction." In *Current Issues in Philosophy of Science,* edited by Herbert Feigl and Grover Maxwell, pages 245–256. New York: Holt, Rinehart and Winston, 1961. Applies two criteria to three classes of inductive rules. Claims this will show "in each of these three classes there is one rule which is superior to all other rules of that class with respect to the purpose the rules of that class are designed to serve." Views this as a pragmatic justification or vindication of the rules (i.e., Reichenbach's straight rule). The three classes of rules: rules of predictive inference, of inverse inference, and of direct inference. The two criteria: the criterion of convergence and the criterion of "invariance with respect to purely linguistic transformations." Formulates the invariance criterion as: "no inductive rule is acceptable if the results it yields are functions of the arbitrary features of the choice of language." Notes that "if the task to be accomplished is the prediction of objective fact, then we do not want to adopt a rule which reflects the arbitrary features of the choice of language in its results." Gives a more precise formulation of the invariance criterion in the last section (section 6). One formulation applies to confirmation functions, the other to inductive rules. Lets $e(A_i, B_i)$ stand for "an inferred value according to a rule R of either a short-run frequency or a limit of a sequence of relative frequencies;" lets A_j and B_j stand for "terms of any language such that, according to the semantical and syntactical rules of the languages containing" $A_i, A_j, B_i, B_j, A_i = A_j$ and $B_i = B_j$. States that if rule R satisfies the criterion of linguistic invariance, then $e(A_i, B_i) = e(A_j, B_j)$. See the comments by Barker (pp. 257–260), rejoinder by Salmon (pp. 260–262), and comments by Rudner (pp. 262–264). Barker claims that the Goodman paradox shows the straight rule violates the invariance criterion because the rule "yields conflicting probabilities for predictions about future emeralds, which prediction we obtain depending on whether the predicate 'grue' or the predicate 'green' happens to be the predicate that we use in our language." Salmon replies that "as given in the paper, the *criterion of linguistic invariance* is not satisfactory; for we must add to it some restriction concerning the type of language to be considered." Claims that if we could show gruelike predicates "essentially involve a temporal reference in a way in which ordinary predicates do not," then this would be grounds for excluding a language with gruelike predicates. Emphasizes that the invariance criterion "cannot be satisfied by any inductive rule as long as we allow complete freedom in defining predicates." Rudner claims that Goodman's paradox shows the invariance criterion is "itself defective as a criterion through being so strong that no theory of inductive inferences in science *could* meet it." Believes the general point is that "any entities of a given kind, *K*, which are in the extension of some predicate, *P*, owe their membership in that extension, in part at least, to *conventional* features of language—in particular to those linguistic conventions . . . which make the predicate correctly applicable to the entities." Also believes that there will be a nonequivalent predicate *Q* that conventionally applies to *K* entities and it will be possible to choose *P* and *Q* so that they both apply to some examined subset of *K* entities and yet applying both predicates to all *K* entities "leads to a contradiction." In short: "no theory of induction is immune from linguistic *variance.*" Concludes that a desideratum "is a theory which will eliminate or minimize unwanted *consequences* of such inevitable variance." Maintains that the straight rule does not minimize or eliminate unwanted consequences. Believes that Goodman's theory in *FFF* "gives at least some valuable clues for discriminating relevant linguistic *conventions which are arbitrary* from ones which are less arbitrary and thus provides us with at least some results relevant to the formulation of the requisite rules." Skyrms (1965) claims that Goodman's paradox does not show the straight rule violates the precise formulation (section 6) of the criterion of linguistic invariance. See Salmon (1963a, 1963b) for an attempt to avoid the Goodman problem by restricting predicates to purely ostensive predicates.

Salmon, Wesley C. "Inductive Inference." In *Philosophy of Science: The Delaware Seminar*, Vol. 2, edited by Bernard Baumrin, pp. 341–370. New York: Interscience Publishers, 1963a. Presents his version of Reichenbach's pragmatic justification (or vindication) of induction. Considers six rules for inferring limits of relative frequencies; rejects a rule if it fails to be asymptotic, regular, or linguistically invariant; argues for rejecting all but induction by enumeration. Formulates the criterion of linguistic invariance as: "given two logically equivalent descriptions (in the same or different languages) of a body of evidence, no rule may permit mutually contradictory conclusions to be drawn on the basis of these statements of evidence." Notes the new riddle as a "remaining problem" because it "can be turned into an argument to the effect that even the rule of induction by enumeration fails to meet the criterion of linguistic invariance." See Smokler and Rohr (1969) for an argument against this criterion.

Salmon, Wesley C. "On Vindicating Induction." *Philosophy of Science* 30 (1963b): 252–261. Defends Reichenbach's rule of induction for inferring the limit of a relative frequency in a sequence from the relative frequency in an initial section of the sequence. Introduces normalizing conditions and a criterion of linguistic invariance as adequacy conditions for rules of induction. Maintains that "probability relations, relations of confirmation, and relations of inductive support are not functions of purely linguistic considerations." Formulates the invariance criterion as a "consistency requirement" that is violated when "an inductive rule permits contradictory conclusions to be derived from the same evidence." States the criterion in terms of two inductive inferences made with the same rule of induction and with premises that only differ purely linguistically: "the conclusion of the one must not contradict the conclusion of the other." Believes that (as it stands) Reichenbach's rule of induction does not satisfy the invariance requirement, and that a version of Goodman's paradox demonstrates this. Thinks the original green-grue paradox "does not actually involve a violation of the criterion of linguistic invariance" because the two premises (observed emeralds green/grue) are equivalent as a result of the definitions of predicates as well as "the synthetic statement that the observations occur prior to the specified time *t.*" Also thinks "it is desirable to characterize positionality more generally" and to avoid a "basic ambiguity in the definition of 'grue' and 'bleen'." Reformulates the paradox with an ordered sequence of objects as the universe, defines "grue" as green and less than or equal to subscript 1000 or blue and greater than subscript 1000, and the premises are conjunctions recording that emeralds with subscripts $1-100$ are green/grue. Believes that if we use an inductive rule and "allow its free application to every type of predicate that can possibly be defined, this is tantamount to allowing the use of other inductive rules besides the one selected." Wants to exclude violations of the invariance criterion "which arise by allowing complete latitude with respect to the admission of predicates" and yet preserve the principle behind it "by refusing to elevate one language with its particular set of predicates to a privileged position." Regards an inductive logic as an extension of a system of deductive logic. Maintains there are two main purposes in developing the system: to be able to express true or false assertions ("a descriptive language") and to "incorporate inductive inference" with an inductive rule. Says "that at some level of language we must provide the reference of terms by means of non-verbal definitions, and we might as well do it at the object language level." Introduces the three parts of an ostensive definition: positive instances, negative instances, and a similarity clause. Defines a purely ostensive predicate as a predicate that can be defined ostensively, whose positive/negative instances can be "indicated non-verbally," and whose positive/negative instances have "an observable resemblance." Notes that purely ostensive predicates are observation predicates and open "in the sense that their definition does not limit the number of individuals to which they may be correctly applied." Believes empirical science needs a language of open observation predicates with empirical reference in order to express descriptive generalizations, and that purely ostensive predicates will do this. Takes the chief inductive aim to be providing a method for establishing "universal or statistical generalizations on the basis of observational evidence," which requires open observation predicates. Proposes a semantic restriction on the interpretation of basic predicates: viz., "that they be interpreted in such a way as to become purely ostensive predicates." Points out that "grue" is not purely ostensive because some grue things do not match other grue things ("they do not look alike"), and so it is "impossible to cite a number of positive instances of grue things and stipulate that anything which resembles them in some observational characteristic is grue." Claims this destroys the grue-green symmetry because "green" can be a basic predicate in the descriptive language of science while "grue" cannot. Notes Reichenbach's view that justifying induction "is a problem in primitive knowledge." Considers a primitive inductive inference to be one with observation statements as premises and a primitive inductive rule as applying only to observation statement premises. Notes that if Reichenbach's rule is a primitive inductive rule, then it must be restricted to purely ostensive predicates, which thereby eliminates Goodman's paradox here. See the reply by Skyrms (1965).

Salmon, Wesley C. "On Vindicating Induction." In *Induction: Some Current Issues,* edited by Henry E. Kyburg and Ernest Nagel, pp. 27–41. Middletown, Connecticut: Wesleyan University Press, 1963c. A paper given at a 1961 conference on inductive logic held at the Wesleyan Center for Advanced Studies. Essentially the same paper as Salmon (1963a). See the comments by Max Black (pp. 42–44); discussion by Wiener, Black, Scriven, Bar-Hillel, Sellars, Nagel, Madden, Braithwaite, Jeffrey, and Salmon (pp. 45–48); and the reply to Black by Salmon (pp. 49–54). Black maintains (in the discussion) that Salmon is using "an absolute notion of direct resemblance" when he claims grue things don't all look alike, and yet "the notion of 'looking alike' is relative to our language": if a Navajo-speaker and an English-speaker confront the same evidence and use the same rule of induction, they could "reach incompatible conclusions." Black maintains that degrees of confirmation are "relative to the conceptual framework of the language." Salmon (in his reply to Black) emphasizes that we should accept the criterion of linguistic invariance because it is a consistency requirement. Replies to Black about "interlinguistic contradictions": he is "quite willing to agree that different conceptual schemes can and should give rise to conflicting conclusions," but that "a conceptual scheme is far more than just a language; different conceptual schemes are not merely different notations or different systems of predicates." Compares an alchemist and a modern chemist drawing conclusions from the same observable phenomena with an English-speaking chemist and a German-speaking chemist drawing conclusions from the same observable phenomena. Claims it is legitimate for the chemist and alchemist to draw different conclusions, but not the English-speaking and German-speaking chemist (unless they also have relevant theoretical differences). Considers Bar-Hillel's claim (in the discussion) that "any inductive rule will lead to contradiction" (as in a detachment rule instead of just degrees of confirmation relative to data). Suggests that Bar-Hillel has something like this in mind: two languages with the same color predicates except for "blue" and "green" in one of the languages and a single-disjunctive "blue-or-green" in the other language; two people examining the same objects; one person (using the language with "blue" and "green") sees that all of the objects are blue, while the other person (using the other language) sees that all of the objects are blue-or-green—which seem like different conclusions from the same observable phenomena via the same rule of induction. Claims they are not using the same premises—"premises which differ purely linguistically"—because they saw the objects differently and so do not have the same data.

Salmon, Wesley C. "Bayes's Theorem and the History of Science." In *Historical and Philosophical Perspectives of Science,* Minnesota Studies in the Philosophy of Science, Vol. V, edited by Roger Stuewer, pp. 68–86. Minneapolis: University of Minnesota Press, 1970. Argues that historical information has "logical functions" in an adequate account of scientific confirmation, and that Bayes's theorem provides an adequate formal schema for the confirmation and disconfirmation of hypotheses. Emphasizes the role of historical information in estimating the prior probabilities in a Bayesian analysis. Comments (pp. 83–85) that the new riddle shows how "there is more to confirmation than confirming instances"; believes that Goodman would view prior probabilities "as somehow based upon linguistic usage"; feels that "a good deal of the experience of the human race becomes embedded in the languages we use" and that the entrenchment solution makes use of this information; thinks that the chapter in which Goodman presents the entrenchment solution "can be read as a tract on the Bayesian approach to confirmation."

Salmon, Wesley C. "Confirmation." *Scientific American* 228 (1973): 75–83. Begins the article by discussing the paradox of the ravens and the grue-bleen paradox. Defines "grue" so that (with midnight, December 31, A.D. 2000 as the critical time) "an object that exists during a period that extends into both the twentieth and the twenty-first century is grue during the entire period if it is green during the twentieth century but changes to blue at the beginning of the twenty-first century and remains blue thereafter." Notes the criticism that "grue" is a positional predicate, and Goodman's reply that "green" is positional if we start with "grue" as basic. Points out that the raven and grue paradoxes have been standard problems in confirmation theory for thirty years, there is an "enormous literature" on them, "every theorist believes he has the definitive answer to each of them," and yet there is no consensus on the correct answers. Note that Goodman claims (1973, p. 359) an object does not have to change from green to blue in order to remain grue.

Salmon, Wesley C. "Russell on Scientific Inference or Will the Real Deductivist Please Stand Up?" In *Bertrand Russell's Philosophy*, edited by George Nakhnikian, pp. 183–208. London: Gerald Duckworth & Co., 1974. Maintains that Russell (1948) actually regarded nondemonstrative inference as deductive inference with suppressed premises. Examines Russell's attempt to find such premises; compares Russell's views with those of Carnap, Popper, and Reichenbach. Section 3, "The Grue Problem," covers Russell's argument that the principle of induction (by enumeration) is false. Claims that Russell posed the new riddle in terms of manufactured classes, took the problem to be the result of using classes defined extensionally, and solved the problem by restricting the principle of induction to classes defined intensionally, i.e., "no explicit reference to *unobserved* members of the class is permitted in the definition." Considers how Russell might respond to Goodman's view about positional predicates by arguing that some descriptive terms (such as color terms) must be ostensively defined. See Salmon (1963) for more on this last point.

Salmon, Wesley C. "Note on Russell's Anticipations." *Russell,* no. 17 (1975): 29. Maintains that Russell independently discovered the grue-bleen paradox and provided a correct solution in *Human Knowledge: Its Scope and Limits* (1948). Notes that Goodman does not mention Russell's solution in *Fact, Fiction and Forecast*. Directs us to the third section of Salmon (1974) for a detailed discussion.

Salmon, Wesley C. "Nelson Goodman: A Philosopher in Search of Bayes's Theorem." In *Reality and Rationality,* forthcoming. Contends that when Goodman was writing *FFF,* he was "essentially a philosopher in search of Bayes's theorem." Points out that Goodman does not mention anything Bayesian in his exchange with Carnap in the late 1940s and that all four editions of *FFF* do not refer to anything Bayesian. Also points out that Goodman wants to use "other relevant knowledge," pay attention to the "raw material" here, and involve overhypotheses when making projectibility judgments, and that a subjective Bayesian wants to do the same thing by invoking prior probabilities. Comments on how Goodman's concept of projectibility involves frequencies and how this is a Reichenbachian idea. Emphasizes that Goodman's theory is incomplete by discussing three scientific examples in which one thing makes another more credible but it is not plain how entrenched predicates could be doing this: e.g., animal test results with saccharin applying to humans. Asks why Goodman has never recognized (and acknowledged in print) the relationship between Bayesian prior probabilities and his view of projectibility. Speculates that Goodman might think the Bayesian approach is wrong, or he might see "no particular gain to be had by dragging Bayes's theorem into the discussion." Emphasizes that Goodman's theory of projectibility and Bayesianism are not (necessarily) in conflict with one another; prefers to view Goodman's grue problem as a special case of a general problem about assigning priors. Gives three reasons why it is worth bringing up Bayes's theorem in connection with Goodman's *FFF:* viz., it is (1) a theorem that (2) provides a precise place for prior probabilities in the confirmation of hypotheses while still (3) allowing that there is more to evaluating prior probabilities than entrenchment rules. Also see Salmon (1970).

Sanford, David H. "Disjunctive Predicates." *American Philosophical Quarterly* 7 (1970): 162–170. Section I: "The Problem." Introduces the problem by showing that Butchvarov must rule out disjunctive qualities because they produce unacceptable consequences for his account of generic universals. Points out that "simple syntactical criteria are ineffective" because we can replace a predicate in disjunctive form by an equivalent predicate in nondisjunctive form, and that it is ineffective to rule out predicates equivalent to predicates in explicit disjunctive form because we can replace a predicate in nondisjunctive form by an equivalent predicate in disjunctive form. Also notes that if we say a predicate equivalent to a predicate of the form "*Q* or *R*" is disjunctive when something *Q* does not have to resemble something *R*, this is ineffective unless we can reply to the claim that these things resemble each other because they are both *Q* and *R*. Considers Searle's criterion: viz., if *G* is nondisjunctive, then "anything which putatively specifies *G* is logically related to everything else which putatively specifies *G*." Believes this criterion rules out too much because it rules out a nondisjunctive predicate like "colored." Observes that "the problem of disjunctive predicates may also be approached via Nelson Goodman's New Riddle of Induction." Points out that it "seems natural to say that 'grue' is a disjunctive predicate and that 'green' is not," and that "the problem is to provide grounds for saying this which do not beg the question." Section II: "Disjoint Predicates." Defines a disjoint area as an area divided into two subareas, where the boundaries of the subareas are completely disjoint. E.g., West and East Pakistan. Gives an analogous definition for a disjoint predicate: viz., if a predicate "can be partitioned into two subpredicates which have no borderline cases in common," then it is a disjoint predicate. E.g., the predicate "red or green." Adds three restrictions in terms of an original predicate "*P*" with subpredicates "*Q*" and "*R*." First: "*P*" must exhaust each of the subpredicates, "*Q*" and "*R*" must be jointly exhaustive of "*P*," and they must be exclusive of each other. Second: neither "*Q*" nor "*R*" can by itself exhaust "*Q*." Third: (in order to deal with problems caused by predicates with no borderline cases) if anything is *Q* if and only if it is *P* and it is *S*, then there is a borderline case of *S*. Notes a consequence of this restriction: "each subpredicate must have a borderline case." Maintains that we should "distinguish what happens to be from what might be" when interpreting these restrictions. Section III: "Disconnected Predicates." Calls the compound area of Colorado and Arizona "a disconnected area" because it can be partitioned into two subareas with no common boundary segments. Defines a "disconnected predicate" as a predicate that can be "partitioned into two subpredicates such that every borderline case of each subpredicate is also a borderline case of the original predicate." Notes that, as things stand, "all disjoint predicates are disconnected." Defines an "exclusively disjunctive predicate" as either a disjoint predicate or a disconnected predicate that is not disjoint because "the subpredicates which result from the partition of a predicate are exclusive to each other." Considers whether "grue" is an exclusively disjunctive predicate. Points out that "grue" is not a disjoint predicate because there can be borderline cases of its subpredicates. Considers whether "grue" is a disconnected predicate. Discusses Goodman's point about defining "green" as a disjunction involving "grue" and "bleen." Believes that if his original definition of "grue" is adequate, then "grue" is a disconnected predicate because the borderline cases of its two disjuncts are borderline cases of "grue." Points out that if we add a condition to his definition—that a borderline case of both of its two disjuncts is grue unless it is a borderline case of "neither green nor blue"—then "grue" is not a disconnected predicate; and that if we add a similar condition to the definition of "bleen," then "bleen" is not a disconnected predicate and "the symmetry of interdefinability between 'grue' and 'bleen' on the one hand and 'green' and 'blue' on the other is restored." Notes that even if we define "grue" and "bleen" so that they are not disconnected predicates, they are disjunctive in a way that "green" and "blue" are not disjunctive. Section IV: "Inclusively Disjunctive Predicates." Considers the way in which "red or hard" is a disjunctive predicate. Discusses a predicate that is not inclusively disjunctive "even though it is equivalent to the disjunction of two overlapping predicates." Introduces the predicate "redange or yellange" to apply to "colors in the spectrum between red and yellow inclusive." Compares "red or hard" with "redange or yellange" and notes that if something is a borderline case of both "red" and "hard," then "what kind of borderline case it is of one is irrelevant to what kind of borderline case it is of the other." Specifies that "a predicate is *split* into subpredicates if it exhausts each of the subpredicates which in turn are jointly exhaustive of it and not exclusive of each other." Says that a predicate "*P*" is inclusively disjunctive if "*P*" can be split into two subpredicates "*Q*" and "*R,*" the subpredicates have borderline cases in common, and something is both a borderline case of "*Q*" and a borderline case of "*R,*" and "what kind of borderline case something is of one subpredicate is irrelevant to what kind of borderline case it is of the other." Notes that "red or hard" is inclusively disjunctive on this definition while "redange or yellange" is not. Section V: "Skew Predicates." Maintains that Wyoming and South Dakota are a skew area, while North and South Dakota are not a skew area. Defines a "skew predicate" as a predicate "*P*", with subpredicates "*Q*" and "*R,*" sub-subpredicates "*T*" and "*U,*" and boundary predicate "*S,*" such that (1) anything is Q if and only if it is both T and S, and anything is R if and only if it is U and not S; (2) the predicates "*T or S*" and "*U or S*" are both inclusively disjunctive predicates; and (3) "if something is a borderline case of one subpredicate and also a borderline case of the boundary predicate, it does not follow that it is a borderline case of the other subpredicate." Claims that exclusively disjunctive predicates are either disjoint, disconnected, or skew predicates. Points out that "grue" is a skew predicate because its subpredicates are incompatible, inclusively disjunctive, and "if something is a borderline case both of 'green and first examined before t' and of 'first examined before $t,$' it does not follow that it is a borderline case of 'blue and not first examined before t.'" Maintains that "green" is not a skew predicate because (when partitioned into "grue and first examined before t," "bleen and not first examined before t") the most important condition is not satisfied: i.e., "a borderline case of 'first examined before t' is a borderline case of 'grue and first examined before t' if and only if it is a borderline case of 'bleen and not first examined before t.'" Admits that it might be possible to partition "green" so that it does satisfy the important condition; suggests it is reasonable to view a predicate as "non-disjunctive" if there is no apparent way of proving the opposite." Section VI: "The New Riddle Of Induction." Believes Goodman's entrenchment rules (*FFF*, chapter IV, first edition) have the correct form but the wrong content. Would have "them refer to the contrast between predicates which are not disjunctive and those which are, rather than Goodman's contrast between well entrenched predicates and those less well entrenched." Believes "disjunctiveness" is more basic than entrenchment. Claims a predicate can be poorly entrenched because disjunctive, but not "disjunctive because it is poorly entrenched." Notes that his view does not depend on "green" and "blue" being more familiar or better entrenched, and that his view "has no direct connection with the possibility of ostensive teaching." Discusses a case in which some people take our predicate "red" to be disjunctive because they use the predicate "vermson" to mean "red or green," and they apply "strong vermson" and "weak vermson" to red things, "medium vermson" to green things. Contends that nonetheless "vermson" is disjoint and "red" is not disjoint because the subpredicates of "vermson" do not have borderline cases in common, while the subpredicates of "red" do have borderline cases in common. Maintains that Goodman could have used a disjoint predicate to make his point. Concludes that he sees no reason to suppose that "grue" being disjunctive "is relative to the language we happen to speak or to the inferences of our forebears." Also see Sanford (1981) and (this volume).

Sanford, David H. "Independent Predicates." *American Philosophical Quarterly* 18 (1981):

171–174. Notes that an apple's red color has nothing "intrinsically" to do with its round shape, and vice versa. Attempts to define "independent predicate" so that we can represent this in terms of "red" and "round" being independent predicates. Introduces the predicate "hupe" to mean "hue and shape." Claims "an adequate definition of independence will show that 'hupe' is a conjunctive predicate, one equivalent to a conjunction of independent predicates." Claims we cannot use similarity (red things are similar to other red things) in defining independence because "our judgments of similarity are too closely related to our judgments of independence" (red or round things are similar to other red or round things). Believes an adequate definition will show "round" is not a disjunctive predicate, while "red or round" is a disjunctive predicate equivalent to a disjunction of independent predicates. Defines the L (logical) independence of two predicates "F" and "G" in terms of it being possibly true (for each conjunct in the following conjunction) that something is F and G, and that something is F and not G, and that something is not F and is G, and that something is not F and not G. Maintains that L-independence is too broad. Considers how to define disjunctive and conjunctive predicates. Notes that syntactic criteria are inadequate and that independence is not a purely syntactic criterion. Points out that if we use the notion of L-independence and regard a predicate as conjunctive if and only if it is equivalent to a conjunction of independent predicates and as inclusively disjunctive if and only if equivalent to a disjunction of independent predicates, then "any predicate whose extensions include at least two things is both disjunctive and conjunctive." Introduces "the notion of the boundary of a predicate's extension" and borderline cases of a predicate, or things on the boundary of a predicate's extension. States that predicates "F" and "G" are exclusive disjuncts of the predicate "H" if "they are each exhausted by 'H' and in turn are jointly exhaustive of it and exclusive of each other." States that a predicate "H" is exclusively disjunctive if it has "F" and "G" as exclusive disjuncts with non-null extensions, and "anything on the boundary of either exclusive disjunct is also on the boundary of the original predicate." Maintains that if predicates are independent, then "the boundaries of their extensions are independent," and that if the boundaries of their extensions are independent, then "they intersect." States two conditions for when two predicates "F" and "G" intersect: first, something is on the boundary of the predicate "F and G" and on the boundary of the predicate "F and not G" and on the boundary of the predicate "not F and G" and on the boundary of the predicate "not F and not G;" second, anything on both the boundary of "F" and the boundary of "G" is on the boundary of "F and G" and on the boundary of "F and not G" and on the boundary of "not F and G" and on the boundary of "not F and not G." Defines two predicates "F" and "G" as minimally independent (M-independent) if and only if they satisfy these two conditions. Notes that the definition of inclusively disjunctive is wrong in Sanford (1970). Discusses how the predicate "W" ("has a mass not less than 100 pounds and not greater than 200 pounds") is equivalent to a conjunction of two M-independent predicates and also equivalent to a disjunction of two M-independent predicates that involve the dimensions of mass in pounds and height in centimeters, and yet "W" is not a conjunctive nor a disjunctive predicate. Believes this is a case of spurious independence because "distinct boundaries of one predicate and distinct boundaries of another *genuinely independent* predicate intersect with each other in exactly one place," not two. Formulates his "final definition of independence" in terms of his accounts of the distinctness of boundaries and the distinctness of intersections. Maintains that if predicates "F" and "G" are genuinely independent, then "each distinct portion of the boundary of 'F' intersects each distinct portion of the boundary of 'G'," and the distinct portions of their boundaries do not intersect more than once. Points out that "two predicates are genuinely independent if and only if their complements are genuinely independent," and that a predicate is "inclusively disjunctive if and only if its complement is conjunctive." Incorporates material from, and attempts to improve on, Sanford (1970). See Sanford (this volume) for his most recent view.

Savage, Leonard J. "Implications of Personal Probability for Induction." *Journal of Philosophy* 64 (1967): 593–607. A major figure in statistics known for his theory of subjective probability and work on Bayesian decision theory. Describes and defends the concept of personal probability. Discusses induction from his personal probability point of view. Doubts that there is a rational basis for our beliefs about the unobserved. Regards Hume's arguments and Goodman's grue and bleen discussion as "correct and realistic." Reports that he sees "no objective grounds" for believing a universal proposition that is not a tautology. Claims that "what we would ordinarily call knowledge of a universal is acceptance with a high probability of a universal with a finite domain or of many such." With regard to all emeralds being green, claims they are if we mean, as a matter of convention, that emeralds are green gemstones; adds that "perhaps geologists mean such a thing by 'emerald' that, for them, there are already nongreen emeralds, or at least the possibility of nongreen ones is not closed by convention."

Scheffler, Israel. "Inductive Inference: A New Approach." *Science* 127 (1958): 177–181. Also in this volume. Aims to "acquaint the scientific reader with the background and the direction of Goodman's investigations, as they bear on the interpretation of induction." Discusses two replies to Hume's challenge about the rational justification of induction. Believes the ordinary language reply (i.e., how we normally use "rational") is inadequate because "not every statement which outstrips available evidence is reasonable, though some are." Refers to the second reply as "the generalization formula." States the generalization formula as "reasonable inductions are those which conform to past regularities." More precisely: we make one prediction instead of its opposite because of "its congruence with a generalization thoroughly in accord with all such evidence, and the correlative disconfirmation of the contrary generalization by the same evidence." Claims that Goodman's work refutes the generalization formula. Introduces Goodman's copper/third son example: if a given piece of copper conducts electricity, this confirms the hypothesis "All copper conducts electricity," but if a given man in a certain room now is a third son, this does not confirm "All the men now in this room are third sons." Notes that both hypotheses are simply generalizations from the evidence statements, and so the generalization formula selects both credible and incredible inductions. Goes on to explain how Goodman shows "we do not even establish that the next specimen of copper conducts electricity, for we can produce a generalization equally supported by the evidence and yielding the prediction it does not." Introduces a gruelike copper hypothesis: "All copper either has been examined prior to t and conducts electricity or has not been examined prior to t and does not conduct electricity." Points out that "for cases assumed new, then, the generalization formula selects no particular inductions at all." Also notes that the situation does not improve as data accumulates because there will be other gruelike copper hypotheses specifying times later than t. Introduces Goodman's term "projectibility" and explains how projectible hypotheses are "generalizations *capable* of receiving support from their positive instances and in turn sanctioning particular inductions." Considers attempts to repair the generalization formula. First: say the formula does not apply to generalizations that refer to time, as the gruelike copper hypothesis does. Claims "the situation is easily reversed." Lets "K" stand for the complicated predicate of the gruelike copper hypothesis and explains how the gruelike hypothesis becomes "All copper has the property *K*" and the normal copper hypothesis becomes "All copper is either such that it has been examined before *t* and has the property *K* or has not been examined before *t* and does not have the property *K*." Second: say the formula must be applied to a generalization in the wider context of other, relevant, well-established generalizations and not in isolation. Introduces the wider generalization "All classes of specimens of the same material are uniform with respect to electrical conductivity" and notes that it discredits the gruelike copper hypothesis. Also introduces a gruelike wider generalization: "All classes of specimens of the same material are uniform with respect to possession of the property *K*." Notes that this hypothesis is equally supported by the same evidence and that it discredits the normal copper hypothesis. Maintains that "we are again face to face with the very problem with which we started." Describes how Goodman uses "pragmatic or historical information" in the form of "the *biographies* of the specific terms or predicates employed in previous inductions." Introduces Goodman's notion of entrenchment and explains how "conducts electricity" is better entrenched than the complicated gruelike predicate because it picks out a class that has been mentioned more often in formulating inductions. Explains Goodman's notion of the degree of projectibility of a hypothesis, how it represents the notion of lawlikeness, and how this solves the general problem of dispositions. Points out that Goodman does not provide an "explanation of entrenchment itself." Also points out that entrenchment criteria will not "lead to the ruling out of unfamiliar predicates, thus stultifying the growth of scientific language." Maintains that unfamiliar predicates can be well entrenched if they are coextensive with well-entrenched predicates, and that they can inherit entrenchment from parent predicates. Adds that "Goodman's criteria provide methods for evaluating *hypotheses,* not predicates." See Scheffler (1963), Part III, "Confirmation," for additional discussion.

Scheffler, Israel. *The Anatomy of Inquiry: Philosophical Studies in the Theory of Science.* New York: Alfred A. Knopf, Inc., 1963. Now in print from Hackett Publishing Co., Indianapolis, Ind., 1981. See Part III, "Confirmation," especially sections 1–2, 7–10. Concerned with formulating "the specific criteria by which some inductions are justified as reasonable, while others are rejected as unreasonable, though both groups outstrip the available evidence." Characterizes the generalization formula as the idea that we make one prediction instead of its opposite because of the prediction's "congruence with a generalization thoroughly in accord with all such evidence, and (hence) the correlative disconfirmation of the contrary generalization by the same evidence." Considers whether this provides "a *criterion* for singling out those predictions regarded as justified at any given time." Examines the "natural view of the generalization formula": i.e., "that instances which *accord with* a generalization in fact *confirm* it, in the sense of *selecting* it as a basis for particular inductions." Notes that "the hypotheses designated by the generalization formula do not uniformly sanction the particular judgments based upon them." Introduces Goodman's example of this: a piece of copper confirms the lawlike hypothesis "All copper conducts electricity" but if a third son is now in a certain room, this does not confirm the accidental hypothesis "All men now in this room are third sons." Takes this to show "that, in addition to all credible or sanctioned particular inductions, the generalization formula also selects certain incredible ones." Claims that Goodman shows "we do not even 'establish' that the next specimen of copper will conduct electricity, for we can produce a generalization equally supported by the evidence and yielding the prediction that it will not": viz., the generalization "All copper has either been examined before *t* and conducts electricity or has not been examined before *t* and does not conduct electricity." Takes this to show "that the generalization formula does not yield any desired induction whatever." Notes that the situation does not change as we accumulate empirical data because it does not matter how many gruelike copper hypotheses have been disconfirmed up to a certain point in time, "we still have (by the generalization formula) contradictory predictions or inductions for every case not yet included in our data." Also notes that the generalization formula is "unrestricted with respect to the predicates entering into the hypotheses in question, except for the general requirement that they be observationally definable." Introduces Goodman's notion of projectibility and claims projectibility criteria will "pick out just those generalizations which are *confirmable*, i.e., *capable* of receiving selective support from their positive instances as against rival hypotheses and, therefore, of sanctioning particular inductions in turn." Considers the view that we can characterize projectibility "by ruling out generalizations making reference to time." Introduces "*K*" for the gruelike copper predicate (examined and conducts or not examined and doesn't conduct) so that the gruelike copper hypothesis becomes "All copper is *K*." Defines "conducts electricity" as "examined before *t* and *K*, or not examined before *t* and not *K*" so that the normal copper hypothesis makes a temporal reference. Considers whether "the generalization formula is being applied too narrowly" and whether it would help to take "account of a wider context of relevant hypotheses." Introduces the generalization "All classes of specimens of the same material are uniform with respect to electrical conductivity" and notes that it conflicts with (and so discredits) the gruelike copper hypothesis. Introduces the analogue, "All classes of specimens of the same material are uniform with respect to being *K*," notes that it is equally well supported, and that it conflicts with (and so discredits) the normal copper hypothesis. Concludes that if we appeal to large hypotheses, this "serves merely to postpone our perplexity." Considers whether there is "a radical shift in reference at *t*" for the predicate "*K*" but not the predicate "conducts electricity." Uses "grue" as an example in which "reference radically shifts with respect to color, at *t*," and so is a temporal predicate. Believes "the trouble with this argument is its failure to acknowledge the *relativity* of the notion of a 'shift in reference'." Points out that "grue" shifts at *t* (from things that are green to others that are not) and that "green" also shifts in reference at *t* (from things that are grue to others that are not). Adds that time reference is not an essential feature of the problem. Shows how the predicate "grue" can be explained without a time reference: e.g., "grue" could apply to anything that has *H* and is green, or that does not have *H* and is blue, where "*H*" could designate "a feature of geographical location, known to us through special information." Also notes that each of the evidence cases has the nontemporal property "of being identical with one or another of them, and this property is, moreover, not possessed by any case beyond the evidence." Maintains that it does not solve anything to translate the generalization formula "into terms of *falsification*" because both the normal copper hypothesis and the gruelike copper hypothesis are "each unfalsified by the evidence to date" and "they conflict for new cases." Argues that we cannot solve anything by appealing to simplicity (the normal copper hypothesis is structurally simpler and less complicated than the gruelike one) because "equivalent hypotheses with extensionally equivalent, though different, predicates are always available, which are as complex or simple as you like, by the standards of internal structural simplicity." Notes how Goodman argues that simplicity "is distinct from both weakness, or safety, and strength." Explains Goodman's entrenchment solution and his definitions of "presumptively projectible hypothesis," "initial projectibility index," and "degree of projectibility." Takes "the most natural objection" to be that Goodman does not provide an explanation of entrenchment itself. Notes that "further explanation is not ruled out" and that Goodman has tried to formulate criteria for selecting projectible hypotheses. Claims it is a misconception to think that Goodman's entrenchment solution might "lead to the ruling out of unfamiliar predicates, thus stultifying the growth of scientific language." Notes that unfamiliar predicates can be as entrenched as any predicates they are coextensive with, that they can inherit entrenchment from parent predicates, and that Goodman's criteria eliminate hypotheses instead of terms. Ends with a discussion of how inductive rules might be seen as exemplifying "more comprehensive accepted principles, and are thus not idiosyncratic." Thinks that Goodman's projectibility rules (favoring entrenched over nonentrenched predicates) exemplify "a kind of conceptual inertia or conservatism which has been remarked also in other contexts, under a variety of labels." Cites Quine on "familiarity of principle" and "a principle of conservation applicable to whole systems of statements." Notes that projectibility "involves a certain principle of conservation with respect to predicates (or their extensions)." Maintains there are two components of "familiarity of principle": viz., "minimum revision" and "maximum extension" of the scheme. Adds "another principle, of *model*-conservation, which operates where scheme-conservation is overridden, perhaps by the demands of systematic simplicity, in meeting an observational challenge or incorporating new data." Believes "one might justify the projectibility principles by pointing out that they are in fact not idiosyncratic" because "they exemplify a comprehensive principle of conceptual conservation, which counsels the preservation of as much of our intellectual equipment as possible, provided the weightier demands of fact and systematization are satisfied." Concludes by noting that Goodman's entrenchment solution "is ostensibly limited to simple universal hypotheses of observational sort" at present and that nonobservational theoretical notions are important in actual scientific theories.

Scheffler, Israel. "Projectibility: A Postscript." *Journal of Philosophy* 79 (1982): 334–336. Makes a number of points about "All emeralds are green" and "All emeralds are grue." Notes that we need to assume they conflict in order to have a problem about choosing between them, and that we are assuming the contrary "if we have positive reason to suppose that all emeralds will have been examined by *t*." Maintains that if we do not have a positive reason to suppose they are exhausted by time *t*, then we are to presume the hypotheses are not exhausted and so they conflict. Argues that if we are correct in presuming they are unexhausted, our choice of the green over the grue hypothesis on the basis of relative entrenchment "enables us to anticipate cases in conflict"; if we are not correct in presuming they are unexhausted, "we lose nothing by such choice since these hypotheses agree, given exhaustion by *t*"; if we presume they are exhausted and this is incorrect, we are not prepared "for cases examined after *t*, until they are actually confronted." Adds that if we presume they are exhausted by *t*, this "is the denial of novelty" because there is always a gruelike predicate with a time *t* "the moment just after the last case examined." Points out that if "All emeralds are grue" is unprojectible, this does not show "All emeralds are green" is projectible because "it may be *blocked* through conflict with an equally well-entrenched hypothesis" that it does not override and vice versa. Considers Zabludowski's (1975) hypothesis "All stones are fusible," which is supposed to be supported, unviolated, unexhausted and as well entrenched as "All emeralds are green." Notes that if these hypotheses conflict, "All emeralds are green" is nonprojectible; and if they do not conflict "All stones are fusible" does not threaten to make "All emeralds are green" nonprojectible. Points out that if we do not assume they conflict and do not assume the contrary, we do not need to choose between the two hypotheses and "we can project them both, treating them as not in conflict unless and until positive reason emerges to persuade us otherwise." Believes this policy is better than "suspension of projection altogether" because the latter policy deprives us of projectible hypotheses when they do not conflict, and if we project both when they do conflict, "future experience, guided by such projection, may itself correct our mistaken presumption of projectibility." Emphasizes that we should consider the no-conflict presumption "part of our preferred policy of facilitating projection," and so "unless positive reason indicates otherwise," we are to presume "All emeralds are green" to be projectible instead of presuming it to be nonprojectible because of its relation with "All stones are fusible." Points out a difference with respect to how "the rule of conflict operates" in the two comparisions: viz., if we do not assume a conflict between the green/grue hypotheses, we do not have a problem about choosing between them, and if we assume there are cases to be examined after *t,* this "underlies and requires discriminating projection" and "it is hardly an assumption we are likely to dispense with unless we have specific reason to assume the contrary for the particular evidence class in question"; but if we assume there is a conflict between the green and fusible hypotheses, this "blocks projection altogether" and provides a reason "for minimizing such assumption, allowing projection fuller scope."

Scheffler, Israel and Goodman, Nelson. "Selective Confirmation and the Ravens: A Reply to Foster." *Journal of Philosophy* 69 (1972): 78–83. A reply to Foster (1971). Consider Foster's projectibility requirement in section IV. Wonder if Foster has actually alleviated the raven paradox because, on his own account, "a black raven but not a thing that is neither black nor a raven would count as evidence that whatever is not black is not a raven." Also wonder about whether "All nonblack things are nonravens" is projectible. Note that even if its predicates are poorly entrenched, this "seems to illustrate no general principle" because "many other privative predicates are well entrenched." Note in addition that a privative predicate "will be as entrenched as any of its coextensive predicates." Emphasize that "ill-entrenchment of predicates does not make a hypothesis unprojectible": i.e., we must consider any conflicting hypotheses and how well entrenched they are. Wonder if "the predicate to be compared for entrenchment should or should not include the logical constant '−'." Also see the reply to Foster by Schwartz (1972).

Schick, Frederic. "Allowing for Understandings." *Journal of Philosophy* 89 (1992): 30–41. Considers ideological, formal, and visceral objections to his views on the logic of action, notably about the role of people's understandings or "the way people put the facts to themselves." Discusses whether there are standards for proper vs. improper, sound vs. unsound, understandings. Brings up Goodman as someone who "studied a special case of this question" with the grue problem. Regards the entrenchment solution as "very narrow" because "it deals with a special question only"—the question of proper descriptions for inferences, not the question of proper descriptions in any context. Goes on to cite Goodman as rejecting the question ("right and wrong has no strict application") in *Ways of Worldmaking*.

Schlesinger, G. *Confirmation and Confirmability.* London: Oxford University Press, 1974. Chapter 2, "Confirmation and Parsimony," discusses the curve-fitting problem from *Scientific Inference* (1931) by Harold Jeffreys: viz., infinitely many equations can fit a finite number of observations, so how do we select the right equation? Argues that we should select the simplest equation or hypothesis. Maintains that the maximizing simplicity principle is the only one able to select a unique hypothesis based on the observations as opposed to extraneous factors. Mentions grue in a footnote on page 43; argues that there are infinitely many "artificially created" gruelike hypotheses and no criterion for selecting one of these over the others, while for natural language hypotheses "we have no problem as their use yields a unique prediction in all cases." Also see Kemeny (1953), Ackermann (1961), Swinburne (1971), Sober (1975),

Glymour (1980), and Turney (1990) for discussions of simplicity and the curve-fitting problem.

Schlesinger, George. *Religion and Scientific Method.* Dordrecht, Holland: D. Reidel, 1977. See chapter 21, "The Principles Underlying Scientific Method," for a discussion of Jeffreys's curve-fitting problem and grue. Stresses the importance of his Principle of Adequacy: "when H and H' are similarly related to all the available evidence, we regard H as more confirmed than H', if and only if, H is more adequate than H'." Claims "the most adequate hypothesis is the one selected with the aid of the only useable guiding rule." Maintains that the "only useable guiding rule" selects a specific hypothesis—the simplest equation for the curve-fitting problem and the green emeralds hypothesis for the new riddle. Essentially the same view as Schlesinger (1974).

Schlesinger, George N. "The Justification of Empirical Reasoning." *Philosophical Quarterly* 29 (1979): 208–219. Develops points from Schlesinger (1974). Claims the adequate hypothesis-selection rule combines straight induction from observations of a past regularity with a simplicity requirement. Argues that only this rule is capable of selecting hypotheses uniquely. Section IV discusses the curve-fitting problem and his simplicity solution from (1974); also considers Goodman's paradox and three solutions to it: Salmon (1963), Barker and Achinstein (1960), and Carnap (1947). These solutions are supposed to illustrate "the fact that hypothesis-selection rules that seem intuitively satisfactory conform to the fundamental principle underlying methodology: to avail oneself of adequate rules which are unique of their kind."

Schlesinger, George. "Strawson on Induction." *Philosophia* 10 (1981): 199–208. Examines Strawson's dissolution of the problem of induction, especially the claim that the rules of inductive reasoning have been adopted as a matter of convention. Develops points from Schlesinger (1974) and (1979). Section IV discusses the curve-fitting problem and Goodman's paradox "to illustrate that a solution which may be advanced with any plausibility at all must be based on the principle that we reject any rule that does not help us to select a particular hypothesis"; essentially the same discussion as Schlesinger (1979).

Schlesinger, George N. "Is It True What Cicero Said about Philosophers?" *Metaphilosophy* 19 (1988): 282–293. Maintains that "common sense and sound intuition provide a fairly effective defense mechanism for the eventual rejection of most inauthentic philosophical propositions." Takes the new riddle as his most dramatic illustration. Claims commonsensical people will assume the future to be like the past, regard green as a unitary color but not grue, let color change or constancy be "determined by inherent appearances," and so expect emeralds to be green in the future. Discusses Carnap's (1947) solution and Goodman's reply in *Fact, Fiction and Forecast.* Discusses Rosenkrantz (1982) in detail to show how hard it is to suppress "common sense and sound intuition."

Schlesinger, George. *The Sweep of Probability.* Notre Dame, Ind.: University of Notre Dame Press, 1991. See chapter IV, section 6, for a discussion of the new riddle. Essentially the same as Schlesinger (1988). Remarks, in comparing the new riddle to Jeffreys's curve-fitting problem, that "it is by no means clear why Goodman's problem, though having had a remarkably higher dramatic impact, presents a serious source of worry."

Schock, Rolf. "Ravens, Grue, and Material Implication." *Dialectica* 38 (1984): 347–350. Claims that the new riddle is "no paradox" and "totally misguided." Considers it nothing more than a "straightforward consequence of material implication": viz., that a material conditional is true when its antecedent is false. Reformulates "all emeralds are green" and "all emeralds are grue" as conjunctions of two material conditionals, one conditional about the color of emeralds before time *t* and one about the color at or later than *t*. Maintains that the former conjuncts are "inductively supported or confirmed in the usual way," but that the latter conjuncts (about after *t*) are conditionals which "have up to now unsatisfiable antecedents." Claims both are confirmed "by the relevant trivially true instantial statements for emeralds and other objects inspected up to now." The two hypotheses are only "trivially true" material implications and so inductively they are "only trivially equal." Views such "trivially based" hypotheses as correct but uninteresting.

Schwartz, Robert. "Confirmation and Conflict." *Journal of Philosophy* 68 (1971): 483–487. Examines "interrelationships among confirmability, projectibility, and lawlikeness." States the current, single projectibility rule from *FFF*. Lists four unprojectible hypotheses according to this rule: e.g., when all of the emeralds examined before *t* are green and they are all square as well, "All emeralds are square" overrides "All emeralds are grund," and so "All emeralds are grund" is unprojectible. Notes that if the evidence were different, these hypotheses could be projectible: e.g., "All emeralds are grund" is projectible when the emeralds examined before *t* are green and round. Believes this shows there are two senses of "projectibility" because "though the rule does provide a principle for choosing among incompatible hypotheses, it does not ensure that projectible hypotheses are always the sort confirmable by their positive instances." Notes that if our evidence consists of green emeralds examined before *t*, this is not enough evidence to confirm "All emeralds are grund" because it still conflicts with hypotheses like "All emeralds are grare" and so it is not projectible. Concludes that "those hypotheses not confirmable by positive instances are incapable of overcoming conflict on the basis of their own evidence." Formulates the second sense of "projectibility" as: a hypothesis is C-projectible if and only if it is supported, unviolated, and unexhausted "and its existing conflicts can be overriden on the basis of each of its positive instances." Considers the claim that lawlike generalizations support counterfactuals, and argues that some (first sense) projectible hypotheses do not support counterfactuals and are not lawlike: e.g., if "All emeralds are green" is projectible, everything on his couch (at *t*) is found to be green, and all emeralds (examined by then) are green, then "All things either on my couch at *t* or an emerald are green" is projectible, and yet does not support counterfactuals (e.g., if this red pillow were either on my couch at *t* or were an emerald . . .) and "does not seem suited for contexts of explanation and prediction where laws are needed." Considers requiring "that a hypothesis be C-projectible if it is to be a law." Believes this might be too strong because there will be reasons for regarding "All emeralds are grund" or "All emerubies are gred" to be laws when the evidence makes them projectible, even though they are not C-projectible: e.g., the emerubies hypothesis will support counterfactuals, will be a consequence of two laws, and might be used to explain and predict in some contexts. Wonders if it might be better to insist "that confirmability on the basis of positive instances is basic to lawlikeness" and to say that "All emeralds are grund" and "All emerubies are gred" are not lawlike hypotheses or only lawlike in "some derived sense."

Schwartz, Robert. "Paradox and Projection." *Philosophy of Science* 39 (1972): 245–248. A reply to Quine (1970 and this volume) and Foster (1971). Notes that "the Quine–Foster solution" to the raven paradox "rests on a supposed projectibility asymmetry between *R are B* and *−B are −R*, the former considered by them projectible, the latter not." States three reasons why this is not the right approach to the paradox: e.g., it is not a general solution because there is no asymmetry with respect to the projectibility of hypotheses and their contrapositives when they have "terms like flexible, flammable, electrically charged, organic." Suggests that if $-B$ and $-R$ are poorly entrenched according to Goodman's account, "perhaps the thing to do is alter the notion of entrenchment" so that a predicate is entrenched "not only when a coextensive predicate is projected, but also when its complement extension is projected." Assumes this is a sound approach. Introduces the current (1970) definition of a non/un/projectible hypothesis. Notes that if we take support to be selectively positive instances, then $-Ba$, $-Ra$ does not support R *are* B and that hypothesis is not projectible; also Ra, Ba does not support $-B$ *are* $-R$ and that hypothesis is not projectible. Claims "this approach to the paradox requires distinguishing what it means to project R *are* B from what it means to project $-B$ *are* $-R$." Considers whether R *are* B is projectible if we use Hempel's satisfaction criterion for support and the evidence is $-Ba$, $-Ra$. Points out that it depends on "how we construe the notion of *conflict* in our rule of projection." That is, R *are* B and R *are* $-B$ conflict only if there are ravens, and so if there are ravens and these hypotheses are equally well entrenched, then they are nonprojectible; and if "we assume that there are no ravens, there is no conflict but, it would seem, neither is there any paradox." Discusses how R *are* B, $-B$ *are* $-R$, and R *are* $-B$ are not projectible when we assume there is a conflict; also discusses how they are projectible when we assume there is not a conflict. Notes that when we assume there is not a conflict, "we can then agree with Hempel and other advocates of the equivalence conditions, that with $(-Ba, -Ra)$ as the only evidence, R *are* B is both confirmed and projectible" and this also sustains "our intuition that this evidence does not warrant the projection of black to *ravens*." Ends by claiming that a satisfaction-criterion theory of projection can indicate "the asymmetrical weight of $(-Ba, -Ra)$ in warranting projections about nonblack things as opposed to ravens" without "distinguishing between the projective content" of R *are* B and $-B$ *are* $-R$ (as in *FFF* and taking support as selectively positive instances). See the reply to Foster by Scheffler and Goodman (1972).

Schwartz, Robert John. "Approximate Truth and Confirmation." *Philosophy of Science* 48 (1981): 606–610. Argues that many acceptable scientific hypotheses are approximately true and obviously projectible, yet on Goodman's view would not count as projectible hypotheses because they are violated and perhaps also unsupported.

Schwartz, Robert; Scheffler, Israel; and Goodman, Nelson. "An Improvement in the Theory of Projectibility." *Journal of Philosophy* 67 (1970): 605–608. Replace the two rules for eliminating unprojectible hypotheses (stated in *FFF*, Second edition, chapter IV, section 4) by one rule that uses the notion of one hypothesis overriding another. Specify that (for supported, unviolated, unexhausted hypotheses) one hypothesis overrides another if they conflict, the former hypothesis is better entrenched than the latter or overridden hypothesis, and the former hypothesis does not conflict with an even better entrenched hypothesis. State the new, revised rule as: "a hypothesis is *projectible* if all conflicting hypotheses are overridden, *unprojectible* if overridden, and *nonprojectible* if in conflict with another hypothesis and neither is overridden." Examine "the effect of different evidence" on whether three hypotheses are unprojectible: "All emeralds are grund," "All emerubies are green," and "All emerubies are gred." Point out how, for example, the hypothesis "All emeralds are grund" is unprojectible when the evidence consists of emeralds examined before t and all of them have been found to be both green and square, how the hypothesis is nonprojectible when all of the emeralds have been found to be green and some of them have been found to be square, and how it is projectible when all of the emeralds have been found to be both green and round. Note some hesitation about regarding "All emeralds are grund" as projectible in this last circumstance, and believe it results from confusing two senses in which a hypothesis is projectible: "a hypothesis is projectible if support normally makes it credible" and "a hypothesis is projectible only when the actual evidence supports and makes it credible." Maintain that while "All emeralds are grund" is "a hypothesis not normally projectible," it can gain "projectibility under sufficiently favorable circumstances." End by giving necessary and sufficient conditions ("subject to the further considerations" in section 5 of chapter IV) for a hypothesis being projectible, unprojectible, or nonprojectible. Also given on page 108 of *FFF*, third or fourth edition. Also see Goodman (1972) for this paper.

Settle, T.W. "The Point of Positive Evidence—Reply to Professor Feyerabend." *British Journal for the Philosophy of Science* 20 (1969): 352–355. A reply to Feyerabend (1968). Maintains that Feyerabend confuses scientific method with induction and that he ignores the role of confirmation in making rational decisions about conducting scientific experiments and, more generally, the role of confirmation in technological pursuits.

Shalkowski, Scott A. "Concepts and Correspondence." *Philosophy and Phenomenological Research* 47 (1987a): 461–474. States and criticizes two arguments Goodman uses in rejecting a correspondence (realist) theory of truth. Calls one argument "The Argument from the Veil of Conceptions" and claims Goodman uses it to support his conventionalism. Discusses grue in connection with premise three of this argument: viz., "realism requires that true sentences of our language give an account of the world that is independent of any descriptions." Views the entrenchment solution—choosing the green over the grue hypothesis on the basis of predicate entrenchment—as a matter of convention because "the world is not sufficient to justify a choice of one over the other." Argues that this conventionality (theorizing with the term 'green' instead of 'grue') is not a problem for realism about truth because "conventionality does not entail indeterminacy of truth, nor does it entail that the world cannot render sentences containing conventionally chosen terms true." See the reply by Elgin (1987) and the response by Shalkowski (1987b).

Shalkowski, Scott A. "Correspondence Revisited." *Philosophy and Phenomenological Research* 47 (1987b): 476–478. A response to Elgin (1987). Maintains that he discussed the grue paradox only to "show where conventionality enters into even a realist account of truth." Claims it is a matter of convention whether we have 'green' or 'grue' or both in our language, but it is not a similar matter of convention with regard to truth conditions. Maintains this sort of conventionality is not a problem for "the objective character of the world or the correspondence theory of truth." Notes that realism does not solve the grue paradox and its consequences are irrelevant to the paradox.

Shirley, Edward S. "An Unnoticed Flaw in Barker and Achinstein's Solution to Goodman's New Riddle of Induction." *Philosophy of Science* 48 (1981): 611–617. A reply to Barker and Achinstein (1960). Argues that Barker and Achinstein misread the definition of "grue" and in consequence they do not show Goodman is wrong about the symmetry between "grue" and "green." Maintains that in Goodman's definition the time t is the time at which an object is examined and not the time or date at which an object exists, and that all of Barker and Achinstein's points involve the latter in the form of dating a future scene in a picture.

Shoemaker, Sydney. "On Projecting the Unprojectible." *Philosophical Review* 84 (1975a): 178–219. Section I. Concerned with justifying our policy of projecting entrenched predicates instead of nonentrenched predicates (i.e., "green" instead of "grue"). Will consider a person, Mr. B, who projects "grue" and ask if this person has an unreasonable or incoherent projective policy. Claims Goodman's theory cannot show this policy is unreasonable because it allows "grue" to be more projectible than "green" in the event that somehow "grue" becomes more entrenched than "green." Section II. Considers whether one prediction (green or grue) will be shown wrong by examining emeralds after time *t*. Argues that if we observe green emeralds after *t*, this does not show Mr. B's grue prediction is wrong. Claims that if a person systematically projects "grue," this "involves expecting generalizations involving grueness which hold up to a certain time to continue to hold after that time," and so this person will not be surprised that these emeralds look the way grue emeralds looked at an earlier time (e.g., reflecting light of a certain wavelength). Emphasizes that "the expectations of a systematic 'grue' and 'bleen' projector will be disappointed only in case the expectations of a systematic 'green' and 'blue' projector will also be disappointed." Section III. Wonders if Mr. B is projecting Goodman's predicate "grue" or a predicate with the same meaning as our predicate "green." Introduces the agreement-after-*t* condition: a person projecting Goodman's predicate will agree with us after time *t* when applying "green," "blue," "grue," and "bleen" to examined objects. Notes that Mr. B's case does not satisfy this condition so far. Section IV. Discusses an inconsistency in the Mr. B case: viz., if Mr. B also projects "is exactly similar in color to," then he will be predicting some blue objects examined after *t* will be the same color as some grue objects examined before *t*. Avoids this problem by introducing Ullian's (1961) term "schmolor" and having Mr. B project "is exactly similar in schmolor to" and other relational schmolor predicates. Believes this does not satisfy the agreement-after-*t* condition. Claims Mr. B will find a new emerald similar in schmolor to previously examined grue (green) things and not to bleen (blue) things because he is committed to certain generalizations about "things indistinguishable by sight." Attempts to gruify more of Mr. B's vocabulary. Introduces "is ingrustinguishable from" and has Mr. B project this predicate instead of "is visually indistinguishable from." Believes this does not satisfy the agreement condition because Mr. B will end up using Mr. A's behavioral criteria for visual indistinguishability as his criteria for ingrustinguishability. Maintains that gruelike predicates "will affect what evidential generalizations are accepted and hence what is taken to be evidence for the instantiation of various properties." Section V. Discusses whether nonobservational predicates are the only predicates that involve accepted generalizations when applied to observed items. Maintains that if we regard ourselves as "reliable visual color detectors," then we are committed to generalizations about things similar (different) in color looking alike (different) to us, e.g., generalizations about things looking green or blue to us. Notes a connection between reliable visual color detectors and the ability to learn color words ostensively: viz., if a person has learned the meaning of "green," then the relevant generalizations, the "Looks-Green propositions," are true in a lawlike way of that person. Believes that if Mr. A now asks Mr. B whether he learned "grue" or "green" ostensively, Mr. B is facing a dilemma because the answer "grue" will show Mr. B did not learn Goodman's term and instead learned another word for our "green," and the answer "green" shows his position is incoherent in that he is supposed to be projecting "grue" and yet his answer commits him to the "Looks-Green" propositions. Section VI. Notes the Mr. B case has been about systematically projecting Goodman's "grue." Defines projecting a term systematically relative to our projective policy. Considers whether Mr. B can satisfy the agreement condition by selectively projecting "grue"— e.g., just in "all emeralds are grue" and generalizations it implies. Argues that if Mr. B adopts the selective policy, there will be an epistemological asymmetry between "green" and "grue" because Mr. B will defend his grue/bleen ascriptions by referring to his green/blue ascriptions and temporal information. Points out that Thomson's objections (1966) will then apply to Mr. B's position. Section VII. Supposes that Mr. A and Mr. B differ in their ability to discriminate between blue or green objects: viz., they agree when both objects have been examined for the first time before *t* or after *t*, but they disagree when one of the objects has been examined before *t* for the first time and the other after *t*. Notes how this will satisfy the agreement condition, and how that is only a necessary condition for Mr. A and B meaning the same thing here. Maintains we also need to consider what explains this agreement. Presents a science fiction explanation in terms of unobserved objects emitting alpha radiation if green and beta radiation if blue, human eyes emitting gamma radiation up until *t*, gamma radiation causing a blue object to start emitting alpha radiation and a green object to start emitting beta radiation, and Mr. B having receptors sensitive to alpha and beta radiation instead of green and blue light. Maintains that any explanation must "involve the supposition that prior to *t*, but not afterward, the first observation of an object makes a permanent change in it, and that the permanent state thus induced influences the way the object acts on the sensory receptors of one of our two men, either Mr. A or Mr. B, but not on the way it acts on the sensory receptors of the other." Argues that if we accept the radiation explanation, then Mr. A and Mr. B are not agreeing about anything or making incompatible predictions before *t* because Mr. A and Mr. B use the grue-green terms to ascribe different properties (light vs. radiation ones). Section VIII. Presents his argument with the Barker and Achinstein (1960) definitions of "grue" and "bleen." Has Mr. B just start applying "grue" to blue things at *t* and "bleen" to green things while he expects "from grue things what he had previously expected (in terms of flavor, say) from similarly shaped and sized blue things, and vice versa." Suggests explaining this in terms of green objects emitting alpha radiation before *t* and beta radiation after (and a similar switch for blue things), but notes that Mr. A and Mr. B would not be agreeing when they each apply "grue" or disagreeing about their predictions for after *t*. Suggests another explanation with an internal timing device set to produce a change at *t* in Mr. B so that blue things will look to him like he recalls green things looking before *t*. Maintains that "such a man will have learned 'grue' as a word for the color green despite the fact that after *t* he will tend (unless corrected) to apply it to blue things." Also notes that if the radiation explanation is correct, then "Mr. B's terms would not even be coextensive with the similarly spelled and pronounced terms in Mr. A's vocabulary" and this would be another reason for believing Mr. A and B do not mean the same thing by their grue-green terms. Section IX. Stipulates that the agreement condition is satisfied. Considers how much gruification is necessary to keep the stipulation coherent along with the claim that Mr. B is systematically projecting "grue." Changes from "grue" to "emeruby," where the predicate applies to emeralds examined before *t* or rubies examined after *t*. Views the case from Mr. A's perspective and argues that if Mr. B's terms mean what Mr. A's terms do, then Mr. B has irrelevant reasons for applying them to objects examined for the first time after *t*, it is only a coincidence that Mr. B correctly applies the terms "emeruby" and "ruby" after *t*, and the agreement between Mr. A and B cannot be explained by the hypothesis that they mean the same thing by these terms. Section X. Considers what the Mr. A–Mr. B case shows about our projective policy and projective vocabulary. Describes an alternative policy just like our policy except that its vocabulary includes gruelike terms with counterparts in our vocabulary. Maintains that the Mr. A–Mr. B case shows it is not intelligible for us to think about adopting this policy instead of our current policy, and so "it also makes no sense to ask for reasons why I should continue to pursue my present policy *rather than* adopting such an alternative policy." Section XI. Imagines a person Omar with an alpha-meter for detecting the property alpha, and who wonders if "alpha" is unprojectible and a gruelike predicate (having "alpha" as its counterpart) is projectible. Maintains that "alpha" is projectible because there are true lawlike generalizations with "alpha." More generally: if Omar has good reasons for thinking that "alpha" has an extension, Omar must think that "alpha" is projectible. Believes that "green" and "blue" are like "alpha" in that "the belief that these terms have extensions is inseparable (for a rational person) from the belief that we ourselves are 'visual color detectors,' and thus inseparable from the belief that there are true lawlike generalizations containing color words, and thus inseparable from the belief that these words are inductively projectible (at least to some appreciable degree)." Maintains that entrenchment is evidence of projectibility when a term is part of another person's vocabulary and, in that case, entrenchment indicates that the term must be translated (if it can be translated) into your idiolect by a term you consider projectible. Also see Shoemaker (1975b), (1980a) and (1980b).

Shoemaker, Sydney. "Phenomenal Similarity." *Critica* 7 (1975b): 3–34. Also in *Identity, Cause, and Mind: Philosophical Essays* by Sydney Shoemaker (Cambridge: Cambridge University Press, 1984), pp. 159–183. Examines "the notion of similarity, first in general, and then as it applies to experiences." Notes that if two things are grue, this does not mean they are similar in an important way. More generally: "it is not true of just any predicate that the things to which it applies are alike, or similar, in virtue of the facts that make it true that the predicate applies to both." Connects projectibility, lawlikeness, and similarity. Points out that Goodman and Quine (1970 and this volume) connect projectible predicates and natural kinds. Regards the following as connected with our belief that "grue" is an unprojectible predicate: grue is not a genuine property, the extension of "grue" is not a natural kind, grue things are not similar to each other because they are grue. Introduces the term "Goodman–Quine account of similarity" for the view that similarity ought to be explained (in part) in terms of projectibility. Notes a problem for this account: the "seeming incompatibility" between "the fact that similarities and dissimilarities are prominent among the immediate deliverances of experience" and the claim that projectibility can partially explain similarity, where we take a Humean view of the projectibility/lawlikeness/causality family of concepts. Starts to explain away this incompatibility by showing how the Goodman–Quine account involves a person's innate quality spaces, and so "likenesses and differences in the ways things look, feel, and sound to the person correspond to similarities and differences between the things themselves," where the similarities involve common projectible properties and the correspondence results from evolution. Goes on to ask how the Goodman–Quine view applies to being immediately aware of similarities between perceptual experiences. Believes this will involve an infinite regress in the form of an "infinite hierarchy of experiences." Notes how to avoid this regress by distinguishing between levels of experiences. Emphasizes another difficulty with an account that involves experiences of experiences: viz., we cannot misperceive relationships between experiences like we misperceive color relationships between physical objects. Considers whether "similarity as a relationship between experiences is unanalyzable," and so cannot be explained in terms of projectibility. Describes properties (of experiences) that are gruelike relative to other properties, and quasi-similarity relations between experiences in virtue of common gruelike properties. Asks what determines that some of the properties are intrinsic, others spurious, and that some of the relations are intrinsic, others quasi. Maintains that if this question can be answered, then similarity is analyzable. Considers whether similarity (taken as unanalyzable) "might be introduced by a private ostensive definition," but notes it "seems to require that the definer already has the notion of similarity." Attacks the idea that it is only a contingent fact "that the intrinsic features of experiences are projectible, and that their intrinsicness has nothing logically to do with their projectibility." Argues that "the only features of experiences that I could hope to name by a private ostensive definition are projectible features," that there is no question "of my naming a feature ostensively and then finding out empirically that it is intrinsic," and that there is an incompatibility between the idea of experience similarity being unanalyzable and the fact that we are immediately aware of intrinsic similarities between experiences (an unanalyzable notion of experience similarity can't be introduced and can't be innate). Suggests that experience similarity can be explained in terms of its causal role. Develops this idea by considering whether an inverted spectrum hypothesis is coherent: viz., that the way colors look to some people "is constantly changing, and that this is compensated for and goes unnoticed because of a systematic memory falsification." Believes that we must understand the similarity of experiences in terms of experiences of similarity. Maintains that experiences are phenomenally similar when "they stand in a relation which is such that if two experiences are related by that relation, and are co-conscious, their joint occurrence yields, or tends to yield, awareness of similarities holding between material things," where the similarities between material things can be explained by the Goodman–Quine account in terms of projectibility. Notes that "experience of similarity" is an intentional expression. Concludes with the contention "that our ability to be aware of experience similarities is implicit in, and is a sort of shadow or reflection of, our ability to be perceptually aware of objective similarities in nature." Emphasizes that if a person or animal cannot be aware of experiences they have, this is not analogous to blindness. Claims they cannot be aware of their experiences because they do not have the necessary concepts. Maintains that there is propositional content to perceptual awareness, and "how this content should be articulated depends on the conceptual sophistication of the creature doing the perceiving." Hopes to show that being aware of perceptual experiences involves being aware of phenomenal similarities/differences between perceptual experiences. Also see Shoemaker (1980a) and (1980b).

Shoemaker, Sydney. "Causality and Properties." In *Time and Cause,* edited by Peter van Inwagen (Dordrecht, Netherlands: D. Reidel Publishing Co., 1980a), pp. 109–135. Also in *Identity, Cause, and Mind: Philosophical Essays* by Sydney Shoemaker (Cambridge: Cambridge University Press, 1984), pp. 206–233. Section I. Claims that "any account of causality as a relation between events should involve, in a central way, reference to the properties of the constituent objects of the events." Section II. Contrasts genuine properties, changes, and similarities with mere-Cambridge ones. Regards grue as a mere-Cambridge similarity. Points out that "not every phrase of the form 'being so and so' stands for a property which something has just in case the corresponding predicate of the form 'is so and so' is true of it." Section III. Considers a theory of properties as causal powers. Claims this is not the same as a theory of properties as dispositional properties. Notes that we distinguish between dispositional and nondispositional properties, and that dispositional properties depend on nondispositional ones. Believes we should distinguish between dispositional and nondispositional predicates, and between powers "and the properties in virtue of which things have the powers they have." Views a power as "a function from circumstances to effects." Thinks the term "dispositional" should be applied to predicates, not properties. Section IV. Maintains that the identity of a property is determined by "its potential for contributing to the causal powers of the things that have it." Illustrates this with the property of being knife-shaped, where this is the shape of a certain knife. Says that something has a conditional power when it "has a power conditionally upon the possession of certain properties": e.g., a knife-shaped object can cut wood (a conditional power) when it is knife-sized and steel. States a sufficient condition for an object having a power conditionally and an identity condition for conditional powers. Expresses his view as "properties are clusters of conditional powers." Regards powers *simpliciter* as special cases of conditional powers. Claims a property is not the meaning of a predicate, and emphasizes the distinction between a concept and what it is a concept of. Section V. Claims that he holds his theory for epistemological reasons. Maintains that if we can explain "how properties are capable of engaging our knowledge, and our language, in the way they do," then a causal theory must be true. Introduces the supposition that the identity of properties consists of "something logically independent of their causal potentialities." Claims it implies we cannot know "various things which we take ourselves to know": e.g., that two things are similar because they have a common property, or that an object has kept the same property over time. Considers a "simplest hypothesis" reply: viz., properties are the best explanation of causal potentialities. Believes this is questionable because the "dissociation of property identity from identity of causal potentiality is really an invitation to eliminate reference to properties altogether." Discusses whether his arguments have established that the causal potentialities of a genuine property "are essential to that property, in the sense of belonging to it in all possible worlds." Suggests that if causal potentialities cannot vary across time, then they cannot vary across possible worlds. Section VI. Discusses how his theory does not apply to mere-Cambridge properties: e.g., two things can be grue "in virtue of having properties that have different potentialities." States a *prima facie* plausible criterion for telling whether something has a genuine or mere-Cambridge nonrelational property at a certain place and time. Bases the criterion on what kind of observations and tests will directly settle the question—ones near or remote from the place and time. Believes that his causal power theory explains why this is a plausible criterion. Section VII. Acknowledges that his account of properties is circular because it explains conditional powers in terms of properties and property identity in terms of sameness of properties. Distinguishes between intrinsic and mere-Cambridge powers. Notes that "power" only refers to an intrinsic power in his account. Believes his account is not empty or vacuous because it is circular. Claims "the notion of a property and the notion of a causal power belong to a system of internally related concepts, no one of which can be explicated without the use of the others." Also in this system: event, similarity, persisting substance. Believes an analysis should chart internal relationships instead of reduce. Section VIII. Notes a strong consequence of his theory: "causal necessity is just a species of logical necessity." Believes true causal laws are necessarily true, but not analytic or a priori. Views them as "necessary a posteriori." Maintains that some clusters of conditional powers are not properties because they lack "a certain kind of causal unity." States a criterion of causal unity: "conditional powers X and Y belong to the same property if and only if it is a consequence of causal laws that either (1) whatever has either of them has the other, or (2) there is some third conditional power such that whatever has it has both X and Y." Discusses how causal unity helps to explain "how knowledge of the causal potentialities of properties can develop empirically." Section IX. Argues against two attempts "to reconcile the claim that the identity of a property is determined by its causal potentialities with the apparent conceivability of worlds in which the causal laws that obtain are different from, and incompatible with, those that obtain in the actual world." Considers one attempt based on contingent, lawlike connections between conditional powers, and another based on a core cluster theory of properties instead of his total cluster theory. Believes the first attempt fails because "it is not possible that there should be a world in which conditional powers that are instantiated in the actual world can be instantiated while actual world properties cannot be instantiated." Believes the second attempt fails because the core cluster theory "makes the modal status of causal connections, their being necessary or contingent, epistemologically indeterminate." Section X. Asks how we can imagine "logically but not causally possible" situations when, according to his theory, there are no such situations. Discusses Kripke's answer to a similar question about imagining that heat is not molecular motion: viz., we are actually imagining that our heat sensations are caused by something else, not that heat is something else. Considers whether conceivability implies possibility, and so it is possible that our heat sensations are caused by something else besides molecular motion. Argues that "conceivability is not conclusive proof of possibility." Distinguishes two uses of "conceivable" and "on both of them it is possible to conceive what is not possible." Section XI. Maintains that singular causal propositions are implicitly general and that "the generality of causal propositions stems from the generality of properties, that is, from the fact that properties are universals." Postscript. Describes a counterexample to his account of properties and revises the account so that "properties are individuated by their possible causes as well as by their possible effects." Also see Shoemaker (1980b).

Shoemaker, Sydney. "Properties, Causation, and Projectibility." In *Applications of Inductive Logic,* edited by L. Jonathan Cohen and Mary Hesse, pp. 291–312. Oxford: Oxford University Press, 1980b. Attempts to clarify the distinction between genuine properties and mere Cambridge properties such as grue. States that a genuine property must be a differential property (Slote, 1970) and that grue is not a differential property because a nongrue emerald could be exactly similar to a grue emerald. Notes how this point depends on the distinction between genuine and mere-Cambridge similarities. Connects the genuine/mere Cambridge distinction with Hume's regularity theory of causation and problem of induction. Claims that a satisfactory account of the distinction will "render intelligible the linkage between genuineness of property (sort, regularity, and so on) and inductive projectibility" as well as "our ability to detect genuine properties and genuine similarities in the world." Believes the distinction can be explained in terms of causality. Briefly presents the view from Shoemaker (1980a) about genuine properties. Maintains that every genuine property "is constituted by its potentialities for contributing to the causal powers of the things that have it" and "that what distinguishes genuine properties like green from mere Cambridge properties like grue is that their possession make a determinate contribution to causal powers." Insists that genuine properties must have some causal potentialities, that it is impossible for two different properties to have all of the same causal potentialities, and that causal potentialities (of genuine properties) cannot change over time. Admits this account is circular; believes this cannot be avoided. Describes enumerative induction as a special case of inference to the best explanation, and an explanation as a set of causal laws and antecedent conditions that implies the regularity, correlation, or uniformity in question. Maintains that if we are entitled to project an observed regularity, this is because "we are entitled to believe that there is a set of causal factors that produced it and that the regularity we have observed is only part of a more extensive regularity produced by those factors." Also maintains that "the explanation of a mere-Cambridge regularity is always in the first instance the explanation of a related genuine one." Adds that properties are universals and that induction can be viewed "as the process of learning about universals by considering their instantiations." Goes on to examine Jackson's view (1975 and this volume) that all consistent predicates are projectible and that illegitimate grue inductions are illegitimate because they violate a counterfactual condition. Asks why this condition must be satisfied in order to apply the straight rule legitimately. Answers that if we wish to be entitled "to believe that the explanation of the observed regularity is appropriately projection-entitling," then this condition must be satisfied. Disputes Jackson's view of cases in which grue inductions satisfy the counterfactual condition. Introduces the notion of pseudoprojectibility for an illegitimate projection that involves a predicate like "grue," and yet is such that we can "legitimately get from its 'premiss' to its conclusion via two definitionally based deductions and a legitimate induction involving the projection of a different predicate" like "green." Believes Jackson's cases are really cases of "grue" being pseudoprojectible, not genuinely projectible. Considers how we know that predicates like "green" are genuinely projectible. Sees this problem as "the problem of how we know, or are justified in believing, that these predicates stand for genuine rather than mere-Cambridge properties." Refers to his views in Shoemaker (1975a). Claims that, for predicates typically learned by ostension, "our belief that a predicate has a meaning and extension is inseparable from our belief that we, or at any rate someone, can reliably detect cases in which that predicate applies." Also claims this involves believing the predicate is projectible and has a genuine property as its nonlinguistic counterpart. Maintains that "in so far as the speakers of a language regard a predicate as projectible, this limits its possible referents to genuine properties." Illustrates this with Barker and Achinstein's (1960) predicate "condulates electricity." Concludes that scepticism about projectibility "reduces to an extreme form of scepticism that threatens to call into question the very meaningfulness of the language in which it is expressed." See the reply by Swinburne (1980). Also see Shoemaker (1980).

Skyrms, Brian. "On Failing to Vindicate Induction." *Philosophy of Science* 32 (1965): 253–268. A reply to Salmon (1963a, 1963b) and critical examination of Reichenbach's pragmatic attempt to justify induction. See section 4, "Wesley Salmon and the Criterion of Linguistic Invariance." Maintains that Goodman's paradox does not violate Salmon's (1963a) formulation of the invariance criterion. Discusses Salmon's version of the paradox and notes that Reichenbach's straight rule assigns the same probability to an emerald being grue as it does to an emerald being green. Also notes that these two conclusions are jointly inconsistent when we assume the class of emeralds is not exhausted before the 1,000th place (i.e., there are more emeralds to examine). Points out that "the criterion of linguistic invariance doesn't say anything about throwing in assumptions." Claims that Salmon "misapprehends the logical force of the Goodman paradox" because he does not appreciate how it "also arises when there are two classes which *by virtue of contingent fact* coincide in part, and fail to coincide in part." Maintains that "the proper symptom of Goodman's Disease is not violation of Salmon's criterion, but inductive inconsistency." Claims that Salmon's definition of a purely ostensive predicate "precludes any attempt to define the physical modalities in terms of our inductive logic," and that its observable resemblance clause is unclear—indeed, if "observable" means "ostensively definable," the definition is circular. Considers whether, on Salmon's definition, the predicate "is 37 inches long" is a purely ostensive predicate. Notes that if we exclude this sort of predicate, then "it is difficult to see how even a theory of concatenated induction built on this basis, could ever form an adequate language for science." Points out that if we are permitted to carry a measuring tape and use it, then we can correctly apply "is 37 inches long" by direct inspection. Also points out that if we are permitted to carry a calendar clock and use it, then we can correctly apply "grue" by direct inspection. Argues that if we exclude a predicate like "satisfier of a prediction made by a certain method *S*," then we will also be excluding a vital step in Reichenbach's pragmatic justification; and if we include a predicate like this, then we can construct a gruelike paradox (see end of section 3). Goes on to argue that "any attempt to cure Goodman's Disease by attacking 'queer' predicates, is doomed to failure." Analyzes the logical form of the Goodman paradox and claims "the paradoxical nature of these cases does not consist in logical contradiction, but simply in the fact that this may be an extremely stupid prediction to make in the circumstances." Believes that, for Reichenbach's probability estimator rule, we can retain the logical force of Goodman's paradox by assuming a Reichenbachian knows, at the time in question, it is contingently true that our observations have exhausted the intersection of the classes denoted by our two predicates and our reference class. Claims the probability estimator rule cannot take this information into account and we will have to reject the claim that our observations have not exhausted our reference class. Calls this the "Badman Paradox." Illustrates it with ordinary, directly observable, ostensively definable, nonpositional, well-entrenched predicates: viz., "block" for the reference class, and "stone" and "green" for the other two classes. Notes that the Goodman and Badman paradoxes violate the Criterion of Inductive Consistency for a probability estimation rule or set of rules, where a rule is consistent "for a given interpretation if and only if for any logically consistent information base the assumption that all the forthcoming estimates are correct is (under that interpretation) consistent with that information base." Suggests that a complete set of estimator rules (a "probability estimator apparatus") should consist of rules connecting observed relative frequencies with posits and also rules "determining which predicates are *projectible* in which *contexts.*" Suggests that the Inductive Consistency Criterion can be a partial test for a complete set of estimator rules if we replace "logically consistent information base" with "information base which we are reasonably sure, on the basis of current physical theory, is physically possible."

Skyrms, Brian. "Nomological Necessity and the Paradoxes of Confirmation." *Philosophy of Science* 33 (1966): 230–249. See section II, "The Paradoxes of Confirmation," p. 233. Claims Hempel (1945) assumes "that positive instances are always confirmatory in the required sense (i.e., that if E is a positive instance of H, then the likelihood of H given E is higher than the likelihood of H on tautological evidence)." Maintains this is an incorrect assumption, and lists eight examples showing that it is: e.g., if we let Fx hold if and only if x is a blade of living grass or x is the cloth on a billiard table, and we let Gx hold if and only if x is green, "does the observation of a green blade of grass lend any support to the assertion that all cloths on billiard tables are green?" See the reply by Hempel (1968); claims that Skyrms's argument about positive instances presupposes the same thing as Goodman's argument about grue hypotheses.

Skyrms, Brian. *Choice and Chance: An Introduction to Inductive Logic.* 3d ed. Belmont, Calif.: Wadsworth Publishing Co., 1986. See chapter III, "The Goodman Paradox and the New Riddle of Induction," for a well-known exposition of the problem and its importance for a system of scientific inductive logic. Emphasizes connections between "the linguistic machinery we use" and the changes we detect in a situation or the regularities we discover in a sequence of events. Considers how "for any prediction whatsoever, we can find a regularity whose projection licenses that prediction"; illustrates this with examples about predicting the color of an object in a box, about extrapolating along curves that fit census data points, and about finding a generating function to continue a series of numbers. Explains how the principle of the uniformity of nature is uninformative without rules for determining projectibility. Also see chapter IV, section 13, "Lawlike and Accidental Conditions," for relevant material.

Slote, Michael Anthony. "Some Thoughts on Goodman's Riddle." *Analysis* 27 (1967): 128–132. Argues that Goodman's riddle can be solved partially by appealing to the notions of a differential property and an inductively vicious property, and by noting how one hypothesis can be more acceptable than another because it posits similarities as opposed to differences and because it is simpler. Claims this solution is limited to differential predicates. See the replies by O'Connor (1967) and Swinburne (1968), and the reply and amplification by Slote (1968). Also chapter 5 of his book *Reason and Scepticism* (1970).

Slote, Michael A. "A General Solution to Goodman's Riddle?" *Analysis* 29 (1968): 55–58. Defends Slote (1967) against criticisms by O'Connor (1967) and Swinburne (1968). Also argues that his previous solution (1967) to the new riddle (limited to differential predicates) can be extended to any predicates. Maintains that Goodmanian predicates are not projectible because they make for generalizations that posit more unnecessary differences and complexity than generalizations with the predicates we actually project.

Slote, Michael A. *Reason and Scepticism.* London: George Allen & Unwin, 1970. Chapter 5 is entitled "The New Riddle of Induction and the External World." Makes use of material from Slote (1967) and Slote (1968). Considers the new riddle as a skeptical problem for his analogical argument for other minds and for his arguments in support of commonsense claims about the external world. Rejects Goodman's entrenchment solution because either it has implausible assumptions or it is epistemologically incomplete. Develops a solution in terms of differences between hypotheses with respect to positing things unlike ones already posited or with respect to positing new kinds of things. Maintains that these sorts of differences can make one hypothesis less simple, and therefore less acceptable, than another.

Slote, Michael A. "Entrenchment and Validity." *Analysis* 34 (1974): 204–207. Argues against the claim that if a predicate is entrenched, then it can be validly projected. Assumes a necessary condition for an inductive methodology being valid, describes creatures who systematically use Goodmanian predicates in making inductive inferences, and introduces their meta-inductive Goodmanian predicate about using an inductive methodology. Maintains that this predicate, even if entrenched, could not be projected over the uses of any valid inductive methodology because thereby the methodology would fail to meet the necessary condition.

Slote, Michael A. "Confirmation and Conservatism." *American Philosophical Quarterly* 18 (1981): 79–84. Argues that there are important connections between methodological conservatism and the actualized predictive power of a hypothesis, and between methodological conservatism and the adoption of a bold hypothesis. Maintains that his view about actualized predictive power supports to some extent Goodman's general view about entrenched predicates.

Small, Kenneth. "Professor Goodman's Puzzle." *Philosophical Review* 70 (1961): 544–552. Provides a precise statement of the interdefinability of "green," "blue," "grue," and "bleen." Notes that he does not include "examined" in his definitions of "grue" and "bleen." Maintains that while one pair of definitions is equivalent to the other, this symmetry does not show the predicates are indistinguishable as far as being qualitative or positional. Claims Goodman's crucial mistake is to say we can start with "grue" and "bleen," and then define the other pair in terms of them and a temporal term. Asks what Goodman could mean by "starting with" here? Claims we do know what it means to start with "green" and "blue" because we know what they mean "independently of any definition," while we do not know this for "grue" and "bleen." Views this as an asymmetry and the interdefinability as just a formal symmetry. Considers a reply: it is enough to have a formal symmetry with dummy predicates because it is just a fact (which could be otherwise) about our language that we know the meanings of certain predicates independently. Objects that formal relations hold between dummy predicates, not predicates, the identity of a predicate is not just a matter of its spelling and pronunciation, and so formal relations are irrelevant—"it is predicates which are projected, not dummy predicates." Explains how this reply concedes "that in order to raise the puzzle it must be conceivable that there be creatures who could independently know what 'grue' and 'bleen' mean in the way we know what 'blue' and 'green' mean." Claims the new riddle depends on a hypothesis about some creatures being able to look at an object and tell whether it is grue or bleen without first telling if the object is green or blue, and if it is before or after time t. Maintains there could not be any creatures like this because the hypothesis (that there are such creatures) is an unintelligible hypothesis. Maintains the hypothesis is unintelligible because by now "grue" and "bleen" have been defined and are predicates in our language, and so a creature could use the spelling and pronunciation associated with the predicates, but not the predicates. Considers another way to identify the creatures' predicates with our "grue" and "bleen." Supposes that we represent the creatures' predicates as "glef" and "brid," and that we note they only apply "glef" to grue things and "brid" to bleen things; also supposes that the creatures note we only apply "blue" to blif things and "green" to gred things, where "blif" means brid before t or glef after, and "gred" means glef before t or brid after. Asks "whether we can establish interconnections among these eight predicates in such a way that 'blue' and 'green' will be qualitative . . . and therefore projectible if and only if 'glef' and 'brid' are." Thinks this will be difficult because we have two pairs of predicates from "different languages spoken by different creatures." Considers what happens at time t: we do not notice any changes, while the creatures (Saturnians) talk and behave as if glef things are now brid, brid things now glef. Notes two situations here: the Saturnians tell us the change is coming, they do not. Thinks we would probably adopt the hypothesis that "Saturnians are capable of detecting certain characteristics of things that we are not capable of detecting," and then say that we have been unable to learn the meanings of "glef" and "brid" and that we will be using "grue" and "bleen" as convenient ways to talk about the extensions of "glef" and "brid." Considers whether knowing the extension is (more or less) knowing the meaning here; replies that, given the extra sense hypothesis, we cannot regard "grue" and "glef" as synonymous because the hypothesis assumes things change while the synonymy says they did not. Thinks the issue is now about a symmetry in which the evidence for one pair of predicates being qualitative is also evidence for the other pair being qualitative (or positional). Believes we will never be in a position to project "glef" and "brid" because these predicates cannot be translated into our language, and so we will have to ask Saturnians about the projectibility of these predicates, and they might tell us they expected changes (one situation) based on a physical theory of theirs. Maintains the "obvious conclusion" here is that "glef"/"brid" projectibility has no connection with "blue"/"green" projectibility because "evidence for the glefness or bridness of something is not evidence for the blueness or greenness of it, and so we could not possibly get contradictory results by trying to project the two pairs of predicates from examined to unexamined cases."

Smokler, Howard. "Goodman's Paradox and the Problem of Rules of Acceptance." *American Philosophical Quarterly* 3 (1966): 71–76. Gives a precise statement of Scheffler's (1958) version of the paradox and notes two of its presuppositions, one about inductive rules as acceptance rules, the other about admissible predicates; shows how to change this version into Goodman's version. Criticizes attempts to ban predicates like "grue," especially Salmon's (1963) attempt to ban "grue" because it is not purely ostensive. Examines Goodman's entrenchment solution to the paradox, but considers it "logically arbitrary." Argues for avoiding the paradox by rejecting rules of acceptance, like Carnap does in his system of confirmation; shows how this option works for both a qualitative and a quantitative notion of confirmation. Considers whether this approach can solve the paradox when degrees of confirmation are taken to be fair betting quotients; believes it can if we realize that predicates like "grue" involve a notion of order and so we should not try to formulate the paradox in a first-order functional calculus but in something like Carnap's coordinate language. Advocates viewing Goodman's paradox as "an independent argument against a conception of inductive logic which makes use of rules of acceptance." See the reply by Williams (1969).

Smokler, Howard and Rohr, David. "Confirmation and Translation." In *Philosophical Logic,* edited by J.W. Davis, D.S. Hockney, and W.K. Wilson, pp. 172–180. Dordrecht, Holland: D. Reidel Publishing Co., 1969. The authors argue against an adequacy condition for analyses of confirmation: viz., that confirmation relations are language-invariant or independent. They state this formally as the General Equivalence Condition; maintain it should be rejected because it conflicts with a more justified condition: viz., the Projectibility Condition stating that "only hypotheses projecting projectible predicates are confirmed by evidence." Contend that projectibility is language dependent in that a predicate may be projectible while its translation is not; argue that all existing definitions of projectibility (e.g., Carnap's, Goodman's, Salmon's) are language dependent. The authors describe a translation case in which the General Equivalence Condition fails if you comply with the language-dependent Projectibility Condition; also comment on how dropping the General Equivalence Condition means "the language in which an inductive inference is stated would be of importance in determining (at least in some cases) whether or not an hypothesis is confirmed by available evidence." See Salmon (1960 and 1963) for a proponent of linguistic invariance.

Sober, Elliott. *Simplicity.* Oxford: Oxford University Press, 1975. Argues that we can measure the simplicity of a hypothesis in terms of how well the hypothesis answers certain kinds of questions. Analyzes simplicity as informativeness relative to one of these questions, and informativeness as the amount of extra information a hypothesis needs to answer one of these questions. Takes these questions to be sets of natural predicates. Considers natural predicates to be "the frame of reference against which our simplicity judgments are made." Speaks of designating or choosing predicates as natural. Develops the natural predicate view in connection with Goodman's green and grue hypotheses. Maintains that if we regard colors as natural and grulers as not, then the green hypothesis is simpler than the grue hypothesis. Allows that "we can imagine a person who has the opposite intuition about which predicates are natural" and so we would expect that person to see the grue hypothesis as simpler than the green one. Applies his theory (pp. 38–40) to heterogeneity hypotheses and their homogeneity counterparts. Takes a change hypothesis to be one kind of heterogeneity hypothesis; notes that the grue hypothesis is a change hypothesis, the green hypothesis is a no-change hypothesis. His theory takes no-change hypotheses to be simpler than their change counterparts, thus agreeing with a common intuition about the role of simplicity in choosing hypotheses. Emphasizes that the designated natural predicate families provide the frame of reference for judging change or not here. Discusses (in chapter 5) Goodman's view about justifying induction and describing it; argues that Goodman fails to take into account that "description becomes justification only when parameters in the description align themselves with goals that we designate as desirable."

Sober, Elliott. "The Evolution of Rationality." *Synthese* 46 (1981): 95–120. Attempts to describe a framework for understanding how rationality could be the result of evolution. Considers three problems for an evolutionary account, one of which involves an analogue of the problem of induction: viz., the problem of distinguishing between rational and irrational methods that are locally equivalent in an environment. Introduces the straight rule, counterinduction rule, and mixed strategy of using the straight rule before 2000 and counterinduction after 2000. Notes that the straight rule and the mixed rule appear to be equally fit because they are locally equivalent in producing the same outputs from the same inputs in the environment where selection has occurred. Introduces a rule that is globally equivalent with the straight rule and involves adding and subtracting integers in connection with the observed proportion. Claims these rule problems are the same as rational hypothesis choice problems such as we have with the green and the grue hypotheses, which "are locally equivalent within the environment in which evidence has been gathered." Maintains that we select the green hypothesis on the basis of simplicity and economy, and that evolutionary processes select from locally and globally equivalent rules on the same basis. Argues that overall fitness consists of internal and external fitness, that input-output equivalence is a matter of external fitness, and that informational economy (e.g., storage, detectors) is a matter of internal fitness. Considers the mixed strategy less economical than the straight rule because it requires a clock (a detector); also considers the adding and subtracting variation on the straight rule less economical because it "requires an adding machine," and this would be "a needless extravagance from the point of view of the economy of nature." Contends that "the simplicity of the straight rule recommends it to natural selection as well as to our own reflective judgments."

Sober, Elliott and Lewontin, Richard C. "Artifact, Cause, and Genic Selection." *Philosophy of Science* 49 (1982): 157–180. Criticize the view that "natural selection is always, or for the most part, selection for and against single genes." Maintain that "genic selection coefficients are artifacts, not causes, of population dynamics." Examine various philosophical implications of their critique, including the distinction between real and pseudoproperties. Claim that "selfish genes and grue emeralds bear a remarkable similarity." Maintain that "grue" does not pick out a real property even though it is defined with predicates that do pick out real properties. Argue that the real/pseudoproperty distinction is not a matter of being independent of human thought and language, of being similar to each other, or of being a better predictor of further characteristics. Claim that real properties are causally efficacious. Present an example in which genotype fitness values do not cause genic fitness values at that time, but do cause changes in genic frequencies at a later time; also present an example in which a grasshopper being green does not cause it to be grue then, but this does cause it to evade a predator at a later time. Emphasize the distinction between two kinds of determination: logical and causal. Note that a predicate may pick out a real property in one context, not in another, and that some predicates might be "globally artifactual" (perhaps "grue"). Also note that their grue-genic selection comparison is not a solution to Goodman's epistemological problems about induction, does not provide an a priori way of making the real/pseudoproperty distinction, does not mean grue will be artifactual given "the truth of any scientific model," or even that causal efficacy "captures the metaphysical distinction at issue." Do maintain that the comparison shows us how we ought to understand "a rather abstract metaphysical issue." Add, in footnote 11, that the comparison also shows how the real problem with "grue" is not that it is a positional, as opposed to purely qualitative, predicate. For more on real properties being causally efficacious, see Elliott Sober, "Why Logically Equivalent Predicates May Pick Out Different Properties," *American Philosophical Quarterly* 19 (1982): 183–189.

Sober, Elliott. "Confirmation and Law-likeness." *Philosophical Review* 97 (1988): 93–98. Argues, contrary to Goodman (1965), that some accidental generalizations can be confirmed by their positive instances; also argues contrary to Goodman (1965) that if some observed positive instances confirm a generalization, then they may not likewise confirm a claim about unobserved instances (e.g., the next instance). Examines Jackson and Pargetter's view (1980) on instance confirmation and presents a counterexample to their nomological condition.

Sollazzo, Gary. "Barker and Achinstein on Goodman." *Philosophical Studies* 23 (1972): 91–97. A reply to Barker and Achinstein (1960). Defends Goodman against two of Barker and Achinstein's arguments that are supposed to show the grue-bleen and the green-blue languages are not symmetrical because Mr. Grue can't do things Mr. Green can, and vice versa. Considers the claim that Mr. Green can always use green paint to represent green objects in a painting, but the same is not true for Mr. Grue using grue paint to represent grue objects. Believes Barker and Achinstein's first argument depends on showing two statements are inconsistent: viz., that (1) Mr. Grue applies "grue" to just those objects Mr. Green would call "green" before 2000 or "blue" after 2000, and that (A) Mr. Grue calls an object in a picture "grue" just when it has been represented with grue paint. Claims these statements are not inconsistent together, but they are along with the statement (A') "that an object in a picture is to be called 'green' when and only when the paint—i.e., pigment—used in representing it is green paint." Believes that statement (A') must be rejected if we accept that (A) Mr. Grue calls an object in a picture "grue" just when it is colored with grue paint and that (1') for Mr. Green the predicate "green" has the same extension as "grue before *t* or bleen after" has for Mr. Grue. Emphasizes that Mr. Grue begins with (A), takes "grue" to be nonpositional, and so does not have to consider the date of scenes in pictures. Notes that, on Goodman's symmetry thesis, we cannot have both "grue" and "green" nonpositional at the same time, and that we decide which is nonpositional on the basis of entrenchment. Believes that Barker and Achinstein start with (A') because they regard "green" as better entrenched than "grue." Claims their additional arguments "fail to empathize sufficiently with Mr. Grue's foreign perspective." Considers one of these arguments: viz., Mr. Grue has to color the grass grue in two scenes (one before *t*, the other after) in pictures, where both pictures are screened off except for the plots of grass, and if he can do this (coloring one plot green, the other blue), Mr. Grue has extrasensory powers. Examines how Barker and Achinstein reply to a counterargument attempting to show that, from Mr. Grue's perspective, Mr. Green must have extrasensory powers: viz., if Mr. Green has to color the grass green in two pictures, one of Harvard Yard in 1959, the other of the Yard in 2001, where he can only view the plots of grass in each picture, then he will use the same paint—green—in both pictures, while Mr. Grue would not. Claims this is not what Goodman's symmetry thesis entails; believes it entails that "Mr. Grue would paint both patches grue just as Mr. Green painted both patches green." Claims this depends on Barker and Achinstein's first argument in that Mr. Grue will not have a problem if (A) is assumed, while he will have a problem if (A') is assumed. Maintains that if "green" and "grue" are interdefinable, then they both cannot be qualitative predicates at the same time, but either can, as a matter of logic, be qualitative while the other is positional. Concludes that Barker and Achinstein fail to show anything wrong with Goodman's position because they take the predicate "grue" to be a positional rival to a qualitative predicate "green." Also see Goodman (1960), Ullian (1961), and Shirley (1981).

Spielman, Stephen. "Review of *Probability and Evidence*." *Journal of Philosophy* 81 (1984): 168–173. A review of Horwich (1982b). Critical of how Horwich deals with measuring degrees of belief and with interpreting probability claims in an "objectivist" manner. Claims Horwich views the grue paradox as an example in which "the swamping of priors cannot account for our judgments about theory preference," and so takes it as an objection to personalists. Claims, however, that there is only a verbal difference here between a personalist account and an objectivist account. Ends by claiming that "elementary logical errors mar Horwich's treatment of Nelson Goodman's paradox of confirmation." Maintains Horwich gives "a peculiar and unclear version of the 'grue' paradox." Argues that Horwich inadequately defines gruelike predicates and erroneously concludes that projectibility comes from a relatively high prior.

Stegmüller, Wolfgang. "Counterfactuals, Dispositions, Natural Laws and Induction." *Kant-Studien* 50 (1958–59): 363–390. Review article in German by a well-known German philosopher of science. Goodman cites this review article as supplementary reading for chapter VII, "Induction," in *Problems and Projects* (1972). In the Introductory Note to the third edition of *FFF*, Goodman says that Stegmüller "has corrected the notion that 'anti-inductivists' of the school of Karl Popper escape the new riddle of induction." Stegmüller also makes this point in an English translation of one of his essays; see chapter 4, "The Problem of Induction: Hume's Challenge and the Contemporary Answers," section 3, pages 91–94, in Volume II of *Collected Papers on Espistemology, Philosophy of Science and History of Philosophy* (Dordrecht, Holland: D. Reidel Publishing Company, 1977).

Stemmer, Nathan. "Three Problems in Induction." *Synthese* 23 (1971): 2872–308. Attempts to solve the paradox of confirmation, resolve questions about the degree of confirmation assigned to universal sentences in Carnapian inductive logics, and define the distinction between projectible and nonprojectible predicates in a general and rigorous way. Describes how to "determine the classes which a species uses for its innate inductive behavior." Calls these "inductive classes" for that species. Describes investigating stimulus generalization experimentally, plotting generalization gradients that represent the degree to which one stimulus generalizes to similar ones, ordering classes of stimuli by their generalization potential for an organism and eventually obtaining the generalization continuum for all normal members of a given species. Introduces three types of predicates: natural, restricted, and artificial. Stipulates that natural predicates denote inductive classes for our species, restricted predicates denote classes with high generalization potentials (so high they are not inductive classes), and artificial predicates denote classes with low generalization potentials (so low they are not inductive classes). For example: is a dog; is a large, squat, brown dog; is a lion or a dog or a triangle or a tree or a white thing or a blue thing, respectively. Distinguishes between regular and irregular classes: the former "ensure many correct inductions," the latter do not. Maintains that the difference between projectible and nonprojectible predicates corresponds to the difference between "natural and restricted predicates on the one hand and artificial predicates on the other hand." Claims natural and restricted predicates denote regular classes, and so "they are *a priori* adequate for use in inductive procedures." Discusses Carnap's (1947) view that purely positional predicates (and perhaps mixed) are not projectible, while purely qualitative predicates are. Argues that Carnap's view is too wide and too narrow: e.g., the purely qualitative predicate "nonblue" is not projectible; the projectible predicate "solar" is not purely qualitative. Notes that Carnap does not consider "why there should be at all an inductively relevant difference between predicates." Points out that Carnap did single out spatio-temporal predicates as making gruelike predicates nonprojectible. Claims that "to achieve this effect an essential use is made of the logical connective 'or'." Maintains that most logical connectives can change natural predicates into artificial ones by changing their a priori degree of regularity. Warns that logical terms are not neutral with respect to induction. See Stemmer (1975) for a modification, and Stemmer (1978, 1979, 1981, 1985) for similar views. See Konyndyk (1980) for criticism of these views.

Stemmer, Nathan. "A Relative Notion of Natural Generalization." *Philosophy of Science* 42 (1975): 46–48. Attempts to correct a defect in Stemmer (1971) where he introduces the notions of a natural and an artificial generalization in order to account for "generalizations that are intuitively confirmed by their positive instances and those that are not intuitively confirmed by such instances." Points out that sometimes logically equivalent sentences end up being different kinds of generalizations: i.e., 'All ravens are black' is a natural generalization while 'All nonblack objects are nonravens' is an artificial generalization. Modifies his 1971 definitions of natural and artificial generalizations so that every sentence logically equivalent to a natural generalization 'All *A* are *B*' is itself a natural generalization "relative to an object that is both *A* and *B,* and every sentence logically equivalent to an artificial generalization 'All *A* are *B*' is itself an artificial generalization relative to an object that is both *A* and *B.*" Now accounts for "intuitive confirmation" in terms of objects intuitively confirming sentences that are natural generalizations relative to those objects, and not confirming sentences that are artificial generalizations relative to those objects.

Stemmer, Nathan. "A Partial Solution to the Goodman Paradox." *Philosophical Studies* 34 (1978): 177–185. Explains why an earlier paper (Stemmer, 1971) does not solve the paradox and proposes a new, albeit partial, solution. Describes a class of intuitively correct, instinctive inductive inferences that use innate generalization classes. Justifies these inferences by appealing to evolutionary theory: instinctive behavior is normally useful or has survival value, and if an instinctive inductive inference is normally useful, then it must be normally reliable. Notes that "the class of grue objects has so far played the same role in evolution as the class of green objects," and so evolution cannot justify choosing the green hypothesis instead of the grue one. Distinguishes between inductive inferences about the past ("All *P* were *Q*") and those about the future ("All *P* will be *Q*"). Claims the Goodman paradox "affects only inductive inferences that refer to the future." Describes a class of intuitively correct, instinctive inductive inferences about the future that use innate generalization classes. Lets an intuitive uniformity be "a uniformity that ensured the reliability of the intuitive inferences" about the past. Justifies the future inferences by assuming the continuity postulate: "the nature of the world will continue to be intuitively uniform." Claims the postulate is only partially supported because all of its evidence belongs to the past, and the world's uniformity has also made some nonintuitive, grue inferences reliable. Emphasizes that the postulate is modest and "merely transfers past generalities into the future." Calls his solution a partial one because this justification depends on the assumed validity of the continuity postulate. Claims that intuitively projectible predicates are predicates "whose extensions are innate generalization classes of humans." Maintains that both Hempel and Goodman's paradoxes have the same cause: making inductive inferences with predicates that are not intuitively projectible. Notes that his solution does not deal with all types of inductive inferences, just an elementary type. Suggests that his solution might be a complete one even if he cannot prove that his postulate is true. Views Goodman's problem as restricted to finding "a criterion for distinguishing between projectible and non-projectible predicates which is justified, as far as possible, by empirical data and plausible conjectures." Also see Stemmer (1979, 1981, 1988) and Konyndyk (1980).

Stemmer, Nathan. "Projectible Predicates." *Synthese* 41 (1979): 375–395. Develops Stemmer (1971, 1975); incorporates Stemmer (1978). Describes instinctive generalizing
behavior in terms of innate generalization classes, their range of application, and
naturally expected properties. States a criterion for intuitively valid inductive inferences
based on this behavior for humans. Considers inferring the elementary hypothesis "All
C are *P*" from a positive instance, and concludes this is intuitively valid if *C* is an innate
generalization class and *P* is a naturally expected property. Formulates a criterion for
distinguishing intuitively projectible and nonprojectible predicates in elementary
hypotheses: the antecedents denote innate generalization classes, the consequents
denote naturally expected properties. Appeals to evolutionary theory in arguing that
intuitively valid inferences (to elementary hypotheses) were frequently reliable, and so
their intuitively projectible predicates "were actually projectible in our terrestrial
environment." Considers inferring "All terrestrial *C*'s were *P*" from a positive instance,
and concludes that if the predicates are intuitively projectible, the instance justifies the
inference. Emphasizes that his conclusions are scientific hypotheses with explanatory
power with regard to our generalizing behavior. Notes that grue and green have played
the same role in evolution and so they do not differ in actual projectibility with
inferences about the past. Claims there is a difference in actual projectibility into the
future with hypotheses like "All *C*'s will be *P*." Introduces the partially supported
continuity postulate: "the nature of the world will continue to be intuitively uniform."
Argues that we ensure unrestricted actual projectibility for intuitively projectible
predicates, and that we justify unrestricted, intuitively valid, elementary inductive
inferences, if we assume this postulate and regard it as stating that "the nature of the
whole universe has the same intuitive uniformity as our terrestrial environment."
Believes that his views so far constitute a partial solution to Goodman's problem; see
Stemmer (1978) for more on this partial solution. Points out that evolutionary theory
actually justifies inferences to "Many terrestrial *C*'s were *P*" and not to "All were."
Discusses how falsifying instances produce restricted antecedent predicates that denote
intuitively nonprojectible subclasses of innate generalization classes. Emphasizes how
restricted predicates depend on our psychological predispositions. Also discusses how
falsifying instances produce expanded consequent predicates that do not denote
intuitively expected properties. Considers whether restricting and expanding had
survival value or were useful. Examines criterial predicates (such as "mammal") that
denote the union of innate generalization classes or restricted classes. Notes how they
are intuitively nonprojectible and yet possibly were actually projectible, and how
determining this depends on knowing about the relevant area of science. Maintains that
his solution to Goodman's problem has more explanatory power than Goodman's
entrenchment solution because it covers "all those successful generalizations that were
made by organisms that lacked a language." Also see Stemmer (1981, 1988) and the
criticism by Konyndyk (1980).

Stemmer, Nathan. "The Objective Confirmation of Hypotheses." *Canadian Journal of
Philosophy* 11 (1981): 395–404. Changes and clarifies points about confirmation from
Stemmer (1971 and 1975). Distinguishes between a subjective and an objective
criterion for confirmation: the former agrees with our feelings or intuitions, the latter
with "what happens in the real world." Attempts to formulate a criterion of objective
confirmation. Claims members of many species have innate dispositions to generalize
using specific classes (innate generalization classes), these dispositions had survival
value or were useful, and so the generalizations were reliable frequently. Considers the
best explanation for this reliability to be that innate generalization classes were highly
uniform: if a member of the class had a property, then very often a large proportion also

had the property. Adds that these classes were uniform "with respect to *biologically important properties*" from an evolutionary point of view. Maintains that his analysis supports the thesis of the uniformity of innate generalization classes (for well-developed species and biologically important properties). Notes that the thesis claims the classes were highly uniform, not that they will be in the future. Also notes that linguistic overgeneralizations do not affect the thesis, and that other types of classes can be highly uniform. Formulates a sufficient condition for the objective confirmation of elementary hypotheses about the past: "if P is an innate generalization class and Q was a biologically important property, then, in the absence of evidence to the contrary, a few elements of P that are Q strongly confirm objectively the hypothesis 'All P were Q'." Claims this condition supports our intuitions about black ravens, nonblack nonravens, and which confirms "All ravens are black." Suggests that it might be a sufficient condition for both objective and subjective confirmation. Admits the condition is only a first step towards a comprehensive theory of confirmation. Emphasizes that it is an important step because children as well as scientists start with these elementary types of hypotheses.

Stemmer, Nathan. "Hume's Two Assumptions." *Dialectica* 42 (1988): 93–103. Claims Hume mentions two assumptions in his discussion of justifying inductive inferences: viz., "that the future will be similar to the past" and "that if certain entities have certain properties, then similar entities have similar properties." Calls these "the futurity assumption" and "the generalization assumption," respectively. Presents a sufficient condition for an intuitively valid inductive inference based on the notion of an innate generalization class; maintains that the condition specifies a basic class of intuitively valid inductive inferences. States a thesis about a great number of these inferences being successful or reliable and a thesis about the earth having "an intuitive uniformity" that makes for this reliability. Regards the first thesis as a weaker yet corresponding form of Hume's generalization assumption. Maintains that evolutionary biology supports these theses; they supposedly explain "the large number of observations which show that humans are born with specific generalizing dispositions." Introduces a postulate about the earth continuing to be "intuitively uniform." Regards this as almost equivalent to Hume's futurity assumption. Claims there is no logical justification for either the first thesis or the postulate, but there is a "scientifically valid" justification for the first thesis: viz., "it is well supported by empirical evidence." Argues against replacing the two (thesis and postulate) by a single assumption.

Stenner, Alfred J. "A Note on 'Grue'." *Philosophical Studies* 18 (1967): 76–78. Argues for a change in Goodman's notion of entrenchment. Maintains that predicates are not simply entrenched but entrenched relative to a culture, and so one predicate is better entrenched than another predicate with respect to a given culture.

Sternberg, Robert J. "Intelligence and Nonentrenchment." *Journal of Educational Psychology* 73 (1981): 1–16. Reports on experiments involving "nonentrenched" or novel kinds of tasks that require learning and thinking within "new conceptual systems." Describes a "projection task" in which a subject is presented with "a description of the color of an object in the present day and in the year 2000." Descriptions can be a green or blue dot, or one of four color words: viz., blue, green, grue, or bleen. For example, one test item presents the word 'green' and then a blue dot, indicating that the object is called green in the present and appears physically blue in the year 2000. Subjects must describe the object in the year 2000 by choosing grue, bleen, or green, with grue being the correct answer. Also describes a projection task about objects on the planet Kyron appearing solid or liquid depending upon whether they are north or south of the planet's equator. Describes a third projection task about four types of people on this planet: some born children will remain so, some born adults will remain so, some born children will become adults, and some born adults will become children. Reports on error rates and solution or response latencies, and correlations between scores on the projection tasks and three ability tests. Claims the projection experiments show that "the abilities required to perform nonentrenched tasks successfully and to process nonentrenched concepts within such tasks appear to be consequential in individual differences in measured intelligence." See Sternberg (1982) and (1983).

Sternberg, Robert J. "Natural, Unnatural, and Supernatural Concepts." *Cognitive Psychology* 14 (1982): 451–488. Concerned with "what makes seemingly natural concepts (such as *green* and *blue*) easier to process (e.g., perceive, remember, or reason with) than seemingly unnatural concepts (such as *grue* and *bleen*)." Considers three hypotheses: viz., natural concepts are better entrenched, natural concepts are simpler to process because they "require fewer conceptual transformations," and natural concepts are simpler and more entrenched than unnatural ones. Describes five experiments asking subjects "to characterize the state of an object at some future time on the basis of information about the state of the object both at that time and at some earlier time." Reports on one "instantiation of the task" that involves the color of an object at a future time and the color words 'green,' 'blue,' 'grue,' and 'bleen.' Also reports on versions involving objects being solids or liquids depending on whether they are north or south of a planet's equator, people being born children or adults and remaining so or changing from one to the other during their life span, and water being in a liquid or solid state at one time or another. Takes solution latency and error rate to be dependent variables. Describes qualitative tests of the entrenchment and simplicity hypotheses for predictions about solution latencies. Claims these tests show that "both entrenchment and simplicity contribute to ease of information processing, but that the effect of simplicity was greater than the effect of entrenchment." See Sternberg (1981 and 1982) and Bokhorst (1986).

Sternberg, Robert J. "Components of Human Intelligence." *Cognition* 15 (1983): 1–48. Describes Sternberg's componential view of human intelligence. Covers the historical and contemporary context, the metatheory or componential framework, the theory itself, and data from tests of the theory. Reviews (pp. 24–31) experiments requiring subjects "to make a projection that characterizes the state of an object at some future time on the basis of incomplete information about the state of the object both at that time and at some earlier time." Calls these "nonentrenched tasks" when they require "novel kinds of thinking in novel domains." Describes one nonentrenched task that presents a subject with "a description of the color of an object in the present day and in the year 2000" and in which the description "could be either physical—a green dot or a blue dot—or verbal—one of four color words, namely, *green, blue, grue,* and *bleen.*" Discusses how measures of response or solution latency on these tasks indicate intelligent performance. See Sternberg (1982) and (1981) for reports of the original experiments.

Stich, Stephen P. and Nisbett, Richard E. "Justification and the Psychology of Reasoning." *Philosophy of Science* 47 (1980): 188–202. Aim to make a case for "the philosophical relevance of recent empirical work on reasoning" by looking at Goodman's "reflective equilibrium" solution to the old riddle of induction. Claim that Goodman's solution involves empirical assumptions about how real people make inductive inferences. Review empirical work indicating that humans "regularly and systematically" accept as valid inductive inferences that are invalid: e.g., they commit the gambler's fallacy, make regression errors, and misjudge covariation. Consider two replies, one appealing to teaching subjects the error of their ways and the other appealing to rules being justified for those subjects but perhaps not us. Present an analysis of justification in terms of epistemic authorities, the expert reflective equilibrum account; modify this analysis to one in which a rule "accords with the reflective inductive practice of the people the speaker takes to be appropriate."

Stillwell, Shelley. "Confirmation, Paradoxes, and Possible Worlds." *British Journal for the Philosophy of Science* 36 (1985): 19–52. Argues that three of Hempel's well-known paradoxes of confirmation do not follow from Nicod's Criterion and the Equivalence Condition. Focuses on the importance of a sentential, as opposed to objectual, interpretation of confirmation. Mentions the new riddle in passing. Notes that Hempel argues for the Equivalence Condition "by claiming that equivalent hypotheses have the same content, and so, are the same hypothesis" and note that this line of argument is open to "Goodman-type examples." In a long footnote (p. 22) maintains that, with a sentential interpretation, one can retain Nicod's Criterion, the Equivalence Condition, and the Reverse Equivalence Condition despite Goodman-type examples. Thinks her remarks "do not touch on" the new riddle, but rather "serve to suggest that the notion of qualitative confirmation may be weak enough to be characterisable in terms of equivalence-type conditions together with" the sentential version of Nicod's Criterion.

Stove, D. C. *The Rationality of Induction.* Oxford: Oxford University Press, 1986. Gives three arguments (chs. V–VII) to prove that induction is justified. Develops and defends these arguments in the rest of the book. Considers the grue problem in chapter VIII, section V. Claims grue is not a problem for his three arguments. Claims, more generally, that grue is only a problem for "the belief that non-deductive logic is *purely formal.*" Discusses Hempel's definition of confirmation and Carnap's theory of logical probability. Points out that Hempel and Carnap believed nondeductive logic was purely formal. Maintains, however, that grue is not a counterexample to Hempel's definition of confirmation. Notes that Hempel defines a classificatory concept, not a comparative one, and so it does not have any consequences about two hypotheses (e.g., the grue and the green) being equally well confirmed (by emeralds observed prior to *t*). Challenges anyone to derive the following from Hempel's definition: "All emeralds observed before 2000 A.D. are green" confirms "Any emerald observed after 2000 A.D. is blue." Also maintains that grue is not a counterexample to Carnap's theory of logical probability. Challenges anyone to derive the following from Carnap's theory: "All emeralds observed before 2000 A.D. are green" is intitially favorably relevant to "Any emerald observed after 2000 A.D. is blue." Considers Armstrong's (1983) gruelike objection to his early logical probability argument from a 1973 article. Claims the objection does not apply to his current arguments because it depends on substituting "grue" for predicate variables or dummy predicates, and the current arguments are not about argument forms or schema with such variables or constants. Views the grue problem as showing only that some inductive inferences are not rational, and his arguments as claiming only (in response to an inductive skeptic) that some are rational. Contends the grue problem shows that, for systematic treatments of inductive inference, we need to restrict the range of predicate variables. Claims inductive logic was only thought to be purely formal because everyone thought (erroneously) deductive logic was purely formal. Acknowledges that the grue problem shows inductive logic is not purely formal. Believes, however, that Goodman's own statement of the grue problem is a "model of non-rigour." Asserts that it is impossible to derive the problem with any meta-principles of confirmation "not able to be shown on other grounds to be false." Denies, in other words, that the confirmation statement " 'All emeralds observed before 2000 A.D. are grue' confirms 'Any emerald observed after 2000 A.D. is grue'" entails the statement "'All emeralds observed before 2000 A.D. are green' confirms 'Any emerald observed after 2000 A.D. is blue'." Wonders why the grue problem has become important. Thinks the main factor has been "the immemorial illusion that logic is nothing if not formal."

Sweigart, John W. and Stewart, John P. "Another Look at *Fact, Fiction and Forecast.*" *Philosophical Studies* 10 (1959): 81–89. A reply to Pap (1955). Argue that Pap does not understand Goodman's treatment of dispositions, possible entities, and projectible hypotheses. Includes an exposition of Goodman's views on these topics.

Swinburne, R.G. "'Grue'." *Analysis* 28 (1968): 123–128. Argues that the new riddle can be solved by distinguishing between primary and secondary tests for applying a predicate to an object, using this as the basis for a distinction between qualitative and locational predicates, and then formulating a projection rule about pairs of predicates that can be used to make conflicting predictions and yet one of the pair is a qualitative predicate (such as "green") while the other is locational. Also comments on Slote (1967) and Wheatley (1967). See the reply by Slote (1968) and also the extended analysis in Swinburne (1969) as well as in his book *An Introduction to Confirmation Theory* (1971).

Swinburne, R. G. "Projectible Predicates." *Analysis* 30 (1969): 1–11. Considers two supported, unviolated, unexhausted hypotheses—"All *A* are *B*" and "All *A* are *C*"—that "lead to conflicting predictions in fields other than that so far studied": viz., we will have conflicting predictions for any *A* that is a *G* if "Every *B* that is *G* is not *H*" and "Every *C* that is *G* is *H*," where "*H*" designates an observable property. Introduces his (1968) rule of projection: if both "All *A* are *B*" and "All *A* are *C*" are supported, unviolated, and unexhausted, and "*B*" is a locational predicate, "*C*" a qualitative predicate, then we should adopt "All *A* are *C*" instead of "All *A* are *B*." Points out that this rule is inadequate because it only applies to a pair of hypotheses with a conflict between qualitative and locational predicates. Notes that it will not help us choose between "All ravens have black backs" and "All ravens have plan-black backs," where something is plan-black if and only if it is black and "situated on a planet more than 80 million miles from its centre of revolution, *e.g.* on the Earth, *or*" not black and not on such a planet. Also notes that it will not help us choose between "All men are trailless" and "All men are grailless," where something is grailless if and only if "it has green hair and a tail, *or* no green hair and no tail." Notes that if the two competing hypotheses "lead to conflicting predictions for *A*'s which are *G*, but the same predictions for *A*'s which are not *G*, the two predicates *B* and *C* will be inter-definable": where *K* and *C* are contraries, and *B* and *J* contraries, something is *B* if and only if either it is *C* and not *G* or *K* and *G*; something is *C* if and only if it is *B* and not *G* or *J* and *G*. Introduces a second rule of projection: "if the primary tests for the application of one of the competing predicates (*B*) to an object, but not for the other (*C*) involve finding out whether it has the property (denoted by *G*) in virtue of which the two hypotheses will yield conflicting predictions, we are to project *C* and not *B*," where a primary test for applying a concept is such that if the test is positive, then the concept applies "of logical necessity." Notes that this rule only applies where "one predicate (*C*) has an epistemological priority to the other (*B*)." Also characterizes circumstances in which this projection rule is wrong: viz., "if hypotheses attributing properties similar to that denoted by *B* to objects having properties similar to that denoted by *A* were in general much better confirmed than hypotheses attributing properties similar to that denoted by *C* to objects having properties similar to that denoted by *A*." Formalizes this in a third projection rule that overrules the second projection rule, allowing *B* to be projected instead of *C*, if and only if A is a member of a class of predicates, B is a member of a class of predicates, and C is a member of a class of predicates such that many hypotheses with antecedent predicates from the A class and consequent predicates from the B class (like "All A are B") are supported, unviolated, and unexhausted while very few hypotheses with antecedent predicates from the A class and consequent predicates from the C class (like "All A are C") are supported, unviolated, and unexhausted. Believes this third rule is elliptical because "any predicate will belong to a very large number of different predicate classes, and its application will vary with the predicates classe to which we ascribe predicates." For example: we can assign the predicate "raven" either to the class of birds or the class of animals with species averaging greater than or equal to two feet in length. Claims we can provide either an empirical or an a priori justification for a way of classifying predicates. Contends that "any empirical justification will in the end require an *a priori* one to back it." Maintains that empirical evidence "consists of evidence showing that this particular method of classification yields successful hypotheses." Notes, in connection with the raven example, there are many supported, unviolated, unexhausted hypotheses "about the appearance and physiology of all birds, attributing predicates to all birds which do not apply to all fishes, all mammals, etc." but there are few supported, unviolated, unexhausted hypotheses "about the appearance and physiology of all members of the class of animals, the average length of members of whose species is more than or equal to 2 ft., which are not also true of members of the class of animals, the average length of members of whose species is less than 2 ft." Claims that empirical evidence in favor of classifying predicates one way rather than another (say the X way rather than the Y) amounts to showing there are, in the field in question, many supported, unviolated, and unexhausted hypotheses that ascribe to all objects characterized by an X-predicate, "a predicate not possessed by many other members of distinct classes of the same level," but few supported, unviolated, and unexhausted hypotheses that ascribe to all objects characterized by a Y-predicate, "predicates not possessed by many other members of distinct classes of the same level." States this in the form of a general rule ($3'$) about preferring one class of predicates to another class of predicates in classifying predicates in order to apply the third projection rule, where the rule involves classes of classes of predicates (e.g., a wider class of predicates having the members of a narrower class of predicates as members), and hypotheses about these classes of classes of predicates. Believes it is clear "that rule ($3'$) instead of removing the unclarity in rule (3) has only taken it one stage further back." That is: just as any predicate may belong to a large number of predicate classes, a predicate class may itself belong to a large number of classes of predicate classes. Maintains that "we can provide empirical justification of our way of classifying predicates at this, as at any other stage, if we can show that if we classify predicates in this way rather than in some rival way, then we get from our data of observation better results (*viz.,* more hypotheses supported, unviolated and unexhausted) in other fields." Points out how this will depend on "our method of classifying methods of classifying methods of classifying predicates." Believes it is clear that "any attempt to reach ultimate empirical justification for the use of some predicate rather than another in some proposed law can only lead to an infinite regress." Argues, however, that "any justification at the final stage must be *a priori*" because we use some information about the world each time we justify a system of classifying predicates, we only have a finite amount of information about the world, and when we use the last information to justify a very general system "the use of the system of classification which was taken for granted in providing this justification cannot receive empirical support." Believes there is only one a priori justification for a system of classifying predicates: viz., "that it seems to us the natural way of classifying." Also believes that whether a predicate is projectible "is determined by empirical data slotted into the system of classification determined by the language and the way in which we have been taught to use it." Acknowledges that "new empirical data can force us to change any system of classification" and gives "an extremely simple illustration" of how we might adopt a new system of classification. Notes, however, that while "any given classification may be overthrown by empirical evidence," it is still true that "the very process of overthrow presupposes other classifications justified *a priori.*" Also acknowledges that "any projection at all among predicates which differ in epistemological priority (apart from any eliminated by rule (1)) could be licensed by some system of classification compatible with data so far available." Asks whether it is "arbitrary that we stick to our present system." Argues that we should adopt "as a fundamental rule of inductive inference the rule that we must never change our system of classifying at will, only allow it to be modified by new empirical data." Points to the fact that we obviously view some projections as right and some as wrong, the fact it seems natural to classify properties in this way, and the fact that "there is no empirical evidence supporting another way."

Swinburne, Richard. *An Introduction to Confirmation Theory.* London: Methuen & Co. Ltd., 1971. Uses material from Swinburne (1968) and (1969). Discusses projectibility on pages 78–81. Says that "of physical necessity all A's are Q" is projectible if its "intrinsic probability" is greater than all other statements of the form "of physical necessity a proportion p of A's are Q" except for the statement "of physical necessity no A's are Q." Notes this also holds for statements of statistical probability. Says that "we can call a hypothesis probjectible in Goodman's sense if its intrinsic probability is not zero." Points out that some universal nomological statements are not projectible, especially those in which "Q" designates "an exact numerical value of a measurement of a quantity which can vary continuously" and those in which either "Q" or "A" is a positional predicate. Notes that "grue" is "the most famous example of a positional predicate." Defines "grue" so that something is grue if and only if it is green at a time before A.D. 2000 or it is blue at or later than A.D. 2000. Claims the grue hypothesis has zero intrinsic probability because "we do not regard such a hypothesis as confirmed when its predictions in the form of observational reports (deduced from the nomological proposition and background evidence) come off." Discusses the new riddle in chapter VII, "Simplicity," pages 100–122. Introduces the new riddle "conflict," notes we obviously want to adopt the green hypothesis, and claims "the task of confirmation theory is to bring out the principle which makes this the simpler and so more probable hypothesis." Points to the obvious rule: viz., the grue hypothesis contains a positional predicate and "nomological propositions containing positional predicates are non-projectible absolutely." Puts this in his terminology: the green hypothesis is simpler, its intrinsic probability is not zero, and so it is "intrinsically more probable than 'all emeralds are grue'." Points out that, on Goodman's account of projectibility, the grue hypothesis is less projectible than the green hypothesis, not absolutely nonprojectible. Also points out that, on Goodman's account, the grue hypothesis could be more projectible than the green hypothesis, thus more probable intrinsically and "more probable on evidence predicted equally accurately by both hypotheses and compatible with them." Believes this is mistaken and we should look for a better account of why the green hypothesis is intrinsically more probable than the green hypothesis. Defends the claim that "green" is essentially qualitative and "grue" is essentially positional. Characterizes a predicate as positional "if in order to find out as certainly as can be found out whether or not it applies to an object we have to find out its relations to some other *particular* thing." Believes this shows that even if "green" and "grue" are interdefinable, "which is positional and which qualitative depends on the meaning of the terms." Believes this shows the rule (nomological propositions with positional predicates are not projectible) is a "transcultural rule." Formulates a more general rule for dealing with conflicts when neither *"B"* nor *"C"* are positional: viz., "in all conflicts between incompatible hypotheses 'all *A*'s are *B*' and 'all *A*'s are *C*', where *'B'* is epistemologically superior to *'C'*, 'all *A*'s are *B*' is simpler and so intrinsically more probable than 'all *A*'s are *C*'." Defines predicate *'B'* being epistemologically superior to predicate *'C'* as: we must get in a position to know whether *"B"* applies to an object in order to find out whether *"C"* applies to the object "as certainly as can be found out," but not conversely. Points out that "green" is epistemologically superior to "grue" and that "black" is superior to "plan-black" (from Swinburne 1969), where "plan-black" means black and located on a planet more than 80 million miles from its center of revolution, or not black and not located on such a planet. Points out that no evidence will confirm the grue hypothesis, but some evidence could confirm "All ravens are plan-black." Notes that, on the more general rule, the green hypothesis has greater intrinsic probability than the grue hypothesis. Also defines one predicate being epistemologically equivalent to another, and one predicate being epistemologically independent of another. Discusses the curve-fitting problem as a case "of conflicting hypotheses whose consequent predicates are epistemologically equivalent." Examines Harold Jeffreys's (1931) solution. Concludes that "our judgements about the relative mathematical simplicity of mathematical equations are dependent on the notation in which those equations are expressed and our familiarity with and understanding of that notation." Believes this applies to "incompatible hypotheses 'all *A*'s are *B*' and 'all *A*'s are *C*' where *'B'* and *'C'* are epistemologically equivalent or epistemologically independent predicates." Claims the simpler hypothesis will be the one providing "a more natural description of objects." Notes that whether a description is more natural "depends on the conceptual scheme with which we have grown up." Discusses Sanford's work (1970) on disjunctive predicates. States the following rule (based on Sanford's "objective account of disjunctiveness"): "All *A*'s are *B*" is simpler than "All *A*'s are *C*" if *"B"* is a non-disjunctive predicate and *"C"* is a disjunctive predicate. Believes this is a useful, transcultural additional rule. Considers whether we can measure familiarity by entrenchment. Argues that, on Goodman's extensional view of meaning, "we cannot even apply Goodman's rules of projection until we have determined by other means what results they will give!" Believes this shows it is impossible, on Goodman's view, to determine the relative simplicity of hypotheses. Suggests changing from "coextensive" to "synonymous." Considers whether, on Goodman's view of adopting a hypothesis, we can caculate how often a predicate has been projected. Believes the view is too vague to evaluate. Asks why using a term in a description doesn't entrench it, and why there isn't a difference in entrenchment for terms projected the same number of times, except that one term appears in unfalisified hypotheses while the other appears in a hypothesis "subsequently falsified." Tries to give a "more realistic, if rather vaguer, picture of the matter" in which the best-entrenched predicates are those appearing in a wide range of nomological propositions accepted by the scientific community, and where the size of the proportion of scientists who accept the propositions, and the eminence of the scientists, are relevant factors. Discusses overhypotheses in chapter XI, pp. 174–179. Reviews Goodman's account of overhypotheses and claims it "needs amendment in one small but important respect." Believes Goodman should change his definition of a positive overhypothesis to: *"H* is a positive overhypothesis of *h* if the antecedent of *H* is a parent predicate of the antecedent of *h*, and the consequent of *H* is an *S*-parent of the consequent predicate of *h."* Notes his definition of an *S*-parent: if "among the classes to which *'Q'* applies is every class, all of whose members belong to the extension of *'R'*," then predicate *"Q"* is an *S*-parent of predicate *"R."* Expresses Goodman's points in his terminology, provides two realistic examples, and discusses how to generalize Goodman's account so that it can deal with statistical overhypotheses.

Swinburne, R. G. "Properties, Causation, and Projectibility: Reply to Shoemaker." In *Applications of Inductive Logic,* edited by L. Jonathan Cohen and Mary Hesse, pp. 313–320. Oxford: Oxford University Press, 1980. A reply to Shoemaker (1980b). Maintains that Shoemaker's strong thesis is incorrect: viz., that genuine properties are just causal powers. Believes Shoemaker does not support this thesis adequately, and that his main arguments "have a strongly verificationist flavour." Discusses, for example, the argument that two different properties cannot have the same causal potentialities because "we could never know whether two objects had the same or different properties." Replies by appealing to the principle of simplicity: if two objects produce a certain effect in certain circumstances, then it is simpler to suppose they do so because they possess a common property as opposed to two different properties. Also believes Shoemaker's thesis is false because we know what properties various objects have, and yet on Shoemaker's thesis we could not. Argues that if we can recognize the powers of objects, then we can recognize when certain changes have occurred, and yet we need to recognize the properties of objects in order to recognize when these changes have occurred—"if properties are nothing but potentialities for contributing to causal powers, we have a vicious infinite regress." Goes on to discuss what else there is to properties besides causal powers, and speculates on why Shoemaker came to adopt his strong thesis. Also see the section with brief comments (pp. 321–332) by Mackie, Mellor, Hesse, and Margalit. Includes replies by Shoemaker and additional remarks by Swinburne, especially about "grue" being unprojectible because it is an intrinsically positional predicate, and not because of Shoemaker's strong thesis about properties.

Teller, Paul. "Goodman's Theory of Projection." *British Journal for the Philosophy of Science* 20 (1969): 219–238. Critically examines Goodman's theory of projection and maintains that "the tenable residue of Goodman's theory is compatible with a version of Bayesian confirmation theory." Argues that it is incomplete and oversimplified to analyze the problem in terms of a projectible/nonprojectible dichotomy rather than in terms of degrees of projectibility, and that Goodman's own discussion (e.g., of adopting hypotheses) is in line with generalizing the dichotomy to grades or degrees. Claims that at best Goodman's theory "can give only crude estimates of projectibility and that probably most of the details have to be supplanted in favour of some alternative approach." Maintains there are difficulties in determining the entrenchment of predicates because of difficulties in determining when predicates are coextensive and when one predicate is the parent of another (and thus difficulties with the method of overhypotheses as well). Notes that it would be circular to resolve these difficulties by relying on a general characterization of inductive methods or general solution to inductive problems. Explores three kinds of solutions: e.g., instead of being coextensive, we might appeal to predicates being synonymous and then appeal to meaning relations between predicates in order to determine when some predicates are parents of others. Also discusses problems with new predicates or theoretical terms in connection with explanatory theories. Points out parallels between Goodman's scheme and a Bayesian approach to confirmation theory, especially a subjective Bayesian approach. Emphasizes that "the prior degree of confirmation, $C(h)$, of a proposition, h, has all the properties of a projectibility index as described by Goodman." Notes that, unlike Carnap's version of a Bayesian approach, a subjective version has a way to fix or estimate prior degrees of confirmation, though of course the estimates may differ from person to person. Considers whether "the projections singled out by such a subjective characterisation will be in accord with past accepted practice and thus form an explication of valid inductive inference in Goodman's sense." Proposes interpreting the confirmation function C so that it is "a summary of the collective standards of rational practice to which most of us generally subscribe," and then letting entrenchment be one possible way to estimate prior degrees of confirmation.

Temple, Dennis. "Grue-Green and Some Mistakes in Confirmation Theory." *Dialectica* 28 (1974): 197–210. Regards the green hypothesis as claiming that every emerald always has been and always will be green, the grue hypothesis as claiming that every emerald will be green until time t and then will change to blue. Argues that whether emeralds will change color is not the kind of question "which can or should be referred to entrenchment or any semantical property of terms or statements." Considers this to be a question about possible causes that requires a line of causal reasoning to support proposed answers. Outlines how to reason from information about observing emeralds to an answer supporting the green hypothesis, and how to reason more conclusively for that answer by systematically investigating the structure of emeralds to determine what makes them green—by developing "some theoretical understanding" of the phenomenon.

Thagard, Paul R. "The Best Explanation: Criteria for Theory Choice." *Journal of Philosophy* 75 (1978): 76–92. Views a criterion as "a standard of judgment which must be weighed against other criteria used in evaluating explanatory hypotheses." Describes three main criteria and "the tensions" between them: viz., consilience (static and dynamic), simplicity, and analogy. Claims that generalizations "can also be inferred as best explanations." Considers induction by simple enumeration to be flawed in a major way because it does not take account of the variety of instances; on the inference to the best explanation view, "the variety of instances is simply a kind of consilience." Points out that the inference to the best explanation view emphasizes pragmatic notions rather than syntactic or semantic ones. Claims "this concern with the pragmatic translates into the avoidance of the notorious paradoxes of confirmation" but says that space does not permit him to discuss how this view deals with Hempel's ravens and Goodman's grue paradox. See Thagard and Nisbett (1982) and Holland, Holyoak, Nisbett, and Thagard (1986).

Thagard, Paul and Nisbett, Richard E. "Variability and Confirmation." *Philosophical Studies* 42 (1982): 379–394. View principles of inductive inference as "content relative." Illustrate this by examining how instances confirm generalizations. Argue that the degree of confirmation here depends primarily on background knowledge "about the kinds of entities and properties the generalization concerns." Maintain that variability is a prime factor here; that is, how well instances confirm 'All F are G' depends on how variable F's are with respect to G's. Present experimental and nonexperimental evidence to support this claim. State the claim more precisely by formulating degree of confirmation as a monotonic, negatively accelerated function of the number of instances where the rate of acceleration mainly depends on variability. Attempt to show that the notion of a kind "possesses some psychological and philosophical respectability." Compare their view with theory choice as choosing the best explanation, Hempel's qualitative confirmation theory, and Bayesian confirmation theory. Recommend "a more empirical approach to inductive logic" that will eliminate "distractions which arise from artificial constructs such as 'grue'." See Holland, Holyoak, Nisbett, and Thagard (1986) for a book-length discussion of this approach.

Thomson, Judith Jarvis. "Grue." *Journal of Philosophy* 63 (1966a): 289–309. Restates the new riddle by supposing mineralogists have reasons to think all beryls are green, putting 'grue' in place of 'green' in these reasons to produce reasons to think all beryls are grue, and then asking why the former reasons are better reasons for the green hypothesis than the latter reasons are for the grue hypothesis. Considers why we should think that the green reasons and the grue reasons provide equally good support for their respective hypotheses; rejects a rule based on the truth-preserving operation of replacing a nonlogical constant everywhere in a hypothesis and the reasons supporting it, and claims that "no one who thinks there is a puzzle about grue can accept this inductive rule." Appeals to a general principle about reasons in trying to establish an asymmetry between 'green' and 'grue' in connection with knowing the color of all beryls examined so far: viz., you can know they are green just by looking at them in good light, but you can know they are grue only by deducing this from two other things you know, that they are green and that they have been examined before the time in question. The general principle about reasons is: if you have found the Xs so far examined to be P and know they are P or Q just because you have deduced this from their being P, then in the absence of an independent reason to think V is responsible for a thing being Q, you have no better reason to think V is responsible for a thing being P or Q than you have to think V is responsible for a thing being P. Appeals to this principle and the asymmetry in trying to show that we do have reason to prefer the green hypothesis to the grue one and so "we are entitled to say it is on balance probable all beryls are green rather than grue." Also considers how to handle "queer subject-terms" by appealing to asymmetries and the general principle. See the comments by Goodman (1966) and the reply by Thomson (1966b).

Thomson, Judith Jarvis. "More Grue." *Journal of Philosophy* 63 (1966b): 528–534. A reply to Goodman (1966), defense of Thomson (1966a). Claims she was not trying to define projectibility or observability; rather she was trying to provide a sufficient condition for inductively preferring one specific hypothesis to another—"All beryls are green" to "All beryls are grue." Maintains that one could not tell whether a beryl is grue simply by looking at it in good light, while one could tell whether it is green by looking at it in a good light; regards this point as merely one step in an argument about knowing about the color of all beryls examined to date. Emphasizes that no one could tell that a beryl is grue just by looking at it in good light; argues that "Goodman has given no ground at all for supposing that a machine could be constructed (or a human being tampered with) in such a way that we could say of it that it now can tell that a thing is grue *just* by taking a good look at it in a good light." Explains how her approach can show "All bits of copper conduct electricity" preferable to "All bits of copper condulate electricity." Considers whether "Copper conducts electricity" is a hypothesis that any scientist would ever project; wonders what we are supposed to imagine is going on with copper if it condulates electricity rather than conducting it; remarks that in connection with the emerald and copper examples, one must "make up word usage, or science, or both, in order to get this puzzle off the ground."

Turney, Peter. "The Curve Fitting Problem: A Solution." *British Journal for the Philosophy of Science* 41 (1990): 509–530. Attempts to provide a justification for the standard solution to the curve-fitting problem: viz., for the given set of data, select the simplest family of equations by looking for the family with the fewest number of parameters. Notes how this involves the criteria of accuracy and simplicity. Defines the instability function of a family of equations for a set of data; notes that its values indicate whether the family is sensitive to, or resists, perturbed data. Proves that the instability function is, for a family of linear regression equations, proportional to the dimension of the parameter vector, which is a measure of complexity. Proves, in other words, that the simplicity of a family is proportional to its stability. Maintains that we should want the simplest family because it will be the most stable; claims that "stability is the ability to resist random perturbations." Maintains that we should want stability because "it leads to repeatable experiments." Views data as both a signal and noise, considers repeating an experiment as an attempt to duplicate the signal part of the data, and claims "a stable theory is less sensitive to noise than an unstable theory." Agrees with Goodman (1971) about simplicity being one test of the truth of a theory. Says accordingly: "to the extent that stability leads to repeatable experiments, stability leads to truth." Points out that simplicity (understood as stability) is also important when extrapolating and interpolating data instead of repeating experiments. Discusses Hume's problem for curve fitting (justifying our standard methods) in terms of assuming a definite error distribution or not, and provides a pragmatic justification (similar to Reichenbach's) that we should. Comments on Schlesinger's (1974) view that simplicity is the only objective criterion for selecting among equally accurate curves; notes this is a rare case and insists that we end up selecting a unique curve by balancing accuracy and simplicity. Formulates Goodman's problem for curve fitting by plotting observations on time and color axes, where the equation for the green theory belongs to a family with one parameter, the equation for the green-before and blue-after theory belongs to a family with three parameters, and the grue theory equation belongs to a family with one paramater. Notes that his measure of instability will not help us here because it depends on "the assumption that we can identify projectible coordinates." Accepts Goodman's entrenchment view of projectibility and sees an entrenched predicate as having "demonstrated its stability, by surviving in our language." Thinks that Mulhall (1989) confuses the intension and extension of "grue."

Ullian, Joseph. "Luck, License, & Lingo." *Journal of Philosophy* 58 (1961a): 731–738. Also in this volume with a postscript. Argues that "if, after digesting Goodman's contributions and coming face to face with his 'new riddle of induction,' one *still* has the gnawing feeling that there is more to be said, then one's anxieties will have shifted to a new location." Describes how Goodman views justifying deductive or inductive inferences: viz., as "codification of the kind of inference in question." Considers whether we can appeal to codification for both kinds of inferences. Notes that deductive inference seems to be organizational while inductive inference "purports to generate fresh knowledge," and so it seems like we should have "less freedom in deciding what predictions to make than in choosing which of our facts to redigest." Responds that "we should have expected to have more lingering qualms in the inductive case, if only because we presumably had more qualms there to begin with." Notes that both Donald Williams and Georg von Wright attempt to justify inductive inference in terms of future cases resembling past cases, and that the new riddle shows these attempts fail because "the crucial question always remains: *resemble in which respects?*" Claims that even if we could "explicate perfectly the idea of a genuine or purely qualitative or *projectible* (from Goodman) predicate, it would be of no help whatsoever for purposes of resurrecting a priori justifications of inductive inferences or policies." Points out that "there is no law of logic (deductive *or* inductive) according to which a distinction may be employed arbitrarily in an argument just because it has been drawn with clarity and precision." Reviews Goodman's entrenchment solution to the problem of defining valid prediction, and considers why the right predicates are the ones that become the well-entrenched predicates. Notes that if we believe we can solve the new riddle by giving an explication, then we would not be asking about the right predicates becoming entrenched. Goes on to discuss the question nonetheless. Mentions large-scale, successful extrapolations in the history of physical science (often by way of analogy) and observes that "we have come to have a very great confidence that concepts which help us in one area of our experience will turn out to be extendible to other areas, and on a very large scale." Believes this is "a very remarkable phenomenon" and "one which couldn't have been counted on." Believes the same thing is true about "simpler concepts, even those as simple as concepts of colors or hues." Marvels at the fact that our basic property concepts "are so uniformly of use in describing and organizing our experience." Emphasizes this point by saying he finds "it remarkable that we get any mileage at all out of our concepts, that we have any use whatsoever for general terms." Asks how general terms "turn out to be of use for us?" Claims it is a "brute" fact that we can learn to use general terms and agree with others in how we use them, and that we "can explain what this ability consists in only up to a point." Believes that we "give too much credit to nature for all this" and that we should remember "concepts and the employment of general terms depend upon classification"—and "one class is as good as another as far as logic is concerned." Points out that "from the vast number of theoretically available alternatives we mark off a relatively small number of (open-ended) classes, which are roughly the same for me as for you, and in terms of them we find it possible to make sense out of our experience." Believes the explanation here "will likely be an evolutionary one:" i.e., "were it not for the evolvement of such a knack we should have had no language, no conceptual power, and very little chance for survival through these many centuries." Maintains that having successfully projectible predicates is "a special case of our having any use for predicates at all." Complains that conventional treatments of induction are too concerned with inference and with simple examples. Calls for more "attention to the actual functioning of language, both plain and specialized." Considers whether different concepts might have been as useful or more useful. Regards this as a question about "how well off we might have been with a basically different conceptual scheme" or "a radically different language." Says that "almost any answer except a shrug of the shoulders seems out of place." Admits that logic does not require "precisely our conceptual structure for the organization of what we call our experience." Ends with a comment on how well we make inductive inferences: viz., we need "the entire fabric of our language" to do that well.

Ullian, J.S. "More on 'Grue' and Grue." *Philosophical Review* 70 (1961b): 386–389. A reply to Barker and Achinstein (1960). Considers how Mr. Grue should represent the color of grass in the year 2001 if he expects it to be grue, the option of using a sample of the color you expect it to have then, and whether we will say he used blue or grue. Claims that "counting blue and not grue as a color is to honor our customary classifications to the extent of begging all the interesting questions here." Views Barker and Achinstein as trying to isolate the positional predicates without paying attention to our customary or ordinary classifications in the form of "the facts of entrenchment." Maintains that it will not help to invoke a criterion for sameness of color, matching, primarily because what matches for one person may not match for another, and so "who is to say that today's green fails to match tomorrow's blue for Mr. Grue?" Introduces the word "shmolor" as a word that functions for Mr. Grue in the way that "color" functions for us, except that there are differences in what counts as a color and as a shmolor. Notes that now we can say something has the shmolor grue at a certain time just in case it is green and the time is before 2000 or it is blue and the time is 2000 or after. Adds that we can now suppose (but do not have to) that Mr. Grue treats objects of the same shmolor as indistinguishable just as we treat objects of the same color as indistinguishable. Claims it is circular to maintain that we classify objects with respect to color in our manner because we label the objects as they really are in the world. Concludes that Barker and Achinstein simply refuse to accept one extension being as good as another for a class as a class "no matter how much (or how little) its description may cut across the boundaries of our ordinary classifications."

Ullian, Joseph S. "On Projectibility." *Nous* 9 (1975): 329–339. A reply to Gottlieb (1975). Sees Gottlieb as criticizing a straw man because Goodman's theory does not equate projectible hypotheses (at a given time) with rationally supported hypotheses. Maintains that Goodman's theory connects beliefs about rational support with the projectibility judgments allowed by a belief corpus. Formulates the connection as: "relative to a belief corpus, a hypothesis may rationally be taken to be supported by its instances iff on the basis of plausible inferences—say, inferences that count as acceptable for nongeniuses —the corpus gives rise to the judgment that it is projectible." Explains how this connection deals with three of Gottlieb's objections: viz., about hypotheses with no true instances, predicates we do not suspect are coextensive, and unformulated hypotheses. Thinks of projectibility as "halfway between plausibility and truth" and believes "we reason plausibly in hopes of reaching the projectible, with the further hope that that will lead us to truth." Says projectibility is to induction (somewhat) as truth is to deduction. Notes a parallel between starting with the right premises (i.e., true premises) for deduction, the right initial corpus for induction. Claims that the right initial corpus must be "accurate enough and broad enough" in various ways because projectibility (at a given time) is a hybrid notion. Explains how it depends on information that is part of some record and probably available (past instances and past projections) and information that is not part of any record and probably unavailable (coextensiveness and conflicting hypotheses). Adds that it is often easy to make projectibility judgments with Goodman's guidelines. Considers Gottlieb's view that predicates should not earn entrenchment from violated hypotheses. Disagrees with this view because it goes against how people actually frame hypotheses, is unneccessary considering how other predicates probably will become better entrenched than the predicates in violated hypotheses, ignores how these predicates can function to "stake out the extensions eventually selected" by their successors, overlooks how these predicates can still function in statistical hypotheses, and leaves us with "nothing to build on" (no earned entrenchment) when all of the predicates come from violated hypotheses and there is nothing to replace them with. Notes that Goodman recognizes there are questions about the best way to measure entrenchment. Goes on to consider Gottlieb's views on degrees of projectibility. Points out that a full theory of inductive inference will "be able to handle a variety of quantitative distinctions in its input and to offer quantitative distinctions in its output." Also points out that Goodman's infant theory only makes qualitative distinctions for one simple kind of hypothesis. Views Gottlieb's fruit-fly case as forcing Goodman's theory to deal with a quantitative issue that it was not designed to deal with. Argues that in the fruit-fly case at least "we can find a certain conditional hypothesis credible, and then await further evidence to determine which of the components is to count as projectible." Explains when, according to Goodman's analysis, those conditionals can be taken as gaining credibility from the evidence. Contrasts this situation with the grue case. Discusses a widespread complaint about Goodman's entrenchment theory: viz., that Goodman does not explain why his theory should work, and so perhaps his theory just happens to make the right distinctions instead of having to. Claims this is a question for another theory to answer, most likely a psychological theory about learning.

Ullian, Joseph S. "Wanton Embedding Revised and Secured." *Journal of Philosophy* 77 (1980): 487–495. A reply to Zabludowski (1977) and Kennedy and Chihara (1977).

Presents a new formulation of the criterion for hypothesis J wantonly embeds the hypothesis H, where "J and H may be regarded as universally quantified conditionals with no free variables." Notes how the original formulation used a body of information, rho, to specify the class of H's unexamined cases. Believes "the wanton-embedding relation should relate hypotheses *simpliciter.*" Maintains that "whether J wantonly embeds H should not vary as evidence increases, nor should it depend on which of H's instances have been examined." Eliminates rho from the current formulation. Claims the Kennedy–Chihara examples depend on adding to rho a statement with a relation like "has the same color as." Points out that wanton embedding can be caused by either the antecedent or the consequent of a hypothesis. Concludes that if J wantonly embeds H, then this depends on whether either the conjunction stating that x is a positive instance of J or the conjunction stating that x is a negative instance of J "yields information concerning the instances of H other than x." Defines, for "formulas of lower predicate calculus without function symbols," the concept of one formula implying another formula essentially: viz., one formula implies another essentially if the former formula does not imply, for any k-ary predicate letter occurring in the latter formula, any result of supplanting a positive number of occurrences of this predicate letter in the latter formula by a new k-ary predicate letter. Also defines the concept of a self-essential formula (i.e., a formula that implies itself essentially). Notes that "only self-essential formulas can be—or can even occur in—essential consequences." Labels a formula "*x-restricted*" if all occurrences of "*x*" in the formula are free, the formula does not contain free variables besides "*x*," and all of the quantifiers of the formula "are restricted to range over the class of objects different from *x*." Notes that "any formula in which no variable other than '*x*' is free is equivalent to an *x*-restricted formula." States the new criterion for wanton embedding: the hypothesis J wantonly embeds the hypothesis H if and only if either the conjunction stating that x is a positive instance of J or the conjunction stating that x is a negative instance of J has an *x*-restricted essential consequence containing the *x*-restricted antecedent of H stating that y is an instance of H. Notes how the new formulation of the criterion shows that each of Zabludowski's (1974) contrived hypotheses wantonly embeds "All M are N." Considers "cases of wanton embedding, on our criterion for it, where the rivalry between H and J may appear innocuous." Points out that if J wantonly embeds H, then "we simply bar J from the circle of H's competitors; H may still succumb to other hypotheses under the basic rule of projectibility." Notes that the relation of wanton embedding is not reflexive, symmetric, transitive, irreflexive, or asymmetric; and that it "is not in general preserved when a predicate (antecedent or consequent) in J or H is replaced by a coextensive one." Argues that no *x*-restricted essential consequence of a formula with all occurrences of "*x*" free, and in which a monadic predicate letter "G" (occurring in the context "Gx") is followed only by variables, can "contain an occurrence of 'G' that is followed by a variable other than '*x*'." Points out how the argument can be generalized. Maintains that neither the green hypothesis nor the grue hypothesis wantonly embeds the other because "x is an emerald and x is green" cannot have an *x*-restricted essential consequence containing "y is an emerald." See the reply by Zabludowski (1982).

Ullian, Joseph S. "The Ninth Inning." *Journal of Philosophy* 79 (1982): 332–334. Follows and replies to Zabludowski (1982). Ninth and final paper in a direct exchange with Zabludowski. Notes that we may regard both "All emeralds are green" and "All stones are fusible" as projectible if we do not have any reason to suppose they conflict. Emphasizes that there is no regress because "we need not *judge* that there is no conflict before judging the hypotheses projectible." Believes that Zabludowski's generalization h^{***} does not compete with "any live hypothesis" because it is violated and so reduces to "All stones are round." Generalization h^{***} is "All stones are round and fusible, or round and not such that some stones that are emeralds are either fusible but not green or green but not fusible, or fusible and such that some stones that are emeralds are either fusible but not green or green but not fusible" in Zabludowski (1975). Notes that h^{***} does conflict with "All emeralds are green," but argues that h^{***} is not a rival to "All emeralds are green" because either h^{***} "reduces to a hypothesis known to be false, or had we somehow mustered grounds for supposing conflict between 'All emeralds are green' and 'All stones are fusible', h^{***} would have reduced to the latter hypothesis and so have been otiose." Admits that his latest criterion for wanton embedding does not block all Zabludowskian hypotheses. Maintains that these contrived hypotheses are obviously not as simple as the hypotheses they are supposed to compete with, and so "it is likely that further plausible auxiliary principles—or perhaps some wider use of the test of wanton embedding itself—would suffice to rule them out as well." Stresses that nonetheless Goodman's projectibility theory does not need these auxiliary principles or a principle of wanton embedding. Comments on the last two paragraphs of Zabludowski (1982). Claims that if a hypothesis wantonly embeds a supposed rival, this alone does not prevent the hypothesis from being projectible; that if two hypotheses wantonly embed each other and so do not compete with each other, "this need not prevent us from choosing between them, since each may have rivals that do not embed it;" and that Zabludowski's h^{***}-like hypothesis is nullified for reasons similar to those cited as nullifying his generalization h^{***}.

Ullian, Joseph and Goodman, Nelson. "Bad Company: A Reply to Mr. Zabludowski and Others." *Journal of Philosophy* 72 (1975): 142–145. A reply to Zabludowski (1974) and, in passing, to Kennedy and Chihara (1975). Maintain that Zabludowski has not produced genuine counterexamples to the *FFF* rule of projectibility; claim his examples either violate conditions for properly applying the rule or a principle about relative simplicity. Emphasize that the *FFF* theory of projectibility is qualitative, not quantitative, and "imposes limits both on what it accepts as input and what it aims at as output." Formulate a principle of admissible (and necessary) information for using the rule: viz., information that the two competing hypotheses are supported and unviolated, that they conflict, and that, regardless of their truth-values, they are "about equally well-entrenched or else a particular one of them is the much better entrenched." Claim that all of Zabludowski's examples involve the assumption (or an "exactly parallel" assumption) that we know some As are not Bs, where "B" is not the antecedent or consequent predicate of either of the competing hypotheses. Note that this assumption violates the principle on admissible information, and so "the rule of projectibility is not applicable to any of them as they are stated." Note that the *FFF* theory only applies to simple universal hypotheses, and that Zabludowski's examples involve hypotheses with obvious differences in simplicity. Believe a principle of wanton embedding will block all of Zabludowski's examples: viz., a hypothesis H cannot compete with any hypothesis "that wantonly embeds H itself within it." State this idea informally in terms of excluding a hypothesis J from being in competition with a hypothesis H "if determination of the positivity or negativity of some of J's instances threatens to depend on and require information about instances of H that are still unexamined." Go on to state this idea formally (using Goodman's analysis of "about") and show how it applies to five of Zabludowski's examples. See the reply by Zabludowski (1975).

Ullian, Joseph and Goodman, Nelson. "Projectibility Unscathed." *Journal of Philosophy* 73 (1976): 527–531. A reply to Zabludowski (1974) and (1976). Consider whether Zabludowski's hypothesis h^{***} shows that a supposedly projectible hypothesis h is not projectible because h^{***} is supported, unviolated, not overridden, and—with h conflicting with the not-overridden yet violated "All A are B" and h^{***} amounting to the not-overridden "All A are C" if h and "All A are C" conflict, otherwise amounting to "All A are B"—h^{***} conflicts with h. Note we cannot simply say that h^{***} is violated when it amounts to the violated "All A are B" because "being violated (like being supported and being unexhausted) is a trait with a noetic component, and it is not in general transmitted from a hypothesis to a hypothesis coextensive with it." Claim "the rascal in the example" is assuming the information we accept at t does not exclude "All A are C" from being in conflict with h. Note that if the information does exclude this, then we would know h^{***} amounts to "All A are B" and so we could regard h^{***} as violated. Maintain that Goodman's theory of projectibility "allows that there are circumstances in which it is plausible to *assume* that two hypotheses conflict, even where guarantee of such conflict is lacking." Claim we can presume two hypotheses conflict "on the basis of our data and other assumptions," not simply on a whim. Do not hold that we can presume anything we do not have any reason to deny. Insist that the principle of admissible information is "a spelling out of such evident facts as that the rules for resolving conflicts operate only when the truth values of the two hypotheses are undetermined." Introduce ¢ as an abbreviation for: h and "All A are C" conflict. Consider what happens if we accept, reject, or neither accept nor reject ¢, and maintain that *"whichever"* way we pass it will thereby render h^{***} otiose": either h^{***} will be identified with "All A are C" or deemed to be violated. Adopt the position of "good, conservative persons of science": the less confident we are that "All A are C" does not conflict with h, the better it would be "to postpone branding of h as projectible until further evidence is available." Go on to consider an extended account of projectibility that applies to degrees of credibility, and makes credibility distinctions among unviolated hypotheses. Argue that if ¢ is plausible because it has a high degree of credibility (say p), then we do not need h^{***} in order to see h is not projectible; and if ¢ has a degree of credibility less than p, then "All A are C" does not show h is not projectible. Note, moreover, that *"h^{***}* has no higher degree of credibility than ¢ does, so its credibility is less than p." Conclude that "h^{***} turns out to be no more credible than a claim that was not credible enough to be deemed plausible," and so if a hypothesis h conflicts with h^{***}, this detracts "little from projectibility of h in the case in question." End by considering Zabludowski's criticisms of the principle of wanton embedding, in particular that the grue hypothesis wantonly embeds the green hypothesis. Maintain that *"none* of the new consequences that he cites is implied differentially with respect to U^* as the principle requires." Believe he has "misconstrued the status of the symbol 'U^*'." Emphasize that 'U^*' is merely an abbreviation for '$U - \{x\}$', and so the sentences derived in Zabludowski's examples actually contain '$U - \{x\}$' and not 'U^*'. Explain how this means each of Zabludowski's new consequences "has the defect that its generalization with respect to 'U' is equally a consequence; so none of them is implied differentially with respect to U^*." See the reply by Zabludowski (1977) as well as by Kennedy and Chihara (1977).

Vickers, John M. "Characteristics of Projectible Predicates." *Journal of Philosophy* 64 (1967): 280–286. Considers how "grue" and gruelike predicates cause problems for a Carnap-style inductive logic aimed at selecting an adequate c-function for a rational agent. Presents the new riddle in terms of an agent using the straight rule to estimate the likelihood of future events, and finding that it assigns "the same likelihood to an unexamined emerald's being grue, hence blue, as to its being green." Denies that the problem is caused by the straight rule instead of "grue." Examines c-functions that make the degree of confirmation depend on a parameter lambda and the relative logical width of a property (i.e., an account of prior probability) and that seem to assign a higher likelihood to an unexamined emerald being green than to it being blue. Constructs a proof to show that, with the same frequencies and logical widths, a *c*-function "that is a mixture of these two measures must assign the same probability to a heretofore unexamined object's being a grue emerald as it does to such an object's being a green emerald." Notes that it is important for Carnapians to define projectibility because they typically deal with grue predicates by insisting inductive logic can only be applied to projectible properties. Examines Jeffrey's (1966) definitions of semantic and pragmatic projectibility. Introduces notation and gives sufficient conditions for a *c*-function being strongly and weakly equivalent to the straight rule for two properties. Argues against Jeffrey's claim that "if green is semantically projectible of emeralds then grue is pragmatically anti-projectible of emeralds." Presents a counterexample to this claim by defining a symmetrical *c*-function whereby, for emeralds, grue and green are semantically projectible, grue is pragmatically projectible, and green is pragmatically anti-projectible. Describes a model for this *c*-function. Claims that green is an inductively static property and so "the semantic projectibility of green does not imply the pragmatic anti-projectibility of grue." Regards a property *P* as inductively static of another property *Q* when the properties in question are independent of the indexical property of having been examined by an indexed time. Points out that green and grue are symmetrical in that "for every *c*-function that pragmatically projects green but not grue, there is a corresponding *c*-function that pragmatically projects grue but not green." Claims that Jeffrey does not "show us why we should prefer a function that projects green over a function that projects grue." Discusses how properties are not inductively static because of a logical relation to examination (such as grue and ordinary objects), and others because of a probabilistic relation (such as being exposed and film, or being virginal and females). Introduces "virwife" to mean a female "who is either an examined nonvirgin or an unexamined virgin." Describes a female population with proportions of examined/unexamined virgins and nonvirgins such that a plausible *c*-function will treat virwife (not virgin) as an inductively static property and pragmatically projectible in this population. Emphasizes that if projectible properties are identified with properties "which are independent of examination," this does not restrict inductive logic to projectible properties: e.g., if the primitive properties in a language are static, this does not mean that only static properties can be expressed in this language because static properties are not closed under Boolean operations.

Vincent, R.H. "Popper on Qualitative Confirmation and Disconfirmation." *Australasian Journal of Philosophy* 40 (1962): 157–166. Attempts to show that Popper's criteria of confirmation have unacceptable consequences and so are themselves unacceptable. Popper's three criteria are in appendix ix of *The Logic of Scientific Discovery:* viz., the criterion of initial qualitative confirmation, of qualitative confirmation, and of relativized confirmation. Argues (on pp. 162–163) that the criterion of relativized confirmation "gives rise to something very much like N. Goodman's riddle of the grue emeralds." Defines 'is grue' to mean 'is green and examined before time *t* or is non-green and not examined before *t*.' Claims that, according to Popper's relativized criterion, a sentence about a particular object being green confirms the hypothesis that all emeralds are grue relative to the information that the object is an emerald and is examined prior to time *t*. Does not know if Popper's criterion of initial confirmation "would give rise to Goodman's result."

Wallace, John R. "Goodman, Logic, Induction." *Journal of Philosophy* 63 (1966a): 310–328. States two principles that are supposed to connect a logical theory with a theory of induction: viz., a theory of induction must, in explicating predicates, follow the principle of the indiscernibility of logical equivalents and the principle of the indiscernibility of definitional equivalents. Claims that if quantification theory is the logical theory connected with Goodman's theory of projectibility, and if it is connected via these two principles, then there are serious difficulties with Goodman's explanations of his key notions—indeed, the explanations "are reduced to absurdity." Argues that the logical equivalents principle makes for difficulties with Goodman's notions of a positive instance, a negative instance, a supported hypothesis, a violated hypothesis, an exhausted hypothesis, an evidence class, and a projective class. Argues that the definitional equivalents principle makes for difficulties with Goodman's notions of eliminating one hypothesis in favor of another, accounting for the entrenchment of complex predicates in terms of their parts, distinguishing between names and predicates, classifying simple universal hypotheses as categorical and hypothetical, and defining the antecedent and consequent predicates of a hypothesis. Concludes that "we do not understand what the theory of projectibility is about." Considers the importance of this divide between logical consequence and inductive confirmation; discusses the situation by relating the two principles to views about translating and communicating. Maintains that we will need a new logical theory "in order to reunite the notions of Goodman's theory with the notion of logical consequence." See comments by Goodman (1966) in the same issue.

Wallace, John R. "Lawlikeness = Truth?" *Journal of Philosophy* 63 (1966b): 780–781. Comments on Wallace (1966a) and Goodman (1966). Argues that Goodman's theory of projectibility is committed to the following equivalence: 'All emeralds are grue emeralds' is true if and only if 'grue emerald' is as well entrenched as 'emerald.' Claims this is "counterintuitive" because it conflates the subjective with the objective in letting entrenchment—"a measure of a kind of force and vivacity that terms have"—also be an indicator of the truth-value of hypotheses. Argues that Goodman's theory is also committed to the following equivalence: 'All emeralds are grue emeralds' is true if and only if 'All emeralds are grue emeralds' is lawlike. Claims this is "absurd" because it means that if this hypothesis "is confirmed by its instances, it is true, and that, if it is not confirmed by its instances, it is false." See the reply by Goodman (1967); also in Goodman (1972).

Watanabe, Satosi. *Knowing and Guessing: A Quantitative Study of Inference and Information.* New York: John Wiley & Sons, Inc., 1969. See chapter 4, "Deduction and Induction," section 4.5, "Classical Paradoxes." Discusses Hempel's paradox of the ravens and Goodman's paradox of the grue emeralds. Claims that Goodman's paradox "can be stripped of its magical appeal rather easily." Maintains that the green and grue hypotheses differ in "*a priori* credibility." Rejects the view that the hypotheses differ in "syntactical construction" because one has time-dependent terms, the other does not. Notes how we can reverse the situation by defining "green" in terms of "grue" and "bleen." Believes that if Goodman found himself in a place ("a primitive tribe") where the predicate "evil spirit" is entrenched, then "all hypotheses formulated in terms of 'evil spirit' would become projectible for him." Evaluates Goodman's entrenchment solution as an explication of "projectible." Acknowledges that it may be extensionally correct. Feels it is less than desirable intensionally because "the phenomenon of entrenchment is so heterogeneous with respect to the other explicated features of inductive inference." Complains that "the linguistic fact of entrenchment is only remotely related to other features of the inductive process." Agrees that a solution will refer to "an extrasyntactical empirical fact." Introduces four instruments that indicate whether an object is a certain color or not: a green meter, blue meter, grue meter, and bleen meter. Claims the grue and bleen meters must have spectrometers and timepieces, while the green and blue meters only need spectrometers. Takes this to mean that "grue" is "operationally time-dependent" and "green" is "operationally time-independent." Points out that the grue meter does not have to contain a timepiece; it does have to be an instrument "whose crucial physical property changes in time in relation to other 'fixed' properties of many physical objects." Considers an objection based on interchanging fixed and changing quantities. Agrees with the common-sensical, basic physics choice of fixed quantities because "any deviation from it makes a coherent understanding of the physical world well-nigh impossible without violating the basic form of our reasoning." Emphasizes that these fixed quantities are "anchored in material objects" and so we have an operational criterion for the asymmetry between "green" and "grue." Claims that a hypothesis with time-independent predicates is preferable to one with time-dependent predicates because "one of the main functions of theory formation resides essentially in identifying some constancy or unity in spatial and temporal varieties." Contends that his criterion is more important than an entrenchment criterion because "it rests on the concept of constancy in time."

Watkins, John. *Science and Scepticism*. Princeton, N.J.: Princeton University Press, 1984. A neo-Popperian account of scientific knowledge. Chapter 8 is on corroboration; one section discusses paradoxes of confirmation such as Goodman's paradox. Views the new riddle as a "sideways proliferation argument" and claims "the trick in this form cannot be played on any scientific theory that relates the behaviour of observed things to that of unobserved things." Maintains there are, however, grue-ish variants of such theories. Considers Bartley's claim (1968) that grue hypotheses are not directed at solving a problem; maintains they are directed at solving the same problem as the original hypotheses, and in posing problems they are connected with "problematicality." Considers whether a grue-ish variant is well corroborated if its original theory is; asks whether the original theory would be well corroborated if the grue-ish theory had come first. Contends that grue-ish theories are not really theories because they are conjunctions whose conjuncts have "no temporal overlap," and so the conjunction does not have any testable consequences already entailed by one of its conjuncts or the other. Thereby denies corroborations to grue-ish "theories." Argues that a similar move— splitting a theory into two parts according to a point of time in the future—will not end up denying corroborations to the real, original theories because they will have "predictions across a span of time."

Watling, J. "Critical Notice of *Fact, Fiction and Forecast*." *Mind* 64 (1955): 267–273. Criticizes Goodman for making no attempt "to discover what it is about counterfactual conditionals and possible entities which makes it difficult for him to accept them." Suggests the solution to the counterfactual conditional problem might be nothing more than "showing that the reasons for asking for an analysis are not good reasons." Claims Goodman's analysis of dispositional terms has an unacceptable consequence: viz., that you can't understand a dispositional term unless you know a property causally connected to the corresponding manifest property. Maintains that Goodman confuses "the question whether our predictions about the future can be justified with the question whether inductive arguments, that is arguments from particular cases to general laws, can be justified." Claims Goodman does not distinguish between whether we can justify predictions and whether we can know predictions are true. Considers Goodman wrong "in arguing that none of our predictions are valid and that we cannot know them to be valid." Claims Goodman proceeds by inventing a new meaning for the term "valid argument" so that it applies to inductive arguments, but wonders why anyone should care if an argument is valid or not in this new meaning. Argues that Goodman supports a Humean notion of validity "by a false analogy with deductive inference." Does not discuss Goodman's entrenchment idea because it "cannot solve any problems about how it is that evidence supports hypotheses or how it is possible to know the future." Concludes that Goodman comes to his conclusions because of "his conviction that reduction is the only method of removing a philosophical difficulty."

Wheatley, Jon. "Entrenchment and Engagement." *Analysis* 27 (1967): 119–127. Rejects Goodman's entrenchment solution as implausible because seemingly arbitrary. Introduces and defines the engagement relation between two sentence types; the relation involves a defeating condition based on the notion of a language change. Claims that the sentence type "*X* is an emerald" engages "*X* is green" but not "*X* is grue." States a rule taking this to be a logically cogent reason for preferring the green hypothesis and eliminating the grue one. See the criticism by Swinburne (1968).

Whiteley, C. H. "Confirmation." *Proceedings of the Aristotelian Society, New Series* 74 (1973–74): 1–14. Argues that an observational datum D confirms a hypothesis H as against not-H to the extent that "the net probability of H as against not-H is increased by the addition of D to our relevant information." Applies this view to Goodman's paradox. Agrees that the data, the observed emeralds, are both consistent with and implied by the grue hypothesis. Maintains that this is not sufficient to confirm the hypothesis. Regards Goodman's argument as fallacious in that "*p* confirms *q*-and-*r*" does not follow from "*p* confirms *q*." Emphasizes that the fallacy still occurs if we express "*q* and *r*" in one expression. Claims that "All emeralds are grue" expresses "two distinct and logically independent statements, assigning to emeralds observed at different times two perceptibly distinct and incompatible properties." Thinks "grue" behaves like "greap," where greap things are green and cheap: the definition of "greap" does not turn the observed green emeralds into confirmation for the hypothesis that all emeralds are greap, and thus all emeralds are cheap. Also compares "grue" to the adjective "piebald," which means having patches of black and white, or other colors, as with the coat of a horse. Maintains that observing some white hairs does not confirm the hypothesis that the horse also has some brown hairs and is piebald because "the hypothesis that some of its hairs are brown does not affect the probability that some others are white." Claims the grue hypothesis and the green emeralds data stand in a similar relation.

Wilder, Hugh T. "Quine on Natural Kinds." *Australasian Journal of Philosophy* 50 (1972): 263–270. A criticism of Quine's claim (1970 and this volume) that the notion of a natural kind will dissolve in each mature branch of science. Maintains that Quine takes the problem to be one of analyzing the notion of comparative similarity. Introduces two conditions for an adequate analysis. One: "the analysandum must be a notion of comparative similarity which does justice to Goodman's notion of projectibility." Two: the analysans "must be non-trivial, in the sense that it must be non-circular." Argues that Quine's notion of comparative similarity meets the first condition because Quine makes an appeal to the principles of natural selection in connection with sciences maturing. Argues that Quine's two sample analyses (from chemistry and zoology) do not meet the second condition because they "appeal to the notion of similarity itself." Contends that Quine does not present any other sample analyses or provide any reasons for supposing future analyses will be adequate.

Wilkerson, T.E. "A Gruesome Note." *Mind* 82 (1973): 276–277. Argues that the new riddle of induction can be solved if we assume all emeralds are green and redefine "grue" to mean either being in a sample and green or not in the sample and blue; then "grue" is seen to be no more projectible than "in the sample."

Williams, Peter M. "Goodman's Paradox and Rules of Acceptance." *Philosophy of Science* 36 (1969): 311–315. A reply to Smokler (1966). Examines the role of Scheffler's generalization formula in versions of Goodman's paradox that take inductive rules to be "rules of acceptance permitting one to assert detached conclusions." Maintains that the generalization formula produces a set of consistent generalizations and that the contradictions in question come from adding a premise after applying the formula. Argues for a restriction on adding premises after using the generalization formula. Claims to block the contradictions by prohibiting the introduction of a self-contradictory premise, a premise inconsistent with the evidence, or a premise that contradicts any generalization you can obtain from the evidence with the generalization formula. Therefore does not view Goodman's paradox as "a crucial argument against rules of acceptance."

Wilson, Fred. "Kuhn and Goodman: Revolutionary vs. Conservative Science." *Philosophical Studies* 44 (1983): 369–380. Provides a schema for the logical structure of a Kuhnian paradigm and explains how it fits Kuhn's views on periods of normal scientific research. Describes the grue problem and Goodman's entrenchment solution. Contends that "Goodman's picture of science generates an account of research that is not essentially different from Kuhn's account of normal scientific research." Compares these two accounts with regard to periods of revolutionary science when scientists must choose to pursue a theory that has not been tested yet and that "has never been projected." Describes how, on Kuhn's account, scientists can use their subjective values; argues that this is a rational means-to-an-end response to a time of crisis. Argues that Goodman's rules (his entrenchment solution) are inefficient and inadequate during a period of scientific revolution because the new theory will not have entrenched concepts, there won't be any overhypotheses to support it, and "since the competitors are equally generic, there are no more generic parent predicates from which the concepts in the new candidate could inherit entrenchment." Concludes that Goodman's rules would actually "forbid the search for radically new paradigms." Regards Goodman's account as "inevitably conservative."

Wilson, Mark. "Maxwell's Condition—Goodman's Problem." *British Journal for the Philosophy of Science* 30 (1979): 107–123. Argues that Maxwell's condition and related principles justify many of our inductive preferences. Claims they do this without isolating a special class of predicates (e.g., purely qualitative predicates) for induction. Notes they do not completely solve Goodman's problem. States Maxwell's condition as "a law of nature must be valid at all points in time and space." Changes Newton's gravitational law so that "the universal gravitational constant changes at a particular time." Calls this deviant Newtonianism. Points out that, with a gruelike definition of gravitational force, the deviant law has the same syntactic form as the usual law and so Maxwell's condition, interpreted as a condition on syntactic form, will not rule it out. Nor will (similarly interpreted) the principle of Special Relativity, which requires a law to hold in every inertial frame. Believes it will be sufficient "to require that all the laws in the theory be invariant under the transformations which represent simply relocations of the coordinate origin within the theory." Puts this quasi-operationally as a restriction on possible experimental results: e.g., "All emeralds are gred" fails to meet Maxwell's Condition because we could (if this hypothesis were true) experimentally determine our location in time by synthesizing an emerald and noting its color. Adds that generally we will have to consider a theory in order to decide whether a hypothesis (embedded in the theory) satisfies Maxwell's Condition. Attempts to formulate a general version of Goodman's query in terms of a theory T and a *G-variant* of T, where the variant is exactly like the original theory except for having gruelike versions of a predicate P where the original theory has predicate P. A gruelike version of P takes the form $(Px \& Rx) \lor (Qx \& -Rx)$. Thinks the general question is about specifying conditions for preferring an original theory to its G-variant when both are confirmed equally by all evidence to date. Shows how special relativity is a G-variant of classical mechanics. Maintains that "in this case we would *not* expect a purely *philosophical* methodology to prefer one theory over the other." Believes we need a theory of confirmation that allows us to order the possible G-variants of a theory in terms of absurdity: e.g., from deviant special relativity at one end point to deviant Newtonianism at the other. Maintains that Maxwell's Condition rules out many G-variants of the hypothesis that all emeralds are green, the principle of Special Relativity rules out a variant based on the velocity of emeralds, and the size variant (emeralds being smaller than six cubic feet and green) is far less absurd than the other variants. Regards the absurdity of a G-variant of current physical theory as proportional "to the 'entrenchment' of the highest order methodological or physical principle that it violates." Points out that Maxwell's Condition and the principle of Special Relativity only apply to laws of physics or laws reducible to laws of physics, not to non-law inductive generalizations about, e.g., the average density of matter in the universe. Uses probability to rule out Goodmanized versions of these generalizations: the Goodmanized density hypothesis is physically possible but extremely unlikely. Believes there are still other G-variants that his principles do not handle. Thinks his general formulation of the problem "makes any crisp listing of *all* relevant 'methodological' principles extremely unlikely." Does not view Maxwell's Condition as an a priori principle equivalent to a principle about the uniformity of nature. Notes that Dirac's gravitational theory violates Maxwell's Condition but does not want to rule it out simply because it does. Does not view Maxwell's Condition as just a well-confirmed law of nature because its importance cannot be attributed solely to its well-confirmed status. Does not see how to specify the times when we would allow a theory to violate Maxwell's Condition. Considers part of the problem to be that "the features which mark a given scientific regularity as a 'law' seem to differ from one historical period to another." Warns against accepting Goodman's theory of projection; wants to consider how it applies to changing from Newtonian mechanics to Einsteinian relativity. Asks why Einstein shouldn't have proposed a deviant relativity theory with gruelike predicates; suspects the answer depends on retaining Maxwell's Condition "as an *unviolated hypothesis* carried over from Newtonian mechanics."

Woodward, James. "Critical Review: Horwich on the Ravens, Projectibility and Induction." *Philosophical Studies* 47 (1985): 409–428. An essay-length review of Horwich (1982b). Section II is about projectibility. Compares Horwich's account of projectibility with Roger Rosenkrantz's "rather more conventional Bayesian treatment" in *Inference, Method and Decision* (1977). Also see Rosenkrantz (1973) and (1981). Considers whether observing green emeralds prior to t confirms the grue hypothesis. Notes that Horwich thinks it does (indeed, that it follows from Bayes's theorem); explains why Rosenkrantz disagrees. Argues that, given his own views on probabilities and confirmation, Horwich must conclude that the grue hypothesis is confirmed by examining a known emerald and finding it to be grue. Sees this as a criticism of Horwich's "general method for determining the support provided by starred positive instances," where a starred positive instance of "All As are Bs" is a known A that is examined and found to be a B. Also argues that, on Horwich's own view, if a starred positive instance of the grue hypothesis confirms the grue hypothesis, then it does not follow that the green hypothesis is confirmed by examining a known emerald and finding it to be green. Claims that Horwich's account of projectibility has counterintuitive results: e.g., the hypothesis "All As are B" can be projectible "even though the prior probability that all sampled As are Bs is *much* lower than the prior probability that all sampled As are Bs and not all unsampled As are Bs and *much* lower than the prior probability that not all sampled As are Bs and all unsampled As are Bs." Considers Horwich's explanation "of why evidence for a theory provides one with reason to believe its predictions." Sees his explanation (in terms of "a restricted version of the consequence condition") as "defective and unnecessary" because high probability hypotheses do not generally satisfy the consequence condition, and Bayesian analyses can explain this in terms of probability relations between the evidence and the hypotheses, and so they do not need to appeal to confirmation conditions.

Zabludowski, Andrzej. "Concerning a Fiction about How Facts Are Forecast." *Journal of Philosophy* 71 (1974): 97–112. Revised version in this volume. Mentions in passing "the causal aspect of the entrenchment theory of induction." Believes that "it is simpler, given our sensory equipment, to depict the world in green" than in grue, and that the entrenchment of predicates "derives from the plausibility of certain inductions." Will argue "that there is no interesting connection at all between which predicates are, or appear, well or ill entrenched and which inductions sound plausible or implausible." Will try to show that "for any inductive generalization (and thus for any credible one, in particular) one can formulate another inductive generalization that is incompatible with the former and whose predicates appear at least as well entrenched." Notes the definitions of projectible/unprojectible hypotheses and states Goodman's theory of projectibility as two rules: "(i) reject a generalization (supported, etc.) if you judge it to be unprojectible; (ii) adopt a generalization if you judge it to be projectible," where adopting a generalization is considering it more credible than all of the conflicting generalizations and rejecting is considering it less credible than some of the conflicting generalizations. Discusses the idea that Goodman's theory is supposed to explain decisions between conflicting hypotheses. Takes two hypotheses as conflicting at a certain time "if one cannot consistently believe that both are true, given the evidence available at that time." Points out that Goodman takes two hypotheses as conflicting when they do not follow from each other and they ascribe different predicates to something and only one of the predicates actually applies. Asks why Goodman's concept is "of any special interest." Notes that he will be interpreting "conflict" as Goodman does and also "as incompatibility on evidence." Section I: "Projectibility." Argues "as an initial exercise" that if a hypothesis is projectible, then it is not true. Assumes his meaning of conflicting hypotheses and lets h be an unviolated, unexhausted hypothesis at t. Supposes that "Ax" and "Bx" are among the best entrenched predicates at t and that "some objects are known at t to fall under both of them and some others are known to fall only under the first," and so "All A are B" is supported and violated at t. Introduces h' as supported at t, unexhausted, unviolated, and incompatible with h, so that h' must be overridden in order for h to be projectible at t. The generalizations h' is "All A are either B or not H," where "H" is the conjunction of h and a tautology or the predicate "x is such that h." Claims that if h' is overridden at t, then its disjunctive consequent predicate is not as well entrenched at t as the corresponding predicate of a rival hypothesis, which means "it is not coextensive with 'Bx', and therefore h is false." Believes this generalizes because there is always "a pair of predicates such that both belong to the best entrenched at t—one as antecedent, the other as consequent—and such that some objects are known at t to fall under both and some are known to fall only under the first." Now assumes Goodman's meaning of conflicting hypotheses and supposes an additional condition: viz., "some objects that fall under the antecedent of *h* also fall under '*Ax*' and either fall under the consequent of *h* but not under '*Bx*' or conversely." Argues that if a hypothesis is projectible, then it is false on Goodman's notion of conflict as well. Lets *h* be "All iron melts at 1535 degrees centigrade," "*Ax*" stand for "*x* is metallic" and "*Bx*" stand for "*x* is yellow"; also lets *h* be "All horses are maned" and "*Ax*" stand for "*x* is a horse" and "*Bx*" stand for "*x* is white." Contends that "just as no hypotheses ever projectible are true, so no hypotheses ever projectible are false" and so "no hypotheses are ever projectible." Argues this by introducing a sentence *s* such that *h* does not follow from *s* or from not *s* on the information we accept at *t*, and by introducing two supported, unexhausted, unviolated cognates of *h** that are incompatible with *h*: "All *A* are either *B*, or not *H* and *S*" and "All *A* are *B*, or not *H* and not *S*," where "*Sx*" is the conjunction of *x* = *x* and *s*. Section II: "Unprojectibility." Maintains that "an immediate corollary" of the previous arguments "is that all those hypotheses whose antecedents or consequents are at a given time less than best entrenched are at that time unprojectible." Notes that, according to the accept/reject criterion, we should reject all supported, unviolated, unexhausted hypotheses with less than best-entrenched antecedents or consequents. And that "a host of predicates occurring in generalizations we in fact find credible do not seem to be better entrenched than any predicates whatever." Concludes that either we constantly adopt thousands of unprojectible generalizations or we regard no predicates as ever less than best entrenched and no supported, unviolated, unexhausted hypotheses as ever unprojectible. Section III: "Projectibility and Unprojectibility Again." Corrects the criterion so that we will reject a generalization "not when we merely *find that there is another* that overrides it—but rather when *there is another that we find* to override it." Corrects the definition of an unprojectible hypothesis so that an unprojectible hypothesis has a rival "to be *judged* at the time in question as overriding." Admits that now his previous arguments are not effective because they do not show that for every (supported, etc.) hypothesis with an antecedent or consequent judged less than best entrenched "there is a particular rival that must be judged as overriding." Also redefines projectibility so that a (supported, etc.) hypothesis is projectible "if it has no rivals (supported, etc.) to be judged at the time in question as not overridden." Assumes his meaning of conflict and argues that any (supported, etc.) hypothesis *h* is still not projectible at *t*. Supposes "*Ax*," "*Bx*," and "*Cx*" are among the best-entrenched predicates at *t*, and we know some objects fall under all three predicates, and some falling under "*Ax*" at *t* do not fall under "*Bx*." Also supposes the information we accept at *t* does not exclude "All *A* are *C*" as true and *h* as false. Introduces a supported, etc., generalization *h*** that is incompatible with *h*: viz., "All *A* are either *B* and *C*, or *B* and *H*, or *C* and not *H*," where "*H*" is still the conjunction of *h* and a tautology. Maintains that *h*** is not overridden at *t* because "its antecedent is ranked at *t* among the best entrenched," being coextensive with either "*Bx*" or "*Cx*." Notes that if either predicate of *h* is less than best entrenched at *t*, then *h*** overrides *h* and *h* is unprojectible at *t*. Assumes Goodman's notion of conflict and argues that *h* is not projectible at *t* because "there is a hypothesis—e.g., *h****—that is supported, etc., at *t* and that must be admitted at *t* to be at that time a non-overridden rival of *h*." Again notes that if either predicate of *h* is less than best entrenched at *t*, then *h* is unprojectible at *t*. The generalization *h**** is "All *A* are *B* and *C*, or *B* and not *K*, or *C* and *K*," where "*K*" stands for "is such that *h'* conflicts with *h*" and *h'* is "All *A* are *C*." Illustrates this with (e.g.) *h* being "All horses are maned" and the predicates "horse," "white," and "denser than water," with "*K*" being "is such that some horses are either maned and not denser than water, or denser than water and not maned." Section IV: "Overhypotheses and Comparative Projectibility." Discusses how Goodman's theory connects the projectibility of "All marbles in bag *B* are red" with an overhypothesis like "Every bagful in stack *S* is uniform in color," where bag *B* is from stack *S* and the predicates of the overhypothesis are parent predicates of the bag *B* hypothesis. Notes that only some supported, unviolated overhypotheses are relevant (e.g., Goodman's "All bagleets are uniform in color" example). Claims the theory has two "troublesome" implications: the projectibility of a hypothesis can be influenced by information that confirms various higher-order hypotheses and yet is "irrelevant to the hypothesis in question," and the projectibility of a hypothesis can be influenced negatively by information that normally confirms it. Corrects these troubles by redefining the concepts of negative and positive overhypothesis. Maintains that the real trouble with Goodman's overhypothesis theory is that "generalizations we in fact find plausible seem to have no advantage in comparative projectibility over many of their most implausible rivals:" e.g., if "All horses are maned" is more projectible than its rival h^{***}, this will be due to appreciably projectible positive overhypotheses and yet it is much easier to find a bizarre overhypothesis like "All species of mammals are either uniform in color and uniform in density, or uniform in color and not such that some horses are either maned but no denser than water or denser than water but not maned, or uniform in density and such that some horses are either maned but not denser than water or denser than water but not maned." See the initial replies by Kennedy and Chihara (1975) and by Ullian and Goodman (1975). The *Journal of Philosophy* eventually published a total of eleven replies (the last in 1982) by Ullian and Goodman, Zabludowski, Kennedy and Chihara, and Scheffler. Also see Kennedy and Chihara (1978).

Zabludowski, Andrzej. "Good or Bad, but Deserved: A Reply to Ullian and Goodman." *Journal of Philosophy* 72 (1975): 779–784. A reply to Ullian and Goodman (1975). Explains his argument that "All emeralds are green" is not projectible because of the rival hypothesis "All stones are either round and fusible or round and not *K* or fusible and *K*," where *K* is the predicate "such that some stones that are emeralds are either fusible but not green or green but not fusible." Notes that he shows these hypotheses conflict by invoking the information "that some stones that are emeralds are green but are not round," and that Ullian and Goodman claim this violates their principle of admissible information. Complains that Goodman simply posits that the green and the grue hypothesis conflict while he shows that the green hypothesis conflicts with his stones hypothesis h^{***}, and yet Goodman's projectibility criterion cannot apply to his pair of hypotheses. Concludes he should just posit that his pair of hypotheses conflict instead of trying to prove they do. Discusses his argument that if a hypothesis is projectible, then it is false; notes that Ullian and Goodman claim his argument is wrong because if hypotheses effectively compete, then "the comparative entrenchment of their predicates does not depend upon their truth value." Claims that some of his examples (e.g., the green hypothesis and h^{***}) are "free of this deficiency." Makes two comments on whether his examples violate the principle of wanton embedding. Agrees that his examples do wantonly embed their rivals, argues that the grue hypothesis wantonly embeds the green hypothesis, and that the green hypothesis wantonly embeds the grue hypothesis. Contends that for "any pair of unviolated generalizations, each wantonly embeds the other; accordingly, each is conspicuously less simple than the other—a dialectical equality in inequality—and each must be eliminated." Ends by claiming that the problems with Goodman's theory of projectibility depend on "the assumption that the difference between plausible and implausible inductive generalizations is a difference between the classes they pick out." Believes we can't solve the new riddle unless we allow "predicates to have, besides extension, also meaning." See the reply by Ullian and Goodman (1976) and further comments by Kennedy and Chihara (1977).

Zabludowski, Andrzej. "Quod Periit, Periit." *Journal of Philosophy* 74 (1977): 541–552. A reply to Ullian and Goodman (1976). Section I: "The Master Argument." Examines Ullian and Goodman's argument about whether $h***$ is a threat to the projectibility of h. Notes that their argument involves the statement ¢ (i.e., h conflicts with "All A are C"), that the statement ¢ has not been determined to be false, and that Ullian and Goodman consider what to say about h if ¢ is true and also if the truth value of ¢ is in question: in the former case we deny that h is projectible because it conflicts with "All A are C," and in the latter case we are undecided about the matter and wait for more evidence. Claims that "the logic of this argument escapes me." Believes the first case is "of no interest" because we are not concerned with showing (e.g.) "the trivial fact that some hypotheses are bound to be denied 'projectibility' even without our involving their queer rivals like $h***$." Asks, in connection with the second case, why we need to know that h conflicts with "All A are C" when we know $h***$ is an equally impressive rival to h. Also points out that if more evidence defeats $h***$, this does not mean h is projectible because h must confront "a whole bunch of $h***$-like rivals" in order to pass Goodman's projectibility test. Maintains that since we do not have a hypothesis in sight that would pass Goodman's test, "nothing can matter less than whether there is a chance that some hypothesis will pass it in some future." Section II: "Conflict." Considers the claim that "All emeralds are green" overrides "All emeralds are grue" and "All emeralds are gred." Points out that this assumes the grue and gred hypotheses conflict (Goodman's meaning of the term) with "All emeralds are green." Claims that if the grue hypothesis conflicts with the green hypothesis, the gred hypothesis must be false; and that if the gred hypothesis conflicts with the green one, the grue hypothesis must be false. Concludes that we do not need to consider entrenchment in order to reject the grue and gred hypotheses. Considers the claim that "All emeralds are green" overrides the grue hypothesis. Argues that we cannot reject the grue hypothesis by appealing to premise (i) and premise (ii)—that the grue hypothesis conflicts with the green hypothesis and that the green hypothesis is well entrenched while the grue hypothesis is not, respectively— because we "cannot adopt the former premise reasonably without making the other superfluous." Considers redefining "conflict" so that two hypotheses conflict if, and only if, "neither follows from the other and they ascribe to something two different predicates of which *at most* one actually applies." Claims this creates a problem for Goodman's rule about accepting a hypothesis if we judge it to be projectible: viz., that we could not accept "All emeralds are green" because it is projectible—the reason being that we must accept "All emeralds are green" in order to consider it projectible. Believes the redefinition retains a circularity. Notes that Ullian and Goodman believe the green hypothesis is projectible now, and so they must be confident that it does not conflict with a hypothesis like "All stones are fusible." Presumes they are confident about this because they believe "that all stones are fusible and all emeralds are green," which means that their belief in the projectibility of the green hypothesis "is founded, in particular, on their belief that the hypothesis is true," which in turn is founded on their belief that the hypothesis is projectible. Section III: "The Theory 'Extended.'" Notes how Ullian and Goodman believe their master argument becomes an even better reply when they extend Goodman's theory of projectibility so that it takes account of degrees of credibility. Points out that the extended theory considers whether one hypothesis overrides another as well as whether a hypothesis is incredible. Maintains he apparently overlooked the fact that "Goodman's entrenchment theory is not intended to defend a generalization like 'All emeralds are green' against such rivals as $h***$: the theory assumes such rivals to be ruled out beforehand." Wonders why the extended theory rules out $h***$ on the basis of reasonable acceptance/rejection standards but not the grue hypothesis; why the theory needs to bring in entrenchment to eliminate the grue hypothesis when it does not need to bring in entrenchment to eliminate $h***$; why it treats $h***$ as more incredible than the grue hypothesis. Notes that $h***$ is equivalent to statement S: All stones are fusible and not all emeralds are green. Doubts that S is more incredible than "All emeralds thus far examined are green but all others blue." Believes that S seems incredible because "its second conjunct sounds incredible." Believes this shows that we cannot judge "All emeralds are green" to be projectible unless we appeal to the fact that "All emeralds are green" is highly credible, which in turn shows that "All emeralds are green" is not highly credible because it is projectible or that we follow Goodman's rule about accepting a generalization if we believe it is projectible. Section IV: "The 'Principle Of Wanton Embedding.'" Considers Ullian and Goodman's point about $U*$ being an abbreviation and whether a sentence is implied differentially with respect to $U*$. Maintains that Ullian and Goodman's own examples (in their 1975 to illustrate the principle of wanton embedding) "are at odds with the proviso in question": viz., that a sentence with the abbreviation $U*$ does not count as differentially implied with respect to $U*$ unless the sentence without the abbreviation does. Attempts to show again that "All emeralds are grue" wantonly embeds "All emeralds are green," and that "All emeralds are green" wantonly embeds "All emeralds are grue." For example: the green hypothesis wantonly embeds the grue hypothesis because, with U being the set of undetermined cases for the grue hypothesis, the conjunction of "x is green," "x is an emerald" and rho implies "If everything belonging to $U - \{x\}$ is green, then all emeralds are green" differentially with respect to $U*$. Concludes with a few comments about whether he misrepresents (in his 1975) the principle of admissible information. Claims that he takes into account "the very argument . . . which was to show Ullian and Goodman's principle at work" (in Ullian and Goodman, 1975) and that "the innocent triviality to which the authors now reduce their 'principle of admissible information' has no connection whatsoever with that eccentric argument." See the reply by Goodman and Ullian (1978).

Zabludowski, Andrzej. "Revised but Not Secured: A Reply to Ullian." *Journal of Philosophy* 79 (1982): 329–332. A reply to Ullian (1980). Criticizes Ullian's 1980 version of the principle of wanton embedding. Lets hypothesis h be "All emeralds are green." Introduces hypothesis h', which results from changing the predicate "Ky" in his hypothesis $h***$ from Zabludowski (1974). Hypothesis $h***$ is "All stones are either round and fusible, or round and not K, or fusible and K." Now lets "Ky" mean "All stones are fusible, and all stones that have not been observed are not green." Claims that h' is supported and unviolated, that its antecedent and consequent predicates are among the best entrenched (the contrived consequent predicate being coextensive with either "round" or "fusible"), and that h' conflicts with h. Points out that h' does not, however, wantonly embed h because it does not use the predicate "emerald" and so "does not 'essentially imply' any formula containing that predicate." Concludes that Ullian's new version of the embedding principle "is of no help to Goodman's projectibility criterion." Modifies Ullian's 1980 definition of wantonly embedding (drawing on earlier definitions) so that h' ends up wantonly embedding h. Claims the modified definition has the same problem as preceding definitions: viz., any hypothesis (e.g., all emeralds are green) wantonly embeds it competitors (e.g., all emeralds are grue). Believes the notion of embedding is "totally wrongheaded." Maintains Ullian is exploiting a feature of $h***$ that you can find in "perfectly decent generalizations": viz., "it contains an occurrence o of a predicate such that at least one argument of o is an occurrence of a variable, but no argument of o is an occurrence of a variable bound by the main quantifier." Notes how this means "a host of decent generalizations are bound to count as 'wantonly embedding' others." Considers Ullian's view that this is not alarming because if a generalization wantonly embeds a rival, this does not mean it cannot be projectible. Supposes that h_1 is a decent generalization with the feature Ullian is exploiting, and that its antecedent denotes a class as well entrenched as any class. Supposes that h_2 is a rival to h_1, that it is like h^{***}, and that it has the same antecedent predicate as h_1. Believes that we do not have an explanation of why we prefer h_1 to h_2 because the rule of projectibility does not eliminate h_2, and h_2 wantonly embeds h_1 and h_1 wantonly embeds h_2. Maintains that if the notion of embedding doesn't explain why we prefer h_2 to h_1, then "its account of what is wrong with h^{***} as a competitor of h does not hold water." See the reply by Ullian (1982) and the discussion by Scheffler (1982).

Zabludowski, Andrzej. "On Induction and Properties." *Pacific Philosophical Quarterly* 72 (1991): 78–85. Argues that Goodman's problem cannot be solved by distinguishing between genuine and pseudo (or Cambridge) properties. Primarily concerned with the views of Bealer (1982) and Shoemaker (1980), and with a criterion like: a supported, unexhausted, unviolated generalization is projectible if and only if both its antecedent and consequent predicates designate genuine properties. Notes that a Goodman nominalist would reject solutions based on properties; argues that, without properties, Goodman nominalists do not have an adequate answer to questions about why a certain predicate applies to some distant object (e.g., an object existing a million years ago). Claims that "one can contrive unviolated and abundantly supported, yet utterly implausible generalizations using predicates that designate perfectly 'genuine' properties." Maintains that Goodman's problem is not simply about predicates designating properties, but also about how they designate (what they mean). Recognizes controversies about properties, predicates designating properties, and identity criteria for properties; claims his argument is, for the most part, neutral with regard to these. Considers "All emeralds are green" and "All emeralds are roundhard," where both are supported, unviolated, and incompatible. Contends that his roundhard generalization does not refute the Bealer–Shoemaker criterion because he can't show that "roundhard" designates a genuine property; also contends that it is not clear that his roundhard generalization does not satisfy the criterion. Proposes a change in the criterion to meet this last point: viz., adds a clause about the evidence available not excluding that the generalization is both true and has the right sort of predicates. Introduces "All emeralds are hardround" and claims that its predicates designate genuine properties. Stipulates that if all emeralds are green, then being hardround = being round, and that if some emeralds are green, then being hardround = being hard. Argues that he is not stipulating one predicate is synonymous with another because you need extra-linguistic information to detect the equivalence, or that he is stipulating a certain statement (either about hard or round things) is a contingently necessary truth. Claims this last error "rests on confusing implication or entailment with necessitation." Maintains that the predicates "roundhard" and "hardround" are "analytically coextensive." Admits that the stipulation introducing "hardround" is peculiar because it cannot be written as an explicit definition without equating properties with sets of possible objects. Discusses how this kind of stipulation does not fit in with Putnam's analysis ("On Properties," his *Philosophical Papers*) of two predicates designating the same property. Also see the appendix to Zabludowski (this volume).

Ziff, Paul. *Epistemic Analysis: A Coherence Theory of Knowledge.* Dordrecht, Holland: D. Reidel Publishing Company, 1984. See chapter XIII, sections 168 and 169. Claims to resolve Goodman's problem of projectible predicates. Describes conflicting predictions about the color of the next snowfall. Introduces the term "grite-*t*" for being white prior to time *t* and not white after it. Distinguishes this term from "grite-*t*-1," "grite-*t*-2," and other terms for being white *n* moments prior to *t* and not white after this *t-n*. Assumes all snowfalls prior to *t* have been white, so none have been any of the grite-*t-n*, thus establishing "the inutility of these conceptions." Maintains that if we suppose grite-*t* is a useful conception, then we must explain how it differs from these predecessors; if we suppose it is on a par with these predecessors, then we do not have anything to explain. Concludes that "considerations of coherence direct us to consign grite-*t* to limbo along with its fellows." Claims this resolution is compatible with Goodman's entrenchment solution; views entrenchment as "merely a manifestation of coherence."

INDEX